SECOND EDITION

The Scientist Practitioner

Research and Accountability in the Age of Managed Care

Steven C. Hayes
University of Nevada, Reno

David H. Barlow
Boston University

Rosemery O. Nelson-Gray
University of North Carolina at Greensboro

Allyn and Bacon

Boston ■ London ■ Toronto ■ Sydney ■ Tokyo ■ Singapore

Vice President, Editor in Chief, Education: Sean W. Wakely
Editorial Assistant: Susan Hutchinson
Marketing Managers: Ellen Dolberg and Brad Parkins
Editorial Production Service: Chestnut Hill Enterprises, Inc
Cover Administrator: Jennifer Hart

Internet: www.abacon.com

Between the time Website information is gathered and published, some sites may have closed. Also, the transcription of URLs can result in typographical errors. The publisher would appreciate notification where these occur so that they may be corrected.

Library of Congress Cataloging-in-Publication Data

Hayes, Steven C.
    The scientist practitioner : research and accountability in the
age of managed care / Steven C. Hayes, David H. Barlow, Rosemery O.
Nelson-Gray.—2nd ed.
      p.   cm.
    Includes bibliographical references and index.
    ISBN 0-205-18098-1 (pbk.)
    1. Clinical psychology—Practice. 2. Clinical psychology–
–Research. 3. Managed mental health care. I. Barlow, David H.
II. Nelson-Gray, Rosemery O. III. Title.
    [DNLM: 1. Psychology, Clinical—methods. 2. Research—methods.
WM 105H418s 1999]
RC467.B36 1999
616.89'023—dc21
DNLM/DLC
for Library of Congress   98-39960
                                                  CIP

Printed in the United States of America

10 9 8 7 6 5 4 3 2 1   03 02 01 00 99 98

To Joseph Cautela (David H. Barlow),
Irving Kessler (Steven C. Hayes),
and in memory of Joseph Wolpe
and Alan O. Ross (Rosemery O. Nelson-Gray)

CONTENTS

PREFACE

The first edition of this text was based on the idea that practitioners could better be brought into the research enterprise in behavioral health and education through the use of single-case designs and clinical replication series. Much has happened in the field in the years that have passed. The health care delivery system has evolved from a cottage industry to a full-scale industrialized system, and the private practice of psychotherapy is under tremendous strain due to this transition. The public sector is privatizing, and the managed care organizations are launched on an effort to reduce unexplained variability between providers and to establish a cycle of quality improvement.

The wheel is very much in spin, but it is very clear that in the emerging world the role of practitioners in the empirical development of the behavioral health care disciplines is even greater than the role we envisioned in 1984. The first wave of managed care organizations emphasized cost containment and "supply side" methods of reducing the utilization of services. Under the pressure of competition, legislation, regulation, litigation, and accreditation, the second generation of managed care is focusing on the delivery of effective and efficient services as a method of achieving market success. There is no better method of determining which treatments are effective and efficient than science, and thus tremendous opportunities exist for scientist-practitioners in these systems. But to take advantage of this opportunity scientist-practitioners need to widen their focus to include prevention, triage, training, supervision, treatment development, program evaluation, and practice guidelines.

In this volume we point to those opportunities and attempt to prepare students to succeed in the era of managed care. In 1984 the appeal was essentially one of values: The field needs the knowledge that scientist practitioners can develop. Today, the appeal is more direct. The empirical abilities of the scientist-practitioner provide economic value to a new age of health care delivery. Particularly at a doctoral level, the tools provided in this volume will help the practitioner compete and win. Fortunately, so too will the people we serve.

We believe that we are witnessing a historic transition, one that will finally marry the economic interests of the delivery system to the development and implementation of an empirical knowledge base. Similar marriages have occurred recently (e.g., in information technology, or biotechnology) and they have resulted in a great leap forward in practical knowledge. If the scientist-practitioners can rise to this challenge, the same result seems possible here.

The authors would like to thank Bette Selwyn, Peggy Hart, J. T. Blackledge, Pamela Love, and Jennifer Gregg for their assistance. We would also like to thank Kirk Strosahl, Group Health Cooperative of Puget Sound, John D. Cone, United States International University, and Rona Levy, University of Washington, for reviews of the manuscript at various stages.

Steven C. Hayes
David H. Barlow
Rosemery O. Nelson-Gray

ABOUT THE AUTHORS
AND CONTRIBUTORS

Steven C. Hayes is Nevada Foundation Professor and chair of the department of psychology at the University of Nevada. An author of 13 books and more than 200 scientific articles, his interests cover basic research, applied research, methodology, and philosophy of science. In 1992 he was listed by the Institute for Scientific Information as the thirtieth "highest impact" psychologist in the world during 1986–1990 based on the citation impact of his writings. Dr. Hayes has been president of Division 25 of the APA, the American Association of Applied and Preventive Psychology, and the Association for Advancement of Behavior Therapy. He was the first secretary-treasurer of the American Psychological Society and is currently cochair of the Practice Guidelines Coalition.

David H. Barlow has published over 400 articles and chapters and 20 books, mostly in the areas of anxiety disorders, sexual problems, and clinical research methodology. Dr. Barlow was formerly professor of psychiatry at the University of Mississippi Medical Center and professor of psychiatry and psychology at Brown University; he initiated psychology internship programs in each setting. He was also Distinguished Professor in the Department of Psychology at the University of Albany, State University of New York. Dr. Barlow has been president of the division of clinical psychology of the APA and of the Association for Advancement of Behavior Therapy. Dr. Barlow is professor of psychology, Research Professor of Psychiatry, Director of clinical training programs and Director of the Center for Anxiety and Related Disorders at Boston University.

Rosemery O. Nelson-Gray is currently professor of psychology and director of clinical training at the University of North Carolina at Greensboro. She received her Ph.D. from the State University of New York at Stony Brook in 1972, after studying with Professor Eysenck in England. She was the founding editor of the journal *Behavior Assessment*. She is a past-president of the Association for Advancement of Behavior Therapy, Division 25 (Experimental Analysis of Behavior) of the APA, and of the Council of the University Directors of Clinical Psychology. She has coauthored two books (*The Scientist Practitioner* and *Conceptual Foundations of Behavioral Assessment*, 1986, Guildford), and has published more than a hundred articles. She has lectured throughout the United States and in Europe and South America. Her current research foci are unipolar depression and personality disorders.

Susan C. Baird, M.A., is a doctoral candidate in clinical psychology at the University of North Carolina at Greensboro. She received a B.A. degree in psychology and German in 1993 from Trinity University in San Antonio, TX. She is currently in the predoctoral internship program at Duke University Medical Center. Her research and clinical interests are personality disorders and evaluating treatment outcome.

William J. Korotitsch earned a bachelor of arts at State University of New York at Albany in 1991, and a master of arts degree at the University of North Carolina at Greensboro in 1997. He is a doctoral candidate in clinical psychology at UNCG, with research interests including cognitive processes in assessment and psychopathology.

CHAPTER

1

The Scientist Practitioner

Introduction

The world of practice is rapidly changing. The revolution in our health care delivery system that is managed care has altered the role of behavioral health care providers almost beyond recognition during the last decade, and these changes continue to occur. As documented below, the days of doctoral-level behavioral health care providers rendering hour after hour of individual psychotherapy or consultation with little or no accountability for their results are largely over. The doctoral-level behavioral health care provider of the present, and particularly the future, will have a new set of responsibilities. These responsibilities will include *developing* mental health and educational programs, *administering* these programs, *training* and *supervising* assessment and intervention within these programs and, most importantly, *evaluating* the effectiveness of behavioral health care and educational programs. Direct service delivery will be limited to times when either the impact of a doctoral-level provider is known to be superior, or most especially when complex and nonresponsive cases demand the development of new methods and new programs.

In meeting these obligations, the doctoral-level practitioner at the beginning of the next century will ultimately fulfill the role of scientist practitioner as envisioned a half century ago. This individual must not only be a superb clinician capable of supervising interventions, and intervening directly in difficult cases, but must also be intimately familiar with the process of evaluating the effectiveness of interventions, whether administered to an individual or an institution. The scientist practitioners of the twenty-first century must adapt the scientific method to the practice settings in which they find themselves, and communicate these findings to policy makers and third-party payers in order to achieve the elusive goal of providing effective and efficient services with accountability. The purpose of this book is to describe in some detail methods of developing, administering, evaluating, and training in the delivery of behavioral health care and education services that will epitomize the role of the scientist practitioner.

Before attempting these ambitious goals, it is important to recognize that attempts to link science and practice in the last half of the twentieth century have largely failed. In psychology as well as other professions, this has resulted in a split between science and practice that has at times threatened to rend professional

1

associations such as the American Psychological Association asunder. At the worst of times, practitioners denied all relevance of scientific methods to their enterprise, and scientists derided the inadequacy and ineffectiveness of practitioners. Since the residue of these wars remains with us to this day, it is important to examine the origins of the scientist–practitioner model and what went wrong. Lessons from this historical prelude should allow us to prevent the repetition of mistakes from the past as professionals adjust to the industrialization of behavioral health care.

Origins and Current Status

Ideally, the label "scientist practitioner" describes three primary and interrelated roles for behavioral health care providers. In the first role, practitioners are *consumers* of new research findings from research centers, usually new assessment or treatment programs that they will put into practice. In the second role, practitioners are *evaluators* of their own interventions and programs using empirical methods and outcomes measures that would increase accountability. In the third role, practitioners are *researchers*, producing new data from their own settings and reporting these data to the applied and scientific community. In these roles the behavioral health care provider earns the title *scientist practitioner.*

What was the origin of the idea underlying the scientist–practitioner model of training? What were the goals that the founders of clinical psychology were attempting to reach and why were leaders in all of the mental health professions as concerned as they were, even in the early 1960s when it seemed that a split between science and practice was developing? Why is the model of a scientist practitioner still the most popular and highly revered model of training for clinical psychologists in North America (Kanfer, 1990; Phillips, 1989; Shakow, 1976; Stricker, 1992) and other countries (Martin, 1989), and increasingly popular in such fields as social work (Bloom & Fisher, 1982; Ivanov, Blythe, & Briar, 1987; Jayaratne & Levy, 1979), despite the seeming failures of this model over the years? To find answers to these questions, one must examine some of the original documents espousing the scientist practitioner as a model for training. The history of the movement is found largely in clinical psychology and closely allied educational fields, although the issues are equally relevant to other practitioners in applied settings.

The remainder of this chapter will trace the origin of the scientist–practitioner model of training as it evolved in clinical psychology and the experiences of all of the behavior-change professions in the ensuing decades that forced reconsideration of this model by some. Practical and philosophical differences that have prevented practitioners from doing research will be described, as well as the unfortunate finding that research findings have had little impact on practice in past years; that is, practitioners stopped "consuming" research. Reasons for the development of this scientist–practitioner split, with the consequence that many practitioners have not been empirical and therefore not accountable, are suggested. Finally, developments that have made the scientific-empirical approach to practice more necessary and highly valued than ever in this era of managed care are described.

Development of
the Scientist–Practitioner Model

Lightner Witmer, David Shakow, and F. C. Thorne

From the very first conceptions of clinical psychology, as articulated by Lightner Witmer, who originated the term "clinical psychology" and formed the first psychological clinic in 1896, science and practice were considered inseparable. "The pure and the applied sciences advance in a single front. What retards the progress of one, retards the progress of the other; what fosters one, fosters the other. But in the final analysis the progress of psychology, as of every other science, will be determined by the value and amount of its contributions to the advancement of the human race" (Witmer, 1907/1996, p. 249).

The idea that a psychologist should be trained as both a scientist and a professional became the policy of the American Psychological Association following a report of an influential committee chaired by David Shakow in 1947 (Shakow, Hilgard, Kelly, Luckey, Sanford, & Shaffer, 1947). While Shakow would go on to make many important contributions during his distinguished career, he remained the foremost spokesperson for this model of training (e.g., Shakow, 1969).

But the ideals of the scientist practitioner were never more clearly laid out than in a paper published in American Psychologist in 1947 by Frederick C. Thorne, entitled "The Clinical Method in Science." Stating what could well be the thesis of this book, Thorne made the following observations on the conduct of clinical practice:

> Formerly, clinical technology was mainly empirical, i.e., based on study and "experience" rather than experiment. To a certain degree therapy must always be empirical since the primary consideration is the welfare of the patient rather than the conduct of a scientific experiment. Perhaps the most significant development, however, is the increasing application of the experimental approach to the individual case and to the clinician's own "experience." Ideally, diagnosis (description) and treatment of each individual case may be regarded as a single and well-controlled experiment. The treatment may be carefully controlled by utilizing single therapeutic factors, observing and recording results systematically, and checking through the use of appropriate quantitative laboratory studies. In addition to the general scientific orientation to the individual case there are frequent opportunities in clinical practice to conduct actual experiments to determine the validity of diagnosis or the efficacy of treatment. For example, a simple experiment may be set up in which a placebo and a specific drug may be administered according to a definite pattern, such as A/B/B/A, with careful recording and mathematical analysis of results. . . . Individual clinicians are encouraged to apply experimental and statistical methods in the analysis of case results and larger scale analyses are made of the experience of the whole clinic over a period of years. Thus the clinician comes to regard each individual case as part of a larger sample. (pp. 159–160)

Unfortunately, Thorne was wrong. This did not represent the development of the practice of clinical psychology or any of the human service professions, at least, prior to the era of managed care. Clinical practice was to remain intuitive and based on experience for many years yet to come. But perhaps Thorne's writings, at the very least, would influence an important group of professionals meeting two years later.

The Boulder Conference

Although clinical psychology has a long history (e.g., Routh, 1994), it is not an exaggeration to say that the birth of clinical psychology, as we know it today, occurred in August of 1949 in Boulder, Colorado. At that time, a total of 71 representatives from training universities, mental health service agencies, and allied professions met daily for the unusually long period of two weeks. This conference was sponsored by the National Institute of Mental Health and the American Psychological Association to arrive at a consensus on the content of training of clinical psychologists. Although a committee of the American Psychological Association, chaired by David Shakow, had recommended a training model emphasizing both science and practice two years earlier (Shakow et al., 1947), the Boulder conference was in a position to have an enormous impact. It brought together for the first time virtually all of the existing clinical psychology training programs with representatives from numerous clinical and governmental agencies. But its participants were most likely unaware that the words "Boulder model" would be mentioned during the ensuing 50 years every time psychologists convened to discuss training, and that any training innovations would be discussed in the context of the conclusions reached during those two weeks in August of 1949. Furthermore, the close interrelationship of the professions comprising the original "mental health team," specifically psychiatric nurses, psychiatric social workers, psychiatrists, and clinical psychologists, was recognized even then. In view of their overriding interest in what was basically the same problem, it was inevitable that considerations of training, and particularly the role of research in training, would be seriously considered by all of these professions. These considerations have had some impact on all professions producing behavioral health care providers as well as other clinical and educational professions, despite the very different history and traditions of these other professions.

The unanimous recommendation at the end of this conference—the validity of the scientist–practitioner model for training—did not reflect the attitudes of all of the participants when the conference began. In the oft-cited report on this conference (Raimy, 1950), it was observed that the role of research in the training of the clinical psychologist was perhaps the most challenging issue debated there. This was true since "neither tradition nor the definition of clinical psychology provides much guidance" (Raimy, 1950, p. 79) because clinical psychology, even at that time, functioned in many different fields—from research planning to full-time psychotherapeutic intervention. Training emphasis then, as now, varied from producing statistically sophisticated therapists to service-oriented practitioners. These opinions were reflected initially by factions who questioned sincerely whether graduate students could be trained in both areas. Then, as now, one faction suggested that emphasis on research training might dilute and weaken the necessary training for competence in diagnosis and treatment. An equally strong faction, seldom heard today, pointed out that as much damage might be done by diluting a good research training with time spent on applied diagnostics and therapy. In retrospect, the underlying rationale for the latter position was quite valid, in that this faction questioned whether anything clinicians did as service workers at the time was effective, or at least had been proved effective. This position was best represented by a quote that has run down through the decades, "Psychotherapy is an undefined technique, applied to unspecified problems, with unpredictable outcome. For this technique we recommend rigorous training" (Raimy, 1950, p. 93). Eysenck's more serious and better documented statement on the lack of proven effects of psychotherapy three years later was to have a more profound impact (Eysenck, 1952), but the same feeling prevailed in 1949.

Five Reasons for "Joint" Training

Against this background, it is very surprising to see that the decision of the conference to recommend the training of clinical psychologists for research and practice, with equal emphasis on both, was not a compromise to resolve a dilemma, but was an almost unanimous consensus of the participants. This unanimity occurred despite the realization that there were considerable risks involved in deciding to train students in both areas and that this model of training was in many aspects a unique experiment in professional training.

The basis for this unanimous recommendation rests on five important considerations, many of which are still relevant today. First, it was decided that students should receive training in both research and practice in order to develop an interest and background in both areas, despite the fact that some might concentrate on only one area during their careers. Thus, every clinical psychologist receiving the doctor of philosophy degree was seen as unique, in that combined training in practice and research enabled one to engage in either research, training, or preferably a combination of the two. Underlying this reason was a further assumption that specialization by a large group of individuals, in this case specialization in either research or practice, had certain well-known tendencies to produce narrowness of thinking and rigidity of action. But, as the conferees noted:

> When, however, persons within the same general field specialize in different aspects, as inevitably happens, cross-fertilization and breadth of approach are likely to characterize such a profession. Whether the four-year doctoral training program, which emphasizes both research and service, will achieve the desired result is a question to be settled by the future. (Raimy, 1950, p. 81)

Second, with a rationale that would find many sympathizers today, the conferees stated, "The manifest lack of dependable knowledge in clinical psychology and personality demands that research be considered a vital part of the field of clinical psychology. Participants at the conference displayed considerable humility with respect to confidence in present techniques" (Raimy, 1950, p. 80). Today it seems we have made superior progress in identifying specific techniques that are effective with specific problems (e.g., Barlow, 1994; Chambless et al., 1996; Roth & Fonagy, 1995), but few would disagree that we still have much to be humble about.

Third, the participants believed that there was no reason that clinical psychology could not find people capable of carrying out both roles. It was noted, even then, that applicants far exceeded the number of slots for training and that preference should be given to the student who showed some potential for combining both functions.

Fourth, it was observed that direct involvement in the clinical process by researchers would bring them into intimate contact with important research issues. This rationale is widely accepted today. Finally, effectively delivered service may provide some of the much needed financial support for the initiation and continuation of research projects. This is more true than ever, since health care delivery systems require new data-based evidence to succeed in the marketplace.

There is no question that the experimental nature of this very different training experience did not escape the conference participants:

> The development of the profession of clinical psychology constitutes something of an educational experiment in that clinical psychologists are being trained both as scientists and as practitioners. Most professions base their practices on one or more sciences and train their future members in a separate professional school. In contrast, clinical psychologists are trained concurrently in both the theoretical (scientific) and applied (clinical) aspects of psychology. This training occurs not in professional schools but in graduate schools of our colleges and universities. (Raimy, 1950, p. v)

What is particularly interesting to note is that the conference participants were not a bit naive about the difficulties inherent in combining both roles or the types of research skills that should comprise the major part of the training effort. A section of the conference report was devoted to enumerating methods whereby research could be made more meaningful and relevant to the trainee. Among the most important was a recommendation that research methodology be taught in the context of significant clinical problems. Indeed, specific clinical research skills suitable for training were suggested that were different in many ways from the research skills suitable for an experimental psychologist. This recognition is best exemplified in the following conclusion:

> Research training for "rat" psychology is probably most efficiently accomplished by lengthy exposure to problems in which rats are the objects of observation and discussion. Nonetheless, the problems of human beings may demand approaches other than those used in studying the lower animals. If rigorous thinking can produce good research in animal psychology, equally rigorous thinking should be possible where humans are concerned. Proper methodology and crucial issues in the field of personality may be more difficult to establish and define; the problems

faced by one field of science are rarely if ever solved by a simple carryover of tech-niques and concepts from another field. (Raimy, 1950, p. 87)

Current attacks on "positivistic" methods in clinical science most often conclude that research must take into consideration the context and experience of practice (Hoshmand & Polkinghorne, 1992) reflecting a concern clearly articulated by the conference participants almost 50 years ago. The conference participants were aware not only of the importance of developing a science that would be particu-larly applicable to clinical problems, but also of the dangers of not developing this approach, as illustrated in the following passage:

> Too often, however, clinical psychologists have been trained in rigorous thinking about nonclinical subject matter and clinical problems have been dismissed as lack-ing in "scientific" respectability. As a result, many clinicians have been unable to bridge the gap between their formal training and scientific thinking on the one hand, and the demands of practice on the other. As time passes and their skills become more satisfying to themselves and to others, the task of thinking systemat-ically and impartially becomes more difficult. (Raimy, 1950, p. 86)

Here the scientist–practitioner gap was clearly anticipated. Fears that this gap would bring about the overspecialization, rigidity, and narrowness of thinking mentioned above were important considerations in producing specific recommen-dations for dual training.

The type of research that the participants thought would be suitable for train-ing and even for dissertation requirements was much broader than one would think after reading reports on the recommendations of this conference in later years. It was thought that one of the important skills forthcoming from this train-ing effort would be an empirical approach to clinical phenomena, where observa-tion and analysis would remain the most important tools for understanding what problems were in need of further investigation and what answers were likely to be permitted by the facts observed. Training in the skills of empirical observation and measurement would help the clinician to separate preconceptions and inferences from observations. This resembles what we have termed the evaluative scientific activity of practitioners designed to increase accountability. While it was stressed that training in statistics and the writing of experimental reports would be an important part of this training, it was recognized that there would be a great deal of variability in the need for data analytic procedures and that a minimal—rather than an optimal—degree of competence was desirable.

There is little question that the Boulder conference did not intend the clinical psychologist to do his or her research in an animal laboratory or even to confine research to the traditional hypothetical-deductive strategy so popular at that time. Indeed, evaluation research and policy research were noted as being particularly important for clinical psychologists—objectives that are crucial in today's man-aged care environment. Even the study of individual cases, a procedure deeply rooted in the case-study method of psychoanalysis (Barlow & Hersen, 1984), was thought to be a legitimate exercise, as noted in the following passage:

> Intensive studies of individual cases might well reveal the significant variables required for an adequate scientific account of personality dynamics and change. The value of the individual case study as legitimate research for an advanced degree has been debated for a number of years. One cannot, however, question the case study as a means of making intimate observations, for getting "close to the data," or "securing clinical phenomena" that demand explanation, and for making dramatically evident our present lack of understanding. (Raimy, 1950, p. 85)

The participants did doubt that a single case study, no matter how brilliantly executed, could satisfy the requirements of a doctoral dissertation, but noted, "However, this question deserves further study before a categorical denial of the suitability of this form of research enterprise is made" (Raimy, 1950, p. 89). This seems a particularly "liberal" position in view of the fact that single case experimental designs, as opposed to clinical case studies, had not yet appeared.

In summary, the recommendations of the Boulder conference did not constitute an overly narrow and rigid set of restrictions on the training of clinical psychologists wherein every clinician would spend equal amounts of time on practice and the production of research, whether they were related or not. Rather, what was recommended was a well-trained clinician, who would combine clinical practice with an empiricism and a research methodology particularly suited for clinical work. Many of these empirical clinicians, but not all, would make substantive contributions to answering the important questions concerning assessment and treatment that would benefit the profession as a whole. The unquestionable rationality of this approach may be one reason for the persistence of this training model in the face of numerous alternatives proposed in recent years, which have not yet impacted to a significant degree on the majority of clinical training programs. In fact, this model has never been more appropriate than in today's managed care environment, where evaluative methodologies are essential to support practice. The question left unanswered is, Why has this model been so slow to be adopted in practice settings?

Subsequent Conferences

The Boulder conference was followed by numerous others, varying in size and scope, and occurring at a frequency of approximately every 2 years. This process was punctuated occasionally by other large conferences, often convened to review the recommendations of the Boulder conference as they applied at that time. Such conferences occurred in Miami Beach in 1958, Chicago in 1965, Vail in 1974, and Gainesville in 1990. At Miami Beach the scientist–practitioner was strongly reaffirmed as the optimal model for training clinical psychologists, describing functions that would be particularly welcome in today's managed care environment:

> In the research and evaluation area, probably lies psychology's greatest and most singular opportunity for contributing to mental health. By improving the scientific

basis for mental health programs and participating in the evaluation of the results of the wide range of mental health services and activities, psychology, along with other disciplines, not only can render the widest possible public health service by investing and sharpening the tools of mental health, but [can] provide administrators, legislators, and the public with the information they need to implement program development. As usually the only members of the mental health team with research training, the clinical psychologist, counseling psychologist, school, and other psychologist, all have a special responsibility in this area for not only utilizing their own research knowledge and skills but for bringing other psychologists and other scientists in on the many problems that lie beyond the competencies of any one psychologist. (Roe, Gustad, Moore, Ross, & Skodak, 1959, p. 38)

These characteristics apply to the practitioner as researcher and evaluator, rather than consumer. Throughout these conferences it is assumed that the clinician would be a consumer of research. Nevertheless, some problems were noted at this time, such as the fact that the Boulder conference had dealt with dual training only as a generality and had not provided guidance on the specifics of implementing this role. At Miami Beach the broad definition of research was reaffirmed, which may have reflected an early realization that the more basic "hypothesis-testing" research strategy was not being integrated successfully with the clinical aspects of training.

What was noteworthy about the next major conference in Chicago in 1965 was the almost defensive reaffirmation of the scientist–practitioner model in terms far stronger than had been used before, accompanied by a dramatic relaxing of the definition of science. This position was accompanied by a frank statement on the difficulties of doing meaningful clinical research. To quote the proceedings:

> The conferees particularly deplored the view, often implicit in the organization of clinical training programs, that clinical psychology is comprised of two separate elements: science and practice. They went on record as viewing science and practice as two facets of the same fundamental entity, declaring that a systematic search for truth can occur in a clinical setting as readily as in a laboratory. The premise leads to the conclusion that training necessarily involves an ongoing, continuous integration of science and practice and that where such integration is achieved, the relative proportions in which the two aspects are present in any particular training program are of secondary importance. (Hoch, Ross, & Winder, 1966, p. 75)

The conferees did conclude, however, that collecting empirical data is only one possible interpretation of research, even within the context of the dissertation. Other examples would be theoretical, historical, evaluative, or scholarly contributions that might not include the collection of data.

Throughout this conference an undercurrent of dissension on the adequacy of the scientist practitioner model was obvious. Warning signals were beginning to appear that the model was not working as hoped and that the model, to once again quote the conference, was not being implemented "with sincere investment and enthusiasm." Opinions to appear in print in the next several years would confirm this suspicion. Bergin, Garfield, and Thompson (1967) were to point out that these recommendations for loosening of the guidelines for dissertation research, contained in the Chicago conference, were startling and an "unambiguous challenge to a tradition which has tended to stultify research in clinical psychology and which has produced many trifling dissertations" (p. 314). They noted that this declaration of independence was a clear expression of the long frustration endured in clinical psychology training, resulting from an exclusive reliance on the experimental model for clinical research. They confessed, however, that they had not been successful in providing greater integration between research and practical training at Columbia University, widely considered a model program at the time.

Disillusionment

In retrospect, these sentiments of frustration and dissatisfaction had really been there all along. The Boulder conference affirmed the logic and integrity of the scientist–practitioner model, but expressed some question whether it could be implemented, noting that the answer was somewhere in the future. At Miami Beach in 1958, the conferees lamented the fact that the Boulder conference had not told them in what specific ways clinicians could do research or researchers could do clinical practice. And Chicago, despite the strongest defense of the model to date, deftly did away with the collection of data as one of the functions of the clinical scientist. Without question, this was shocking!

But the Chicago conference, with its glossy prose and optimistic views of the future, communicated through its inherent contradictions the frustration and pessimism evident at that time. In fact, science and practice were not integrated, and some thought this would never happen. As early as 1961, the Joint Commission on Mental Illness and Health published a report on its alarm over the developing scientist–practitioner split, particularly in view of the growing necessity for the development of new assessment and treatment procedures at that time. For, if there was one thing that most empirical clinicians and researchers agreed upon, it was that therapeutic procedures were still largely unproved (Eysenck, 1965). In a landmark book on psychotherapy research, Bergin and Strupp (1972) concluded, after interviewing leading researchers in the field of behavior change, that traditional hypothesis-testing, group-comparison research was simply not applicable to clinical problems. Their major criticism of this approach was the exaggerated importance accorded to problems of methodology and a lack of emphasis on socially important behavior change. As Bergin and Strupp observed, the kinds of effects interesting to clinicians should be so readily observable that resorting to statistical significance should not be necessary. And yet, this was an essential component of traditional research on psychotherapy and psychopathology at that time.

Professional Training in Professional Schools

Vague concerns arose from time to time in the report of the Boulder conference (Raimy, 1950). These concerns revolved around potential problems with training in the methods of science when so much time had to be devoted to professional training itself, particularly since many students were not interested in science. Ten years later, in Miami Beach in 1958, the conferees observed that the notion of a professional degree was brought up from time to time, but generally evoked little interest. Nevertheless, within 10 years of that conference the first professional degree in psychology, the doctor of psychology (Psy.D.) program at the University of Illinois, was established (Peterson, 1968). This program, and others that followed, including independent or "free-standing" professional schools of psychology, were based on multiple sources of dissatisfaction with traditional training. Among these dissatisfactions were political and logistical issues, as articulated so clearly by Albee (1970). Albee noted that psychology did not have its own captive training sites—such as hospitals for medical schools or schools for colleges of education—and therefore had to rely on other professions for practical training. Furthermore, the political control of training programs was often in the hands of experimental psychologists. Nevertheless, topping the list of reasons put forth by the founders of this movement was the incompatibility of the scientist and the professional. In a controversial but highly regarded article on the uncertain future of clinical psychology, Albee (1970) observed that one of the most serious problems for the scientist–practitioner psychologist "has been the requirement that he play the incompatible game of science" (p. 1075). Albee then detailed his view of the essentially conflicting types of research that are relevant to science and clinical work. "The clinician, including the clinical psychologist, often must engage in life history research rather than experimentation" (p. 1076). This statement reflected Albee's belief, at the time, that the causes and maintaining factors of most psychological problems lay in childhood and only longitudinal study could elucidate these causes.

In his proclamation of the first doctor of psychology program at the University of Illinois, Donald Peterson, one of the most eloquent defenders of this alternative training model (Peterson, 1976a; 1976b), noted that the number of clinical psychologists generally interested in both research and service appeared to be very small and that the professional degree recognized the reality that most students wanted to be professionals rather than scientists. To do this properly and to teach the abundance of knowledge and skills required of the thoroughly trained professional in the 1970s, the competing activity of research training would have to be sharply curtailed or eliminated. As Peterson observed, "Our students now spend three-sevenths of their time doing dissertation research and studying languages. That is an intolerably ineffective use of expensive resources for people who are planning to enter careers of professional service" (Peterson, 1968, p. 511). The clear implication of this statement is that research training has no more relevance for the professional than learning foreign languages.

Continuing a tradition begun in Chicago in 1965, the doctoral dissertation became the primary target for those questioning the relevance of research. Adler (1972) observed that the research techniques utilized in most dissertations "are those of obsolete research methodology essentially inapplicable to the illumination of meaningful social and clinical issues" (p. 72). Adler proposed that any research in the new doctor of psychology program would be submitted to the test of relevance for practice regardless of the methodology. Stricker (1973), echoing a broad consensus of the times, reiterated Bergin and Strupp's observations on the peripheral and trivial nature of most dissertations that were making little or no contribution to knowledge. In 1973 Stricker remembered the recommendations for a dramatic broadening of the definitions of research made in Chicago in 1965, but observed that these recommended changes had no parallel in the halls of our universities where "business appears to go on as usual."

Yet another major conference on training in clinical psychology, the Vail conference, took place for a week during July of 1973. Recommendations from this conference (Korman, 1976) went far beyond previous conferences in explicitly endorsing the creation of doctor of psychology degrees and downplaying the scientist–practitioner model as the one appropriate model for training clinical psychologists. While noting that some programs may wish to retain the Ph.D. and, by implication, the traditional scientist–practitioner model, recommendations for research training included a reaffirmation and extension of those recommendations made in Chicago 8 years earlier, calling for greatly increased flexibility in dissertation research criteria. This included a wider range of possible dissertation chairs, persons presumably with less "traditional" research interests. For the first time in the history of these conferences on psychology training, no section describing recommended research training was included. Remarks on research are confined to those that advocate greatly increased flexibility and relevance in doctoral dissertation research. As Stricker (1975) observed, "The recommendations emanating from this conference were often contradictory and inconsistent, making rejection by mainstream psychology seem inevitable and perhaps throwing out a few promising babies along with the bath water" (p. 1063), but the devaluation of the scientist–practitioner role during this conference was the culmination of a train of thought stretching back years.

This devaluation received a boost from economic and health care policy trends in the late 1970s and early 1980s. As presented more fully in Chapter 2, the rapid growth of health insurance, including coverage for mental health, had the effect of expanding considerably the fee for service market for the delivery of behavioral health care at that time. This, in turn, increased demand for training in the provision of these services across professions and at all levels of training from bachelors to doctoral level. In view of this demand and the ready availability of reimbursement, market pressures favored flexible practitioners who could operate in any number of clinical settings. The market seemed to have little need for those who could bring to bear the scientific underpinnings of practice to clinical and educational programs.

All of this began to change in the late 1980s and particularly the 1990s as behavioral health care costs skyrocketed and the payers of behavioral health care, mostly government and industry, decided that these costs must be "managed." The first generation of managed care emphasized cost containment and "supply side" methods of reducing the utilization of services (Manderscheid & Henderson, 1996; Sobel, 1995). But increasingly, payers of these services have also emphasized an increase in the quality of behavioral health care; that is, individuals under care must demonstrate an alleviation of behavioral problems and a return to functioning. The quality imperative has proved to be a particularly difficult goal to achieve for reasons described in succeeding chapters, but an attempt to deliver services that are *both* effective and efficient is now the hallmark of "Generation II" of managed care (Strosahl, 1994, 1996). This is the change that has brought the scientist–practitioner model back to center stage in behavioral health care.

The Scientist–Practitioner Model Reaffirmed

Few psychologists reconsidering the role of research in the training process over the decades have held any illusions concerning the success of the scientist–practitioner model as it has been implemented. In an insightful and personal statement on the issue as early as 1966, Garfield concluded that all of the major discontents and confusions within clinical psychology could be traced to the uniqueness of the "Boulder experiment," as opposed to failure of the model as implemented.

Garfield attributed this failure to a lack of adequate role models for psychologists in training. "Unfortunately, they are not given an integrated model with which to identify, but are confronted instead by two apparently conflicting models—the scientific research model and the clinical practitioner model. As I see it, the Boulder model is really not available to them . . . " (Garfield, 1966, p. 357). The biggest disappointment of this failure, according to Garfield, was the observation that practicing psychologists "have contributed so little to a better understanding of what is involved in modifying personality and behavior and in contributing to newer and more efficient ways of helping people with problems of adjustment" (p. 358).

But far from seeking alternative models or abandoning research training, Garfield concluded at that time that it was more important than ever that this be made workable. Echoing the Joint Commission on Mental Illness and Health (1961), where the dimensions of our ignorance about assessment, therapy, prevention, and other aspects of psychological intervention were observed, Garfield concluded that there are few fields that need research as badly as clinical psychology. In this respect, the lack of research activity by Ph.D. psychologists was a social and professional tragedy. What was most needed to temper this tragedy was the production of a clinical psychologist who could solve significant problems, devise new techniques, and evaluate both these new procedures as well as adaptations of older ones. This could be accomplished only through a true integration of research and practice and the devising of clinical research procedures that would be fully appropriate to the clinical situation.

Today, in the era of managed care, this type of professional is needed more than ever. Yet the challenge of putting research and practice together remains large. The recommendations for developing a research methodology applicable to the clinic were made with equal intensity at Boulder in 1949 and at every conference since, without any discernible change in the products of the graduate schools of clinical psychology. Despite progress in recent years, the need for applied research and for clinically relevant methods to do it are as vital now as they were in 1966, when Garfield observed that most clinical psychologist students saw research solely as a hurdle to overcome before hanging up their shingles to practice psychotherapy.

Garfield was not the only one who strongly reaffirmed the scientist–practitioner model during this period and after (e.g., Proshansky, 1972; Schover, 1980; Tyler & Speisman, 1967; Wollersheim, 1974). Surveys of practicing psychologists conducted during this period overwhelmingly reaffirmed the scientist–practitioner model of training as unique and appropriate. Perry warned in 1979 against relying on others for the production of new knowledge that would form the basis of any further advance in the practice of clinical psychology. Perry quoted Ericksen (1966), "Insofar as professional psychology becomes pinched off from scientific psychology, it will be taking one clear backward step toward becoming a second-class service technology" (Ericksen, 1966, p. 953). Professional schools of psychology, particularly those with no university affiliation, were seen as a move in this direction. The same situation in medicine in 1910 provoked a radical restructuring of medical education from a varied series of "free-standing" schools to a strong affirmation that medical education could be administered properly only in the context of the university (Flexner, 1910).

While many others defended the scientist–practitioner model, none did it better than the chair of the committee that put forth the original recommendation for this model in 1947. Approaching the end of his distinguished career as a clinical psychologist, David Shakow (1976) concluded that the viability of the scientist–practitioner model "derives fundamentally from the recognition by clinical psychologists that in the scientist–practitioner model they have captured most adequately the underlying motivation that led them to select psychology as a life work which is other-understanding through self-understanding by way of science" (p. 554). Shakow challenged training programs to ask themselves, "How well do the programs develop persons who can examine evidence critically, who are concerned with the advancement of knowledge, and who, if necessary, can carry on activities directed at the acquisition of this knowledge?" (p. 560).

The value of this training was affirmed once again at the most recent conference on scientist–practitioner training in Gainesville, Florida, in 1990 (Belar & Perry, 1992). Reflecting on a common misunderstanding of the scientist–practitioner, delegates to this conference concluded that many psychologists have misunderstood this model, assuming that one is not acting as a scientist unless he or she publishes in scientific journals. Rather, the integration of scientific methods into practice is the hallmark of the model, and the basic requirement of scientific practice is that results need to be communicable. In fact, occasional surveys suggest that if research is defined more broadly, psychologists trained in the Boulder model have positive attitudes toward research and remain involved in some form of research or evaluative activity, even if they don't publish the results (Barrom, Shadish, & Montgomery, 1988).

In the face of an overwhelming reaffirmation of the importance of producing scientist–practitioners, the practical issues basic to this deeply philosophical confrontation were often overlooked. For example, there is nothing in the arguments of those advocating professional schools of psychology that would preclude scientific training as an integral part of clinical work, let alone program development and evaluation. Even those advocating the abandonment of the scientist–practitioner model in favor of a professional model at the time (e.g., Peterson, 1976b), did not advocate a lack of acquaintance with research methodology. Others (e.g., Stricker, 1975; 1992) emphasized more frequent and intensive clinical learning experiences rather than a deemphasis on research. Naturally, research that competed with these clinical practice experiences would have a lower priority. But, ever since the Boulder conference, everyone writing about ideal training has advocated a clinical research methodology that does not compete with clinical work, but rather is directly related to clinical work and the acquisition of new knowledge about clinical intervention. Developments in managed care have greatly expanded the role of the scientist practitioner beyond routine direct clinical work to the provision of accountability for clinical and educational interventions in whatever form they are administered. These developments have created imperatives for the reintegration of science into practice.

A Historical Perspective on the Scientist–Practitioner Split

Ideal Model: Inadequate Methods

The high ideal so often espoused—that all practitioners will participate in the research process and advance our knowledge—has not happened at this time, as noted above. The appropriate research strategies and methodology to reach this ideal, recommended in the Boulder conference, and in every conference and paper on the subject since that time, have not been forthcoming. The true integration of research and practice so long envisioned has not occurred due primarily to two factors: (a) the almost universally acknowledged inadequacies of traditional research methodology to address issues important to practice, and (b) the lack of a clear link between empiricism and professional success in the practice context. In this section, we will consider the first of these two factors. The second factor will be addressed later, particularly in Chapters 2 and 4.

Every recommendation that has been made since 1949, while endorsing greater integration of research and practice and the development of new research methodology, has been unable to outline specifically what this would entail. And each training conference or each well-thought-out observation published individually has lamented previous efforts for not specifying how research could be accomplished in practice. Leitenberg observed as early as 1974, as did Garfield in 1966, that the scientist–practitioner model had never really been tested in clinical psychology because the research methodology taught to our students involved an approach that had been developed in laboratories of experimental psychology and was inappropriate to the subject at hand. To a large extent, this is still true today.

The overriding consequence of the lack of an appropriate research methodology for practice has been a disillusionment with research on the part of professionals in training in all health and educational fields, a disillusionment fueled by the economic trends of the 1970s and 1980s. The often noted observation that research training is viewed as a hurdle to be circumvented, if possible, on the way to the professional degree, and the observation that relatively few trained practitioners with the inclination or skills to do research are doing any research at all, confirms the general disillusionment. It is not the idea that was wrong, but rather the inability to develop the tools to implement the idea in a practice context where use of these tools is essential. Ironically, the rise of managed care is making traditional group comparison research methods more practically relevant as one part of program development and evaluation. Even there, however, it is important to build treatment development on the observations and realities of practitioners, and for that new methods are needed.

This state of affairs is not limited to North America. In an important survey of clinical psychologists and clinical psychology training programs in Australia and the United Kingdom, Martin (1989) found that the scientist–practitioner model was strongly endorsed in these countries. But data collected from systematic surveys revealed that the ideals of this model had not been successfully implemented, much to the frustration of programs and practitioners alike. Martin suggested that the major obstacle was the dearth of training in appropriate applied methodologies suitable to practice situations, such as program evaluation and time-series methodologies. This point of view was underscored in the United Kingdom by Watts (1992) in his presidential address to the British Psychological Society.

This issue was well described early on in the well-known survey of leading psychologists and psychiatrists conducted by Bergin and Strupp in the early 1970s (Bergin & Strupp, 1972). This survey substantiated the comments from individual leaders in the field that the research approach itself was the major reason that students in the behavior-change field did not have a scientific methodology that was appropriate to applied problems. Bergin and Strupp concluded:

> Among researchers as well as statisticians, there is a growing disaffection from traditional experimental designs and statistical procedures which are held inappropriate to the subject matter under study. This judgment applies with particular force to research in the area of therapeutic change, and our emphasis on the value of experimental case studies underscores this point. We strongly agree that most of the standard experimental designs and statistical procedures have exerted, and are continuing to exert, a constricting effect on fruitful inquiry, and they serve to perpetuate an unwarranted overemphasis on methodology. More accurately, the exaggerated importance accorded experimental and statistical dicta cannot be blamed on the techniques proper—after all, they are merely tools—but their veneration mirrors a prevailing philosophy among behavioral scientists which subordinates problems to methodology. The insidious effects of this trend are tellingly illustrated by the typical graduate student who is often more interested in the details of a factorial design than in the problem he sets out to study; worse, the selection of a problem is dictated by the experimental design. Needless to say, the student's approach faithfully reflects the convictions and teachings of his mentors. (Bergin & Strupp, 1972, p. 440)

Today these concerns tend to be expressed in terms of the limited applicability of traditional research methods, particularly large clinical trials, to practice situations (APA Task Force on Psychological Intervention Guidelines, 1995; Barlow, 1996a; 1996b). In the typical clinical trial, interventions, whether drug or psychological, that are thought to be appropriate for a particular psychological disorder are tested for their efficacy. The intervention thought to be effective is usually administered to a large group of patients, and the results are compared to the results from other interventions, placebo controls, whether drug or psychosocial, or no treatment, in a suitably matched large group of patients. Since at least 20 or 30 patients—and often hundreds—must complete treatment as well as a suitable follow-up period, these clinical trials often take years to complete. Such issues as the homogeneity of patient populations in these clinical trials, the assumed lack of comorbidity, and the supposed rigid application of treatment protocols lead practitioners to believe that the results of clinical trials evaluating the efficacy of treatment are not applicable to their practice. Furthermore, we are only now beginning to research the actual dissemination of empirically supported treatments, so empirical evidence on these concerns has been very limited.

These concerns, of course, are not new. Throughout the 1960s, particularly at the major conferences, there is an undercurrent of disaffection with traditional research methodology emanating from the experimental laboratories. In fact, as we have seen, as far back as 1949 the participants at the Boulder conference also recognized that traditional experimental research approaches were probably not fully adequate for use by the majority of clinicians in studying clinical problems. But with the emphasis on promulgating the scientist–practitioner role, little attention was paid to the specific limitations of traditional research strategies for applied problems, nor were detailed suggestions forthcoming on what alternatives were available. With the widespread realization of limitations of traditional research methodology, an analysis of the specific inadequacies of these procedures as applied to clinical and educational problems began (Barlow & Hersen, 1984; Bergin & Strupp, 1972). Among these were practical and ethical limitations to conducting clinical trials on the part of practitioners, as well as other characteristics of traditional research methodology that limited the relevance of traditional research findings to practice. We will briefly review some of these specific issues, beginning with practical factors that preclude practitioners from carrying out clinical trials and related clinical research. In the following section, we will review factors that limit the applicability of clinical research to the practice setting.

Why Practitioners Have Not Done Research

With some exceptions, research strategies utilized in clinical trials emanate from the laboratories of experimental psychology. These strategies emphasize data collected from large groups of subjects, usually animals, which are then analyzed either within or between large groups. The historical origins of this approach have been described in Barlow and Hersen (1984), but applying this approach to clinical or educational practice poses enormous practical difficulties for erstwhile applied researchers. As noted above, this strategy requires, among other things, the matching of large numbers of clients who are relatively homogeneous. For example, if one were studying the efficacy of a particular intervention for patients with generalized anxiety disorder, one would need approximately 20 such patients matched on relevant background variables such as severity of the problem as well as other variables thought to be pertinent in the particular experiment, such as age, sex, personality characteristics, history of previous treatment, and the like. Ideally, these patients would be treated at approximately the same time. The simplest type of experiment would involve treating one group of 10 of these patients and examining the effects in comparison to a second untreated group of 10. More sophisticated factorial experiments looking at the interaction of treatments with organismic variables thought to interact with treatment, such as ages of patients or severity of problems, would require in some cases far more than these two basic groups, greatly increasing the number of subjects required. Following tradition, the minimum number of subjects per group is approximately 10, although methodologists generally prefer a far greater number to allow one to determine the effects of a given intervention over and above the considerable intersubject variability that inevitably occurs in such an effort.

As many young researchers have discovered, the activities associated with this type of effort, such as gathering and analyzing data, following patients, paying experimental therapists, and simply recruiting the patients, may take years. This is one reason that much of this research, particularly in the context of doctoral dissertations, has been carried out with readily available, large pools of subjects such as college sophomores. But the effects of these interventions on college sophomores or other analogue populations will not necessarily be the same as the effects on clinical populations (e.g., Barlow, 1994; Mathews, 1978), making the relevance of such efforts questionable in many cases.

This is further complicated by tremendous advances in the technology of assessing specific behavioral problems in recent years. As noted earlier in this chapter, an applied researcher must spend much of his or her time keeping up with sophisticated advances in measurement procedures, often requiring intimate knowledge of physiological monitoring equipment and computer technology. For example, clinical research on sexual problems now requires a sophisticated laboratory, expensive physiological monitoring equipment, the potential for assaying biochemical samples in some instances, and data-reduction procedures that have become so complex that specific software packages are now available. To set up such a laboratory, taking advantage of the recent advances in objective measurement of sexual arousal, takes the better part of a year and costs many thousands of dollars. Similarly, in the field of anxiety disorders, rather complex verifiable behavioral observations of the consequences of anxiety, along with portable physiological equipment capable of measuring the physiological component of anxiety in the client's natural environment, have become very important parts of the assessment of anxiety in clinical research centers dealing with these disorders. In addition, new assessment procedures and strategies are developing continually, and meaningful clinical research efforts must incorporate these advances in assessment to ensure the greatest relevance of the data from these studies. In clinical practice, on the other hand, where the emphasis is on dealing with an individual, a family, or a small group of individuals, these sorts of efforts are very difficult to mount, even if one had the necessary funds, equipment, and space to carry them out. And yet, some quantifiable assessment is essential, as recent developments in outcomes assessment in the context of managed care have reaffirmed.

Practitioners must be concerned also with the ethical implications of any research efforts. In applied research settings, most of which are connected with large universities or medical schools, committees exist to determine if risks are inherent in the research procedures and, if so, whether the benefits of the research to the individuals participating and to society at large outweigh the risks. This problem is most apparent in withholding treatment from clients in the control group when one is dealing with therapy-outcome research. This cannot be done without careful consideration of the risks involved. Of course, in most instances there is no evidence that the treatment works in the first place, which forms the basis for conducting research on its efficacy. Therefore, one could argue that withholding an unproved treatment from a control group might be less of a risk than applying this same treatment to the experimental group. But, in the area of clinical practice, where the goal is always to relieve human suffering in the individual, intervening with some treatment, however inadequate or unproved, will always be preferable to leaving a distressed client to his or her own resources.

In addition to these marked practical differences, there are obvious procedural and philosophical differences between practice and research. The goal of the practitioner necessarily must be to get patients better as quickly as possible. The nature, length, and intensity of any intervention is tailored to the individual client and his or her individual problem. But in research on behavior-change procedures, patients are randomly assigned to fixed treatment conditions, most often in the absence of any individual behavioral analysis that might result in variations of the treatment offered. In addition, practitioners will alter therapeutic strategies as soon as it seems reasonable and beneficial to the client, based on some ongoing monitoring of the program, however informal. In research, on the other hand, treatment must continue irrespective of individual progress, since the comparisons made at a posttest will examine data from those who do not improve as a result of the fixed treatment protocol, and average the results in with those who improve in order to look at overall differences among the treated and control groups. In most cases, if this research using traditional methodology is conducted properly, those evaluating the therapy and in a position to make changes in the therapeutic protocol will not even be aware of a specific individual's success or failure, because they will be blind to the assignment of clients to conditions. For these reasons, professionals seldom act as scientists in the sense of researchers or evaluators conducting large clinical trials.

A final reason for a lack of research is that it takes time, and many practice settings are quite demanding. Different aspirations may be practical in different settings. In the present volume, we distinguish between general practice settings in which there is little interest in empirical work, and work inside formal health delivery systems in which empirical work may pay off quickly for the organization. We will address both of these contexts in the chapters that follow. For example, even in the most practically oriented general practice settings, clinical replication series are needed and mountable (see Chapter 9), while in formal health care delivery systems science can help these systems succeed in a competitive market (see Chapter 4).

Why Practitioners Have Not Consumed Research Findings

These practical and strategic issues are not the only factors inhibiting practitioners from an involvement with science. If this were the case, practitioners would certainly participate with enthusiasm where possible and where resources allowed, for the results at least would be directly applicable to their work. Furthermore, practitioners would eagerly await research findings from major research centers that would help them improve their individual practice. But other more important limitations exist that diminish the relevance of research to practice settings. In the last analysis, it is these issues, more than any other factors, that have accounted for the scientist–practitioner split and led to a lack of interest among professional students in research and research methodology as well as a subsequent deemphasis on research training in graduate and professional schools.

Statistical versus Clinical Significance   One of the strongest and most pervasive traditions accompanying traditional experimental methodology has been a reliance on statistical significance to determine the existence of the effects of various interventions. This reliance on statistical significance has come under sweeping attack, even in basic research where investigators have been concerned that statistical determinations hide important sources of variability and lead investigators to assume that experimental effects are important if they reach statistical significance; even though they may, in fact, be very weak. This is particularly true if the number of organisms or observations within the experiment are very large. For example, Meehl (1978) considers that this approach to the basic science of psychology has produced "low grade ore" or very weak and unreliable findings that are often difficult to replicate, given the large intersubject variability inherent in psychological experiments. In some cases an experimental effect will reach statistical significance, most often defined as the .05 level of probability that the results would occur assuming only chance, while attempts at replication might indicate that there is a .25 probability that the results would have occurred assuming that only chance was responsible. Meehl (1978) concluded that this reliance on statistical significance was one of the "worst things that ever happened in the history of psychology" (p. 817).

The important issue in this controversy is the size of the experimental effect with which one is dealing, since statistical significance, even when properly interpreted, bears no relation to the importance of or the size of the effect. The noted experimentalist S. S. Stevens observed, "Can no one recognize a decisive result without a significance test?" (1958, p. 853). These arguments have been elaborated over the years by many leading experimental theorists such as Bakan (1966), Cronbach (1975), Cronbach and Snow (1977), and Tyler (1931) and more recently by clinical scientists (Jacobson, Follette, & Revenstorf, 1984; Jacobson & Truax, 1991). In one of the more comprehensive discussions of this issue from a basic experimental point of view, Carver (1978) recommended abandoning all statistical significance testing and reverting to alternative ways of evaluating research results. These strategies would involve more direct observation of the data, including strength of effect and replication. Using educational research as his starting point, Carver suggested that researchers should ignore statistical significance testing when designing research since a study with results that cannot be meaningfully interpreted without looking at the *p* values is a poorly designed study.

One of the problems lies in the word *significant*. A statistically significant result can be very trivial indeed and be very far from the usual meaning of the word *significant*. And yet, once one achieves statistical significance, typically it is simply reported in a journal or book, with most consumers of research assuming that the result is truly significant or clinically important.

When these procedures are used in applied research, particularly to determine if the results of an intervention are effective, the problems are multiplied and compounded. The major issue here is that the practitioner is always concerned with the individual, and statistical significance says nothing about improvement in an individual patient undergoing that treatment (Barlow, 1981). This is best illustrated by referring once again to our simple, between-group, experimental comparison of a treatment for clients with generalized anxiety disorder. For example, if anxiety were reliably measured on a 0 to 100 scale, with 100 representing severe anxiety, a treatment that improved each patient in a group of individuals with GAD from 80 to 75 would be statistically significant if patients with GAD in the control group remained at 80. But this improvement would be of little use to the clinician, since the patients in the treatment group would probably not notice the improvement themselves and would certainly still be very anxious. An improvement of 40 or 50 points might be necessary before both the clinician and the client considered the change clinically important (Barlow & Hersen; 1984; Chassan, 1960). Statisticians will quickly point out, of course, that this problem is easily correctable by setting a different criterion for "effectiveness." More recently, clinical scientists such as Neil Jacobson and his colleagues (Jacobson & Truax, 1991) have proposed some strategies to be reviewed briefly in Chapter 3 that accomplish this goal.

In fact, this intersubject variability can also account for a tendency to underestimate clinical effectiveness of a given treatment when relying on statistical significance to determine the presence of an effect. For example, a given treatment might be quite effective for a few patients, while the remaining patients do not show substantial improvement, or even deteriorate somewhat. Statistically, then, the experimental group does not differ from the control group, whose members are relatively unchanged. When broad divergence such as this occurs among clients in response to an intervention, as is often the case in clinical research (Bergin & Lambert, 1978), statistical treatments will average out the clinical effect along with changes due to unwanted sources of variability. These problems have been referred to generally as clinical versus statistical significance (Barlow & Hersen, 1984; Hersen & Barlow, 1976).

Some have attempted to correct for the problem in determining the size of effect statistically by using such techniques as percentage of variance accounted for (Hays, 1963). But, as Yeaton and Sechrest (1981) point out, these procedures do little to help the clinician attempting to interpret clinical research, because even procedures shown to account for a large percentage of the variance in the group as a whole may be quite ineffective for some specific patients in the group.

More recently, a statistical technique called "meta-analysis" has been applied to psychotherapy research, beginning with the pioneering efforts of Smith, Glass, and Miller (1980). In conducting a meta-analysis, one calculates the effect size of an intervention. An effect size is basically a comparison of the amount of change or the size of an effect in the group receiving the intervention versus a control group that receives an alternative intervention or perhaps no intervention. In a meta-analysis the results from many studies testing the efficacy of a specific intervention, or perhaps a more general intervention such as psychotherapy, are summated. Effect sizes are typically calculated using a common metric—the common metric being a standard score (known as a Z score). For example, an effect size of 1.0 indicates that an average patient in the group receiving the intervention would be at the 84 percentile of scores for patients in the comparison group. These calculations assume that scores from patients in all groups are normally distributed. An effect size of 2.0 would indicate that the average treated person was at the 97th percentile in scores in the untreated group. But as Jacobson and Truax (1991) point out, effect sizes can also be unrelated to clinical significance. For example, if the variability is very low in a group of treated patients, such that each patient in the group improves a little bit whereas each patient in the comparison group remains relatively stable, one could obtain a very large effect size but a clinically insignificant finding. On the other hand, as Rosenthal (1995) has pointed out, sometimes relatively small effect sizes can be extremely clinically significant if one is, for example, talking about an intervention across tens of thousands of individuals in the population that could be shown to save two to three hundred lives. Rosenthal cites the example of the Physicians Aspirin Study in which those patients taking aspirin on a regular basis evidenced a 1% advantage over those taking placebo in the prevention of heart attacks and deaths from heart attacks. But since the number of patients in the aspirin and placebo groups was each approximately 11,000, this accounted for almost 100 lives.

In recent years, scientists conducting clinical trials have become more aware of this problem and have begun to report results in terms of percentages of patients reaching a certain clinical criterion such as "high endstate functioning" which, in many studies, is analogous of being symptom-free or "cured" (Barlow, 1994). But a firm convention has yet to be adopted in many areas of research.

The Average Client   In 1865 one of the first great scientist practitioners, the physician and researcher Claude Bernard, castigated a colleague interested in studying the properties of urine (Bernard, 1957). This colleague proposed collecting specimens, from urinals in a centrally located train station, to determine properties of the average European urine. Bernard countered that this would tell us very little about urine or the individuals providing the samples. Despite Bernard's warning, this tradition has continued in research, limiting the relevance of this type of research to practitioners interested in an individual client (Barlow & Hersen, 1984; Hersen & Barlow, 1976; Sidman, 1960). This critical issue is the averaging of results. To take our example again, 10 patients homogeneous with generalized anxiety disorder would bring very different histories, personality variables, comorbid disorders, and environmental situations to the treatment setting and will respond in varying ways to treatment. That is, some clients will improve and others will not. This is because any group of patients chosen for an experimental investigation will very seldom reach the degree of homogeneity that would lead to a relatively uniform response among all members of the group. In fact, as Kiesler (1966, 1971) pointed out several years ago in what he called the patient uniformity myth, patients are most often heterogeneous, as described above. This makes it very difficult, if not impossible, to generalize results obtained from the average response of the group as a whole to an individual client walking into the therapist's office. Therefore, the practitioner cannot know if a treatment that reached statistical significance (or evidenced a substantial effect size) will be effective with his or her particular patient.

These problems, of course, have their origins in traditional research methodology and, in particular, the improper use of sampling theory (Fisher, 1925; Hays, 1963). Sampling theory dictates that if one is going to make adequate inferences about the population with which one is working, then one should randomly sample this population and then apply a particular therapeutic technique to a randomly assigned subgroup of this random sample. Any effects that one then achieves could be said to apply, at some level of probability, to the population as a whole and to other random samples taken from it.

Translating this into applied research, one would have to determine all of the relevant characteristics of the disorder of interest. This would yield the "conceptual population" (e.g., all persons with panic disorder). All clients with these characteristics would then need to be identified. This would yield the "known population" or that group for whom the probability of being selected is one divided by the number in the known population. One would then have to draw a random sample from this known population and randomly assign subjects to a control group or a treatment group. If one found a statistically significant effect then, theoretically, one would conclude that the treatment would be generally effective with people having this disorder and that similar results would be obtained with other random samples. In other words, if all the methodological requirements are in place, the results will not only have internal validity (an unambiguous relation between an independent and dependent variable) but also external validity (generalizability to other conditions, populations, or situations). But applied researchers discovered long ago that there are many practical problems with this model.

First, while great progress has been made in the clarity of our conceptual populations, known populations are not isomorphic with them. For example, while we can define exactly what we mean by "panic disorder" we do not know who has this disorder and who does not. A person with panic disorder who is wealthy will probably not be known to a researcher drawing a sample from a county hospital. A male with panic disorder may be more reluctant to seek treatment than a female. Usually we can only guess what the factors may be that distinguish potential subjects who are detected from those who are not, and usually the importance of these factors to clinical outcome are also unknown. This means that it is impossible to characterize the exact relationship between conceptual and known populations.

Second, even within the more limited group that is known, random selection is not possible. Clients will agree or not agree to come into therapy, and the sources of this agreement or disagreement are themselves usually not known.

Third, random assignment is often not possible. Clients may refuse certain treatments, or may drop out once they are assigned. Even if the rates of dropout are the same, the reasons may differ, and thus bias the groups in undetectable ways. For example, clients in a demanding treatment group may drop out because it is too demanding. Clients in a control group may drop out because treatment is not demanding enough. If the researcher has assessment devices already in place, these reasons (and thus the nonequivalence of the resulting groups) might at least be detected, but there are myriad possible reasons for dropout and one can never be sure that all possible sources have been examined.

Finally, even if all the requirements had been met, the result will necessarily apply only to other random samples from the known population. Clients seek out clinicians for many nonrandom reasons (reputation, location, position, fee structure, referrals, and so on), and there is nothing that ensures that results with a random sample will apply to specific nonrandom samples such as these. Thus, there is no guarantee of external validity as a statistical must in the practical world that applies research results.

Applied researchers understand these problems and have dealt with them in a number of ways. The most common strategy seems to be trying to obtain a homogeneous sample—that is, a large patient group who would be very much alike on all relevant characteristics (Barlow & Hersen, 1984). This strategy admits that the conceptual and known population may differ, but it attempts to make the results more applicable by highly refining the conceptual population. There are two desirable effects this might have. First, differences in responding among the clients in the group might be reduced somewhat and the effects of the treatment, if they existed, would become more clear. Second, in view of our inability to randomly sample and assign, it seeks external validity based on the more practical principle of logical generalization (Edgington, 1966, 1967). If a patient group is highly specified, it is logical that these results might generalize to other persons with the same characteristics.

The homogeneous sample strategy makes implementation of the research model all the more impractical in real-world clinical settings, however, since highly refined groups are difficult to assemble. Furthermore, its possible benefits have usually not appeared. Research experience has shown that even these small groups of homogeneous patients vary greatly in their responses to treatment, producing a large amount of intersubject variability that necessitates statistical determination of an effect. Meanwhile, the great restriction of population characteristics prevents the researcher from examining empirically whether the refined group is in fact, and not just in theory, different than a more heterogeneous group of clients, such as might be seen in a general clinical practice.

The applicability of the principle of logical generalization is likewise limited because the next patient walking into a practitioner's office is unlikely to be identical to anybody in the homogeneous sample. It would be more practical for practitioners to judge the similarity of their patients to those experimental patients showing varying degrees of improvement and to determine which of their clients are most like those that showed marked improvement among the experimental clients. This procedure will be discussed in greater detail in Chapter 3.

Research Has Little Influence on Practice

In many ways, the prevailing experimental strategy growing out of the traditional research methodology of treating large groups of subjects, determining the average results, calculating statistical significance in comparison to some control group, and then inferring that these results indicate that a treatment may be effective for any individual client seen by a practitioner has served to widen the scientist–practitioner gap. Practitioners have been disillusioned as to the relevance of traditional clinical research in contributing to their effectiveness with individual clients with complex human problems (e.g., Cohen, Sargent, & Sechrest, 1986).

This was true even as early as the 1960s and early 1970s, as is most evident in comments from leading clinicians surveyed by Bergin and Strupp (1972). Most prominent among these comments is the oft-noted quote from Matarazzo, " . . . even after 15 years, few of my research findings affect my practice. Psychological science per se doesn't guide me one bit. I still read avidly, but this is of little direct practical help. My clinical experience is the only thing that has helped me in my practice to date . . . " (Bergin & Strupp, 1972, p. 340). People were less surprised with Carl Rogers, who took the same position; but erstwhile scientist practitioners were still a bit shaken when, in 1969, he advocated abandoning formal research in psychotherapy altogether (as cited in Bergin & Strupp, 1972). It was not a large inferential leap to assume that many clinicians who have not achieved this prominence, but are nevertheless trained in the scientist–practitioner model, suffered an equal lack of influence from research.

As noted throughout this chapter, this state of affairs is not unique to the human service field or the area of behavior change in particular. For example, in the field of rehabilitation medicine, Schindele (1981) describes in some detail how the same limitations in experimental research methodology, described above, severely limit the usefulness and applicability of research in rehabilitation to the practice of rehabilitation medicine.

Where Did Practitioners Get Their Techniques?

Since it seems clear that applied research has had little influence on practice, the question arises, where did practitioners get their techniques and procedures during the last several decades? Every day thousands of people entered professional settings with a variety of complaints representing the full range of psychological, educational, social, or medical problems. These problems were assessed, the problem was formulated, and the intervention was conceptualized and delivered.

As did Matarazzo when he was in training (Bergin & Strupp, 1972), practitioners reported learning their procedures from watching their teachers. Subsequently, these practitioners may have altered the therapeutic procedures learned in professional school, based on their own trial-and-error experience (Hoshmand & Polkinghorne, 1992). Very often these procedures are described in the context of systems or theories that in turn arose out of the trial-and-error experience of previous practitioners who had elaborated their approaches into systems. Since some clients always get better, no matter what one does, there is ample opportunity for practitioners to commit a cognitive error and attribute their success to their particular procedure (Dawes, 1994) and to discount failures for one reason or another, such as lack of motivation of the client.

Those early practitioners who could communicate their theories clearly, or who presented new and exciting principles, tended to attract many followers. If these same people wrote prolifically and/or gave numerous workshops, then their procedures would be far more likely to be adopted through sheer exposure than would procedures of those who gave fewer workshops or wrote very little about what they were doing. That practitioners are more influenced by workshops, conversations with colleagues, and manuscripts describing clinical innovations than by research has been verified in a number of surveys (e.g., Beutler, Williams, & Wakefield, 1993; Cohen, 1979). But it seems that these procedures are rarely applied in quite the same way as they were demonstrated. The same trial-and-error experience engaged in continuously by practitioners, as well as conversations with colleagues, would ensure that new variations or twists of the original procedures would be implemented and would vary from practitioner to practitioner. Thus, any patient with some psychopathology, for example, walking into a therapist's office 10 years ago, might receive a variety of treatments for exactly the same condition, ranging from primal scream therapy through long-term daily sessions of psychoanalysis or short-term rational emotive therapy, depending on which office the client enters. Even today, in the era of managed care and brief treatments, great variability exists in therapeutic approaches as a function of settings and clinicians (I. O. M., 1992). Unfortunately, the client would be unlikely to benefit from many of the more radical versions of the hundreds of different types of psychotherapy developed over the years if they are practiced with theoretical purity.

But few procedures were practiced with theoretical purity, to the great advantage of millions seeking help from psychotherapy. Fortunately, given our inadequate data base, therapists continued to innovate and often hit upon successful procedures. For example, therapists from psychoanalytic, behavioral, and rational emotive schools, treating agoraphobia, would all recommend in vivo exposure as part of the treatment, albeit for different theoretical reasons, and in the context of a variety of additional procedures. And chances are that the clients experiencing all of these treatments would benefit (Barlow, 1988; Barlow & Hersen, 1984). Similar statements could be made about educational or rehabilitation practices, and the like.

The emergence of clinical practice guidelines or "best practice" procedures (Chambless et al., 1996; Dobson & Craig, 1998; Hayes, 1998; Hayes, Follette, Dawes, & Grady, 1995) has greatly changed this custom, as articulated in subsequent chapters. These methods have arisen in an attempt to correct the enormous variability in practice patterns around the country and to provide, ideally, a more scientific and economically feasible base for practice.

The Future: Clinical Practice in the Era of Managed Care

As psychologists and other mental health professionals anguished over the scientist–practitioner split and brainstormed methods for closing the gap, a revolution was brewing during the 1980s. As the costs of providing health care— including behavioral health care—spiraled, governments and policy makers began to look more closely at the provision of behavioral health care with an eye to holding down costs while ostensibly maintaining quality in terms of the effectiveness of the health care delivery system. More than 124 million persons are now covered by private managed behavioral health care plans (Oos & Stair, 1996). While this has severely disrupted the clinical practice patterns of many behavioral health care providers, it has, in an ironic way, underscored the true spirit of the recommendations from the Boulder conference held back in 1949. For whatever the goals of managed care in the United States, it is providing a new context for the provision of behavioral health care services. This new context, which is beginning to go beyond mere reduction of costs to an emphasis on effectiveness and efficiency of interventions, is forcing practitioners to reexamine the relevance of empirical methods to their success as practitioners.

Practitioners are now being held accountable for their efficiency and effectiveness by having to demonstrate, in an empirical fashion, the outcomes of their work. Health delivery systems are increasingly interested in the development and management of programs based on the best available evidence. To accommodate this revolution in the delivery of behavioral health care, large clinical trials have become more responsive to the needs of practitioners. One way in which they have become more responsive is by reporting results in terms of clinical significance rather than statistical significance and by highlighting results from individuals rather than the group average. In addition, researchers are now more interested in showing that treatment delivery models improve overall clinical outcomes in a cost-effective manner in the context of actual delivery systems.

More importantly, practitioners themselves have decided that they must invent new methods and strategies to be accountable in today's managed care environment. In so doing, they are beginning to extend the all-important results gleaned from large clinical trials and make them relevant to their own practice settings, much as was envisioned almost 50 years ago.

This new context makes empiricism of direct *practical* relevance to doctoral-level practitioners. It is dramatically changing the linkage between research and practice. Single case research is now of relevance not merely because it is possible or practical in an applied setting, but also because it is a useful step in the development of innovative treatment programs. In the first edition of this volume we argued, as we have again in this edition, that the scientist–practitioner model required new methods to be implemented. But the mere availability of these methods did not produce their regular use. In today's environment the use of empirical methods is linked to the economic success of a large section of the economy, and thus to the economic success of scientist practitioners themselves. Those professionals best able to develop effective and efficient approaches to health care delivery will be greatly rewarded, and science is the best system yet devised to accomplish such ends. Even group comparison methods, which we argued above have often been impractical outside of large, funded clinical trials, are now of more practical relevance in the practice environment, at least in modified form, as a final step in the research and development efforts of behavioral health care firms. The consumption of research findings is being institutionalized in the form of empirically based practice guidelines, which are increasingly evident in managed behavioral health care (Hayes, 1998; Hayes et al., 1995). These changes have come so rapidly, however, that many professionals and many training programs are not yet fully prepared for them.

The successful experiences of practitioners must be observed, verified, and accumulated through empirical practice and accountability. The theoretical and research developments in applied research centers that hold out so much promise for dealing with the variety of severe behavioral and emotional problems must be tested in ways that will influence and be relevant to practitioners. Attention must be paid to the absolute amount of improvement or the size of effect, with an emphasis on changes within the individual in his or her own particular environment. Without the development of a cumulative body of knowledge on the effects of various interventions in the human services, we are doomed to a series of never-ending fads and promises. Traditional scientific methodology alone is not appropriate to answer the major questions relevant to applied settings. In addition, an alternative scientific and empirical approach directly relevant to practice settings is needed. Before describing these approaches, it is essential to put them in context by outlining both the revolution in practice in the United States that is managed care, and the consequences of this revolution for our science and our practice and the role of the scientist practitioner.

2 Managed Care, the Scientist Practitioner, and the Future of Behavioral Health Care Delivery

Introduction

The revolution in the delivery of health care is upon us. Everyone agrees that the delivery of health care in general—and mental or behavioral health care specifically—has emerged from a cottage industry to a major commercial activity. Large international corporations who have organized the delivery of health care into competitive markets dominate this activity. In a very short time these companies have created a multibillion dollar industry. While these trends encompass a bewildering array of business and organizational strategies, the totality of the system under which most of us are now operating has come to be known as managed care (Cummings, 1986; 1992; Trabin & Freeman, 1995). The overriding goals of managed care, in the eyes of policy makers, are to increase effectiveness and efficiency in the delivery of health care. To achieve this goal, practitioners and the entities in which they operate are increasingly required to develop more effective ways to achieve measurable outcomes (e.g., reduction in distress and increased adaptive functioning) in an efficient and time-constrained manner, and to be held accountable for those outcomes. The overriding purpose of this book is to assist practitioners in reaching those goals, thereby enabling them to compete successfully within today's systems of behavioral health care.

In this chapter we will review, briefly, the origins of managed care as it has evolved in the context of behavioral health care, and the types of organizational structures for delivering this care that currently exist. We will then describe likely future developments in these systems of care and the consequences for practitioners in clinical settings. We will also attempt to predict the roles that clinicians and practitioners are likely to play in these emerging systems.

While some disagreement inevitably exists over the shape of these systems, it is very clear to everyone that clinicians and practitioners will have to learn to (a) demonstrate to third-party payers and policy makers that their practices are effective and efficient, and (b) increasingly develop more effective and efficient techniques. In other words, they will have to integrate scientific and empirical approaches into their practice and function as true scientist practitioners. Thus, emerging health care delivery systems are providing a context in which the skills of the scientist practitioner will not only be important, but will be necessary to compete effectively in the marketplace. We will conclude this chapter with an analysis of why we need new models of training to make behavioral health care providers relevant to today's health care delivery systems.

Behavioral Health Care: The Past

For decades the predominant behavioral health care system in our society was the fee-for-service arrangement. In this system, any provider, such as a mental health clinician licensed to provide mental health services in a given state, would compete for referrals and charge a fee for every service provided. In behavioral health care, these services were most typically an hour of psychotherapy, or perhaps the administration of a psychological test, or a psychotropic drug. Many (but by no means all) individuals were able to purchase health insurance to cover part or all of these costs; specifically, the health insurance was called indemnity-based health insurance. This insurance simply paid for the health-related service (or a portion thereof) either through reimbursing the patient, or through direct payments to the health service provider.

If any cost controls existed in these plans, they were structured in the form of limits on benefits, often referred to as "benefit design." For example, an indemnity plan might limit reimbursement to a maximum number of psychotherapy sessions per year (e.g., 20); limit the total dollar amount reimbursable within a year; and/or require a copayment (e.g., 20% to 50% of the cost). Typically, some combination of the above strategies was employed to design mental health benefits. Inherent in this system was the notion that patients could choose any eligible provider they wished. Thus each provider (or clinic) basically ran its own business. Drum (1995) has likened this system to the prevalence of the small family farms so common in the first half of this century, prior to the era of the industrialization of agriculture.

It is also important to recognize that health insurance is a relatively recent development in our society, beginning approximately 50 years ago. Benefits for behavioral health care in the form of insurance benefits for outpatient psychotherapy became widespread only in the past 20 or 25 years. In that relatively short period of time, mental health practitioners have designed their practices and training institutions on the assumption that these benefits would remain in place indefinitely. However, these benefits could not remain in place for a simple reason: cost escalation.

The insurance companies or government entities paying the bills are known collectively as "third-party payers" (with the patients and the providers the first and second parties). One consequence of indemnity-based health insurance was that third-party payers became increasingly subject to any escalation in costs that occurred. Cost escalation was relatively unconstrained, since the contingencies operating in this system did not encourage efficiency or effectiveness. If patients stayed in therapy as long as the provider felt it was necessary, providers would benefit, since third-party payers would usually reimburse for this amount without information on the need for treatment or its outcome. It was not uncommon for therapy to continue until the mental health benefit was exhausted.

A number of factors have made this system for delivering behavioral health care all but obsolete (Cummings, 1995; Drum, 1995; Strosahl, 1994; Trabin & Freeman, 1995). In the 1980s costs for behavioral health care began skyrocketing. For example, within a five-year period, from 1987 to 1992, the average yearly premium for mental health and substance abuse, for employees of businesses providing health insurance as a fringe benefit, had increased from $163 per employee to $318, an increase of nearly 100% (Shoor, 1993; Strosahl, 1994). Why did these costs skyrocket? The answers are complex, but several factors can be identified. To take one example, during the last two decades benefits available for behavioral health care problems have increased. Sometimes these benefits were mandated by state and federal legislative initiatives in order to ensure that psychological problems were covered to approximately the same extent as medical or physical problems. Among the most costly benefits were inpatient stays for behavioral health care, in which the average length of stay was in the 25- to 30-day range, with many individuals staying much longer. These contingencies resulted in the rapid proliferation of private (and profitable) psychiatric hospitals and addiction treatment centers. In addition, and in part as a response to these increasingly available third-party benefits, the number of behavioral health care training programs also increased. Thus, large numbers of psychologists, psychiatrists, social workers, marriage and family therapists, chemical-dependency counselors, and other groups, began delivering services, many of whom were eligible to receive fees from third-party payers. Also, long-term psychotherapy as well as counseling for personal growth have been popular in some areas of the country. But these services are expensive, and employers and others began questioning the effectiveness of these interventions (Trabin & Freeman, 1995). Psychotherapy services became more normalized and important in the culture, resulting in additional demand. Fees for psychotherapists rose as more providers functioned essentially as small businesses, totally dependent on hourly fees for their services. New and more expensive technology (e.g., new drugs, psychological and biological assessment procedures) entered into the system. All of these factors produced an unacceptably rapid increase in the costs of behavioral health care.

The typical response of indemnity-based health insurance companies faced with escalating costs was to maintain their profits by charging higher and higher premiums to businesses and individuals purchasing their policies. But it wasn't long before both government payers (e.g., Medicare and Medicaid), as well as business and industry, were unable to absorb any further increases in costs without risking bankruptcy or, in the case of corporations, interfering with their ability to compete in world markets, thereby endangering their very existence. A frantic search began for methods to manage behavioral health care costs.

The Industrialization of Health Care

The idea of "managing" health care delivery is not particularly new. As Cummings (1995) points out, for example, the Kaiser-Permanente Health Plan was founded nearly 50 years ago, with strong labor union participation. Since the labor unions were actually purchasing the health care benefits in this plan, they would meet regularly with providers in the plan in an attempt to make sure that quality care was being offered within the context of realistic costs. In other words, they would informally "manage" their health care benefits. But it was the unacceptably spiraling health care costs of the 1980s that lead to the urgent conclusion that these services had to be aggressively managed on a national scale. The basic premise of managed health care delivery systems is that considerable cost savings will result if the necessary and appropriate care is delivered in a timely, effective, and efficient manner by those least costly providers with the requisite expertise in administering the procedures needed.

Several factors presaged efforts to manage health care delivery (Trabin & Freeman, 1995). In 1973 Congress passed the *Health Maintenance Organization* (HMO) *Act* that did much to legitimize a very different method of delivering these services. While the initial purpose of HMOs (to be described more fully below) was to encourage the promotion of health, and the prevention of disease and disorder, the utility of this approach as a method of managing costs was also apparent. *Employee assistance programs* (EAPs) were also a forerunner of managed health care problems. EAP programs began in the 1950s as a health service provided by large companies to identify problems of alcohol abuse in the early stages, and to arrange for appropriate referral of employees with this problem. The idea was that early identification and treatment would alleviate lost productivity from that employee, and that personnel in the EAP would know the best referral source for the employee—something employees would be unlikely to find out for themselves. To accomplish this, EAPs created an informal network of providers in whom they had confidence and would refer employees to these providers.

Utilization review companies began in the 1970s. The purpose of these companies was to reduce health care costs for large employers such as national corporations or government entities, including various branches of the uniformed services and the U.S. postal service, by "monitoring" the utilization of health services on a concurrent basis. Typically providers in health care facilities such as hospitals would have to speak to a representative of the utilization review company, usually a registered nurse, to receive "authorization" to continue treating the patient, admit the patient into the hospital, and so forth. Reimbursement to the health care providers would then be contingent on meeting certain utilization criteria (Trabin & Freeman, 1995).

In 1982, Congress approved the concept of *diagnostic related groups* (DRGs) for Medicare and Medicaid recipients. The idea behind DRGs was that, given a certain medical diagnosis—for example, pneumonia—the cost of effective treatment could be predicted with some accuracy. Guided by these data, the government reimbursed hospitals and other health care organizations only for the *average* cost of treating that particular diagnostic problem, and not for the actual costs incurred. Interestingly, psychological disorders (including addictive disorders) were initially excluded from the DRG formulas due to an absence of adequate data on the cost of treatment. Consequently, while nonpsychiatric hospitals were beginning to feel the effects of belt-tightening, private psychiatric and chemical dependency hospitals continued to be reimbursed on a cost-plus basis. These facilities flourished for a time in the 1980s as a result, growing by as much as 40% (Cummings, 1995; Trabin & Freeman, 1995).

The spiraling of behavioral health care costs soon brought the forces of managed care to bear on these costs with a vengeance. This occurred when it was discovered that the health care industry, including the behavioral health care industry, could be organized into a structured and market-driven entity, and that profits would accrue to those organizations who could effectively accomplish these goals. Thus, managed care companies also began to share in the profits derived from health care that were previously divided only among (a) providers, (b) facilities (such as hospitals), and (c) insurance companies (Drum, 1995). Much of this "profit shifting" has been at the expense of providers and to the benefit of managed care companies.

There is now no doubt that managed care companies have been effective in reducing the rapid increase in health care costs, particularly behavioral health care costs, and with little overall decrease in quality (see Mechanic, 1996, for a review). As a result, the reach of this industry is expanding rapidly, rising, by some estimates, at a rate of approximately 20% a year (Cummings, 1995). In a span of less than a decade managed care has risen from a minor player to the dominant force in private health care plans (Oos & Stair, 1996), and an increasingly important force in the public sector (Frank, McGuire, Notman, & Woodward, 1996). We are witnessing nothing less than the industrialization of health care delivery (Cummings & Hayes, 1996).

The growing pains of managed care have closely followed the usual trends in any transition from cottage industry to full industrialization (Hayes, 1998). An extended analogy will help to understand the factors involved. The computer industry provides an example that is recent enough to be memorable and yet old enough to be well along in its development.

In the early stages of industrialization, *vendors proliferate and consumers are confused.* Computer companies literally sprang up overnight in garages, offering a bewildering array of features that varied a great deal from machine to machine. Consumers had a hard time knowing whether, say, Radio Shack's operating system was better than Commodore's or MS-DOS; whether a tape drive was better than a floppy drive; or whether an Intel chip was better than a Motorola chip. In the confusion, *poor quality products succeed but then die out.* A vendor in the computer industry could buy cheap components from Taiwan, take out an ad, and be an instant computer company. As the poor reliability of these machines became known, consumer satisfaction plummeted, the cost of returns and repairs soared, and additional purchases shrank. Many initial successes became failures. As products become better understood, *vendors and product lines are consolidated.* The computer industry went through a tremendous shakeout as Microsoft outwitted IBM in operating systems, Apple stumbled, and the number of major word processing programs shrank from a dozen to only two or three. After consolidation, in both software and hardware only a handful of vendors were left as major players. Finally, in a mature marketplace, *known firms offer known commodities of known quality, cost, and value.* The computer industry is just entering this phase. The risk to the consumer is much lower now since it is hard to make a major mistake. There is variability in features, quality, and cost, but it occurs within a known range and provides choice to the consumer who may, for example, forgo cutting-edge technology or extended guarantees in exchange for a lower price, or who may require the state of the art at a higher price.

The managed care industry is proceeding rapidly through this same developmental sequence. Vendors did indeed proliferate chaotically. For example, from 1975 to 1995 the number of HMOs increased from 166 to 600 (Group Health Association of America, 1995). Predictably, consumers were confused. In November 1996 a Louis Harris poll showed that 55% of the U. S. Population had no understanding at all of what "managed care" meant and almost half did not know what a "health maintenance organization" was (Gannett News Service, 1996). There is wide agreement that quality was uneven and not the general emphasis of the early stages of managed care (Manderscheid & Henderson, 1996). The behavioral health care industry now is undergoing a major shakeout (e.g., Belar, 1995). Small managed care companies are being swallowed up by larger ones, and large companies merge with one another, all in the quest for market share and domination. Many visionaries, such as Nick Cummings (1992; 1995) and others, believe that managed care is in a transition to a more efficient and effective behavioral health service delivery system that will emphasize quality of services as much as cost. Essentially, that prediction fits the usual pattern of industrialization in which eventually "known firms offer known commodities of known quality, cost, and value." Whether, or how quickly, "Generation II" of managed care will arrive remains to be seen, but history suggests that processes of industrialization, once begun, are rarely diverted despite the wishes of those whose interests have been harmed.

Regardless of one's opinion about managed care, it is likely to be with us for many years. Thus, it seems important to review briefly the variety of initiatives designed to manage behavioral health care in the current environment. As we do so, it will be useful to understand how these systems compete in the marketplace. Our computer metaphor will provide additional help.

The value of a computer is a combination of the capabilities of the machine, its reliability, and cost. Initial decisions to buy a given computer are made both by end users and by others (e.g., middle management) who determine that a given machine has adequate value. Additional purchases of given computers depend in part upon the satisfaction of end users, and other purchasers, with the machines. If manufacturers can save money without lowering quality, value goes up. It is risky, however, for manufactures to try to make money by lowering the quality of the product. If the machines are unreliable and consumer satisfaction goes down, repurchases will go down as well and costs to the manufacturer may go up as machines are returned for repair. The trick is to offer the capabilities consumers want, at a lower cost than competitors, while increasing or at least maintaining quality.

These same market forces are at play in managed behavioral health care. Managed care organizations (MCOs) must offer services that consumers want, and at a competitive cost. Initial buying decisions are made both by employees, who want certain kinds of capabilities within a given cost range, and by employers (who usually put a given MCO on an approved list and pay part of the costs of the coverage). Whether patients reenroll depends in part upon the satisfaction of both the employers and employees with the value of the coverage provided. If MCOs can save money without lowering quality, value goes up. It is risky, however, for MCOs to try to make money by lowering the quality of the product. If the service is poor quality, health outcomes are not achieved, consumer satisfaction goes down, reenrollment goes down as well, and costs to the provider may go up as clients who were not treated effectively continue to demand services for continuing problems. As in the computer industry, the strategy is to offer services consumers want, at a lower cost than competitors, while increasing or at least maintaining quality. Thus, the major components to keep track of in analyzing the systems we will describe are the following: initial cost to the consumer or employer, initial cost to the MCO, health outcomes produced, outcomes produced relevant to the workplace, consumer satisfaction, employer satisfaction, costs of additional demands for services, and reenrollment. These components together determine the business success of behavioral health care delivery systems.

Current Behavioral Health Care Delivery Systems

A bewildering array of strategies for organizing the delivery of health care currently exists (Giles, 1993). We have already talked about utilization review and the kind of pretreatment assessment or precertification of patients that would be involved in EAP. Other managed care strategies focus on providers and involve credentialing and contracting with certain numbers of providers (panels), who are then offered ongoing continuing education in behavioral health care procedures to best develop their skills. Still other strategies involve developing a system of outcomes measures that allows providers to be assessed or "profiled" on their effectiveness and efficiency. The idea here is that the most effective and efficient providers will receive the bulk of the referrals within the system of managed care. We will elaborate on some of these strategies below, as we cover the highlights of current systems and strategies and how they differ from the traditional fee-for-service arrangement. We will then move on to describe the likely future organization of health care delivery systems in general, and behavioral health care delivery in particular.

HMOs, PPOs, and IPAs

Basic types of health care delivery systems and their functions are outlined in Table 2.1 (Strosahl, 1994). Most people are now familiar with HMOs, wherein individuals or, more usually, employers such as corporations or public agencies

TABLE 2.1   Managed Mental Health Characteristics: Delivery System Design

Strategy	Function
1. Health maintenance organization (HMO); usually prepaid benefit designs, makes extensive use of capitation model	1. Reduce cost through prevention, low rate of hospitalization, briefer outpatient care, medical cost offset
2. Preferred provider organization (PPO); usually based in copayment benefit design	1. Payer-provider agreement reduces session costs, ensures referral volume 2. Helps utilization review
3. Individual practice association (IPA); uses prepaid health care or copayment benefit designs	1. Group contract shifts cost control incentive to provider group 2. Helps utilization review
4. Employee assistance program (EAP); usually limited to 1 to 3 free visits per referral	1. Deflects use away from expensive mental health services 2. Streamlines referral process 3. Acts as proxy for company in focusing treatment, reducing disability time 4. Emphasizes prevention and early identification to reduce intensity of secondary treatment

.contract with an HMO to provide all health services for employees of the organization for a set fee per year. The fee is usually based on the number of employees in the organization as well as their characteristics, such as age and sex. This allows the HMO to predict the approximate amount of health care the employees will need. The HMO then typically sets a prepaid price per person, which is referred to as capitation, usually expressed on a per month basis. For example, an MCO organized as an HMO might bid $3.00 per person per month for behavioral health care to a corporation with 50,000 employees or $150,000 per month to cover inpatient and outpatient mental health and substance abuse treatment, administrative costs, and profits (Giles, 1993). Clearly, the less services provided in this arrangement, the greater the profit. In the most usual situation, the HMO might be competing with several other health care organizations to provide services to a specific corporation or agency. Therefore, it will attempt to bid the lowest cost per employee. On the other hand, the corporation and its employees are interested in quality and service, as well as price, and will take these factors into account in choosing a health plan. The HMO takes a risk in that the provisions of too much service will result in financial loss. Thus, in theory, it is in the interest of the HMO to keep people healthy and prevent the provisions of costly health services. Most other MCOs now engage in this type of risk-assuming contracting, although the type of delivery system may differ.

HMOs are often organized as fully integrated staff models, where all providers, including behavioral health care providers, are salaried and work in a small number of locations. These health care professionals provide services only to patients who have contracted with the HMO. Health care providers working for the HMO are rewarded in a variety of ways for keeping patients healthy and/or providing the least amount of necessary service. Historically, behavioral health benefits and services have often been sparse in full-service HMOs. This is changing, and for several reasons that make sense—given our computer-purchase analogy described earlier. HMOs and the entities purchasing care have begun to realize that providing more adequate behavioral health care not only reduces future utilization for psychological problems but also *offsets* costs for medical care, since patients with psychological disorders and problems who are adequately treated utilize *less* medical care. This *cost offset* phenomenon is and will continue to be one of the most powerful arguments for providing effective behavioral health care services (Quirk et al., 1995). In addition, behavioral health care is valued by both consumers and employers, and thus poor-quality behavioral health care can reduce the market competitiveness of given HMOs.

Some HMOs are organized in a "blended" model in which salaried staff are backed up by an independent network of providers. The clear trend is toward a full capitation model in which behavioral health care and primary medical care are fully integrated (Giles, 1993; Quirk et al., 1995; Strosahl, 1994) either directly in an HMO, or by an integrated system in which there are separate components fully accountable to the whole system. In theory, this model provides better quality and cost control, and HMOs are one of the fastest growing segments of the industry.

A second type of delivery system is referred to as *a preferred provider organization* (PPO). The emphasis is to actively manage the delivery of health care on the part of a specific group of health care providers (the panel) who have been authorized or certified by the PPO to deliver services to their patients. PPOs differ from HMOs principally in the method of reimbursement (Giles, 1993). PPOs typically reimburse their panel of providers on a fee-for-service basis, although the provision of services is heavily "managed," to ensure that only appropriate care is delivered. Also, patients have the option of using one or another (preferred) provider or, perhaps, a nonparticipating provider, in which case their copayments would typically be substantially higher. Providers in turn can avoid working as fully salaried employees of an organization, as they would in staff model HMOs. This arrangement is attractive to providers because they are assured, for the most part, a steady flow of patients, albeit at a somewhat lower level of reimbursement then they might receive under the old unmanaged fee-for-service system. Providers must also agree to participate in all efforts to manage the delivery of care, including utilization review (Feldman & Fitzpatrick, 1992).

Much like HMOs, MCOs organized to deliver services as PPOs bid on contracts from corporations and agencies to provide health services and, in turn, contract with a group of practitioners to provide those services. Alternatively, some MCOs might simply agree to administer the program with the object of reducing costs, without assuming any financial risk in the event of cost overruns on service delivery. When this happens it is termed an "administrative services only" (ASO) arrangement.

Practitioners join these organizations or "panels" of providers in order to continue receiving referrals. In exchange, they typically agree to provide less service than they might ordinarily, and at a lower price. The provision of services is actively managed or monitored by the PPO using a variety of procedures, as exemplified in Table 2.2. Thus, limits typically exist on the benefits available within these plans. For example, there is a cap on the number of sessions of outpatient therapy and/or the amount of copayment required by the patient is greater as the number of sessions increases. In addition, many of these plans have a "gatekeeper" physician or behavioral health care professional who determines beforehand (precertifies) whether it is necessary to refer the patient to more specialized care. This reduces the likelihood of patients seeking out and sometimes receiving more specialized and more expensive care on their own, when a lower level of care or no care at all might be adequate.

The problem with PPOs considered as a business model is that consistent quality is hard to obtain. A number of MCOs have begun to deal with this through practice guidelines, in which providers are treated much like staff in an HMO. That is, providers are told not just how much they will receive, but which kinds of services they should deliver. This is one of the primary ways that empirical evidence is being forced into the health delivery system by MCOs (Dobson & Craig, 1998; Hayes, 1998). A second problem with PPOs is that some cost-saving measures (e.g., session caps) have competitive and sometimes cost disadvantages. In many large cities, arbitrary treatment limits are increasingly being reduced, since both employers and employees are irritated by them. If the services being denied influence the employee's performance, employers may see possible economic benefit in changing the approved list of providers. Furthermore, arbitrary service limitations can produce cost shifting (e.g., to primary care or to the emergency room), or increase costs due to denied necessary treatment. Arbitrary service caps thus can impose both a competitive and a cost disadvantage.

The major advantage of PPOs as a business model is that they allow health care delivery systems to provide full-service delivery systems without large initial investments. Many hospitals or regional medical entities, as they enter into managed care arrangements or launch their own MCOs, simply do not have the expertise in behavioral health to provide needed services, and contracting with a PPO solves that problem. More recently, PPOs have helped small and medium-sized MCOs deal with the bewildering array of regulations and accreditation requirements that are springing up in behavioral health care delivery.

As reflected in Table 2.1, providers may also organize themselves into *individual practice associations (IPAs)*, who contract directly with companies or other groups for the provision of health services. In these organizations, the procedures bypass existing MCOs. As we will see below, this is very much a developing trend that has as its goal to return some of the "profits" currently flowing to MCOs and

TABLE 2.2   **Managed Mental Health Characteristics: Practitioner and Facility Monitoring**

Strategy	Function
1. Precertification	1. Allows front-end control of treatment planning
	2. Controls unnecessary tests and treatment
	3. Matches level of care to level of need
2. Mandatory review session limits	1. Identifies high-risk situations early
	2. Mid-point review limits length of treatment
	3. Stops ineffective treatment
3. Post-hoc utilization review	1. Places client/therapist at risk for unnecessary treatment costs by requiring treatment matching
4. Practice profiling	1. Identifies therapists who are consistent outliers
	2. Triggers practice management strategies to bring costs down

their executives back to the health care providers themselves. Sometimes it is even claimed that an IPA is not "managed care" at all, because the contract is between a pool of employees and specific providers working at a given point of service. But IPAs are not really a different organizational arrangement. They cut out the intermediary—at least at first—but most IPAs are structured similarly to HMOs in that they bid on contracts on a capitated basis. In essence, the providers themselves are at risk for service delivery needs. In addition, because of increased regulation, litigation, and the greater risks capitation presents to small groups of providers with a small number of contracts, there are strong pressures on IPAs to grow into larger and larger systems. As they do so, the management functions that formerly resided in MCOs are essentially recreated "in house," since any large system requires sophisticated forms of management. In some cases, IPAs have even "outsourced" these centralized functions back to MCOs, who pick up core billing and management functions for a fee. In this arrangement, IPAs essentially begin to blend into a variant of staff model HMOs, but ones owned by the staffs themselves.

IPAs are recent, but they are already evolving. In response to varying needs, for example, group practices of specific types of professionals (e.g., psychologists) are increasingly adding a variety of health care professionals (e.g., nurses) to the team, becoming what has been called an integrated delivery system (Cummings, 1997). As an indication of the trend, Nicholas Cummings, whose "BioDyne" was one of the most successful early behavioral health PPOs, is now busy organizing a new "carve in" company that integrates behavioral health care and primary care.

This hybridization of behavioral health care delivery systems shows that managed care is not a simple, specific organizational structure, but rather an approach to cost and quality based on an industrial model. The trends toward management, consolidation, and integration seem to occur regardless of where one starts, simply because market forces move systems in that direction. In the modern era, even provider-managed delivery systems tend to become forms of "managed care" in this sense due to the exigencies of the marketplace.

Utilization, Review, Clinical Practice Guidelines, and Practice Profiling

Within these organizational structures exists an overlapping set of strategies to effectively manage care, some of which we have touched on. Using a term that has entered the vocabulary of all health care providers, *the utilization of services* is continually reviewed (utilization review—UR) particularly within a PPO structure. As noted in Table 2.2, in the case of behavioral health care, this will occur after a certain preset number of sessions and/or after treatment is completed. The utilization reviewer must then authorize additional treatment or decide, after the fact, whether the treatment rendered was appropriate and should be reimbursed. Utilization review forces the behavioral health care provider to conform as closely as possible to any standards or practice guidelines provided by the PPO for the condition under treatment. Because of difficulties with denying payment for treatment already delivered, most utilization review is now prospective or concurrent, wherein authorization is provided beforehand to provide appropriate services.

Recognizing the great variability in care among members of networks, MCOs began promulgating guidelines often referred to as *clinical practice guidelines* or "best practice plans" that standardized treatment to some extent beyond simply limiting costs of services and number of sessions allowed. These plans actually began to articulate, based on some existing criteria, the optimal ways of assessing and treating the variety of problems (e.g., lower back pain) presenting to clinical settings. In the case of behavioral health care, early plans coming from MCOs simply specified the number of sessions allowable for certain conditions, such as depression or attention deficit/hyperactivity disorder (ADHD), based strictly on economic considerations. However, it wasn't long before independent contractors, or the plans themselves, began putting together clinical practice guidelines specifying the most efficient and effective interventions and/or patient treatment matching strategies based on existing scientific evidence. It also became apparent that surprisingly few mental health professionals were adequately trained to be accountable for their practice by producing the kinds of outcomes data that would demonstrate their efficiency and effectiveness. This was found to be true even for doctoral-level psychologists trained in programs adhering to a scientist–practitioner model. Lack of accountability has proved to be a severe disadvantage in today's marketplace since, in the absence of these data, psychologists have been unable to persuade health care administrators in MCOs that what they were doing was effective.

In the late 1980s the federal government, with its substantial interest in health care, also began requesting the construction of clinical practice guidelines to decrease variability in the manner in which various health care problems were treated from setting to setting and practitioner to practitioner. Presumably, since this variability was substantial, some methods of treatment were effective and many were ineffective. This, in turn, prompted an even greater interest in identifying treatments with some evidence for effectiveness, particularly brief treatments. Thus, further impetus was given to establishing the validity of interventions with medical or behavioral problems as determined by clinical trials and other strategies of clinical science. Best practice standards are now a part of most utilization review activities within MCOs. Since clinical practice guidelines are likely to play a more substantial role in the years to come, a more detailed description of the development of these plans will be provided in Chapter 4.

Finally, managed care organizations are increasingly monitoring the clinicians in their systems to ascertain the costs each clinician incurs in providing services and, more importantly, the effectiveness with which each provider treats the problem and returns the patient to normal functioning. This is called *practice profiling* and, theoretically, allows MCOs to pick and choose among the most effective health care providers, dropping those who are more expensive and/or less effective from their lists. Since this kind of action may engender lawsuits on the part of providers dropped from panels, the more usual consequence of practice profiling is to differentially refer patients to those providers within the system with the best practice profiles. Few, if any, referrals go to other providers on the panel.

Managed Behavioral "Carve-Out" Programs

MCOs realized early on that managing behavioral health care resulted in a very different set of difficult problems compared to managing health care for more traditional medical problems. It is for this reason that mental disorders were initially excluded in the 1980s from the diagnostic-related groups' provisions mentioned above. And yet, spiraling costs and other factors operating in the 1980s made the need to manage behavioral health care apparent. To accomplish this goal effectively, behavioral health care was carved out of traditional health care and managed separately (Cummings, 1995; Drum, 1995). Most, but not all, PPOs are carve out plans, for example.

David Drum (1995) has organized the nature of current behavioral health care carve-out systems and contrasted these current systems to pre-carve-out indemnity care systems in Table 2.3. In this table one can see how health care delivery systems compete for clients, how patients initiate care if they feel they are in need, the range of services provided under the different systems, and the all-important consideration of identifying the "customer" of the health service provider. Among behavioral health care providers, the shift to first-generation carve-out systems such as PPOs and focused behavioral health care HMOs had

TABLE 2.3   Changes in the Service Delivery System

Behavioral Healthcare Systems (Category/Type)	Competition for Clients	Insured's Authority to Initiate Care	Range of Services	Provider's Customer
A. Pre-carve-out systems: unmanaged indemnified care 1. Indemnification-based fee for service (FFS) 2. Qualified participation networks (QPN)	Independent providers compete via reputation/visibility for free-choice clients.	Virtually unrestricted.	Provider and insurer had only marginal responsibility for assuring availability of needed services.	Patient is customer, and provider primarily must satisfactorily serve patient.
B. First-generation carve-out systems: managed care organizations (MCOs) 3. PPOs with open client selection of network providers 4. Managed care networks with gatekeeping and provider surveillance 5. Managed care hierachical networks with anchor practice groups 6. Managed care in-house staff systems	Organizations compete for right to serve client populations, decreasing the number of free-choice clients. 3. Competes with other network-approved providers and to some extent with non-network providers. 4. Competes with other network preferred providers, based increasingly on performance criteria profiling. 5. Competes with other high-performing providers and anchor groups. 6. Takes only those patients under contract to MCO.	As MCOs evolve, greater restrictions are placed on patients' authority to initiate care. Increasingly, patients must go through a gatekeeper or to a specific practice group to determine necessity and duration of care.	MCO is responsible for assuring range of services offered; covers managed benefit plans or EAP services offered. MCOs achieve this by establishing provider networks and entering into contracts with health care entities to create a contractually based care system.	Under MCOs, the provider has both the patient and the MCO as customers. Provider must satisfactorily serve both the MCO's customer and the payer. MCO must satisfactorily serve the insuring corporation and its benefit manager.

TABLE 2.3   Continued

Behavioral Healthcare Systems (Category/Type)	Competition for Clients	Insured's Authority to Initiate Care	Range of Services	Provider's Customer
C. Second-generation carve-out systems: provider-initiated health care organizations (PCOs)	Competition for clients increasingly occurs at agency/system level and for large groups of clients.	Patient authority to initiate reimbursable care is usually limited to in-group/system providers and to care deemed necessary. If patient accesses care outside system, severe cost penalties are incurred.	PCO responsible for establishing a comprehensive care system or linking to a larger provider-based care system. PCO establishes a contractually linked care system with the provider/investor often owning facilities, MSO, and group practices.	Under PCO, provider has to satisfy both patient and PCO as customers. The PCO in turn is concerned with satisfying the payer/insuring corporation and its benefit manager.
7. Practice associations with contracting capability	7. Competes with MCO and other practice associations (IPAs, GPWWs, & MSOs).			
8. Group practices with risk-contracting capability	8. Competes with MCOs, group practices, and health care corporations.			
9. Integrated facility/provider organizations with risk-contracting capability	9. Competes with MCOs, HMOs, hospitals, local and national health care corporations.			
10. Health care system with integrated facility/provider groups and provider networks with risk-contracting and insurance managed care, and carve-in capability	10. Competes with MCOs, HMOs, local and national health care corporations.			

devastating consequences. Providers lost access to potential patients whose care was under the direction of a specific MCO. Thus, independent behavioral health care providers were in the uneasy position of either going out of business for lack of referrals (and many have during the 1990s), or joining an MCO network and accepting lower fees and controls over services provided in order to receive sufficient referrals to stay in business. Because there is generally an oversupply of behavioral health care providers, practitioner profiling, as described above, further restricts referrals to those providers in the network who are not efficient or effective. Thus, even those providers who are able to gain access to a panel or network are not assured of sufficient referrals to survive.

As Drum (1995) points out in Table 2.3, the competition for patients has now shifted from the individual practitioner, carefully building his or her reputation over the years in order to attract patients, to the organization or MCO to which the practitioner belongs. These MCOs, then, end up competing with each other for contracts with large groups of clients, usually employees of a specific company or agency. In the process, patients have lost much of their ability to seek out health care wherever and whenever they feel it is necessary. Rather, most patients go through a gatekeeper of some sort, usually a primary care physician, or perhaps a behavioral health care provider who is part of an EAP, to determine if subsequent referrals are necessary.

The major problem with carve-out arrangements is that they do not hold providers or the MCO accountable for the true cost of care, and they tend to produce lower consumer satisfaction. When services are denied, the immediate cost of care goes down but, as noted earlier, costs often shift to more expensive outlets (e.g., the emergency room). Carve outs could function like a computer maker selling cheap "no name" machines: The cost was initially low, but so, too, was the value. As a result, carve-out arrangements are beginning to decrease somewhat in favor of fully integrated or "carve-in" systems where behavioral health care and medical care are fully integrated once again. Even if the actual provision of behavioral health care services is not part of primary care, in carve-in systems the behavioral health care providers are held accountable for the total cost to the delivery system. Carve outs do offer the considerable advantage, however, of developing and maintaining expertise in the details of behavioral health care delivery systems. Because of the increased costs of accreditation and regulation, small MCOs in physical medicine may use carve outs more for their expertise in these areas than for cost savings per se.

Problems with Managed Care

Changes in health care delivery have not been evolutionary; they are revolutionary, and they affect the manner in which every behavioral health care provider practices and the types of services offered to every patient seeking care. Furthermore, as is often the case in the beginnings of any endeavor, there have been enormous problems associated with the implementation of managed care practices. Since the purpose of any corporation is to maximize profits for shareholders, in these early stages of operation managed care companies have sought to maximize income, often at the expense of quality. Consumer confusion about the nature and quality of services delivered opened a wide door for poor business practices to proliferate. In some cases, managed care companies have compromised services available for certain conditions to levels that are well below the levels of services that most health care practitioners would recommend.

As a result, regulation, legislation, and litigation are becoming increasingly important parts of the landscape of managed care (Mechanic, 1996). To take one example from obstetrics, in 1996 the U.S. Congress passed a law preventing MCOs from requiring new mothers to leave the hospital sooner than 48 hours after a routine vaginal delivery. Similar kinds of restrictions have been put in place for other conditions, although companies differ greatly in their policies and procedures on managing care, and their standards are continually changing. In this regard, the operations of current-generation MCOs have been likened to the operations of large capitalistic corporations in the nineteenth century. In those years, companies engaged in cutthroat competition to maximize profits, including such tactics as abusing their workers (including young children), requiring long hours at low wages, abusing their customers by turning out shoddy products or services, and abusing their competitors by striving for monopolies such that competition would disappear, to the detriment of the consumer and the worker. Over the decades, government, workers, and consumers responded with a variety of regulatory actions and other measures to counter these destructive tendencies. While no one would suggest that MCOs have gone to those extremes, many think that greatly increased regulation of the industry is required, and regulatory actions have increased substantially in the last few years (Mechanic, 1996). In addition, several states have modified their laws to allow MCOs to be sued more readily, hoping that litigation will cut back on abusive practices (Verhovek, 1997).

In addition to regulation and legislation, accreditation and quality ratings are becoming increasingly important to MCOs. In the United States, over the last few years, the National Committee for Quality Assurance (NCQA) has come from nowhere to being fundamentally important to many MCOs. In some states, MCOs cannot offer plans that are not accredited. NCQA fully approves only about 15% of the plans it inspects, and its requirements continue to stiffen. For example, in 1998 behavioral health care plans accredited by NCQA must have implemented at least some scientifically based standards of care. NCQA and the major trade associations in the industry (e.g., The HMO Group and the American Managed Behavior Health Association) are developing methods of monitoring the quality of MCOs in order to provide more objective ratings to consumers. Some large corporations (e.g., Xerox, General Electric) are beginning to rate HMOs and to encourage employees to select higher-quality plans. Formal measures of client satisfaction are being developed (Marshall, Hays, Sherbourne, & Wells, 1993) that are contributing to these developments.

As the health care industry matures, the customer (the employer, employees, or the individual patient) will be better able to choose intelligently among alternative health care plans. If the system works as intended, both price and quality will be factors in any choice, and the unbridled emphasis on reducing costs alone will greatly diminish. Since managed care companies have been highly effective in reducing the spiraling of health care costs (Cummings, 1995), most company executives currently recognize that competition for customers in the coming years will be based to a much greater extent on quality of services provided.

Difficulties with MCOs have not been restricted to an overemphasis on cost reduction, however. Some providers have objected to the very structure of MCOs, particularly those that closely review and monitor their work. Since individuals employed as utilization reviewers are often less qualified by virtue of education and training to make clinical judgments than the providers they are reviewing, substantial tension has arisen among MCOs and providers on their panels. Communication between these two groups of professionals has often degenerated into name-calling and recriminations. As MCOs gained increasing market share, providers soon realized that their very survival depended on cooperating more fully with these companies. But few providers would agree with MCO policies on the delivery of care in all cases, with most thinking that these policies put the patient at a disadvantage, at least some of the time. Part of this problem, as we shall see, lies in the difficulty behavioral health care providers have had in demonstrating to policy makers and MCOs that their interventions have been effective, since they have lacked the necessary measures of outcome and the empirical evidence validating their interventions to convince health care policy makers that all but minimal services were really necessary.

The Future

Most people in the field agree that the current generation of managed care organizations will not last and that the field will evolve to counteract shortcomings and abuses, while at the same time reining in costs. Nick Cummings, a former president of the American Psychological Association and a founder of one of the original behavioral carve-out MCOs, has made some cogent predictions on the types of evolution that will occur in this field (Cummings, 1995; Cummings & Hayes, 1996), predictions that are shared to some extent by others (e.g., Quirk et al., 1995; Strosahl, 1996; Trabin & Freeman, 1995). First, Cummings believes that behavioral health carve outs will disappear and that behavioral health care will be reintegrated with more traditional health care for physical disorders and diseases. He suggests that this will be the case because we have now learned how to manage behavioral health care and, therefore, carving it out as a separate entity is no longer necessary. The other economic factor prompting this change is the finding that the provision of adequate behavioral health care is likely to be effective if problems are recognized early, when patients first present to their primary care practitioner. The provision of behavioral health care at this time will also reduce the costs of subsequent medical and surgical procedures by identifying those patients whose physical complaints are largely emotional in origin. In this regard, the recent discoveries that behavioral health care directly impacts the prognosis and course of physical problems will be of increasing importance. For example, psychosocial procedures increase longevity and even cure rates of individuals suffering from cancer (e.g., Fawzy, Fawzy, Arndt, & Pasnau, 1995; Spiegel, Bloom, Kaemer, & Gottheil, 1989), and they reduce mortality following myocardial infarctions (Frasure-Smith, 1991). Thus, as noted, one of the principal outcomes of behavioral health care would be to offset medical costs, and Cummings predicts that this medical cost offset will become one of the most important factors in determining the value of behavioral health care.

Cummings also predicts that the role of behavioral health care professionals will change substantially. For example, doctoral-level psychologists (as well as psychiatrists) are likely to become managers, researchers, and supervisors of therapy in any integrated behavioral care system. Professionals with lesser training, such as those with master's degrees, will administer most routine therapy. He notes "empirically derived treatment protocols will enable master's-trained therapists to provide routine care" (1995, p. 31), with doctoral-level personnel, such as psychologists, called in to provide direct services only on the more complex and difficult cases.

In Cummings's view and in ours, one of the principal roles for doctoral-level personnel, such as psychologists, would be to design future behavior health care systems and carry out the necessary outcomes research and quality control monitoring that will provide the most efficient and effective care to patients. This will require knowledge of research and program evaluation strategies as they relate directly to the provision of care to both individual patients and groups of patients across the health care delivery system. Doctoral-level psychologists will also be responsible for effecting useful triaging systems in which the problems and health concerns of patients are quickly and efficiently identified, allowing appropriate referral for intervention. Doctoral-level personnel will, as they have been, be responsible for innovating and evaluating new approaches to assessment and intervention that take into consideration matching and intensity of treatment to specific patient problems. Finally, doctoral-level personnel will continue to treat the more severe and intractable cases who are not responsive to more standardized intervention (Barlow & Barlow, 1995). But the function here will be not just routine service delivery, but rather analytic as these high-level personnel attempt to ascertain *why* initial treatment failed so that future cases with similar presenting characteristics can be integrated back into the treatment system. We will discuss this model in more detail in Chapter 4.

In another important prediction that is already beginning to come true, Cummings suggests that community consortia will emerge that will resemble purchasing alliances of buyers seeking the best possible health care services for their groups. These purchasing alliances will have considerable power to effect change among MCOs and their successors in that they will demand both quality as well as price from any MCO to whom they allocate their substantial business. As Trabin and Freeman (1995) point out, some states are beginning an attempt to integrate their public mental health systems into private systems, thereby developing large purchasing alliances.

Finally, Cummings predicts that MCOs in the future will be community accountable health care networks (CAHNs) that will be comprehensive and provide all health services—outpatient, inpatient, and partial care. Cummings envisions that the CAHN will be an exclusive provider organization. In other words, all patients will be required to seek out health service from within a specified network of providers. It is also likely that the providers themselves will become full-time employees of these organizations as opposed to simply contracting with them along with several other MCOs, as is currently the case. The CAHNs will be reimbursed through methods of capitation described earlier such that they assume the bulk of the financial risk. Strong community-based purchasing alliances will once again ensure that the price is neither too low, which would mean insufficient quality in the delivery of care, nor too high. To monitor quality, CAHNs will form boards or oversight committees comprised of employers, provider representatives, and members of the community. Also, it is envisioned that these CAHNs will be owned by the providers themselves. The providers will then hire the necessary financial and administrative expertise to run them successfully. Thus, these systems will be essentially provider run, fully capitated, and integrated HMOs.

The beginnings of this type of system can be seen in Table 2.3. The basic difference between the second-generation systems and the first-generation systems in this table is that they are run by the providers themselves, thereby cutting out the intermediaries—the MCOs—who, at the current time, are reaping most of the profits. In this way the providers share proportionally in the profits but will also assume all of the risks in the type of contracting they will provide.

In what may be an example of this future plan, Steve Wetzell formed what he calls a business health care action group that is essentially a purchasing alliance in Minnesota. In 1995 this group was comprised of 250,000 members, which was 10% of the market in the Minneapolis–St. Paul area. He notes that the prevailing managed care model has the employer contracting directly with the MCO plan who in turn contracts with networks of providers. Problems with this model, some of which have been articulated above, include the fact that one result is the assembling of large overlapping networks such that individual practitioners might

---

TABLE 2.4   Where We Are Going Next

- Direct contracts with competing care systems
- Care system incorporates:
    1. Full continuum of care
    2. Risk sharing
    3. Accountability
    4. Continuous quality improvement
- Care system competes based on:
    1. Quality
    2. Cost
    3. Service

belong to several plans, if they qualify. These health plans then seek to maximize premiums and minimize provider payments. Furthermore, the providers are not sufficiently accountable since they don't own or advocate the plan. This system is also inefficient since different plans impose different rules, the network of providers are often unstable as providers are dropped or move from one plan to another, and the types of data produced by the plans for purposes of improving effectiveness and efficiency are fragmented.

Wetzell's vision for the future is a competing care system model, presented in Table 2.4 and Figure 2.1, wherein providers basically band together to form their own comprehensive care systems. These systems would include inpatient and outpatient care, as well as laboratory or assessment services and contracts with administrative entities to provide support services. Thus, the providers would basically own the plans. In turn, the employers would basically provide to their employees vouchers with which to shop among competing plans. In this way, the providers would advocate their own product, and presumably the networks would be more stable. But with patients making the decision themselves rather than employers, the market would be driven more directly by consumers and become more truly competitive.

COMPETING CARE SYSTEM MODEL

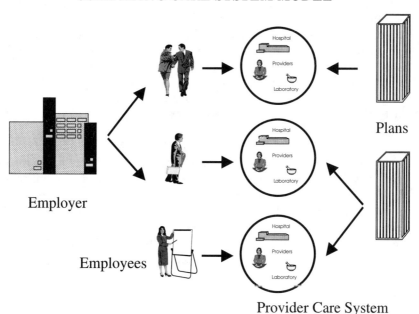

FIGURE 2.1   One model of the evolving world of health care delivery systems.
Figure is redrawn and slightly modified from Drum, 1995.

This is, of course, just one of several possible arrangements, but it does encompass some of Cummings's vision of community-wide integrative care systems and large purchasing alliances in which consumers develop more clout in shaping their own health care, including behavioral health care.

Conclusion

In this chapter we have reviewed the ongoing revolution in behavioral health care delivery and speculated on the future of these systems into the next century. The future organization of health care delivery will most likely be in the form of capitated and fully integrated HMOs that are either staff model or staff model equivalent. These entities will emphasize integrative, preventive care including preventive behavioral health care focusing on areas such as smoking reduction and other health risk behaviors, appropriate child care, early intervention with emerging behavioral problems in children, and spousal abuse. In addition, intervention will focus on early manifestations of the variety of psychological disorders that only become more severe (and more expensive to treat) with time. As these entities become more mature, the emphasis on reduced treatment to accomplish cost reduction so prevalent today is being lessened as it becomes clear that the provision of poor quality services is more expensive in the long run. In fully integrated plans it will also be more risky to undertreat in the hopes that the patient will be shifted back to the primary medical plan—if the condition reemerges due to poor quality treatment, as is the case in current "carve-out" systems. At this point, the emphasis on benefit limits such as limited numbers of sessions should be reduced as it becomes more clear, based on valid outcomes assessments and other empirical scientific approaches to behavioral health care, how to deliver the highest-quality service at the lowest price.

Of substantial importance is the future of mental health professionals such as doctoral-level psychologists in these emerging systems. The bedrock of these systems is accountability to the customer, whether it be the employer organization, or the patients themselves, and the constant development of more effective and efficient models of care. To accomplish accountability, health care organizations must produce verifiable outcomes that demonstrate both quality and efficacy of behavioral health care as well as cost effectiveness. To accomplish system development, a continuous process of measurement, analysis, innovation, implementation, and evaluation is needed. In both cases, in order to participate in a mature industrialized behavioral health care delivery system, mental health practitioners are going to have to adapt empirical methodologies to the practice setting. In other words, they must truly become scientist practitioners.

3 Current Research Strategies and the Role of the Practitioner

Introduction

Before examining the role of the practitioner in the development of applied research and the new research challenges of managed care, it is important to consider the contributions made to the field of behavior change by applied research methodology. We have seen in Chapter 1 that practitioners, for the most part, neither do research nor evaluate their procedures, and that applied research has so far had relatively little influence on usual and customary practice; that is, practitioners do not readily consume research findings. Nevertheless, this is an exciting period in the development of behavior change procedures, and applied research has made notable progress. While the dissemination and influence of research findings on practitioners may still be somewhat limited, the contribution of research to the clinical knowledge base is substantial and growing. Furthermore, the rise of managed care promises new institutional and economic reasons to expect greater dissemination and influence of the existing research base.

The development and evaluation of new and more effective behavior-change procedures is a young field that began gaining momentum only in the 1960s and 1970s. During this time, systematic research has progressed on a number of problems across the health, mental health, and educational fields. Often this research has been carried out by closely knit groups of investigators in applied research centers around the world who meet and communicate frequently to compare notes. These are the research specialists who have made a career of applied investigation.

Progress has been uneven in the development of effective behavior-change procedures. More has been discovered about dealing with some problems, such as anxiety disorders or conduct disorders in the classroom, than with others. Only certain questions have been addressed, a much smaller list has been answered, while many others have been largely ignored. As we will see over the next chapters, we are answering some questions, and these answers are contributing to our knowledge, but we are leaving unanswered some of the questions that would make this knowledge relevant to practitioners working in applied settings, particularly managed care settings.

There are many problem areas that are appropriate examples with which to examine the strengths and weaknesses of current research efforts and the critical role that could be played in the research process by practitioners. Problems such as depression, marital disorders, or attention deficit/hyperactivity disorder could serve as examples, because research has progressed in a similar fashion in many of these areas. One area that is particularly appropriate, however, is the problem of panic disorder with agoraphobia (PDA), because research is reasonably well advanced, and because a number of new intervention techniques have recently emerged.

This chapter will review briefly the progression of research in PDA, looking at advances that have been made that have contributed to our fund of knowledge. We will then consider the issue of the proven efficacy of psychosocial treatments more generally, based on the current research program. We will examine questions that have been answered, as well as questions that traditional applied research methods have not answered. One major question that has not been answered concerns the feasibility of implementing new treatments and the generality of effectiveness of new treatments across patients in applied settings, a question particularly relevant to managed care settings. We will suggest that difficulties with this question and its many corollaries have contributed to the weak influence of research on practice and the relative lack of interest of practitioners in the research process. This thorny issue will be illustrated in the context of PDA. We will propose that solutions to these problems will require more research participation by the practice base of the behavioral health professions, and we will examine several alternative models that have been proposed to address this issue.

Research on Panic Disorder with Agoraphobia

The Development of Fear-Reduction Procedures

In panic disorder with agoraphobia, the strengths and weaknesses of traditional clinical research are readily apparent. Radically new treatments, both psychosocial and drug, for fear, panic, phobia, and anxiety have been developed during the last 25 years. The emergence of these treatments has influenced practice and also, quite independently, stimulated research. This research has contributed to our basic knowledge about treatments for PDA but has left important questions unanswered.

As late as the 1960s there were no psychosocial treatments with proven effectiveness for PDA. Reflecting the state of knowledge at that time, most clinicians were reluctant to ask patients with agoraphobia to expose themselves to fear-provoking situations, since it was thought that the resulting anxiety might be harmful in some way. This state of affairs began to change in 1958 with the publication of Joseph Wolpe's influential work *Psychotherapy by Reciprocal Inhibition*. In this book Wolpe described a new treatment for fear and anxiety in general—and phobia in particular—called *systematic desensitization*. In fact, Wolpe treated 210 consecutive cases, many of whom suffered from phobic disorders. His demonstration that 90% of these cases were much improved or cured, and his specification of both the nature of the problem treated as well as the procedures involved in systematic desensitization sparked a whole generation of research on fear-reduction procedures (Barlow, 1988). These procedures also attracted wide attention among practicing clinicians always on the lookout for new and more effective therapeutic strategies to use with their patients. Since this series was derived directly from

Wolpe's private practice, and also described a rather straightforward therapeutic technique that could easily be incorporated into the armamentarium of practicing therapists, it is not surprising that clinicians took note. It was not long before numerous workshops and other practical guides were available for clinicians interested in learning more about the procedure. Wolpe specified rather clearly the presenting clinical problems as well as the processes of systematic desensitization. He also reported the percentage of patients reaching a well-defined criterion of success and described characteristics of those who failed. In so doing he fulfilled most of the necessary ingredients of a clinical replication series. The increasing relevance of clinical replication series to the clinical research effort as well as the powerful influence of these series on practice will be reviewed below.

Treating Agoraphobia

Systematic desensitization, as it was originally described, was carried out almost entirely in imagination. In this procedure, patients were asked to imagine feared situations or objects while engaged in some anxiety-inhibiting state such as relaxation. Early clinical trials with agoraphobic patients (as contrasted to patients with specific phobia) suggested that this technique was not more effective than traditional psychotherapy. Furthermore, overall improvement with PDA was small for both approaches (Barlow, 1988; Emmelkamp, 1982; Gelder & Marks, 1966; Marks, 1971). In the mid 1960s, clinical experiments, often using single case designs, began to appear evaluating the therapeutic benefits of encouraging patients with agoraphobia to expose themselves directly to real-life fear provoking situations (e.g., Agras, Leitenberg, & Barlow 1968). Since that time, clinical investigators have clearly demonstrated that real-life exposure or "exposure in vivo" is an essential component of any successful treatment for agoraphobia. Therapeutic techniques incorporating this process are substantially more effective than any number of credible alternative psychotherapeutic procedures (Barlow, 1988, 1994; Chambless & Gillis, 1994; Mavissakalian & Barlow, 1981; O'Brien & Barlow, 1984; Telch & Lucas, 1994). The effectiveness of exposure-based strategies is also supported indirectly by the well-documented observation that patients with agoraphobia do not improve over time without treatment. This phenomenon was first demonstrated by Agras, Chapin, and Oliveau (1972), who followed a group of agoraphobic patients for five years before exposure-based treatments were widely available and found no improvement in the absence of treatment. Subsequent studies have demonstrated the chronicity of anxiety disorders in general (Barlow, 1988).

During the late 1970s and 1980s, after the effectiveness of exposure-based procedures had been established for PDA, a number of studies commenced on the optimal manner of administering exposure-based treatments. Such issues as the intensity of exposure to feared situations, the importance of the presence of a therapist during exposure exercises, the addition of anxiety-reducing procedures such as relaxation or distraction techniques, and other variables were evaluated. Most of these evaluations took place in the context of large between-group comparisons (Barlow, 1988). Generally, findings indicated that gradual self-paced exposure seemed to have some advantage over more intensive exposure in that attrition rates were reduced, excessive dependence on the therapist did not occur, and improvement continued at the end of treatment. Some studies also indicated that intensive in vivo exposure was associated with a higher relapse rate than less intensive treatments (e.g., Jannson & Ost, 1982), although this result was not found in every study (e.g., Chambless, 1990). Follow-up studies of agoraphobic patients treated with exposure-based procedures revealed that for most patients significant effects were maintained or even enhanced over long periods, particularly when treatment was more gradual and self-paced. For example, several studies have indicated that gains are maintained for periods of 4 years or more (Burns, Thorpe, & Cavallaro, 1986; Jannson, Jerremalm, & Ost, 1986; Jannson & Ost, 1982).

Despite the gratifying results from large clinical trials, most investigators recognized the limitation of exposure-based procedures. Attrition rates were often high, although they were reduced somewhat by careful introduction to the treatment and less intense self-paced exposure-based procedures (Barlow, 1988; Barlow, Hayes, & Nelson, 1984; Jannson & Ost, 1982). Report of success rates of 60% to 75% reflected the fact that 25% to 40% of agoraphobic patients who completed treatment failed to benefit to any significant degree. Also, a substantial percentage of the remaining 60% to 75% may not have reached clinically meaningful levels of functioning. For example, Marks (1971) reported that only 3 of 65 patients or 4.6% were completely symptom-free at four-year follow-up. Typically residual symptomatology in the form of anticipatory anxiety, avoidance, and panic attacks was not uncommon (Michelson & Marchione, 1991). In summary, exposure treatments were proved to be effective interventions for PDA based on large clinical trials, and the results were maintained over time, but many people did not benefit, and many of those who did benefit were left with residual symptoms.

Treating Panic

During the 1980s psychologically orientated clinicians increasingly realized that exposure-based treatments targeted agoraphobic avoidance, but ignored what had come to be considered the central feature of PDA—panic attacks (Barlow, 1988; Barlow, 1994). During this period, we attempted to develop a cognitive-behavioral treatment designed to target panic attacks directly (e.g., Barlow, 1988; Barlow & Craske, 1994). At the heart of this treatment, referred to as panic-control treatment (PCT), is systematic structured exposure to feared internal sensations. While developing this approach, we devised a variety of ways to elicit feared internal sensations in the office, including sensations of depersonalization and derealization. To this basic strategy we added a strong cognitive therapy component as well as a breathing retraining module. At the same time, David Clark and his colleagues from Oxford were developing a similar treatment, placing somewhat more emphasis on the cognitive component (e.g., Clark et al., 1994).

Initially, preliminary results from open clinical trials suggested significant improvement as a result of this innovation (e.g., Shear, Ball, & Fitzpatrick, 1991). In the first large-scale controlled study of this approach (Barlow, Craske, Cerny, & Klosko, 1989), PCT, either combined with progressive muscle relaxation or administered independently, was significantly more effective than progressive muscle relaxation alone or waiting-list control procedures. Using intent-to-treat analysis, which would include all subjects entering the study (even if they dropped out along the way), fully 80% of those patients in the PCT group were panic-free at the end of treatment. In this trial, only panic disorder patients with no more than mild agoraphobic avoidance were included to fully test the panic-reduction properties of this psychosocial treatment.

In a related study, Klosko, Barlow, Tassinari, and Cerny (1990) compared the efficacy of PCT with that of alprazolam (Xanax), placebo, and a waiting-list control condition in 57 patients with panic disorder with no more than mild agoraphobic avoidance. Once again at posttreatment 87% of PCT patients were panic-free compared with 50% for alprazolam patients, 36% for placebo patients, and 33% for the waiting-list control group. PCT was significantly more effective than alprazolam, placebo, and waiting-list control groups on panic-free status (Barlow & Brown, 1995). Subsequently, other studies have replicated the effectiveness of this psychosocial procedure for panic disorder (Clark et al., 1994; Telch et al., 1993). Additional studies reported that the therapeutic effects of this treatment were maintained at follow-ups of one to two years (Craske et al., 1991; Clark et al., 1994; Côté, Gauthier, & LaBerge, 1992). Barlow and Lehman (1996) report on 12 clinical trials evaluating cognitive-behavioral approaches for panic disorder, almost all of which demonstrated the effectiveness of this procedure, usually in comparison to some other credible psychosocial treatment, a drug placebo, and/or a waiting-list control group. At present, large-scale clinical trials are underway testing the separate and combined effects of these approaches with proven pharmacological treatments (e.g., Barlow, 1996b).

The Establishment of Psychosocial Treatments with Proven Efficacy

The systematic progression of clinical research, usually in the form of large clinical trials, has established the effectiveness of psychosocial treatments for PDA. This evidence has been accepted by government agencies such as the National Institute of Mental Health (Wolfe & Maser, 1994), the National Health Service in the United Kingdom (Roth & Fonagy, 1995), and other groups whose task it is to ascertain effective psychosocial treatments.

Advances emanating from our research have not been limited to the development of effective psychosocial treatments for PDA. Over the past 20 years, systematic clinical research, most often in the form of large clinical trials, has established the efficacy of a number of well-defined psychosocial interventions for specific disorders. For example, Andrews, Crino, Hunt, Lampe, and Page (1993; see Barlow, 1994), utilizing meta-analytic methodology, identified average effect sizes and subject numbers associated with studies carried out on pharmacological treatments during the 1980s (Quality Assurance Project, 1983; 1984; 1985). These effect sizes, and the studies that produced them, were designated by the World Health Organization

(WHO) as sufficient such that the drug treatments evaluated in these studies were placed on the WHO list of essential drug treatments. Andrews et al. then compared the effect sizes in these successful pharmacological treatments to the effect sizes in studies of psychosocial treatments for a variety of disorders. In addition, the authors applied stringent criteria to studies of psychosocial treatment before determining that an effective psychosocial treatment exists. Those criteria included (a) the existence of at least three independent studies from different centers, (b) sufficient specification of the psychosocial treatment in each published study to allow replication, (c) clear diagnosis of the target clinical disorder, and (d) the ability to calculate the effects and standard deviation compared to a well-matched "placebo" psychosocial condition. Using these criteria, the authors identified 29 trials across six disorders that were included in the meta-analyses, all of which compared a psychosocial treatment to a credible alternative psychosocial treatment or placebo. The results, displayed in Figure 3.1, showed that psychosocial treatments were

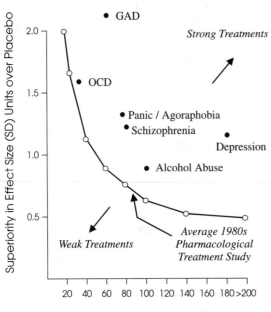

FIGURE 3.1   Superiority in effect size (SD) units over placebo for a variety of conditions. The curve with open circles shows the average effect sizes for pharmacological treatment studies published in the 1980s. The free-standing filled circles show the results for a meta-analysis of well-controlled studies of psychosocial interventions.

Redrawn from Andrews et al., 1993 (submitted for publication).

comparatively effective for a number of disorders, including alcohol abuse and dependence, major depressive disorder, panic disorder, generalized anxiety disorder, obsessive-compulsive disorder, and even schizophrenia (in combination with medication).

Recently the Division of Clinical Psychology of the American Psychological Association appointed the Task Force on Promotion and Dissemination of Psychological Procedures (Task Force, 1995). The goal of the Task Force was to identify effective treatments for specific psychological disorders based on current evidence, and make recommendations on more effective ways to disseminate these approaches. The Task Force first summarized some of the literature on the efficacy of different psychotherapeutic approaches. Although the initial list of treatments was not the product of an exhaustive review of the literature, this list provides documentation at a glance of the current status of psychosocial treatment. Both the criteria used and the list of treatments have now been updated (Chambless et al., 1996). Using strict methodological criteria, the Task Force classified treatments into the categories "well-established treatments," "probably efficacious treatments," and "experimental treatments." Criteria for defining "well-established treatments" and "probably efficacious treatments" in the updated report are presented in Table 3.1.

The Task Force identified a number of effective psychosocial techniques for the treatment of various mental disorders. Table 3.2 from the updated report gives an overview of some of the most effective psychosocial treatments for common psychological disorders.

In an important development, Roth and Fonagy (1995) reviewed the status of psychological treatments in a commissioned report to the National Health Service (NHS) of the UK. The purpose of this report was to create policy regarding the delivery of psychosocial treatments within the NHS; in other words, to move toward a requirement that treatments with proven efficacy be considered as first-line interventions. Similar to the APA Task Force, the NHS report concluded that psychosocial interventions, particularly cognitive-behavioral approaches and interpersonal psychotherapy (IPT), have proved efficacy for a number of disorders, including anxiety disorders, depression, eating disorders, psychotic disorders, and personality disorders.

Questions Answered by Current Research

As is demonstrated by the example of research on PDA, over the past 20 years it is clear that programs of systematic clinical research have occasioned a number of significant advances in our knowledge. First, we have accumulated considerable information on the general efficacy of well-specified and manualized psychosocial treatments when compared to no treatment or some credible alternative interventions. Second, component analyses of the necessary and sufficient conditions for the efficacy of these procedures have been undertaken. This has resulted in more streamlined and more powerful psychosocial procedures that in many cases are at least as effective or even more effective than existing pharmacological treatments

TABLE 3.1   Criteria for Empirically Validated Treatments

Well-Established Treatments

I. At least two good between-group design experiments demonstrating efficacy in one or more of the following ways:

   A. Superior to pill or psychological placebo or to another treatment

   B. Equivalent to an already established treatment in experiments with adequate statistical power (about 30 per group; cf. Kazdin & Bass, 1989)

OR

II. A large series of single case design experiments (n > 9) demonstrating efficacy. These experiments must have:

   A. Used good experimental designs, and

   B. Compared the intervention to another treatment as in I. A.

FURTHER CRITERIA FOR BOTH I AND II:

III. Experiments must be conducted with treatment manuals.

IV. Characteristics of the client samples must be clearly specified.

V. Effects must have been demonstrated by at least two different investigators or investigatory teams.

Probably Efficacious Treatments

I. Two experiments showing that the treatment is more effective than a waiting-list control group

OR

II. One or more experiments meeting the Well-Established Treatment Criteria I, III, and IV, but not V

OR

III. A small series of single case design experiments (n > 3) otherwise meeting Well-Established Treatment Criteria II, III, and IV

(Barlow, 1994). Third, some of the mechanisms of action present in many of these procedures have been explicated, although our knowledge is generally less well developed in this area. For example, experiencing or "emotionally processing" fear structures, using exposure-based procedures, and the resulting cognitive and emotional change seem to be important components of psychosocial anxiety-reduction techniques (Barlow, 1988; Barlow, Chorpita, & Turovsky, 1995). This research, in turn, has increased our knowledge of the nature of anxiety and panic.

TABLE 3.2   **Examples of Empirically Validated Treatments**

Well-Established Treatments	Citation for Efficacy Evidence
ANXIETY AND STRESS:	
Cognitive behavior therapy for panic disorder with and without agoraphobia	Barlow et al. (1989) Clark et al. (1994)
Cognitive behavior therapy for generalized anxiety disorder	Butler et al. (1991) Borkovec et al. (1987)
Group cognitive behavioral therapy for social phobia	Heimberg et al. (1990) Mattick & Peters (1988)
Exposure treatment for agoraphobia	Trull et al. (1988)
Exposure treatment for social phobia	Feske & Chambless (1995)
Exposure and response prevention for obsessive-compulsive disorder	Balkom et al. (1994)
Stress inoculation training for coping with stressors	Saunders et al. (in press)
Systematic desensitization for simple phobia	Kazdin & Wilcoxon (1976)
DEPRESSION:	
Cognitive therapy for depression	Dobson (1989)
Interpersonal therapy for depression	DiMascio et al. (1979) Elkin et al. (1989)
HEALTH PROBLEMS:	
Behavior therapy for headache	Blanchard et al. (1987) Holroyd & Penzien (1990)
Cognitive behavior therapy for irritable bowel syndrome	Blanchard et al. (1980) Lynch & Zamble (1989)
Cognitive behavior therapy for chronic pain	Keefe et al. (1992) Turner & Clancy (1988)
Cognitive behavior therapy for bulimia	Agras et al. (1989) Thackwray et al. (1993)
Interpersonal therapy for bulimia	Fairburn et al. (1993) Wilfley et al. (1993)
PROBLEMS OF CHILDHOOD:	
Behavior modification for enuresis	Houts et al. (1994)
Parent-training programs for children with oppositional behavior	Walter & Gilmore (1973) Wells & Egan (1988)
MARTIAL DISCORD:	
Behavioral marital therapy	Azrin, Bersalel et al. (1980) Jacobson & Follette (1985)
SEXUAL DYSFUNCTION:	
Behavior therapy for female orgasmic dysfunction and male erectile dysfunction	LoPiccolo & Stock (1986) Auerbach & Kilmann (1977)
OTHER:	
Family education programs for schizophrenia	Hogarty et al. (1986) Falloon et al. (1985)
Behavior modification for developmentally disabled individuals	Scotti et al. (1991) Kazdin (1977)
Token economy programs	Liberman (1972)

(continued)

TABLE 3.2   Continued

Probably Efficacious Treatments	Citation for Efficacy Evidence
ANXIETY:	
Applied relaxation for panic disorder	Ost (1988)
Applied relaxation for generalized anxiety disorder	Barlow et al., 1992
Exposure treatment for PTSD	Borkovec & Costello, 1993
	Foa et al. (1991)
Exposure treatment for simple phobia	Keane et al. (1989)
	Leitenberg & Callahan (1973)
Stress inoculation training for PTSD	Ost et al. (1991)
Group exposure and response prevention for obsessive-compulsive disorder	Foa et al. (1991)
	Fals-Stewart et al. (1993)
Relapse prevention program for obsessive-compulsive disorder	Hiss et al. (1994)
CHEMICAL ABUSE AND DEPENDENCE:	
Behavior therapy for cocaine abuse	Higgins et al. (1993)
Brief dynamic therapy for opiate dependence	Woody et al. (1990)
Cognitive therapy for opiate dependence	Woody et al. (1990)
Cognitive behavior therapy for benzodiazepine withdrawal in panic disorder patients	Otto et al. (1993)
	Spiegel et al. (1994)
DEPRESSION:	
Brief dynamic therapy	Gallagher-Thompson & Steffen (1994)
Cognitive therapy for geriatric patients	Scogin & McElreath (1994)
Psychoeducational treatment	Lewinsohn et al. (1989)
Reminiscence therapy for geriatric	Arean et al. (1993)
	Scogin & McElreath (1994)
Self-control therapy	Fuchs & Rehm (1977)
	Rehm et al. (1979)
HEALTH PROBLEMS:	
Behavior therapy for childhood obesity	Epstein et al. (1994)
	Wheeler & Hess (1976)
Group cognitive behavior therapy for bulimia	Mitchell et al. (1990)
MARTIAL DISCORD:	
Emotionally focused couples therapy	Johnson & Greenberg (1985)
Insight-oriented marital therapy	Snyder et al. (1989, 1991)
PROBLEMS OF CHILDHOOD:	
Behavior modification of encopresis	O'Brien et al. (1986)
Family anxiety management training for anxiety disorders	Barrett et al. (in press)
OTHER:	
Behavior modification for sex offenders	Marshall et al. (1991)
Dialectical behavior therapy for borderline personality disorder	Linehan et al. (1991)
Habit reversal and control techniques	Azrin, Nunn, & Frantz (1980)
	Azrin, Nunn, & Frantz-Renshaw (1980)

Most of the psychotherapy outcome studies comprising the modern era of systematic research have been carried out using traditional clinical research methodology. These methods are effective in answering some clinical questions, but they de-emphasize others. Advances in clinical science have not overcome the enormous barriers separating science and practice. We will briefly address some of the problems and their sources in the present chapter, while the others will be addressed more extensively later.

The applied question that practitioners need to have answered was clearly stated almost 30 years ago by Gordon Paul: "What treatment, by whom, is most effective for this individual with that specific problem, and under which set of circumstances, and how does that come about?" (Paul, 1969). While a great deal of progress has been made, we still do not know nearly enough about how to link research knowledge to individual clients, individual practitioners, and specific contexts. Doing so will require more knowledge about the important functional characteristics of clients, practitioners, and settings, and the development of theoretical systems adequate to organize those characteristics into a coherent whole. We also know little about how to give away the knowledge that we do have: how to disseminate, train, supervise, and ensure consistent quality in services delivered. We still have work to do in distinguishing clinically important change from change that is reliable but relatively unimportant. A number of practical issues are also not being adequately addressed, including how to prevent problems, how to predict treatment responsiveness, and how to make interventions maximally efficient.

Some of these problems are encouraged by the present structure of clinical outcome research, particularly because of its enormous reliance on group comparison designs with syndromal entities. Consider, for example, the reliance on inferential statistics considered only at the group level of analysis. This has lead to an unfortunate and unwarranted emphasis on statistical "significance" (p values) as the outcome of greatest importance (Hunter, 1997; Loftus, 1996). For example, the most usual method of reporting the results of group comparison outcome studies is to note that certain psychosocial procedures are significantly more effective statistically than no treatment or alternative forms of treatment. Put more precisely, using the .05 level of probability, there were less than five chances in 100 of obtaining differences this large assuming that only chance factors were operating. This can be important information, but it does not translate into the clinical significance of the treatment, nor into the size of the effect it produces, and often seems to deflect attention away from these issues (Hunter, 1997).

During the 1980s clinical investigators began correcting for this deficit in several ways. Many studies began estimating the percentage of individual patients reaching a certain clinical criterion, usually designated as "clinical responder" status. Thus, we arrived at the oft-cited summary statistic that 60% to 75% of patients with PDA showed some "clinical benefit" from in vivo exposure procedures (Barlow, 1988; Clum, 1989; Jannson & Ost, 1982). Similarly, using meta-analytic procedures described in Chapter 1, other investigators (e.g., Jacobson, Wilson, & Tupper, 1988; Trull, Nietzel, & Main, 1988) demonstrated that effect sizes from exposure-based modalities were substantially greater than no treatment or comparative treatments. While not a substitute for appropriate estimates of clinical significance, effect sizes convey some idea of the extent of behavior change after treatment.

The enormous emphasis on internal validity in the current research approach has tended to de-emphasize the equally important issues of external validity: the degree to which research knowledge will generalize to other settings. The ultimate applied question framed by Paul is, first and foremost, a question about external validity: A practitioner needs to know how to turn research knowledge into specific treatment recommendations for a specific client. In most applied areas, we know relatively little about how to group clients in ways that predict treatment outcome (Hayes, Nelson, & Jarrett, 1987). Furthermore, we know relatively little about how to disseminate our effective treatments to the practice base. This latter problem is a highly significant one and justifies a more extended discussion.

Problems with Dissemination of Effective Psychosocial Treatments

In Chapter 1 we discussed the lack of influence of traditional clinical research findings on practice. That is, practitioners seemed reluctant to take advantage of the accumulating evidence from clinical research, particularly in the form of large clinical trials. Now, evidence has accumulated that individuals suffering from a number of psychological disorders are substantially disadvantaged by the scientist–practitioner split. In the case of panic disorder with agoraphobia, for example and as previously reviewed, psychotherapy researchers from all theoretical persuasions have concluded that structured exposure-based exercises are a necessary part of effective treatment. Nevertheless, three recent surveys reported that a large percentage of phobic individuals are being treated with general counseling, hospitalization, or medication, while only 15% to 38% are receiving psychosocial interventions that have been shown to be effective (Breier, Charney, & Heninger, 1986; Goisman et al., 1993; Taylor, King, Margraf, et al., 1989). See Table 3.3.

TABLE 3.3   **Utilization of Effective Psychosocial Treatments in Cases of Panic and Phobic Disorders**

Study	Sample Size	**Percent Receiving Effective Psychosocial Treatment**
Taylor et al. (1989)	794	15% (counseling and hospitalization: 50%)
Breier et al. (1986)	60	16%
Goisman et al. (1993)	231	38% (medication: 93%)

Adapted from: "Psychological Interventions in the Era of Managed Competition," by D. H. Barlow (1994). *Clinical Psychology: Science and Practice,* 1 (2), 109–122.

Moreover, national probability samples indicate that only approximately one out of three individuals with phobia are receiving any treatment at all, let alone an effective one (Regier et al., 1993). It seems clear from these data that psychosocial procedures with proven effectiveness are simply not available to the majority of individuals who would benefit from them.

Some might conclude that this state of affairs will be self-correcting, since new clinicians progressing through our training programs will surely have developed the expertise to administer these effective interventions. Unfortunately, this assumption seems to have no basis in fact. The Task Force from the Division of Clinical Psychology, previously cited, also collected data on the extent of training in empirically validated treatments ongoing in doctoral clinical training programs (Crits-Christoph, Frank, Chambless, Brody, & Karp, 1995). These data indicate that relatively few students in organized clinical psychology programs are being taught these interventions. Table 3.4 presents the percentage of American Psychological Association doctoral programs that offer training in empirically validated treatments. Ten out of the 18 treatments listed in Table 3.4 are taught in courses, or supervised during clinical work in less than 50% of the doctoral programs. Less than 30% of the programs offer training in well-established treatments, such as family therapy for schizophrenia, cognitive behavioral therapy for social phobia, and interpersonal psychotherapy. Only cognitive therapy for depression reaches 80% of the students, at least by being mentioned in course work or supervised to some extent in clinical situations. Furthermore, these data are likely to be an *overestimate* based on reporting biases. There is no reason to think that the data would be different in training programs for the other mental health professions.

Unanswered Questions: How Effective Is Treatment?

The appalling lack of influence of traditional clinical research on practice is due in large part to questions of vital interest to practitioners left unanswered by our clinical research efforts. Among these questions are the following: How effective are these procedures, for whom will they work, and with whom will they fail? Related questions involve the generalizability and maintenance of the effects of these treatments, and their impact in a variety of settings and practice contexts.

One reason we do not know the answers to these questions now is that our traditional research approach generally does not address them. For example, in order to know who improves *due to treatment*, we need to know something more than pre and post scores on a large number of individuals. Improvement in these scores for any given individual could easily be due to extraneous factors, or even to measurement error—not to the effect of treatment per se. Considered at the level of the group, random assignment holds such things equal across groups, but the very nature of the question "who improves due to treatment" requires that we distinguish the effect of treatment *at the level of the individual*, not merely the group.

Other areas of ignorance come not from the weaknesses of group comparison approaches per se, but from the politics of research programs. Funding for large research centers is usually based on a technological model of treatment

TABLE 3.4   Percentage of APA Doctoral Programs That Offer Training in Empirically Validated Treatments

Well-Established Treatments	Taught in Course	Supervised Clinical Work
Beck's cognitive therapy for depression	89.6	80.0
Behavior modification for developmentally disabled individuals	34.1	36.3
Behavior modification for enuresis and encopresis	45.2	40.0
Behavior therapy for headache and for irritable bowel syndrome	38.5	40.7
Behavior therapy for female orgasmic dysfunction and male erectile dysfunction	38.5	27.4
Behavioral marital therapy	57.0	60.7
Cognitive behavior therapy for chronic pain	47.4	46.7
Cognitive behavior therapy for panic disorder with and without agoraphobia	64.4	69.6
Cognitive behavior therapy for generalized anxiety disorder	69.6	77.0
Exposure treatment for phobias (agoraphobia, social phobia, simple phobia) and PTSD	64.4	59.3
Exposure and response prevention for obsessive-compulsive disorder	58.5	48.1
Family education programs for schizophrenia	24.4	22.2
Group cognitive behavioral therapy for social phobia	24.4	19.3
Interpersonal therapy for bulimia	20.7	31.9

Probably Efficacious Treatments	Taught in Course	Supervised Clinical Work
Klerman and Weissman's interpersonal therapy for depression	25.9	16.3
Parent-training programs for children with oppositional behavior	57.8	60.0
Systematic desensitization for simple phobia	68.9	62.2
Token economy programs	45.2	25.2
Applied relaxation for panic disorder	65.9	72.6
Brief dynamic therapies	65.9	61.5
Behavior modification for sex offenders	23.7	27.4
Dialectical behavior therapy for borderline personality disorder	17.0	16.3
Emotionally focused couples therapy	39.3	46.7
Habit reversal and control techniques	41.5	35.6
Lewinsohn's psychoeducational treatment for depression	36.3	6.3

development that was borrowed from the FDA for use with pharmacotherapy. In drug research, what is most at issue is "Is this drug safe and effective for a given condition." If the answer is "yes," the treatment can be delivered in a consistent manner merely by following the prescribing instructions on the physician's insert. Costs can be precisely specified. The drug is highly specified via chemical formula.

Psychosocial interventions are not like drugs. Their precise components are hard to stipulate, practitioners must often be thoroughly trained to deliver them, quality is hard to assess and maintain, their feasibility is crucial, and their costs may be hard to specify. Researchers are now virtually required to solve some of these problems in funded research. It is expected, for example, that treatment will be specified through manuals or other means (Wilson, 1995), and measures of treatment adherence and competence will be developed (Waltz, Addis, Koerner, & Jacobson, 1993). Other problems that go beyond the usual technological approach, however—including feasibility, disseminability, and cost-effectiveness—are generally underresearched. In practice settings the importance of such questions is immediately and unavoidably evident.

Problems in Applying Research Results to Practice Situations

At the most basic level, it would seem one might answer the question, "How effective is a treatment?" by looking at percentages of success based on some clearly specified criterion of success in between-group comparison studies. But even this question is very difficult to answer from research that has been reported thus far, although, as mentioned above, the progression of research on effective psychosocial treatments has advanced considerably in recent years. To estimate the percentage of individuals improved, one must look at those groups within a controlled clinical trial that have received a relatively unadulterated form of the treatment; that is, the treatment should have been delivered in roughly the same fashion as one would expect it to be delivered clinically. This precludes, for example, crossover designs where patients receive one treatment for half of the experiment and then "cross over" to receive another treatment for the second half of the experiment. This also precludes, to some extent, designs where there are groups of clients receiving only one component of the treatment. To take one example, a therapist might administer intensive in vivo exposure to patients with agoraphobia, without instructions to practice between sessions, an aspect that seems very important in the context of these treatments (Barlow, 1988). Of course, interventions administered in research settings are often delivered in an ideal fashion, with many experimental assistants ensuring that the details of treatment are delivered precisely. These conditions do not obtain in typical applied settings.

For these reasons, there are very few instances in which interventions have been delivered to large-enough groups of clients, in the manner described above, such that determination of percentage of success would be useful (other difficulties notwithstanding for the moment). To take one early example, an important and widely cited study at the time was reported by Emmelkamp & Kuipers (1979), who lumped together a number of their experiments in which patients with agoraphobia received different versions of exposure-based procedures, depending on what experiment they were in. These versions included imaginal exposure, instructions to practice, supervised practice, cognitive restructuring, and the like. Some clients received only one component, other received different components or a combination of components, depending on the purpose of the experiment. All were treated, of course, in a predetermined number of sessions and in accordance with other experimental design requirements in force at the time. Those patients who responded to a letter asking for follow-up information 4 years after they finished their particular experiment were included in this analysis. The criterion for "success" was movement of 2 points on a 9-point, self-rated, global rating scale of improvement on the "main phobia." Naturally, these reports are subject to the usual distortions of self-report of progress. The data indicate that 75% of the respondents had met the criteria of achieving and maintaining at least a 2-point improvement after 4 years.

Obviously, some clients must have improved more than 2 points, but from this study, and most reports of its kind, it is not clear who improved, with what particular characteristics and, more importantly, who failed. Furthermore, as Garfield (1981) pointed out, at the time, improvement of 2 points on a 9-point scale, vague as this criterion is, can mean relatively little improvement for at least some clients. For example, in one follow-up study, where these data were reported, only 18% of a group of 56 patients with PDA were "symptom-free" at follow-up, although 83% had met the criteria for "improvement" (McPherson, Brougham, & McLaren, 1980). More recent "longitudinal" follow-up strategies, where the fate of specific individuals is determined over time, rather than the average response of the group, confirms that the average response, assessed cross-sectionally, can be misleading (Brown & Barlow, 1995).

There are other limitations to the interpretation of these data. For example, the Emmelkamp and Kuipers (1979) data were concerned solely with clients seen in the Netherlands by either Emmelkamp or one of his colleagues. Similarly, those data reported by McPherson, Brougham, and McLaren (1980) were for clients all locally seen and followed up only by telephone. Thus, the generality of these findings across clinical centers is uncertain. Finally, to reiterate, these figures are gleaned, for the most part, from controlled experiments where treatment was delivered in an artificial manner to conform to experimental requirements (e.g., a specific number of sessions, exposure only during sessions rather than between, no imaginal exposure, etc.). This is quite different from the usual delivery of these treatments in clinical settings. Furthermore, as noted above, reports of *individual* clinical success and failure are often not reported.

Unfortunately, this difficulty with controlled clinical trials continues. One large ongoing study at four different clinical research sites is testing the separate and combined effects of PCT and drug treatments for PDA. In this study there are five distinct experimental conditions to which patients are randomly assigned. In three of the experimental conditions or groups, PCT is administered either alone, in combination with drug, or in combination with placebo. In the remaining two groups, the drug is administered alone or placebo alone.

To determine percent of success from a given treatment, a clinician might examine results from the PCT or drug conditions administered alone or the combination treatment, depending on which treatment he or she might be considering for the next individual patient coming into the office. The clinician might assume that the results from PCT alone, for example, would provide a good estimate of the expected clinical effects from this approach, if this were the treatment being considered. But the rather rigid application of these treatments, as dictated by the detailed methodological requirements of the clinical trial, also make these treatments somewhat unrepresentative of how they might be delivered in a more flexible practice setting. For example, all patients in this trial received 11 sessions of PCT, and only 11 sessions, unless they dropped out prior to completion of the treatment. Treatment was delivered based on a detailed manual that prohibited interactions that were "off task" or not relevant to the treatment. Thus, if the patient was experiencing a particular life crisis that he or she wished to discuss, a rationale would be offered (gently) that it would be very important to continue on with the treatment although we could discuss the life crisis at a somewhat later time. If, in the judgment of the clinician and the patient, the life crisis required immediate attention, the patient would have to be dropped from the study, since treatment could no longer be administered in the prescribed manner. In addition, a very large number of assessment procedures were administered in this trial to examine in detail the workings of the individual treatments and their relative effects. But these measures, in both their number and complexity, would be impractical and unrealistic in a clinical setting. The difficulty is, of course, that these detailed assessment procedures alone might contribute to the effects of treatment in some unknown way; that is, they might be "reactive."

Another major factor raising questions about the applicability of results from this clinical trial to practice situations involves the selection of patients. In this particular study patients first had to meet detailed inclusion criteria, since the target disorder under study was panic disorder with no more than mild agoraphobia. Patients had to meet criteria for panic disorder, but were excluded if agoraphobic avoidance was more than moderate. As many as 50% of the patients otherwise meeting criteria for panic disorder were excluded on this basis alone. In addition, since patients had to be willing to be randomized to either drug or nondrug treatment, these individuals had to meet medical criteria that would allow them to take a tricyclic antidepressant, the drug under study. A number of patients who might have benefited from PCT did not get into the study because they failed to meet these medical criteria. Finally, and perhaps most importantly, patients had to agree to be randomly assigned to one condition or the other, meaning that they would be willing to enter either the psychosocial treatment, the drug treatment, or combination, and that, possibly, they would be taking placebo medication. A large number of patients who had a clear preference for either psychosocial or drug treatment refused to enter the experiment because they did not wish to receive the alternative treatment. Similarly, a number of patients did not wish to be placed on placebo medications. For all of these reasons, fully 80% of patients otherwise meeting criteria for PDA could not participate in this study for one reason or another.

Obviously, this result raises substantial questions about the generality of this study to the "average" individual patient with PDA.

Effects of Treatment on the Individual

These issues also raise serious questions about the effectiveness of these procedures with an individual patient walking into an individual therapist's office. Will this particular patient be one of the approximately 12% who drop out of exposure-based treatments (Jansson & Ost, 1982), or perhaps one of the 30% who not only fail to improve, but perhaps deteriorate a bit? What are the patient characteristics that are associated with improvement, with no improvement, or with deterioration? Perhaps just as important, what are the patient characteristics and the characteristics of the patient's situation that predict marked improvement to the point of "cure," versus minimal to moderate improvement in the neighborhood of 2 points on a 9-point scale? As noted in the first chapter, traditional research is not designed to provide answers to these questions, despite the overriding importance of these answers to practitioners.

As a result, even with the major contribution to knowledge of traditional clinical research in the area of anxiety disorders, practitioners still are unable to predict with any certainty the effectiveness of these procedures with their own individual patients. It is likely that if clinicians experience two or three failures in a row they may give up on an intervention, such as exposure-based therapy, in favor of some other recent innovation. Thus, research and practice continue in parallel.

This, of course, is not a newly discovered issue. It has been raised many times in many contexts. For example, several decades ago both Kiesler (1971) and Paul (1969), from the standpoint of traditional comparative outcome research, called for much greater attention to organismic variables (i.e., individual differences) and their interaction with the effects of various treatments. More recently Greenfield (1989) and Persons (1991) have highlighted, once again, the somewhat artificial nature of clinical trials and the necessity to make clinical research more realistic and generalizable. But, as evidence from the current status of clinical research suggests, traditional research strategies seldom accomplish these particular goals.

Consider this partial list of unanswered questions: (a) How effective is a therapeutic procedure? That is, how many people with a specific problem will improve to what extent? (b) What causes greater, as opposed to lesser, degrees of success, and what causes failure? (c) Will an otherwise successful intervention in a research setting generalize to other individuals in a practice setting? It is unlikely that practitioners will be seriously influenced by research, despite impressive contributions to our knowledge, until answers to these questions are forthcoming.

Alternative Models of Research

Recognizing the lack of influence of traditional research on practice, many skilled theorists and investigators attempted early on to adapt research methodology or research practices to applied settings so that the data produced from the research efforts will be more meaningful and relevant. Sechrest (1975) suggested that practitioners become more involved in research in an administrative and participatory way. For example, clinicians could assist in planning or could make clinical records available. Also, clinicians could act as judges in clinical research projects. Sechrest did not suggest how the unanswered questions above might be answered, however.

In 1971, Kiesler described a series of questions of more interest to "artisans" (practitioners) than to scientists, such as who gets chosen for therapy, who drops out, and who succeeds or fails, recognizing, even then, the narrow focus of traditional research. But Kiesler did not propose new strategies to answer these questions, suggesting instead that client and therapist variables thought to be important by clinicians could be plugged into grand factorial designs. Such studies would be enormous, and enormously costly, and in decades since the recommendation was made there are virtually no examples of their being implemented.

Quasi-Experimental Designs

Realizing that traditional experimental designs were often impractical in applied settings, Campbell and his associates originated quasi-experimental designs (Campbell & Stanley, 1963; Cook & Campbell, 1979). This strategy, developed particularly in the context of social policy research, involves an adaptation of traditional research designs such that causal inferences are still possible, albeit with an explicit recognition of those factors that pose threats to the validity of the causal inferences. The major difference between quasi-experiments and more traditional experimental methodology is that the quasi-experiments do not use random assignment to groups to create the comparisons from which treatment-caused change is inferred. Instead, " . . . the comparisons depend on non-equivalent groups that differ from each other in many ways other than the presence of a treatment whose effects are being tested. The task confronting persons who try to interpret the results from quasi-experiments is basically one of separating the effects of a treatment from those due to the initial noncomparability between the average units in each treatment group; only the effects of the treatment are of research interest" (Cook & Campbell, 1979, p. 6).

Basically, there are two kinds of quasi-experimental designs. One is a variation of the more traditional randomized, between-group comparison, termed *nonequivalent group design*. In this design the assignment to groups is not randomized, and therefore the groups are not directly comparable in one or more ways (in addition to the administration of the independent variable or treatment). The second is an interrupted time-series design in which the effects of a treatment are inferred by comparing measures taken at several points before the introduction of a treatment with measures taken at several points afterward. In a well-known example, the effects of a new tough crackdown on speeding in one state were evaluated by looking at traffic fatalities for a lengthy period before and after the introduction of the law. As noted in Barlow and Hersen (1984), this latter quasi-experimental design has much in common logically with some of the single case experimental designs used in studying the effects of interventions on behavior change, particularly the withdrawal design.

A monumental contribution of this work to research in any context is the elucidation and specification of the specific threats to internal and external validity proposed originally by Campbell (1959) and elaborated by Campbell and Stanley (1963) and Cook and Campbell (1979). What becomes clear from their analysis is that levels of inference or conclusions from an experiment are on a continuum, with increasing threats to the inferences or conclusions one can draw as one moves further away from tightly controlled experimental designs. For example, in research on psychosocial interventions, as one moves from the traditional randomized group-comparison or single case experimental design toward the uncontrolled case study, one will be less and less confident about the cause of any effects one observes. With these threats in mind, well-specified conclusions can be drawn even from the individual case study, when properly conducted, and there are many strategies available to reduce the threats to internal validity occurring in the typical uncontrolled case studies or series of cases (e.g., Kazdin, 1981).

Highlighting the Individual

Kiesler (1971) cogently observed that the science of behavior change looks for laws applying to individuals generally. The differences between research traditions have not so much to do with the nomothetic purposes of science as they do with the strategy used to reach these nomothetic generalizations. Traditional research methods concentrate on a level of analysis that emphasizes general tendencies against the measured but unanalyzed background of individual variability. Practitioners, however, see *individuals,* either singly or in groups. Individual variability (e.g., in the need for certain treatments, in the response to particular treatments) is part of their foreground concern. There is a lack of fit between the two that is inherent.

Consideration of the state of our knowledge, discussed above, would seem to point to the necessity for a new emphasis on the individual in applied research in order to address some of the unanswered questions. This emphasis would highlight the effects of various interventions on individual clients, examining client-treatment interaction, client-treatment matching, and other aspects of a particular individual's response to treatment and what this response can tell us about other individuals who will experience the same treatment. It is the importance of this issue that distinguishes the area of human services from other areas of science. This is the one single factor that requires substantial alterations in, and additions to, the way we do science. But a methodology that highlights the individual and, at the same time, maintains the integrity of an empirical and scientific approach to the study of human behavior has been slow in developing.

Deviant-Case Analysis

One creative approach, proposed by Alan Ross in 1963 and elaborated on somewhat later (Ross, 1981), is called *deviant-case analysis.* The essential feature of this method is the intensive study of individuals (participating in research employing traditional randomized group designs) who differ markedly from the group average. Ross proposes that this be done immediately after the experiment is finished, preferably by the experimenter or a collaborating clinician, so as not to lose contact with the patients participating in the experiment. Ross notes that this would be a much less expensive strategy than gathering detailed information on every single subject participating in a traditional experiment. Yet, this strategy would yield a great deal of data and, ultimately, knowledge, on the variety of patterns of individual responses to a given fixed intervention.

In this way, at least within the context of traditional research, some information on the generalizability of findings from experimental patients to patients entering the practitioner's office would be available through the process of *logical generalization* (Barlow & Hersen, 1984; Edgington, 1966). This simply refers to the process of deciding, on logical grounds, how similar the experimental subjects are to the ones seen by the practitioner. Thus, practitioners reading reports on deviant-case analyses, subsequent to reports of the major research findings, could decide when to use the procedures and with whom, depending on the similarity of the patients they are seeing to those in the deviant-case analyses. Deviant-case analyses, then, would not involve practitioners in the research process as researchers or evaluators, but should ensure, at the very least, that they would consume research findings. This strategy will form an important part of our recommendations outlined below.

Single Case Designs for Practitioners

Within the area of applied research, a methodology capable of determining the effects of interventions in individuals and the reasons for these effects has evolved (e.g., Barlow & Hersen, 1984; Jones, 1993). For example, much of the research in the problem area of PDA, previously discussed, has utilized this methodology, most often termed *single case experimental design* or time-series methodology. We will use both terms primarily because the former, although widely adopted, can mistakenly suggest that these designs never require multiple subjects; the latter focuses attention more on the intensive data analytic method these designs employ but is not as widely used. This methodology has been helpful in determining effective and efficient components of interventions in those experiments where component analysis is the goal, as well as ascertaining basic mechanisms of action of given interventions. Usually this is done through careful introduction and withdrawal of various components of a given intervention in the manner described in Chapters 5 through 8 of this book.

A major advance in our applied research efforts has been practitioners' increasing use of single case experimental strategies in applied settings to determine the effectiveness of treatment or, on occasion, of active ingredients within a treatment across a small series of patients. Nevertheless, the overwhelming majority of research activity involving single case experimental designs to date continues to be carried out in applied research centers rather than in the offices of practitioners. In part this may be due to the relative unfamiliarity of this experimental approach and some of the perceived practical difficulties thought to conflict with the implementation of research of any kind in an applied setting (Agras, Kazdin, & Wilson, 1979; Barlow, 1994). Among many limitations, often mentioned are ethical and practical difficulties. These include, but are not limited to, imposing baseline phases on patients who may require immediate treatment, or withdrawing presumably active ingredients from the treatment package of a patient who has been doing better. This, of course, is a common characteristic of the withdrawal type of single case experimental design often reported in the literature (Barlow & Hersen, 1984; also see Chapter 6). Single case experimentation shares other difficulties with more traditional between-group comparisons when used by practitioners, including the increasing complexity of necessary dependent variables, such as sophisticated ambulatory physiological measures of clinical phenomena. Few practitioners would be expected to have on hand this state-of-the-art measurement instrumentation (e.g., Hofmann & Barlow, in press).

Some of the major obstacles to practitioners' doing research with individuals in their settings are practical. Thus, modifications in single case experimental designs have been proposed that make it possible for practitioners to use these tools to establish functionally analytic relationships and participate in the research process as researchers and evaluators (Barlow, 1981; Hayes, 1981; Hilliard, 1993; Jones, 1993). These developments include the use of practical and realistic outcomes measures easily employed in the offices or settings of most practitioners, and the modification of experimental strategies or the organization of new strategies so that ethical and practical problems preventing their use in applied settings are overcome. A description of these strategies, along with the presentation of realistic and practical measures easily employed by practitioners, will form the major part of this book.

Perhaps as important, the rise of managed care presents new opportunities for the practical conduct and implementation of applied research. In that context, single case designs, clinical replication series, group comparison designs, and program evaluation strategies are all relevant and needed. By including all these components into an integrated system, a research engine for science-based practice results. In the following chapter, a model of research involvement in integrated managed behavioral health care systems will be presented. We will return to the issue of applied research in general practice settings, including private practice, following a description of time-series methods practitioners can use to generate data relevant to applied issues (Chapters 5–8).

4 Opportunities for Integrating the Scientist Practitioner into a System of Managed Behavioral Health Care Delivery

Introduction

Scientist practitioners are not yet fully connected to the opportunities the changing environment in health care delivery presents, and they may seem to envision a future that is quite similar to the past. We think the changes will be more dramatic and that those scientist practitioners prepared to use their skills in new ways are most likely to prosper. The purpose of this chapter is to develop a comprehensive model of applied research and science-based practice in integrated, managed systems of behavioral health care delivery. Our goal is to define a set of professional roles, public needs, and practical economic benefits that can marry the skills of scientist practitioners and an industrialized health care delivery system.

The key to this marriage is the mutual benefits that it promises to the stakeholders in behavioral health care delivery. Scientist practitioners have an opportunity for significant advancements in knowledge, for the development and delivery of quality clinical services, and for an increase in the need for their analytic skills. The health care delivery system has an opportunity for an increase in the perceived and real value of their services for the public, and thus the economic success that may be possible. The government, employers, and the public see the possibility of better-quality services at a lower overall cost.

In what follows we will consider behavioral health from a systems perspective, beginning long before a client seeks out assistance for a behavioral problem. All components of this model are being implemented in some segments of the industry today, but so far as we know no system yet exists that integrates them all. In many areas, this model is forward looking. Yet the forces are clearly in place to move the health care delivery system in this direction, which promises better health care for society at large. If scientist practitioners rise to the challenge, they will have a major role in determining the direction that is followed.

An Integrated System of Science-Based Practice

A model of science-based practice in the era of managed care is shown in Figure 4.1. This model is presented for two reasons: First, it helps describe the logical components of health care delivery that can be researched and developed by scientist–practitioners. In that aspect, the model is meant to make the domains

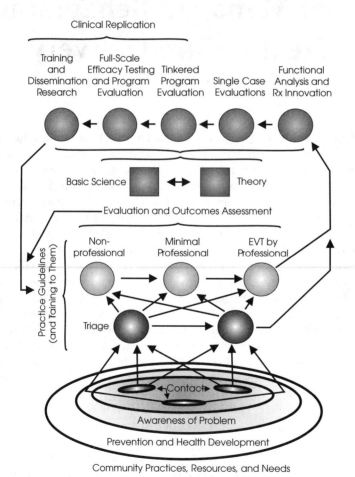

An Integrated System of Science-Based Practice

FIGURE 4.1   An integrated model of science-based practice in managed behavioral health care.

more coherent, rather than to prescribe certain kinds of actions. Second, the model suggests specific ways that scientist practitioners can use their skills to develop and evaluate the behavioral health care delivery system. In that aspect, the model is more prescriptive and helps place the scientific methods that are described in this book into a larger and more coherent context.

The model begins at the bottom of the figure, and moves up, beginning with the largest circle representing the entire community and its practices, resources, and needs. In the context of those practices, resources, and needs, there are nascent health care needs, long before there are known and treated behavioral health problems.

Prevention and Health Development

Behavioral health problems do not emerge in whole cloth, and they do not visit people randomly. They develop over time, in certain people in certain settings. If it is cheaper and easier to prevent a problem in the first place, than to treat it once it occurs, then there are economic contingencies in the modern world of health care delivery to promote an early interest in prevention and health development.

It has long been recognized that primary prevention—the prevention of a disorder prior to its occurrence (Kessler & Albee, 1975)—could sometimes save human and economic costs as compared to even fairly effective intervention after the fact. For example, solving drug problems after they occur is difficult, expensive, and time-consuming (Rice, Kelman, & Miller, 1991), while some drug-prevention programs are known to reduce the incidence of this difficult-to-treat problem (e.g., Botvin & Tortu, 1988). Similarly, some health problems—AIDS for example—are currently impossible to cure but can be prevented through behavioral means (Leigh & Stall, 1993). The federal government is now putting increased funding into prevention, and models have been developed of national research programs in this area (Coie, Watt, West, Hawkins, Asarnow, Markman, Ramey, Shure, & Long, 1993).

There are several difficulties that primary prevention has faced, however, particularly in behavioral health areas (Albee & Ryan-Finn, 1993). Prevention research is inherently longitudinal, is relatively difficult to conduct, and has been chronically underfunded. Perhaps more importantly, the results of prevention research have not been of immediate economic relevance to a specific economic sector, but only to society at large. This put a huge drag on the practical importance of prevention. Even if prevention programs could prevent behavioral disorders, who would pay for them, especially once the era of big government programs faded?

Increasingly, consolidated managed care systems begin to provide an answer to this question. So long as delivery systems were paid on the basis of services delivered, not lives covered, there was no incentive to prevent behavioral disorders. So long as the health care coverage was divided among hundreds or thousands of firms, movement of consumers between plans made prevention programs economically uninteresting for a given company, even when they were effective, because the payback time exceeded the likely consumer retention interval. Both of these factors are rapidly changing as indemnity insurance coverage disappears and the industry consolidates. Consolidation is leading to huge MCOs. For example, in 1997 the top five PPOs covered over 85,000,000 lives (The National Psychologist, 1997). Only six months later, mergers had produced two huge companies, Magellan and Options, that together covered 90 million lives—over 60% of the market. As the size of MCOs increases and the number of firms decreases, there is a reduction of movement between health care plans by consumers. This in turn makes the investment in prevention one that might pay off financially for MCOs. Adding major impetus to this process, beginning in 1998 the National Committee for Quality Assurance (NCQA), the major accrediting body in managed care, began implementing preventative care standards as part of their accreditation criteria. Thus, for the first time, prevention programs not only *could* work in the abstract, but increasingly they are both required and potentially economically helpful for the industry.

Scientist practitioners have a great deal to contribute to this area, and the resources to develop the knowledge base are growing both within the federal government and within managed care. But prevention is not merely a different focus: It is also a different level of analysis and a different way of thinking about problems. Thus, taking advantage of this opportunity will require conceptual readjustment.

Psychotherapists tend to address and treat social and behavioral problems (drug abuse, AIDS, teenage pregnancy) as they occur at the level of the individual. Prevention and health development cannot be approached in this fashion for two reasons. First, approaching prevention one individual at a time means that large segments of the total population are now individual clients. This is a costly and unworkable approach. Society can hardly afford to place a psychological nanny in every home. The alternative in prevention is a public health model, based largely on epidemiology. Epidemiologists study the incidence, prevalence, and distribution of diseases and other health-related problems in specified populations in an effort to control these problems on a community-wide or population-wide basis (Lilienfeld & Stolley, 1994). The concepts epidemiologists have developed to work with this level of analysis provide a powerful and workable set of concepts, particularly when combined with the experimental rigor and active intervention orientation of scientist practitioners. We will explore some of these concepts briefly below.

Second, prevention is not necessarily problem focused in a fashion that would be recognized by psychotherapists as relevant to mental health. Prevention researchers have long recognized (Joffe, Albee, & Kelly, 1984) that prevention does not involve merely removing the unhealthy goads to problematic behavior (e.g., stress, abuse)—an approach that is somewhat similar to traditional mental health approaches. Prevention programs are often also constructive. They are designed to create competencies and coping skills that are prophylactic, even when unhealthy goads to problematic behavior exist. This can lead to areas of interest that would be surprising to psychotherapists. Developing academic skills in children, for example, prevents a wide number of negative behavioral health outcomes (Biglan, 1995), and yet the dividing line between clinical and educational interventions is traditionally great. Once the shift from a problem orientation to a health focus is made, however, the experimental and active intervention orientation of scientist practitioners can lead to important insights.

Prevention and the Metaphor of Epidemiology

To understand how prevention can involve not just a change in domain but also a change in level of analysis, it is helpful to examine briefly the concepts that have been useful in a public health approach to infectious physical illness. These can be divided into three broad categories (Lilienfeld & Stolley, 1994): host factors (e.g., immunity), agent factors (e.g., virulence, mode of transmission), and environmental factors (e.g., crowding, hygiene). We will explore three of these specific concepts from public health (there are many others) to show how there are parallels in the world of behavior health when a population-based epidemiological model is adopted.

Immunity   There are several kinds of immunity, but two seem most relevant here. *Acquired immunity* is the ability of a host to fend off disease as the result of previous exposure. For example, smallpox vaccination ultimately eliminated that dreaded disease from the globe, based on the fact that restricted smallpox infections increased antibodies that made later major infection impossible. Similarly, in the behavioral health area, training in positive cognitive and behavioral approaches tends to reduce the later incidence of serious depression in adolescents with some depressive tendencies (Clarke, Hawkins, Murphy, Sheeber, Lewinsohn, & Seeley, 1995).

   Group immunity protects vulnerable members in a group based on the strength of others in that group. For instance, if all but a few in a community are immunized against whooping cough, those who are not immunized will nevertheless be protected from infection. Similarly, involvement in prosocial groups by children and adolescents tends to reduce drug abuse (see Miller, 1997, for a review), presumably because children are less exposed to negative models.

Virulence   *Virulence* refers to the strength or power of an agent to invoke a full-fledged disease in a particular host once exposed or infected (Last, 1988). A virulent organism will produce demonstrable disease in a greater percentage of infected people than will a less virulent organism. Some treatment programs have fallen victim to the virulence of behavioral disorders themselves. For example, group therapy for certain kinds of juvenile violence, drug abuse, and crime can *increase* the prevalence of these problems by creating a social context in which children are exposed to poor behavioral models (Biglan, 1995).

Mode of Transmission   *Mode of transmission* refers to the substrate through which infectious agents operate (Last, 1988). These different modes of transmission have major implications for the propagation of a disease (Timmreck, 1994). If the AIDS virus were airborne rather than propagated by bodily fluids, the very existence of human civilization might have been threatened. Similarly, the behavioral disorders that seem to propagate readily by the mass media (e.g., drug abuse, violence toward women) seem to present a particularly difficult challenge to modern society and to the treatment community.

The science of prevention has built on this epidemiological level of analysis, focusing on the risk factors and protective factors that are precursors of dysfunction (Coie et al., 1993). As the examples we have presented show, thinking about prevention leads to a broad, systems-level focus that is all too unusual among psychotherapists and scientist practitioners. A change in focus is needed, because it is clear that the importance of prevention is growing. It is not too difficult to imagine a time in which communities with the active involvement of the health care delivery industry will mount prevention programs of a very broad and general sort in behavioral health. The key in making this transition will be changes within the industry (e.g., consolidation) combined with the development of prevention models of proven effectiveness as measured against real health care cost savings. This is not mere speculation. For example, in some large cities, managed care companies are already involved in such things as school programs to reduce gang violence (a surprisingly large source of emergency room trauma episodes—and thus health care costs—in some urban communities).

The first place that prevention programs are most likely to take off, however, is in specific high-risk populations. Focusing on at-risk populations has the benefit of narrowing the population of greatest need, and thus can be mounted using more limited resources.

A study by Clarke et al. (1995) provides an excellent example. These researchers screened a few thousand high school students using a self-report instrument known to predict depressive episodes. Students who were at risk for depression were randomly assigned to either a treatment or control condition. The experimental program was a class that taught, over fifteen 45-minute sessions, healthy cognitive and behavioral approaches to depressive thoughts and other psychological challenges. In the control condition students continued with any preexisting intervention or were able to seek out new interventions during the study period, and these episodes of care were monitored. One year later, the incidence of depression in the treatment group was one-half that of the control group in this at-risk population. Confirming the at-risk nature of this group, depressive episodes in the control subjects occurred at nearly four times the frequency observed in community samples.

Detection and Awareness

The next, smaller circle in Figure 4.1 refers to the awareness by individuals in the community that they have a behavioral problem, if prevention and health development have not avoided the problem occurrence. Because most forms of behavioral disorders are developmental and historical, it makes great sense to detect and treat behavioral problems early, before they become severe or chronic, and before they become broadly disruptive of functioning. Thus, it is important for the community to know how to detect early warning signs, and to help persons in need get into contact with health care resources. This general area is sometimes called "secondary prevention," which refers to early diagnosis and treatment of a disorder.

In an era of managed care, early detection and awareness is not just the sensible and humane thing to do, it may also be the less costly thing to do. For example, untreated depression is known to lead to much higher health care utilization and costs (Von Korff & Marshall, 1992). Yet even extremely limited interventions for depression are known to have great benefits, provided the program is delivered early in the depressive process (Robinson, Wischman, & DelVento, 1997). In order for treatment to occur early, however, the community must know and understand something about the nature of behavioral disorders and their treatment.

Unfortunately, the models of mental and behavioral health presented by the culture often are distorted. For example, Hyler, Gabbard, and Schneider (1991) examined how behavioral disorders were presented in film and were able to identify several stereotypes that were commonly used, none of which seem accurate: (1) rebellious free spirit, (2) homicidal maniac, (3) out-of-control seductress, (4) member of society with a special, enlightened insight, (5) narcissistic parasite, and (6) zoo creature on display. Common behavioral disorders are often mischaracterized in the culture. For example, suicide is commonly said to occur primarily in depressed people, an idea that is known to be false (Chiles & Strosahl, 1995); schizophrenia is characterized as a "split personality," when that is a misunderstanding based on mere etymology; agoraphobia is said to be a fear of marketplaces, when it is much more than that.

Community and media programs to improve awareness of behavioral health issues are known to have a significant and lasting positive impact. For example, when the British Broadcasting Company showed a concentrated series of several ten-minute segments on mental health issues, the majority of adults in Britain became aware of the series, and of those (a) nearly half reported that they had tried new ways of tackling their problems, (b) three-quarters knew people who had similar problems, and (c) over a third had tried to help others in new ways (Barker, Pistrang, Shapiro, Davies, & Shaw, 1993). Media education programs of this kind not only increase knowledge about behavioral problems, and reduce stigmatization, they also are known to make it more likely that people will seek out needed psychological services for behavioral problems (Fonnebo & Sogaard, 1995).

Educational programs to improve awareness about mental health issues have also been evaluated in the schools. In one particularly well-designed study, for example, it was shown that a brief educational program in a high school significantly increased knowledge of common mental problems, and increased the likelihood that students would be willing to seek help for them (Battaglia, Coverdale, & Bushong, 1990).

What is not yet known is whether such programs can reduce the overall effectiveness and efficiency of behavioral health care delivery considered from a systems perspective. Early detection must be relatively specific in order to be efficient. If everyone became convinced that they had a behavioral health problem requiring intervention, for example, the impact on the health care delivery system would be quite negative even though more people would receive needed early intervention.

The goal is early and *accurate* detection of problems that are more treatable when detected early; excessively high error rates (false positives or false negatives) will doom an early detection and awareness program.

One efficient way early detection and awareness training might be done is to target persons in the community who are particularly likely to observe disordered behavior, such as police, bartenders, and the like. For example, in Reno several large casinos train blackjack dealers to recognize out-of-control compulsive gamblers and to refer these to community agencies for gambling addicts.

A great deal of research needs to be done to understand how to promote effective and efficient detection of nascent behavioral health problems, and the era of managed care makes that research of great potential importance. Scientist–practitioners are people with the proper background to develop and evaluate effective programs of this kind.

Reaching the Point of Contact

The smaller horizontal circles in Figure 4.1 refer to various points of contact with the health delivery system. When a person, spouse, or parent becomes aware of a self behavioral problem or one in others, he or she may seek out points of contact for information or assistance. Mental health professionals often seem to assume that this primary point of contact is or could be the specialty behavioral health care delivery system, but that is far from the truth. The overwhelming majority of behavioral health problems lead to points of contact in primary medical care, the schools, churches or synagogues, social agencies, the criminal justice system, employment settings, tribal leaders or traditional healers, and so on—*not* to mental health specialists.

In the era of fee-for-service health care delivery, mental health practitioners with good reputations could prosper merely by opening an office and developing a referral network. In the era of industrialized health care delivery, a more proactive posture is needed—particularly by highly trained doctoral-level providers— to produce added value to the health delivery system and to document this fact. Scientist practitioners need to help develop delivery systems that properly (a) channel difficult behavioral problems into the health care delivery system, and (b) provide where possible effective responses at the point of contact. Doing so requires a better working relationship between common points of contact and the skills and abilities of scientist practitioners.

Primary medical care is a classic example. Psychologists have a long history of involvement in medical and surgical facilities (Cummings, 1992). Yet this early involvement did not lead to a more integrated delivery system. Instead, mental health care was usually delivered in a specialty model. Psychologists and psychiatrists had their own offices in their own facilities. This failure to integrate behavioral health care into the larger system of health care delivery has had major negative consequences. First, many behavioral health problems present in primary care, but behavioral health care specialists are usually absent from these facilities. Over 25% of primary care patients experience mood disorders, almost 20% present with one or more anxiety disorders, and 5% suffer from probable alcohol abuse or dependence

(Spitzer, Williams, Kroenke, Linger, deGruy, Hahn, Brody, & Johnson, 1994). Second, many physical health problems involve behavioral components in their origin or treatment, but it is uncommon for these components to be addressed. For example, only 49% of patients referred for a sigmoidoscopy to screen for colorectal cancer attend the screening, in part out of fear about the procedure (Cockburn, Thomas, McLaughlin, & Reading, 1995).

In the era of managed care, the value provided by the skills of scientist practitioners needs to be seen in the context of health care delivery more generally. It makes political, economic, and practical sense to go where the problems are, instead of the other way around. This is especially true given that a body of evidence exists showing that behavioral health care delivery can significantly reduce overall health care costs (Cummings, 1991).

Churches and synagogues provide another good example, of several that could be described. Churches and synagogues provide a traditional source of counsel and comfort in dealing with behavioral problems, with greatly reduced stigma and resistance to psychological suggestions (Pargament, Falgout, Ensing, Reilly, Silverman, Van Haitsma, Olsen, & Warren, 1991). Churches and synagogues also have a long tradition of volunteer work, and involvement with health problems. Helping these systems be more effective in referral and assistance can be a very cost-effective way of improving overall health care (see Pargament et al., 1991, for a particularly good, data-based model). Churches may be an especially important way to reach minority groups, such as African Americans (Thomas, Crouse Quinn, Billingsley, and Caldwell, 1994), with preventative, educational, detection, or early intervention programs. Like other points of contact outside of specialty behavioral health care clinics (e.g., worksites, the criminal justice system), churches and synagogues have historically been largely ignored by scientist–practitioners as an important part of the de facto health care delivery system.

Triage

The arrows in Figure 4.1 leading from different points of contact to and among different centers with triage functions convey the idea that when services cannot be fully delivered in an initial point-of-contact setting, referrals are made to aspects of a more specialized behavioral health care delivery system. The first component of that system is likely to be triage: the systematic use of assessment to determine treatment needs.

There has long been a recognized need for greater treatment utility of assessment (Hayes et al., 1987). This, in combination with the economic interest of managed care firms in both producing and tracking better clinical outcomes, has lead to an explosion of interest in assessment systems that match clients to type and level of care. Some of these systems are based on comprehensive, scientifically based matching models (e.g., Beutler, 1991; Howard, Moras, Brill, Martinovich, & Lutz, in press), while others are more intuitive. Many commercial firms have sprung up to market such assessment systems to managed care companies. Interestingly many of the assessment and treatment assignment systems being offered to MCOs include both initial and outcomes assessment—an approach very much in line with the thinking of scientist practitioners. We will address some of these areas of assessment in Chapters 11 through 13.

The economic interests of MCOs will dictate to some degree how the general area of assessment and triage develops, but this influence seems likely to be positive, not negative. For far too long, assessment devices have been evaluated for "quality" without significant regard for their ultimate practical impact on clinical and functional outcomes. MCOs seem unlikely to support assessment for assessment's sake since this adds a cost without a benefit. Rather, managed care firms are developing batteries, devices, and assessment units that will quickly differentiate among different levels of health care need. Existing syndromal nosologies have limited value in this area. Researchers have also paid too little attention to the full range of treatment options that different kinds of clients may need, a topic to which we now turn.

Levels of Empirically Supported Clinical Care

As was noted in Chapter 1, the history of psychotherapy lead in the 1970s and 1980s to an enormous increase in doctoral-level providers, particularly in psychology. Even in the 1990s, doctoral programs continue to turn out graduates who, in the words of Nick Cummings, "want a shingle, a couch, and a Mercedes in the driveway" (Cummings & Hayes, 1996, p. 10). Psychology, for example, became overcommitted to psychotherapy delivery, weakening many hard-won prizes in that process: assessment, career counseling, consultation, child development, and so on (Hayes & Heiby, 1996).

The weakness of that strategy was revealed by the advent of managed care. MCOs were well aware of the literature showing that nondoctoral providers were generally as effective as doctoral-level professionals (Christensen & Jacobson, 1994), and the number of master's level providers hired by MCOs exploded. Doctoral-level scientist practitioners do have many skills to offer, including treatment delivery, but these skills must be integrated into a stepped care model in which the level of intervention fits the clinical need based on the best available evidence.

The three spheres above triage in Figure 4.1 represent some of these levels. Some clinical needs can be satisfied using books, videotapes, self-help groups, and other interventions that do not require the presence of a professional. Others may require qualified interventions by staff with limited forms of training, such as phone calls from caseworkers. Others will require the intervention of professionals, generally at the master's level or at the doctoral level when that is known to be helpful. All of these methods should be empirically validated and refined in a process of evaluation and continuous quality improvement. In what follows, we will review some of the evidence that a stepped care model is useful and can produce high-quality outcomes at a lower cost.

Self-Help Groups   An excellent example of ways that clinical benefit can be produced with limited or even no professional intervention is self-help groups (Powell, 1994). Over 7 million people are in self-help groups in the United States, about half lead by professionals and about half not (Lieberman & Snowden, 1993). The widespread view that self-help groups are mostly a white, male, middle-class phenomenon appears to be incorrect. Although referrals come more from these groups, actual attendance is greater among females and minority group members (Humphreys, Mavis, & Stofflemayr, 1991). The research on self-help groups is still limited, but they often appear to produce significant clinical impact (e.g., Lieberman & Videka-Sherman, 1986) at greatly reduced cost (e.g., Peterson, Abrams, Elder, & Beaudin, 1985). Indeed, "low tech" solutions can be wildly more effective on a cost basis than "high tech" solutions (Marks, 1992).

Bibliotherapy   The clinical impact of books, tapes, and computer programs is another, perhaps even more dramatic, example of the possible benefit of very limited interventions. Most clinicians at least occasionally used bibliotherapy as an adjunct to treatment (Starker, 1988). Meta-analyses of the best available studies show that bibliotherapy can be quite effective, even when used without other forms of intervention, with average effect sizes approaching 0.8 (Gould & Clum, 1993). Even fairly well-controlled studies (e.g., Jamison & Scogin, 1995; Lidren, Watkins, Gould, Clum, Asterino, & Tulloch, 1994) have yielded positive results and good maintenance with a wide variety of clinical disorders from depression, to panic, to sexual dysfunction.

The existing literature directly comparing individual or group intervention with bibliotherapy, while small, has not shown a significant advantage for professional intervention (Gould & Clum, 1993). The literature comparing different modalities of bibliotherapy is limited, but it appears that videotaped interventions combined with written materials are particularly helpful (Gould & Clum, 1993). Computer-based programs have also been shown to be helpful, including some that mimic the responses of actual professionals (Bloom, 1992).

An example of the use of bibliotherapy is provided by Kashima, Baker, and Landren (1988). Parents were taught how to improve the self-care skills of their disabled children. Sixty-one families were randomly assigned to receive this training by videotape or by a professional trainer. Live training produced slightly higher knowledge of behavioral principles, but otherwise the results were the same.

A second example is a study by Lidren et al. (1994) evaluating Clum's (1990) cognitive behavioral self-help book for panic-disordered clients as compared to a cognitive behavioral group therapy. The study showed that both were effective as compared to a waiting-list control, and equally so.

Bibliotherapy is not universally effective, however. It is known, for example, that clients differ widely in their views on its possible value, and that treatment outcome is much better with clients who expect to be helped by bibliotherapy (Ogles, Lambert, & Craig, 1991). Thus, it probably should not be used with subjects who are uncertain about its possible value.

Professionals should not be threatened by the rise of minimal nonprofessional intervention technologies such as bibliotherapy or self-help, for three reasons. Most importantly, the goal of clinical science is alleviation of human suffering, and thus any technology that is effective and efficient is desirable. In addition, the development of limited and inexpensive intervention technologies permits the allocation of other resources toward areas of greater professional need. Finally, it is the scientist practitioners who will develop and disseminate much of the technology (e.g., bibliotherapy) used without major professional involvement.

Minimal Professional Interventions   At another level of complexity, some interventions are being developed that require only limited training. For example, Robinson, Wischman, and DelVento, 1997, have developed an effective approach to the treatment of depression in primary care that relies mainly on a brief meeting with a nurse and follow-up phone calls by a caseworker. This program is supervised and monitored by psychologists and psychiatrists, but the actual intervention requires very little time from doctoral- or even master's-level professionals.

The role of the scientist practitioner in this kind of treatment is to develop and to test these technologies, to integrate them into delivery systems, to disseminate them, train others in their use, provide appropriate supervision, and to help evaluate their impact in the actual clinical environment. Again, although the role is not the direct delivery of services, these kinds of interventions should not threaten scientist–practitioners, for all the reasons mentioned earlier.

Empirically Supported Treatments by Professionals   Some treatment technologies—perhaps many—require not just limited training but more extensive professional preparation at the master's or doctoral level. Few technicians are likely to be proficient in cognitive behavioral therapies, for example, because the concepts are many and are often complex. When a person has clinical needs that can best be addressed through empirically validated treatments delivered by professionals, then they must receive such treatments. The goal of efficiency cannot be allowed to overwhelm the even more important goal of effectiveness, and the movement toward quality clinical outcomes in managed care would mean nothing if this point is ignored. If master's level providers can do a good job supplying this care, however, undoubtedly they will be used in large part. This may be uncomfortable for some doctoral-level providers, but it also means a more efficient system that is less costly to all. If data exist showing that doctoral-level providers should be used, however, then they must be used.

These levels of care (nonprofessional, minimal professional, and professional) together define what is currently known in a population-based, empirical approach to clinical intervention. The outcomes from such treatment must be evaluated, as is shown in Figure 4.1, but they constitute the known core of clinical intervention. If we were to stop here the role of scientist practitioners in an industrialized health care delivery system would be important but somewhat limited, and that indeed is the impression of many scientist practitioners as they look at Generation I of managed care.

What makes that impression misleading and opens the door for so many additional opportunities is the following. It has been estimated that overall only about 35% of the clients deemed eligible to receive an empirically validated treatment will improve to the point that they no longer demand services for the same problem (Cummings & Hayes, 1996). In addition, many disorders and behavioral problems have no empirically validated treatments available. Taken together, this means that a large number of current clients will ultimately require more than population-based clinical care, as evidenced by our existing knowledge base. It is the next steps where the value added by scientist practitioners is most obvious: Someone must learn to increase the percentage of treatment responders by devising, testing, and disseminating new and more effective approaches. It is here that the training of doctoral-level scientist practitioners is unique. No one else has the mix of clinical, methodological, and analytical skills adequate to this task.

Treatment Development, Evaluation, and Dissemination

If it is true that the majority of current clients need more from the behavioral health care delivery system than current knowledge provides, there is a huge population of persons with whom to work directly. In such cases (e.g., treatment failures, complex cases), the goal of treatment delivery by the best-trained professionals is not merely the clinical gains of the individual client, but the development of knowledge that will allow similar clients in the future to be treated in a more cost-effective manner by the health care delivery system.

In the first edition of this book, we laid out how this process of knowledge development could occur in the practice environment. In the fee-for-service world of health care delivery, however, the actual incentives for knowledge development were largely intrinsic and abstract. In the era of managed care, the industry itself has a direct economic interest in the continuous development of knowledge. This interest is every bit as direct as the interest a car manufacturer has in a new gearbox that is better and cheaper, or that a computer manufacturer has in a disk drive that does not require repairs. For this direct interest to be tapped, however, scientist–practitioners must have and must use the tools to develop and test more effective and efficient approaches—which is precisely what the rest of this volume is all about. The spheres and boxes at the top of Figure 4.1 represent a model of empirically based treatment development aimed at those clients for whom the existing knowledge base is inadequate.

Functional Analysis and Treatment Innovation   A great deal has been written about how to evaluate new clinical technologies, but relatively little about how to think of them in the first place. New and truly innovative treatments rarely emerge from common sense, precisely because that source *is* common and, thus, already available. Sometimes innovations emerge accidentally, but more often they seem to come from the dynamic interplay between a detailed knowledge of the discipline and a detailed knowledge of an individual suffering human life. Scientist practitioners need to understand current clinical innovations, the relevance of basic processes, and theoretical development (the boxes in Figure 4.1). The broader, deeper, richer, and more multifaceted the clinician's knowledge base, the more creative insights and connections may emerge in analyzing possible sources of human suffering. Thus, the proper context for treatment innovation is twofold: thorough and broad training in the content of the behavioral sciences, and deep contact with the clinical realities.

There is a more provocative way to say this. Increasingly, treatment innovation requires *uncommon* sense. Any conceptual scheme that is known and thoroughly explored is, almost by definition, less likely over time to be the source of real treatment innovation. Consider, for example, how the field has fractured into comfortable subareas, such as treatment approaches, syndromal categories, or demographic groups. It seems unlikely that these comfortable conceptual schemes will produce maximum treatment innovation over time. Indeed, their dominance may be one reason that less progress has been made in the development of more functional groupings and a better understanding of basic processes of behavior change (Hayes & Follette, 1992).

Perhaps no better system of developing treatment innovations has been derived than functional analysis (Haynes & O'Brien, 1990). Classical functional analysis has the following components (Hayes & Follette, 1992):

1. Identify potentially relevant characteristics of the individual client, his or her behavior, and the context in which it occurs via broad assessment. It is this step in which a deep contact with the clinical situation is most important.
2. Organize the information collected in Step 1 into a preliminary analysis of the client's difficulties in terms of basic principles so as to identify important causal relationships that might be changed. It is this step in which a deep contact with the discipline is important.
3. Gather additional information based on Step 2 and begin to finalize the conceptual analysis.
4. Devise an intervention based on Step 3 that will modify the variables identified.

Single Case Designs   The first four steps are a kind of "conceptual functional analysis." The next two are empirical:

5. Systematically implement treatment and assess change in a scientifically sound manner.
6. If the outcome is unacceptable, recycle back to Step 2 or 3.

Thus, the next step in treatment development is a series of tests of the theoretical and technical innovations generated. Chapters 5 through 8 of this volume will explain in great detail how to accomplish this step.

Tinkered Program Development   When the scientist practitioner has developed an innovative approach that seems to help with some segment of a previously difficult or unresponsive subpopulation, more full-scale program development begins, but still with a great deal of tinkering and modification. The scientist practitioner will probably want to test out any positive results with other, similar clients, since the goal of empirical analysis in a managed care environment is the development of knowledge applicable to subpopulations, not merely to individuals one at a time.

One of the primary ways to conduct this phase of program development is through clinical replication, though as is shown in Figure 4.1 that method is useful (a) as a technology is being developed, (b) as a program evaluation strategy for well-developed methods, and (c) as a way of examining dissemination. We will cover the method and role of clinical replication in Chapter 9.

During the early phase of development and testing, technological precision (e.g., manual development, development of adherence measures) is necessary for scientific purposes, and this will become a major component of program development. However, the ultimate goal of treatment development in a practical setting is not merely technological precision, but also functional generalization. In the world of industrialized health care delivery, high degrees of technological precision will be justified as a permanent aspect of treatment only when the benefits and costs warrant (e.g., with severe and costly patients). Thus, there should also be a systematic examination of how best to simplify the technology and prepare it for system implementation. Because of the practical realities of managed care, dissemination and transportability is fundamental even to this relatively early step of treatment development; it is not saved for last.

A list of factors to consider in treatment development is shown in Table 4.1. This table is a modified version of one developed by William Miller in response to several federal initiatives at the National Institute on Drug Abuse and the National Institute of Mental Health to foster treatment development. By examining the various rows and columns, one can develop a fairly detailed list of steps that need to be taken. We will discuss most of these steps later in the book.

"Stage I" of treatment development covers the three steps we have discussed: functional analysis, single case analysis, and tinkered program evaluation. In this stage there is a great deal of movement back and forth between theoretical models, technological innovation, and clinical outcome. In the psychopharmacological area, pharmaceutical companies, who have a financial interest in treatment innovation, largely fund Stage I research. Until quite recently there was no parallel in the psychosocial area. Now, however, the federal government has begun funding Stage I research. In addition, the research and development arms of the managed care industry are blossoming, with over twenty large in-house research centers already formed, covering more than 20 million lives (Wagner, 1997). As the industry consolidates, the financial interest in treatment development as a method of quality improvement grows.

Full-Scale Efficacy Testing and Program Evaluation   When the program development phase and the processes of tinkering are concluded, it is time to evaluate full-scale implementation of the program. Many of the details of this phase are found under the Stage II column of Table 4.1. These topics will also be addressed in Chapters 9 and 10, when clinical replication and program evaluation are

TABLE 4.1   Steps in New Treatment Development

Stages of Treatment Development Research:

Stage Ia = Feasibility testing, early development, refinement, and testing of treatment procedures
Stage Ib = Tinkered program development and pilot testing of treatment outcome
Stage II = Efficacy testing; may include a formal pilot-efficacy testing phase
Stage III = Transferability testing; effectiveness and dissemination testing

Typical Components of Stage:	Ia	Ib	II	III
TREATMENT METHOD				
Specify theoretical rationale (theory of the disorder)	✓	✓	✓	✓
Specify causal chain (theory of treatment; mechanisms)	✓	✓	✓	✓
Demonstrate feasibility; e.g., acceptability, safety		✓	✓	✓
Specify process measures (operationalize causal chain)		✓	✓	✓
Establish reliability of process measures			✓	✓
Provide provisional therapist manual specifying procedures		✓	✓	✓
Specify pilot testing procedures (if applicable)		✓	✓	✓
Specify whether and which procedures will be modified, and the basis for the modification	✓			
Provide completed therapist manual specifying procedures			✓	✓
THERAPISTS				
Specify inclusion criteria (requirements)/how measured		✓	✓	✓
Justify any exclusion criteria for therapists		✓	✓	✓
Establish availability of needed therapists		✓	✓	✓
Specify assessment measures administered to therapists		✓	✓	✓
Provide descriptive data for therapists			✓	✓
Specify procedures for assigning cases to therapists		✓	✓	✓
Specify procedures for training and certifying therapists		✓	✓	✓
Establish reliability of therapist adherence measures			✓	✓
Specify therapist competency measures and reliability			✓	✓
Specify dissemination strategies and their feasibility				✓
Specify measures of diffusion, adoption				✓
Provide training outcome data			✓	✓

TABLE 4.1   **Continued**

Typical Components of Stage:	Ia	Ib	II	III
CLIENT/PARTICIPANTS				
Identify target population (heterogeneity/homogeneity)	✓	✓	✓	✓
Specify inclusion criteria		✓	✓	✓
Justify any exclusion criteria		✓	✓	✓
Address gender/minority representation	✓	✓	✓	✓
Establish capability to recruit the needed sample		✓	✓	✓
Document retention rate in treatment			✓	✓
Specify client measures and their reliability		✓	✓	✓
Provide descriptive data for client sample			✓	✓
Report client predictors of response to treatment			✓	✓
DESIGN AND ANALYSIS				
Specify outcome measures	✓	✓	✓	✓
Establish reliability of outcome measures		✓	✓	✓
Report outcome data			✓	✓
Report process-outcome linkage data (causal chain)			✓	✓
Specify control conditions (experimental/quasi-experimental)		✓	✓	✓
Specify *a priori* hypotheses (outcome, predictors, process, etc.)		✓	✓	✓
Specify analysis plan to test hypotheses		✓	✓	✓
Demonstrate necessary statistical power for analyses			✓	✓
Indicate whether tailored pilot phase will precede formal trial			✓	
Specify efficacy/safety monitoring point for the decision to continue or stop treatment development along this line			✓	
Specify criteria and procedures for decision to continue or stop treatment development along this line			✓	

examined. The lion's share of federal funding in the evaluation of behavioral health care treatment is Stage II research.

Traditional group comparison methods and randomized clinical trials are the most common methods of Stage II research. We have not covered these methods in the present volume, since they are so widely covered elsewhere.

Training and Dissemination Research   It is not enough to develop and test treatments; they must also be disseminated. Many of the details of this phase are found under the Stage III column of Table 4.1. Stage III research is perhaps the least well developed in psychosocial areas. Part of the lack of development may be methodological and conceptual, rather than practical.

The point of Stage III research is the examination of the broad impact of an intervention technology as it is used in general clinical settings. In the pharmacological area, Stage III data are collected in the field as medical practitioners use the new technology and report observed effects and side effects to the Food and Drug Administration. No such mechanism exists in the psychosocial area, and perhaps as a result, dissemination research is usually thought of as large multi-site, multi-million dollar research studies. But there are other methods by which to accomplish the analytic goal.

As is shown in Figure 4.1, clinical replication research is itself a kind of Stage III research, and one that makes maximum use of the variability inherent in different settings, clinicians, and client groups. We will describe this method in detail in Chapter 9.

In addition it is quite possible to research dissemination and training methods directly by varying these methods experimentally. For example, clinicians can be randomly assigned to receive certain kinds of training, and the impact of this dissemination on client outcome can be examined. Strosahl, Hayes, Bergin, and Romano (1998) termed this approach a "manipulated training research method" of dissemination research and provided an experimental example. They assigned 17 master's-level therapists and one psychologist in a staff model HMO either to receive a one-year training program in acceptance and commitment therapy (ACT; Hayes, Strosahl, & Wilson, in press; Hayes, 1987) or to receive no additional training (those not receiving training = 10; receiving training = 8). Clinicians continued to receive general clinical referrals of all kinds. Prior to training, both therapist groups had all of their clients assess at baseline and again 5 months later. This was repeated after training. Results indicated that after training, clients of ACT trained therapists reported significantly better coping than the clients of untrained therapists, were referred significantly less frequently for medication evaluations, and were more likely to have completed treatment in the 5 months following initiation of treatment.

In this approach to dissemination research, what is being evaluated is not the impact of a specific technology when it is used, but the impact of the dissemination of a technology per se. For example, Strosahl et al. (1998) did not require that clinicians use ACT with all their clients, which in any case would probably have been inappropriate since many of the cases may not have fit the underlying therapeutic technology. Nevertheless, the improved outcomes for clients show that the clinicians took advantage of the training—an important outcome, especially since training has so seldom been shown to improve clinical competence (Dawes, 1994).

Another worthwhile variant of Stage III research is the "benchmarking" research strategy (McFall, 1996). In this approach, treatments of known efficacy are implemented in clinical service settings, and a point-by-point comparison is made of the outcomes obtained in research clinics versus service clinics. A good example is provided by Wade, Treat, and Stuart (1998), who applied the MAP treatment protocol for panic disorder (Barlow & Craske, 1994) to 110 clients at a community clinic. The results closely paralleled the original research studies, which considerably enhances the clinical importance of the original data.

The federal government, seeing the need for Stage III research, has begun to focus more on this kind of project. As the health care industry develops, it is also a major focus of industry research and development (Wagner, 1997). But perhaps the greatest growing force for dissemination is the development of practice guidelines, which we will discuss in some detail; this is fitting emphasis, given its importance to scientist–practitioners.

Practice Guidelines

With the growing realization that we have effective psychosocial treatments, as well as effective drug treatments, for a number of psychological disorders, there has emerged, among policy makers, the new strategy called "best practices" or "clinical practice guidelines" described briefly in Chapter 2 (Barlow, 1994). The overriding goal of these types of efforts is to correct the enormous variability in treatment delivery wherein any number of patients might receive ineffective treatments, or treatments with no proven efficacy for a given disorder, despite the fact that effective treatments exist. These clinical practice guidelines, which had their origins in medical disorders, have now rapidly spread to the full range of psychological disorders.

In a variety of subtle ways, these guidelines are assuming the force of law. For example, in several states within the United States, practitioners who can demonstrate that they have followed relevant clinical practice guidelines would be immune from malpractice litigation. Conversely, those practitioners who strayed too far from these guidelines would be subject to costly litigation in the event of certain adverse outcomes. The National Committee for Quality Assurance (NCQA) is now requiring MCOs to implement empirically based clinical practice guidelines.

Over the past 10 years, guidelines have proliferated, with some coming from professional societies such as the American Psychiatric Association (APA, 1993), others from government agencies such as the AHCPR (Depression Guideline Panel, 1993), and yet others from managed care companies or private groups. As noted in Chapter 2, many of these guidelines, particularly in the latter group, have been little more than transparent cost-cutting tools that, most likely, are more harmful than beneficial to patients. But scientific organizations are becoming more interested in practice guidelines and their implications. For example, in June of 1991 the American Association of Applied and Preventive Psychology brought together 25 professional associations in Washington, D.C., for the First Summit of Applied Psychological Science Organizations. The summit adopted the four resolutions shown in Table 4.2. These resolutions show how far organized applied psychology as a whole had moved, by the early 1990s, in the direction of the kind of science-based practice we envisioned some years ago (Barlow, Hayes, & Nelson, 1984). The second summit the following year explicitly called for scientifically based practice guidelines, scientific standards for continuing education, dissemination of empirically based treatments, and a national clinical database.

TABLE 4.2   **Resolutions of the First Summit of Applied Psychological Science Organizations**

A. Establishment of a Structure for the Certification of Effective Procedures

Applied psychological science should establish processes and procedures that will identify effective intervention, prevention, and assessment techniques on which practice can be based, including methods for:

1. the construction of a broad, current, and relevant database,

2. provisional identification of effectiveness, and

3. achievement of consensus on effectiveness.

The goal of these methods is the certification of effective procedures.

B. Dissemination, Education, and Psychological Knowledge

Applied psychological science should promote and evaluate new and effective methods for disseminating empirically validated applied and preventive intervention and assessment procedures, and should facilitate the integration of these procedures into practice.

C. The Reaffirmation of Scientific Values in Psychological Application

Practice in psychology entails a commitment to the consumption and utilization of psychological research and the continued evaluation of procedures within the context of applied needs. When prevention, assessment, or intervention procedures go beyond existing scientific knowledge, systematic evaluation is especially necessary.

D. Involvement in the Research Process: The Scientist–Practitioner

Practitioners and applied researchers should be intimately involved in the process of developing and identifying effective applied procedures. Scientist–practitioners are involved in the research and discovery process by suggesting research problems, evaluating the effectiveness of procedures in the practice setting, and providing feedback.

A number of applied psychological science organizations, such as the Division of Clinical Psychology Task Force report reviewed in the last chapter, have launched initiatives in these areas in the 1990s. Recently, the American Psychological Association (APA) completed work on a template for developing clinical practice guidelines intended to cover mental disorders and psychosocial aspects of physical disorders. The APA undertook this task in view of the methodological expertise available within the association, but also because of its experience, decades previously, with a similar issue. At that time psychological tests were proliferating, without a template or set of scientific criteria on which to base the development of those tests. In response, APA, in cooperation with the American Educational Research Association and the National Council on Measurement in Education, in 1966 developed the first version of the well-known *Standards for Educational and Psychological Tests and Manuals* (APA, 1966). The purpose was to delineate the scientific criteria of reliability and validity that any psychological test would have to meet to be credible and useful. This document has become the standard in the field and is widely used by professionals, policy makers, and courts to determine the adequacy of various psychological tests.

In an attempt to create a similar document for clinical practice guidelines, a broadly representative task force with methodological expertise in this area has written a template for developing guidelines covering interventions for mental disorders and psychosocial aspects of physical disorders. This template was accepted as an official APA document in February of 1995. Although APA developed the template because of psychology's interest and expertise in methodological considerations, the task force recommends that actual guidelines be constructed by interdisciplinary panels and be useful to practitioners from all mental health disciplines. The task force also suggests that with minor modifications the framework of the template should be applicable to other health care interventions, although that was not its primary purpose.

The template also notes that most current guidelines are disorder-based, and this is likely to continue to be the case. Policy makers and most health care professionals are no longer interested in broad general questions such as "Do drugs work?" or "Does psychotherapy work?" This is because all treatment decisions are made in the context of the presenting problem, and treatment will necessarily differ somewhat from disorder to disorder. Indeed, accumulating evidence on the effectiveness of interventions is almost all disorder-based. More importantly, this template serves as a model of the types of research and clinical efforts necessary to evaluate interventions and write subsequent clinical practice guidelines. As such, it extends the integrated model of applied research proposed by Agras and Berkowitz (1980) by delineating the role of practitioners in providing important evidence for these guidelines.

As noted above, the template requires that clinical practice guidelines be constructed on the basis of two simultaneous considerations or *axes.* The first axis suggests a rigorous assessment of scientific evidence based on results from systematic evaluations of the intervention in a controlled clinical research context. Evidence from these types of evaluations has come to be considered under the heading of the *efficacy* of an intervention. The most powerful methodological tools for determining efficacy are randomized clinical trials in which a given intervention is demonstrated to be better than some credible alternative approach. Despite this emphasis on hard scientific evidence, two other important contributions to the efficacy axis, as noted by the template, are quantified clinical observations collected by clinicians seeing a series of patients with a given disorder and the clinical wisdom accompanying such experience; in other words, clinical replication series.

The second consideration, given equal weight in the template, concerns the applicability and feasibility of the intervention in the local setting where it is delivered, as well as a determination of the generalizability of an intervention with established efficacy. While some policy makers have chosen the word *effectiveness* to describe this set of considerations, as mentioned above, the APA task force preferred the less redundant and less confusing term *clinical utility.*

The clinical utility axis reflects the necessity to evaluate the extent to which a given intervention, regardless of the efficacy that may have been established in the clinical research setting, will be effective in the practice setting in which it is typically applied. It also reflects the ability, and perhaps the willingness, of practitioners to use the intervention in question as well as, more importantly, the inclination of patients to accept the intervention.

Basically three major factors are considered under the heading of clinical utility: feasibility, generalizability, and cost-effectiveness. *Feasibility*, referring as it does to the extent to which treatment can be delivered to patients in specific settings in which they will be treated, encompasses the following guidelines, quoted in their entirety.

Guideline 4.0. The Panel should evaluate the acceptability of the intervention to patients who will receive the service. There are many reasons why patients would prefer not to receive some treatments regardless of demonstrated efficacy. These reasons may include such factors as pain, cost, duration, fear, side-effects, and adverse reactions. **Guideline 4.1.** In the context of relatively equal efficacy, patient choice is an important factor in recommending one intervention over the other. There is some evidence that patient choice will increase the clinical utility of a given intervention. In addition, the unwillingness of a patient to accept a specific treatment may preclude the administration of an intervention, regardless of efficacy. **Guideline 4.2.** The Panel should evaluate evidence on the likelihood of compliance with an intervention by the patients who will receive the service. Interventions require in and out of session activity on the part of the patient. If it has been shown that patients are unable or unwilling to comply with treatment requirements despite the best efforts of the therapist, the intervention will not be effective. Examples of this concern include the patient's unwillingness to self-monitor activities, to engage in new behaviors, or to take medications regularly, when these are integral parts of treatment.

Guideline 5.0. The Panel should evaluate the ease of dissemination of the intervention. Guideline 5.1. The Panel should evaluate the availability of practitioners who possess satisfactory competence in the administration of the intervention. Interventions require differing levels of training and skill to achieve optimal effects. Clinical utility may be affected if the availability of competent practitioners is severely limited. Therefore, the Panel should take into account the requirements for training, as well as the availability of opportunities to reach a level of satisfactory competence with the intervention. Current lack of available practitioners or training opportunities should not lead a panel to discount the utility of a promising treatment. Instead the panel should encourage expanded opportunities for appropriate training. **Guideline 5.2.** The Panel should take into account the cost of administering the intervention. Some interventions require costly technology or the support of additional personnel or resources.

The second factor, *generalizability*, echoes the theme made throughout this book. That is, the results from traditional clinical research methodology in the form of randomized clinical trials are very important for establishing efficacy, but the results may not necessarily "generalize" to the practice situation due to the variety of constraints present in tightly controlled clinical trials. Thus evaluating the generality of the efficacy of an intervention across patients, settings, and therapists is a crucial step in the research process. To accomplish this goal, the template specifies the following guidelines, which should form a necessary component of any clinical practice directive.

Guideline 6.0. The Panel should take into account the breadth of patient variables when evaluating patient characteristics in the intervention. Variability in responding among broadly defined groups of patients may contribute to knowledge of patient to treatment matching, which is an important consideration in clinical settings. **Guideline 6.1.** The Panel should be guided by research and cultural expertise addressing issues regarding the cultural background of the patient when evaluating the intervention. Interventions that are of demonstrable efficacy with one ethnic group may not be equally applicable to patients from other ethnic or cultural groups. In the absence of relevant research, caution must be exercised in generalizing to patients with varied cultural backgrounds. Provisions should be made for cultural input whenever treatment guidelines are applied to diverse populations. **Guideline 6.2.** The Panel should consider research addressing the issue of the sex (biological characteristics) and gender (social characteristics) of the patient. Interventions that are of demonstrable efficacy with male patients may not be applicable to female patients in the absence of an equivalent data base. For example, men and women often have different thresholds for entering treatment for alcoholism (because of greater perceived stigma for women). Males and females metabolize drugs in different ways. Therefore results from studies on men may not generalize to women and vice versa. **Guideline 6.3.** The Panel should evaluate research and relevant clinical consensus concerning the developmental level of the patient. Interventions that are of demonstrable efficacy with middle-aged patients may not be equally applicable for children or geriatric patients. For example, interventions that require complex verbal behavior are not appropriate for most young children. **Guideline 6.4.** The Panel should consider whether data or relevant clinical consensus exist on other relevant patient characteristics when evaluating the intervention. Patient characteristics such as, but not limited to, SES, geographical location, religion, sexual orientation, and physical condition may play an important role in determining the clinical utility of an intervention.

Guideline 7.0. The Panel should evaluate data on the efficacy of treatment when administered by therapists who differ on a number of relevant dimensions. **Guideline 7.1.** Therapist training, skill, and experience should be evaluated as a factor in treatment outcome. **Guideline 7.2.** Therapist personal characteristics such as, but not limited to, gender and ethnicity should be evaluated as a factor in treatment outcome. **Guideline 7.3.** Interactions between therapists' characteristics such as those listed above and patient characteristics should be evaluated as these relate to treatment outcome.

Guideline 8.0. The Panel should evaluate data on treatment robustness when evaluating the intervention. A well-designed efficacy study often makes use of a highly structured approach to treatment whereas treatment as offered in the practice setting rarely conforms to this level of structure. A treatment's clinical utility may vary with alterations in administration from the specified treatment protocol. Data relevant to issues such as adhering to a protocol, differing time frames for delivering treatment, and the possibility of interrupting treatment to address family crises should be addressed. **Guideline 8.1.** The Panel should evaluate data pertaining to the setting in which an intervention is offered. An intervention with proven effectiveness in one setting, such as an institution, home, school, day treatment, clinic or office, may vary in effectiveness when it is offered in an alternative setting.

Additional guidelines address the important issue of determining cost-effectiveness.

Most of the data relevant to the clinical utility axis must be collected in actual practice situations. It is also noted that while some of the issues might be evaluated in the context of randomized controlled clinical trials, "more often data will be in the form of quantified clinical observations (clinical replication series) . . . " Thus a role has now clearly been laid out and endorsed by the American Psychological Association for the formal participation of practitioners in the research process. In so doing, APA fulfills an essential role.

Furthermore, the value of clinical replication series is not limited to contributions to the clinical utility axis. Note that quantified clinical observations (clinical replication series) also contribute in a substantial manner to the internal validity or efficacy of an intervention. The purpose of the efficacy axis is to evaluate whether a beneficial effect for treatment can be demonstrated. In other words, in a controlled clinical context is the intervention more effective than alternative interventions or no treatment? This, of course, is an essential step in the validation of any clinical intervention, and the usual randomized controlled clinical trials are the major tool; but, clinical replication series also have a substantial role in this process as outlined in some of the guidelines from this efficacy axis.

Guideline 1.0. All interventions should be subject to empirical confirmation. Such confirmation is necessary regardless of the theoretical derivation of the intervention. At present, many empirically based investigations have been completed or are underway to test the efficacy of psychotherapeutic and pharmacological interventions.

Guideline 2.0. Efforts should be made to generate systematic compilations of clinical consensus by sampling opinions across recognized interdisciplinary groups of experts. Such efforts probably inspire greater confidence than unsystematic clinical opinion, but still fall short of judgments based on carefully controlled empirical evaluation.

Guideline 3.0. Each intervention should be subjected to an increasingly stringent set of methodologies designed to enhance confidence in the efficacy of that intervention. Panels developing recommendations for specific interventions should consider the level of technological advancement in the research producing the available data base. **Guideline 3.1.** Quantified clinical observation represents an initial step in the systematic evaluation of treatment efficacy. In this procedure, sometimes referred to as clinical replication series, the extent of the clinical efficacy of an intervention is "tested" with a series of patients. The intervention is applied in the practice setting and quantifiable observations are made in regard to clinical efficacy of the intervention across a large number of diverse patients with a given disorder. These clinical observations may then form the basis for further systematic evaluation. **Guideline 3.2.** Randomized controlled trials represent more stringent means of evaluating treatment efficacy. In essence, patients are randomly assigned to conditions so as to reduce the likelihood that the groups differ prior to treatment with respect to characteristics that could influence subsequent status. Within this category, three subcategories represent increasingly stringent tests of efficacy: (a) The first question of interest is often whether treatment is better than doing nothing at all. In point of fact, it is often difficult to operationalize doing nothing, so assessment-only or wait-list controls are typically used despite the limitations inherent to these approaches. Such comparisons allow not only a determination of whether an intervention has any efficacy at all, but also whether it has any adverse effects. It is often an important part of the treatment evaluation process. (b) A number of factors are known to be common to all treatments; the second question of interest is then whether the intervention being studied offers any benefit over and above the application of these factors. In evaluating a psychological intervention, the usual strategy involves creating a credible comparison treatment appropriate to the clinical trial. In pharmacological evaluation, the appropriate strategy is the double blind placebo controlled trial. Both strategies have their advantages and disadvantages, their strengths and weaknesses, and the results must be carefully examined. (c) Because the ultimate goal is to maximize efficacy, the third point of interest involves how the treatment in question compares with alternative interventions, either pharmacological or psychosocial, known or believed to be effective. The outcomes of these comparisons will guide the field toward the maximally effective intervention(s). As the process of evaluating efficacy advances, studies will be added to the available database, thereby providing multiple sources for these comparisons. Progress also requires systematic review of these replications. Ideally research will address the important issue of patient/treatment matching within problem areas. Some individuals with a given problem may respond better to some treatments than to other treatments, whereas others with that problem may respond differently. It is possible that such patient/treatment matching will maximize efficacy. Progress also requires systematic review of these replications. Reviews may include statistically sophisticated techniques for compiling results, such as meta-analysis, in addition to criticism based upon the application of the logic of experimental design. However, panels cannot and should not rely solely on the results of meta-analytic strategies since the results may be influenced by the variable quality of the studies included in the analyses. A number of issues need to be considered in designing and evaluating any of these levels of evidence. They include: (1) Outcome measures used to ascertain efficacy must assess appropriate dimensions of the psychological disorder as determined by a consensus of clinical practitioners, clinical scientists, patients, and third-party payers. (2) Assessment batteries should be broad-based so as to include satisfactory measures of life functioning including social and occupational functioning, measures of family or couple functioning, and subjective well being as determined by a consensus of experts working in the area. (3) Efforts should be made to assess patient satisfaction with treatment, as well as any untoward iatrogenic effects of treatment or side effects of treatment. (4) Description of outcome should specify clinical significance (i.e., actual clinical benefit) in addition to any reports of statistical significance. The full range of responses to the intervention should be reported, including such outcomes as (a) functioning within normal limits, (b) much improved but not functioning within normal limits, (c) improvement, (d) no change, and (e) deterioration. The mandate for a particular intervention is enhanced if it normalizes functioning. (5) The treatment should be described in considerable detail such that it can be carried out consistently across clinical settings. (6) Procedures should be instituted to ascertain if the treatment was adequately delivered and received. These determinations of treatment integrity should be assessed by determining (A) was the treatment, as delivered, adequate in terms of quantity and quality? (This factor is typically assessed using validated treatment adherence instruments, as well as ratings of overall competence). (B) Did the treatment have the specific intended effect? This measure of construct validity (sometimes referred to as "manipulation check") would include such factors as cognition actually changing in cognitive therapy or interpersonal relationships changing in IPT. (7) All studies should report intent to treat data specifying attrition due to drop out or refusal. (8) There should be adequate long-term follow-up studies of treatment.

Notice particularly in guideline 3.0 that methodologies for establishing efficacy are arranged hierarchically based on the capability of the specified methodologies to establish efficacy. In this regard the largest role is accorded to randomized
clinical trials that are expressly designed to establish efficacy of the particular intervention. But ranked just below randomized clinical trials are clinical replication
series where the extent of clinical change associated with a given intervention is
evaluated across a large series of patients. Information from this effort can contribute substantially to the design of randomized controlled trials, thus furthering
the evaluation of the intervention.

Finally, the APA task force also noted that once clinical practice guidelines are
constructed they should be evaluated for reliability and validity just as any other
psychological tool or instrument. The specific guidelines specifying the nature of
this evaluation follow.

**Guideline 17.0. The Panel should specify methods of evaluating the psychological
intervention guideline. Guideline 17.1.** Recommendations for evaluating the reliability
of the guidelines should be detailed. Ascertaining whether the guidelines are interpreted
and applied consistently by practitioners comprises one assessment of reliability. If
resources permit, one could ascertain whether other groups of experts, given the same
evidence and methods for guideline development, would come up with essentially the
same conclusions. Typically, reliability would be approximated by independent review of
the guidelines by alternative groups with equivalent expertise. **Guideline 17.2.** Recommendations for evaluating the validity of the guideline should be detailed. The validity of
the guideline may be evaluated retrospectively by independent consideration of the substance and quality of evidence cited, the methods chosen to evaluate the evidence, as well
as the relationship between the evidence and the ultimate recommendations. The guideline may be evaluated prospectively by determining whether it leads to better therapeutic outcomes in the target populations.

As this discussion shows, a great deal of progress has been made in the development of a structure within which practice guidelines can be constructed and
implemented. In a number of health areas, methods for rating and gathering
empirical evidence for clinical practice guidelines are maturing (e.g., Hadorn,
Baker, Hodges, & Hicks, 1996). If we turn the clock back 20 years, scientific practice
guidelines in mental health would be out of the question. The research was still too
limited, and the results were still too ambiguous to be useful. The depth of knowledge needed for completely adequate practice guidelines is impressive and is a tes-
tament to the scientific progress of the field.

In Figure 4.1 the result of program development and testing are practice
guidelines. Because of the structure of managed care, practice guidelines provide a
key means of ensuring some degree of quality control. Once practice guidelines
exist, however, they themselves must be tested to see if clinical quality improves

when the guidelines are developed. If so, training in and supervision of the guidelines will be needed. If these guidelines become linked to accreditation criteria for the industry, a powerful economic force will be brought behind the use of scientific knowledge in the practice setting.

Some of this is already happening. The National Committee for Quality Assurance (NCQA), one of two major accrediting bodies in managed care, is now requiring the use of at least two empirically based behavioral health practice guidelines in order for managed care firms to be accredited. In another development, a national coalition of managed care firms and professional and scientific associations called the Practice Guidelines Coalition (PGC) (Hayes, 1997, 1998) has been formed to produce short, clinical-friendly, multiple-disciplinary, evidence-based practice guidelines. How these changes will work out in practice is not known, but what is clear is that the industrialization of health care delivery seems to lead directly to practice guidelines. This is not surprising, given that quality control has been a major focus of all modern industrial systems in all areas of the economy over the last few decades.

In essence, then, the goal of an integrated system of science-based practice in managed care settings is the development of systems of treatment delivery that gradually ensure a positive clinical response from a greater and greater proportion of clients, using treatment resources that are as inexpensive as possible. The goal of most treatment delivery by doctoral-level scientist–practitioners will increasingly be to develop a great enough knowledge base that treatment services at this level are not as frequently needed. It is this combination of intellectual resources, clinical need, and economic interest that has a chance to revolutionize the role of scientist practitioners in the health care delivery system.

Nicholas Cummings has described this process clearly (Cummings & Hayes, 1996, p. 11):

> The doctoral-level psychologists will be developing the protocols, and testing the protocols. The goal will always be to raise that 30 percent of protocol responsive cases to 40, to 50, to 60, hopefully to 90. There's a level at which we might get alarmingly close to the cookbook stage. That is far off and there will always be room for clinical judgment. But we have to make room for master's level providers. This is going to surprise you. Group practices owned by doctoral practitioners have more non-doctoral people than group practices owned by managed care companies. Once he or she is at risk, [the] psychologist sees the light and says, "Why should I be putting a Mercedes engine on a bicycle?" And so they gear the level of training to the task that has to be done.

The era of managed care presents great challenges to scientist practitioners, but it also presents great opportunities. Scientist practitioners seem best positioned to develop treatment programs, to evaluate these programs, to supervise less-trained providers in these empirically established technologies, and to pick up the pieces when empirically validated treatments are not enough with complex cases (Belar, 1995). To do all of this will take every ounce of creativity, clinical skill, methodological ability, and theoretical knowledge that the field possesses. If scientist practitioners do not rise to this challenge and show their ability to add actual value to the delivery system commensurate to their salary costs, the behavioral health care industry will simply move along without them. We now turn to some of the methods that will allow scientist practitioners to serve their needed roles.

5 The Essentials of Time-Series Methodology

Introduction

When a practitioner is asked to intervene to help produce beneficial change, several factors are usually in place. An individual or group of individuals are facing significant problems. The clients usually have particular goals in mind and often have an idea about the source of their difficulties. These problems are usually sufficiently long-standing that routine methods of change guided by the client's implicit models of health and of dysfunction have already been attempted by the client and have failed. Sometimes more formal change efforts guided by more technical or scientific interpretations have been attempted by professionals, and these too have failed to solve the problem fully.

If the situation is fairly routine, then analysis of the case suggests that there is a known intervention for a problem that appears to be understood. Ideally, this intervention is also known on empirical grounds to be effective with problems of this kind. In this situation, the primary empirical task is one of evaluation, both of the impact of treatment on this individual and perhaps of the impact of the larger program or system of which this service delivery is a part. Even a routine applied case presents the opportunity and the need for an evaluation of the impact of existing procedures, as compared to methods of behavior change that have already been attempted, and for the development of clinical replication series. The value of evaluation in these cases is not merely one of justifying the value of intervention— it is developing rules of generalization that will allow the field to know which treatment is most likely to work for which client. Without the involvement of the practice community, that key clinical question will simply never be answered.

If the problem is complex and resistant to treatment, the task is one not merely of evaluation but also of more sophisticated forms of case analysis and perhaps technique development. When empirically validated treatments are unavailable or when they fail, it is the job of the scientist practitioner to learn how to help. In the emerging world of empirically based practice in managed care settings, there is a strong economic interest in doing so, because for every treatment-resistant client who appears, dozens more are bound to follow, clogging the system and confounding other clinicians. Case analysis, technique development, and evaluation in these situations is needed, not just to treat this particular case but to find a way to succeed with cases like it.

Time-series methodology (single case designs) is a set of strategies that scientist–practitioners may employ in both of these situations. These strategies all build upon both the needs of the applied setting and the model of decision making being used informally by clients and practitioners.

In time-series approaches, the practitioner formalizes the measurement of relevant psychological events and repeats these assessments over time. The pattern of behavior that emerges is carefully examined and several questions are asked of the data: Is the problem constant? How bad is it? Is it getting worse or better? This series of measurements over time and questions asked of it are not *fundamentally* different from the implicit actions taken by a client with a problem, or of most practitioners treating that problem. The practical requirement that the practitioner systematically assess the problem is simply translated into the empirical requirement that formal, systematic, repeated measurements be taken. This change is not trivial in its impact, because the formality of repeated measurement insulates the practitioner from certain key errors of judgment that are common to human decisions.

The practitioner then analyzes the problem and examines what behavior change strategies the client has already tried in order to achieve the desired goal. This analysis differs from the informal change attempts of clients or of change attempts by less empirical practitioners, in that it is informed by the scientific literature and may involve structured tests of hypotheses.

The practitioner then specifies an intervention. The practical suggestion that specific treatments be designed to fit client needs is modified only slightly in time-series methodology. Treatments must fit a scientific interpretation of the problem and be specified well enough that the treatment can be disseminated and adherence to the treatment plan can be assessed.

The scientist practitioner then implements an intervention in a way that allows relatively unambiguous examination of its impact. What is new is that the practical recommendation that practitioners determine if their treatments are actually benefiting the client is translated into the requirement that design strategies be recognized, they be modified appropriately so as to demonstrate and replicate significant effects, and that compliance with the specified intervention be monitored.

As can be seen in this overview, time-series methodology is a formal but flexible analytic strategy that systematically builds upon the natural decision methods of clients and practitioners alike. Indeed, it can be argued that good practitioners are already doing evaluations of potential scientific value with most clients they see, if they follow the highest standards of good professional practice. We will argue throughout the next several chapters that good mental health practice seems often to involve an implicit type of time-series methodology in that the logic of the two enterprises is so similar. It is this fit that makes time-series methods almost uniquely suited to research and evaluation in the practical clinical environment.

The connection between the natural analytic strategies of clients and practitioners on the one hand, and formal time-series methods on the other, emphasizes a more general point that we will return to several times in the next few chapters. Research and evaluation does not stand in isolation from human decision making. Methodologists often overemphasize the distinctions, and thereby produce methodological systems that seem quite foreign to practitioners and consumers alike.

Methodologists are by nature conservative, in part because they make their reputations by being able to argue logically that certain controls would produce some additional judgmental precision. Commonly, the *cost* or *practicality* of these controls, compared to their benefits, is often not given adequate consideration.

In the abstract, methodological purity is a nice thing to have. There are many ways to make errors in human judgment, and if cost or practicality is not a factor, it is nice to have the help. But this book is about research and evaluation in the real world of practical work. In that world, cost and practicality *are* factors. By appreciating how methodological controls really work, we can adopt a more flexible approach in which weaknesses in one area, which may be dictated by the realities of the applied environment, are made up for by strengths in other areas. Some of these strengths may also come from the applied environment itself, such as frequent access to real problems or the opportunity for frequent replication.

It is our intention in this chapter to lay the groundwork for the use of time-series methodology for research and evaluation in applied settings. We will approach the issue from a flexible, practical point of view that emphasizes the scientific credibility of the overall enterprise, rather than emphasizing methodology in a vacuum.

Repeated Measurement and the Individual Level of Analysis

The fundamental core of time-series methodology, as is denoted by this name, is repeated measurement over time of the client's psychological activity and its context. These activities could include overt behaviors, thoughts, feelings, bodily sensations, memories, or physiological reactions. We will use the term "behavior" to refer to all of these. Contextual features could include motivational factors, physiological factors, history, family patterns, behavioral repertoire, contingencies, cognitive schemas, and a host of similar factors that are used to detect the sources of current behavior. In contrast to some group-comparison research designs, in which only a few measurements are taken (e.g., a single-measurement pretreatment and another posttreatment), time-series methodology relies on the frequent assessment of behavior and its context across time. From these frequent measurements, estimates can be drawn of the level of occurrence of important behavior, its apparent trends, and the degree of variability in the behavior of interest around this level and trend. These estimates are then used to detect sources of behavioral influence and to determine the impact of treatment.

The Purpose of Science: Distinguishing Sources of Variability

The need to determine level, trend, and variability around level and trend comes from the way that time-series methods approach the central purpose of applied science. All psychological research is designed to distinguish three sources of variability in measurement: measurement error, extraneous variability, and intervention-related variability.

Measurement Error   This kind of variability is produced by inconsistency in the measurement procedures themselves. Such variability might be thought of as artificial, in that the behavior itself is not varying—it only appears that way. For example, suppose we measure the degree of anxiety felt by a client in response to certain standardized imagined scenes. Suppose further that during one presentation the scenes are read in a very strained voice by the therapist and in another they are read in a very calm tone, and that anxiety ratings track these differences. Unless the practitioner is aware of the inconsistency in the measurement process, it may be concluded erroneously that the client is sometimes more anxious than other times. In fact, the client is only reporting more or less anxiety under uncontrolled and variable measurement conditions.

Extraneous Variability   This kind of variability is produced by impactful variables that were not manipulated or specifically controlled by the analyst. Usually these variables are not even formally measured or known to have occurred.

For example, a client may be ill one day and feeling well the next, and behavior may track these differences. A depressed person may begin to feel better when a troublesome relative moves away. A drug addict may suddenly stop using drugs upon learning that she is pregnant. Unlike the previous example, these are all *real* differences in behavior, but they are due to variables (i.e., illness, change in family circumstances, pregnancy) that the analyst did not manipulate and may not even have assessed.

It is impossible to avoid the presence of extraneous variables of this kind. Behavior does not occur in a vacuum; extraneous variability can be of differing kinds, and can present differing analytical problems.

One type occurs when extraneous variables are varying frequently throughout but not in a known and systematic fashion, what might be termed *background extraneous variability*. This may lead to an enormous amount of variability in the data as particular variables occur and fail to occur. Essentially you might think of this as a kind of static that will disguise the effects of other variables, much as radio static can make it impossible to hear the actual program. Background extraneous variability makes a successful empirical analysis more difficult, because the "signal-to-noise ratio" of information is reduced.

Another kind of problem occurs when some extraneous variable happens to coincide with treatment. *Coincidental extraneous variability* occurs when some strong extraneous variable presents itself simultaneously with the introduction of treatment or other important changes in treatment conditions. For example, the pregnant drug addict just mentioned may enter a drug treatment program immediately before learning of the pregnancy. An immediate reduction in drug use may mimic a strong treatment response, but instead it could be a response entirely produced by the attempt of the mother to avoid harm to her child.

Sometimes extraneous variables are inherently related to treatment. An example of such *inherent extraneous variability* might be that of a depressed and socially withdrawn person entering into an intensive treatment for depression. The client may improve in part because the social context of therapy provides needed social contact and concern, not because of any specific characteristics of the intervention. Yet it is not possible to remove social contact and concern from the treatment—it is an inherent property. This case is really a matter of specifying the functionally important units of intervention, and designing controls to help establish mechanisms of action. Concern with this kind of extraneous variability is central when theoretical processes or mechanisms of action are important to identify.

Sometimes behavior may be changing due to a systematically varying extraneous variable. An example of *systematic extraneous variability* might be the gradual increase in the physical abilities of children caused by maturation. Changes due to systematic extraneous variables tend themselves to be systematic and thus to be more readily separable from those effects that are due specifically to treatment.

Of all these kinds of extraneous variables, the most critical is coincidental extraneous variability because it is the kind that is most readily confused with treatment. Controlling for coincidental extraneous variability is one of the driving forces for time-series experimental designs. All of these designs are sensitive to the possibility of such coincidental arrangements and attempt to deal with them by making the probability of repeated coincidences unlikely.

Intervention-Related Variability   The third source of variability is that produced by the treatment itself. It is this impact that the practitioner usually wishes to assess. It is important to underline, however, that an ability to see the impact of treatment is dependent upon an ability to separate it from variability due to measurement error and extraneous variables. Essentially, when we have weeded out alternative sources of variability, we are left with the treatment effects. Thus, all forms of applied science boil down to a simple task: to distinguish intervention-related variability from measurement error and extraneous variability.

Variability in Group Comparison and Time-Series Approaches

In group-comparison approaches, variability between subjects within specified groups or conditions is used as a simultaneous estimate of measurement error and extraneous variability. Variability between subjects within groups is sometimes called "error" in a statistical sense, but error in that sense includes both *real* variability due to extraneous factors and *false* variability due to inconsistent measurement (the latter being what we are calling "measurement error" in a more specific sense). Using variability between subjects as an estimate of measurement error and extraneous variability is logical because subjects within particular groups have supposedly been treated in exactly the same manner by the researcher: Variability within the group must therefore be due to something else.

In group-comparison approaches, intervention-related variability is estimated by various methods of calculating the central tendency of scores within a group. Statistical inference essentially creates a kind of rubber ruler that is stretched harder the more variability there is between subjects within groups. This stretched ruler is then applied to the difference between groups on measures of central tendency. The logic is that the greater the measurement error and extraneous variability, the larger the distance has to be between groups to be unlikely, if one assumes that only chance is operating.

The core logic of group-comparison approaches is shown diagrammatically in Figure 5.1. It is an impeccable logic, but there are many questions of importance to the applied environment that are not addressed adequately by this logic.

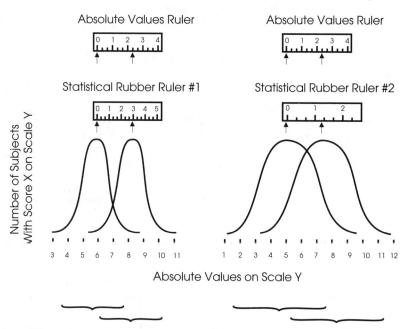

FIGURE 5.1   In group-comparison research the degree of variability between subjects within groups is the source of estimates of measurement error and extraneous variability. In this graph, greater variability between subjects within groups is represented by the greater spread shown in the distributions of scores on the right. Distances between groups must be larger to be statistically significant the more such sources of variability are present. Thus, for example, while the absolute value of the difference between the means of the scores for the groups is the same for those two groups on the left as it is for those on the right, those on the left may be statistically significant, while those on the right are not.

In time-series research, a series of measures are taken repeatedly. These series can be characterized in various ways. A given series of measurement occasions will have an overall *level:* some average or general value of the measure. It will have a *trend:* a direction of change from the beginning of the series to the end. Trends are usually characterized linearly, but they need not be. A series of adjusted levels and trends can be generated in a variety of ways over successive subcomponents of a data series (e.g., see Janosky, 1992) and combined to characterize its *course.* In essence "course" is just a more flexible way to characterize a trend, so we will use the term "trend" to refer both to linear trends and to curves fit over time to the changing course of data (e.g., Knox, Albano, & Barlow, 1996). Finally, each of these measures of central tendency also occur in the context of the *variability* around them. A graphical presentation of these concepts is shown in Figure 5.2.

Variability around level and trend is used to establish the presence and impact of measurement error and extraneous variability. When a condition is

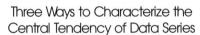

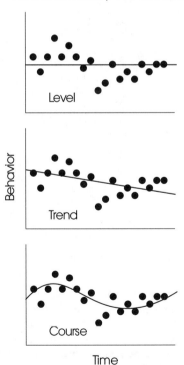

FIGURE 5.2   Three ways of characterizing the central tendency of a data series: level, trend, and course.

changed, changes in level and trend (the time-series analog to central tendency measures in group-comparison designs) are examined against the background of the estimate of measurement error and extraneous variability. The logic is essentially similar to group-comparison approaches: The greater the measurement error and extraneous variability, the larger the distance has to be between estimates of level and trend to be important. Thus, repeated measurement is essential to time-series designs, because repeated measurement allows an estimation of the three sources of variability that need to be distinguished in research. The core logic of time-series approaches is shown diagrammatically in Figure 5.3.

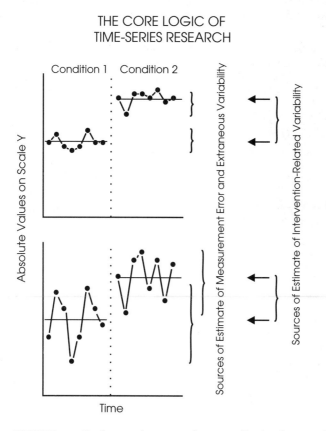

FIGURE 5.3   In time-series research, normally the degree of variability within conditions around estimates of level and trend is the source of estimates of measurement error and extraneous variability. The more such sources of variability are present, the more difference between the central tendency of compared conditions must be large to be viewed as significant. Thus, for example, while the absolute value of the difference between the levels in each condition is the same for those data in the top half of the figure as it is for those in the bottom, the data in the top half of the figure may be taken to be more important than those on the bottom.

An Example of Level of Analysis: Who Improved Due to Treatment?

Whether one is doing time-series research or group-comparison research, the full determination of who improved due to treatment requires repeated measurement. In the clinical arena this is well known. Practical clinical guides exhort clinicians to "examine regularly and consistently whether therapy is being helpful" (e.g., Zaro, Barach, Nedelmann, & Dreiblatt, 1977, p. 157). In most areas of human functioning, no practitioner would be satisfied with only one or two assessments of a client over a period of time that included both the determination of client needs and the design, implementation, and conclusion of treatment. Suppose, for example, your physician happened to take your blood pressure one day and it showed readings that would indicate high blood pressure. If, at that point, your physician failed even to take a second reading and proceeded to lay out a several-month course of intrusive treatment, you should be concerned. If your physician further informed you that no additional assessments of your blood pressure would be taken until the treatment had run a several-month course, and that the physician intended to remain "blind" until then, it would be time to find a new physician. For methodological reasons, this is the approach pursued in common applied research designs using group-comparison methods, and within its intended scope it is a defensible approach. For the practitioner, however, this type of decision making is out of the question.

The need for repeated measurement in order to detect who improved due to treatment comes from a more profound source: This question *requires the separation of measurement error, extraneous variability, and intervention-related variability at the level of the individual.* Understanding the importance of different levels of analysis makes a huge difference to the applied researcher.

Asking "who" improved "due to" treatment is the same as asking which individuals have high intervention-related variability in the context of known degrees of measurement error and extraneous variability for that individual. This point is often missed in discussions of the relative advantages and disadvantages of time-series versus group-comparison approaches. For example, in the typical group-comparison design in which a premeasure and postmeasure are taken for subjects in both experimental and control groups, measurement error and other extraneous variables are totally inseparable from the treatment effect for any given individual. The three sources of variability are separated only at the level of the group, because variability between subjects within specified groups is the source of estimates of measurement error and extraneous variability, while differences between measures of the central tendency of the group is the source of estimates of intervention-related variability. Thus, if Patient A improves 25% on a particular behavioral measure from pre to post, it could be due to measurement error, extraneous variability, treatment-related variability, or combinations of all three. We have no way of knowing.

Figure 5.4 shows the problem. Suppose, sitting on Mt. Olympus, we knew that Patient A had a depression score that varied over time due to extraneous factors as shown in the top of the figure. Suppose, further, that there is no measurement error nor treatment effect for Patient A: Variability is real but due entirely to

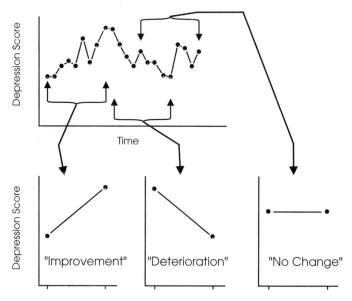

FIGURE 5.4   Traditional pre–post studies do not allow treatment responders to be identified at the level of the individual because separation of the three sources of variability only occurs at the group level. In this example, any type of response could be produced from extraneous variability alone. Identification of individual treatment responders at a minimum requires repeated measurement in order to estimate sources of variability at the individual level of analysis.

variables neither known nor manipulated by the experimenter. Measures are taken once a week.

This patient agrees to be part of a two-month-long study. Figure 5.5 shows three distinct patterns of results, using pre–post measure across an eight-week period. The client could appear to improve, deteriorate, or stay the same, depending on when the study begins and ends. From Mt. Olympus we can know these changes are all due to things happening in the Patient A's life, not to treatment. The researcher is not so lucky. At the level of the individual, nothing can be said from data of these kind about the source of variability.

This is not a problem in group-comparison approaches so long as the researcher sticks to questions that these methods are designed to answer. Knowing who improved due to treatment is not such a question.

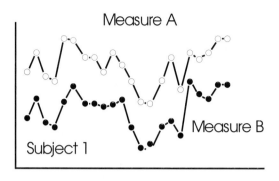

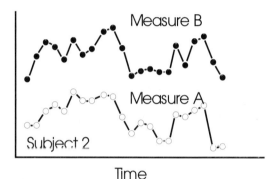

FIGURE 5.5 Two subjects from a hypothetical study of covariation between two measures considered first at the level of the individual versus first at the level of the group. These two measures correlate very highly within these two subjects across time (above .90 in each case), but if levels vary randomly, cross-sectional analysis (across people at any single time) will not reveal this relationship.

The domination of methodological tools at the group level of analysis has sometimes disguised the need to distinguish questions that are appropriate at given levels. Times-series designs are often hard for researchers to understand for this reason. Researchers are used to answering questions using familiar methods, and if those methods do not fit the question, that lack of fit is often hard to detect.

Here is an example of a level-of-analysis problem in the area of assessment. Suppose a practitioner wants to know if a readily obtained measure will track client improvement or deterioration as well as a more arduous measure. To ask this question 100 clients with this problem are recruited and given both measures. The resulting scores are correlated, and when the two measures correlate weakly to moderately, the practitioner is discouraged. This is an entirely typical approach (and result!) but it is not yet time for the practitioner's tears. The question the practitioner wanted to ask has not yet really been asked because the method of answering the question did not fit the level of analysis of the question itself.

The cross-sectional strategy employed examined only covariation between individuals at a given time to see if the measures were related. But this relation was not the relation the practitioner wanted to know about! The practitioner wanted to know if, in general, changes in one measure over time predicted changes in another for these clients. This question is one that requires first an answer at the individual level and then a nomothetic generalization built upon that foundation.

To see the point, imagine that the method was changed so that all 100 clients were assessed repeatedly using both measures. Figure 5.5 shows an idealized version of the resulting data, using only two subjects to make the conceptual point. If the absolute level of each measure is highly variable, but the relationship between them is not, measures can be highly correlated at the level of the individual but not at the level of the group. In these two subjects, for example, Subject 1 is high on Measure A and moderately low on Measure B; Subject 2 is high on Measure B and low on Measure B. If the absolute level of Measure A and B is highly variable and relatively independent across clients, correlations taken across the group at any of the 23 measurement occasions will be low. But suppose these two subjects are characteristic of the group: If so, the two measures could be *highly* correlated across time for virtually every individual and *still be weakly correlated in all cross-sectional analysis.* Indeed, one can readily construct data sets in which the two measures are correlated perfectly for every individual across time and not at all for the group. This is not a mere abstraction. Research has shown that answers to basic questions about covariation among measures (e.g., the relation between attitude and overt behavior) differ very widely depending on whether the questions were asked at the group or individual level (e.g., Epstein, 1979, 1980, 1983; Lamiell, l980, 1981; Lamiell, Trierweiler, & Foss, 1983).

Why would the absolute levels of two measures related within individuals across time be highly variable and relatively independent across individuals? Consider the area of sexual arousal to get a sense of how that could happen. Suppose ten women are asked "how aroused are you looking at this picture?" Their physiological arousal as measured by vaginal blood flow is also recorded. One woman might call a 70% increase in blood flow "somewhat" aroused, the other may call the same thing "very" aroused, while still another who has confused signs of sexual high arousal with those of disgust might call the same thing "not at all aroused." Taken across all women, this difference will greatly reduce the relation between these two measures of sexual arousal. Yet the measures could still be highly related within individuals across time. The first woman might call a 40% increase "a little bit" aroused; the second might call it "somewhat" aroused; and the third might now call it "aroused." In fact, research on this precise question with males has shown significantly higher covariation between sexual arousal measures when the relation is first calculated at the individual level of analysis and then collapsed into a nomothetic generalization, as opposed to the relation itself being assessed at the level of the group (Turner & Hayes, 1996). Note that this difference has nothing to do with the number of subjects; it has to do with detection of sources of variability at the level of the individual or the group.

This problem of level of analysis is one reason researchers have had such a hard time developing reasonable decision rules for the application of given treatments based on assessment—what has been termed the "treatment utility" of assessment (Hayes, Nelson, & Jarrett, 1987). Group comparison studies in treatment matching can be enormously expensive. Project MATCH, for example, studied the impact of matching treatments to clients in substance abuse, and cost more than $20,000,000. Unfortunately, virtually no significant results were found (Project MATCH Research Group, 1997). Correlational studies matching patient variables to outcomes are not as difficult or as expensive to do, but they are often hard to replicate. It now should be clear why: Outcome at the level of the individual may be the result of all three sources of variability. This is not a problem if these three sources are distinguished at the level of the individual, otherwise all three sources of variability are mixed together statistically in a fashion only the person on Mt. Olympus could disentangle.

Appreciation for the level of analysis of different questions has profound implications for evaluation and research. The research design must fit the research question. Practitioners work with clients, not epidemiological entities. Thus whatever is done at the group level of analysis (and a great many important questions reside there), it seems important that clinical work also be built from a strong base in the intensive analysis of client outcomes.

Quality of Measurement

As will be discussed in Chapters 11 through 13, the quality of measurement is the cornerstone of all applied work. This point is recognized in rules of good professional practice, but it has been hidden due to the way it has been discussed. For example, practitioners may be advised to "try to become sensitive to the client." Stated in another manner, this advice is a call for sensitive measurement. Clinicians may be told to "distinguish mere symptoms from the essence of a problem." Stated in another manner, this advice is a call for the assessment of functionally important units of behavior over relatively unimportant topographical features. Good practitioners are often said to be able to discern subtle indicants of client progress and to know how to elicit these cues. This is another way of saying that practitioners should be good at informally measuring client behavior and arranging conditions in which these measures can be taken. An emphasis on securing repeated measures of real quality is nothing more than a more systematic way of doing what applied workers attempt to do anyway.

As will be noted later, good measurement systems can be taken under consistent conditions in order to minimize measurement error. Their administration and scoring is standardized. It is especially important that any condition that might reasonably be expected to influence the measure cannot be allowed to covary with treatment. Usually the best way to protect against this is to keep the measurement procedure as standard as is possible on such dimensions as the time of assessment, the assessor, implicit demands on the client, and the like.

While both of the preceding points regarding the need for quality measures and the need for standardization of measurement are clinically sensible, practitioners often react against this advice. Sometimes this reaction comes because practitioners become increasingly confident in their unaided clinical judgment, and any standardization seems intrusive or unnecessary. Unfortunately, several decades of decision research show that experience almost always produces confidence, but is not assured to produce competence (Dawes, 1994; Dawes, Faust, & Meehl, 1989). This is a fundamental judgment error. Experience alone tends to produce competence only if the task that is being practiced provides clear, immediate, and accurate feedback. Shooting basketballs, typing, or playing a guitar will improve with practice alone; whether or not the performance is effective will be immediately clear. But applied psychological work is rarely like that: The effects are often delayed, ambiguous, and hard to detect. Unsystematic measurement is particularly unlikely to improve with experience alone because it is not being calibrated against clear, immediate, and accurate feedback.

At one time, systematic measurement was difficult and time-consuming. Now there are a number of widely available client assessment and tracking software packages that will administer assessment instruments, score them, and even remind the practitioner when another administration is due. Many practitioners are still in the habit, however, of "winging it." Even if inexpensive solutions were not now available, the ease that comes from winging it would be illusory. Increasingly, as noted in an earlier chapter, clinicians and educators are being required by managed care firms, insurance companies, institutional regulations, or quality assurance committees to specify applied goals and measures of them. Systematic measurement under these conditions can protect the professional's interest with a cost in time and effort that is less than that required by the attempt to defend shortcuts. In addition to pressure from outside sources, the push for quality measurement seems required by the ethics of intervention in applied settings. Anyone who has worked in the applied arena is aware of how easy it is for clients and practitioners alike to deceive themselves. Unfortunately, practitioners are also human; the capacity for self-deception is not significantly diminished by possession of an advanced degree. Without systematic measurement, it is quite easy for a practitioner to claim, in good conscience, that a client is improving when in fact this is not true.

Several additional guidelines can be offered for the practitioner conducting repeated measurement in the context of time-series methodology.

Start Your Measurement Early

The first phase of all applied interventions is a period of assessment. Sometimes this phase may be very short (for example, in crisis intervention), and other times the phase may be quite extended. It is important for the use of time-series methods in applied settings that systematic measurement begin almost immediately, usually before the assessment period ends. The reason for this is simple. In applied settings, where clients are paying for services or have limited services available, the practitioner does not have the luxury of obtaining extended measurement when that would delay significantly the onset of treatment. If systematic assessment waits until the end of the assessment period, it becomes impossible to obtain a baseline against which to evaluate the effects of intervention. Several time-series design elements do not require a baseline, but many powerful ones do, and there is no need to throw away the potential for their use due simply to delays in measurement.

Fortunately, the applied needs of the assessment phase itself can be supported by the use of early repeated measurement. In the beginning of this phase, the practitioner is exploring various alternative formulations. Many measures exist that are appropriate for exploratory work and, if they are implemented with an eye toward their future use, they can be turned into systematic measures useful throughout the course of intervention. For example, suppose a client comes in who is extremely anxious. Interviewing during the first session may indicate several possible sources of this anxiety. Rather than wait until it is clear exactly what is producing the anxiety, the practitioner could develop several possible measures at the end of the first session. The clinician might ask the client to record in a diary whenever he or she experiences a significant degree of anxiety. Similarly, a card-sort procedure might rapidly be developed that contains several possible dimensions contributing to the discomfort. A structured interview such as the Anxiety Disorders Interview Schedule-IV might be arranged (DiNardo, Brown, & Barlow, 1994). Standardized self-report inventories might be administered.

As time goes on, and the case becomes clearer, some of these measures will probably turn out to be irrelevant, and these can then be dropped. If, however, several measures have been taken, it is likely that at least some of them will continue to be valuable.

There are applied advantages to this as well. Often the collection of systematic measures reveals that apparent problems are really not problems or at least are not problems to the imagined degree. Human judgments are greatly influenced by certain factors such as confirmatory bias, failure to attend to base rates, or the tendency to form illusory correlations between infrequent events. Such cognitive errors can have notable applied impact. For example, a child can be called "hyperactive" because a parent suggested it to a teacher who then "observed" the expected behavior, because a few notable occasions in which compliance was a problem have been inappropriately generalized, or because a school physician tends to call all problem children by that name. When systematic measures are taken, these cognitive errors are harder to make and easier to detect.

Early systematic measurement may reveal patterns in the nature of the difficulty that can suggest possible avenues of remediation. Finally, by starting measurement early, it is possible to develop even more adequate measures that coincide more directly with the practical needs of a particular applied situation. These points are often driven home when practitioners fail to develop measures until the last minute. After completing an evaluation based on more informal procedures, a practitioner may begin systematic measurement and treatment simultaneously. It is not uncommon to find that the measurement process shows that the intervention was based on an inadequate picture of the situation. These kinds of false starts are destructive in an applied sense and minimize any potential scientific value that the case may have.

If the practitioner has started measurement early, often the assessment phase will conclude with an adequate baseline already in hand. The possibility of obtaining an adequate baseline is also increased by the range of measures taken early in assessment.

Take As Many Measures As Is Reasonable and Practical

If time allows it, good practitioners generally explore a client's problems broadly so as to ensure that the eventual intervention is sensitive to the range of client needs. To the extent that measurement systems can be designed that are cheap and unobtrusive, this advice translates into the recommendation that practitioners explore the reasonable avenues of measurement. Assessment can be thought of as a funnel (Nelson & Barlow, 1981). While the initial assessment is quite broad, the information gained from it increasingly tends to narrow the applied focus. The early use of multiple measures is a critical parallel to this natural process. For example, suppose a client comes into outpatient therapy seeking treatment for depression. In the first session the clinician may notice that the client is engaging in a number of self-derogatory statements. Rather than wait for a complete picture to emerge, the clinician may begin to keep track of the number of unprompted self-derogatory statements. Later, as the session proceeds, it may become clear that the client's thinking shows several cognitive errors characteristic of depressed clients. Measures designed to tap into these dimensions can be implemented. For example, the clinician may send the client home with the request to fill out a self-report measure of automatic depressive thoughts.

Through this type of strategy a large number of measures will be generated from which only the most useful and appropriate will ultimately be retained. Obviously, it is possible to burden clients with unnecessary or excessive measurement procedures. In reality it seems to be more of a fear on the part of practitioners than a common, real-life problem. If the clinician is convinced that a given measure has potential value, clients will sense this and will usually experience it as supportive, not excessive. The key is to keep assessment linked to the applied purposes at hand, and to use measures that fit the demands of the practical situation.

Use Available Measures

While the quality of measurement is the cornerstone of time-series evaluation, this does not mean that all measures must be of the highest quality. Often, the practitioner does not know what to measure or exactly how to measure it. In some practical situations it may be difficult or even impossible to obtain measures of extremely high quality due to restrictions caused by limited time, limited access, or cost restrictions. Some measures used in applied research are presently impractical for ongoing applied intervention. Over time, this problem has lessened as applied researchers have learned to do more with less. For example, most long self-report questionnaires now have short forms available that often do just about as good a job as the full instrument. Indeed, advances in computer technology have made it much easier to use and manage high-quality and rapid assessment. In some areas, however (e.g., the assessment of sexual arousal), it is still difficult or expensive.

Rather than abandon the attempt to be systematic because measurement procedures cannot meet some arbitrarily high standard, it is better to take the best measures practically possible while simultaneously recognizing any compromises or limitations. The power of time-series methods derives largely from an emphasis on replication. No single case is a "critical experiment." It is the overall picture that is important. Thus, while the contribution of a given analysis may be limited due to deficiencies in measurement, it may contribute to an overall sequence of cases that are valuable and scientifically meaningful.

The willingness to use the best measures practically possible, even if they are not perfect, has other benefits. In the process of attempting systematic evaluation, methods may be discovered that will allow more precise evaluation in the future. Similarly, the difficulty in securing adequate measures, while uncomfortable, may motivate a search for better measurement systems. This is precisely why many shorter assessment devices have been developed over the last decade. The biggest reason to be practical, however, is because systematic measurement reduces the capacity for applied self-deception. If we fail to take systematic measures and rely instead upon intuitive procedures, the overall quality of assessment is almost certainly decreased at the same time that the concept of measurement is put out of mind.

Take Measures Frequently

A final recommendation can be made about the process of repeated measurement. More frequent measures, so long as the frequency still has applied meaning, generally allow a greater degree of precision in a time-series analysis. This happens because infrequent measures allow only a delayed assessment of variability around a given level and trend, and because more frequent measures provide more opportunities for the detection of extraneous factors or measurement error. In addition, the number of design options is increased when measures are relatively infrequent.

It is also possible to take measures too frequently, however. Measures may be intrusive or are susceptible to factors such as practice or fatigue. Measures can be lengthy, difficult, or costly. Usually the solution for these problems is to take some practical measures frequently (those that are easy to implement, fairly unobtrusive, and likely to be agreed to by the client) and supplement these with measures that can be taken only infrequently. Especially if the measures are related, the more frequent measurement will tend to validate and support the less frequent measurement and vice versa. For example, a rehabilitation therapist working with a stroke victim in a rehabilitation center may not be able to do a comprehensive evaluation of the client's motor skills frequently. These comprehensive motor assessments take several hours and require skilled evaluators. The clinician could, however, take a simple range-of-motion measure on a particular limb being worked on, which could then tend to validate at least part of the infrequently taken overall assessment, and vice versa.

Frequency should be fitted to the problem at hand. In general, measures should be taken at the frequency that could be useful in detecting real changes in the phenomenon being measured. For example, reading performance does not change significantly on an hourly basis. Evaluating the impact of a reading program with hourly reading measures would be useless overkill. Weekly progress might be more meaningful.

Many additional points need to be considered about specific measurement devices or strategies. We make additional measurement recommendations in Chapters 11 through 13.

Specifying the Intervention

A critical component of any applied intervention is the degree to which "the techniques making up a particular . . . application are completely identified and described" (Baer, Wolf, & Risley, 1968, p. 95). Any deficiencies in this step will threaten an ability to replicate effects that are achieved. Replication is the mechanism through which the external validity or general usefulness of time-series methodology is demonstrated, so any imprecision in this area can be quite costly.

It is useful to think about why we replicate empirical studies. A superficially correct but false answer is that we replicate research to see if doing the same thing leads to the same results. Scientists do not replicate investigations to see if the exact same conditions will produce the same effects; this is, instead, something scientists hold as an a priori assumption. If the conditions are *exactly* the same, in a determined world the effects should be the same. Rather, we replicate research to see if doing what a researcher says was done is functionally doing the same thing. The issue is the functional adequacy of verbal specification of events.

One is tempted to solve the problem of specifying treatment by literally specifying *everything* that was done. A few moments' reflection shows that this is impossible. An educational practitioner would spend a lifetime specifying everything that happened in a single school day. A clinician could do the same with just a few therapy sessions. It is just not possible to specify every comment, every look, every temperature variation, every sound, every item of clothing, every movement, and so on. The specification of an intervention is thus not an endless listing of all conditions present. Rather, it is an approximation: a verbal rule that summarizes the apparently critical components of the intervention, which professionals can use as a guide for action. Whether that rule is adequate or inadequate can become entirely clear only in the process of attempts to replicate.

Researchers have spent a great deal of effort increasing the adequacy of specification of interventions over the last twenty years, and especially the last decade. Early research on psychotherapy gave only general descriptions of treatment conditions and the philosophy or approach (the "school") of the therapist (VandenBos, 1980). In the 1970s researchers became more interested in measuring and demonstrating treatment integrity and in controlling other variables that might impact on treatment outcome (VandenBos, 1980). Especially in the 1980s treatments became more adequately manualized, and measures of treatment integrity and therapist competence have become more sophisticated (Luborsky & DeRubeis, 1984). While even these steps cannot substitute for an adequate program of replication itself, they make replication more likely and more useful. In addition to the "small revolution" (Luborsky & DeRubeis, 1984) of treatment manuals, these manuals are increasingly being linked to scientifically based practice guidelines (Hayes, Follette, Dawes, & Grady, 1995). This means that practitioners increasingly can turn to empirically validated and thoroughly manualized interventions in major areas of actual practice.

The purpose of treatment manuals is to "achieve a reasonable degree of uniform quality and consistency of therapist performance" (Butler & Strupp, 1991, p. 528). Manuals are most useful when the target population is well specified, the treatment procedures can be clearly stated, and procedures are relatively consistent across clients (Teasdale, 1988). The last requirement is becoming less of a restriction as more flexible manuals are constructed. The earliest manuals were focused on fairly specific problems and generally were written by behavior therapists (Wolpe, 1969). Over time, researchers have learned how to develop manuals that are clear, and yet apply to complex or conditional interventions (e.g., Butler & Strupp, 1991). In addition, applied psychologists are learning to specify treatment in such a way that a wider range of unexpected situations can be handled in a manner consistent with the treatment approach—what has been termed the "procedural descriptiveness" of the manual (Thomas, Bastien, Stuebe, Bronson, & Yaffe, 1987).

Quite complex intervention approaches can be tested if they are sufficiently specified so as to tap into the components of intervention that determine their effectiveness. Conversely, no empirical approach will save a practitioner's favorite intervention principles if, in fact, these principles are so vague as to be uninterpretable by others.

Assessing Treatment Adherence and Competence

Specification of treatment is not enough. Practitioners must also show that treatment was delivered as specified, and was done so competently (Waltz, Addis, Koerner, & Jacobson, 1993). The logic of assessment of treatment integrity is simple. If in an empirical study it cannot be shown that the actual treatment given fit the description of the treatment given, we have little reason to believe that replicating that described treatment will functionally be doing the same thing as was originally done—and that is the whole purpose of replication.

Treatment adherence measures usually specify certain key components of the approach that must be done. Sometimes the measure also specifies certain actions that *cannot* be done, according to the approach. Treatment competence measures usually involve rating scales applied by thoroughly trained experts in the approach, who assess whether the treatment is delivered in a manner that is smooth, coherent, sensitive, and effective.

The best measures of treatment adherence and competence go beyond unstructured judgments by the therapist or clients involved, assess multiple sessions, assess the major components of intervention, and distinguish between effective and superficial implementation (Moncher & Prinz, 1991). If a practitioner videotapes, audiotapes, or otherwise records what was done in applied work fairly detailed measures of treatment adherence and competence can be utilized. This degree of effort is probably likely only when actually publishing data from the practice setting, but in fact treatment adherence and competence assessment are arguably important in supervision and training as well. Apparently no actual empirical work has yet been done on the applied impact of the use of treatment adherence or competence measurement, however, and much remains to be done in the development of simplified and practical adherence and competence measures.

Establishing the Degree of Variability in Repeated Measures

An estimate of the degree of variability in the client's behavior (as repeatedly measured) is critical in time-series methodology. It is in the context of this estimate that determinations are made about the level and trend in the behavior, and predictions are drawn about the future course of the behavior. This variability (also termed intrasubject variability) is the background against which we evaluate all the facts about treatment using time-series approaches.

The reason repeated measurement is necessary to identify treatment-related variability can be restated in these terms. The goal of applied intervention is to improve client functioning. "Improvement" is essentially a matter of intrasubject variation. The only way to estimate intrasubject variability is to take repeated measurements within an individual across time, to assess the variability directly, and to attempt to distinguish treatment-related improvement from other sources of variation. Differences between people are just not the same as differences within people. Reliance on infrequent measurement of many individuals is not a shortcut to a determination of individual improvement.

This logical fact is fairly easy to demonstrate. For example, the top of Figure 5.6 shows a situation in which intrasubject variability is nonexistent and yet intersubject variability is high. The bottom of Figure 5.6 shows that intrasubject variability can be high when intersubject variability is low.

These patterns are not as improbable as they might at first seem. Many behavioral patterns associated with weather, weekends, or major holidays vary as much or more within people than across people. Conversely, many behavioral traits, skills, areas of achievement, or intellectual performances show the opposite pattern. If the top graph in Figure 5.6 were, say, a comprehensive assessment of knowledge of psychology, the scores probably would not change much from day to day within people, but they would certainly vary widely across people.

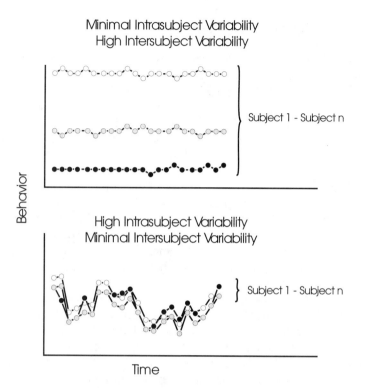

FIGURE 5.6   **An example of the logical independence of intrasubject and intersubject variability.** In the top figure, intersubject variability is high and intrasubject variability is low. In the bottom figure, the reverse is true. Intrasubject variability, therefore, cannot be estimated by knowledge of intersubject variability alone.

When variability within subject is assessed with many subjects, both types of variability are known. The reverse is not true. Regardless of how many subjects are assessed infrequently, variability within a client cannot be derived from this information. Regardless, then, of the methodology chosen, the estimation of intrasubject variability is an essential component of applied research.

What Is Stability?

Estimating the degree of intrasubject variability occurs along two continua. One is based solely on a physical dimension. If we have a series of events measured along some physical dimension, we can speak of the degree of variability in that set of data. For example, data could be said to be highly variable when the standard deviation from the mean is high and relatively stable when the standard deviations are low. The concept of variability as a purely physical property, however, has its limitations. Estimates of variability have meaning only because of the use to which these estimates will be put. For example, physicists would be appalled at the degree of variability (in purely physical terms) shown in the behavior of animals in operant chambers. These same basic operant researchers, in turn, would be troubled by the degree of physical variability tolerated in applied research. For the purposes of measuring the speed of light, physicists cannot tolerate even the most infinitesimal degree of physical variability. For measuring the effect of a particular schedule of reinforcement, much more physical variability may be tolerable. Thus, the second continuum used to evaluate variability is its analytic utility. This is not a purely physical quality. Rather, it is an evaluation of that physical quality relative to a methodological task at hand. We will use the term "stability" to refer to that property.

What then is an acceptably small degree of variability in the problems or performances being measured? The logic of time-series methodology and of applied work generally suggests that data must be stable in the following sense: The influences of measurement error and extraneous variables are sufficiently limited or sufficiently clear so as to enable a clear statement about the effects of the independent variable at its expected strength. In other words, the degree of underlying variability seen cannot eliminate an ability to see expected effects.

Others have at times used the word "stability" to mean that the data have no trend and that the degree of physical variability is small. This definition of stability is problematic for several reasons. For one, as we have just argued, variability criteria based solely on absolute physical dimensions are arbitrary. Another difficulty is that this use of the term confuses the issue of trend with the issue of variability around that trend. Behavior that has no trend and minimal physical variability is stationary. It can be shown, however, that nonstationary data can still be stable in the functional sense defined above.

Practitioners very often do not see stationarity in their clients' behavior. Clients may be gradually deteriorating or gradually improving, and intervention may still be required. The mere presence of a trend does not mean that the data are not stable, however. Trends may be due to the consistent effect of some extraneous variable, such as maturation. As long as the extraneous variable does not covary systematically with treatment, treatment effects can be distinguished from the background extraneous variables causing the steady trend.

There is the misperception that stationary data are *necessarily* less influenced by extraneous variables. This is not logically necessary, since a lack of trend can itself be the product of extraneous variables. For example, two extraneous variables could be present that canceled each other out. Say that a clinician was interested in the social functioning of a withdrawn child. Maturational effects might be improving the ability of the child to interact socially while the deterioration produced by social isolation might be working in the opposite direction. It is conceivable that these two variables could cancel each other out so evenly as to produce a lack of a trend in the behavior of interest. Any intervention with this child, however, would be an intervention in the context of the effects of social isolation and maturation. Conversely, imagine this same case with the effect of maturation removed (as might occur with an adult, for example). The resulting trend could be a gradual deterioration. Intervention in this instance would occur in the context of the gradual effect of social isolation. In both cases, baseline controls for extraneous variables but it does not eliminate them. Thus, both cases have equal scientific status in the abstract, even though there is a trend in one case and not the other. Thus, stationarity does not relieve us from the duty to control for or to identify important extraneous variables, nor is it necessary for time-series evaluation to achieve stationarity in measurement.

Throughout the sections that follow, we will use the word "stable" in the functional sense just defined. Most of the recommendations made by other methodologists, which use a more limited sense of the term, are equally valid when the word has been defined more functionally. With the exception of the definition, the rules remain intact.

Let us return then to the question of how much variability can be tolerated in the data or, stated differently, how we can know when our measures are stable. Since we cannot rely purely on physical components of variability to answer this question, the answer can only be stated conditionally. To put it bluntly, it all *depends.* It depends on (a) our knowledge of the treatment and its effects; (b) on our knowledge of the particular behavior, disorder, or deficiency, and its known course or its response to treatment; (c) on our knowledge of a particular measure that we have used of the behavior and how sensitive it is to actual changes that occur; and (d) on our knowledge of the effects of external conditions and extraneous variables involved in this particular intervention with this particular client in this particular situation. Fortunately, practitioners are in the best position to make this judgment.

The most crucial variable in determining stability is how large a change we expect to find. For example, consider the data shown in Figure 5.7. If the expected outcome is that shown in the top part of the figure, then the first phase is far too variable for our purposes. The data overlap completely, and the shift in level is minimal. If, conversely, we anticipate the effects in the bottom part of Figure 5.7, then these same data are perfectly adequate. The effect of treatment is relatively sudden, the level difference is large, and the overlap is small. The more we expect or require large and relatively rapid treatment effects, the more physical variability can still be considered stable. Similarly, if intervention is itself likely to reduce the degree of variability in the data, in addition to impacting on the level or trend in the data, then more physical variability can still be considered stable.

Indeed, there are some circumstances in which variability itself is a reasonable target. For example, a manic-depressive may on average have a normal mood—it is the variability in mood that is abnormal. When variability is itself the target, again the degree of change must be considered. Examine the data in Figure 5.8. The baseline is inadequate if the effects we hope for are those on the top right. If we hope to see the effects shown on the bottom, the baseline is probably sufficiently stable.

All of this means that stability requires some knowledge about the problem being treated. Sometimes none of these questions concerning the likely effects of an intervention can be answered with certainty. There are two things to be said in this

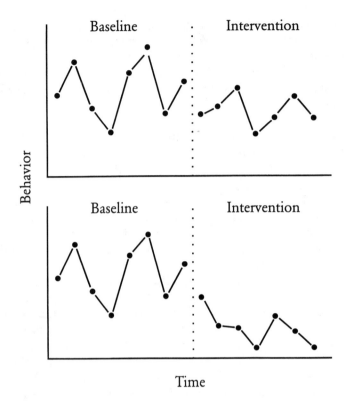

FIGURE 5.7   An example of how data with the same amount of variability can be nonstable or stable, depending upon the expected results. If the results at the top are expected, the data are nonstable. If the results at the bottom are expected, the data are stable.

case: First, the lower the degree of variability in a physical sense the better, so it makes sense to try to eliminate sources of variability if possible so that a clearer picture might be seen. Second, while there may not be a good basis to predict the outcome there usually is a good basis to state what outcomes are acceptable. In other words, instead of thinking of anticipated effects as a prediction of what will happen, they can be thought of as a statement of the minimum change that would be satisfactory. This does not seem to require so much a prediction of future events as a statement of current values. If data are not sufficiently stable to see the effects of minimally acceptable outcomes, the practitioner may wish to consider the ethics of intervention. There is another way to state the situation when data are not sufficiently stable to see the effects of acceptable outcomes: We will not be able to see a reasonable treatment effect even if it is found. But all interventions have costs and risks in addition to possible benefits. Not all cases should be treated. If we will not be able to see a reasonable treatment effect even if it is found, then intervention probably is not necessary.

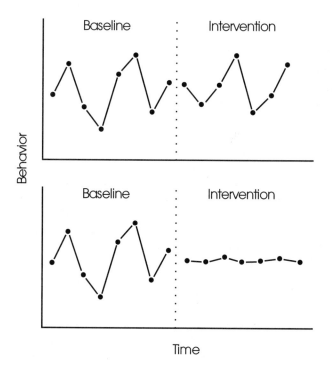

FIGURE 5.8 **Another example of how the adequacy of baseline is a relative concept.** In this case, the unusual target for treatment is a reduction in variability itself. If the results at the top are expected, the stability shown in baseline is inadequate. If the results at the bottom are expected, the baseline is adequate.

The Amount of Data Needed to Assess Stability

A related question to the one of stability is that of the number of data points needed to estimate stability. One data point provides a minimal estimate of level, but not trend, nor variability. Two data points provide a minimal estimate of level and of trend, but again they provide no estimate of variability around level and trend. Finally, with three data points, an estimate—however minimal—is provided of level, trend, and variability around that level and trend.

As a scientific matter, the more data points that are collected beyond three data points the better. There is no real maximum. But in the applied world the benefits of increased data must always be weighed against their various costs. Estimates that are based on a few data points are defensible under several conditions. First, if the degree of variability seen is extremely low (for example, if three data points in a row were on or near the same exact score), then the need for a larger sample might be mitigated. Similarly, if the effects expected are very large, then the number of data points in the estimates of stability might be correspondingly reduced. When there is a disorder that we know a great deal about and where there is a known course, then a small sample (or even one measurement) may suffice to indicate the level and trend in the behavior. If the measure is of extremely high quality, then fewer data points may be needed. For example, one or two positive laboratory results from a good-quality laboratory will usually be enough to convince a physician that a patient has AIDS. The measures are of high quality, and a great deal is known about the normal course of this disease.

Because so many factors are involved, there is no absolute answer to the number of data points needed to estimate stability. Indeed, as in practice itself, there are few absolute answers anywhere in time-series methodology. Just as in any applied situation, when you are in the dark you need more information to be sure where you are. To the extent that you are not in the dark about the effects that are anticipated, or the quality of the measure, or the course of the behavior, to that extent you can cut corners on the number of measurements required.

Ideally, estimates of stability are similarly based throughout the course of the study. That is, the amount of data collected, and the degree of variability taken to be acceptable in the data, should ideally not vary widely from phase to phase. This is not a hard and fast rule, however. Sometimes we are forced to base our estimates of stability in some phases on far fewer data points than there are in others. As will be discussed in subsequent chapters, this can produce a distortion in our ability to discern actual effects. As elsewhere, when compromises need to be made, the solution is to replicate the effects and provide additional control elsewhere that compensate for weaknesses.

What to Do When Data Are Not Stable

There are basically four things that a practitioner can do when faced with data that are unstable: analyze sources of variability, wait and see, examine the unit of analysis, or proceed anyway.

Analyze Sources of Variability   One of the main advantages of collecting systematic individual data is the way that this highlights potential sources of control over the phenomena of interest. If, for example, baseline data show several periods in which the client was functioning at a level that would be acceptable after treatment, then the obvious thing to do is to attempt to discern what it is about those periods that is producing improved functioning.

There are three methods to use when attempting to analyze sources of variability. First, *possible effects due to measurement error* should be explored. Any inconsistency in the measurement process could easily produce excessively variable data. If this false variability is removed, the picture may become clear. The second strategy is to examine the data and attempt to *identify major extraneous variables that might produce the instability.* These can be then controlled or eliminated, more or less one at a time, until stability emerges. Often this process will give hints about the best way to intervene.

For example, Figure 5.9 shows the hypothetical record of a child in school who is said to be "hyperactive." It is not uncommon in such a situation to find that, despite the reports of teachers or others, the child is not always troublesome, distracted, or off-task. Instead there are often distinct periods when the child's on-task behavior reaches dramatically low levels, and the common cognitive errors amplify this pattern in the minds of parents or teachers into a relatively constant one. In this hypothetical case, the practitioner has determined that the child usually meets or exceeds the average levels of on-task behavior in the classroom, but there are times when on-task behavior degrades dramatically. The obvious thing to do is to attempt to see what it is about these days that distinguishes them from others. On examination it may be determined that these days are associated with an inadequate breakfast, inadequate sleep, visits by a relative, difficult school tasks, tests, or some other extraneous condition.

If the extraneous variable can be identified, it may be possible to manipulate it directly or indirectly, or to establish an intervention that makes sense in light of its impact. For example, the child might be put into a school breakfast program, or taught how to request help appropriately with difficult tasks. If the variable is one that cannot be manipulated, the practitioner can at least organize the data points with relevance to the extraneous variable. For example, suppose the child is from a broken home and generally shows school problems only when staying with his father. These data may be quite stable when organized into with-mother days and with-father days, as is shown in Figure 5.10. Essentially, this strategy turned the data into a kind of natural alternative treatments design (see Chapter 7), in which

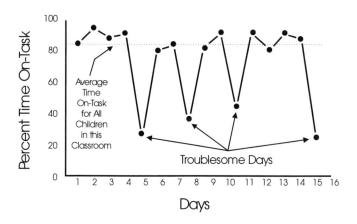

FIGURE 5.9   An example of how systematic, repeated measurement sets the occasion for analyzing extraneous sources of variability. The child's behavior is problematic only on days 5, 8, 11, and 16. If the source of control over the behavior on these days can be identified, treatment might be greatly aided.

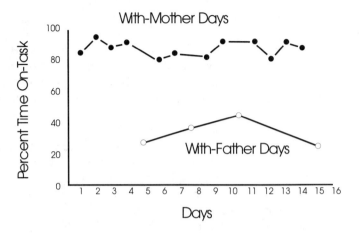

FIGURE 5.10   When the child behavior is graphed in terms of major extraneous conditions, the apparent instability disappears.

only one natural condition is a treatment target. The source of variability may not necessarily be removed—it may turn out that the practitioner cannot really change the home situation (e.g., due to an uncooperative parent) and there may be nothing (e.g., abuse) happening to demand that it be changed. At least, however, it can be statistically controlled for analytic purposes.

The final method of analyzing sources of variability is to create a consistent environment in an attempt to control all possible extraneous variables. This is essentially the strategy chosen by those who do laboratory research, and in a limited way a parallel condition can be created in some relatively controlled applied settings (e.g., inpatient facilities). As a result of controlling for all conceivable variables, stability may emerge, but the cost is often too high for those in applied settings.

Wait and See   A second major strategy when data are excessively variable is to wait for a more stable pattern to emerge. Often stability is temporarily disturbed by extraneous factors. This is particularly likely in baseline when, for example, clients may expect sudden change, may be attempting to improve their situations, may be examining their difficulties more systematically than previously, and so on. Clinicians often note that merely the commitment to enter into psychotherapy "stirs things up." Clients may become much more emotional, for example. A client reporting a difficulty for the first time may be surprised to find herself or himself forcing the story out through tears. "I didn't realize I was so upset about this" is not an uncommon report early in therapy. Conversely, some clients commonly discover "instant cures" in the early phases of intervention. A disturbed couple coming into treatment for the first time may feel great relief just because each partner is willing to come, for example. A more defensive client may suddenly "feel better" as a means of avoiding confrontation with a difficult problem.

All of this means that the applied picture may be unstable at first but then settle down because these processes of change tend to be too superficial to last. The emotionality may diminish, the disturbed couple may begin to fight once again, and the avoidant defenses may prove to be false. For such reasons, the hypothetical pattern shown in Figure 5.11 is not uncommon. Essentially, this advice can be summarized this way: If the picture is unclear, wait a while to see if clarity emerges. As the picture becomes clearer, it may be more obvious whether or not treatment is necessary. This is not arbitrary and abstract advice; it is linked to practical realities. Practitioners should not normally proceed if the picture is so confused that it is not even clear that intervention is needed, or on what. When data are unstable in a functional sense, that is what is meant, and in this situation wait and see is a reasonable option to consider.

Examine the Unit of Analysis   A third major strategy when data are excessively variable is to examine the temporal unit of analysis. Measures are often collected in a particular temporal unit due to matters of convenience and not to practically defensible considerations. For example, clients are often asked to self-record in hourly or daily blocks, or assessment may be taken at treatment sessions. The more meaningful unit of analysis may be much larger—say, weekly or monthly. If the actual phenomenon makes more sense in larger temporal units, then the data may be blocked or intrasubject-averaged. One way in which this is accomplished is simply by calculating the mean for the data appearing during set blocks of time. The data shown in Figure 5.12 reveal what often occurs when data are blocked or intraclient-averaged. The top graph shows the raw records for a psychotherapy client coming into therapy twice a week and recording data session by session. The bottom graph shows those same data ranged into weekly blocks (i.e., blocks of two sessions). The data are much more clear in the lower than the upper graph.

When there are sufficient data points in each phase it is possible to use more statistically sophisticated forms of blocking. For example, Janosky (1992)

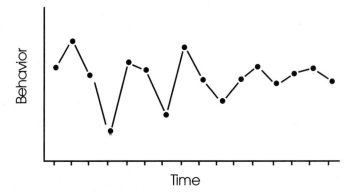

FIGURE 5.11   **It is not uncommon to see unstable data become stable over time.**

FIGURE 5.12   An example of the effect of blocking or intrasubject averaging. In the top graph, raw data are graphed from therapy sessions held twice weekly. In the bottom, weekly averages are graphed. The bottom shows a much clearer and more stable pattern. Intrasubject averaging should be done only when the temporal unit of analysis is too small relative to the phenomenon being examined.

recommends the use of a nonparametric sequential smoothing algorithms such as those available in SPSS or other popular statistical packages. An example of the application of this procedure is shown in Figure 5.13, taken from a study by Knox, Albano, and Barlow (1996). In this figure, the frequency of compulsions in four children is shown. The compulsions vary widely across days. The smoothed curve figure shows what amounts to a continuously revised measure of central tendency. By combining both data sources on one graph, this approach highlights the changing level and trend in each phase (the smoothed curve) while still allowing the variability around that measure of central tendency to be observed.

It is important that practitioners not deceive themselves by these processes. The variability in the behavior itself is not changed by the way that we choose to examine our data. Put another way, blocking will often reduce the variability in data but it will never reduce the variability in behavior. Nevertheless, variability in behavior need not always be highlighted. This might be better understood by

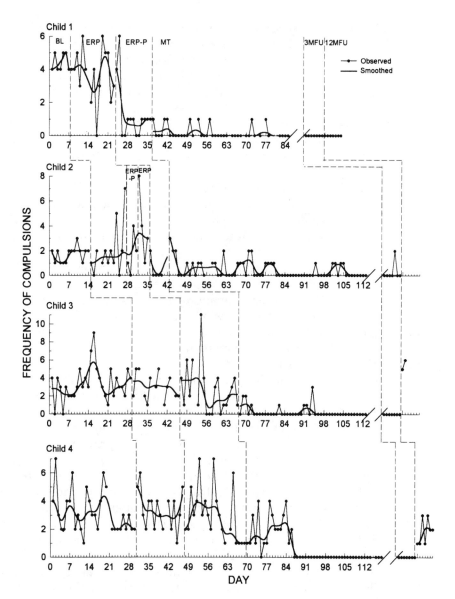

FIGURE 5.13   An example of the presentation of data both in smoothed and raw form.
These data show the frequency of compulsions in four children across baseline ("BL"),
exposure and response prevention ("ERP"), exposure and response prevention plus
parental involvement ("ERP-P"), and maintenance ("MT") phases and at 3- and 12-month
follow-ups. This method of data presentation allows both the course of each condition
and variability around that course to be seen.

The figure is taken from Knox, L. S., Albano, A. M., & Barlow, D. H. (1996). Parental involvement in the
treatment of childhood obsessive-compulsive disorders: A multiple baseline examination incorporating
parents.

Behavior Therapy, 27, 93–115 and is used with permission of the Association for Advancement of Behavior Therapy.

examining a similar measurement situation. Suppose an instructor wished to assess the level of performance of a student. An essay exam might be given in which several specific questions are asked. Each of these questions will be scored, but the total performance on the exam will consist of the sum of scores on the individual questions. If the teacher is keeping track of trends in a student's scoring, probably the trends will be calculated across several overall tests—not over dozens of specific essay questions arranged in sequence. A practitioner considering the use of intraclient blocking faces a situation much like that. Because we do not really care about the variability in answers to individual questions, blocking is natural and sensible.

Consider a similar case in which a married couple has come in for treatment. The clinician may ask each partner to record the number of pleasing and displeasing things done by the other. These records will undoubtedly be collected daily, not because daily records are the best picture of marital functioning, but because the clients will better be able to keep track of their records that way. Marital arguments, for example, are probably not best viewed on a daily basis. All couples probably have some bad days. Seeing the forest and not just individual trees may be easier if a larger temporal unit is used. Thus, the average level of disturbance over several days or even longer periods may be a more meaningful unit of analysis. Despite the claims of some purists, it is no more dangerous to collect these data into larger and more meaningful units than it is to record a test based on overall performance.

The key issue, practically, is the same one methodologically: We should select units of analysis based on their meaningfulness. One way to think of this is to consider the smallest unit that could possibly lead to the practitioner's reacting to apparent improvement or deterioration. This is probably the meaningful unit of measurement and the one that should be used in data presentations.

There *is* a danger, however, when blocking or intrasubject averaging is used on a completely post hoc basis with no applied justification. The danger is that the particular temporal unit chosen might just happen to lead to stable data because of a chance coincidence between this unit and the variability observed. Replicating findings based on blocked data with additional clients can guard against this possibility. If these additional clients can be evaluated successfully using the same blocking interval, then the practitioner may be more confident that the interval chosen is appropriate. In questionable circumstances it is always best to maintain the smaller temporal unit at the data collection phase so that the inherent variability in the behavior can be viewed in a more fine-grained way. The case of the instructor giving an essay examination can illustrate the point. While it may not be useful to consider the student's performance on a question-by-question basis for the purpose of determining the trends in performance, the examination itself must be scored question-by-question. The instructor might notice that the performance on a particular question is quite poor, while the performance on another question is quite good. This may be due to the quality of the lecture covering that material, to the quality of the background reading, or to other events that may give clues about how best to instruct the student. In a similar manner, blocked data may be best for viewing the overall impact of a program, but it is often advisable to retain and perhaps even to present the data collected in smaller temporal units in addition to the larger ones.

Proceed Anyway   A final strategy that a practitioner can take when faced with excessively variable data is simply to proceed anyway. This advice should be followed only when there is some real need to proceed, such as immediate applied demands. The advice to proceed anyway is not a call for "sloppy" clinical work or for inadequate evaluation. Rather, it is a recognition that sometimes corners must be cut due to practical realities. It is better to attempt an evaluation despite the corners being cut than to abandon all hope of an evaluation due to a failure to meet some arbitrary standard. Often, in the attempt to analyze a case despite the high variability in the data, something may be learned which may assist the clinician in future cases. At times the intervention may have such a powerful effect that an unexpectedly clear picture may emerge despite seemingly excessive variability. In any case, by collecting systematic data the practitioner is being responsible and will be able to account for his efforts to those who may require this information, including the client.

Accountability: The Continuity of Case Studies and Single Case Experimentation

The purposes of time-series methodology range from accountability to the production of new scientific knowledge. Essentially, up to this point the focus has been on measuring client progress and specifying treatment. These elements are central to any attempt to be accountable. If you look up accountability in the dictionary you will find that the word comes from a root word meaning "to count." Giving an account implies reporting the facts: the count. An account has other meanings too, such as the statement of a relation. In the same way, pure accountability in the applied environment sets the stage for more complex goals. As you move beyond accountability, not only can you say what you did, you can say something about what it means.

When you do this, you begin to go beyond the case-study level to the single case experimental level. You move from mere description to an analysis, which is a continuum. Later we will explore how pure accountability efforts can be combined to support the development of scientific knowledge. Similarly, in Chapters 6 through 10 we will explore ways that the professional can increase scientific output in the analysis of individual cases. For instance, one of the most natural clinical designs is the A/B (a period of baseline followed by a period of treatment). This design in itself is not usually an experimental design. Yet it can easily form the basis of experimental designs, with very little additional effort. Once we are accountable it is only a small step to the creation of scientific knowledge. It requires two additional steps: replication and the creative use of single case design elements.

This entire book is built on accountability, yet you will not see a separate chapter on accountability, or even on case studies. This is because we feel that time-series methodology should be viewed as a whole. There is no clear dividing line between the uses to which it is put.

The next three elements of time-series methodology, however, primarily apply when the goal goes beyond simple accountability. Thus, they are most relevant when the applied scientific role of the scientist-practitioner requires not just the implementation of treatment procedures of known effectiveness and documentation of their impact (as in cases of program evaluation, clinical replications series, or routine evaluation) but also the development of new knowledge. This happens most often when the case is complex or treatment-resistant and there is a need to develop and evaluate new procedures or approaches.

Replication

The logic of all time-series analysis requires replication of effects. In the applied setting this requirement is increased because of the methodological compromises often forced there. Furthermore, generalizability of our knowledge depends on many systematic replications of effects across many clients and settings.

There are two areas where replication is important. One is replication within a single evaluation. Often this is replication within a subject, while at other times it involves replication across several subjects. Time-series research depends on the principle of unlikely successive coincidences. A single coincidence is rarely thought of as unlikely. As the number of coincidental effects increases, our confidence in the reality of the effects seen increases. Ways of replicating effects in this way will be discussed in Chapters 6 through 9.

The second type of replication that is critical to the success of time-series methodology is replication across clients. When a particular effect has been seen in a particular individual and a rule or description has been derived to explain the important conditions, we usually have little confidence that this description is, in fact, adequate. As other practitioners use this description to guide their attempts to treat similar cases, the adequacy of the description will be tested. It is only in this process that errors in our ability to describe the actual functionally important variables will appear. This is the process of clinical replication.

An Attitude of Investigative Play

Undoubtedly the biggest difference between group-comparison research and time-series methodology is the overall approach encouraged. Time-series research should be a dynamic, interactive enterprise in which the design is always tentative, always ready to change as significant questions arise in the process. There should be an attitude of investigative play. The practitioner should have decided on a general strategy to follow in evaluating a particular applied question. This strategy, however, is not a detailed statement of such things as a length of phases, sequence of conditions, and the like. To follow such a course means that the practitioner cannot respond to the demands of the situation as they arise. This is simply not good practice. For example, clinical guides often advise clinicians to "be prepared to alter your style if dealing with a client in response to new information" and "be prepared to have many of your hypotheses disproved" (Zaro, Baruch, Nedelmann, & Dreiblatt, 1977, p. 28). A practicing clinician cannot afford to go into a treatment session (much less a whole series of sessions) with an absolute commitment to follow a particular course of action.

One of the common mistakes made by professionals attempting to do time-series evaluations is to attempt to use time-series tools as they have been taught to use group-comparison procedures. This virtually eliminates the applied environment as an appropriate place to do science. Clients' data often do not conform to the preset mold; they often do not confirm preset hypotheses. When unanticipated effects are seen, the practitioner must be ready to abandon previous ideas and to let the client's data be the guide. In group-comparison research, however, the design is planned in detail beforehand and then carried out. Indeed, it is often recommended that there be no possibility of evaluating client progress during the course of the intervention itself. Probably the most extreme example of this is double-blind research, most often used to test out new drugs. While this may be appropriate for endeavors that are specifically research oriented, it is inappropriate for those attempting to combine scientific and applied goals.

One way of increasing the attitude of investigative play is to graph data frequently and in several different ways. Just as good practitioners often examine their case notes and assessment materials between client visits, the examination of client data allows detection of interesting patterns or leads that need to be followed. By adopting such an intellectual stance, unexpected or even undesirable data patterns can often be clues on how best to treat this client and how to interpret particular behavioral phenomena.

Thus, an attitude of investigative play means approaching the task in such a way that the practitioner finds some intrinsic enjoyment or value in the investigation—that is, the careful search for an answer to the client's problems. As in all games, there are certain set rules and expected outcomes. The practitioner "wins" the game by learning how to be of help. The kind of play involved in applied exploration is not something that diminishes the seriousness of the task. To the contrary, it supports the practitioner in following leads that are presented and in maintaining a commitment to excellence.

If, in the process of exploration, a particular phenomenon emerges or a particular anomaly occurs, a good practitioner (and a good scientist) will pursue it and use it. Suppose, for example, a client drops out of therapy for a time. Instead of being seen as something that has interfered with an ongoing evaluation, it might be used as a period during which the maintenance of treatment gains can be assessed. Similarly, if a client shows some real difficulty in the course of treatment, it could be viewed as an opportunity to learn more about the phenomenon rather than as an interference with some preset notion about how the case would proceed.

Knowledge of Design Elements

It is our claim that the logic of applied decision making and that of single case design is very close, and often identical. If so, the practitioner with knowledge of design elements will usually be able to fit design tools to practical needs. It is to these tools that we now turn.

6 Within-Series Elements

Introduction

In this chapter we will begin to identify the logical structure of time-series methods. As we develop specific ways of designing applied evaluations using these methods, we will be able to compare them to the implicit logic of clinical and educational practice.

We will argue that comparing both reveals that practitioners already use most of the logical elements of time-series methodology, although rarely self-consciously. This similarity in approach and logic has two effects. First, it means that often the task of scientist–practitioners is not so much to change their methods of clinical investigation in order to conduct empirically meaningful evaluations, but merely to recognize and make explicit the scientific logic of practical work. Second, the relatively close fits permits practitioners to use these design elements deliberately to improve their applied decision making, to document clinical effects, or to develop new clinical programs without a great deal of difficulty or interference with the practical demands of applied setting.

Because the purpose of this book is to examine scientific methods in the context of the practical applied environment, we will not spend much time on methodological requirements that would improve the quality of knowledge but would interfere in an obvious and significant way with service goals. Such conflicts are possible, but they are usually avoidable without a significant compromise of either practical or scientific purposes. In addition, the self-discipline and rigor produced by an effort to be systematic have many applied benefits.

In this chapter, and those that follow, we will emphasize the logic of single case design elements, not the form of completed designs. The creative use of time-series methodology in the exploration of applied phenomena can be enhanced by emphasizing design elements or tools rather than numerous completed designs. For example, designs such as an A/B/A or B/C/B have often been described as separate designs even though their basic logical structures are identical. In fact, all single case designs are built from a small set of building blocks. There are potentially as many specific single case designs as there are designs for brick buildings, and the core elements of each are as simple. Nothing characterizes the practical applied environment so much as rapid change and unexpected demands. Completed designs can be fairly elaborate structures, and many things can occur in the context of applied work that makes adherence to specific designs difficult or even impossible. By emphasizing design elements, the scientific practitioner is ready to go with the applied flow, without having to abandon a reasonable analytic approach.

In the next three chapters we will attempt to distill all time-series work into a few core elements, organized by the nature of their estimates of stability and the logic of their data comparisons. In this way, we hope that we can underline the similarity between the logical units of time-series methods on the one hand and strategies of applied decision making on the other. Just as a practitioner may need to switch intervention strategies as the actual needs and responses of the client are better known, so, too, the practitioner conducting time-series evaluations must be aware of the range of logical design alternatives available at any moment and be prepared to take advantage of new opportunities.

There are three fundamentally different kinds of time-series design elements— within, between, and combined-series elements—organized by their logical structure and the nature of the comparisons they engender. By far the best known are the within-series elements. (The other two types will be described in the next two chapters.)

In within-series elements, the sources of information are changes observed within a series of data points organized across time and taken on a single measure or related set of measures. Each data point is seen in the context of those that immediately precede and follow it; that is, the series of interest is built in real time. Groups of data points are collected together according to the consistency of the specifiable conditions under which they were collected. Each consistent condition constitutes a "phase" in the sequential series. Like the individual scores themselves, in within-series elements specific phases are evaluated in the context of the phases that precede and follow them—that is, in real time.

There are two groups of elements based on this strategy: simple phase changes and complex phase changes. In this chapter we will describe the logic of each of these types and delineate the specific elements that utilize their logic. We will start by describing the simple phase change, and then we will point out how it may actually be used in a clinical case. Following this, we will describe the complex phase-change elements.

The Simple Phase-Change Element

The cornerstone of many of the popular time-series strategies is the simple phase change. This element consists of:

1. Establishment of the level, trend, and degree of variability around level and trend seen within a series of data points organized across time and taken under similar conditions,
2. A systematic change in the conditions impinging upon the client while maintaining consistency of measurement procedures, and

3. Examination of concomitant changes in the level, trend, and degree of variability around level and trend seen within a series of data points organized across time and taken under the new conditions.

This strategy is a "within-series" strategy in that systematic changes seen within a series of data points across time are examined. A within-series effect is observed when:

1. A change in the conditions impinging upon the client
2. Leads to major changes in the level or trend of the data series (or, in rare cases, to changes in variability),
3. Considered in the context of the degree of stability of the data in the phases being compared.

What we are doing in a simple phase change is using the first phase (in combination with everything we know from other sources) to determine the nature of the phenomena of interest and to project its course into the future. Against that background, we then examine the patterns shown in the second phase. If there are major changes in the expected patterns, then we suspect that an effect has occurred.

Probably the most common example of a simple phase change occurs when data are repeatedly collected during a baseline period and continue to be collected during a subsequent treatment period. This is termed an "A/B design." By tradition, A always refers to baseline, B to the first identified treatment or treatment element, C to the second identified treatment or element, and so on. If the level, trend, or stability of the data shown in phase A changes when phase B is implemented, B may be responsible, and thus our confidence that treatment B produces an effect increases incrementally. How much it increases is a function of many factors. We will discuss these in more detail later.

Even a single simple phase change can accomplish many desirable goals. First, it allows the practitioner to be accountable. This is important on several grounds, from the demands of third-party payers, to professional and ethical requirements. The cornerstone of "accountability" is being able to give an accurate report (an "account") of just what the practitioner did and just what progress the client has made. A simple phase change can help do just that.

Second, even this simple design element will begin to allow statements to be made about the likelihood that improvement is due to treatment. Suppose, for example, that an A/B design seems to show a clear treatment effect. If we know that this treatment has been shown to be effective in controlled experimental work with other clients, our confidence increases that the apparent treatment effect with this client is real. That is, the known effectiveness of the intervention makes it more plausible to account for the observed pattern by an appeal to an impact of the intervention.

At times, the level of knowledge obtained from an A/B may approach that of an experimental analysis based on replicated findings. Suppose, for example, that we know based on other information that a particular behavior is resistant to change and rarely, if ever, improves spontaneously. Suppose, further, that a long and steady baseline is present. Dramatic effects following treatment implementation may yield knowledge that approaches a level of confidence appropriate to more controlled experiments.

To take a readily understandable example from physical medicine, it might be of worldwide interest if a patient who was undeniably HIV positive over many measurement occasions suddenly became permanently HIV negative following the implementation of an innovative treatment. This finding would have to be replicated in others, of course, but if the measurements were carefully done and documented it would not be dismissed out of hand on the ground that it was probably due to extraneous factors. We have enough experience with the virus causing AIDS to know that extraneous factors rarely, if ever, lead to spontaneous elimination of the infection once it is well established. This does not mean that the treatment certainly was responsible, but it makes it reasonably likely.

Note also that very few scientists would dismiss the importance of such a finding on the grounds that the treatment effects, even if real, are idiosyncratic. They may indeed be idiosyncratic, but the history of applied science shows that generally applicable treatments can often be built from specific effects with specific individuals. Even a few positive treatment cases would give scientists a better leverage point in this deadly war with the virus that causes AIDS. Even an idiosyncratic finding, if real, helps reveal the nature of the disorder. The great interest shown in the handful of cases who have remained healthy for decades despite being HIV positive is a clear demonstration of the possible general scientific value of even a small number of specific instances.

Examples from mental health or educational areas of the same kind of situation might be the social withdrawal of a chronic schizophrenic or the educational limitations of the moderately mentally retarded. These kinds of behavioral phenomena rarely change spontaneously and permanently. Sudden, major, and permanent improvement following treatment in such areas might be quite convincing, even if the demonstration were based only on an A/B design.

In most cases, however, a single simple phase change will need to be bolstered by replication, within the same client, across clients, or (most often) in both domains. Time-series methodology is built upon *replication* as the source of ultimate confidence in the knowledge produced. It is this relatively incremental, bottom-up approach that makes time-series approaches so relevant to the applied environment. An effect can be replicated in many different ways, as we will see in this and subsequent chapters, and no one experimental analysis needs to be perfect to be valuable as part of a larger program of research and evaluation.

One common way to replicate findings is to repeat the phase change, but now in reverse order. To continue with our example of an A/B design, this strategy would yield an A/B/A design. If the behavioral changes associated with the first phase change now are altered in a coherent fashion with the second phase change, then our confidence in the effect increases incrementally. This simple phase-change process could be repeated indefinitely. Like a child throwing a light switch on and off, the researcher would be quickly persuaded by a consistent and contingent relationship between changes in the conditions influencing a client and changes in the client's observed behavior. Each specific sequence of simple phase changes would form a specific design defined by their number, type, and sequence—for example, A/B/A/B or B/A/B. Two different treatments can be compared in exactly the same manner—for example, B/C/B or C/B/C/B. All of these specific forms are identical in terms of their analytic logic, although the certainty of knowledge that each may yield differs, and the specific kinds of questions one is asking with a given simple phase change design may vary.

The evaluation of effects in all within-series designs is based on an examination of patterns of changes in the level, trend, and variability shown in the data. These changes can be of different magnitudes, latencies, and consistency. Figure 6.1 presents several examples of changes in these various characteristics representing improvement. The most dramatic changes are those that are (a) of large magnitude, (b) closely related in time to the phase change, and (c) consistent throughout the phase.

To get a sense of how these factors can combine, consider each of the 12 graphs in Figure 6.1. Graph A shows a change in level only. The change is sudden and steady. Depending on what we know about the behavior of interest, such a change will probably be viewed as large and unexpected, relative to the background variability. This effect thus seems fairly strong.

Graph B shows a similar effect, except that the change is somewhat more gradual. Here the effect is slightly less clear because of the less sudden change, but the magnitude is equally large and steady and the effect is nearly as believable. In Graph C, a sudden change in both level and trend occurs, which makes the change even more dramatic than that seen in Graph A.

Graph D shows only a sudden change in variability. Variability per se is rarely a target of intervention, and in the applied environment many extraneous factors can cause sudden changes in variability. If variability were the target, the effect shown in Graph D is noticeable, but it would probably need to be replicated before much confidence in the effect would be possible.

Graph E shows a delayed change in variability, which is even weaker. Few conclusions can be drawn from these data.

Graph F provides little or no evidence of behavior change associated with the phase change. There is a change in level, but since the trend is exactly the same, this change is probably due to the arbitrary division of the same data series with a known trend into different phases.

Graph G is similar to Graph B, except the trend continues and the variability is greater. The constancy of trend is somewhat positive but it is based on only a few additional data points. More importantly, the increased variability weakens the conclusion that any change had occurred, even though the central tendencies shown in the data series for Graphs G and B are similar.

Graph H is similar to Graph A, except variability is greater. This weakens the comparison, but the effect is still so sudden, consistent, and large that the effect seems fairly clear. Note, for example, that there is no overlap between the data in the two phases.

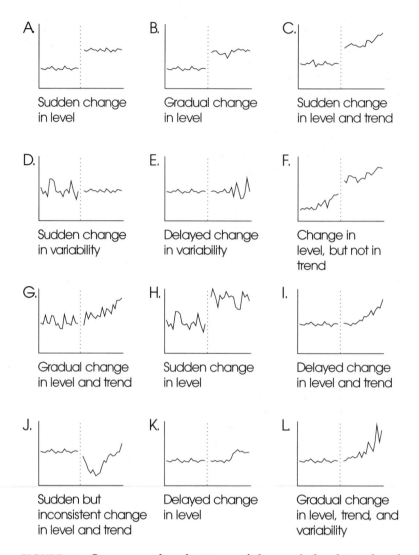

FIGURE 6.1   **Some examples of patterns of changes in level, trend, and variability in a simple phase change.**

All the other graphs (Graphs I through L) are relatively weak because of inconsistent or delayed effects. Through replication, all of these could be shown to be real effects, but the incremental determination that an effect probably did occur would be quite tentative for data such as these.

When we have determined that a change has probably occurred, this does not mean that we can conclude that the change in the conditions (the change in "phase") was responsible for it. The most critical difficulty is that we would never know what would have happened had we not changed phases as we did. Were this not true, we would be able, with a single pre- and a single postdata point, to determine whether or not a particular intervention had worked with a client. What we are relying on is the plausibility of the overall picture that is shown.

There are many factors that could threaten the internal validity of changes that are seen. Internal validity refers to the extent to which the effects seen are due to the stated treatment (Campbell & Stanley, 1963; Cook & Campbell, 1979). Table 6.1 summarizes some of the possible reasons for an apparent effect due to a phase change other than the actual change in the manipulated conditions. In phase-change designs with individual clients, there are three basic issues: Did something in the client's world happen to coincide with the phase change? Is the assessment device consistently applied? Are there effects due to time or repeated assessment that began to occur near the phase change? There are several other threats to internal validity, but most of these apply primarily to group-comparison approaches.

Distinguishing these effects from effects due to a phase change is a primary goal of the various controls used in time-series methodology. The major strategy is to replicate the effects, while allowing other factors (e.g., number of assessments, timing of the phase change) to vary systematically. In the design options that follow, we will periodically point out how this goal is accomplished.

Using the Simple Phase Change

The simple phase change provides an example of the manner in which time-series methodology fits the logic of good applied practice. In this section we will describe the sequence of events faced by a practitioner in a practical situation. Using the

TABLE 6.1   **Major Alternative Explanations for Effects Seen in a Time Series**

1. Coincidental events	Real extraneous events in the client's world happened to coincide with changes in conditions so as to mimic effects due to a phase change (e.g., implementation of treatment).
2. Time alone	Processes such as maturation, learning, or other gradual effects associated with time alone mimic effects due to a phase change.
3. Assessment	Repeated assessment itself causes systematic changes in the client's behavior that mimic effects due to a phase change.
4. Instrument drift	Changes in the measurement instrument itself produce pseudo changes that mimic effects due to a phase change.
5. Regression to the mean	The tendency for scores to show a central tendency mimics effects due to a phase change.

example of a psychotherapist treating a simple case, we will attempt to show how the simple phase change can be used to develop knowledge in such a single case.

This example is a bit artificial, because we will assume many facts of the case in order to proceed with the example. In actual work it is rare that the applied question will be completely obvious as the practitioner begins to work with the client (whether that client is an individual, group, agency, or system). The practitioner must approach the case as a process of investigation, exploration, and evaluation. For that reason, all of the design tools and approaches should be available for use as specific questions arise. The practitioner should not have decided a priori, for example, that a simple phase change is the design tool that will be used with a particular client regardless of the needs that occur as the work proceeds.

Establishing the First Phase (e.g., Baseline)

Typically, a therapeutic relationship begins with a period of assessment. This assessment serves two functions. It helps reveal the nature of the client's situation, and it allows the practitioner to determine whether or not the problem is deteriorating, improving, or is stationary. If the guidelines described in Chapter 5 have been followed, usually when the initial evaluation period ends at least a short baseline will be in hand. If not, it is usually wise to wait until an adequate baseline is established. This advice can be stated in terms more relevant to the practical situation: Ideally, intervention should occur only when the practitioner can be relatively confident that intervention is warranted. That is exactly what an "adequate baseline" means.

Sometimes, however, we must proceed immediately to intervention well before a thorough assessment is completed. This is particularly likely when the client is in crisis, the problems are especially severe, or the context of the client contact provides other assurance that intervention is needed (e.g., the client has been referred by a reliable colleague or agency). In these cases, the practitioner can rely on methods other than a quantitatively sufficient baseline for the adequacy of the evaluation and analysis. The guidelines offered here apply as well to the situations in which intervention has proceeded before a baseline has been obtained as they do to the more usual case when a thorough assessment period is possible.

Several recommendations have been offered as to the adequacy of obtained baselines (or first phases in general). One consideration is the length of the phase. This issue applies to the length of any phase in a within-series strategy. The purpose of repeated assessment is to enable the establishment of adequate estimates of level, trend, and stability of the client's behavior of interest over time and situation. In the absence of other information, it is impossible even to separate these three aspects of data until a minimum of three measurement points have been collected. If one data point is collected, no estimates of trend will be possible and the data will by definition be stable. When two data points have been collected, an estimate of level is available, but variability and trend will be indistinguishable. It is only when three data points have been collected that level, trend, and variability around level and trend can begin to be separated. More data points are usually highly desirable, of course.

The suggestion that phases include at least three data points is not an absolute one, but it is also not an artificial one. In the normal applied situation, it is difficult to know whether or not the picture that the client is presenting at any given point in time is representative, or if the problem is rapidly improving or deteriorating. These questions are as important to good practice as they are to time-series methodology. The suggestion that at least three data points be collected can be translated into the more usual applied advice to know where you are and where you are going with a particular client.

Sometimes, however, various considerations modify the recommendation for several data points in a particular phase. There may be other information available on the problem being measured that makes several assessment occasions less important. For example, the disorder may have a known history or course, such as the social withdrawal of a chronic schizophrenic, or the AIDS example used earlier. In this situation it may not be as important to assess the stability of the behavior because, on other grounds, we expect that it will be fairly stable. If the assessment devices themselves are strong in such an instance, and thus measurement error is not an issue, even a single pre- and postdata point may be meaningful.

At other times, we may have access to an archival baseline, such as records from previous therapists, or reports from individuals in the client's environment about past adjustment. In these situations, even a single data point may confirm what is already suspected or known, based on the availability of other quality sources of information, and the treatment may then proceed. Indeed, if the archival baseline is clear, it is often not practical, as an applied matter, for the scientist practitioner to delay intervention. For example, Montgomery (1993) treated the aggressive behavior of an institutionalized male who was severely retarded and chronically aggressive. In order to create a more extended baseline, the staff reports of aggressive episodes were carefully scored. The researcher could have created an entirely new baseline, but this would have meant waiting for many new aggressive episodes, with the continuing possibility that the staff or client would be injured. Such a demand might have been better from a purely scientific point of view, but it would move the practitioner out of an applied role into a more purely research role.

At first glance it might seem to be lethal to the single case experimental analysis of a case to proceed without an extended baseline, or with only an archival baseline. In fact it is not, because the practitioner has many other design tools available to make up for short phases. For example, the simple phase change might be repeated later within the same client, or the effects might be replicated with others. All of this is not to say that phases consisting of many data points are not desirable. They are, and often the applied situation will naturally produce long phases. For example, if the case is particularly complex or unclear, but not yet in crisis, an extended assessment period is common. Certainly in the treatment phase it is not unusual for phases to be lengthy. Particularly if assessment data are collected frequently, the situation in which very few data points are available can often be avoided.

A second consideration is the stability of baseline. All of the earlier comments (Chapter 5) apply here. There is one possible addition to those recommendations.

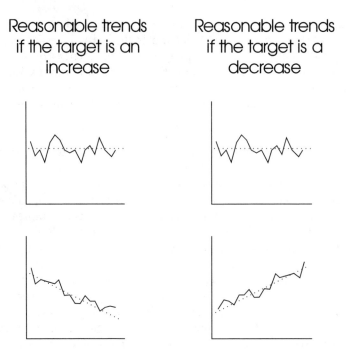

FIGURE 6.2 Adequate baseline trends, depending upon the goals of intervention.

If it is difficult to obtain stability within a phase, it may be possible to use a design that is more robust in this regard. An example might be the alternating-treatments design, which will be discussed later in Chapter 7, on between-series strategies.

A final consideration is the level and the trend shown in the first phase. The level must be such that the following phase makes sense. For example, if the client is in baseline, the level of problem behavior must be such that a subsequent treatment phase is warranted. Furthermore, the trend shown in the first phase should also be one that justifies a phase change. When the following phase is expected to produce increases in the data, then either a declining or a flat trend is highly desirable. If decreases are expected, then rising or flat trends are beneficial. Examples of these patterns are shown in Figure 6.2.

These are not rigid rules, and they are not arbitrary. In terms of logic, they mimic good clinical and educational practice. If a client were to come in who had a rapidly improving situation before treatment had even begun, then most practitioners would recommend putting off intervention until the need for it became clearer. All treatment has costs and risks. Iatrogenic effects (deterioration due to treatment) are always possible. It makes no sense to intervene if the behavior is already improving at about the same rate that could be hoped for in treatment. If the client is improving, but is improving slowly, and treatment is expected to accelerate that improvement noticeably, then intervention might be justifiable. The rule of thumb is similar to that offered in the case of stability in Chapter 5: If treatment effects would not be clearly distinguishable from baseline even if the treatment effects are as large as expected or as hoped for, based on the literature or practical experience, then the baseline is not adequate. Stated in applied terms, treatment is not warranted when, even if it is successful, it will not be evident that it is successful. It is not necessary, however, that the client not be improving at all before intervention occurs. If the behavior is improving but is improving more slowly than would be evident if treatment succeeds, then the baseline is adequate for the purposes of single case analysis.

The suggestion that stationary or deteriorating baselines are most desirable before intervention is thus not an artificial or slightly sadistic desire to see unfortunate client circumstances in order to accomplish research purposes. No practitioner *wants* clients to be worsening. Rather, it is a recognition that there are conditions under which treatment is not warranted, either as an applied matter or as an empirical matter. The logic of time-series designs in this area and that of good practice is the same. Stated in other words, the considerations about adequate baselines are exactly the same kinds of considerations that lead utilization review boards, managed care organizations, or third-party payers to look first for evidence of a problem that is not improving on its own before treatment is implemented.

All of these considerations about baseline actually apply to any phase in a within-series strategy, including the first in a simple phase change. The logic of the simple phase change (and complex phase changes) is the same whether one is going from a condition that one has arbitrarily termed "baseline" to one termed "treatment," or vice versa, or whether one is going from one treatment to another. After all, a baseline period is really a type of treatment. It is the treatment that the world happens to be applying to the client at that particular time.

Implementing the Second Phase (e.g., Treatment)

Once the first phase (for example, the baseline phase) has been established, then it is possible to move to a second phase. We are assuming that baseline has now been collected and treatment is ready to begin.

Before treatment begins, the practitioner may wish to consider whether there are variables that need to be controlled before intervention. For example, the practitioner may suspect that the client will be highly susceptible to social influences and that almost any kind of well-justified intervention will work due to a placebo or social-demand effect. This may be important in helping us understand the characteristics of the client—for example, in determining whether or not the problem seen is itself due to the client's suggestibility. It may also be important in that it will prevent us from using a more difficult, costly, or risky intervention with the client if that is not necessary. Under these conditions the practitioner may wish to begin not with treatment, but with a variant of it that will eliminate these possible alternative explanations for any effects that might be seen.

An example from one of our own cases seems relevant. A depressed client had entered an inpatient facility for depression during the summer every year for the last four years. The treatment team suspected that part of the problem came from the lack of support she felt from an uninvolved husband when their small children were home from school during the summer vacation. Although psychoactive medication had always worked fairly quickly, antidepressant drugs are costly and can have significant side effects. It seemed possible that improvement in the past may have been due not to pharmacotherapy but to nonspecific factors. The hospital stay may have provided relief from a difficult situation, for example, and the implementation of treatment by an involved and caring team may have reassured the client. To test this, the client was prescribed a placebo with an official-sounding name on the label. Like clockwork, the client improved as she had in previous years and returned home. Because of the implications of this effect, follow-up outpatient treatment for the first time focused more on couples therapy than medication checks. Essentially, what the treatment team did was to test a kind of modified baseline condition before first launching into a full implementation of treatment.

As this example shows, controlling for important variables before beginning formal treatment is often part of good clinical and educational decision making and may even fit in with legal requirements, such as the requirement that the least restrictive alternative treatment available be implemented first. If, when the less restrictive intervention is put in place, a strong effect is seen, then there is no need to go on to a more difficult treatment. Conversely, if no effect occurs when certain factors are controlled, then an alternative explanation for any subsequent effects will have been eliminated, the case may be better understood, and the logic of time-series methodology will allow an intervention phase to begin. (Why an ineffective phase can be followed by treatment will be discussed in more detail shortly.)

Another consideration is that treatment ideally should begin—at full force if possible. When one is going from one phase to another, it is desirable for the difference between the two phases to be maximal. Gradual shifts between phases can minimize apparent differences between them. This has been pointed to as a major deficit in single case experimental designs in the practical setting because often clinical interventions are inherently gradual (Thomas, 1978). Where implementation must be gradual, however, time-series approaches still apply. It is just that the analysis that results will probably be more conservative and in need of replication because real treatment results will probably also be gradual—they will look more like Graph I in Figure 6.1 than Graph A. Gradual implementation can cause false negatives (Type II errors—falsely concluding that treatment did not work in this situation), but false positives (Type I errors—falsely concluding that treatment worked in this situation) are less likely. Whether this is a bad thing depends in part on which error would be more costly in a given situation.

Acting on Results

When the second phase is implemented, there are logically only three possible outcomes: no apparent improvement, deterioration, or improvement.

No Improvement   If there is no change, there are at least three reasonable courses of action. One is to wait for a period of time to see if treatment will have a delayed effect. If it does, the first phase-change data comparison will (due to the delay) not be a strong one, but it can be replicated later. The second alternative is to try a totally different type of treatment. A third course is to add or subtract elements from the treatment package.

The logic of these last two recommendations should be discussed. If a phase produces no change in the data, then it is reasonable to assume that the behavior of interest has not been altered by the treatment condition. To the extent that this can be assumed, there is no impediment to moving on to another treatment or adding an element to treatment that might be more effective. Essentially this makes the first treatment phase part of baseline. Consider the data shown in Figure 6.3, for example. Since Intervention B added nothing, the B phase can be considered (with caution) part of the Baseline or A phase. There is a tendency to think of baseline as a vacuum, but of course it is not. Baseline is just a name for all the things in the world of the client that surround the behavior as it is. Some of these things are relevant to the behavior, but most probably are not. An ineffective B phase can thus be thought of as baseline with the addition of yet another irrelevant variable. Viewed that way, the client is still in baseline. (This is written, "A = B".)

Of course, it is possible that an ineffective treatment produced a changed state of affairs that now interacts in some way with subsequent treatment. For example, suppose we teach a retarded child to imitate, but find that this does not improve social skills. Suppose we then mainstream the child into a normal classroom, and find an increase in social skills. It could be that the ability to imitate was critical to the impact of the normal classroom, but its effect was not apparent until appropriate models were more readily available. These kinds of possibilities can be assessed and detected in a program of replication. Because of such possibilities, the plausibility of equivalence between baseline and ineffective treatment phases is jeopardized as phases are added. An A=B=C=E=F/G/F/G design, where nothing

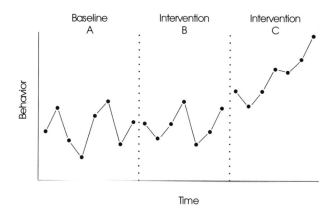

FIGURE 6.3   **A hypothetical example of an A = B/C design.** This is normally considered functionally equivalent to a simple phase change, because B is thought to be part of the first phase.

works until G, seems inherently weak unless a very coherent rationale can be provided for the failure of so many interventions compared to the apparent effectiveness of G.

An example of such a situation is shown in a study by Cope, Moy, and Grossnickle (1988). In this study, McDonald's restaurants promoted the use of seat belts with an advertising campaign (B), accompanied by the distribution of instructive stickers for children asking them to "Make It Click" (C). These two interventions were tried repeatedly. Finally, an incentive program was implemented giving away soft drinks for drivers who arrived at McDonald's with their seat belts fastened. The results are shown in Figure 6.4. The design could be described as an A=B=C=B=C=B/D/A. There is a lot of evidence that purely antecedent approaches such as those used in phases B and C tend to be relatively ineffective in the regulation of socially important behavior if they are not combined with other, more direct forms of social intervention (Biglan, 1995). Thus, it is not very surprising that the data showed that only the incentive program made a difference. Because the impact of advertising on such behavior is known to be weak, the result seems quite believable, even though so many ineffective phases were included.

The solution to possible order, interactive, or carryover effects is to replicate systematically any effects ultimately found in designs of this kind. For example, in the study just described, incentive programs might be tested directly (an A/D/A/D design might be a good way to do this). Similarly, in our earlier examples the effects of interventions found to be effective could be tested with very similar clients.

These three possible paths (wait, try a new treatment, change the old treatment) are the same courses of action that seem advisable on applied grounds. Sometimes treatment will work if the practitioner sticks with it, but if still no change is apparent, a responsible professional will try something else. In the applied situation, if the first treatment produced no effect, returning immediately to a major reassessment of the client (e.g., returning to baseline) is an option, but it is more likely that other interventions will be tried, especially if the initial assessment phase was careful in the first place. In the same way, the logic of single case experimental design would permit a return to baseline following an ineffective

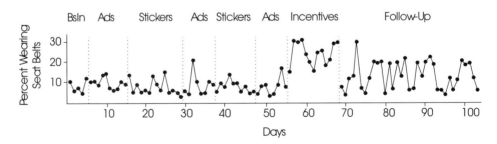

FIGURE 6.4   An example of an A = B = C = B = C = B/D/A design (redrawn from Cope, Moy, & Grossnickle, 1988).

treatment phase, but it does not require it if other plausible treatment alternatives are available.

Deterioration   If the treatment produces deterioration, then the course both clinically and methodologically is clear. The treatment should be terminated. At this point, the behavior could once again improve (or at least stop its deterioration) or it could continue to deteriorate. If it does the former, then the clinician will have documented an iatrogenic effect of treatment that is itself often a significant contribution to clinical knowledge. Iatrogenic effects have long been documented in applied literature (such as that of psychotherapy, Bergin & Strupp, 1972). Unfortunately, relatively little is known about our treatment failures. They tend to be hidden in the "error variance" of group-comparison studies. The present approach may allow the experimental documentation of negative findings, since it goes beyond affirming the null hypothesis to documenting actual deterioration. If individual client characteristics can be related to such deterioration, an important (if unpleasant) contribution to the applied literature can be made. Conversely, if the behavior continues to worsen when treatment is withdrawn, then it may be that the intervention was not responsible for the deterioration.

Improvement   The last possible effect during the second phase is that improvement could be seen. If so, there are several possibilities that present themselves. If the improvement is less than maximal, the practitioner may wish to add to the treatment or change the treatment to try to produce an even more rapid improvement. This parallels the suggestion made in going from the first phase to the second phase—namely, that if improvement exists that is substantially less than that desired, it is possible to move into a subsequent phase. A more likely course of action is to continue with the successful treatment. The clinician could choose to continue this until the successful conclusion of the case. If so, the end result would be an A/B or a "case-study" design.

The A/B design may itself often make a contribution to the clinical literature. These cases can be accumulated into series that can be analyzed as a clinical replication series, as will be discussed in Chapter 9. This is an extremely useful option and is part of the core of empirical clinical practice. In addition, if the client has another similar problem or if the problem occurs in several different situations, or if another similar client is available, then it is possible to apply the same treatment to these other problems, situations, or clients, and secure experimental design in this way. This is termed a multiple baseline and is discussed in Chapter 8. A final course of action is also available: to withdraw the treatments or to implement a treatment placebo. If improvement then slows or actually reverses, one can conclude that a treatment effect is likely.

Withdrawal Strategies

The use of the withdrawal is a powerful tool. Since the use of this strategy was probably overemphasized in the early literature on single case designs, several difficulties were highlighted that were sometimes mistakenly taken to be characteristic more generally of a time-series approach.

There are many potential problems with the withdrawal of an apparently effective treatment. On the face of it, it appears as though the purpose of withdrawal is to produce a deterioration in the client's performance. Cast in this way, it obviously raises ethical issues, since the client is coming to treatment to get better. If the client were to see the withdrawal as arbitrary it would certainly raise issues in terms of client fees, possible morale problems, and possible neutralization of subsequent effects due to these difficulties. When other persons are involved in treatment (such as treatment staff or the client's family), withdrawal may lead to a lack of cooperation on the part of others.

There are many counterarguments. First, if the treatment is known to be effective, then withdrawal is not necessary. If it is *not* known to be effective with this client, then withdrawal may serve an important applied function, since good practice requires the avoidance of the unnecessary use of ineffective treatment. Physicians recognize this issue in the common practice of "drug holidays." Drug holidays are nothing more than scheduled periods of withdrawal in which the opportunity presents itself for the assessment of the continued need for pharmacological treatment. It is not the purpose of a drug holiday to produce client deterioration. The main purpose is to avoid unnecessary intervention.

Second, relatively few interventions are such that treatment per se can be continued indefinitely. Eventually there will be a treatment withdrawal; the issue is just a matter of timing. Viewed this way, withdrawal allows the assessment of maintenance of treatment effects.

Third, withdrawals are often created by clients naturally in the course of treatment. Clients may go on vacations, become ill, temporarily drop out of treatment, move away for a period of time, be unable to attend treatment sessions due to competing situations, and the like. These can be encompassed in ongoing applied evaluations by examining the data taken during or after these periods, but before reimplementation of active treatment. These "natural withdrawals" are not as methodologically desirable as withdrawals determined by the practitioner. They are more likely to reflect variables that might impact on the behavior of interest. For example, a client may drop out of treatment for reasons that also will produce deterioration in the target behavior. Therefore, practitioners should always specify the reasons for treatment withdrawal, and should view the results with caution. If the withdrawals are occurring naturally, they should investigate the reasons for the withdrawal and stress considerable care and need for replication when presenting the cases. Nevertheless, natural withdrawals can aid in an analysis of treatment effects.

Fourth, withdrawals need not be long and drawn out. Even a very short withdrawal, if it is accompanied by a clear change in the behavior seen, can increase the practitioner's confidence substantially in the treatment effects. The slight delay in treatment that withdrawal imposes should be weighed against the methodological and applied value.

Fifth, a good rationale will often help minimize problems of withdrawals. An absolutely honest rationale may often work quite well. A client may be told, for example, that treatment has apparently been fairly successful so far, but that it is not entirely clear that there continues to be a need for it. In that context, it seems wise to take a short breather and see where things go. This is merely an applied statement of the evaluative situation.

Sixth, withdrawals are often naturally produced by the practitioner in the course of treatment itself by a change of problem focus. The practitioner may, after a period of some progress on a particular issue, turn to other issues of importance. During this time, assessment of these other issues may be occurring that might constitute a kind of natural baseline for the original problem. This is a "withdrawal" in much the same way that the period of assessment, when the client comes in for treatment, is considered to be baseline, even though active initial assessment is ongoing

Finally, treatment withdrawals can often have a clear clinical benefit for clients. Three outcomes are likely during a withdrawal. The behavior may level off, continue to improve, or deteriorate. If it levels off or continues to improve, then the client may be convinced that treatment has indeed been successful and that the problem is now more fully under control. Conversely, if the behavior deteriorates, the client may (if the rationale for the withdrawal has been appropriately handled) see this as confirmation that treatment is necessary and worthwhile.

The withdrawal phase need not be thought of only as a return to baseline. It might include the use of placebos or control conditions. This advice might seem strange at first. Logically, if a particular phase change (e.g., A/B) has been effective, then replication would seem to require conducting the phase change in reverse order (B/A) rather than going to a variant of baseline (B/A'). In fact, however, it is impossible to "go back to baseline" in a literal sense. The second baseline phase in an A/B/A, for example, is baseline in the context of an immediately preceding A/B sequence. Suppose B consisted of attention from a teacher for a given behavior. The return to baseline is now a type of extinction phase—it is not literally a return to the first phase. For this reason, there are many possible explanations if the behavior during the second baseline phase differs from the first—it does not automatically mean that the first phase-change result was due to extraneous factors.

The use of placebos relies on the idea that the second baseline must be *functionally* similar to the first, not necessarily identical in form. A placebo condition and a baseline condition are thought to be functionally equivalent, by definition, even though they are not formally the same. The actual data may not bear out this assumption, of course, but if they do, then functional equivalence is confirmed. Conversely, if a second baseline phase is shown to differ from the first, additional analysis would be needed to find out why.

The Third Phase

If the practitioner has returned to the first condition (following an improvement seen during the second), three outcomes are once again logically possible: no change, deterioration, or improvement. If the behavior deteriorates, then the practitioner would probably reimplement treatment until the case was successfully concluded (e.g., an A/B/A/B design). Other options are available, such as determining the effective components of treatment through an interaction design element. These more complex design options will be described below.

If the behavior shows continued improvement, then several options are available. If the improvement continues at a noticeably lower rate than that seen in the earlier phase, then the practitioner may wish to reimplement treatment. This parallels the recommendation made about the shift from the baseline phase. If the rate of improvement seen continues to be high, then the practitioner could wait to see if improvement will continue or will slow. Sometimes the behavior will soon stop improving or may even deteriorate, perhaps due to a short-lived carryover effect from the second phase. If it does not, there seems to be little applied need to intervene further, because the problem is solved. The practitioner can allow the case to continue to a successful conclusion and store these data. This becomes an A/B design with what amounts to an unusual follow-up phase (the second baseline phase) in which the behavior continued to improve. The sequence can be repeated with other clients as was suggested above with an A/B design. If the effect replicates, then the practitioner would be in the enviable position of having documented a treatment so strong that once delivered it continues to produce improvement even when withdrawn. This is not really as implausible as it may sound. Many treatments are thought to produce relatively permanent changes in the client's environment. For example, a client who has received therapy that established more successful relationships with other people will then live in a much different world than before. Another alternative in this situation would be to apply the same treatment to a different behavior in the same individual or the same behavior in different situations. Once again, this would produce a multiple baseline (Chapter 8).

If no change is seen when the second phase is withdrawn—that is, if the behavior neither deteriorates nor continues to improve—then all of the options just described remain open. Reimplementation, however, is particularly attractive.

Much of the early work on single case designs emphasized the need for a withdrawal phase and for a clear "reversal" of the behavioral patterns seen. This harkens back to the time when these designs were used primarily in the context of animal operant work. In the animal laboratory, there was often an assumption that current behavior is primarily a function of immediately present environmental variables. Demonstrating this required repeatedly returning to the same behavioral level when the same external conditions were in force. Under these assumptions, if, in the second return to baseline phase, the behavior failed to look very much like the data in the first baseline phase (in terms of level, stability, and trend), then experimental control would not have been thought to be demonstrated. This view can be traced to the core idea that independent variables must lead to predictable steady states of behavior.

It is only the history of single case methodology that leads researchers to focus on predictable steady states, not the logic of the design elements themselves. The practitioner usually does not assume that the current level of behavior is primarily a function of the immediately present environmental variables. Usually the assumption is quite explicit that the current level of behavior is heavily influenced by history or by other variables not under practitioner or client control (e.g., under-lying physical processes). Further, the practitioner is not usually interested in pre-dictable steady states of activity as much as in predictable states of behavioral change. For example, the target may be client *improvement* rather than a specific level of attainment.

Several graphical means can be used to focus attention on states of change rather than arbitrary levels. It is possible, for example, to use log linear scales of behavior that emphasize relative amounts of change rather than absolute values. Similarly, it is quite easy to plot data in terms of its change from an established trend rather than in terms of its absolute value.

The data shown in Figure 6.5 may help make the point. The top third of the figure shows an A/B/A/B sequence in which withdrawal produces less improve-ment but no deterioration in the behavior of interest. At first glance, the effects are weak, but the graphical method hides the consistency of changes in rates of improvement. The middle third of the figure draws in trend lines for each phase, and projects the trend into the next phase. This allows an identification of the degree to which data deviate from trends established in previous phases. The bot-tom graph in the figure shows the data plotted as a difference score from the trend established in the previous phase (plus the first-phase data for reference). When plotted in terms of improvement (i.e., in terms of a change from the predicted pat-tern), a more classic pattern emerges in the bottom graph. This does not necessar-ily mean that the bottom graph is the "right" way to present the information. These different graphical forms simply emphasize different objective qualities of the data. All are "correct." The point is that the top figure, which appears to show a pattern that some might say does not demonstrate a clear effect, actually does show a clear effect when the data are thought of in terms of improvement rather than simple absolute levels of responding.

Defining Phases in Applied Situations

Single case designs emerged from the learning laboratory. In these controlled situ-ations it was quite clear when a given intervention was present or absent because "present" meant "physically present." That is not true in many applied situations.

For example, suppose a client's depression is recorded daily. It takes 3 weeks to establish an adequate baseline, and the client is then treated in weekly out-patient psychotherapy sessions. The sessions last about an hour. Occasionally weekly sessions are missed, so the actual gap between therapy sessions varies. After 12 weeks, treatment is withdrawn for 3 weeks, and then reimplemented for another 12 weeks.

The question is this: When is treatment "present" and "absent"? The ready answer is that it was not present for 3 weeks, then it was for 12, then it was not for 3, and then it was again for 12. But that easy answer could be fairly arbitrary. The client is only *physically* present in treatment for, at most, 1 hour a week. Daily ratings of depression occur that same day, and then the next, and then the next. The

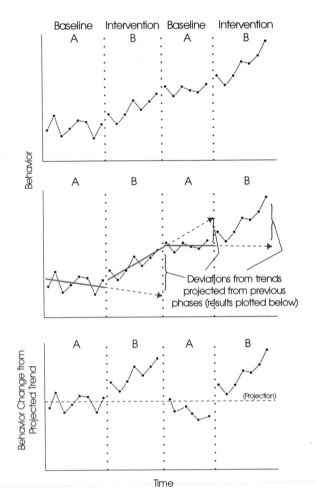

FIGURE 6.5   An example of different ways of looking at data when a withdrawal is not associated with a return to a previous behavioral level. The middle graph projects the trends set in each phase. The bottom graph plots the data in terms of a change from the trend set in the previous phase. The straight horizontal line in the bottom graph represents the trends set by the previous phases. Both versions are equally correct, but the bottom one makes more obvious the control exerted by treatment over improvement or deterioration relative to the established trend.

farther the ratings get from actual treatment sessions, the more plausible it is to call the score a "baseline" score, but the cutoff is not sudden nor is it obvious. There is a continuum.

In our hypothetical example, the session gaps during the treatment phase could occasionally be 2 or even 3 weeks. Note, however, by the time unplanned inter-sessions gaps are 3 weeks long, what is being called "in treatment" in one situation is "baseline" in another. Two-week gaps are in the middle. Thus, when we examine the meaning of a "treatment phase" or "baseline phase" in the applied setting, often what we find is a continuum that is then organized into categorical terms such as "treatment" and "baseline."

There are several implications of this way of thinking about phases in outpatient or similar settings. First, the researcher should try to apply phase labels consistently. If a client misses several sessions it might be more appropriate to view the resulting data as a kind of natural return to baseline than active treatment. Second, phase-change designs are stronger analytically when some components of treatment (e.g., homework) are actively present during each phase. This allows the ambiguity of the phase labels to be reduced. Finally, data that result from a phase-change design should be interpreted in terms of the actual variables manipulated, not the global labels for those manipulations. For example, suppose in a study done in the usual outpatient setting the first few data points in a "return to baseline phase" are indistinguishable from those in treatment. This may be expected if there really is no physical distinction between these first few data points and inter-session data in "treatment."

There is a final implication of the continuous nature of phases in many applied settings: It is possible to use this fact to create a new design option called the periodic treatments design (PTD). We will describe this option later in the chapter.

The Pre–Post AB

One design variant of a simple phase change is the pre–post A/B. It is simply an A/B design in which the baseline and treatment measures are taken before and after a therapy regimen. A pre–post A/B is probably one of the least intrusive design options available.

A pre–post A/B is inherently weaker than a normal A/B because so much time will intervene between the two phases. Even small trends in baseline can reduce the degree to which the second phase can be said to be due to treatment since a small trend projected over time can produce apparent phase changes. Pre–post A/B designs are most often used as part of a clinical replication series, and in this case their weaknesses within subject are made up for to a degree by their between-subject strengths.

An Example of a Simple Phase Change

An example of a simple phase-change design is shown in Figure 6.6. This study (Tustin, 1995) examined the effects of different request methods on the stereotypic behavior (e.g., body rocking and hand flapping) of an autistic man in a vocational center. Tustin noticed that this man seemed to engage in these behaviors most often when a request was made to change work tasks. The usual method was to make the request immediately preceding the change, to provide new materials, remove the old materials, and praise compliance. In a modified method, the request was made minutes before the change, and new materials were provided, but the old ones were not

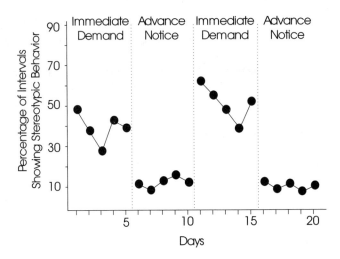

FIGURE 6.6   An example of a simple phase-change design element (redrawn from Tustin, 1995).

removed for at least two minutes, and compliance was praised. The data showed quite clearly that stereotypic behavior was far higher when requests were immediate, compared to the advance-notice method of structuring activity transitions.

Complex Phase-Change Elements

The simple phase change is designed to answer relatively simple questions, such as whether or not a treatment works or whether or not one treatment works better than another. The logic of a phase change may be utilized in more complex ways. In these complex phase-change strategies, there is an overall integrative logic to a particular sequence of phases changes.

Interaction Element

The interaction element is a sequence of phase changes that is designed to assess the contributions of one or more treatment elements. For example, suppose a treatment approach consisted of two distinguishable elements (B and C). Suppose, further, that this package had been shown to be effective, perhaps utilizing an A/B + C/A design. The relative contributions of the elements could be determined by systematically adding or subtracting one of the elements from the other. A number of specific sequences are possible (e.g., B/B + C/B; C/B + C/C; B + C/C/B + C; B + C/B/B + C). Just as with a simple phase change, the number of times that the element is added or subtracted is indefinite.

The logic of an interaction element is identical to a simple phase change. In fact, it is really a form of a simple phase change, but the question is a bit more complex. It is asking what is the combined effect of treatment components compared to one alone. You can see that the logic is the same if you were to write the designation for an A/B/A design with the equally correct designation A/A + B/A.

Typically, the interaction element is combined with other design elements that allow the practitioner to determine whether or not the treatment element or treatment package works at all (e.g., A/B/A/B/B + C/B). At times, however, this may be known already and the interaction element may occur by itself.

The attempt to discern the active components of treatment for a given client is important both practically and scientifically. Practitioners have at times tended to ignore component analyses of treatment packages, perhaps in hopes that something in a larger package will be helpful. Clearly, however, a client has a right to expect that treatment will consist of essential elements. If treatment packages are left in their combined form indefinitely, then a great deal of superstitious behavior on the part of practitioners is possible. For example, early medical treatments often consisted of complicated regimens in which active elements were mixed with unnecessary ones. Persons might be advised to avoid malaria by staying away from night air, shutting all windows, wearing a radium vest, and drinking potions, when in fact the only critical issue was to keep mosquitoes out of the house (a side effect of closing the windows). Some components of the effective package might even have been quite harmful (e.g., the radium vest).

At times, particular elements of treatment may have implications for our understanding of the needs of the individual client or of the nature of the disorder itself. By alternating these specific components, it may be possible to ascertain the nature of the disorder to a greater degree, which might then lead to greater understanding and to important treatment advances. If we know, for example, that only closing the windows has an effect, it might help us find the true cause of the disease (i.e., mosquitoes).

Interaction design elements usually emerge in two ways in practice. In the first instance, a treatment package is working. The question arises whether the effect would continue if an element of the package were removed. Usually this question is examined before an entirely satisfactory state has been achieved. Otherwise, removal of elements is assessing maintenance of effects, not their production.

For example, suppose an educator develops a new math program. It consists of a new self-paced curriculum, special quizzes to provide regular and detailed feedback, teacher praise and support, and peer tutoring. If math skills are now gained more rapidly, it may be worthwhile to remove an element (say, peer tutoring) and see if this improved rate of gain will continue. If it does not, reimplementation will allow a second assessment of the original package. This is an example of an A/B + C/B/B + C design (where B represents the whole package, except peer tutoring).

If no change occurs when the element is withdrawn, others could be withdrawn until some decrement is noticed. The final element could then be reintroduced. The logic of this is the same as that described earlier regarding an A = B/C sequence. In the present example, suppose we view peer tutoring, quizzes, teacher praise, and a new curriculum as separate elements. Suppose we implement the whole package, and show an effect. Suppose we then withdraw peer tutoring, and no change occurs, and then withdraw teacher praise, and again no change occurs. Then we withdraw the quizzes, and progress slows, so we reimplement the quizzes. This complicated example of an interaction element could be written this way: $A/B + C + D + E = B + C + D = B + C/B/B + C$. Our point is that interaction elements can be embedded in a larger sequence of package construction and dismantling in order to identify the effective components of complex interventions.

The second major way an interaction element naturally arises in practice occurs when a treatment approach has an effect that is not maximal. We may then decide to add an element that might increase the effect. If it does, a brief withdrawal (and reimplementation so as to end on the best package) will document the effect. To return to our earlier example, suppose our new self-paced curriculum alone produces an effect, but that it is not maximal. We add quizzes and get clear improvement. The quizzes are then withdrawn and reimplemented. The resulting design is an $A/B/B + C/B/B + C$.

Note that the interaction element alone does not show the effect of treatment relative to baseline. For that, other elements need to be added. For example, the refined package could now be tested against baseline with others (e.g., in an $A/B + C/A/B + C$ design). The present example also demonstrates how interaction elements will naturally tend to distill complex packages and build up simpler ones into maximally efficient units.

Interaction elements seem to be particularly common in time-series comparisons using groups as the subject of interest (e.g., Cope & Allred, 1991; Cope, Allred, & Morsell, 1991; Goltz, Citera, Jensen, Favero, & Komaki, 1989; Pfiffner & O'Leary, 1987). They are less commonly seen using single subjects as a focus (see Hayes & Cone, 1977; White, Mathews, & Fawcett, 1989, for examples), perhaps because the analysis is fairly fine grained, and it thus requires a fair amount of stability to be useful.

White et al. (1989) provide example of the use of the interaction element. They examined the effect of contingencies for wheelchair push-ups designed to avoid the development of pressure sores in disabled children. Wheelchair push-ups were automatically recorded by a computer. After a baseline, two subjects were exposed to an alarm-avoidance contingency (B), a beeper prompt (C), or a combination. An interaction design element was combined with a multiple baseline component. The design for one subject was $A/B + C/B/B + C/B/B + C/C/B + C$, and for the other was $A/B + C/C/B + C/C/B + C$. Each component (B and C) was more effective than baseline, but for both children the combined (B + C) condition was the most effective overall.

Combining Simple Phase Changes to Compare Two Different Treatments

A simple phase change that compares two different treatments makes sense only if it is known that at least one of the treatments is effective in the first place. If this is not known, a comparison of the two treatments may show only that one treatment works better than the other. Both may actually be ineffective or even harmful. We cannot know this for certain until comparisons are made to baseline performance.

One way to accomplish treatment comparison goals and to document the effectiveness of treatment is to combine an A/B/A with an A/C/A. The resulting A/B/A/C/A sequence allows us to determine both whether or not B and C are effective and, though the comparison is not elegant, to generate some data on whether or not B is more effective than C. This last question is not answered in an elegant manner because noncontiguous data are being compared, namely the data in the B phase with those in the C phase, and order effects are also possible. Typically, the order-effect problem is handled by conducting a similar analysis with other subjects, but with a reversal of the sequencing of the two treatments. For example, another client may receive an A/C/A/B/A sequence. The need to control for order effects emerges because order is completely confounded with the two different treatments. For instance, the second treatment may not work as well as the first, precisely because it is the second treatment, not because it is treatment B or treatment C. The patterns shown must be consistent when controls are added for order.

In evaluating the data emerging from time-series evaluations, data that are closer together in time are more easily compared than those that are separated by larger temporal intervals. Many extraneous variables are more likely to occur given a longer temporal interval than a shorter one. For example, maturation or learning-related changes are not likely over short intervals but become more likely as time goes on. For this reason, comparisons of data that are contiguous are stronger than comparisons of those that are further apart in time.

This fact influences strongly the logic of single case experimental designs. An attempt is usually made to arrange conditions in such a way that the more critical comparisons are being made in contiguous conditions. As with most of the rules guiding single case experimentation, this is a matter of degree and not an absolute issue. Several designs, including an A/B/A/C/A, violate aspects of this rule. When it is violated, attempts are typically made to control for some of the threats that it raises. Controlling for order effects in the A/B/A/C/A design is an example.

The considerations involved in conducting such a sequence mimic very closely those that were described earlier for the simple phase change. Clearly, however, many patterns of data outcome could undermine an original intention to conduct an A/B/A/C/A analysis. For example, if the data in the second baseline phase failed to show a slowing of improvement established in the first treatment, then it would make no sense to implement a second type of treatment.

The point here is that these designs tend to emerge naturally in the course of treatment. It is a mistake to decide beforehand to follow a particular sequence of phases rather than to allow the information being collected from the client to guide the emerging design in a dynamic and interactive way.

Sometimes a simple phase change for a given treatment will then justify a more direct treatment comparison. For example, an A/B/A might be followed by a B/C/B/C sequence, resulting in an A/B/A/B/C/B/C (to control for order effects, an A/C/A/C/B/C/B would also be needed with additional clients). In this case, the first four phases established the effectiveness of one treatment. This can then be used as a kind of benchmark against which to evaluate a second treatment (the last four phases). It is fairly common to see a researcher proceed from an A/B directly into multiple treatment comparisons, such as an A/B/C/B/C sequence (e.g., Haring & Kennedy, 1990). Usually this is not the best arrangement since the "benchmark" against which a second treatment is being evaluated is an unreplicated simple phase change. Another alternative sometimes seen is an A/B/C/A/B/C (e.g., Hayden, Wheeler, Carnine, 1989). In this arrangement the A/B relation is replicated, which strengthens the design, but order effects still must be controlled.

An example of an A/B/A/C/A design is given by Harmon, Nelson, and Hayes (1980). In this study, conditions were compared that were designed to improve depressed clients' mood (B) or their activity (C). The purpose of the study was to answer the question: Do people get into a depressed mood because they do less, or do they do less because of their mood? A well-known side effect of self-monitoring is reactivity. This side effect was used to increase mood or activity specifically. Clients were given timers that buzzed periodically throughout the day. During one condition, they immediately rated their mood. During another condition they rated pleasant activity. During baseline, no frequent ratings were made. Overall ratings of mood and activity were also taken at the end of each day throughout the entire study. Nine depressed clients took part (all were also in a weekly therapy group). Three each completed A/B/A/C/A sequences, three completed A/C/A/B/A sequences, and three were in baseline-only throughout. The data of interest are whether measures of mood improve when pleasant activity is increased and if measures of pleasant activity improve when mood is improved.

Figure 6.7 shows that mood improves when pleasant activity increases, regardless of the sequence. Note also that activity does not increase as much when mood is increased, again regardless of order. Thus, we can conclude that improvements in mood are more likely to follow changes in activity than vice versa. Because the same effects are shown in different clients experiencing the conditions in reversed order, order effects are ruled out. This study also demonstrates the use of a baseline-only control, which will be discussed in Chapter 8.

Changing Criterion Element

This element (Hall, 1971; Hall & Fox, 1977; Hartmann & Hall, 1976) is based on a fundamentally different type of reasoning than the elements that have been described thus far. It emerges when it is possible arbitrarily to specify the pattern that a given behavior should show in a particular period, and to change the source of that specification repeatedly. If the behavior repeatedly and closely tracks the specification, then it is reasonable to believe that the source of the specification is responsible for the changes.

Usually, this design is used when particular criteria specify the level that behavior must reach. These criteria could be such things as goals, contingencies, posted expectations, or the performance of others. For example, a clinician may ask

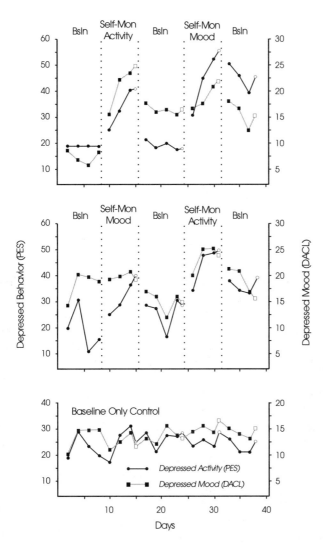

FIGURE 6.7 An example of an A/B/A/C/A design (redrawn from Harmon, Nelson, & Hayes, 1980; the solid data points are blocks of two days).

a socially withdrawn client to strike up at least two conversations per week. After a period of time this criterion may be changed (e.g., to four per week) and the degree to which the behavior then tracks the new criterion can be determined. Similarly, the criteria could be the minimum performance needed to achieve some desired consequence. These criteria could logically be tied to variability or trend as easily as to level, though level is by far the most common.

Figure 6.8 shows hypothetical data for a socially withdrawn client. As part of the treatment, specific goals for the number of social contacts with others are repeatedly

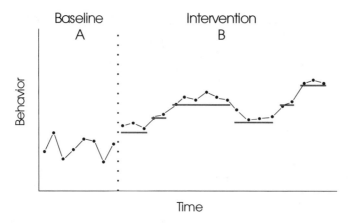

FIGURE 6.8   A hypothetical example of a changing-criterion design.

set. If the data shown in Figure 6.8 resulted, a reasonably strong case could be made for a treatment effect because of the close relationship between the criteria, which are modified by the practitioner, and the resulting behavior of the client.

Because the source of information about treatment effects in a changing criterion design element is the relationship between repeated changes in the criteria and similar changes in the behavior itself, it is important that the criteria changes not mimic common behavioral patterns that might occur naturally. There are at least four things to consider. First is the number of criterion shifts. If only one or two criterion shifts are made, then there will naturally be relatively little information about the correspondence between the criterion and behavior. This is basically the same issue as that of the number of replications in a simple phase change. Each criterion shift provides an opportunity for a replication of the effect seen. At the absolute minimum, of course, at least two criteria are required, but most studies using this design have used four or more criterion shifts.

A second issue is the length of the subphase in which a single criterion is in force. In some versions of this design, researchers have left the criterion in force for a very short period of time. The problem with this is that it does not enable a clear assessment of the correspondence between the criterion and the behavior. The level, trend, and variability of the observed behavior are all important determinants of correspondence. If extremely short subphases are utilized, it is impossible to assess all of these sources of information.

In addition to recommending that the criteria be held for a sufficiently long period of time to determine correspondence, it is also important that the criteria be shifted at irregular intervals. Many behavior-change patterns approximate a gradual increase or decrease in behavior. If criterion shifts are regular, and especially if the length of the subphases is short, the resulting expected behavior pattern will be a gradual and steady increase or decrease. It is better to have some subphases somewhat longer than others so that any cyclic or periodic changes in the behavior will not coincide with criterion shifts.

A third method of increasing the likelihood of detecting a relationship between behavior and criteria is to alter the magnitude of the criterion shifts themselves. Often the changing-criterion design element is used when gradual improvement is expected. It may not be possible or even advisable to shift a criterion in a dramatic way, but to the extent reasonable, the magnitude of criterion shifts should not be consistent. Just as with the length of the subphases, it is desirable to have some criterion shifts greater than others.

A final method of increasing the precision of the design is to change the direction of the criterion shifts. If it is possible to do so, the relaxation of a stringent criterion allows a kind of reversal, very much like an A/B/A/B design. In this case, however, instead of baseline, the reversal consists of a return to an earlier criterion level.

Figure 6.9 shows an example of a series of planned criterion shifts when the level of the behavior is being used to identify the criteria. Notice that this planned series alters the length, magnitude, and direction of criteria changes. Just as with phase changes more generally, it is important that the changes fit into the clinical routine, but it is also important to be mindful of the reasons why the criteria were shifted. The clinician should not go into the case with an expected series of criterion shifts. Rather, the appropriate criterion shifts should merge in the context of therapy with an eye toward variability in magnitude, length, and direction.

If the criterion shifts are heavily influenced by particular client behaviors, it is important to identify that source of control in the description of the procedure. For example, if the criteria are shifted only when the client requests that they be made more stringent, then a shift seen in the behavior might be due to the same factors that led the client to request the shift and not to the criterion itself. As with other phase-change designs, the solution to this seems to be to allow the natural tendency to shift criteria at particular times but to rely on replication, articulation of the reasons for the shift, and some arbitrary shifts when possible.

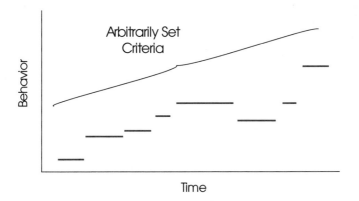

FIGURE 6.9 **An example of ways to vary criteria so as to avoid excessive regularity in a changing-criterion design.**

Belles and Bradlyn (1987) provide a good example of a changing criterion design that uses most of the methods of control the design element allows. The goal was to reduce the smoking rate of a long-time smoker, who smoked several packs a day. The client recorded the number of cigarettes smoked each day (with reliability checks by a spouse). After a baseline period, goals were set by the therapist for the maximum number of cigarettes to be smoked. If the criterion was exceeded, the client sent a $25 check to a disliked charity. For each day that the criterion was not exceeded, $3 went into a fund that could be used to purchase desirable items.

The data are shown in Figure 6.10. Except for one short slip (days 70–75), the subject's smoking precisely tracked the criterion levels set by the therapist. After approximately 3 months, the client had reduced his smoking to five cigarettes per day, which was the client's final goal. This level was maintained for 3 years of follow up.

Belles and Bradlyn used all of the available criterion-related control procedures in their study: Each criterion was left in place for at least three days, and the length of time, magnitude, and direction of criterion shifts varied. Because of this careful approach, the precise fit between criterion shifts and the observed behavior makes it clear that the changes seen were due to treatment.

What is different in the changing criterion as compared to the simple phase change and its variations is that we have some prior expectation of the specific patterns that should be seen in a particular phase or subphase. The changing-criterion design has been most popular when used with behaviors that tend to change gradually. It is particularly well suited to situations in which the client is learning new things in a gradual way or is gradually eliminating a problematic behavior. It does

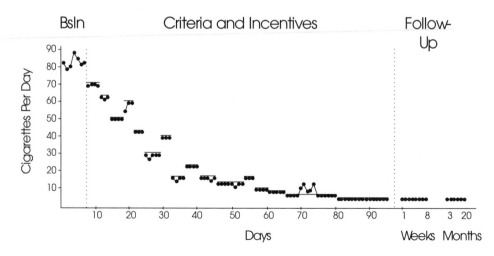

FIGURE 6.10 **An example of a changing-criterion design (redrawn from Belles and Bradlyn, 1987).**

not require any withdrawal of treatment and, in fact, is logically useful even when no baseline assessment phases are obtained.

The main difficulty in the analysis of data in the changing-criterion design is that there is no well-agreed-upon method for determining whether or not the behavior seen fits the series of specifiable criteria. If the data are quite variable and, in particular, if some of the days violate the set criterion in a particular phase, then it will be difficult to determine whether the behavior is tracking the criteria. Similarly, if the criterion is not changed for a period of time and yet there is a trend in the behavior, then this would undermine the conclusion that the behavior is tracking the criteria. If the criteria are stable, then ideally the behavior seen should also be stable. The four recommendations given earlier will greatly diminish the problem of determining the degree of correspondence (as is shown in the Belles and Bradlyn data). Additional analytic aids may be needed, however. One possibility is to present the data (and not the criteria) to persons skilled in time-series methodology and ask them to guess when criteria were changed and by how much. It is then possible to check the correspondence between the hypothesized and actual criteria. Once a hit is defined, the rates of hits and misses expected due to chance alone can be determined and compared to the obtained values with, say, a chi square. The point is that the obviousness of correspondence between the criteria and obtained data is itself measurable.

The other weakness of the changing-criterion design is that it is only applicable when a criterion is a component of treatment. In many cases it is not possible or even desirable to set specific criteria for change. In these situations, other designs are more appropriate.

Parametric Design Element

At times the practitioner is interested in the relative effectiveness of several variations of a particular treatment arranged along some kind of continuum. For example, the clinician may be interested in the effectiveness of a particular amount of therapist self-disclosure. Each of these values of a particular treatment could be considered to be a distinct treatment, and the design options already described could be used to test the parameters of a given intervention. The parametric nature of the comparisons, however, opens up additional options.

One common strategy that is quite popular in the basic experimental literature is to increase the parameter of interest and then to decrease it. This parametric design has been used at least since the 1920s in the investigation of the psychological effects of drugs (Darrow, 1929). Boren (1953) first noted the value of using ascending and descending values in parametric designs, while Sidman (1960) first detailed its definition, strengths, and weaknesses.

By using systematically varied values in an ascending-descending sequence, each value of the intervention is replicated so that the nature of the relationship between treatment parameters and outcome can be obtained. For example, suppose four different levels of a particular treatment were being compared (let's call them B, B', B'', B'''). One sequence that would test the relative impact of these treatment variations would be an A/B/B′/B″/B‴/B″/B′/B/A sequence. If at any point the clinician wished to investigate particular parameters more closely, it would be possible to add alternations of that value to other values of interest (e.g., B′/B″/B′/B″).

The difference in this design element compared to any phase change component is that we have some a priori reason to believe that the conditions are closely related, differing only on a specifiable parameter. To the extent that this belief is true, it strengthens the logical structure of the design and because of that allows somewhat weaker controls in phase sequencing to be used. Consider an A/B/B′/B″/B‴/B″/B′/B/A sequence. If the variations of B were unrelated treatments, this sequence would be described this way: A/B/C/D/E/D/C/B/A. This phase sequence is weak because not all treatments are compared to baseline, and specific phase changes are replicated only in different contexts. Considered as a parametric element, however, the sequence is more logical because the phase changes are matters of quantity and their relative values can be precisely specified. If the parameter is of importance we expect to see an orderly relation between gradual changes in this quantifiable parameter and behavior.

In some ways this is similar to the logic of a changing-criterion design in which expectations about the impact of treatment drawn from our knowledge of the criterion allow us more flexibility in phase sequencing. It differs from the changing criterion in that the data are evaluated in the normal manner and not in terms of correspondence to a criterion.

The prime example of the use of such a design is in an attempt to relate drug dosage levels to a therapeutic response. The parametric design element is a fairly standard model in practice-based drug research (Baumeister & Sevin, 1990) because the treatment variable is so readily quantifiable and because specific dosages of drugs are known to produce very large differences in both desired outcomes and side effects. Researchers often try various levels of the drug to see if an orderly dose-response relationship may emerge. Parametric designs are also useful, however, when the specific values of any variable are known to have widely differing effects, depending on subject characteristics. For example, some stimulus variables impact upon older persons differently than younger persons, but in a fashion that is not readily specificiable a priori. Parametric designs are especially useful in such circumstances (Olton & Markowska, 1988). The relationship need not be linear. Figure 6.11 shows some idealized data from such a design. The top of the graph shows a linear relationship between treatment value (e.g., dosage level) and outcome. The bottom shows a curvilinear relationship. Both are fairly convincing.

Note, however, that the patterns are replicated—that is, each value shows a specific and replicable pattern. When this is not true, the design cannot fully distinguish order effects from treatment effects (e.g., Aman, Teehan, White, & Turbott, 1989).

Kornet, Goosen, and Van Ree (1991) provide an example of a parametric design. These researchers were interested in the effects of naltrexone on the consumption of freely available alcohol. The data shown in Figure 6.12 are the mean values consisting of the difference in the amount of alcohol consumed following a

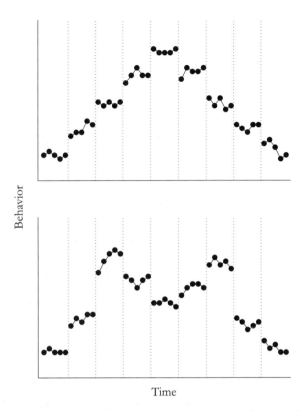

FIGURE 6.11   **Two hypothetical examples of results from a parametric design.**

placebo versus naltrexone. Naltrexone reduced total ethanol consumed in an orderly, dose-dependent fashion.

Periodic Treatments Design Element

The periodic treatments design (PTD) draws upon the observation that treatments are not continuously present in many applied settings. When treatment is delivered in discrete sessions (e.g., in outpatient psychotherapy settings), it is possible to divide data not just on the basis of the continuous presence of treatment, but on the basis of the degree of relevance between a given set of data points and treatment sessions. It is called a periodic treatments design because the source of evidence for an effect is the consistent relationship between the periodicity of treatment sessions and the periodicity of behavior change.

The approach is applicable when the meaningful unit of measurement is fairly high relative to the frequency of treatment sessions. It is particularly relevant when treatment sessions occur somewhat irregularly so that normal periodicity (e.g., weekly variations in activities) cannot mimic true treatment effects. The principle behind a PTD is this: If there is a consistent relationship between the

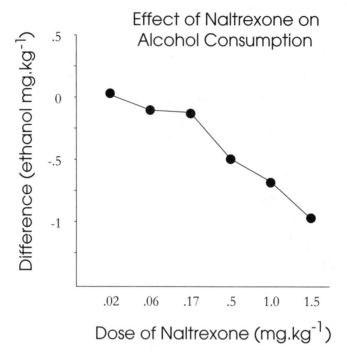

FIGURE 6.12   An example of a parametric design. These are mean data consisting of the difference between the consumption of freely available alcohol following administration of a placebo or naltrexone (redrawn from part of Figure 3 in Kornet, Goosen, & Van Ree, 1991).

occurrence of treatment sessions and accelerated improvement within a data series, the sessions can be said to be responsible.

Figure 6.13 shows hypothetical data that are meant to exemplify the principle. The top half of the figure shows the hypothetical record of positive self-statements of a depressed, self-deprecating client, self-recorded daily. Arrows on the abscissa show days when the client saw a psychotherapist for therapy sessions. Note that the treatment sessions occur at varying intervals, but that in each case improvement accelerates following them. This periodicity cannot be accounted for on the basis of time alone, since there is no consistent relationship between time and improvement. It seems that the treatment sessions themselves are responsible.

Without further experimental work we would not know exactly what about the treatment sessions produced improvement, but this is not different than any initial therapy evaluation. The effects could be due to nonspecific factors (e.g., the value of any kind of therapeutic attention) or to specific therapeutic variables. This same criticism applies to any design, single subject or otherwise, in which treatment is compared to no treatment.

The PTD is not limited to situations in which immediate and dramatic effects occur after treatment. The essential move in this design is to view time from treatment sessions as a continuous treatment-related variable. The exact shape of the function between treatment and behavioral result is an empirical matter. What the PTD does is to treat treatment relevance as a continuous variable and then to relate that to treatment outcome, also a continuous variable. Delayed effects, if consistently shown, could also be related to treatment.

The relationship between treatment and improvement is made more obvious in the bottom half of Figure 6.13, in part by recasting this continuous variable as a digital one, and furthermore by presenting the data in a form that accentuates relative improvement over absolute value. First, the data between each treatment session have been divided into two equal halves. The data for the first half of each

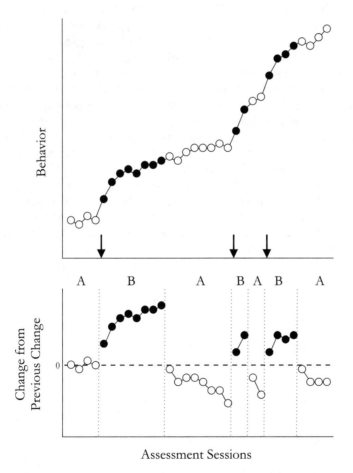

FIGURE 6.13   A hypothetical example of a periodic treatments design. The top figure would normally be considered a B-only design. If we consider "treatment" and "baseline" to be time close to, or removed from, treatment sessions, the data can be divided into conditions (closed versus open circles). When these data are recalculated in terms of the change from the trend established by the preceding "phase," the bottom version is formed (the horizontal line represents the trend set in the previous phase).

such period are shown with solid circles; those for the second half are unfilled. In the bottom figure, each of these periods is now treated as a "phase" and the data are graphed as they were earlier in Figure 6.5: as a deviation from the trend established in the previous phase. This yields a clear picture, and one that is interpretable as a kind of phase-change design.

As this example reveals, a PTD draws on the logic of within-series designs, but it adds in the notion of a treatment continuum. A PTD can be pushed back into a digital form, but the design logic actually does not demand it. Periodicity could be examined in other ways. For example, data points could be assigned treatment relevance values based on the time since the preceding session and correlated with relative improvement scores.

The data shown in Figure 6.14 are from a person with a clinically significant fear of snakes (a fear made suddenly important to her because of her plan to marry a nature photographer who liked to vacation in the Everglades). Two extended exposure sessions (each several hours long) were used to treat this fear. The data shown are the degree of approach shown toward fearful pictures in a visual avoidance measure known to correlate with other forms of behavioral approach toward snakes (Hayes, Nelson, Willis, & Akamatsu, 1982). The client improved immediately and dramatically following exposure. Gains neither deteriorated nor improved after this initial effect. Because the improvement is tightly related to treatment sessions, the most reasonable explanation is that the treatment sessions are responsible for the improvement shown.

The PTD is a design option that fits easily into many forms of practice. Next to a pre–post A/B design, probably no design option is less intrusive in applied settings. Irregular treatment sessions are not uncommon. If the measures taken are frequent relative to treatment and the treatment effects are large and consistent, a PTD should make them visible.

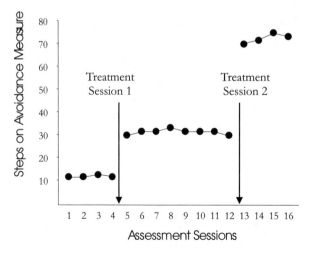

FIGURE 6.14   A case example of the periodic treatments effect.

Follow-Up

Regardless of the particular kind of strategy used to evaluate the single case, the practitioner can and probably should include a follow-up phase. The follow-up phase amounts to an extension of the final-treatment phase.

Even though treatment is no longer in force, the assumption is that if treatment has been effective, it will be maintained during follow-up. In a sense this is very similar to placebo interventions that follow baseline. You might recall that earlier in the chapter we described how phases that are equivalent to baseline can be considered to be part of baseline. In the same way, behavioral patterns that continue after the termination of treatment are generally considered to be part of the treatment phase—that is, a long-term result of treatment.

There are logical difficulties with some of these assumptions for particular single case designs. For example, if several different phases preceded follow-up, it may be that any maintenance that is shown is due to the entire sequence of phases and not to the final treatment. This is the problem of multiple treatment. The difficulties here are no different than the difficulties presented for the interpretation of any phase in a single subject design. The answer is also similar: replication. If maintenance is only shown when a particular sequence is present, then sequence is important.

Evaluating the Results
of Within-Series Strategies

How do we know that the data that result from a within-series evaluation are meaningful? The field has developed largely based upon visual inspection of the data. It is known, based on numerous studies (see Parsonson & Baer, 1992, for a review), that even experienced single case researchers will disagree about the meaning of some data patterns when they are examined visually. In that context it may seem remarkable that some of the best proven applied procedures have emerged from the single case research tradition (Chambless et al., 1996). In fact, however, the two facts may be related.

The very ambiguity of visual inspection procedures tends to focus the analyst toward rules of evidence that emphasize nonarbitrary characteristics of the findings. This may actually protect researchers from overemphasizing weak or questionable effects. Table 6.2 summarizes a few of the rules that seem to guide visual inspection. If a finding meets all of these rules—even if determined only by visual inspection—it would probably be both reliable and important. Conversely, if the effects are of such a size, immediacy, or consistency, the person relying on visual inspection cannot hide these factors behind mathematical assumptions and algorithms. The weakness of the data is evident.

In group-comparison designs, statistical inferential tools are well developed and, in part because of the way these designs arrive at estimates of measurement error and extraneous variability, they are relied upon quite heavily. The adequacy

TABLE 6.2   Some Common Rules in Evaluating Time-Series Data

1. Evaluate effects relative to background variability in the dimension involved in the comparison (i.e., level, trend, or variability itself).

2. The more replications of the effect, the more believable.

3. The more consistent the effect, the more believable.

4. The larger the magnitude of the effect (given background variability and previous knowledge about the behavior), the more believable.

5. The more immediate the effect, the more believable.

6. The more the effect is based on contiguous comparisons, the more believable.

7. Effects that conceptually rule out alternative explanations are more believable.

8. Effects that are based on carefully specified and controlled conditions are more believable.

of traditional statistical inferential tools in the detection of important and clinically significant findings in group comparison research is not assured (e.g., see Jacobson & Truax, 1991), but the applicability of these tools is fairly clear.

Application of traditional statistical inferential procedures to single case designs is controversial. Many statistical procedures are invalidated if the data are autocorrelated, for example (meaning that it is possible to predict a given score from the scores that precede and follow it). Autocorrelation is probably overestimated, especially in small sample sizes (Huitema & McKean, 1991), but it is clearly a problem in some data sets that emerge from time-series designs.

A number of solutions have been proposed (Busk & Marascuilo, 1992; Yarnold, 1992). There seems to be agreement, for example, that some nonparametric procedures—such as the randomization test—apply to some forms of time-series data provided that certain rules of instituting phase changes are followed (Edgington, 1992). When the assumptions of parametric analyses are not violated, common tools such as t tests seem directly applicable to single case data. Others have suggested using meta-analytic procedures to combine single case findings (Busk & Serlin, 1992). Econometric statistical analytical tools apply directly to single case data, but at times the assumptions that need to be met are difficult. For example, some forms of statistical comparisons drawn from these procedures cannot be modeled properly if there are fewer than 50 data points per phase.

At the present time it is probably fair to say that inferential statistics are more available that ever before for single subject data, especially because of the wide availability of statistical packages (McCleary & Welsh, 1992), but that they are still controversial and are used only occasionally. The field is rapidly developing, however, and new tools are constantly being added.

Unfortunately, even if inferential statistical analyses are done, we still cannot be sure if our judgments will lead us to effective action, even though we may feel more certain about them. From a pragmatic point of view, it is most important that analytic procedures be adopted that guide the analyst toward decisions that work, not just decisions that are consistent. While it is well known that well-designed mathematical algorithms can beat clinical judgment in almost all instances (Dawes, 1994), this applies only when predictions are being made to definable, known criteria. Statistical inferential tools are generally based on a form of decision theory linked to sampling theory, in which we do not have a known outcome being modeled mathematically. The value of these tools is more controversial.

The usual argument for the *necessity* of statistical inference goes this way:

1. Science demands valid judgments.
2. If judgments are to be valid, they must be reliable.
3. Different judges disagree; therefore, their judgments are unreliable.
4. If they are unreliable, the judgments are also invalid.
5. Judgments made solely on the basis of statistical inferential tools are reliable.
6. Therefore, judgments made on the basis of statistical inference are valid.

Several logical errors occur here. Even if validity requires reliability (which in at least some circumstances is arguable; see Hayes, Nelson, & Jarrett, 1987), reliability does not imply validity. If we determined the validity of effects by the shoe size of the authors, we would have perfect reliability, but presumably no validity. Ultimately it should be shown, therefore, that judgments aided by inferential statistics actually are better; that they improve our ability to predict or to control phenomena. With single case designs, no such data yet exist. When they do, we will then know how helpful statistical inference is to the practitioner using time-series designs.

In the meantime, the practitioner should watch developments in this area, since the picture is changing rapidly. Increasingly, statistical procedures are being developed for the analysis of single case studies. But even without these tools the long tradition of research in this area suggests that valid and replicable results can be detected using visual inspection.

7 Between-Series Elements

Introduction

In within-series strategies, assessment of level, trend, and variability around level and trend is made within a series of measurements taken across real time, and then organized by conditions, or phases. Because these estimates are made within phases, it is essential that several measurements be taken successively under a given condition (e.g., baseline, or a given treatment) before another condition is instituted. Another way to group data points is to do so first by condition and then by time. Suppose, for example, you notice that an acquaintance responds quite differently to different greetings you give. Sometimes when you see him you use an informal greeting. Invariably, he smiles and returns the greeting. Other times you use a more formal greeting, and then he only nods grimly. Common sense will quickly tell you that your greeting style is responsible for the differences, but note that no stable sequence of three or more measurements in the same condition (i.e., a phase of formal or informal greeting) is required. Are you mistaken in the logic of your conclusion? No, what you have done intuitively is to combine his reactions first by greeting condition and then across time within condition, rather than to do it by successive measurements alone. You have created two series across time (the responses to your formal and your informal greeting), and the differences between these two series provide the evidence of a difference.

This is the logic of between-series design elements. They do not need to contain phases (although phase-change elements can be added as the overall design is constructed) because the estimates of level, trend, and stability are organized by condition and then across time, not by time alone. There are two basic types of between-series design elements: the alternating-treatments design and the simultaneous-treatments design.

The Alternating-Treatments Design

The logic of the alternating-treatments design element (ATD) is based simply on the rapid and random (or semirandom) alternation of two or more conditions (Barlow & Hayes, 1979). By "rapid" is meant that the frequency of possible alternation is about as great as the frequency of the meaningful unit of measurement. If, for example, the clinical phenomenon is best measured in weekly units, there should be a possibility of a change in condition about once a week. The alternations are usually done randomly, but with a limit on the number of times a given condition can be in force sequentially (thus the phrase "semirandomly"). The ATD is also sometimes called the "multi-element" design (Ulman & Sulzer-Azaroff, 1975). Recently, this term has increased in popularity, though ATD still seems to be the more common one.

In the ATD, a single data point associated with one condition may be preceded and followed by measurements associated with other conditions. Because of this, there is no opportunity to assess level, trend, course, and variability within consistent phases. Rather, these assessments are obtained within conditions, by arranging data points sequentially associated with a condition or treatment each into a separate series. If there is a clear separation between such series, differences among conditions are inferred.

The idea of a rapid alternation of conditions is not a new one, but the essential logic of it was long clouded because of the connection between this design and multiple or mixed schedules of reinforcement in the animal operant literature and the apparent relevance of this design alternative only to comparisons between schedules of reinforcement. The ATD, one of the most powerful and applicable design elements in all of time-series methodology, was greatly underused because its essential nature and practical uses were hidden by this historical artifact. The ATD has now assumed its rightful place as a popular method of applied analysis and evaluation, however, and dozens of articles are published each year using this design in every imaginable area of human research.

Consider the following example that emerged naturally in the treatment of a clinical case. The design has some problems, which will be instructive later, but it also demonstrates the logical structure of an ATD. While supervising a student therapist we noticed that an alternation of conditions was naturally occurring. When the student was uncomfortable, he would move back from the client and would tend to be more formal, cold, and predictable. At other times he would lean toward the client and would be more spontaneous, warm, and self-disclosing. What emerged in his clients was a predictable pattern: Clients quieted down and became more defensive when the therapist was leaning back, but more open and self-disclosing when he was leaning forward.

This somewhat whimsical example illustrates the essential logic of the design element. Suppose the therapist took the small additional step of deliberately and randomly scheduling the "lean back" and "lean forward" periods and the client behaved as shown in Figure 7.1. Because of the consistently higher level of self-disclosure shown in the "lean forward" condition, we would conclude that the therapist's behavior was controlling the client's reactions. With additional controls (mentioned later) we might be able to show specifically what it was about the therapist's actions that was critical.

Note that the comparison is made *between* these two data series. Any changes shown within each series are unanalyzed and may be due to extraneous factors, such as history, maturation, and the like. In the ATD itself, there are no phases,

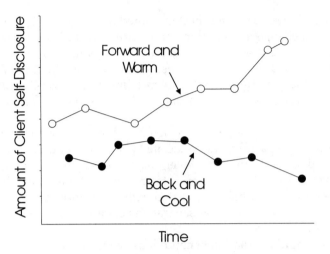

FIGURE 7.1   A hypothetical example of the use of an ATD to assess the effects of therapist behavior on client self-disclosure.

although by random assignment sometimes there may be three or more data points in a row in the same condition. One could think of this as an extremely rapid A/B/A/B design, but the two differ significantly. First, as we have already noted, the nature of the assessment of variability, level, and trend differs. Second, the nature of treatment comparisons differ. Third, an ATD can incorporate three or even more conditions. A within-series comparison is difficult with three or more conditions, and considerable thought must be given to the specific sequence of phases (e.g., an A/B/A/C/A). Finally, the control problems that the two design elements present differ. In an ATD, order effects are less likely (because the order is highly variable due to rapid, random alternation), but multiple treatment interference is more likely for the same reason. Multiple treatment interference occurs when the effect of one treatment is different in the presence of another treatment from what it is in its absence. Such interference is not always undesirable, as we will discuss later, but it is known to occur with ATDs, particularly when there is minimal or no delay between alternations of conditions (McGonigle, Rojahn, Dixon, & Strain, 1987).

Although we have termed this design element the "alternating treatments design," it should be clear that "treatments" is used here to refer to the conditions in force, not necessarily to therapy. Baseline conditions can be alternated with specific interventions as easily as two or more distinct therapies can be alternated. Whether this is needed depends upon the specific question being asked. If the question is "does therapy B work?" then baseline either must be alternated with B, or other design elements must also be used—such as a baseline phase both before and after the ATD element. For example, Figure 7.1 does not show that therapist behavior (i.e., leaning forward and being warm) increased client self-disclosure over doing nothing in particular; that would require a baseline condition. It shows only that self-disclosure increased as compared to what occurred when the therapist leaned back and acted more formally. Similarly, the apparent upward trend in the lean forward condition over time does not show that the client is improving relative to doing nothing special. The trend within series could be due entirely to extraneous factors. If this information is important, baseline conditions would be needed either as part of the ATD or as part of a phase-change strategy.

Types of Comparisons Possible with an ATD

The ATD can be used either alone or in combination with other design elements. It can be used to answer many questions that emerge in the applied environment. An ATD can compare treatment and no treatment, or two treatments to each other (alone or as compared also to baseline). It can also be used to examine the components of treatment, or nonspecific factors. Its most popular use, however, is the comparison of two or more treatments.

Two or more treatments can be compared without baseline in an ATD if they are of known effectiveness and it is only their relative effectiveness that is primarily at issue. In clinical case management it is usually a good idea to collect a baseline even in these conditions, however, to make sure that a treatment effect occurred. When treatments are not of known effectiveness, a baseline is a necessity.

A representative study comparing two treatments and a baseline is provided by Jordan, Singh, and Repp (1989). In this study, two methods of reducing stereotypical behavior (e.g., rocking, hand-flapping) in retarded subjects were examined: gentle teaching (the use of social bonding and gentle persuasion with the developmentally disabled) and visual screening (covering the client's eyes for a few seconds following stereotypic behavior, thus reducing visual stimulation including that provided by these movements). A portion of the data for one of the subjects is shown in Figure 7.2. After a baseline period, visual screening produced a dramatic reduction in stereotypy. Gentle teaching had only a transient effect.

One of the earliest examples of the use of an ATD not merely examined the effect of two treatments but also showed how to control for therapist variables. Agras, Leitenberg, Barlow, and Thomson (1969) examined the effect of therapist praise on a severely claustrophobic client. The subject was a 50-year-old female whose symptoms intensified following the death of her husband some 7 years before being admitted as a research patient in a psychiatric unit. When admitted, the patient was unable to remain in a closed room for longer than 1 minute without experiencing considerable anxiety. As a consequence of this disorder, the patient's activities were seriously restricted.

During the study, the patient was asked, four times daily, to remain inside a small room until she felt she had to come out. Time in the room was the dependent measure. During the first four data points representing treatment (see Figure 7.3), the patient kept her hand on the doorknob. Before the fifth treatment data point (sixth block of sessions), the patient took her hand off the doorknob, resulting in a considerable drop in times.

During treatment, two therapists alternated sessions with one another. One therapist administered social praise contingent on the patient's remaining in the

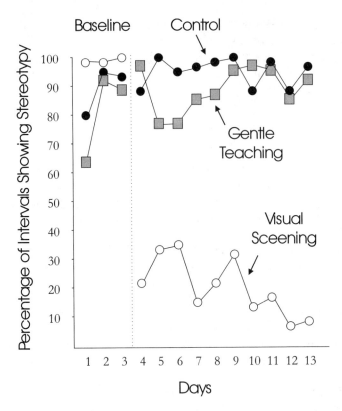

FIGURE 7.2   An example of the use of an ATD to assess the effects of two treatments, compared to a baseline. Note that baseline is included both as a phase and in the ATD itself. (Redrawn from Jordan, Singh, and Repp, 1989. Phases unimportant to the current point in between and after the phases shown have been removed. Note that in the baseline phase no treatments are in effect: The different data points come from arbitrary assignment).

room for an increasing period of time. The second therapist maintained a pleasant relationship but did not praise her in any way for time spent in the room. In the second experimental phase the therapists switched roles, but returned to their original roles in the third phase. The data indicate that praise consistently increased performance relative to no praise. Note, however, that no firm statements can be made about the effect of these two exposure treatments relative to no treatment (no exposure) except relative to a one-point baseline.

Another clinical example shows that the ATD can be used to study the additive effects of treatment components as well as of two entirely different treatment regimens. Hayes, Hussian, Turner, Anderson, and Grubb (1983) treated a 38-year-old female with a driving phobia. The phobia had progressed to the point at which even driving a few blocks would create intense anxiety attacks. After a short baseline, sessions of systematic desensitization were begun, either with or without cog-

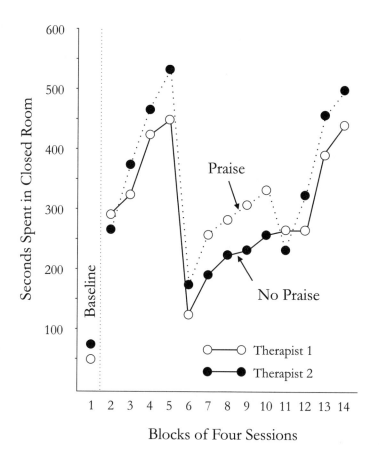

FIGURE 7.3   In this classic case, two therapists alternated in praising or not praising performance during exposure for claustrophobic behavior. The sudden decrease in block 6 came because the client was asked not to hold on to the doorknob while in the closed room (redrawn from Agras, Leitenberg, Barlow, & Thomson, 1969).

nitive coping training being added. As can be seen in Figure 7.4, the coping plus desensitization package worked better than desensitization alone.

Even more analytic studies would be possible using the same approach. For example, the role of a variety of "nonspecific" factors could be assessed using an ATD. A treatment protocol could be followed in exactly the same way each session, except that therapist warmth or some other such nonspecific variable could be alternated. The ATD can also be useful in assessment, as is described later.

Advantages of an ATD

The ATD element has a number of distinct advantages (Barlow & Hayes, 1979; Ulman & Sulzer-Azaroff, 1975). First, it does not require withdrawal of treatment, or if one is used in the ATD itself, it need not be lengthy. If two or more therapies

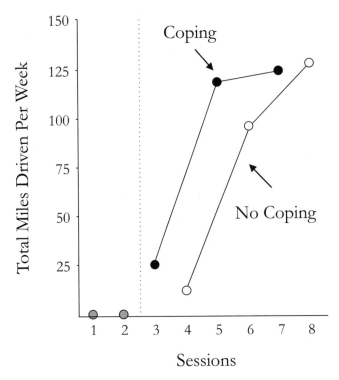

FIGURE 7.4 **The effects of desensitization with or without cognitive coping on miles driven by a driving phobic.**

are being compared, the question "which one works best?" can be answered without a withdrawal phase at all. The lack of a need for treatment withdrawal is a distinct advantage for an ATD. It limits the practical and ethical problems posed by the absence of treatment that might otherwise occur (see Chapter 6).

Occasionally, a primitive type of an ATD emerges naturally. Just as there are natural withdrawals as in a phase-change design, there are natural alternations with baseline as in an ATD. Suppose treatment occurs every other week, but measures are taken every week. You could think of this as an ATD, in which the therapy weeks and baseline weeks are being alternated. Notice the similarity between this logic and that of the PTD. This variant of the ATD is probably one of the least intrusive design alternatives available for single case evaluations.

A second advantage of an ATD is that treatment comparison can usually be made more quickly than in a withdrawal design. A minimally adequate within-series design examining the impact of treatment compared to no treatment requires a relatively stable baseline (using at least three, and usually more, data points), followed by treatment and baseline phases (A/B/A). An ATD can be more efficient because estimates of trend and variability are being taken concurrently, not sequentially.

This rapidity allows an ATD to be used in circumstances that are not well suited to phase-change designs. One such situation occurs when measurement is cumbersome, lengthy, costly, aversive, or necessarily infrequent. For example, suppose a stroke victim is being treated in a physical rehabilitation center. A complete work-up of the patient's physical and muscular functioning may require several hours of careful testing by two or more professionals. Obviously, such a complete work-up cannot be done frequently. Suppose it was possible to do it only once a month. If an A/B/A/B design were being used, and if at least three data points were taken in each phase, it would require 12 months to ask the simplest kind of question (Does treatment work?). With an ATD, the minimum time period would be reduced considerably. Suppose a measure is taken at the very beginning, then after 1 month of treatment, then after 1 month of maintenance, and then after 1 more month of treatment.

Suppose the data shown in Figure 7.5 are the result. In only about one-third the time we could begin to assess whether treatment was effective. This is because the entire data set provides some estimate of the degree of measurement error and extraneous variability. With only two data points in each series, we cannot distinguish variability from trend. In an ATD, however, assessment of variability is

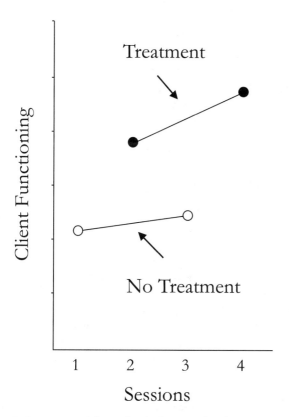

FIGURE 7.5 **A hypothetical example of an ATD when measures are extremely infrequent.**

drawn in part from all of the data, not just those with a single series. Thus, a pattern such as that shown in Figure 7.5 could be caused by variability only if it were very large and happened to coincide perfectly with treatment alternation. With such a small number of data points, this is not a completely unreasonable possibility, but the data might still be reasonably convincing, particularly if the measures used are known not to vary readily.

There is another advantage of the rapid conclusions possible with an ATD: It can be used in a single therapy session. Few other designs allow this. For example, one of our students told a client in desensitization to occasionally prepare for some of the scenes by repeating a comforting statement to herself. When it was pointed out that this accidental alternation allowed a test of the role of cognitive coping on rapidity of progress, the anxiety data for each scene were reexamined. During the first treatment session, anxiety was much lower following the coping statement, an effect that was then deliberately replicated in several subsequent sessions (Hayes et al., 1983). The point of this is that conclusions were possible in a single therapy session. There are some situations, such as in crisis intervention, where this may be a distinct advantage. This example also illustrates how ATDs emerge naturally in clinical practice.

Another advantage of the ATD is the possibility of proceeding without a formal baseline phase. Problems with unstable or improving baselines, for example, can be assessed using an ATD because the design is relatively insensitive to background trends. Suppose, for example, that we are examining a behavior that is continuously changing, perhaps due to maturation. In such a situation, all conditions are likely to be associated with improvement. In a phase-change design this presents special problems because trends are measured in blocks of time (phases) and then compared to those blocks before and after. This is an inherently crude comparison, and treatments must be quite effective to show improvement beyond an already improving baseline. In an ATD, consistent increases in improvement will be easily noticeable, even against the background of a constantly changing baseline.

Perhaps for this reason the ATD is one of the most popular methods of time-series analysis in educational contexts (e.g., Rousseau, Tam, & Ramnarain, 1993; Van Houten, 1993), where rising baselines and background trends are common. Many other behaviors (e.g., physical abilities) do tend to show continuous transition, and the ATD is particularly useful for their analysis.

The top of Figure 7.6 presents a hypothetical example in which every data point represents an improvement over the previous one. Despite the very strong trend in both, the superiority of B over A is notable and reliable.

Note, however, that a strong background trend in an ATD means that the various series will not be very far apart visually. It is not possible to draw two lines in which every data point represents an improvement over the previous one using raw scores without drawing the lines close to each other, regardless of the units along the ordinate or the rate of improvement shown. This is a problem only because it takes experience with ATD results to learn when effects are large or small; the immediate impression is not necessarily a good guide.

There are ways to focus the data presentation on the most relevant variables if there are strong background trends. If we plot each data point for the data shown

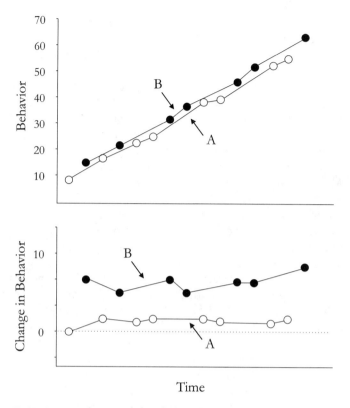

FIGURE 7.6   An example of ATD data in which each data point improves on the preceding one. The raw scores are shown in the top graph. Regardless of the ordinate values or rate of improvement, such situations will pull the curves close together, even if the rate of improvement is much greater in one series. The bottom graph shows the same data graphed as improvement. Here larger ordinate spacing will readily show the magnitude of the difference.

in the top of Figure 7.6 as a difference score from the previous data point, the graph at the bottom of Figure 7.6 results. This graph is more dramatic to untrained eyes, even though it is merely a representation of the data in the top of the figure. Graphical displays should be selected to focus attention on the important aspect of the data.

Considerations in the Use of an ATD

Several issues must be considered before using an ATD. Some of the more important dimensions are the following:

Should There Be an Attempt to Use Discriminative Stimuli?   Distinct discriminative stimuli associated with each of the alternating conditions are not required in an ATD (somewhat like a mixed schedule in the operant literature, Reynolds, 1968). In most situations, such stimuli are difficult if not impossible to avoid, because the differences between treatment conditions are obvious in most forms of intervention. There are times when a discriminative stimulus should and can be avoided, however. For example, ATDs have been used successfully to compare active drugs to placebos (e.g., Silverstein & Allison, 1994) and in such an instance it is important that the placebos appear to be identical. The logic of the design will still allow the comparison between each data series to be made, since reliable differences can be produced by the impact of treatment.

Even though discriminative stimuli are not required in an ATD, they are often quite useful. Multiple treatment interference in ATDs is increased by the lack of discriminability between treatment conditions, especially if one intervention switches over immediately to another (McGonigle et al., 1987). As a result, some researchers (especially those working with the developmentally disabled, for whom discriminability may be more of an issue) have been careful to assign a readily identifiable signal to each treatment so that the client can easily discriminate which treatment condition is in effect (e.g., Jordan et al., 1989). One advantage of clear cues is that, after experience with the cues and the conditions they signal, clients may begin to react in part to the cues themselves, thus tending to pull apart the data for each condition. This is why conditional cues are so popular in animal work, where the consistent reactions that result are analytically useful. Through the use of cues, even treatments that are topographically very similar can be compared. Simply describing the treatment in effect might be a good way to signal changing conditions, particularly since someone would most likely describe these conditions in the normal use of this procedure in the natural environment.

If the alternation of conditions is also associated with the alternation of stimuli, then additional considerations emerge. Take, for example, our earlier illustration of the lean forward and be warm versus lean back and be cool case study. It could be that the client's responses would be controlled not by the therapist's responses (warm versus cool) but by the therapist posture itself, independent of its association with therapist reactions. This is entirely plausible. It may be harder to self-disclose to a person leaning back from you, regardless of how the person then responds.

In such situations, the potential effect of the stimuli per se should be controlled. One way to do this is to reverse the association between the stimuli and treatment, either with another client or with the original client in a subsequent phase. The stimuli should be counterbalanced. For example, the clinician could lean back and be warm. If the client then gradually starts to self-disclose more when the therapist leans back, the suspected impact of the therapist affect will be confirmed. The use of this control was shown earlier in the example of the claustrophobic praised for approach (Agras et al., 1969). Because the differences could have been due to therapist effects, and not to praise per se, the conditions were reversed twice during the course of therapy (see Figure 7.3).

This control is necessary only when the signaling or discriminative stimuli arbitrarily related to what is thought to be the active elements of treatment could reasonably have an impact on their own. If they are not arbitrary, such a control is not needed or possible. For example, suppose two verbal psychotherapies are compared. The nature of the verbal interchange may be a stimulus, but it is impossible to reverse it because the stimulus necessarily is part of the intervention. Similarly, if the stimuli are very unlikely to affect outcome, it is not essential to counterbalance them. For example, if colored lights were used to signal an intervention, such control may be unnecessary (although perhaps still desirable) if lights per se are unlikely to influence the behavior of interest.

It is probably likely that the clinician will at least consider counterbalancing when it is most needed. This is true because the use of signals usually requires some deliberate planning. Counterbalancing usually occurs after a clear difference between treatments has emerged, since this is a control condition. There is usually no reason to control for possible interpretations of a treatment effect until such an effect occurs. The exception are those cases in which the stimuli associated with treatment are known to be impactful. For example, if multiple therapists are used and therapist effects are likely, then therapists could be randomized across interventions from the very beginning, rather than associated with a given treatment and then counterbalanced. If the treatment impact is strong, this alternative may be useful because it could shorten the analysis.

How Many Alternations Are Needed?   The minimum number of alternations is two, but a larger number is highly desirable. The more frequent the alternations, the more opportunities there are for the series to diverge or overlap. Since the fundamental comparison in an ATD is the degree of divergence and overlap between the series, increasing these opportunities increases the precision of the analysis.

The frequency of alternation is limited by several factors. First, alternation can occur no more often than the meaningful unit of measurement. The word *meaningful* is meant to convey the importance of temporal measurement units that are appropriate to the task. (You may recall the discussion of this issue as it related to intrasubject averaging in Chapter 5.) For example, if the nature of the behavior is such that it is most meaningful when viewed as a weekly average, then weekly alternations are the most rapid that could be done. It would be foolish to present the data in, say, daily units, just so that more rapid alternation is possible. The measurement frequency should be dictated by the nature of the behavior, not the design.

A second limitation on alternation frequency is that alternation should occur less frequently if treatment is inherently long lasting. Some treatments are known to have effects that linger for considerable periods of time (e.g., drugs with long half-lives). If they are analyzed with an ATD, the frequency of measurement and alternation should be adjusted to fit appropriate time frames. For example, suppose an active drug with a long half-life and a placebo were compared using very rapid alternation. The two data series would be virtually certain to be similar since the drug would be present at high levels in both cases.

No threat to internal validity is caused by this process. If alternation is too rapid for the treatment at hand, it will decrease the likelihood of detecting an effect. Any clear differences actually found are unaffected.

The "rapidity" of alternation in an ATD is relative to the behavior and its proper unit of measurement, not to real time. In Chapter 5 we suggested that a meaningful unit of measurement is the smallest temporal unit in which a change of importance to treatment could be detected. If for a given behavior the minimal time to show an initial effect is 1 month, then conditions should alternate no more often than 1 month. In this context, monthly alternation would be, by definition, rapid.

How Should Treatments Be Alternated?   Knowing how treatments should be alternated requires an understanding of threats to the validity of an ATD or of the ability of the ATD to answer the question being asked. Foremost among the questions is the magnitude of multiple-treatment interference existing in the ATD.

Multiple-treatment interference (Campbell & Stanley, 1963) or condition-change interactions (Ulman & Sulzer-Azaroff, 1975) pose the question: Will the results of Treatment B in an ATD where it is alternated with Treatment C be the same as when Treatment B is applied in isolation?

Applied research and clinical practice more generally are fraught with treatment interference in the usual sense of interactions with extraneous factors. Our clients are experiencing a variety of events before and between treatment interventions. One client may have recently lost a family member, another flunked an exam, a third had sexual intercourse, and a fourth been threatened on the way to a session. It is quite possible that clients exposed to these different situations will respond differently to treatment than otherwise would have been the case. Putting aside measurement error, such extraneous factors are responsible for the intersubject variability seen in comparing two treatments.

ATDs attempt to control for extraneous factors by dividing each subject in two and administering two or more treatments within approximately the same period of time. The results may be affected by interaction with events occurring in the environment, but these are fairly well controlled.

The special problem posed by the ATD is the degree to which one experimental treatment impacts on another. There are three concerns: sequential confounding, carryover effects, and an alternation effect (Barlow & Hayes, 1979; Ulman & Sulzer-Azaroff, 1975).

Sequential confounding refers to the fact that Treatment C may be different following Treatment B. In an A/B/A/C/A design, for example, we do not trust the comparison of B and C because any differences may be due to order effects. It may not really be B versus C, it may be first versus second. This is why an A/B/A/C/A must be coupled with an A/C/A/B/A, to control for order.

The solution proposed for this in an ATD is random or semirandom sequencing. If many alternations are possible, and the results are consistent throughout the two series, it becomes extremely unlikely that a particular sequence could be responsible for the differences. Consider the following sequence: BCCBCBBCBCBBBCCBCCBCCCB. If the beginning and later sections of the two series continue to show consistent differences, despite random sequencing, order effects are unlikely to be responsible. If they are, however, the data will not replicate, and we will know soon enough.

Carryover or *contextual effects* refer to the influence of one treatment on an adjacent treatment, irrespective of overall sequencing. The presence of treatments in close temporal proximity may lead to contrast (the effects of the two treatments pull apart because of their close proximity) and induction (the effects of the two treatments become more similar because of their close proximity) (Reynolds, 1968; Ulman & Sulzer-Azaroff, 1975).

For example, a mild punisher may be effective when applied alone. When even stronger punishers are also used, however, the greater suppression in the strong punishment condition may be associated with a loss of suppression in the mild condition.

There are several ways to reduce carryover effects. Random sequencing of conditions helps control for some simple kinds of carryover. Suppose we were to claim that Treatment B will always act to increase the behavior shown in the following period. Since both B and C will be next about as often, this will tend to distribute the carryover effects and still allow a reliable comparison of the two treatments.

The use of shorter treatment periods and longer separation between treatment sessions are also valuable. Strong multiple-treatment interference is usually shown when the separation between sessions is minimal.

There are several reasons why carryover may not present a major problem in most applied situations. First, within the normal range of treatment alternation there apparently are no examples of contrast reversing the relative positions of two treatments. It is the absolute value of the impact of treatment that varies or the degree of difference between two treatments. For example, suppose Treatment B leads to better performance than Treatment C. In an ATD, B may be even better and C even worse than usual, but carryover has not yet been shown to make C better than B (although with extremely rapid alternation such an outcome could theoretically occur).

Within limits, this property of contrast permits an ATD to be used as a kind of methodological magnifying glass. A magnifying glass distorts the world, but it does so in order to help us to see the world. The differences seen are real differences, though they may appear larger than they "really are." Clear differences seen in a properly controlled ATD are real differences. As long as we remember that a between-series design asks about differences between series and not about the nature of the individual series itself, our conclusions will not be jeopardized.

Alternation effects are a subset of carryover effects in which the schedule of alternation itself produces and impact: In essence the design becomes an independent variable. In rare instances, the contrast effect produced by rapid alternation has been used as a mode of clinical intervention. For example, rapidly alternating the targets of sexual fantasy has been used to help clarify a sexually confused patient's arousal preferences (Leonard & Hayes, 1983).

It is possible to assess directly the extent to which such carryover effects are present. Sidman (1960) suggests two methods. One is termed *independent verification,* which essentially entails conducting a controlled experiment in which one or the other of the component treatments in the ATD is administered independently.

For example, two treatments might be compared through an ATD in a direct replication across three subjects. Three more subjects might then receive baseline, followed by Treatment B, in an A/B fashion. The second treatment could be administered to a third trio of subjects in the same manner. Any differences that occur between the treatment administered in an ATD or independently could be due to carryover effects. Alternatively, these subjects could receive Treatment B alone, followed by an ATD alternating Treatments B and C, returning to Treatment B alone. Three additional subjects could receive Treatment C in the same manner. Trends and levels of behavior during either treatment alone versus the same treatment in the ATD could be compared.

A more elegant method is termed *functional manipulation* by Sidman (1960). In this procedure, the strength or intensity of one of the components is changed. For example, if one is comparing extended exposure and a gradual, structured approach to a feared object, the amount of exposure could be doubled at one point. Changes in fear behavior occurring during the second unchanged treatment (structured approach) could be attributed to carryover effects.

Some uses of an ATD as part of a larger structured design automatically provide an assessment of carryover. Wacker, McMahon, Steege, Berg, Sasso, and Melloy (1990) suggest what they termed a "sequential alternating treatments design." In this approach, two treatments alternate, but in different contexts, behaviors, or people. After an apparent difference is shown, one treatment is applied to both series, followed by the other treatment. Extensions of this approach have been recommended for the analysis of sequential clinical cases (Houlihan, Jones, Sloane, & Cook, 1992).

Alternation Recommendations   The bottom line of this discussion is that it is desirable to alternate randomly or semirandomly and to keep a careful eye on possible carryover effects. If they are likely to be present and are thought to be a problem, alternation might be slowed somewhat and treatments separated into distinct sessions.

At times, even random alternation will by chance lead to short phases of three more sessions of the same type in a sequence. If the number of possible alternations is very high, this may not be a problem. In many applied situations, however, the practitioner does not have unlimited possibilities to alternate conditions. Since the comparisons are made between series, phases of the same treatment are to be avoided. The solution is to put an upper limit on the number of possible sequential treatment sessions of the same type. For example, the treatments could be alternated randomly (say, by the flip of a coin) but with no more than three of the same type in a row. This semirandom method of treatment assignment complicates (but does not eliminate) the applicability of randomization tests in the statistical analysis of ATD results, however.

Natural Alternation   There are times when treatment alternation occurs naturally. Two examples were given earlier: the alternation in coping instructions in a desensitization paradigm, and the lean-forward-lean-back case. The problem with natural alternation is that it is particularly likely to be influenced by events that will also influence the behavior of interest. For example, the therapist may be leaning back and reacting coolly because of the content of the client's speech, not vice versa.

The same issue was raised earlier with regard to within-series designs. Natural alternation is useful, but practitioners should state the reasons for the alternation, if known, and should interpret the results very cautiously. Even better, a period of deliberate alternation should be included. If both the natural and deliberate alternation lead to the same outcome, the results are considerably strengthened.

One form of natural alternation is practically ubiquitous in situations in which treatment is confined to short periods (e.g., therapy sessions), and measurement occurs more often. For example, suppose a client is receiving outpatient therapy in 1-hour-per-week sessions. Suppose further that measures are taken immediately before and after the treatment session. The pre- and post-session data could be separated into two series, and treated as an ATD. In some situations, this pre–post version of an ATD may provide meaningful data. For example, exposure-based treatments with phobic clients often produce fairly large gains immediately after a treatment session. If a client had repeatedly improved from pre-session to post-session, and if the gains were stable, a pattern like that shown in the top of Figure 7.5 would be seen, where A is the pre- and B the post-measure (see Thyer & Curtis, 1982).

A modification of this approach is possible if measures are more frequent. Suppose there are meaningful daily measures in the same situation, for example. The week could be divided into the half-week period immediately after and immediately before therapy. Measures collected during these two periods could be gathered into two series and compared.

The weakness of these approaches is that alternation is not random and correlation with extraneous variables is possible. For instance, it is possible that deficits in performance immediately before treatment are due to the impending session; improvement afterward may be due to elation over the fact that therapy is concluded for another week. This weakness can be mitigated somewhat if the timing of therapy is randomized. The reader might recognize the logic of this as essentially the same as a PTD (see Chapter 6) but cast in ATD form. Despite the difficulties, a pre–post ATD can provide meaningful data particularly as a form of accountability in applied settings.

Is a Baseline Needed?   A baseline is not required by an ATD, but it can be quite useful. All baselines allow both a description of client functioning and a prediction about future course. If an ATD is done comparing two treatments (after a baseline), this will allow some assessment of the impact of treatment per se (essentially an A/B design), as well as of the differential treatment effects (from the ATD phase). If baseline can also be continued in the ATD phase, an elegant comparison is possible. Any sources of influence that might have coincided with the ATD phase can be ruled out as the cause of improvement during treatment.

An alternative is to withdraw treatment after the ATD phase, or to multiple-baseline the ATD phase. These combinations build upon the logical structure of these other design units and do not need a special analysis.

How Many Series Can Be Compared?   An ATD weakens as the number of series increases, because the time between the same intervention increases, the number of trials of a given intervention decreases, and sources of multiple-treatment interference increase. This makes it less likely that a result will be found, but it does not jeopardize any clear results that are seen.

One way to arrive at an upper limit is to consider the number of data points that are likely to be collected before termination and then decide (based on knowledge about the stability of the behavior and the likely magnitude of effect) how many data points would be needed at a minimum in each series. Two is the absolute lowest value, but four or more are more common. Then divide the second number into the first. That will give the upper bounds on the possible number of different series. An example of an ATD with four data series will be shown later. There are many examples in the literature of comparisons between four or even five data series, although the precision of the design is often harmed if the differences are not large in these cases. In most routine situations, three should probably be treated as a likely upper limit.

How Much Overlap Is Acceptable?   In evaluating the ATD (or STD for that matter, see below), the degree of divergence and overlap between the series is the data of interest. No clear standards have emerged in evaluating between-series results beyond the guidance produced by statistical inferential tools (discussed later). If there is no overlap between the series, and several data points are in each series, then few would doubt the effect. If there is overlap, the issue becomes more complex.

First, is the percentage of overlap small relative to the number of data points? If it is small (say 10–20%), then the differences are more likely to be real. This is particularly so if the number of data points is large, if the magnitude of the divergence is large, and if the magnitude (as well as percentage) of overlap is small. Second, is the behavior known to be fairly stable? If so, the results will probably be more reliable. If the behavior is extremely variable, chance alone can produce divergent series, especially if the number of alternations is small. Third, is there a trend in divergence and convergence? If there are additional design tools they may help interpret the finding.

An example is shown in Figure 7.7. These are the data from an airplane-phobic client in the study mentioned earlier on the effect of cognitive coping on progress in desensitization (Hayes et al., 1983). Notice that there is a clear convergence as the two series progress. The orderliness of the data suggested that the results from the cognitive coping were generalizing to the untreated scenes. Alternating a reminder *not* to use the coping statements with the usual statements then tested this possibility. The data once again diverged. When the original conditions were then reinstated the data converged once more. This shows that the conver-

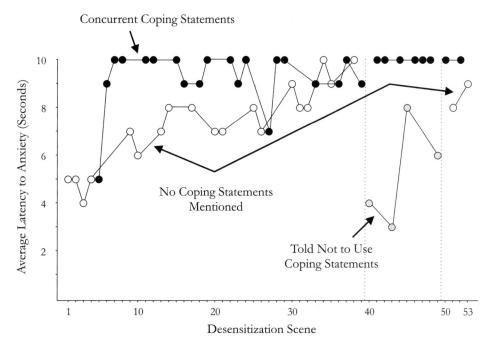

FIGURE 7.7   An example of series convergence in an ATD. The treatment generalized during the ATD to the untreated series, as was shown when the possible generalization was deliberately disrupted in a subsequent phase change (redrawn from Hayes et al., 1985).

gence was a form of systematic generalization, rather that a lack of difference between the two conditions. Parenthetically, this is also a good example of the combination of design elements to answer specific questions. This particular design does not even have a name, but it is a logical extension of design tools we have already discussed.

Providing a Rationale   The use of an ATD in actual clinical practice may at first seem cumbersome. In fact, it is not. Some practitioners worry that clients will think it is odd or arbitrary to alternate treatment rapidly. Usually, the truth works as a beautifully effective rationale. For example, suppose an anxious and socially withdrawn client were to be treated with exposure and social skills training. This client might be told:

> Well, it appears as though there are two aspects to your problem. On the one hand, you are having quite a hard time facing feared situations. On the other hand, you also seem to need to take better control of your relationships with others. Rather than work on only one aspect of your problem, I think we should work on both fronts. I've found it to be quite helpful with others in the past. I think we need to work on both managing and facing your fear and learning to be more assertive.

What I'd like to propose is that we concentrate sometimes on anxiety management and sometimes on learning new skills. I'm not sure which will be most helpful, and in this way we'll cover all the bases. If, later on, it appears that one approach is better than another is, we could then concentrate on that.

Naturally, a real rationale would be subtler, but this gives the basic idea. Clients are usually very receptive to such an approach if the clinician is convinced of the value of it.

Often no need for a special rationale exists because clients will not notice the ATD. Clients do not necessarily expect consistent therapy sessions. For example, if the clinician wants to compare two treatments, usually it is because both seem relevant. If it seems that way to the practitioner, it may also seem that way to the client.

Unusual Types of ATDs

ATDs across Behaviors or Settings   An unusual form of the ATD can be used to document the effect of a single treatment if it can be applied to several problem behaviors or to behaviors in several problem situations, or combinations of both. For example, suppose a client has spasticity in both an arm and a leg and each seems amenable to treatment by EMG biofeedback. The biofeedback treatment could be applied randomly to each area in turn. Separate measures could be taken on each bodily measure. This creates, in effect, a separate ATD for each measure as the treatment is alternated between the arm and leg.

Figure 7.8 shows an example of what might result. The top graph is a kind of ATD in which treatment of the arm is alternated with a placebo (treatment of the leg), while the reverse is true of the lower graph.

There are several possible advantages in this use of the ATD. It evaluates the effect of treatment without any withdrawal, yet allows fairly strong statements about the effects of treatment. This is permitted because the specific effects allow intervention with one behavior to be a kind of baseline (or placebo) for another. Another advantage of this design is that it does not require that the behaviors be completely independent. To the extent that they are not independent, the series will draw closer together, but as long as there is consistent differential effectiveness, the series will diverge. This is the same point made earlier about the relatively robust nature of an ATD when background trends exist. The one requirement of this use of the ATD is that it must not be likely that treatment of one behavior makes the other worse. In that case, iatrogenic effects could mimic treatment effects. Wacker et al. (1990) have provided several additional examples of the use of this approach.

The Use of an ATD as an Idiographic Assessment Procedure   The rapidity of conclusions possible with an ATD offers another interesting use of the design—as an assessment procedure. In many areas, practitioners are told to distinguish between closely related types of problems, or clients, and to apply different treatments to each. For example, a person with a social skills problem might be thought

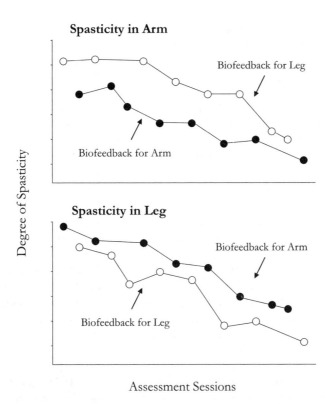

FIGURE 7.8   A hypothetical example of an ATD across behaviors.

to be suffering from excess anxiety (requiring anxiety-relief procedures), or deficit skills (requiring direct skill training). Similarly, a depressed person might be too withdrawn, think irrationally, and have learned to use mood as a method of social control of others. These kinds of assessment distinctions are notoriously difficult to make, and often they are merely logically (not empirically) based (Hayes, Nelson, & Jarrett, 1987). The empirical clinician can use an ATD to make these decisions in a way that not only is empirical, but is individually tailored to the client.

For example, McKnight, Nelson, Hayes, and Jarrett (1984) rapidly alternated cognitive therapy and social skills therapy for a group of depressed clients. Importantly, those who improved best following a specific treatment in the early part of therapy continued to do so throughout. This means that a clinician could conduct an ATD for a short time, determine the best treatment, and then throw all treatment resources into this condition. This basic strategy has been described by earlier researchers (e.g., Kazdin, 1982; Kazdin & Hartmann, 1978).

Sometimes ATDs are used in an initial analog assessment phase that allows a functional analysis of the problem. Treatment that is linked to this analysis is then evaluated using other means. A study by Steege, Wacker, Cigrand, Berg, Novak, Reimers, Sasso, and DeRaad (1990) provides an example. The self-injurious behavior

(SIB) of two severely multiply handicapped children was examined. SIB has been shown to be controlled by different variables in different individuals, including social attention, sensory stimulation, and escape from demands, or combinations of these (Iwata, Dorsey, Slifer, Bauman, & Richman, 1982). The treatment implications vary widely for the different causes of this disturbing and dangerous behavior. For example, if the behavior is maintained by sensory stimulation, removal of this stimulation or the establishment of more appropriate methods of producing such stimulation might be effective. Conversely, if the behavior is maintained by escape from task demands, teaching tolerance for the task and more appropriate methods of regulating social demands might be tried. Thus, it is important to know why SIB is occurring before attempting to treat it.

Steege et al. (1990) exposed their clients to several conditions in separate 10-minutes sessions each day for several days: being alone in a classroom (making sensory stimulation for SIB freely available), social attention contingent upon SIB, reinforcement of appropriate behavior, and making task demands with a brief break contingent upon SIB. The data for one of the children is shown in the upper half of Figure 7.9. After an initial period, SIB was far higher under the task demand conditions than under the others, suggesting that the behavior was maintained by the negative reinforcement of task withdrawal when SIB occurred. Based on this interpretation, a treatment was designed in which task demands were delayed briefly only when the child pushed a button that played the message "stop." Conversely, SIB lead not to withdrawal of task demands but to guided physical compliance with the task. This treatment was evaluated using a within-series design, as is shown in the lower half of Figure 7.9. The assessment results were clearly confirmed.

A similar approach can be followed in an integrated time-series design, using different types of treatment during the ATD (which may be proceeded by a baseline phase if desired), and then throwing all treatment resources into the most successful condition. This basic strategy was described by earlier researchers (e.g., Kazdin, 1982; Kazdin & Hartmann, 1978), and has been used frequently in the applied literature. In this design, the baseline allows a statement of the problem, the ATD allows an individual assessment of which treatment is most likely to work, and the final phases allow a check on whether the treatment is, in fact, associated with further improvement. This approach has become very popular in the developmental disabilities literature because a common method of functional analysis uses the approach (Iwata et al., 1982). Clients are first brought into a laboratory setting, and several different contingencies are compared using an ATD (in this wing of the literature, for historical reasons, the term "multi-element design" seems particularly common as a way of describing the ATD phase). This experimental analysis is then tied to a treatment strategy that is implemented in the natural environment.

The Assessment of Natural Stimuli

The ATD can be used to assess the effects of different stimulus conditions that are components of other tasks. A somewhat whimsical example is a study examining whether baseball batters can hit balls with more visible seams (Osborne, Rudrud,

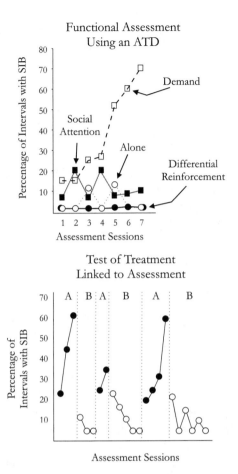

FIGURE 7.9   An example of the use of an ATD as an assessment device. The behavior was functionally analyzed in the top graph, and a treatment based on this analysis was implemented in a simple phase change in the bottom graph (redrawn from Steege et al., 1990).

& Zezoney, 1990; by the way, they can). Many research situations include stimuli that themselves could influence performance (the room, the clothing of laboratory assistants, and so on). Clinical situations include similar factors (e.g., the therapist, the therapeutic setting). The ATD allows an extremely rapid assessment of the effects of such variables.

Van Houten, Van Houten, and Malenfant (1994) provide a more clinical example of this same use of the design. In their study, the alcohol consumption of patrons in a bar was examined when drinks were made with the normal amount of alcohol, or with half that amount. Over several sessions both were compared using an ATD. Even though drinks were freely available, all subjects consumed less alcohol when drinks were "weak," compared to when they were "strong." This suggests that limits on the amount of alcohol in drinks may be an effective way to reduce the known risks associated with alcohol consumption.

The Statistical Analysis of the ATD

The ATD is one of the few single case designs with well-developed and readily applicable inferential statistics (Onghena & Edgington, 1994). The major requirement for use of the test (called a randomization test) is the random assignment of conditions to occasions. A number of software packages are available for calculation of the test (Onghena & Edgington, 1994), and the use of this test seems to be noncontroversial among statisticians. One complicating factor is that the test is most easily used when alternation is truly random. Limiting the number of times that a condition can be in force consecutively makes the test much more complicated or can even make it inapplicable.

The Simultaneous-Treatment Design

The only other true between-series design element is the simultaneous-treatment design (Browning, 1967). The STD is a more generic term for a *concurrent schedule* (Reynolds, 1968). The implication that a distinct schedule of reinforcement is attached to each "treatment" produces the same unnecessary narrowness as the mixed or multiple schedule does for an ATD. Browning's (1967) term, simultaneous-treatment design, seems more descriptive and suitable. Both terms adequately describe the fundamental characteristic of this design—the concurrent or simultaneous application of two or more treatments in a single case. This contrasts with the fast alternation of two or more treatments in the ATD.

One of the best examples of an STD continues to be Browning's original study (1967). Browning first obtained a baseline on the number of incidences of grandiose bragging in a 9-year-old emotionally disturbed boy. Six staff members who worked in the boy's residential cottage participated in the simultaneous application of three treatments: (a) positive interest and praise contingent on bragging, (b) contingent verbal admonishment, and (c) ignoring. At any one time, two of the staff were assigned to each condition. The boy was free to approach any of the staff members. What is of interest here is how much time the boy spent with staff members who were responding in a given way. To control for possible differential effects with individual staff, each team administered each treatment for one week in a counterbalanced order. For example, the second group of two therapists admonished the first week, ignored the second week, and praised the third week. The idea is that the boy "would seek out and brag to the most reinforcing staff and shift to different staff on successive weeks as they switched to S's preferred reinforcement contingency" (Browning, 1967, p. 241).

The data from Browning's subject (see Figure 7.10) indicate a preference for verbal admonishment, as indicated by frequency and duration of bragging and a

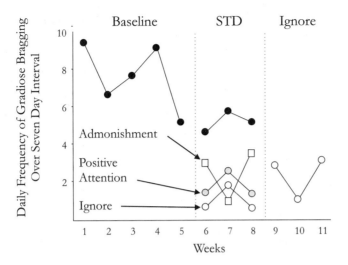

FIGURE 7.10 An example of a simultaneous treatment design as an assessment device. The behavior was functionally analyzed in the STD phase, and the most effective treatment was applied in the final treatment phase (redrawn from Browning, 1967).

lack of preference for ignoring. Thus, ignoring became the treatment of choice and was continued by all staff. There may be instances, however, when preference for a treatment may have little relation to its effectiveness.

In an STD, then, the treatments are available simultaneously. The subject chooses which one is applied. It is unlikely that the client will be equally exposed to each treatment. The very structure of an STD ensures that the client will not be equally exposed to all treatments except in the event that the two treatments are equally preferred.

Because of this limited focus, an STD is not designed for the general evaluation of treatment outcome. Rather, it is useful in the assessment of preference, be it for identification of meaningful consequences, assessing clinical behavior, or identifying treatment preferences.

Many current issues in clinical science are issues of preference, however, and an STD may be useful in addressing them. For example, a clinician working with a child may use an STD to determine which consequences are most preferred. This consequence could then be used as part of a treatment program. Basic questions about the nature of consequence, or about side effects produced by them have been asked using an STD (e.g., Mace, McCurdy, & Quigley, 1990).

An interesting applied example of an STD, combined with other elements, is shown in a study by Carter, Kindstedt, and Melin (1995). They examined the effect of several popular sales promotion activities on both thefts and sales of grocery store items. Groups of several products with roughly equivalent sales and thefts were monitored twice weekly. After a baseline, two promotion approaches—a 10% price reduction (with red sales tags) and increased exposure (produced by shelf placement)—were randomly assigned to groups of items and compared to the normal sales conditions. After a few weeks, baseline was reinstituted for all items.

This design is an STD, sandwiched in between baseline phases. The design is an STD because all conditions are continuously available during the intervention phase, and the measure is of consumer choices (to buy and to steal). By adding baseline phases, initial item preferences are controlled.

For the sake of simplicity of presentation, the data for only the combined and control conditions are shown in Figure 7.11, but in fact the study included data for each of the individual sales promotion conditions as well (price reduction and increased exposure). Thus, four conditions were simultaneously compared, and the logic of this study could have included several other intervention conditions without difficulty.

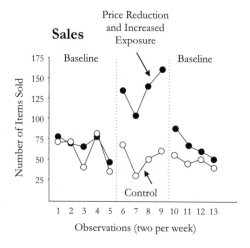

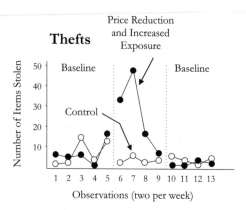

FIGURE 7.11   An applied example of an STD. The effects of popular sales promotions methods on sales and thefts in a grocery store were examined (redrawn from Carter, Kindstedt, & Melin, 1995).

The combined condition almost doubled sales, as is shown in the top half of Figure 7.11. Unfortunately, these commonly used promotional procedures increased thefts even more: In week seven, thefts almost reached 50% of sales for the items in the combined intervention group (see bottom half of Figure 7.11). This carefully controlled use of the STD shows how it can measure choice behavior, and how it can be combined with other design elements. The STD is a design element with much wider applicability than it has yet obtained in the applied environment.

8 Combined-Series Elements and the Integrated Use of Research Tools

Introduction

There are several design strategies that combine both between-series and within-series elements into a logically distinct and coordinated whole. These are what we term *combined-series elements*. Combined-series elements are not just the logically consistent combination of design elements in which each element stands as an independent unit. Combinations of this sort are very important, but they require no special categorization or nomenclature. We will address these at the end of the chapter. Conversely, true combined-series design elements result in unique logic characteristics that go well beyond the characteristics of the individual components. It is these new elements that we will address in the beginning of this chapter.

The Multiple Baseline

The most common combined-series design element is the multiple baseline; indeed this design element has become probably the most popular tool in the single case approach generally. The multiple baseline consists of a coordinated series of two or more replicated simple phase changes in several different data series arranged by person, behavior, time period, situation, or any combination of these, in which the phase changes occur at different points in real time and after different first-phase lengths such that behavior changes are generally seen in interrupted series before phase changes are made in uninterrupted series. By arranging for the phase change to occur in this way, several simple phase changes are elevated into a much stronger whole.

The term *multiple baseline* is something of a misnomer, since any specific phase change might be examined in this way, whether or not an actual baseline is involved. The term *multiple phase change* is clearer and more descriptive, but the older term is probably too firmly entrenched to make a change in terminology worth the confusion. The important point to remember is that, despite its name, any series of phase changes can be arranged in this way, whether or not one of the phases is a baseline. For example, several B/C phase changes could easily be collected into a multiple baseline. To make sense of the term, it may help to recall that, in a sense, the first phase in a simple phase change is always a kind of "baseline" for the second phase, whether or not the first phase is a baseline in the sense of "no treatment."

The purpose of a multiple baseline is to control for the principal weaknesses of the simple phase change. In a simple phase change, it is very rare that the change in behavior will be sudden enough or large enough, and that the knowledge about the stability of the behavior will be strong, enough to conclude firmly that any differences seen are due to the phase change and not to measurement error or to extraneous variables. The first phase provides some protection against assessment-related effects (e.g., instrument drift or reactivity) and time-related processes (e.g., maturation), but the protection is by no means complete (see Chapter 6). The multiple baseline strengthens the protections against effects of this kind. The most lethal difficulty with a single, simple phase change is the possibility that some impactful extraneous event may have coincided with the timing of the change in conditions. There is usually no way to rule this out, and it is the main reason that a simple phase change is generally thought to be pre-experimental until it is replicated (e.g., in an A/B/A/B). As noted throughout the book, however, the A/B, or case study, is on a continuum with single case experimental designs and can make a crucial contribution to science.

The multiple baseline is particularly useful in ruling out the threat posed by possible extraneous variables to the internal validity of an effect shown in a simple phase change. It does this, as will be discussed below, by attempting to replicate the phase change in more than one series, and by using each subsequent series as a control condition for the earlier interrupted series.

The different data series can be *any* that are likely to be functionally independent and that are likely also to respond to the same treatment. The different series can be created in different clients, with different behaviors, in different settings, or any combination of these. The specific phase change must, however, be functionally identical in each series. Typically, the same first condition must yield to the same second condition, because it is alternative explanations for a specific phase change effect that are being eliminated by this design element.

The Logic of the Multiple Baseline

An example of a multiple baseline might be as follows: Suppose you were examining the effects of peer mentoring on the math performance of high school sophomores. Rather than implement the program across all the available classes of 10th graders in a given school, you might choose to stagger the implementation in such a way that each of the classes serves as a control for the others. Often this is the most practical for other reasons (e.g., personnel requirements of the program implementation), but it also produces special experimental characteristics.

Suppose that the data shown in Figure 8.1 resulted. As noted earlier, the change seen in the first phase would not normally be particularly convincing (the behavior has a very well known course, giving us strong reason to believe that the trend set in the first phase will always normally continue). By replicating the results in other series the strength of our conviction would increase, but the multiple baseline arranges the replication of phase changes in a unique way so that specific between-series comparisons are possible in addition to the within-series comparisons made in any simple phase change. The data shown in Figure 8.1 are fairly convincing for that reason.

Figure 8.2 shows the sequence of comparisons in a typical three-series multiple baseline, using the same data shown in Figure 8.1. The sequence of the compar-

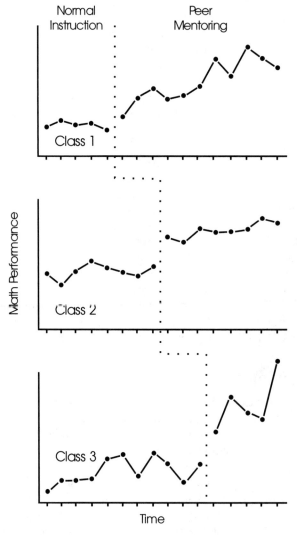

FIGURE 8.1   A hypothetical example of a multiple baseline.

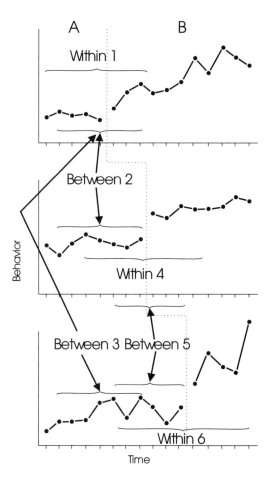

FIGURE 8.2   The within- and between-series comparisons in a multiple baseline, using the hypothetical data from Figure 8.1. The numbers refer to the normal sequence of comparisons. By staggering the phase change after different phase lengths and at different points in real time, several between-series comparisons are possible, which helps control for the weaknesses of a simple phase change.

isons is indicated by the number; the type by the label "within" or "between." The first comparison ("Within 1") is the within-series comparison at the first-phase change. For this comparison, the considerations in determining if an effect may have taken place are identical to those discussed earlier for simple phase changes generally (Chapter 6). In this specific case, the relatively clear change in level and trend, in the context of fairly low variability around level and trend, leads to the conclusion that an effect seems likely. Two additional comparisons can then be made between the first and second, and first and third, series. Since both the second and third series are uninterrupted, they provide a between-series, "baseline-only" control for the effect seen when the first series is interrupted. If the apparent effect seen in the first series ("Within 1") was due to assessment or time-related changes, for example, these changes should have also been seen in the series two and three since they were exposed to just as much assessment over just as long a period of time. But the comparisons "Between 2" and "Between 3" do not support the view that significant changes occurred in the uninterrupted series. The different lengths of the first phase in each series allow a control for some of the threats to the validity of a single, simple phase change.

The next comparison is made at the phase change for series two ("Within 4"). If an effect also occurs here, but not previously in this same series, it provides some control for extraneous events in real time (i.e., a relative moved out, the boss resigned, an illness occurred) that might have produced the effect in the first series. Because of the nature of this control, it is important that the phase change in the second series occur at a different point in real time than the change in the first.

If the data series are being collected simultaneously, then having different first-phase lengths will naturally lead to this. It could be possible, however, to start one series earlier than the other, and ultimately change both series at the same time (but with different lengths of baselines). This is undesirable since it reduces considerably the control provided by the second phase change.

When the second phase change occurs, once again the uninterrupted series is examined for concomitant effects ("Between 5"). This between-series comparison replicates the controls provided by the earlier between-series comparisons ("Between 2" and "Between 3"). Finally, the phase change on the third series ("Within 6") replicates the control provided by the earlier phase changes ("Within 1" and "Within 4"). Thus, a total of six primary comparisons are made in a typical three-series, multiple baseline: three within-series comparisons and three between. If all the results are supportive, as in this case for example, the combination of interlocked comparisons used in a multiple baseline provides strong evidence of an effect, and controls well for the weaknesses in each of the simple phase changes considered separately.

When to Implement a Multiple Baseline

A multiple baseline can be used at any point in a design containing multiple series. It is most common at the beginning of a design, but it could easily be used later. The shaded section of Figure 8.3 provides an example. Treatment was implemented all at once in each series but withdrawn in a multiple baseline fashion. The advantage of this, compared simply to a simple series of A/B/A sequences (see Figure 8.3), is that it (a) provides three additional between-series comparisons (Between 1, Between 2, and Between 3 in the figure), and (b) strengthens the effect of the three withdrawals by "unconfounding" them with events in real time.

Sometimes a multiple-baseline element is repeated in a single design, either to replicate the entire comparison or to conduct another comparison. This strategy is particularly useful when the first comparison raises a question that then can be asked using the second phase as baseline for a third. For example, suppose an

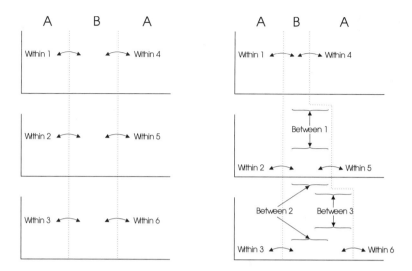

FIGURE 8.3 Demonstration of how a multiple baseline can add to the strength of an analysis regardless of where it occurs. The figure on the left is strong, but the one on the right is even stronger because it adds three between-series comparisons (Between 1–3) to the six within-series comparisons (Within 1–6).

employee exercise program has included feedback about the amount of exercise performed by each shift. This program has been evaluated by implementing the program in a staggered fashion across shifts, and has shown reliable changes in employee fitness. The program manager, however, notes that the employees seem to be claiming that they do more exercise than they really do, apparently in order to make their shift look good. The manager decides to continue the program but now to give feedback to employees about the actual fitness of their shift as measured by cardiovascular measures. In this way, the manager reasons, employee faking or "just going through the motions" will not have any payoff.

This sequence would be described as an A/B + C/B + D, where B is the exercise program, and C and D are the types of feedback given to the shifts. An A/B + C/B + D design is essentially two different, unreplicated phase changes. It is like two separate A/B designs put together, as would be the case with an A/B/C sequence. Such a sequence is usually quite weak, because the effects of C cannot be compared to A in an unambiguous fashion. In addition, any delayed effects of B are confounded with effects of C. By arranging these same three phases in a multiple baseline, however, the weaknesses would be largely resolved.

Figure 8.4 shows the options the manager could use in implementing the third phase. The top of the figure shows one type of sequential multiple baseline. It is useful, but it presents a problem. Note that phase B + D always occurs after a set amount of phase B + C. It is possible that treatment B + C has a delayed effect, such that effects increase after a set amount of time. This is not totally implausible. Many interventions take a period of time really to take hold (or to fall apart). Such effects

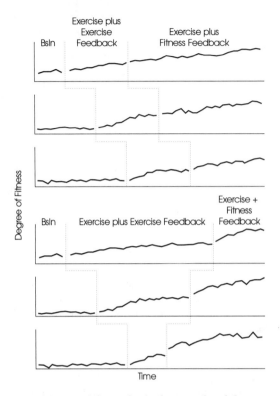

FIGURE 8.4 A hypothetical example of the sequencing of two multiple-baseline elements. The top of the figure presents a problem because the third phase is always implemented after second phases of the same length. The bottom arrangement is stronger and more convincing.

could mimic an effect for fitness feedback (B + D). This would probably be discovered when the order was reversed in another set of subjects (see below), but there is another alternative, shown at the bottom of the figure. Arrangements such as these are stronger because they control for phase length (and events that might correlate with phase length such as maturation) as well as controlling for coincidental events in real time. The overall repeated multiple baseline allows us to conclude that fitness feedback is probably better than exercise feedback in motivating employee health changes.

To strengthen this conclusion, the entire program could be replicated, with the fitness feedback now occurring first, or additional simple phase changes within each shift could confirm the effects. This is needed because the third phase could have an effect due to the fact that it is novel, or follows the second phase.

A multiple-baseline design element is applicable in principle whenever there are several data series that may be independent (we say "may be" because if they are shown not to be, then other design options can be pursued). It is often used when withdrawal of treatment is not possible, or when treatment effects are detectable using a simple phase change but are too slow to analyze readily using withdrawals.

A study by Croce (1990) provides an example. The effects of exercise are often incremental and gradual. Conversely, body weight and fitness are often extraordinarily stable without intervention. The combination of these two factors makes even gradual improvement readily evaluated using a multiple baseline. Croce examined the effects of an aerobic fitness program with three obese retarded adults. The data are shown in Figure 8.5. In this case, the effects of intervention are obvious and persuasive. These same changes may have been more difficult to see in an A/B/A or similar design.

Staggering Phase Changes

If one series has an initial phase that is only slightly shorter than the next, it limits the precision of the between-series comparisons in a multiple baseline. For that reason, fairly large overlaps are desirable. They often emerge naturally in applied work.

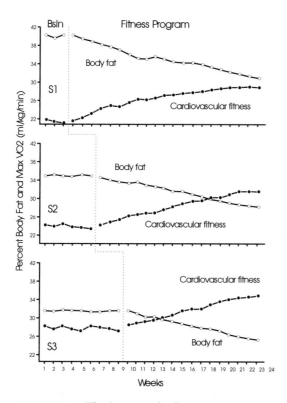

FIGURE 8.5   The impact of a fitness program on the body fat and cardiovascular fitness of three retarded adults (redrawn from Croce, 1990).

The timing of phase shifts is quite important. Recall that the purpose of a multiple baseline is to control for alternative explanations for an effect seen in a simple phase change. If there is no effect, there is no reason to control for these alternative explanations. Thus, the most important rule governing the timing of phase changes is that they should be repeated only when a reasonably clear effect has apparently been shown in the interrupted series. Ideally, the intervention effect with the first series will even have stabilized before the next series is interrupted (Poling & Grossett, 1986), although in the applied setting any clear effect is usually all that is expected.

Consider the data shown in Figure 8.6 as an example of when happens when the second series is interrupted too soon. At first this pattern may look reasonable, but a closer look shows that the effects for the first-phase change have not yet been shown before the phase change on the second series is implemented (cover the last five data points in the first series, and this can be seen clearly). This is a fairly serious flaw in most instances, because we are not then sure if the change in the first

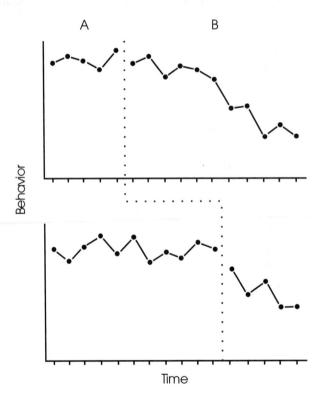

FIGURE 8.6   **An example of improper timing of a phase change in a multiple baseline.** The phase change in the second series occurs before an effect has been shown in the first series. This weakens the analysis considerably because the whole purpose of the between-series comparisons in a multiple baseline is to control for alternative explanations for observed within-series effects (see Figure 8.2).

series was a side effect of whatever caused the change in the second. It is even possible that an extraneous variable produced both changes.

This means that the precise sequencing of phase shifts must not be rigidly planned beforehand. The idealized patterns shown earlier might lead the reader to suppose that a practitioner could carefully lay out the timing of phase shifts before even beginning an evaluation. In fact, the client lays these out by the results shown. In a sense, the client is in charge of the design options; the practitioner is responsible for recognizing them and choosing the best one.

The Number of Series Needed

No absolute rule can be given about the number of phase-shift replications required between series in a multiple-baseline element. The number of baselines used in the literature has varied, from two to up to nine or more (Clark, Boyd, & Macrae, 1975). The logic of the maneuver applies as well to a single replication as to several, however, and it is the logic that defines the design element. Thus, once again we are faced with a continuum in which additional replications strengthen our confidence but no hard and fast line can be drawn between each step. Thus, the clinician should not feel as though the element is useless when only two series are compared, though more are desirable.

If strong results are produced in two series, the phase change has been replicated once, and a single, between-series comparison has provided some control for assessment of time-related effects and coincidental extraneous factors. Other things being equal, an A/B/A might be as powerful, since it too replicates a phase change once. In some ways, however, the multiple baseline may be more powerful, because the phase change is replicated exactly. In an A/B/A, the replication of the A/B phase change is produced by an opposite phase change: B/A. This is often quite reasonable, but at times it is not. For example, if A is baseline and B is a program of reinforcement for performance increases, the second A phase may be thought of as extinction, not just as baseline. A decrease in performance in the second A phase may thus be due to the side effects of withdrawal of reinforcement in the B/A sequence (e.g., behavioral effects may be caused by extinction-elicited aggression or emotional responding), not to the functional equivalence of the A/B and B/A phase changes. The difference is a matter of the functional process involved, not merely the pattern of responses seen, since the side effects of extinction may produce behavioral patterns that mimic a true replication of baseline. By contrast, in a multiple baseline the sequence in each phase change is the same, and thus the replication it provides carries fewer assumptions about the equivalence of the two phase changes. Partly for these reasons, a multiple baseline across three or more series is powerful indeed when properly conducted and when clear patterns are evident.

If several series are compared in the usual way, the design can become too long. This is because the need to wait for clear effects after a phase change extends the first phase in the remaining series that much more. In an applied setting, the extension is especially troublesome if the first phase is truly baseline. Long baselines for purely analytic purposes raise significant ethical problems (e.g., the applied need to begin treatment). There are other problems caused by excessively long phases as well, such as possible rigidity in the client's behavior, morale problems, and the like.

One solution is to shift two or more series at the same time. Suppose nine series were compared, for example. Three phase shifts across groups of three series each would accomplish the multiple baseline more rapidly than nine separate staggered phase changes. This is shown in Figure 8.7. Notice that the top arrangement allows relatively small amounts of overlap. If phase changes are contingent on the behavioral patterns seen, the possibility exists for very long baseline phases indeed. In addition, treatment is in force for only a short time in the last few series.

If many series are compared, the chances of some inconsistency between data series increase accordingly. There are no hard and fast rules about how many in a sequence of data series can fail to show an effect, but in general the practitioner is wise to view the failure to see consistency as an opportunity to analyze its sources. If the failure to replicate can be understood by subsequent analyses, the entire pic-

FIGURE 8.7   An example of alternatives for staggering phase changes when many series exist. Normally the bottom alternative will be more practical.

ture is strengthened. This is particularly elegant if the same principles that explain the effects seen in some series can also explain the sources of a failure to replicate in others. For example, suppose cognitive therapy is used in a multiple baseline with several depressed individuals. Suppose most of the patients show clear effects, but some do not, and further that those who did *not* improve did not practice the skills being taught. This might actually strengthen the conceptual point being made by the multiple baseline (that active participation in cognitive therapy is helpful), especially if other procedures were instituted with treatment failures that lead to better practice and then to improvement in depression. This general analytic strategy is fairly common in studies using multiple baselines (e.g., Chadwick & Lowe, 1990).

Multiple baselines across people are probably particularly prone to the problem of inconsistency of results since the historical determinants of treatment response can vary so widely in these designs. If it is known that multiple variables are involved that make it difficult to predict specific treatment responsiveness, future research can use different design options to explore these idiosyncrasies. For example, some researchers have used a multiple baseline across persons but have implemented multiple treatments using an alternating treatments design to evaluate the effectiveness of several different intervention strategies. This allows idiosyncratic treatment responses that might occur to a single treatment to be seen in the larger context of treatment impact more generally. A study by Stern, Fowler, and Kohler (1988) provides an example of the method. In this study the inappropriate school behavior of two children was reduced by assigning them either the role of a peer monitor, or that of a point earner working with a peer monitor. The positive impact of both roles was clear, as is shown in Figure 8.8. Even if one of the roles were less effective, however, this design would provide meaningful data.

It is not as critical that the second phase of a multiple phase change be of varying lengths. The primary between-series comparisons are between the interrupted and uninterrupted series, not between interrupted and formerly interrupted series (see Figure 8.2). It is more elegant to continue the second phase until all the phase changes have occurred, however, primarily because long second phases provide a useful test of maintenance effects.

Interdependence of Series

Much has been made of the need to avoid the multiple baseline when the specific series are interdependent (e.g., Kazdin & Kopel, 1975). If a phase change in a multiple baseline is accompanied by behavior change not only within series, but also between series, it is difficult to distinguish uncontrolled effects from true treatment effects. Leitenberg made this point some time ago:

> If general effects on multiple behaviors were observed after treatment had been applied to only one, there would be no way to clearly interpret the results. Such results may reflect a specific therapeutic effect and subsequent response generalization, or they may reflect non-specific therapeutic effects having little to do with the specific treatment procedure under investigation. (1973, p. 95)

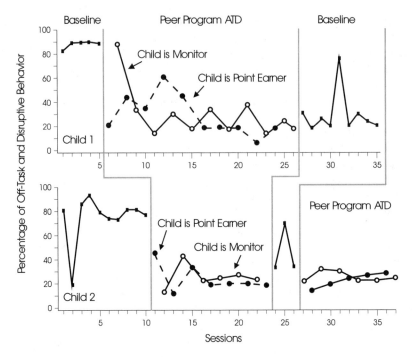

FIGURE 8.8 An example of the use of an alternating treatments component as part of a multiple baseline across persons (redrawn and slightly modified from Stern, Fowler, & Kohler, 1988).

While this argument is sound, possible interdependence of data series is not a problem or weakness of a multiple baseline: rather such interdependence provides analytic opportunities that cannot be pursued without design changes.

Independence of data need not be *assumed* in multiple baselines. Rather it is being *tested*. Often, no clear statement can be made a priori about the independence of data series. Indeed, it is often not desirable that series be independent in an applied sense. Practitioners often hope that changes in one problem area or domain will generalize to other problem areas or domains.

Suppose a clinician is treating a person with multiple phobias. Measures are taken on each, and after a time treatment is begun on one. As it improves, suppose the other phobias also improve. The clinician should immediately abandon the earlier design decision and explore this unexpected but potentially quite exciting finding. One way to do this might be to withdraw treatment for a brief period. If all the phobias then slow their rate of improvement, experimental evidence of a general therapeutic effect would have been obtained. Put another way, lack of independence is not so much a problem as it is an opportunity to study generalization effects.

This opportunity can be pursued only if time-series methodology is viewed in a creative, dynamic way. As we have emphasized repeatedly, the practitioner should never be committed to a specific analytic design. Rather, tentative decisions are made pending the data themselves, and then they are allowed to change as the practical question changes. This is precisely what is advised in good practice more generally.

Some degree of interdependence between series can actually be tolerated in a multiple phase change, particularly if it is not strong or if several series are available (Kazdin, 1980). Suppose, for example, that a strong increase in the treated series is associated with a slight increase in the untreated series. If this untreated series stabilizes and then improves rapidly when specifically treated, few would argue that no effect has been shown. Similarly, if several series show the effect and one or two others show interdependent patterns, usually the most likely conclusion is that the effect is real but that not all the series are independent. If this seems softheaded, consider how unlikely it would be to get strong phase-change effects in several series by chance alone. Usually, this is quite unlikely, thus not every series need show perfect results.

Ineffective Phase Changes

Sometimes an intervention is attempted that shows no effect in the first leg of a multiple baseline. In this situation, two basic alternative strategies are possible. Sometimes it is important to see if an effect will be shown in the remaining series. For instance, a treatment might be thought to be effective for three different types of behaviors. When no effect is shown on one behavior, the practitioner may still believe that the intervention would work with the remaining behaviors. Rather than continue to work on the first behavior, the multiple baseline across behaviors might be extended to the second series. If an effect is shown there, an opportunity is provided to investigate the differential responsiveness of the behaviors.

A more common alternative, discussed in Chapter 6, would be to go on to another condition (e.g., in an A = B/C sequence). This third condition could then be implemented in the other series (e.g., those still in the A phase). If this seems to violate the rule that a multiple baseline must compare the same phase change in each series, recall that an A = B/C is considered functionally equivalent to an A/C. That is, as long as no effect is shown (A = B), we are still thought to be in baseline. This is not necessarily true, but in a sense, this type of multiple baseline tests that assumption since A/C phase changes are implemented on the remaining series. If an A = B/C is not equivalent to an A/C, then the effects should differ. If they do, the option is opened for studying the role of B in the eventual outcome of C.

At times, ineffective phases are expected in a multiple baseline. When it is important to control for possible alternative explanations for a simple phase change, it is sometimes useful to try this condition first in one of the series. The multiple baseline can also incorporate this approach.

Heterogeneity versus Homogeneity of Series

Originally, Baer et al. (1968) suggested that multiple baselines should be done across series of the same type. Thus, a multiple baseline could be done with a similar behavior in two or more clients (across people); with two or more behaviors in one client (across behaviors); or with the same behavior, done by the same person, in two or more time periods or settings (across settings). In addition, Baer et al. argued that all other factors must be held constant. This usually occurs naturally in multiple baselines across behavior and settings, since the same individual is involved (although it would still be possible to mix, say, settings and behaviors), but not in multiple baselines across persons unless the people are in the same settings at the same times and being treated for the same behaviors. Other researchers have also emphasized the need for both the homogeneity and environmental constancy of data series in a multiple baseline (Harris & Jenson, 1985).

The logic of this position is as follows: If the same environmental characteristics are present for several data series, then the uninterrupted series provides an elegant control for the possible role of extraneous variables in the effects seen in the interrupted series. Consider a multiple baseline across several clinical cases. The within-series changes seen when intervention begins in Case 1 are simultaneously compared with changes in the uninterrupted series in Cases 2, 3, and so on. At this point in Case 1, a set of extraneous, nontreatment-related events are always present. If these same extraneous events are also present at the same time in Case 2 and Case 3, and yet performance is stable in these other cases, then these particular events are to some degree ruled out as the source of any change seen at the point of intervention in Case 1.

The logic of the multiple baseline design element, however, does not require this restriction, as we will discuss in the next section on the natural multiple baseline. Any combination of series can be used, as long as the phase change is identical. For instance, a multiple baseline could be implemented across Behavior A in Setting Z, Behavior B in Setting Y, and Behavior C in Setting X. Equally logical, but more unusual, a multiple baseline could be conducted across Behavior C in Person X, Behavior B in Person Y, and Behavior A in Person Z.

The specific series that are selected allow some statements to be made about likely areas of generalization for the effects seen, and thus selection of data series is hardly arbitrary. If several clients with the same disorder were used, and if strong and consistent data were used, it makes it more likely that effects will generalize across people with that behavioral problem. If results are replicated across settings, then results in one setting are more likely to generalize to another for similar clients. Mixing types of series (person, behavior, setting) provides a more ambitious program of the testing of generalization. In other words, some depth is being traded away in exchange for increased breadth. If heterogeneous series are selected with a clear rationale in mind (e.g., if two seemingly different behaviors are examined in several cases because the researcher believes that the behaviors are functionally similar) the results of a multiple baseline using heterogeneous series may carry important conceptual implications for the functional lines of fracture among phenomena.

Whether or not it is wise to examine heterogeneous series depends upon the generality of the rationale for selecting them and the consistency of the results obtained. If the results are highly general, knowledge will probably advance most rapidly with replication across different types of series selected with a coherent rationale in mind. If the results are very specific, tests using the same kinds of series may reduce the likelihood that we will falsely reject effective interventions. In other words, the use of heterogeneous data series increases the risk of a Type II error, in which an effective intervention is falsely viewed as ineffective, but it increases the applied impact of positive results that are found. Type II errors are more likely because it is quite possible to have effective interventions that nevertheless do not generalize across a wide variety of problems, settings, or people. This failure of generalization means that heterogeneous data series are more likely to fail to replicate, and thus lead to the conclusion from a multiple baseline analysis that intervention is ineffective. Homogeneous data series decrease the Type II error risk, provided that the particular phenomenon selected for analysis is a proper target for the intervention at issue.

If treatment effects *do* replicate across heterogeneous series, however, treatment impact has been assessed in a way that provides some test of the external validity or generality of findings. This can be a valuable service since external validity is so important to practitioners. Empirically validated procedures are only useful to practitioners if the applicability of these procedures is known to be high.

Sometimes different series are selected because the research suspects that effects will *not* replicate in the same way. An example is a study by Haring and Kennedy (1990). In this interesting study, two methods of reducing stereotypic behavior (rocking, vocalizing, spitting) in developmentally disabled children were examined in two contexts. The treatments consisted of a time-out period and the differential reinforcement of other behavior (DRO). The contexts were during a classroom task, and during leisure activity. The two interventions might be expected to work differently in these contexts. Time out from a school task may not be nearly so aversive as time out from leisure, for example.

The two variables were manipulated in an A/B/C/B/C/B in one context and an A/C/B/C/B/C in the other, with a multiple baseline overlap between the two. The data are shown in Figure 8.9. DRO and time out worked in an exactly opposite manner in the two contexts, as expected. In this highly unusual case, the multiple baseline and within-series components are used as they are—not because it is expected that each data series will confirm the other, but because it is expected on theoretical grounds that they will not.

The Natural Multiple Baseline

Natural multiple baselines are formed as an inherent by-product of practice. No self-conscious effort is made to collect data series simultaneously, or to delay intervention for purely scientific reasons. There are several ways such natural multiple baselines can emerge.

The multiple baseline across people is probably one of the clearest examples of a natural design element that arises in practice. Nothing could be more natural to practical work than an A/B done with a client in need. This kind of simple phase change can readily form the basis of a natural multiple baseline across persons if several identical A/Bs are done with several clients, usually (but not

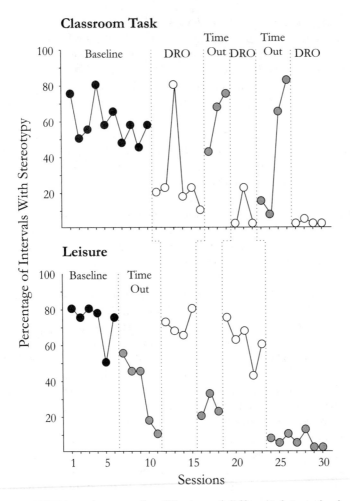

FIGURE 8.9   **An example of the use of different data series in a combined design in which they are expected not to operate in the same manner (redrawn from Haring & Kennedy, 1990).**

necessarily) with similar problems. If individual clients have widely differing lengths of baseline, a multiple baseline is formed. Different cases often do have different baselines due to case complexities or to matters of convenience. Thus, sequential cases often lead to a multiple baseline across people. Similarly, multiple baselines often form naturally across behaviors or problem settings due to the tendency for practitioners to tackle subsets of problems sequentially rather than all problems at once.

Some researchers have argued that saving cases, with perhaps periods of months or even years separating each, violates the logic of multiple baselines (Harris & Jenson, 1985). We disagree, and for several reasons (Hayes, 1985).

Control of Variables   There are two primary difficulties with a natural multiple baseline, such as a multiple baseline across several cases, compared to the more formal type recommended by Baer et al. (1968). The first difficulty is the one we discussed in the previous section. If several clients are being seen at the same time in the same place, then a more formal multiple baseline across persons may allow a slightly more elegant control of environmental variables. Establishing some degree of environmental constancy increases the likelihood that extraneous variables that may have produced an effect for the first person at the point of intervention are simultaneously present for the other clients. In a sense, extraneous variables are not just randomized, they are controlled to some degree across cases. In a simultaneous multiple baseline across persons, if a terrible snowstorm occurred just as the second condition was implemented for Person 1, it also occurred at the corresponding moment for Persons 2 or 3. In a natural multiple baseline across cases, this added form of control is not present.

This may not be very important. For one thing, even in the best of circumstances, extraneous variables are never truly the *same* across persons. For example, the snowstorm may be positive for Person 2 who is a skier, but negative for Person 1 who has had an injury due to slipping on ice. In a functional sense, the only way to be in the "same" environment as another person is to *be* the other person. Thus, even in a simultaneous multiple baseline across persons we do not know if the functionally important aspects of the environment have been held constant across people.

The multiple baseline protects against extraneous variables and measurement error in two different ways. The first set of extraneous variables or sources of measurement error are those environmental, situational, or measurement variables that occur in a fashion unrelated to the time and nature of assessment. All time series designs control for these in the same way: by the principle of unlikely successive coincidences. If such extraneous or measurement variables produced the beneficial change seen when a series of simple phase changes occur, one would have to explain the coincidence between these variables and the onset of treatment in other series as well.

The second set of extraneous variables and sources of measurement error varies systematically with the time and nature of assessment. For example, the amount of time in baseline, the timing of maturation, or the amount of repeated assessment are all extraneous variables that vary systematically with longer or shorter baselines. Observer drift is a source of measurement error that increases gradually over time, and this is also systematically related to phase lengths. All multiple baselines, whether natural or prearranged, control for these variables by arranging for both interrupted and uninterrupted series spread over the same time frame such that changes are seen in interrupted series before uninterrupted series are changed.

This second method of control is important because the principle of unlikely successive coincidences provide no protection against this second set of variables. For example, stroke victims often gradually reacquire some lost behavioral functions due to the natural course of the recovery process in brain injury. If a practitioner were doing an analysis of a rehabilitation program for stroke victims, it would be invalid to fail to control for this well-known source of behavioral improvement. Mere time in baseline is not such a control because the recovery process will vary systematically with it. Rather, controls are needed that unconfound time in baseline with such impactful time-related variables. That is exactly what a multiple baseline does, and it does it equally well in natural as compared to prearranged multiple baselines.

Source of the Phase Shift   The second problem with natural multiple baselines—indeed, of all natural time series designs—is more severe. It was touched upon in the earlier discussion of natural withdrawals. If the clinician is allowing the case itself to determine the exact length of baseline, there is the danger that the same factor that indicated it is time to change phases is correlated with processes that produced the behavior change seen. The main practical protections against this difficulty are the following. Perhaps the most important is repeated replication, both by the practitioner and by others. For example, when several cases are included in natural multiple baselines, the reasons for phase shifts are likely to vary considerably. As others replicate the findings, this is further controlled. A second source of protection is information. Researchers should report in detail why each phase change occurred when it did for each client in a time-series design. Recall that when research is replicated it is only the generality of the report of research that is formally tested. With reports that detail why phase changes occurred, those using the research will not be able to test their generality adequately. Third, researchers should stress caution in writing up time-series reports when natural phase changes occur, so that other researchers will be properly primed to examine this important issue. Fourth, all case analyses attempted should be reported. Especially in a multiple baseline across persons, it is fraudulent to include just a select few cases that fit an expected pattern. If the effect is not seen in some of the cases, the practitioner should attempt to find out why (indeed this seems required by standards of good practice). A careful examination of possible differences between individuals that might account for variable results may lead to treatment solutions for nonresponsive clients. Data showing subsequent positive response in previous failures would increase our knowledge about mechanisms producing change and about boundary conditions of a given treatment. Fifth, when possible, other design tools should be used to strengthen any weak analyses that could be influenced by nonarbitrary sources of phase-change decisions. Finally, some relatively arbitrary phase changes should be included when the analysis permits it. For example, in a natural multiple baseline it may be possible to include one or two cases in which treatment was begun for relatively arbitrary reasons. If the same pattern is seen in all cases, the possible relevance of systematic sources of phases shifts will be reduced.

The Assessment Burden

Some forms of multiple baseline can produce excessive assessment burdens. Normally, assessment frequency should be constant throughout a study because assessment itself is a possible source of behavior change or variability. But some multiple baselines can yield very long baseline phases, even in the practical setting.

For example, a practitioner may be working on multiple problems one at a time. Progress in one area may be slow, meaning that the other behaviors remain in baseline for extended periods. While fairly frequent assessment may be useful near the point at which behavior is targeted for change, it may be overkill in stable baseline phases that will not be interrupted for some time.

A solution is to assess frequently at the beginning of the study, and before and during the interruption of series, but less frequently in uninterrupted series that will not be intervened upon for some time (especially if the data are quite stable and are known to be unlikely to change without intervention). This approach is called the "multiple probe" technique (Horner & Baer, 1978). It has been particularly popular in educational settings, probably because sudden improvements in educational domains are fairly unlikely without explicit teaching in those areas. An example will be presented later (see Figure 8.11).

Questions to Ask Using the Multiple Baseline

The multiple baseline is an extremely flexible analytic tool. It allows the practitioners to answer a wide variety of applied questions, including (1) Does a treatment work? (2) Does one treatment work better than another, given that it is known they both work? (3) Does one treatment work, does another treatment work, and which one works better? (4) Are there specific elements within a successful treatment that make it work? (5) What is the optimal level of treatment? Answering these various questions requires no fundamentally different approach. Rather, responses depend upon the specific sequence of phase comparisons, using this analytic tool.

Types of Multiple Baselines

Probably because of their good fit with the applied situation, multiple baselines are very popular. An examination of studies published in the *Journal of Applied Behavior Analysis* from 1981 to 1985, for example, showed that "the multiple baseline design was used as the primary experimental design element in JABA studies by more than a two-to-one margin over the reversal design, the next most used design strategy" (Cooper, Heron, & Heward, 1987, p. 218).

It is common to arrange multiple baselines into "types" based on the kind of data series being compared. As we have discussed, this is somewhat artificial, since any combination of factors can be used to form data series, depending on the question being asked and the domains the researcher is interested in generalizing across. Nevertheless, there are a few characteristics worth mentioning about these different "types" of multiple baselines.

Multiple Baseline across Settings   Many practitioners assume that treatment delivered in one setting or at one time will generalize to other settings or other times. Perhaps for that reason, there is something nonobvious and slightly disconcerting about multiple baselines done across time or settings. In this approach, several series are created by behavior shown in particular times or in particular settings. Intervention occurs in one series and is examined against the controls provided by other times or settings.

This design seems to be used most often in educational or institutional settings, particularly with children (e.g., Fehr & Beckwith, 1989; Nelson, Smith, & Dodd, 1992; Paniagua, Morrison, & Black, 1990). It is much less common in adult psychotherapy situations, perhaps because psychotherapy itself is to some degree based on the assumption that treatment in one setting will generalize to others. This assumption is probably often incorrect, however, and the multiple baseline across settings or time automatically tests its applicability.

Multiple Baseline across Behaviors   It is rare to encounter persons in need who have isolated, solitary problems. More commonly, difficulties in one area are associated with difficulties in other areas. This fact, combined with the depressing reality that even effective interventions are often shockingly specific and limited in their effects, means that the opportunities for multiple baselines across behaviors abounds in the applied setting. The multiple baseline design across behaviors has been used for almost every kind of applied problem: memory retraining (Benedict, Brandt, & Bergey, 1993; Franzen & Harris, 1993), agoraphobia (Franklin, 1989), self-injurious behavior (Konarski & Johnson, 1989), and writing skills for learning-disabled students (Dowis & Schloss, 1992), just to name a few. It has also been used with many applied populations, including the deaf (Rasing & Duker, 1992, 1993), mentally retarded (Sisson & Dixon, 1986), nursing home residents (Praderas & MacDonald, 1986), brain-injured adults (Burke & Lewis, 1986), and autistic children (Ingenmey & VanHouten, 1991).

The multiple baseline across behaviors design reduces ethical concerns related to delaying treatment to a client, since treatment can proceed quickly to a problem area. It seems especially useful when the withdrawal of treatment is not possible. It is applicable not only when there are multiple problems, but also sometimes when one particularly problematic behavior can be broken down into smaller components.

Multiple Baseline across Persons   The multiple baseline across persons design has been especially popular when a given behavior is to be altered across many clients (Kazdin, 1994). Indeed, this design element fits fairly well within syndromal thinking, and it seems to be increasingly frequently used there. There are many examples of this design in the literature (e.g., Camarata, 1993; DeVries, Burnette, & Redmon, 1991; Ollendick, Hagopian, & Huntzinger, 1991; Taras, Matson, & Leary, 1988).

The multiple baseline across persons design is probably the closest time-series designs ever to come to group comparison design thinking. Inevitably, extensive replications across people reveal a fair amount of variability. People are individuals, and very few interventions work in the same way for everyone. This means, probably more so than with any other design, the researcher must be ready to stop everything and pursue the meaning of individual differences. Thus, it is common that what starts out to be a multiple baseline across people ends up being more complicated.

The Crossover Design

The crossover is used to add between-series comparisons to a within-series element. In it, two concurrent phase changes occur, one in the reverse order of the other, each on a separate series. For example, a B/C sequence might be conducted on one behavior and a C/B sequence on another. By changing phases at the same time, in the same place, after phases of the same length in each series, obvious external sources of influence are kept equivalent in each series. If consistent within-series effects are shown in each series (e.g., if B is greater than C in each case), the likelihood of the effect is increased beyond that of the component simple phase changes, were the series not synchronized in this way. This design element has been widely used in pharmacological studies (e.g., Singh & Aman, 1981).

Crossovers will occasionally emerge naturally in clinical or educational settings. Suppose a client comes in with two problems. One problem is in need of immediate treatment, and treatment begins while baseline is collected on the second problem. After a time, treatment is stopped on Problem 1 and simultaneously begun on Problem 2. This is a natural crossover, created by a shift in problem focus.

The crossover elements can be used to strengthen any within-series design elements so long as more than one series is available (e.g., there are two problems). Rather than conduct the same sequence on each series, the sequences can be timed in a crossover fashion. Figure 8.10 provides an example. Note that the patterns, while relatively weak in each series, are made more believable by the crossover and the two between-series comparisons it enables, because an extraneous variable would have to have exactly opposite effects on each series to produce the result. The main advantage of a crossover is that it is a very simple design element that can be added without great cost to other design components. It is not an especially strong element in and of itself, but it does strengthen other elements.

The Constant-Series Control

Many times there are problems that are repeatedly assessed and left in a single condition throughout (usually baseline). These data can be examined as a type of between-series comparison (e.g., Brownell, Barlow, & Hayes, 1977; Hayes, Johnson, & Cone, 1975; O'Reilly, Green, & Braunling-McMorrow, 1990) and can be combined with other within-series comparisons.

The logic of this comparison is identical to the between-series comparisons made in a multiple-baseline design (see Figure 8.2). Changes occurring elsewhere and not in the control series are more likely to have been produced by treatment (cf. Campbell & Stanley's, 1963, equivalent time-samples design).

The purpose of the constant-series control is to reduce the likelihood that extraneous events, cyclical effects, and the like could have been responsible for the changes seen. If they were, the reasoning goes, why didn't the constant series also change in the same way? For this to be a sensible point, it is important that the constant series could reasonably be expected to be susceptible to an extraneous source

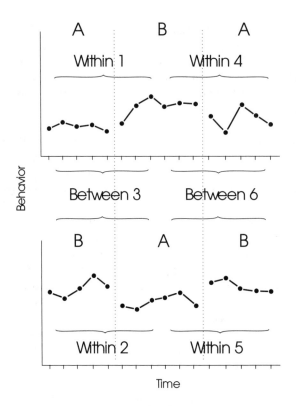

FIGURE 8.10 **An example of a crossover and its logic.** Each series shows a fairly weak treatment effect, but the crossover arrangement makes the effect much more convincing because of the simultaneous acceleration and deceleration across series revealed in the between-series comparisons.

of influence. For example, if the constant-series control was the gender identity of a transsexual and the treated series was the client's depressed mood, the lack of changes in the constant series would add little to the analysis because gender identity is notoriously stable.

The most common type of constant-series control is the use of baseline only when several series are available. If the practitioner has been comparing, say, baseline to treatment in one series, the remaining series might produce a natural baseline-only control. Sometimes this series is used to assess generalization. Often in the practical environment it may be targeted for treatment, but be untreated for practical reasons (e.g., the client decided that therapy was finished).

A study by O'Reilly, Green, and Braunling-McMorrow (1990) provides an example of a baseline-only constant series control. O'Reilly et al. were attempting to change the accident-prone actions of brain-injured individuals. A written safety checklist that listed but did not specifically prompt hazard remediation was prepared for each of several areas of the home. If improvement was not maximal in a given area, individualized task analyses were prepared that prompted change in areas that still required remediation.

The data for one of the subjects are shown in Figure 8.11. There is very little evidence of generalization across responses and the baseline-only constant-series control provides additional evidence that training was responsible for the improvements seen. Changes produced by a written safety checklist were immediate and

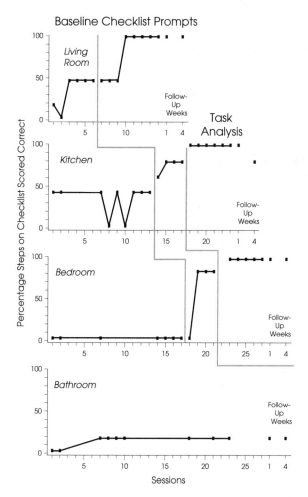

FIGURE 8.11   An example of the baseline-only version of a constant-series control. Three areas in the home have been targeted for intervention with a head-injured woman. One area of the home (the bathroom, shown at the bottom) remains as a baseline-only control.

(Figure redrawn from O'Reilly, Green, & Braunling-McMorrow, 1990. The figure has been simplified to eliminate details not necessary to its use here, such as distinctions between probes and other data types. See original article.)

stable, but they were quite specific for this subject. Some areas of the home required specific prompting to reach maximal levels. Note also the use of the multiple probe technique discussed earlier.

Baseline is not the only type of constant-series control that might be used. Sometimes only treatment has been implemented: what has been called a "B-only" design (cf. Browning & Stover, 1971). A treatment-only control can be helpful in much the same way as a baseline-only control, and in addition controls for unlikely order effects (e.g., that treatment will work only after a formal baseline).

The constant-series control, like all elements that use more than one series, can be applied to any type of series: those organized by person, problem, situation, time of day, or any combination of these. Different series are relevant to different questions, and they emerge in different ways. For example, consider the use of constant-series controls across people. This element provides a home for those cases in which only treatment is given and those in which treatment is never given. As anchors in a series of cases they provide additional control and precision to the analysis.

Constant-series controls emerge very naturally in the course of applied practice. For example, a client may have multiple problems. A practitioner may immediately launch into treatment of some problems. These may be particularly severe, or they may be particularly obvious so that the practitioner might move into treatment, perhaps even in the first session, without feeling the need for additional assessment before beginning. These would form a treatment-only control. Other problems may remain on the back burner. They are clearly problems and they are being repeatedly measured, but needs in other areas are being pursued while their treatment is being postponed. These would form a baseline-only control. These two constant series elements would make a contribution to whatever is done on the other problems. Suppose that the only actual analysis done is an A/B on a third problem. The combination of a treatment-only control, a baseline-only control, and an A/B could elevate a collection of weak (but nonintrusive) design elements into a meaningful design if the resultant data were clear.

The True Reversal

Treatment withdrawal is often termed "a reversal," and it is common to hear a design that includes a withdrawal (e.g., an A/B/A/B) called a "reversal design." Actually, while the data themselves are sometimes expected to reverse when a withdrawal is implemented, the design itself is not a reversal.

Leitenberg (1973) originally made the distinction between reversal and withdrawal designs. A reversal design is one in which, instead of being withdrawn, treatment is deliberately reversed. For example, if a child is being encouraged to play with peers, she may then be encouraged to play with adults and not with peers (e.g., Allen, Hart, Buell, Harris, & Wolf, 1964). While the reversal is not necessarily a combined-series design, it usually is one because separate measures are often kept on two targets. The true reversal is seldom seen in applied situations, both for ethical reasons and because many interventions are not "reversible."

Conclusion

Combined-series design elements put together between- and within-series elements in a new way, with an identifiable and distinct logic. They are new design units, built from other design units.

Various design elements can also be combined in a manner that does not involve new logical units. This second type of combination occurs in practice when the tools we have already described are sequenced in a particular way to attempt to analyze applied phenomena. It is to this that we now turn.

Combining Single Case Design Elements

Throughout this book we have repeatedly emphasized that time-series elements are not completed structures that are simply laid on top of professional activities. Properly used, these designs are the results of creative strategies used to solve applied problems. Design elements should be combined as the need for them emerges, not because they do or do not fit an expected pattern or named design. It is quite possible to create designs that literally have no name, as would be the case with a particular combination of elements never before used. There is no special vulnerability in using a "new design" in such a situation as long as the design elements are used appropriately.

Two issues are of central importance in the combination of design elements in the analysis of particular clinical issues: What is the question that needs to be answered, and what design tools fit the specifics of the situation that can answer the question? Of course, asking a question properly with design elements does not mean that a clear answer will be forthcoming. The variability and lack of experimental control inherent in applied situations often produces ambiguous answers even to well-crafted questions. But if even a small portion of clinical questions leads to clear answers, the frequency of empirical analysis that is possible in the applied setting makes scientific progress highly likely.

Which Design Element to Use

Table 8.1 presents some clinically important questions and examples of the various design elements useful in each situation. Within any row of this table, various elements can be combined to address a given clinical question. As different questions arise different elements can be used by drawing from the different rows.

Consider the first question, Does a treatment work? Several additional questions then need to be answered in a particular situation in order to arrive at reasonable design options that fit the situation. Panel 8.1 presents a flowchart that summarizes some of the major options for Row 1 of the table. Notice that there is almost always an option that could work in a given situation. Sometimes, there are several options.

When there are several options, it may be beneficial to employ redundant design elements. For example, in Row 1 of Table 8.1, there are several within-, between-, and combined-series options. It might be possible to combine several of

TABLE 8.1 Examples of the Use of Design Elements to Answer Specific Types of Clinical Questions

Clinical Question	Design Type		
	Within Series	Between Series	Combined Series
Does a treatment work?	A/B/A/B... B/A/B/A... A/B (see combined designs) Periodic treatments design Changing criterion design	ATD comparing A and B ATD across behaviors or situations	Multiple baseline across settings behaviors, or persons comparing A and B Replicated crossovers comparing A and B
Does one treatment work better than another, given that we already know they work?	B/C/B/C.... C/B/C/B....	ATD comparing B and C	Replicated crossovers comparing B and C Multiple baselines comparing B and C and controlling for order
Does one treatment work, does another work, and which works better?	A/B/A/C/A combined with A/C/A/B/A Or combine any element from Row 1 with any element from Row 2	ATD comparing A and B and C	Multiple baseline comparing A, B and C and controlling for order
Are there elements within a successful treatment that make it work?	Interaction element: B/B+C/B or B+C/B/B+C/C or C/B+C/C or B+C/C/B+C	ATD comparing, for example, B and B+C	Multiple baseline comparing B and B+C, and C and B+C Replicated crossovers comparing B and B+C, and C and B+C
Does the client prefer one treatment over another?		Simultaneous treatments design comparing B and C	
Does a treatment work and if so, what part of it makes it work?	Combine any elements from Rows 1 or 3 with any element from Row 4		
What level of treatment is optimal?	Parametric design	ATD comparing B and B'	Multiple baseline comparing B and B' and controlling for order Replicated crossovers comparing B and B'

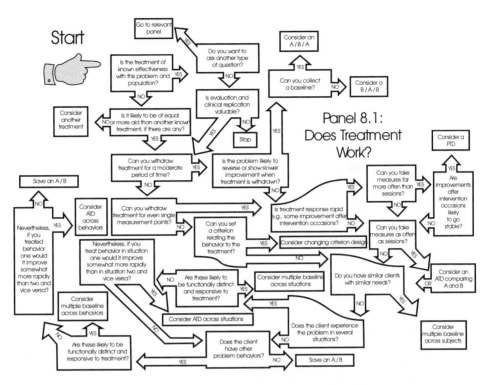

Start

Go to relevant panel

Do you want to ask another type of question?

Is the treatment of known effectiveness with this problem and population? — YES

NO

Is evaluation and clinical replication valuable?

Consider another treatment ← NO — Is it likely to be of equal or more aid than another known treatment, if there are any? — YES

Stop

Consider an A / B / A — YES

Can you collect a baseline? — NO — Consider a B / A / B

**Panel 8.1:
Does Treatment
Work?**

Consider a PTD

Can you withdraw treatment for a moderate period of time? — YES — Is the problem likely to reverse or show slower improvement when treatment is withdrawn?

NO

Save an A / B

Consider ATD across behaviors

Can you withdraw treatment for even single measurement points? — NO

Nevertheless, if you treated behavior one would it improve somewhat more rapidly than two and vice versa? — YES

Can you set a criterion relating the behavior to the treatment? — YES

Nevertheless, if you treat behavior in situation one would it improve somewhat more rapidly than in situation two and vice versa?

Are these likely to be functionally distinct and responsive to treatment? — YES

Are these likely to be functionally distinct and responsive to treatment? — YES

Consider multiple baseline across behaviors

NO

Consider ATD across situations

Does the client have other problem behaviors? — NO

YES

Can you take measures for more often than sessions? — YES — Are improvements after intervention occasions likely to go stable? — YES

NO

Is treatment response rapid (e.g., some improvement after intervention occasions)? — NO

Can you take measures as often as sessions? — NO

Consider changing criterion design

Consider multiple baseline across situations — YES

Do you have similar clients with similar needs? — NO

Consider an ATD comparing A and B — OR

Consider multiple baseline across subjects

Does the client experience the problem in several situations? — NO

Save an A / B

PANEL 8.1.   A flowchart describing how to select design alternatives when the question is whether or not treatment works.

these elements. Consider a simple case. Suppose a therapist is working to reduce the frequency of negative self-verbalizations in a chronically depressed client using cognitive therapy. Suppose the original plan is to do an A/B/A/B with each (see the top of Figure 8.12) This is reasonable, but what if the treatment is so effective it causes improvement that does not slow with treatment withdrawal? It would cost very little to stagger phases across clients (see the middle of Figure 8.12). That way, a simple multiple baseline would be formed that would allow an analysis of irreversible rates of improvement. Suppose, however, that the treatment only works with some people, and it causes irreversible improvement. A multiple baseline will not solve this problem. One possibility is to conduct an ATD in the treatment phases (bottom of Figure 8.12). That way the effects can be documented at the level of the individual. If the treatment only works with some people, this can be ascertained.

Thus, the use of multiple tools increases the flexibility and precision of the analysis. We are not suggesting that such an elaborate design is needed or even desirable in most situations. The point is that the practitioner should consider the use of redundant design tools when it is practical and when the individual advantages of each may be needed. The practitioner needs constantly to be aware of emerging design options and to set things up so that the design can react and change as the

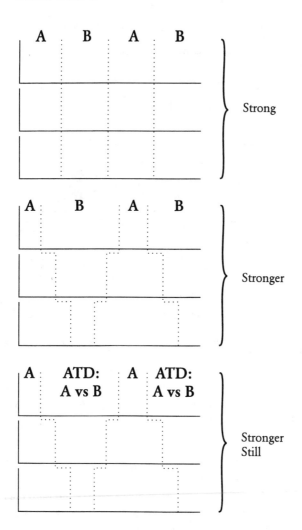

FIGURE 8.12   An example of increasing the strength of comparisons through the use of multiple design elements.

data come in. Table 8.1 may provide a structure for this. The practitioner should monitor the nature of questions that emerge (i.e., What row are we now in? What row are we likely to be in later?) and consider the options in each row. Which fit best? If more than one fits, can they be combined? What are the costs and benefits?

Panel 8.2 shows another flowchart, this one aimed at Rows 2 and 3 of Table 8.1. There are many other questions that could bear on the options selected, but this chart summarizes some of the major ones. Panels 8.1 and 8.2 mimic the decision-making process an experienced empirical practitioner would follow.

A concrete example may be worthwhile. Consider the answers to each of the following questions. Given these answers, ask yourself what the best design

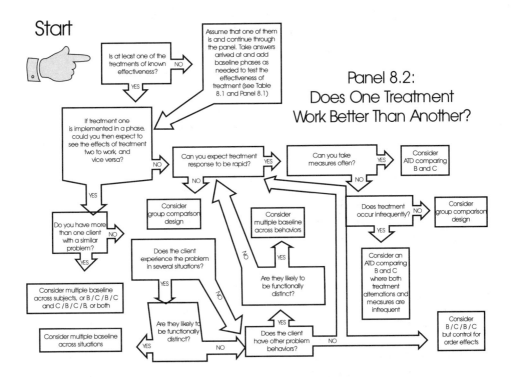

PANEL 8.2. A flowchart describing how to select design alternatives when the question is whether or not one treatment works better than another.

option would be to answer the question: Does a given treatment B work better than doing nothing extra at all?

1. Do I have time to take a relatively extended baseline? **YES**
2. Are my measures extraordinarily frequent (relative to treatment frequency)? **NO**
3. Are my measures extraordinarily infrequent (relative to treatment frequency)? **NO**
4. Do I expect gains to reverse or slow noticeably if treatment is withdrawn? **YES**
5. Can I withdraw treatment entirely at least for a short time? **NO**
6. Does the client have several problems that might respond to this same treatment and are they likely to be independent? **YES**
7. Does the client's problem occur in several discrete settings or times and is response in one area likely to be independent from response in another? **NO**
8. Do I see several clients with this problem each year? **YES**
9. Do I set, and can I repeatedly change, specific goals or criteria as a major part of treatment? **NO**
10. Are order effects likely? **YES**

11. Do I expect fairly rapid improvement? **MAYBE**
12. Are there strong background trends in the target problem that are likely to be there whether treatment is in place? **NO**
13. Are the data likely to be very stable? **PROBABLY NOT**
14. Are very large individual differences in response to treatment likely? **YES**

Working through this list of questions, several items stand out. Although a baseline is available (1), withdrawal is not (5). A simple phase change will probably not apply since it could not go beyond a simple A/B. Although there are several clients available (8), large individual differences are expected (14), so a multiple baseline across clients would be dangerous. There are several problems available that might respond to the same treatment (6), however. A multiple baseline across behaviors replicated across several clients seems to fit the situation. By randomly generating answers to this list of questions and using the two panels, the reader can develop his or her skills to a point at which good design options are intuitively available in almost any conceivable situation.

Stretching the Guidelines

The design options in this volume are not "all-or-none" devices. This book has taken a very liberal stance about the essential continuity between elegant, absolutely defensible design options and imperfect but possibly valuable ones. How far can the basics be liberalized? Different elements can be stretched to different degrees.

Repeated Measurement

Without repeated measurement, there cannot be a series of data points with which to evaluate variability around level and trend. Few situations will allow simple pre–post measurement to be of any use in single case methodology. There are a few exceptions, however,

Sometimes we know so much about the stability and course of a particular phenomenon that even single data points are useful. Examples are hard to find in the behavioral sciences, but they occur regularly in medicine. Suppose we are treating a client with AIDS and produce a complete remission. Even a single observation of a dramatic reversal would be potentially worthwhile because we know so much about the expected nature and course of the disorder

Systematic Measurement

Even more basically, suppose measurement is unsystematic, perhaps anecdotal. In most situations anecdotal information is not scientifically useful except as a basis for the formation of research ideas and hypotheses. Even here, however, there are occasions when unsystematic information might be useful. It may be, for example, that a particular constellation of factors should not be possible, given a particular point of view. Unsystematic data, collected even once, might call this into question if that constellation is apparent. Suppose, for example, it was claimed that true transsexuals never change their sex-role identity. Suppose further that it is clear from anecdotal evidence that a client once fit the definition of a transsexual, but has since changed his identity. This anecdote might provide important and worthwhile evidence. Similarly, someone might claim that all depressed married women are angry at their husbands. If even one client does not show this pattern, an anecdotal report of it may be meaningful.

The methodological rules we have described should not be thought of in legalistic ways. The overall strategy is more important than individual guidelines. The long-term research program is more important than any individual rule violation. This point deserves some additional discussion.

The Purpose of the Methodology

The products of science are systematic statements of relations among events that are based on verifiable experience. Unlike purely experiential disciplines (e.g., mysticism) that eschew the development of verbal rules or laws as an important output, or purely social enterprises (e.g., law) that develop rules without the requirement that they be based on verifiable experience, science attempts to walk a middle line between the two.

Scientific methodology is nothing more than a set of guidelines that permits others to have access to the experiences that support particular statements. In a sense, methodology is a way we isolate ourselves from the capacity we have to deceive ourselves. It is all too easy to see things in a particular way because of our hopes, expectations, wishes, desires, fears, and so on. Practitioners are well aware of this, of course. Cautions about "countertransference" and the like are due to this same concern.

Methodology is valuable to the extent that it does this. It is not a matter of following rules for rules' sake. There is no hidden vault containing "rules of scientific methodology." Nor is it a matter simply of logic or carefully crafted argument. Methodological rules can be logical and still be poor rules if they do not orient the researcher toward what is essential and workable. For example, the logic of null hypothesis statistical testing is elegant, but there is a growing concern expressed in some of our best scientific journals (e.g., Loftus, 1996) that this logic does not orient researchers toward the critical analytic issues. Our point here is that all the rules contained in this book should be taken with a grain of salt. Some of our sensible-sounding recommendations may ultimately turn out not to be very helpful. Logic will not decide this—the progress of the field will—and the only way to decide is to test it.

It is quite possible to assess methodological recommendations empirically. For example, no one has yet done a study to see if the use of single case elements makes clinical success more or less likely overall. It seems that it might, and yet this is ultimately an empirical question.

The answer to the question, "How far can we stretch the methodology?" is then clear: until the methodology no longer makes a contribution. It is not clear how far that will be. For certain rule violations, nature may extract a high price. For others, the cost may be low. Applied disciplines need more experience with the integration of practice and empirical evaluation before we will know how liberal we can be. It seems better simply to do as rigorous a job as we can than to set excessively narrow standards and give up in disgust because they cannot be met.

The Contribution of "Case Studies"

At some point, enough methodological niceties are missed so that an analysis is no longer viewed as a single case experimental design. It is often then called a case study, although we have subsumed both of these under the rubric "time-series methodology." Case studies range from purely anecdotal reports to well-crafted, simple, phase-change designs. The issues they present differ, depending on their exact nature.

In this text, nonexperimental designs (e.g., A/B designs) have not been clearly distinguished from their more elaborate counterparts. This is because there is a continuum of the degree to which designs are "experimental." The distinctions between them are dependent on a host of factors, and weaker forms can become stronger through various means. For example, we have pointed to a number of ways A/B designs can be integrated into more sophisticated analyses (such as a multiple baseline) and we are about to address another such use in the next chapter (clinical replication series).

The case study is of use because it is part and parcel of a general methodological approach. It blends smoothly into more and more sophisticated analyses. Without an interest in case analysis, the entire methodological structure we are advocating is seriously weakened.

Traditional research methodologists have tended to put case studies into a very separate (and lower) class. Their functions are seen as quite limited. Case studies are said to be of use primarily because they suggest hypotheses, for example. While this is surely so, it can amount to damnation by faint praise because virtually anything can suggest hypotheses. Such a view discourages practitioners from analyzing their cases. Without this beginning, where will more elaborate analyses come from?

If case studies are thought of as anecdotal case reports, then it is true that they have a very limited scientific function. Once repeated and systematic measurement is in place and interventions are specified, however, the role expands considerably. The practitioner attempting this type of case analysis will not be certain (before the case is concluded) what the level of scientific product will be. The opportunities abound, as we have argued, to raise the level of knowledge, while simultaneously meeting client needs. Even those analyses that end up at a lower level (e.g., a B-only, an A/B) will form a foundation for clinical replication series or for additional empirical work. These are critical functions on their own, and by encouraging case studies, we increase the likelihood of even more meaningful output. In this sense, an openness to case analysis is virtually a cornerstone of applied research methodology in practice settings. We will see one area in which this is true in the next chapter.

9 Research in General Practice Settings: Production and Consumption of Clinical Replication Series

Introduction

If practitioners could be brought into the research enterprise, it would do at least two important things: (a) it would increase the rate of discovery and treatment development as the hypotheses of practitioners were turned into empirically tested events, and (b) it would multiply by an enormous factor the number of replications of findings initially discovered in either applied research centers or other clinical settings. Innovative research in the clinical environment is both important and possible, especially with the institutional support that managed care settings can provide. The methods described in Chapters 5 through 8 are the primary tools that practitioners can use to evaluate nascent technologies.

Even without the use of the general practice setting for innovation, however, there is a tremendous need for clinical replication merely to evaluate the general impact of applied procedures, and no way to fill that need without accessing the practice setting. Thus, in the present chapter we will begin an examination of production and consumption of research in the general practice environment, paying special attention to the conduct and consumption of clinical replication series. This method is one of the most powerful tools that practitioners have to assess the efficacy and generalizability of treatment technologies.

Clinical Replication Series

Clinical replication is a missing link in our current system of clinical research production. For clinical research to be useful to practitioners we must know what kinds of client are most likely to respond to what kinds of treatments. This question will never be adequately answered in major research centers, however. First, the number of clients needed to address such questions is much too large. Second, research specialists do not and cannot make their careers on extensive processes of replication. Only practitioners have the client flow and practical interest that formal clinical replication series demand.

Clinical replication is a framework that can incorporate the findings of practitioners gleaned from both single case experimental designs as well as from empirical case studies, if measures are carefully taken. These observations are then arranged in a series. The purpose of this series is to direct attention to both successes and failures, defined clinically rather than statistically, in a series of individual patients receiving a given treatment, as well as to test the generalizability of an intervention to a practice setting. One of the hallmarks of clinical replication is a keystone to single case designs generally, but it acquires special force in this context: *intensive local observation* (Cronbach, 1975).

Intensive Local Observation

Describing this now well-known recommendation, Cronbach (1975) noted:

> An observer collecting data in one particular situation is in a position to appraise a practice or proposition in that setting, observing effects in context. In trying to describe and account for what happened, he will give attention to whatever variables were controlled. But he will give equally careful attention to uncontrolled conditions, to personal characteristics, and to events that occurred during treatment and measurement. As he goes from situation to situation, his first task is to describe and interpret the effect anew in each locale, perhaps taking into account factors unique to that locale. . . . As results accumulate, a person who seeks understanding will do his best to trace how the uncontrolled factors could have caused local departures from the modal effect. That is, generalization comes late and the exception is taken as seriously as the rule. (pp. 124–125)

At the heart of this process is a full realization by practitioners and researchers alike of the types of inferences that can be made from data such as these and of the specific threats to internal and external validity accompanying these efforts.

Cronbach's thinking emerges out of an intellectual history in social science, and particularly in educational research, that adheres to the notion that the tightly controlled, fixed-condition, traditional experimentation borrowed from the physical sciences cannot answer all of the important social science questions (e.g., Campbell, 1959; McGuire, 1973; Snow, 1974). While this position has had its champions in psychology, Cronbach (1975) makes the very specific observation that our science is incapable of determining the generalizability of laws established in our research centers to practice settings, for reasons mentioned above. One important reason is the inability to detect patient-treatment interactions.

> The experimental strategy dominant in psychology since 1950 has only limited ability to detect interactions. Typically, the investigator delimits the range of situations considered in his research program by fixing many aspects of the conditions under which the subject is observed. The interactions of any fixed aspect are thereby con-

cealed, being pulled into the main effect or into the interactions of other variables. (Cronbach, 1975, p. 123)

And again,

> The investigator who employs a factorial design can detect some interactions of those conditions he allows to vary, but sizable interactions are likely to be suppressed just because any interaction that does not produce a significant F ratio is treated as non-existent. (p. 124)

To take our typical example once again in applied research, suppose we wish to conduct a 2 × 2 factorial experiment on anxiety disorders where, for example, two levels of intensity of the same treatment are administered to either male or female patients with anxiety. Suppose, further, that after this experiment we were able to say that while more intense treatment is not significantly better for males than less intense treatment, more intense treatment is better for females. This might give evidence for a simple interaction between intensity of treatment and gender. But, as any practitioner knows, this would be merely scratching the surface of individual differences. Other important variables that might interact with treatment include the gender of the therapist, the age of the patient, the social class of the patient, the patient's method of coping with the experience of anxiety (such as persevering in the presence of the anxiety response versus seeking support from others for a period of time), and, perhaps most important, the nature of the family support system and the role this plays in the anxiety response. And we have not even mentioned occupation, number and intensity of stressors in the environment, personality style, intensity, chronicity, and so on and on.

Mischel (1973) has argued that research in personality must become the study of higher-order interactions, and Campbell (1973) points out further the need to reflect on what it means to establish empirical generalizations in a world in which most effects are interactive. Within this context, testing only for the null hypothesis, as Cronbach points out, encourages a disregard for all other individual observations made in the course of the experiment. Depending on the particular applied situation, an applied investigator might observe a very marked interaction between response to treatment and level of support within the family of the patient, but if this were not being tested specifically, it would be unlikely to be reported in any journal article.

Returning to the example of PDA that we developed in Chapter 3, it now becomes clear why the answers to the questions so important to practitioners, such as how effective is the procedure and with whom will it work, have not been answered. These questions cannot be fully answered using traditional research methodology, nor even with single case methodology if too narrowly applied. The complexity of the human condition will preclude any attempt at experimentally establishing generalization. The number of person/treatment interactions present in an applied setting can never be tested adequately in clinical research centers through the use of group factorial designs, even if other weaknesses, such as sampling deficiencies, reliance on statistical significance, averaging, and differences between research and practice settings, were not present. Yet results from the applied research centers on the whys and hows of treatment, so evident in recent advances in our knowledge of psychosocial treatments for mental disorders, will advance our understanding very little without information on the applicability of these procedures.

In applied research, the answers to these unanswered questions must come from practitioners themselves in collaboration with research centers. It is, in fact, the unique ability of practitioners to observe extent of effect, successes, failures, and interactions that makes them the focal point in the process of intensive local observation as well as, in the last analysis, full-fledged partners in the scientific process. If properly developed, this process could be the way in which practitioners fulfill the role of scientist–practitioner so long envisioned in our training centers. This is so for a simple reason: Only in the process of dissemination and use in the applied environment can the impact and applicability of our procedures be assessed. In marked contrast to most controlled experimental research, it is remarkable how impactful research of this kind has been on the behavior of clinicians.

The Process of Clinical Replication

Clinical replication was earlier defined as " . . . the administration of a treatment package (containing two or more distinct treatment procedures) by the same investigator or group of investigators. These procedures would be administered in a specific setting to a series of patients presenting similar combinations of multiple behavioral and emotional problems, which usually cluster together" (Hersen & Barlow, 1976, p. 336). In retrospect, this definition is a bit stiff. It is enough to say that clinical replication is a process wherein practitioners using a clearly defined set of procedures (a "treatment") intervene with a series of cases that have a well-specified and measured problem regularly encountered in applied settings. In the course of this series, the practitioner observes and records successes and failures, analyzing, where possible, the reasons for these individual variations (or intersubject variability). This process embodies all of the functions of intensive local observation, as Cronbach (1975) described it, and takes advantage of the strength of practitioners, specifically their observational skills, in the most important context of all: the treatment setting.

This process, of course, is not new to our clinics and educational centers. It goes on continually, and occasionally the results of such an effort are published. When series are published, they often have an enormous impact on practitioners, although most typically these reports are held in low regard by applied researchers and other scientists, because they do not usually contain the customary experimental controls. But the fact that these series have been influential, at least to practitioners, suggests that they are providing information not obtainable elsewhere. This section will emphasize clinical replication as a strategy to answer the unanswered questions concerning generality of effectiveness and feasibility of administration of a given procedure.

Masters and Johnson Series

An example of one of the more famous clinical replication series was published by Masters and Johnson (1970). This series led to the wide adoption of sex therapy by practitioners. Despite many inadequacies outlined below, this effort is a good example of the potential of the intensive local observation process within a clinical replication series to answer the unanswered questions on patient-treatment interactions and generalizability of the effects of treatment. In this series, Masters and Johnson described uncontrolled conditions occurring during treatment and patient characteristics that seemed to have had some influence on outcome. Furthermore, detailed accounts of reasons for failures were described, and therefore made available to practitioners for comparison with their own patients presenting with sexual dysfunction. Finally, answers to the general question concerning the extent of effectiveness of these procedures were provided in a preliminary way, subject to several serious limitations that resulted in an overstatement of the effectiveness of these procedures.

This series, of course, has many drawbacks and limitations that decrease its usefulness in communicating to practitioners answers to the unanswered questions. For example, Masters and Johnson report failure rates rather than success rates, which tends to obscure the degree of clinical improvement obtained in those cases where improvement was noted, a problem not far removed from the issue of clinical versus statistical significance. Furthermore, intervention procedures are not always as clearly outlined as it might seem. Numerous departures from the standard program are apparently a common tactic (Wincze & Carey, 1991; Zilbergeld & Evans, 1980), but not well described. In addition, assessment of change is not always carried out by methods that would receive wide agreement from practicing clinicians. Many more measures that are practical and therefore easily used by clinicians are now available. Because of the importance of this series, a detailed description of limitations as well as suggestions on how it could have been improved will be presented below.

In view of the enormous influence of this series, it must be noted that its publication seems to have had at least two unintended deleterious effects. First, other practitioners adopting these procedures, and therefore in a position to provide numerous additional data on their generalizability as well as patient-treatment interactions, have either failed to report their results in a useful way or have failed to obtain results at all. For example, Kaplan (1979; 1987), another experienced sex therapist who has written widely and seen numerous cases, did not report results on her series, nor did she describe in any detail patient-treatment interactions or the extent of success or failure among patients.

Second, a more intriguing deleterious effect seems to be the inhibition of further scientific exploration of why treatment is effective and how treatment is effective. The rationale seems to be that this series was so successful that major research efforts would be wasted, since it is difficult to improve on the therapy as practiced. This may account, in large part, for the fact that our knowledge of the nature and treatment of sexual dysfunction is not nearly as far along as our knowledge of other problem areas such as clinical phobia and depression (Barlow, 1994; Wincze

& Carey, 1991). And yet this knowledge of the nature of psychopathology, or a fuller understanding of the problem at hand—as well as the process of behavior change—is essential if we are to maximize improvement for every individual. For example, while there are several early studies demonstrating that sex therapy is more effective than no treatment (e.g., Obler, 1973), there are few, if any, studies indicating that Masters and Johnson–style sex therapy is better than other reasonable alternatives that might involve different behavior-change processes (Crowe, Gillan, & Golombok, 1981; Marks, 1981; Wincze & Carey, 1991).

Even within the Masters and Johnson series, different rates of success and failure are reported for specific problems. For example, the treatment of premature ejaculation is substantially more successful than the treatment for primary erectile dysfunction, where there is considerable room for improvement. In summary, these procedures seem successful for some forms of sexual dysfunction, but we need more research into the mechanisms of action of these treatments, a component analysis of the treatment package, and a better understanding of the nature of sexual dysfunction. These deleterious effects just described seem directly tied to the enormous influence of this clinical replication series on both practitioners and researchers. This influence, in turn, is caused by the ability of this series to answer important questions for practitioners.

Other Clinical Replication Series

Other examples of extremely influential series of this type can be found in the very beginnings of the development of the newly effective procedures for clinical phobia described above. As noted in Chapter 1, Wolpe's (1958) series of 210 phobics and other anxiety-based disorders, reporting success rates approaching 90%, had a large impact on clinical practice, which in turn contributed to the subsequent illuminating and extremely useful course of clinical research.

Other important and new clinical procedures, widely adopted by practitioners, have been largely influenced by clinical replication series. Biofeedback, which originated in the laboratories of experimental psychology, became popular with practitioners for treating some somatic disorders after early clinical reports, many of which were unsystematic case studies. In one instance, thermal biofeedback enjoyed wide application in the late 1960s and early 1970s after reports of its use by Elmer Green, who only later published an uncontrolled clinical trial (Sargent, Green, & Walters, 1972). The use of thermal biofeedback then increased substantially, to the point at which it became a standard tool of many practitioners. This is a good example of the power and influence of this type of effort, since years of subsequent research failed to demonstrate the effectiveness of thermal biofeedback or biofeedback, in general, over and above relaxation procedures in most circumstances (e.g., Katkin, Fitzgerald, & Shapiro, 1978; Silver & Blanchard, 1978). (However, see Blanchard, Andrasik, Neff, Arena, Ahles, Jurish, Pallmeyer, Saunders, Teders, Barron, & Rodichok, 1982.)

Once again, the power of clinical replication series, in terms of their influence on practitioners, is due in large part to the ability of these series to answer questions relevant to practitioners. But experimental analysis of other, more basic questions can occur simultaneously with, or in the context of, clinical replication series. These efforts are best carried out in clinical research centers or through the judicious use of single case experiments by practitioners within clinical replication series. Thus, as we noted in Chapter 4, the clinical replication series is relevant to all of the major questions in the evaluation and dissemination of treatment technologies. Attempts to address, simultaneously, all of the important scientific questions concerning behavior-change procedures should help to check unbridled acceptance of unproven procedures, a problem that has plagued the human services down through the years.

There is now wide recognition of the necessity for clinical replication to fully answer questions relevant to our clinical research efforts. For example, professional societies and government agencies responsible for the recent proliferation of clinical practice guidelines described in Chapter 4 point out that these guidelines must consider the applicability and feasibility of the intervention in the local setting where it is delivered. This is in contrast to a rigorous assessment of scientific evidence based on results from systematic evaluations of the intervention in a controlled clinical research context. The word chosen by some policy makers and researchers to describe information relevant to the former goal is "effectiveness" of an intervention (Seligman, 1995), although the American Psychological Association has recently chosen the less redundant and less confusing term, "clinical utility." In contrast, the term used to describe more rigorous scientific assessment of an intervention is "efficacy." Clinical replication, with strong underlying awareness of the threats to internal and external validity and the level of inferences that can be drawn, can bring the practitioner back into a position of true partnership with the researcher and ensure a contribution by the practitioner to science.

Guidelines for Conducting Clinical Replication Series

Ideally, based on existing models of the progression of applied research, demonstrations of the clinical utility or field effectiveness of research should follow and expand upon careful confirmation of the efficacy of an intervention. The designs we have already reviewed, and relevant group comparison methods, are used to accomplish this task. After experimental verification of the efficacy of a treatment—followed perhaps by component analyses of the necessary and sufficient conditions for a treatment to be effective—studies on the generality, feasibility, and clinical utility of the intervention would begin. In this sequence of events, utilizing clinical replication series furthers an analysis of reasons for failure and of modifications to the intervention to promote generality of effectiveness.

Nevertheless, it is recognized that the world, including the scientific world, does not always proceed in such an orderly fashion, and that many major clinical replication series have appeared prior to the research necessary to demonstrate, first, the efficacy of the intervention when compared against no treatment or some good attention placebo, and, second, the component analysis. In other words, in the most usual case a treatment is developed by an innovative practitioner, based on some familiarity with prior research and theory and/or intuitive judgments concerning the necessary components of an effective intervention. This is followed by a systematic "research-dismantling" strategy wherein the components of treatment are further refined, improved, and often reassembled. Frequently this results in a treatment that bears little resemblance to the original one. For example, Wolpe's (1958) series, as described in Chapter 3, sparked the substantial thrust of research on fear reduction that eventually resulted in an intervention based on in vivo exposure and cognitive behavioral approaches bearing little resemblance to systematic desensitization in imagination.

We would suggest that a clinical replication series to establish feasibility and generality of findings following efficacy research is preferable; and in many ways it is the ideal progression of research, which is one reason we are addressing these matters so late in the present volume. Nevertheless, innovative practitioners who feel that they have developed an effective intervention for a difficult problem will undoubtedly proceed with a clinical replication series and, in some cases, this will be of considerable value to the scientific community if it is ultimately published. It should be stated at this point that there are also grave dangers associated with the publication of "innovative" clinical replication series, particularly if the guidelines described below are not followed.

The history of the human services, and all health-related fields, is replete with dramatic but untested "miracle cures" that seem to have worked in one setting with one practitioner, but were later proved useless. Some of these procedures were actually dangerous. Thus, the guidelines described below should be followed since this will rule out some threats to internal validity, or to the degree of confidence that one has in the actual efficacy of the treatment as opposed to alternative explanations. The value of these innovative series would be greatly increased, of course, by the presence within the series of single case experimentation demonstrating the efficacy of treatment and elucidating the important components of treatment through a component analysis. Thus, the guidelines to be described below apply equally to an initial innovative clinical series, particularly with experimental analyses embedded within it, or to one that is attempting to establish generality of findings after an efficacy-building progression of research.

Questions Addressed by Clinical Replication

There are several unanswered questions that can be particularly well addressed by clinical replication. First, using a well-defined, clinically significant criterion of improvement and applying an intervention in its most powerful form, how many of a series of patients improve? It would be important, of course, to answer this and subsequent questions in as many different settings as possible to establish maximum generality of findings. Second, how many patients show limited improvement that would not be judged clinically significant by practitioners, who would then be forced to consider additional or alternative interventions? Third, how many people fail to improve or perhaps even deteriorate during administration of the intervention? Fourth, what are the reasons for limited improvement or deterioration?

Paying close attention to nonclinical improvement and failures, as well as successes, the practitioner in the process of clinical replication will "try to describe and account for what happened" (Cronbach, 1975, p. 124) by looking at similarities and differences among failures and successes along a number of dimensions. Such dimensions would include, but not be limited to, procedural differences in the application of the intervention (e.g., successful patients may have been seen more frequently than nonsuccessful patients, or sophisticated technology that may enhance the intervention is present in one setting but not another). It is also possible that different therapists applying apparently similar procedures will produce different rates of success. While a search for therapist variables that may influence outcome has not been fruitful as of yet (Christensen & Jacobson, 1994), it is entirely plausible that some therapist variables might show up in the context of a large clinical replication series. For example, therapists who are more competent at administering the treatment protocol in a coherent and structured manner, as determined by assessing quality of therapy, seem to produce a better outcome during treatment of depression by interpersonal psychotherapy (Frank et al., 1991; Frank & Spanier, 1995).

Most practitioners and researchers will look for differences among the patients themselves, assuming that the parameters of the intervention and the practitioner are relatively constant across a series, to find important clues to account for differential response. For example, severity of presenting problems or disorders may well affect not only short-term and long-term response to treatment but also relative responsiveness to different treatments (e.g., Brown & Barlow, 1995; Elkin et al., 1995). In a recent series from our own setting, the simultaneous administration of high-potency benzodiazepines during the early stages of treatment seems to be associated with poorer long-term outcome at a 2-year follow-up point in a large sample of patients with PDA (Brown & Barlow, 1995) when compared to those individuals who were not taking high-potency benzodiazepines. Other investigators are looking to behavioral traits such as treatment "resistance" (Beutler et al., 1991), or "perfectionism" (Blatt, 1995; see also Garfield, 1994).

Definition of Patients

The first guideline concerns the selection and definition of patients. Clearly, little will be communicated from a clinical replication series if a practitioner defines patients very vaguely—for example, "neurotics" or "learning disabled." Classification of patients based on objective, detailed descriptions is essential before one can begin to talk about the effects of treatment, including successes and failures. Within the area of mental disorder, the advent of the DSM system is seen by most as a significant advance in the empirical description and initial classification of emotional and behavioral problems (Barlow, 1991), and this shorthand notation may often suffice. But nothing will be lost and much will be gained by as clear and detailed a description of the presenting problem and background variables as is possible, particularly if the components described are of potential theoretical or functional significance.

One interesting source of such variables occurs when practitioners see a large number of patients in one particular category. Over time, practitioners may exclude certain patients from their treatment, based on their ideas about who will benefit and who will fail. These clinical intuitions are often based on extremely valuable clinical experience derived from informal clinical replication series that are continually going on in every practitioner's setting. For example, a practitioner treating agoraphobics may have observed in the past that two or three patients addicted to narcotics (to take an extreme example) did not benefit from treatment. Therefore, he or she will treat no further patients with narcotic addictions. The difficulty with unexamined selection criteria is that the systematic observations of failures will then be lost to the community of practitioners at large once the results of a clinical replication series are reported. It is preferable to deal with all patients who meet a widely agreed-upon criterion of problem definition, but to keep track of the variable thought to be of importance (e.g., addiction to narcotics). This would allow systematic observation of failures or partial successes to be reported and would provide a formal test of practitioner's ideas.

Of course, many patients seeking out treatment in frontline practitioner settings may not meet criteria for DSM-IV disorders, and others will meet the criteria for disorders about which little is known. In these cases, clear descriptions of the patients' presenting problems and other relevant characteristics will be all the more important. After all, many of the disorders in the DSM system are loose syndromal collections, not functional disease processes, and it seems likely that a variety of discrete functional processes are gathered under given syndromal labels (Follette, Houts, & Hayes, 1992).

Definition of Intervention

The second requirement is the existence of a clearly defined, replicable, intervention procedure. That is, a procedure must be described in enough detail that other experienced and qualified practitioners could apply it after some initial acquaintance with the procedural details of intervention. Very seldom was this guideline fulfilled in clinical research or reports of clinical replication series prior to the 1980s. However, in the 1980s it became necessary for efficacy research purposes to specify in greater detail the psychotherapeutic procedures under evaluation. As was discussed in Chapter 5, to accomplish this, therapeutic interventions were manualized so that multiple therapists involved in the clinical trials administered approximately the same intervention. Treatment adherence instruments were then developed such that audiotapes or videotapes of the intervention could be scored to determine if therapists were, in fact, adhering to the treatment protocol. This process ensured that a well-defined "independent variable" existed in these large clinical trials attempting to demonstrate the efficacy of one intervention or another.

The rigidity with which these manuals are followed in efficacy studies may limit the generalizability of findings from large clinical trials, but the manuals themselves have proved very useful to clinicians wishing to acquaint themselves with new psychosocial treatments with recognized efficacy. Furthermore, clinical replication series are an important source of information about the generalizability of manuals themselves. A very recent step has been to make these manuals available to practitioners on the front lines, who then apply them in a flexible and clinically sensitive manner on the intuitively sensible assumption that "flexibility" will produce more positive therapeutic results.

Interestingly, this assumption has been difficult to prove. For example, Jacobson et al. (1989) found no differences in outcome after marital therapy delivered in a highly structured manner versus more flexibly, although the flexible delivery showed a nonsignificant trend to be a bit better at a 6-month follow-up. In another study specifically testing this hypothesis with 120 phobic patients, the results were, counterintuitively, quite the opposite in that standardized therapy proved significantly more successful than flexible therapy (Schulte, Kunzel, Pepping, & Schulte-Bahranberg, 1992). Wilson (1996) outlines an important research agenda examining the use or misuse of these structured programs in clinical practice. In any case, manualized interventions, however applied, will then lend themselves very well to the accumulation of clinical replication series in forthcoming practice research networks. Clearly described procedures rather than vague references to "psychotherapy" or "physical therapy" will entice practitioners to take those few steps necessary to become further acquainted with a successful procedure.

Adequate, Realistic, and Practical Measures

As with time-series methodology more generally, a third guideline requires that measures of change must be reliable and valid and should be as nonreactive as possible. Guidelines and examples for these types of measurement are described in Chapters 11 through 13.

These measures of change must also yield reliable estimates of the extent of success. This is necessary in order to differentiate improvement that is clinically significant and important from change that might be in the positive direction, but is not sufficient from the point of view of either the patient or the practitioner, necessitating additional efforts to achieve clinically important change. Even more importantly, the appropriate measures must be realistic, practical, and brief so that they lend themselves to use in busy practice settings. Typically these measures should assess not only symptomatic functioning but also patient satisfaction and functional impairment. At present there is a great deal of ongoing activity with the goal of developing uniform outcomes measures that will be applicable in newly developed practice research networks. Most likely these measures will be "online" so that practitioners, supplied with the appropriate software, can enter data directly that is then transmitted to the data processing center of the practice research network or managed care company. Perhaps the best example to date is the work of Ken Howard and associates (e.g., Howard, Moras, Brill, Martinovich, & Lutz, in press) who have developed standardized outcomes assessments to profile individual responses to a variety of interventions.

Observation of Failures

Fourth, and finally, in any clinical replication series, the investigators must attend to failures as well as to limited success in their patients, and engage in intensive local observation in an attempt to determine factors associated with this differential response. In this way, practitioners will determine various procedural and patient variables, particularly in combination, associated with nonresponse or relapse.

These four factors just described comprise the guidelines for a successful, scientifically important, clinical replication series. In essence, clinical replication series build on the basic approach of single case experimental designs, as reviewed in Chapters 5 through 8, but apply these in a simplified manner focused on an evaluation of the generality of treatment impact.

A number of well-done clinical replication series have been reported. Early influential series include Lemere and Voegtlin on adversive approaches to the treatment of alcoholism (e.g., Lemere & Voegtlin, 1950); the influential Wolpe series (1958) referred to above; and the Maletzky (1980; 1991) series on paraphilias. More recent series include a particularly well done clinical replication reported by Morin, Stone, McDonald, and Jones (1994) describing the treatment of 100 consecutive patients with insomnia, as well as reports on treating childhood obesity (Israel, Silverman, & Solotar, 1986). Another well-done recent report described the treatment with cognitive behavior therapy of 38 patients presenting with severe endogenous depression (Thase, Simons, Cahalane, & McGeary, 1991). In order to illustrate these guidelines in the next section, we will examine their presence or absence in one of the best-known clinical replication series, Masters and Johnson.

The Masters and Johnson Series

As noted above, this series has been, in all likelihood, the single most influential piece of work ever published for practitioners who deal with sexual problems. One book, describing direct behavioral interventions for the varieties of sexual dysfunction in a large population of males and females, literally revolutionized the treatment of these problems, such that probably very few psychosocial practitioners today treat sexual dysfunction without some use of these procedures. While these direct behavioral procedures have been integrated into other theoretical systems (e.g., Kaplan, 1987), and a variety of explanations have been made for success, they still comprise the primary set of intervention procedures for these problems. Thus, no chapter on clinical replication could avoid an examination of this important work. Nevertheless, while there are considerable strengths to this series, a review based on the guidelines above reveals that there are also several distinct weaknesses that limit the amount of information available to practitioners.

Selection

First, because of the way the program was set up, and because of some a priori decisions made by the investigators, the patients were highly selected. Some of the criteria included having the time and financial resources to travel to St. Louis and spend two weeks away from home, family, and employment. Referral from some authority—such as health professionals, clergy, and so on—was also necessary, as well as some ascertainment that the married couple otherwise had a stable marriage, communicated well, and were both strongly interested in participating in the program. Questions were also asked of the referring authority about the adaptation of the couple to their community. Finally, the couple, before coming to St. Louis, had to agree to cooperate with the program for 5 years following its termination. Obviously, this produced a very highly restricted group of people, which limits the ability to generalize the results to the more usual flow of patients presenting with this problem in a more typical setting.

On the other hand, the cases that were treated are most often richly and thoroughly described, such that practitioners can readily identify similar cases presented in their clinics. Furthermore, from the point of view of contributing to the research process and suggesting etiological contributions of various factors, numerous data gleaned from the individual histories and experiences during treatment are provided and broken down into various categories. These factors are then related to treatment outcome. For example, the seeming contribution of religious orthodoxy to impotence in males and the fact that patients falling in this category failed most often during treatment for their impotence represents the first time that the potential salience of this issue was recognized.

Intervention

This area has caused considerable difficulty in the years following Masters and Johnson's 1970 report. There seem to be several reasons for this. First, the authors do describe their treatment procedures extremely well. In fact, the clarity of their intervention programs for the various dysfunctions, as described, is undoubtedly one of the reasons that their program has been so widely adopted. Nevertheless, there is accumulating evidence that these therapists may have actually introduced a considerable number of additional clinical procedures and tactics as they tried to do the best they could for their patients. Hints of this have occurred in the various books describing their intervention (cf. Barlow, 1980; Zilbergeld & Evans, 1980). There is, of course, nothing at all wrong with this tactic; in fact, any clinician who does not employ additional procedures if they seem appropriate could be questioned. But, for our purposes, it seems that many of these procedures were not described. Zilbergeld and Evans (1980) attribute the failure of many sex therapists to approach the rate of success reported by Masters and Johnson to this deficit in communication.

Measures

In this area, Masters and Johnson also deserve considerable credit. But, on the other hand, problems have emerged in the way they reported their data—problems that limit its usefulness to practitioners. Attempting to be as conservative as they could in their reports, certainly an admirable goal, they decided upon the now well-known failure rates rather than success rates. This means that after choosing an arbitrary criterion (for example, providing orgasmic opportunity for the female partner in at least 50% of attempts at sexual intercourse, in the case of premature ejaculation), Masters and Johnson reported their results in terms of patients who initially failed to reach this criterion. They reasoned that since relapses might occur, one could not talk of success until the 5-year follow-up. Although they did conduct the 5-year follow-up on people they could reach, and reported the results, the primary statistics communicated around the world were initial failure rates. Fortunately, sexual dysfunction is a rather straightforward problem, observable by both the patient and the partner, and the direct interviews of both partners to ascertain sexual functioning would seem to be an adequate basis for determining success or failure in these cases. Furthermore, except for secondary impotence in males, relapse rates over the 5 years, in those patients who could be reached, seemed minimal. Nevertheless, this dichotomous manner of reporting results obscures degrees of improvement that are to be found in any clinical series and precludes detailed analysis of those patients who did well from those who improved minimally. For example, there were probably some patients with premature ejaculation who were able to provide orgasmic experiences for their partner (assuming one agrees that this is a reasonable criterion) 80% of the time or more. Perhaps another group ranged from 40% to 60% of the time, and yet a third group ranged from 20% to 40%. Even the third group can be said to have improved somewhat if the baseline was zero. More important, one patient reaching the level of 45% would be classified as a failure while the next, reaching 55%, would be a success. A far more preferable system would be to report the range of responses and proceed with an analysis to provide more information to practitioners on the type of response likely from patients walking into their office. Of course, the provision of base rates of sexual functioning using these criteria would also be of considerable assistance so one could judge how far each patient, or the group as a whole, moved in relation to the criteria. These base rates were not provided.

Analysis of Failures

Here Masters and Johnson make perhaps their greatest contribution. They recognize the importance of documenting failures in the development of comprehensive and effective treatments, and repeatedly report on factors that seem to influence failure. In some excellent examples, as in the case of secondary impotence described above, failures are described in tabular form as a function of clinically important factors. The influences of religious orthodoxy have already been mentioned. Furthermore, Masters and Johnson devote a full chapter at the end of their book to a description of treatment failures. Nevertheless, in retrospect, the information could have been more systematic. For example, presumed causes of failure are not provided in any kind of an organized way for other categories of sexual dysfunction. Again, the chapter on treatment failures is really just a summary of selected cases of failure in which the authors discuss or describe the occasional idiosyncratic marital problem or procedural errors on the part of the therapist that seem to be associated with a therapeutic failure. It is not clear how representative these cases are in the context of all failures in their series. And, as in most series discussed thus far, Masters and Johnson did not systematically analyze the reasons for failure using appropriate time-series methodology. However, the documentation of factors associated with failure is certainly a first step.

Summary

One can question the figures of percentage failure, or the after-5-years percentage of success, in relation to the total number of people seen. Using one of many possible strategies in determining their results, Masters and Johnson chose to report only known failures at follow-up. That is, those who, upon interview, either immediately after treatment or after 5 years, were determined to have failed or to have relapsed. But they excluded from follow-up approximately 30% of the patients who could not be reached. Many reports of outcome of a given intervention routinely include these data in the category of failures; and this, of course, might change quite dramatically some of the failure rates, depending on the distribution of these unreachable patients in the various categories. Masters and Johnson cannot really be faulted for this, it is simply a matter of choosing one strategy over the other, and they do make it clear just how they compiled these results. But the results, even with their highly selected sample, might look considerably worse. If results had been communicated rather than the more restricted and more positive failure rates that were reported, the impact of the series on practitioners might have been somewhat different, and some of the frustrations being voiced by many who cannot seem to replicate Masters and Johnson's success might not have occurred.

Examining Failures

One of the best early examples of an analysis of failures coming out of a specialty clinic or clinical research center is Foa's (1979) description of 10 individuals with severe, obsessive-compulsive disorder (OCD). These patients did not respond to her otherwise successful program consisting of exposure and response prevention for compulsive rituals.

Patients with severe OCD, of course, always report an overwhelming fear of contamination or catastrophe. Rituals of various kinds, usually washing or checking, are then carried out to prevent this catastrophe or contamination from occurring or spreading (e.g., excessive washing, checking locks, requesting reassurance, etc.).

In the best tradition of intensive local observation, Foa observed two factors that seemed to differentiate very clearly the 10 failures from the majority of successes. The first she termed *overvalued ideation*. Most individuals with OCD state, when asked directly, that their fears are irrational or senseless, and report that it would be unlikely that the consequences would occur despite the fact that they feel compelled to behave as if a real danger exists. In contrast, four of Foa's 10 failures reported strong beliefs that their underlying fears were, in fact, realistic and that their rituals actually did prevent the occurrence of disastrous consequences. For example, one patient was afraid of inflicting mental retardation on her son through her own contact with retarded people. Another feared contracting tetanus from contact with sharp objects, while still another feared contact with leukemia germs that would cause the death of her husband and children.

Elaborating on the cognitive processes in this last case, Foa describes a woman with above-average intelligence who reported sitting in a beauty parlor one day and hearing the woman sitting next to her tell the beautician that she had just come back from the children's hospital, where she had visited her grandson who had leukemia. The patient immediately left, registered in a hotel, and washed for three days. Her reasons for this were that she would transmit leukemia germs to her husband and children, if she was in contact with them, and they would then die. She reported that although she could transmit them to her family, she was immune to these germs herself. She was asked if she had talked to specialists about the rationality of these thoughts and she mentioned that she had talked to several specialists: "They all tried to assure me that there are no leukemia germs, but medicine is not that advanced; I am convinced that I know something that the doctors have not yet discovered. There are definitely germs that carry leukemia" (Foa, 1979, p. 170). All four of these patients described by Foa were unable to admit some irrationality in these fears. Once again, the more usual case might say something like, "Yes, I know there are no leukemia germs, and that I can't really transmit it, but the fear still overwhelms me and I'm compelled to wash so that I'll feel more comfortable around my family."

In another four patients, Foa observed a second characteristic that seemed to differentiate these failures from more successful patients: the presence of severe depression. Specifically, on a rating scale of 0–8, the mean depression rating for all patients was 4.8 before treatment and 2.8 after treatment. But these four patients who failed manifested severe depression, with a mean of 7.8 on this scale. One patient had severe psychomotor retardation, which prevented her from carrying out routine household chores. The other three were agitated depressives with frequent crying spells. Of the 10 failures, two additional patients displayed combinations of both overvalued ideation and depression.

Since Foa collected multiple self-report measures during treatment, she was able to identify possible reasons why these patients did not do as well. Specifically, the former two groups failed to show habituation while being exposed repeatedly to their fear-producing situations. That is, these patients reported little or no decrement in anxiety during exposure trials when compared to the typical patient. Although the patients with depression, as compared to the patients with overvalued ideation, demonstrated slightly different patterns, neither showed the habituation that seems necessary for successful response to treatment. In an important step, Foa reported that at least some of the depressive individuals later responded to treatment after first being treated for their depression.

Subsequently, researchers, including Foa herself, have followed up on these clinical observations. Overvalued ideation continues to be a very important clinical characteristic for purposes of predicting treatment outcome in this disorder. For example, recognizing research in this area, DSM-IV adopted the specifier "with poor insight" to characterize the 10% or so of patients with this disorder who seem unable to discriminate their obsessions as in any way unrealistic or irrational. This has proved a very useful finding for clinicians. On the other hand, subsequent reports examining the clinical outcome of patients with comorbid mood disorders have not confirmed the importance of this clinical characteristic as a predictor of outcome, as long as the mood disorder is not the principal or more severe diagnosis (Brown, Antony, & Barlow, 1995; Foa et al., 1983).

In summary, we can learn from this interesting series that analysis of failures is comprised of three loosely related steps. First, factors associated with failure or minimal success are identified in the context of a clinical replication series. Naturally, not all factors identified will turn out to be important as in the Foa series. Second, attention is drawn to these factors, and prospective replication occurs in the same clinic as well as other clinics. Third, and most importantly, an experimental analysis, preferably using time-series methodology, can be undertaken—both by the practitioner as well as in more sophisticated research centers—to determine and verify the precise course of failure.

Statistical Approaches for Predicting Success and Failure

Recognizing the necessity of determining patient-treatment interaction, clinical researchers have occasionally employed a somewhat different strategy to address the issue of predicting individual responses to treatment. The strategies and procedures necessary to produce this type of report have been around for decades and have been used occasionally as a supplemental analysis in traditional between-group outcome studies. This strategy involves treating a large number of patients in a clinical replication format, examining overall outcome, and then attempting to identify factors associated with outcome based on predetermined criteria, usually scores on psychological tests (e.g., Brown & Barlow, 1995). These predictions are made statistically, using such procedures as multiple regression, discriminant function analysis, and measures to determine percentage of variance accounted for (e.g., eta squared). Some investigators, in an effort to determine even more complex factors or chronologically arranged combinations of factors associated with success or failure, have resorted to complex correlational analyses, such as structured equation modeling (see special issue of the *Journal of Consulting and Clinical Psychology*, June 1994). The basic purpose in most of these procedures is to make probabilistic statements about factors associated with success or failure in subsequent patients undergoing a specific treatment.

One early example of this type of effort with continuing relevance for practitioners was published—in the area of psychological treatment of headaches—by Blanchard, Andrasik, and associates (Blanchard, Andrasik, Neff, Arena, Ahles, Jurish, Pallmeyer, Saunders, Teders, Barron, & Rodichok, 1982). It formed the basis for an even larger series of 250 headache patients reported in 1985 (Blanchard et al., 1985). This example will be used to illustrate these procedures and to provide a context for comments on the relationship of these procedures to intensive local observation and time-series methodology, as well as updated, more sophisticated quantitative efforts.

Specifically, 91 patients with chronic headaches were treated with a combination of relaxation and biofeedback in a typical clinical replication format. There were no control groups or comparison groups, nor was there any component analysis of treatment strategies usually associated with traditional outcome research. In setting the stage for this analysis, Blanchard et al. noted that the two principal nonpharmacological treatments for headaches are varieties of biofeedback training and relaxation training. Furthermore, numerous controlled, direct comparisons of these two procedures have shown them generally to be equally efficacious. Finally, they observed that direct, controlled comparisons of biofeedback and/or relaxation, in comparison to some controlled condition in the treatment of headache, have been adequately studied or even overstudied, with almost all studies showing that either one of these two treatments is superior to no treatment. Thus, this series represents the ideal implementation of a clinical replication strategy following experimental verification of the efficacy of a treatment.

Different types of headaches were represented among the 91 patients. Thirty-three had tension headaches, 30 had migraine headaches, and 28 combined tension and migraine. Since relaxation is much cheaper, more efficient, and easier to administer than biofeedback, the strategy of the study was to apply relaxation first to all patients, regardless of type of headache, for 10 sessions. Biofeedback was then introduced only for those patients who did not show substantial reduction in headache activity from relaxation therapy. These patients received 12 sessions of either thermal biofeedback for vascular headaches or frontal EMG biofeedback for tension headaches. The notion here is that biofeedback would be administered only to relaxation "nonresponders" to determine if it indeed would be worth the greatly increased cost to put one of these nonresponders through a biofeedback regimen. Naturally, this strategy also allows the investigators to speculate on the mechanisms of action underlying each of these treatments because, if biofeedback works for a relaxation nonresponder, perhaps a different mechanism of action underlies the effectiveness of these procedures.

Since the primary goal of this project was research, a more rigorous and systematic approach to measurement and treatment was observed than is likely to occur in a practitioner's setting. First, all patients were required to complete a 4-week baseline period during which daily ratings of headache were made and numerous psychological tests were administered. Second, the patients, interventions, and measures were exceptionally well described and defined, fulfilling the first three guidelines for clinical replication. Patients presenting with headaches were subjected to extensive diagnostic procedures, including neurological examination, and the categorization of headache type was made by up-to-date, state-of-the-art procedures. Treatment, consisting of relaxation, followed in some cases by one or another type of biofeedback, was standardized to the extent that every step was recorded in a manual; thus, these treatments could be carried out by relatively inexperienced students. Finally, the most up-to-date and sophisticated subjective and physiological assessment of headaches and the various factors thought to be associated with headaches (e.g., background tension and anxiety) were measured—once again, far more extensively than would be likely or even desirable in practice.

The manner in which these measures were quantified allowed Blanchard et al. to set very specific criteria for improvement, a necessary first step for analyzing failures. These criteria were based on data from a validated headache diary and specified a ratio of reduction in headache activity relative to baseline headache activity, referred to as a *headache index*. Patients had to achieve a 50% reduction in headache activity before being considered much improved. Patients not reaching this criterion during the initial relaxation phase were assigned to one of the biofeedback conditions. This "headache index," of course, could be used by any practitioner, making it a very valuable assessment of success or failure.

Although the usual statistical analyses were performed assessing pre–post changes for each treatment, a more stringent and clinically meaningful test of the efficacy of relaxation was calculated to examine the frequency with which individual patients experienced useful reductions in headache activity. This analysis demonstrated that 52% of tension headache patients demonstrated at least a 50% reduction in headache activity, while only 25.8% of patients with vascular headache showed this type of improvement. Numbers of patients falling in the categories of unimproved or worse (defined as less than 20% improvement) or slightly improved (defined as 20% to 49% improvement) were also provided. Similar calculations were made for the biofeedback procedures. Overall, relaxation therapy alone produced significant improvement for all three headache groups, with tension headaches responding most favorably, as described above. Biofeedback led to further significant reduction in headache activity for all who received it, with combined migraine and tension headache patients responding most favorably. In the end, after both treatments had been administered to all who qualified, 73% of tension headache patients and 52% of vascular headache patients were much improved (defined as at least a 50% reduction in headache activity).

Before treatment, a number of psychological tests or inventories were administered. These included the MMPI, the Beck Depression Inventory, the State Trait Anxiety Inventory, and a variety of others. Stepwise multiple regressions were calculated using the psychological test scores alone and also combining these test scores with headache diagnosis to predict average posttreatment headache index score. In addition, in order to conduct a discriminant function analysis, the groups were divided into those who were much improved (50% or greater reduction in headache response) and those who did not meet this criterion, again using the psychological test scores alone as predictors, and then combining the scores with headache diagnosis. This analysis allowed a determination of which two or three test scores would best predict significant improvement.

Considering the multiple regression analysis first, overall results revealed that approximately 32% of the variance in end-of-treatment headache index scores could be predicted after relaxation, and 44% of the variance after biofeedback, using the standard psychological test scores. Specifically, several scales of the MMPI and the life-events scale from the Holmes and Rahe Social Readjustment Rating Scale contributed to the prediction of postrelaxation headache index for all patients. However, different psychological tests turn out to be predictive when one attempts to forecast the response of distinct types of headaches. Specifically, 40.8%, 32.8%, and 26.1% of the variance can be predicted in the final headache index for tension, migraine, and combined headache respectively. While this is considered high by current standards of research, it is unlikely to communicate much to the practitioner concerning predictions of response to treatment in individual patients.

Predictions from multiple regression equations, as Blanchard et al. (1982) point out, are much less useful than discriminant function analyses (described below), for determining generality of findings, including predictors of success. Multiple regression, involving as it does a series of correlations between predetermined predictor variables and response to treatment followed by an analysis of the percentage of variance accounted for, leaves no room for assessment of a clinically significant response to a given treatment and the predictors that might be associated with that clinical response.

To take the "best" example above, the psychological tests would account for 40.8% of the variance in predicting response to treatment of those subjects in the study with tension headache (and this is quite high for a psychological study). Assuming for a moment that one could infer to the population of tension headache sufferers (and to the individual patient in the practitioner's office) from this sample, then one could say that if this one headache sufferer presented a certain pattern of test results, there is a 40% chance he or she would "respond" to relaxation. Whether this response would be clinically meaningful could not be specified. Furthermore, the figure of 40.8% represents the "average" response of 31 subjects in this group. Problems in generalizing from this hypothetical average to an individual patient have been described before (Barlow & Hersen, 1984). For this reason, as well as others, procedures involving the determination of percentage of variance accounted for are very weak methods for determining strength or generality of effectiveness of a treatment. Much the same can be said for other correlational procedures, such as structural equation modeling, that do not consider individual successes or failures.

Blanchard et al. suggest, quite reasonably, that canonical discriminant function may have considerably more clinical utility, since predetermined clinical criteria of success or failure can be entered into this calculation and predictions can then be made on whether a patient will succeed or fail based on these criteria. In this particular study, the criterion, as mentioned above, was at least a 50% reduction on the headache index. Once again, in deference to the practitioner who may wish to use these data, the authors leave the actual classification calculations in manageable form so that practitioners can apply them to their own individual patients. Basically, this calculation reveals that of all patients finishing relaxation, 61.8% could be classified correctly as either successes or failures based on some combination of three of the psychological tests or their subscales. The investigators limited the analyses to three tests rather than the whole battery in the interest of the potential applicability of these procedures to clinical situations. That is, it is easier for a clinician to give three tests rather than a whole battery.

One difficulty with this approach, of course, is the psychological test or subscales that turn out to be the important predictors. In many cases these differ widely from group to group. For example, for the vascular headache group treated by biofeedback, three MMPI subscales were the best predictors of outcome. On the other hand, for all patients finishing relaxation, two calculations from the Life Events Scale and the State Anxiety subscale of the State Trait Anxiety Inventory cluster together as most effective predictors. As the investigators themselves point out, these combinations of test scores defy easy characterization. They conclude that it would probably be naive to expect the same test to predict results for different patients groups and for different treatments. Thus, the generality of these predictors is far from a given fact, despite the large N.

In a more recent example of this type of research endeavor, Brown and Barlow (1995) examined a number of clinical features that have relevance to the prediction of short- and long-term treatment response in patients with panic disorder (with no or minimal agoraphobic avoidance). As was the case in Blanchard et al. (1982), the Brown and Barlow (1995) study did not include any control or comparison groups. In this investigation, the clinical response of 63 patients who completed a 12-session cognitive-behavioral treatment program for panic disorder (Craske & Barlow, 1993) was evaluated at posttreatment and 24-month follow-up. Unlike the Blanchard et al. (1982), Brown and Barlow (1995) selected and analyzed variables with more intuitive conceptual and clinical relevance to the prediction of treatment outcome.

Consistent with the typical practice in panic disorder treatment outcome research, Brown and Barlow (1995) used two categorical measures to signify clinically significant improvement: (1) *panic-free status:* a report of no panic attacks in the month prior to the posttreatment or follow-up interview; and (2) *high endstate status:* a report of no panic attacks in the past month, and a rating of 2 ("slightly disturbing—not really disabling") or below on a 0–8 clinical severity rating scale of panic disorder (assigned by the independent evaluator conducting the clinical interview). Similar to the outcomes of other recent treatment studies of panic disorder (e.g., Clark, Salkovskis, Hackmann, Middleton, Anastaiades, & Gelder, 1994), the percentage of patients achieving panic-free and high endstate status at posttreatment was 68.3% and 39.7%, respectively. These rates increased to 74.6% and 57.1% for panic-free and high endstate status, respectively, at a 24-month follow-up. Change in patients' use of psychotropic medication is another important index of outcome in the treatment of anxiety disorders. At pretreatment, 44.4% of patients were using psychotropic medications (the vast majority were using Xanax). By the end of treatment, this rate had declined to 23.8%, which is noteworthy because, for research purposes, patients using medications had been instructed to remain on a stable dosage during the active treatment phase of the study. This decline was still evident at a 24-month follow-up (25.4%).

Two dimensional variables were analyzed to determine if they were predictive of short- or long-term treatment outcome: duration of panic disorder, and pretreatment clinical severity of panic disorder (based on the 0–8 clinical severity scale assigned by the independent evaluator following the pretreatment clinical interview). The impact of these variables was examined using analyses of variance (ANOVAs) in which duration and clinical severity were used as dependent measures and categorical measures of outcome (i.e., panic-free status, high endstate status) were used as grouping variables. Analyses of the duration variable were not significant, indicating that the length of time patients had been experiencing panic was not associated with either short- or long-term outcome, based on the categorical measures of panic-free status and high endstate status. In addition, pretreatment clinical severity of panic disorder was not associated with high endstate status or panic-free status at posttreatment. However, there was a significant association between pretreatment clinical severity and both high endstate and panic-free status at 24-month follow-up. Specifically, patients who failed to meet criteria for high endstate status and panic-free status at 24-month follow-up had been assigned significantly higher clinical severity ratings for their panic disorder at pretreatment. The fact that this relationship was found only at a 24-month follow-up suggests that patients with more severe symptomatology were just as responsive to treatment in the short term, but were either less able to maintain these treatment gains or more apt to experience marked fluctuations in symptoms over the longer term.

In another interesting result, it was found that patients who were using medication during the active phase of treatment evidenced a poorer outcome than patients not using medications, at both posttreatment and a 24-month follow-up (based on ANOVAs in which dimensional measures of treatment outcome were used as dependent variables and medication use/nonuse was used as the grouping variable). This result was still evident when differences in pretreatment severity were controlled for statistically (additional analyses had indicated that patients using medication were more symptomatic than patients not taking medication on some pretreatment measures). Although many previous studies had failed to detect this relationship (cf. Clum, 1989), this finding was consistent with the long-held clinical wisdom and theoretical opinion that psychosocial and drug treatments for panic disorder may have conflicting mechanisms of action. For instance, these results could be taken in support of the position that certain medications, such as the benzodiazepines, block the mechanisms of action of cognitive-behavioral therapy for panic disorder by preventing the evocation of anxiety that is necessary for emotional processing to occur (Barlow, 1988; Foa & Kozak, 1986). On the other hand, Brown and Barlow (1995) proposed that any negative effects of medication during treatment could also be more psychological in nature. Specifically, these authors speculated that the use of medication during treatment could mitigate the ability of patients to attribute any positive changes in their symptoms to the efficacy of psychosocial therapy and their competency in applying newly learned techniques. If this were the case, then these patients may not garner the same sense of personal control over their symptoms as do unmedicated patients who would be more apt to attribute the alleviation of their symptoms to the successful application of the techniques of psychosocial treatment. In the Brown and Barlow (1995) study, this interpretation seemed more likely because the majority of patients using medication were on very low, nontherapeutic dosages or were using the drugs on a practice research network (PRN) basis.

While conceptually there is much to recommend these kinds of statistical approaches to predicting success and failure, the best application of these methods is likely to occur when treatment-related variability can be identified at the level of the individual. Improvement seen in any given case can be due to some combination of treatment, extraneous factors (e.g., changes in life situation, physical disease, and so on), and inconsistent measurement processes. Even if measurement is carefully controlled, mere improvement does not mean improvement due to treatment. If these statistical procedures are based only on extensive but not intensive data, treatment-related improvement and improvement due to other factors are mixed together in the correlations obtained, which will almost necessarily reduce the degree to which replication of relations can be expected. As readers should now understand, the best way to identify treatment-related variability at the level of the individual is through the use of single case designs, some forms of which can readily be built into group comparisons. Thus, clinical replication series that add some of the controls discussed in the previous chapters have a better chance of finding replicable and meaningful results.

Conclusions

Several similarities and differences should be apparent between these efforts and the more usual analyses of successes and failures carried out in an applied setting. In the applied setting, the practitioner will examine a number of dimensions in the search for predictors of success and failure, including patient variables, therapist variables, other idiosyncrasies of the treatment situation, and perhaps procedural variables relative to the administration of treatment. He or she will not limit himself or herself to a couple of tests or other factors with little logical relation to the problem at hand, as in the Blanchard et al. series. The practitioner will then attempt to identify those factors that seem associated with success or failure. This, of course, should lead, presumably, to more prospective observation and tests of factors thought to be associated with failure in subsequent patients and replication in other clinics. The statistical approach, on the other hand, typically concludes in advance which variables will be examined as predictors without the first step of intensive local observation. Usually these predictors are limited or are very narrowly construed. The Blanchard et al. series is a good example, with its use of psychological tests or inventories. While Blanchard et al. used these in a sensible fashion, often, in other studies, these are multiplied ad infinitum. These tests, representing as they do answers to questions on a paper-and-pencil inventory administered once before treatment begins, have not proved reliable predictors in the past, and even Blanchard et al. admit that the results do not make much sense.

Foa's clinical observation of overvalued ideation, repeatedly assessed over the course of treatment, would seem a more intuitively reasonable predictor than a score on a subscale of the MMPI. Medication use and clinical severity, as in Brown and Barlow, also would seem to be more practical. Other more direct observations of patient behaviors during treatment might also prove to be stronger predictors than one-shot psychological tests. Of course, specifying predictors right from the start does have the advantage of being prospective, and certainly the investigators cannot be accused of introducing some systematic clinician bias into the identification of important predictive factors.

A second major difference is the reliance on a probabilistic statement, as evidenced in the Blanchard et al. and Brown & Barlow series, with the provision of figures on the "likelihood" of a patient's responding in a specific way, given certain test configurations or other pretreatment indices, versus the more individualized type of prediction made thus far in more usual clinical replication series. For example, Foa (1979) identified four individuals who were severely depressed, four with overvalued ideation, and two with both, who were complete failures in her series. Pending further replication and analysis, as outlined in the last section, the practitioner can then determine the extent to which a patient he or she is seeing is similar to one of the Foa patients.

The two series also report discrimination of successes from failures *on the average;* although, as noted above, this discrimination was done with far greater accuracy than is usually the case. A practitioner looking at the Blanchard et al. series with its 40% rate of incorrect classifications, would have to gamble that his or her patient would respond as did one of the correctly classified subjects. Since these subjects are not described much beyond headache type and response on the subscale of various tests, the practitioner would not have much to go on. More detailed individual analysis might examine the 15% to 40% of the patients incorrectly classified on the basis of the various predictors. Were there any apparent differences from those correctly classified? Of course, there is no reason one could not do both types of analyses. But we would suggest that it would be extremely important not to lose sight of the individual as one strives to make clinically relevant predictors available to the practitioner who is seeing individuals.

Both series reported above and other clinical replication series previously described were initial efforts in the analysis of successes and failures that have the advantage of attempting a prospective analysis, but they have the disadvantage of choosing as predictors variables that were not discovered in a clinically relevant fashion through intensive local observation or are otherwise narrowly construed. Nevertheless, this effort would not be complete by any means without further attempts to determine reasons for failure, so that treatments can be adapted and tailored to all patients experiencing distress. For example, while conclusive statements cannot be drawn from Brown and Barlow's (1995) findings as to the reasons why concurrent medication use may have interfered with the effects of psychosocial treatment, these data highlight research directions that may lead to more powerful treatments and predictors of treatment response. For example, detailed analyses of therapeutic process measures could be performed in future studies, particularly with individual cases, to examine the various factors that could account for these outcomes. Regarding the conceptual analysis of why concurrent medication use may hinder psychosocial treatment of panic disorder, measures of anxiety evocation (and habituation) to therapeutic procedures (e.g., interoceptive or situational exposure) and measures of self-efficacy or personal control could be obtained throughout the active treatment phase to determine whether these measures are associated with treatment outcome as a function of medication use/nonuse. Potentially, these findings would have important ramifications on the delivery of drug and psychosocial treatments (e.g., at what point should patients participating in psychosocial treatment be discontinued from their medications?).

Creating a Structure for Clinical Replication: Practice Research Networks

Practice research networks (PRNs) are an innovative attempt to link the practice environment of the production of clinical replication data. The first of these networks has been established by the American Psychiatric Association and is referred to as the Association's Clinical Outcomes Research Network (ACORN) (APA, 1993; McIntyre, 1994). This network will consist of approximately 1,000 clinicians. The goal of the network is to collect data from the cooperating clinicians and to conduct a broad range of studies on the effectiveness of various clinical practice guidelines as well as health service delivery issues, including mental health policy and financing issues. The type of information collected would include the following: (1) diagnosis and basic demographic information from patients, functional status, past history and treatment history; (2) the evaluation process (procedures and results); (3) the treatment recommended and received (nature and intensity of psychotherapy, medication dosage, and length of treatment); (4) the clinical course of the disorder; and (5) other important variables (e.g., insurance status, site of treatment and the like). A related goal would be to evaluate the cost-effectiveness of typical assessment and intervention practices. Since participation in this practice research network is voluntary, the American Psychiatric Association has designed the program so that no member of the network would be expected to spend more than 15 minutes per day in various activities associated with the network, such as providing information regarding various protocols and the like. Most likely the entire network will be "on-line" to facilitate data collection and analysis.

At the present time, several other large-scale practice research networks are in formation. The Practice Directorate of the American Psychological Association in collaboration with the Committee to Advance Psychological Practice (CAPP) have put out a request for proposals from various companies with the capability of collecting practical and realistic outcomes measures appropriate in clinical practice settings. The American Psychiatric Association has a functioning practice research network with over 500 clinicians, and is increasing it to over 1,500. Similarly the state of Pennsylvania, through the Pennsylvania Psychological Association, and the state of Massachusetts, through the Mental Health Corporation of Massachusetts (an organization of over 90 mental health clinics in the state), have initiated large practice research networks. Standardized, realistic measures of clinical outcome, as will be described in Chapter 11, are in place in these networks. In all of them it is envisioned that eventually all clinicians participating in these large practice research networks will be on-line to a central data monitoring facility. In this way important information on outcomes and other aspects of service delivery will be readily available for analysis and rapid dissemination.

The establishment of practice research networks should do much to fulfill ambitions first articulated over a decade ago (e.g., Barlow, 1981; Barlow, Hayes, & Nelson, 1984) to establish a national or international data base from practitioners operating in front-line applied settings. In so doing, the reach of clinical research centers will be extended to the very settings that are most relevant to their work. More importantly, practitioners who should benefit from developments in clinical research centers will participate directly in validating newly developed knowledge and procedures emanating from these settings.

Guidelines for Consuming Clinical Replication Data

To this point we have discussed guidelines for producing clinical replication series. In this section we present guidelines for consuming these findings. The concept of logical generalization suggests the overall approach that would allow practitioners to make reasonable inferences about the relevance of clinical replication series to their own work.

Table 9.1 presents a checklist of important dimensions for practitioners to consider in consuming research. There are many questions to consider. By going through the list while examining a given study or clinical replication series, it is possible to get a sense of its strengths and weaknesses.

Patient Description

First, ask yourself if the patients are described in detail. If they are described in detail, examine your own patients and see if they seem similar in respects that you think are probably important (or which you may know to be important) to treatment outcome. Studies that give relatively little detail about the individual subjects may still be valid. Studies that use very different subjects may also be valid. However, they will be so only to the extent that the phenomena that are identified are of such power and generality that issues of patient characteristics are relatively unimportant. This may often be true, so you should not reject research out of hand, for

TABLE 9.1   **A Checklist of Important Dimensions for Practitioners to Consider in the Consumption of Clinical Research**

In all cases, a *Yes* indicates greater likelihood of generalization to your situation:

1. Are the clients described in detail? Does your client seem similar to those in the series in most or all important respects?

2. Are the procedures used described in detail sufficient for you to do what was done in all important respects?

3. Does the series specify the conditions (therapist, therapy environment) under which intervention was applied? Are they similar to your own? Are there therapist effects?

4. Are measures taken repeatedly across time so that an adequate individual sample is obtained?

5. Are several different measures taken if there is not one universally accepted measure?

6. Are individual characteristics identified that are related to treatment outcome? Do your clients share the favorable characteristics?

7. If the results are reported in group form, is the percentage of individuals showing the effect reported? Is it high? Are individual data shown?

8. Have the results been replicated? Several times? By others?

9. Are the effects (and differences between effects) strong and clinically meaningful?

10. Does the study experimentally test factors that account for success or failure? If so, are the favorable conditions present in your situation?

11. Have you tried the procedures with your clients? Did you achieve similar results?

example, because it used college students or clinical patients who are poorly described. The point is simply to think this issue through as you examine the research findings. Some problems seem to be quite similar across patients (or even species). Others show a great deal of individual variability. If your problem is of the latter type, patient description and similarity are much more important.

Procedural Description

You should then ask yourself if the procedures used are described in detail sufficient for you to administer all components of the treatment that you have reason to believe are important to treatment outcome. On this basis, large sections of the applied literature must be questioned. Whatever the value may be, for example, in philosophical discourse about clinical phenomena and interventions, it is extremely unlikely that it will generalize consistently to individual practitioners if it is stated (as it usually is) in such a way as to allow ambiguous conclusions or different conclusions to be drawn about what was actually done. The role of such discussions may be important in generating more specific techniques, principles, and procedures that then may have a degree of external validity. Nevertheless, it is only when procedures are described in detail that they can possibly have a hope of generality, since it is the rules themselves (not the literal findings) that are being generalized to a new situation. This area is probably one in which the differences between reliability and generality are most obvious. Many studies on clinical techniques show obvious effects but do such a poor job of treatment description that any hope of generality is lost.

Intervention Conditions

Then examine the conditions under which the treatment was applied. What kinds of therapists were used? What was the therapy environment like? Do you have any reason to believe that these factors might have a strong impact on the outcome of treatment? If you do, are these factors similar to the ones that exist in your own situation? Only when you have thought through these kinds of issues can you assume that even demonstrably effective techniques used on patients similar to your own will be likely to be effective when you use them. Studies that include several therapists allow an examination of therapist effects. If none is shown, and the therapists spanned a range of characteristics, then this alleviates the concern a bit. If any therapist effects are shown, the goodness of fit between you and the most effective therapists is more critical. If all of the therapists are similar (e.g., all are students or therapists in training), the lack of therapist effects is less meaningful. You should recognize that several single case designs done by different investigators constitute a kind of assessment of therapist effects.

Repeated Measurement

Were measures taken repeatedly across time albeit realistic and practical measures so that an adequate individual sample is obtained? You as an individual practitioner could not think of intervening with an individual patient until you are fairly sure of the need for intervention. A single assessment may not be enough. Paradoxically, you may be quite willing to take seriously the claims that a particular intervention is effective when a single preassessment has been compared to a single postassessment in several patients. We've already analyzed the logical difficulty with this. If repeated measures are taken, it is usually important that they be presented individually and not just as an aggregate across patients. Among other things, this allows you to assess in considerable detail the goodness of fit between your patient's problems and the individuals in the reported research.

Number and Type of Measures

Are several different realistic and practical measures taken if there is not one universally accepted measure? In many clinical areas the identification of patient problems is not at all a clear-cut matter. Even in fairly well-defined syndromes such as depression, no single universally accepted measure has emerged to define the disorder. It is risky to assume, for example, that someone who has defined a depressive disorder based on low rates of activity is talking about the same characteristics that define your patient. If several measures have been taken and the results are parallel with these several measures, there is a greater likelihood that the findings will apply to patients of yours who are similar on some of those measures. Thus, studies with multiple measures are more likely to generalize to other situations.

Identification of Successes and Failures

Did the individual study examine which patient characteristics were related to treatment outcome? If it did, what was found? Is your patient one who shares the characteristics of those who were treated most successfully? The need for this kind of analysis has already been discussed. Essentially, studies of this sort have generated data-based guesses about rules of generality. Note, however, that the concerns noted earlier apply here. The relationship should be replicable and strong enough to be meaningful. The characteristics identified should be specific and meaningful.

Individual Data

If the results are reported in group form, is the percentage of individuals showing the effect reported? Is it high? Are individual data shown? If you look for data on the effect of interventions on individuals, as recommended here, you will usually be disappointed. The methodological posture we have adopted is currently quite atypical in clinical science. Although the support for this point of view is growing, the huge preponderance of clinical research still clings to some of the worst aspects of group-comparison approaches. Recently, however, many researchers have begun to indicate a box score about how many individuals in a given group showed the effect. For example, a study in which 90% of the patients seemed to improve is probably more likely to generalize to your individual patient than one that revealed an impact of similar magnitude but with only, say, 60% of the patients tested.

Replication

Have the results been replicated? How many times? By whom? Every time a finding is replicated, generalizability increases. If the replications are done by several different persons in several different settings and if the findings are relatively consistent, then this is one of the more powerful indications that these findings may apply to your situation. Unfortunately, the picture is often not clear. A finding may have been replicated in a few settings, but not in others. If it has been replicated at all, it is quite likely that something is effective about it. The difference in results between studies is due to structural differences between them. The failure to replicate in some settings helps us identify the boundary conditions—the limits of generality. The practitioner must assess whether the conditions he or she is facing are more like the studies that replicated the finding or those that did not.

Strength of Effects

Are the effects strong? In the usual study, we often examine the level of statistical significance and forget the magnitude of the effect shown. It is logical, however, that strong effects will be more generalizable than weak ones. In part, this may be due to issues discussed earlier. Strong effects, for example, will tend to be shown in many (if not all) patients. Thus, the individual consistency is likely to be much higher. This consistency itself implies a kind of generality of findings.

Experimental Analysis of Reasons for Success or Failure

Does the study experimentally test patient or situational differences that might relate to the impact of treatment? If so, do your patients or situations show the favorable conditions indicated? This advice has been analyzed in some detail previously as the third step in analyzing failures. If a study identifies the boundary conditions of an effect, or conditions that maximize impact, it is providing a richer, more detailed set of rules to guide others. This amounts to a type of experimental test of generality. The decision rules that result seem particularly likely to generalize because of their level of specificity about variables of proven importance.

Testing It Yourself

Have you tried out the procedures with your patients? Did you achieve similar results in the past? There is no better way to know that research findings apply to your situation than to attempt to apply them. The advice offered throughout the rest of this book is that practitioners view themselves as scientists as well. Without these skills, practitioners cannot fully determine the effectiveness of treatment and, therefore, the applicability of treatment. The feedback to the system is reduced, and treatments might be accepted that are weak (or rejected though worthwhile). If a treatment is applied to one's own practice in the context of systematic evaluation, over time the truth about applicability will emerge.

Application of the Principles to Clinical Practice

This section has been written primarily from the standpoint of the consumer of research. Throughout, it was presented in terms of the consumption of *others'* research. Yet, when practitioners begin to be more empirical, they are themselves producing evaluations. They are then capable of "consuming" their own evaluations. And all the same rules apply. (Just because we ourselves did it does not mean that the standards change.) If it sounds strange to "consume your own evaluations," translate this statement into normal clinical language. *What it means is simply learning from your own practice.* Look again at Table 9.1, but this time with the set, "These are the things I should do in order to maximize the likelihood that what I learn with one patient will transfer to others." Suddenly the guidelines jump out not as drug prescriptions, but as *rules of good practice.*

Consider each point again: *Describing the patients in detail.* What is this but good assessment, careful taking of histories, sensitivity to subtle but critical patient characteristics, and the like? *Describing the procedures and conditions in detail.* What is this but a careful and detailed treatment plan? *Repeated measurement.* Are you carefully assessing the patient's problems and progress in treatment? *Multiple measures.* Are you doing a fairly broad assessment? Are you keeping your eye on the overall functioning and well-being of your patient? *Identification of successes.* Are you careful to ensure that the treatment fits the specific needs and strengths of the individual patient? *Individual data.* Are you assessing and working for the progress of each and every one of your patients or are you content to say only that overall you do well? *Replication.* Are you using procedures that are likely to work? *Strong effects.* Have you met your treatment goals? *Limitations.* If therapy is not working, do you stop, reassess, and try to determine why it isn't? *Testing it yourself.* Has this intervention worked for you? *Internal validity.* Are you really responsible for change? Was the treatment really needed? Are you utilizing resources appropriately?

The rules to be followed in assessing generalizability closely parallel rules to be followed in good practice. The language differs slightly—the message is the same. Another way you could say this is that the kind of knowledge that is based on the highest standards of practice is the kind of knowledge that is likely to generalize. Unfortunately, it is all too easy to take shortcuts. Much of our knowledge is not based on the highest standards of practice. The recommendations made here, and described in this book, can be seen as guidelines to ensure that practitioners produce and consume knowledge that is consistent with these standards.

10 Program Evaluation

Introduction

If the course suggested in this volume has been followed, at this point a specific population may have been identified that has a given set of problems and that may respond positively to an intervention of interest. These interventions may have been drawn from the existing literature, or they may be the result of treatment innovation evaluated through the use of single case designs. In the era of managed care, both of these kinds of programs ultimately require population-based analyses.

The goal of single case analysis is to identify the processes that operate at the level of the individual *in order that generalizations can be made about collections of individuals.* No experimental science exists that studies the truly unique, because the methods and concepts of science itself depend upon classes of events. Similarly, there is no need for a science of Sally and a science of Bob. Rather, by grounding applied psychological science in the intensive study of individuals we allow fundamental behavioral processes to be seen that suggest how best to combine individuals into functionally distinct populations of people and problems with distinct treatment needs.

As such populations are identified, the questions at issue move to another level. Instead of asking questions about individual psychological processes, we become interested in more epidemiological issues: How many such people exist? If they are treated with intervention z, how many will improve and by how much on average?

The behavioral sciences are enormously sophisticated about asking and answering some of these questions. In part this sophistication comes from the use of data analytic tools (e.g., inferential statistics) that first emerged in agricultural contexts where questions about populations (of seeds, for example) are always the questions of importance. Our analytic methods have driven our experimental methods, even when moving to an epidemiological or group level of analysis is premature. But there is a time and a place for group comparison research, and in the model of system development we have described, now is the time and place.

Few readers of this volume will be completely ignorant about how to conduct intervention research using group designs. Because the literature on these topics is so voluminous and well known, we will not cover these designs here. Rather, we wish to affirm their importance when questions of treatment outcome move to questions about populations of people.

This is not to say that group comparison designs need to be conducted in the traditional manner when moving to population-based research questions. Clinical replication series show that large collections of people can be gathered effectively in the context of traditional psychological practice. The intensive quality of time-series designs is still enormously useful, even in randomized clinical trials, since they allow researchers to begin to separate out sources of variability at the level of the individual and thus to identify true treatment responders in a larger population. But the development of large behavioral health care delivery systems has made traditional group comparison research much more relevant to the actual practice environment. Group comparison clinical research is feasible when hundreds or thousands of clients of a given type are part of a single health care delivery system. The need for population-based research to improve the effectiveness and efficiency of health care delivery makes obvious the relevance of clinical research to the ultimate financial success of managed care organizations.

This is why most large managed care firms have large and growing research and development arms. Many of these centers are populated by researchers trained in epidemiological approaches, but increasingly these firms are developing and testing new behavioral health technology. This is a hugely important new opportunity for scientist practitioners to impact health care delivery. The research and development centers in managed care firms allow the design and implementation of applied studies with sample sizes that dwarf psychosocial research done up to this point: literally tens of thousands of cases. In addition, because business firms are used to evaluation research, the barriers to research in some settings are often not encountered to the same degree. Indeed, in some large managed care firms, clinical research contracts (for example, from federal funding sources) are even viewed as a source of new revenue, as well as a means to improve quality and cost effectiveness within the delivery system.

The analysis of population-based delivery systems requires that we move our questions and concepts to another level of analysis. New terms and concepts are required because program evaluation and population-based research is not merely clinical evaluation writ large. Instead of a functional analysis of an individual we need to think of the subgroups of people in a population that have a particular problem, and how that population need can best be met.

Thinking about health problems in these terms represents a different level of analysis, and yet mature health delivery systems must think in such systems terms to survive and prosper. A number of factors determine the overall functioning of health care programs other than the usual issues of the clinical efficacy of those programs. We also need to know the context, process, and content of health delivery systems. We need to ask whether a program meets a health need, covers those who need it and not others, reaches those consumers for whom it is designed, and is delivered according to plan. We need to know whether delivery of an intervention in the rough and tumble world of practice has the same outcomes as it does in highly controlled settings. We may need to know whether clients and others are happy with the services delivered, and whether the overall cost of the program is reasonable relative to its outcomes.

These various issues are all considered under the rubric *program evaluation* (Rossi & Freeman, 1989; Shadish, Cook, & Leviton, 1991). Program evaluation is not just a method; it is an orientation toward the kinds of questions that are thought to be of importance. When we begin to think of behavioral health programs in systems terms, suddenly a whole host of new and interesting issues emerge. One of the first such issues is that we need to assess systematically the nature and scope of a problem. This is termed *needs assessment.*

Needs Assessment

Before we evaluate the impact of a program, we need to consider whether a program is really needed at all. Covered populations may differ greatly in their behavioral health needs. For example, rural populations in the United States are more likely to contain the elderly, or chronically ill (Cordes, 1989). A health care delivery system in a rural area may thus need more services for gerontological depression, say, than might be expected in an urban population, or there might need to be more attention to the overlap between physical and behavioral health care. There might be a greater need for home-based delivery systems to reach those who cannot travel to take advantage of centralized services.

Identifying the mere existence of a problem is not usually difficult since even one case of a given problem documents a need. The bigger problem is assessing the relative rates of health problems and the amount and kind of resources needed to ameliorate these problems. In this phase of program evaluation in managed care settings, detailed data need to be collected on the covered population, and on the services they need, want, and would utilize to produce desirable health outcomes.

Needs assessment would often be a simple matter of interviewing covered consumers were it not for the fact that (a) reports of this kind are often invalid (Deaux & Callaghan, 1984), (b) needs can be quite indirect, and (c) there can be many stakeholders in given health programs. For example, a health care system may have high costs in its emergency room because of teenage violence and the resulting need for emergency medical treatment. Teenage violence in a given area may be caused by a lack of parenting skills, poverty, weaknesses in family support systems, an absence of youth clubs, poor schools, friction based on religious or racial intolerance, or a host of similar problems. In such an instance, simple interviews of persons covered by the health delivery system would be very unlikely to suggest how health delivery costs could be reduced. Few people would probably relate religious differences to emergency room visits, for example, and yet a small amount of intervention relying on community churches might yield big benefits for the health delivery system if that factor were identified.

As a result of the indirect and multiple sources of health problems, a wide variety of data focusing on many constituencies is needed to document the extent and distribution of particular health problems and the contextual conditions that foster it. In behavioral health care settings, needs assessment may involve a very broad assessment of consumers, employers, practitioners, agencies, groups, family, and the community. It involves a careful analysis of the functioning of the existing health delivery system and its high cost areas. A full assessment of the extent and nature of a problem such as high emergency room use could be quite complex, even when the key indicators that might be used to assess changes in these problems are not (e.g., gun and knife wounds in the emergency room might be a readily available measure of the success of a program designed to reduce teen violence).

When the extent and nature of a problem is known, the specific targets of prevention and intervention need to be specified. Usually, the target is the covered population with the specified need, that is, those with a given health condition. But the target of intervention may be broader than that. For example, it is common to target at-risk populations: segments of a covered population with a relatively high probability of either having or developing a given health condition.

Targeting at-risk populations, or populations already at need, is no mean feat. Identification systems must be developed that are both sensitive (that is, persons not at risk are properly excluded) and specific (persons who are at risk are included). Logically, these two properties often conflict with each other. The more "false positives" are avoided, the more "false negatives" tend to occur. Whether targeting systems emphasize one or the other error is often determined by the dynamics of the health delivery system and the problem at issue. For example, less sensitive targeting systems may still be cost-effective when the problem at issue can be avoided or treated easily but would likely be costly if not treated. In the physical health area, vaccination against infectious disease may be an example. In the behavioral health area, an example might be the considerable impact on later violence and health-risk behavior (e.g., smoking) from fairly simple early elementary school interventions (Patterson, 1997). In such cases, the "at-risk population" may even be defined to include virtually everyone, as it often is in the case of, say, vaccination against infectious diseases.

The dynamics of the public health issue in the case of vaccination support a relatively insensitive method since there is often no significant benefit and some potential harm to targeted vaccination versus universal vaccination, and cost is low. It is much more common, however, for it to be important that behavioral health care targeting be sensitive. Behavioral health interventions are often costly, and health systems must deliver these services only to those truly in need. If the associated costs of *lack* of treatment are high, it is equally important that targeting be specific. For example, untreated agoraphobics may frequently demand and receive expensive emergency room treatment or cardiological assessments for "heart problems." It may not save a health system money to fail to identify all the agoraphobic clients they can and get them into treatment, on the false grounds that there is no benefit in artificially increasing demand for behavioral programs. Actively encouraging use of needed programs may save a great deal of money elsewhere in the health delivery system.

In addition to sensitivity and specificity, targeting systems must be practical, both financially and technically. When we have such a system, it is possible to identify the incidence and prevalence of the problem, and to begin to relate risk factors to these dimensions. *Incidence* refers to the number of new instances of a particular problem that occur in a particular area. In other words, we become concerned with the incidence and prevalence of problems in a population, and the delivery of services in a cost-effective manner that will reduce rates of incidence and prevalence during a particular time period. *Prevalence* refers to the total number of such cases with a given condition in a specified area and time. Both of these numbers are often expressed as rates: the proportion of the specified population affected. For example, the yearly incidence of AIDS in a given area may be 1 per 1,000 adults, while the prevalence may to 10 per 1,000 adults. The two measures are highly related but somewhat distinct. For example, behavioral interventions for AIDS immediately target the incidence of AIDS. Safe sex or needle exchange will not cure the infected, but it may reduce the rate of new cases. Conversely, drug treatments for the infected may attempt to find ways to eliminate the virus that causes AIDS, thus targeting prevalence.

Health delivery systems must assess not only the need for services, but also the demand for services. The two can be quite different. Services can be demanded that are not needed or needed that are not demanded. For example, rape prevention programs among males are clearly needed, but are rarely demanded. Indeed, it seems likely that males who want to be part of such programs are less likely to need them than other males, since an interest in rape prevention shows a degree of sensitivity toward others that may be prophylactic. Conversely, weight-reduction medications may be demanded and used by normally weighted adolescents, even though they are not needed and may even be dangerous. As this example of diet drugs shows, our health delivery system is particularly oriented toward patient demand. Patients who demand services have a high likelihood of receiving at least something. Since health delivery systems usually work best when demand and need are at least roughly linked, needs assessment should normally include an assessment of client demand.

Program Goals and Content

When a need has been adequately identified, it is important to specify the morals, values, goals, actions, and barriers that will constitute the program and its outcomes. We will define each of these terms. *Morals* (which comes from a word meaning "manners") are the social conventions of a group. *Values* are the outcomes that particular individuals or subgroups view as positive or negative. Physical health delivery systems often have successfully avoided issues of values and morals since the promotion of physical health and life is so universally adopted. That is, the value of a healthy and long life is usually implicit or assumed. The progress of medical interventions has raised values and moral issues even here, however, and as a society we now actively debate how much medical intervention is warranted in the final weeks or months of life.

Behavioral health interventions have never avoided these issues. For example, whereas treatment of homosexuality was once considered moral and needed, it is now considered virtually immoral to target this sexual preference for change. In less dramatic a fashion, any behavioral health program raises issues of morals and values. What is the purpose of the program (the level of values)? Does society agree with this purpose (the moral level)? Do clients or professionals agree with this purpose (the values level)? For example, a program for survivors of sexual abuse might be designed to relieve anxiety, or to increase the client's ability to experience or tolerate memories of the original trauma, or to increase the capacity for intimacy, or to enhance the client's ability to confront perpetrators of the abuse. These values and moral issues must be faced directly as part of program evaluation, in part because they determine the entire purpose of the program itself.

Once the global purpose of the program is known, these general values can be turned into both concrete goals that might be achieved and the means to achieve them. Values are general directions and can usually never be fully reached (when, for example, has the "capacity for intimacy" been fully reached? No matter how great that capacity, isn't it possible to have greater capacity still?). *Goals* are the concrete, measurable, and achievable outcomes or objectives of the program. For example, if the valued outcome of our program for survivors of sexual abuse is reduced anxiety, the concrete goal might be a reduction by at least 50% of the amount of state anxiety as measured by a given anxiety inventory. It is critical that goals and objectives be specific and concrete, because this allows for the program actually to be evaluated in a fashion that is linked to its purpose. Ideally, the specification of goals is part of program development itself, in which program developers are regularly asking themselves in a highly specific way how they will know if the program is successful. If properly done, the phase of goal specification will result also in the major component of the outcome-assessment package to be used in the evaluation of program impact.

Actions are the specific tasks that program staff intend to accomplish to achieve the program goals: deliver a therapy, write a patient manual, set up a self-help group, or what have you. Designing and implementing an intervention is often a major focus of professional programs (e.g., case conceptualization, functional analysis, practica in therapy delivery) but often scaling interventions up to a program level is difficult. These actions hopefully have been informed by the iterative process of treatment development described throughout this book. Whether based on theory, technology, or common sense, it is important that program actions be highly specific so that these actions themselves may be assessed, as will be discussed later.

Barriers are the contextual and situational features that must be modified so that program actions can be taken successfully. For example, our program for survivors of sexual abuse may consist of a twelve-week group therapy program that follows a carefully constructed therapy manual. It may not be possible to deliver these program actions, however, without reducing the stigma involved in admitting to a history of sexual abuse. A targeted media campaign, using well-known entertainment figures who are willing to admit to an abuse history, might be used to remove the barriers to program participation.

Monitoring of Program Processes

When a program has been designed and implemented to meet a need, it must be monitored internally so that it is known who it reaches, what it contains, and how it functions in the context of an organization. These kinds of questions are addressed through what has been called "process analyses" (Schalock & Thornton, 1988). Logically, the process assessments are linked to—but separate from— program outcome per se. Services must be used to be effective, for example, but they may be used and ineffective.

Program Use

Appropriate use of services is desirable not just for altruistic reasons but also because it may create important program outcomes such as client functioning, satisfaction, or reduction of costs elsewhere in the health care delivery system. Many factors influence participation and use of services. For example, it is known that minority clients access psychotherapy at relatively low rates (Padgett, Patrick, Burns, & Schlesinger, 1994), but they tend to stay in therapy longer if minority therapists are available (Sue, 1995). Similarly, physical distances or lack of transportation may influence program participation (Human & Wasem, 1991). Particular cultural or religious groups may have strong beliefs about the meaning of mental health problems or the acceptability of certain treatments for them (Hunter & Windle, 1991). Insurance coverage is an enormously important factor determining participation in health care (Landerman, Burns, Swartz, Wagner, & George, 1994).

Gross measures of participation are not enough for program evaluation purposes. It is also important to show that those who participated needed the care delivered, and others did not. The sensitivity and specificity of program participation is termed "utilization" (Tischler, 1990). Utilization review has long been used by insurance companies to reduce health care costs by demanding data on the appropriateness of service delivery. Quite apart from the immediate cost-control purposes of utilization review, it is important to document the functioning of a program. Indeed, utilization assessment is *more* likely to be accurate and useful for program evaluation purposes if it is *not* linked to immediate cost control. For example, clinicians often "diagnose up" in order to justify more extensive treatment when utilization review is linked to treatment access or reimbursement. But this very process undermines the ability to assess the sensitivity and specificity of the program utilization, and thus distorts the program evaluation itself. Utilization evaluation that does not have immediate financial- or access-control purposes is less likely to be distorted in this fashion.

Program Delivery

Once the client has accessed a behavioral health program, we must assess how the program itself was delivered: Were the program actions actually taken as specified? A program may be well designed in principle, but impossible to deliver as specified. For example, the program may call for professional skills that are beyond program staff. The program may be poorly specified and thus be delivered in a variable fashion, even by careful program staff members. The program may be poorly supervised and may be delivered in a diluted or distorted form. Effective program delivery requires that accurate and feasible assessment and feedback systems be built in, so as to correct for program inefficiencies.

In psychotherapy research, it has become commonplace to construct fairly elaborate measures of treatment adherence and competence, especially linked to well-defined and manualized psychotherapy protocols. Adherence and competence are logically linked but are distinct. *Adherence* means the degree to which specified therapy activities occurred. *Competence* is more complex.

> We use the term competence to refer to the level of skill shown by the therapist in delivering the treatment. By skill we mean the extent to which the therapists conducting the interventions took relevant aspects of the therapeutic context into account and responded to these contextual variables appropriately. Relevant aspects of the context include, but are by no means limited to (a) Client variables such as degree of impairment; (b) the particular problems manifested by a given client; (c) the client's life situation and life stress; (d) and factors such as stage in therapy, degree of improvement already achieved and appropriate sensitivity to the timing of interventions within a therapy session. (Waltz, Addis, Koerner, & Jacobson, 1993, p. 620)

Many of the available adherence and competence instruments are highly specific to particular treatments and can be very expensive to implement. This may be appropriate in the context of treatment outcome research, because it is theoretically and scientifically important to distinguish treatment effects that are due to specific factors. Less expensive forms of delivery assessment are often used in program evaluation (e.g., client reports of the kinds of interventions delivered), because the purpose of assessment in this area is more an issue of program management.

Some of the greatest improvements in the cost effectiveness of health care systems have come from changes in the *mode* of delivery: where, when, and by whom given services are delivered. For example, outpatient surgery has reduced the cost of surgical interventions. Similarly, community care, self-help, or even computer-delivered treatment is often as effective as traditional mental health treatment but is far less expensive (Marks, 1992)

Assessing Program Outcomes

We will consider three basic types of program outcomes: direct effectiveness measures; indirect effectiveness measures, including client satisfaction and social validity; and cost outcomes. Each is critical to the functioning of health delivery systems.

Direct Effectiveness Measures

The behavioral sciences are expert in the development of direct-effectiveness measures that are used to measure the relative effectiveness (e.g., is treatment x better than treatment y or than no treatment?) and marginal effectiveness (how much treatment delivered at what scale would be most effective?) of a program (Rossi & Berk, 1990). If the process of goal specification has been followed carefully, this domain of program evaluation should be relatively straightforward. In the three chapters that follow we will review in detail some of the measures that are commonly used to assess clinical change.

The major change from traditional clinical assessment to the evaluation of program outcomes in this area is that the relevant constituencies (and thus the values and goals) may include more than a mental health specialist and a client. For example, the employer who is paying for the health coverage may be interested in work productivity, family members may be interested in social functioning, and government may be interested in the regulation of crime, violence, or social risk. Because the history of empirical clinical psychology has been formed largely around patient–therapist dyads, many of the measures appropriate to this larger set of outcomes are still relatively poorly developed compared to, say, measures of anxiety or depression.

Indirect Effectiveness Measures: Client Satisfaction

Broadly speaking, client satisfaction measures program performance relative to consumer expectations (Oliva, Oliver, & Bearden, 1995). It is a critically important, if indirect, outcome for most health care programs in the era of industrialized health care (Marshall, Hays, Sherbourne, & Wells, 1993), and for two major reasons. First, client satisfaction ratings correlate with medically relevant outcomes such as compliance with pharmacotherapy regimens (Sherbourne, Hays, Orday, Dimatteo, & Kravitz, 1992). Second, clients who are satisfied are less likely to request changes in the assignment of primary physicians, to sue providers, or to disenroll in health plans (Marshall et al., 1993). Thus, client satisfaction provides a broad, readily available, and crucially important measure of program functioning, but it is relatively less common in mental health research.

There are two major approaches to the measurement of client satisfaction: (1) global satisfaction, or (2) satisfaction with reference to specific dimensions of health care such as access, competence, time spent waiting, or the quality of communication with health care professionals. In general, the two approaches correlate highly (Marshall et al., 1993), but the more specific measures may provide additional information for administrators interested in improving their system of delivery in particular domains.

Generally client satisfaction measures are collected during or after a session of care delivery (e.g., at the end of a psychotherapy session), because compliance with this kind of request for information is higher in the context of face-to-face interactions than with follow-up mail-in requests. Client satisfaction can be gathered continuously after each visit or at the end of a course of therapy. There is some research indicating that measures of satisfaction taken in the first few sessions of psychotherapy predict clinical outcomes and ultimate client satisfaction (Strupp, 1987). Thus, frequent and early assessment of client satisfaction is not uncommon in the managed care industry. We will have more to say about client satisfaction measures in Chapter 12.

Indirect Effectiveness Measures: Social Validity

In addition to client satisfaction, program evaluation may involve the assessment of the satisfaction of others in the community with the major aspects of health care programs such as the appropriateness of the program values, goals, or procedures, or the significance of the effects observed. This approach to the validation of applied programs has been termed "social validity" (Wolf, 1978), and in the applied area it has assumed increasing importance (Schwartz & Baer, 1991).

In some ways, you can think of social validity as a superordinate concept that includes client satisfaction as one dimension or aspect (Test, 1994). In the health care system, the relevant audience for a given program is not just the person actually receiving the specific service but also those who pay for the services ("indirect consumers" such as employers or parents), those who interact regularly with the person receiving the service, and taxpayers and members of the larger community members who benefit from a healthy population (Test, 1994). Consider, for example, the stake that employers have in health care plans. These plans are paid for by employers not merely because health care coverage is necessary to recruit and retain good-quality employees, but also because in principle these plans should make it more likely that employees come to work and function well while they are there, thus increasing the productivity of the company. Thus, it is reasonable to assess the functioning of a health care program not just by client satisfaction, but also by the achievement of the goals of the various stakeholders involved—such as employers—and by the satisfaction of these stakeholders.

Assessing Costs

In the age of managed care, at issue are not just the clinical efficacy of the program but also its financial efficacy (Pallack, 1995). Formal analyses of the benefits and costs of treatment have been part of behavioral health research for some time (see Weisbrod, Test, & Stein, 1980, for one of the first elaborate examples) but only about one in 20 studies on therapeutic outcome in the modern era have reported even the most rudimentary forms of cost data (Yates, 1994).

The resistance to cost analyses is in part a recognition of the inherent difficulty and even arbitrariness involved in turning clinical comparisons into cost comparisons (Wilson, 1995), but it is probably also a result of the implicit belief that cost relates in a fairly uniform way to therapeutic activity and therapeutic outcome. In some areas of human functioning, those assumptions are reasonable. In general, the more ditchdiggers working, the more ditch will be dug. The bigger the backhoe, the bigger the cost, and the faster the ditch will be dug. But therapy is not necessarily like that. A self-help group or a well-timed and well-crafted book or videotape might be about as effective in some circumstances as an expensive and highly trained therapist, and in such circumstances the low-tech solution might be wildly more effective on a cost basis than the high-tech solution (Marks, 1992). Cost analysis is also somewhat foreign to mental health disciplines, and conducting such analyses requires planning and effort, which may be an additional barrier.

The resistance to cost analysis may also be based on perceived values issues. For example, some mental health workers have equated cost analyses with a lack of empathy and caring for clients (Book, 1991). But value conflicts do not seem to be inherent. A concern for cost can serve the larger goal of better health care for a greater number of people—hardly a cold and uncaring approach. Cost containment can translate into increased access to health care (Vandenbos, 1983). If tremendous resources are poured upon the lucky few, at a cost of fewer available resources for the many less fortunate, avoidance of cost analyses in order to promote "clinical empathy" may be a formula for greater human suffering. In addition, from a professional point of view, behavioral health may have a great deal to gain by cost analyses, since it is known that psychological suffering greatly increases the utilization of expensive inpatient and outpatient primary medical care (Manning & Wells, 1992).

Types of Cost Analyses

There are two major types of cost analyses in behavioral health (Yates, 1994). In the primary type, the degree of clinical improvement seen with therapy (a nonmonetary measure) is expressed in terms of the monetary resources used to accomplish these outcomes. This is called *cost-effectiveness*. It allows researchers to calculate how much clinical impact is produced by a given amount of resources, or to determine which of two methods uses fewer resources at a given level of clinical outcome. Often these values are expressed as ratios, and the ratios are used to compare various treatments: For example, one could calculate how much money on average is needed to produce a ten-point decrement in a Beck Depression Inventory for cognitive-behavior therapy versus Prozac.

It is not always easy to specify program cost. When all the resources used to mount a program are listed, they still have to be turned into a numerical value. Actual money spent is the usual method, but there are others. For example, *opportunity cost* expresses the cost of resources compared to what the same resource would have been used for, had the program not been mounted (Schalock & Thornton, 1988). From the points of view of administrators with limited resources the true cost of a program is the abandoned alternative uses for those resources.

While cost-effectiveness is a major step forward in the kind of data needed to manage a health care system, it has a major weakness. In principle, cost-effectiveness is quite specific on the cost side of the ratio, but it is inherently vague on the positive outcome side. This is because improvement is (a) expressed in nonmonetary terms, and (b) is typically focused on a fairly specific clinical goal. The limits of this approach can be seen when one begins to think more in system terms. For example, Prozac may lead to a higher dropout rate than cognitive-behavior therapy, and more of the clients dropping out may later demand emergency medical services.

Cognitive-behavior therapy may lead to great gains in employment than Prozac or vice versa. Prozac may produce sexual dysfunction (a fairly common side effect), which in turn may lead to medical visits.

As managed mental health programs have gone beyond mental health carve-out firms, in which cost alone dominated, managed care administrators have had to begin to think more in terms of the total integrated health system—of which behavioral health is merely one part. Cost effectiveness data can only go so far in integrating the wide number of variables that have to be considered, because it is inherently difficult to combine disparate nonmonetary outcomes.

Cost-benefit analysis provides one solution. In this approach, both cost and benefits are examined using a numerical (usually monetary) metric. Suppose we wish to conduct a cost-benefit analysis of a psychosocial treatment program for panic disorder. We might estimate the dollar benefit of decreased tardiness or absence at work and combine this with the dollar benefit of higher social functioning, and then compare these values to the dollar costs of the treatment minus the cost savings due to reduced use of medical visits for psychological (but seemingly physical) problems. What would result is a ratio of benefits to costs, all expressed in monetary terms.

Cost-benefit analysis is a powerful tool that allows complex systems to be modeled and compared using a single metric, but it too has serious difficulties. It is very difficult to turn all outcomes into monetary values, and there is no well agreed upon methods for doing so in most areas of behavioral health. What is the monetary value of, say, a ten-point reduction in a Beck Depression Inventory? Indeed, there is something disconcerting about forcing such "intangible" benefits into dollars-and-cents terms. Furthermore, there is no agreement about which costs and benefits to "monetize." Should benefits to society at large be equally weighted with, say, benefits to the managed care corporation?

One way cost-benefit analysis is sometimes done is to compare the cost of treatment to the longer-term costs already built into the system. In effect, reduced costs becomes a measure of clinical benefit. This kind of metric is common in politically charged issues, since the public may be more willing to pay for a service once if it is convinced that the alternative is even higher costs later. For example, the effect of education on reduced need for future prisons might be calculated, and that metric might be used to fight for a new state educational initiative. Frank, Klein, and Jacobs (1982) provide an example of this approach. The cost of an independent living program for geriatric mental hospital patients was compared to the baseline pattern of hospitalization and discharge. For every nickel invested in the experimental program, it was projected that a dollar would be saved in eventual hospital costs.

Because of their inherent complexity as more factors are considered, in the behavioral health field, most cost analyses to date have focused on a limited set of comparisons. O'Farrell, Choquette, Cutter, Brown, Bayog, McCourt, Lowe, Chan, and Deneault (1996) provide an example. With a group of thirty alcoholics, the cost-benefit analysis focused on the effect of behavioral marital therapy (BMT) with and without relapse prevention (RP) on reductions from baseline in the health and legal costs associated with these clients' alcoholism. Additional cost-effectiveness analysis compared clinical improvements in the number of days abstinent per unit cost of the two conditions, and in the impact on marital adjustment.

Both treatments produce greater reductions in health and legal costs than the cost of the therapy actually delivered (behavioral marital therapy alone or with relapse prevention); that is, their cost-benefit ratios were positive. Because the combined program was considerably more expensive and the outcomes on drinking were similar, when just the impact on drinking was examined behavioral marital therapy alone had a cost benefit that was about three times as large as behavioral marital therapy with relapse prevention. When the impact on *both* drinking and marital adjustment was considered, however, the two treatments were about equally cost effective. This shows how important it is to consider which outcomes and costs are included in a cost-benefit analysis. To get a total view of the impact of treatment, many costs and benefits could be included, but it is both conceptually and practically more difficult as more factors are added. At the present stage of development, even relatively straightforward cost analyses can be of considerable importance in behavioral health.

In one sense, complex cost-benefit thinking is already concretely instantiated in the financial bottom line of fully capitated managed care organizations, particularly when session caps and other artificial cost-reduction strategies are removed and when adequate competition exists. Over the long run, a managed care firm will tend to survive if the relative benefits to the patients and others involved in the selection and payment of the managed care company (benefits that are surely complex and dynamic) are sufficiently great to lead to a premium payment that is greater than the total cost of doing business.

Unfortunately, markets are not necessarily mature, competitive, and free. At least over the short run, for example, it is quite possible to make a great deal of money by shifting costs to the public sector, by hiding the poor quality of the health services delivered, or by reducing needed services to a higher cost segment of the covered population. Thus, we cannot be sure that the complexity inherent in a financial bottom line adequately represents the total strengths and weaknesses of a health delivery system, especially as it will be felt in the long run. Distortions of program values and integrity in the name of financial success my be made less likely (not more likely) by careful cost analyses, however, because the long-term negative impact of such practices can be more readily modeled and seen by system administrators. Ultimately, morals and values have an impact on the financial bottom line, as is becoming more apparent in the backlash against some of the most abusive practices of the nascent managed care industry.

Psychologists and other behavioral health specialists will increasingly be held to account not only for the clinical effectiveness of their procedures, but also for their financial viability as part of the health care industry itself. If mental health experts are not willing to rise to this challenge, there are surely other fields that will, and the ability of behavioral health professionals to control their destiny will be reduced accordingly.

Evaluation Design

All the well-known tools of group comparison research can be used in program evaluation. For example, clients identified to be in the population of need might be randomly assigned to an experimental program versus treatment as usual. Client acceptance of evaluation research seems to be relatively high in managed care systems, perhaps because these systems routinely evaluate services with consumer surveys or phone sampling. Group-comparison treatment outcome research had traditionally been confined to funded clinical laboratories, but the industrialization of behavioral health care has created new structures in which these designs can be mounted and are fiscally relevant.

The topic of group comparison designs goes beyond the scope of this volume, but it should be immediately clear that all of the tools of time-series design can also be used in program evaluation. The trick is simply to think of the population as the individual being intensively analyzed. Other than the shift of levels of analysis, and the specific program evaluation issues addressed above, all the design concerns previously discussed in Chapters 5 through 8 apply without modification. For example, suppose a new anxiety program were implemented in several clinics to reduce the frequency of emergency room visits by clinic patients for panic. It would be no great challenge to implement the program in a multiple-based, across-clinics fashion, and to evaluate the impact accordingly.

The Use of Program Evaluation Techniques

There are many examples of evaluation methods that have impacted the behavioral health care system. A classic example is an analysis of the impact of mental health care conducted in the Kaiser Permanente Health Plan by Cummings and Follette (1976). This evaluation was one of the first to show that emotionally distressed people tend to overutilize medical services, and that even minimal behavioral health care services could greatly reduce these offset costs.

Kiesler and Simkins (1991) provide another example. In this study, a very notable rise in affective disorders in insured patients was documented and traced to efforts by clinicians to attempt to receive higher reimbursement rates for a more severe condition.

A widely followed example is provided by a radical decentralization of state-provided mental health services in the state of Washington. The enabling legislation, passed in 1989, mandated that the systems changes be carefully evaluated. A team of researchers from the University of Washington was brought in and contracted to perform the task.

As in most real-world evaluations, some of the original design features (see Perry, Hoff, & Gaither, 1994, for a partial description) were compromised by a series of constraints (see Gilchrist, Allen, Brown, Cox, Semke, Thomas, Jemelka, Perry, & Sutphen-Mroz, 1994). The overall results showed that the new law did not result in unwanted decreases in services, but did result in more continuity of care. Perry and

Hanig (1994) describe the immediate impact of the evaluation, which included substantial increases in state funding and further policy changes to support what was perceived to be the successful impact of the reform philosophy. This is an interesting impact, since a common source of resistance to program evaluation is the perception by clinicians that it is likely to lead to decreased program resources.

Ethical Issues

Several important ethical issues arise in the use of data for practical evaluation in real-world practice settings. Unless these issues are properly viewed, they can present significant barriers to the use of scientific tools in practical settings. The biggest source of ethical difficulties comes from the mixture of scientific and practical goals.

Is Scientific Methodology Ethically Defensible in Practice?

Society has always been ambivalent about science. The pursuit of knowledge is frightening because it implies a willingness to enter unknown and perhaps undesirable places. The motivation and sense of balance of the scientist is thought to be critical. Knowledge is a genie that, once let out, is difficult indeed to return to the bottle.

These very human worries are reflected in such disparate arenas as the biblical story of Creation (in which humankind's fall from grace is caused by eating from the tree of knowledge); movies about "mad scientists" who pursue knowledge at the expense of human values; or current concerns about the dehumanizing effects of computers, genetic engineering, or test-tube babies. The point is not that these worries are unjustified. The point is that our ambivalence about science must be recognized, and placed in proper perspective. Restraints on the pursuit of knowledge must be applied only to situations that warrant it.

Society has generated a large number of rules to protect human subjects. These include procedural protections, such as the submission of research proposals to human-subjects committees, as well as specific mandated activities on the part of a researcher, such as the acquisition from the subjects of informed and written consent to the research procedures involved. Quite apart from the formal legal requirements that surround the term "research," there are a number of informal requirements as well. These can range from the ethical practices in a particular applied profession (such as the standards set forth by the American Psychological Association) to the individual, idiosyncratic application of ethical and moral guidelines to these activities. Should these protections be applied to clients who are treated in an empirical way by empirical practitioners? Does the kind of methodology advocated here turn clients into human subjects, and therefore psychological practice into formal research?

If it does, the whole purpose of this book is unattainable. Practitioners could not function if their routine professional work was seen as formal research, with all of the additional protections that implies. There seems to be, however, an important difference between research and clinical evaluation.

The Distinction between Research and Evaluation

A good deal has been written about this distinction, but advances in evaluation procedures and recent changes in the protection provided to human subjects have produced an environment in which this issue is particularly critical. First, we should examine the verbal distinctions we make between research and treatment, and second, the functional importance of these variables and the societal mechanisms that have sprung up around them.

The dictionary defines *research* as the careful hunting for facts or the truth. This sense of research is clearly quite compatible with treatment. After all, successful treatment involves a kind of investigation of the world of the particular client. This sense of the word *research* is not what people are talking about when they talk of protection for human subjects. Over the years, research has come to mean a search for objective facts in which regard for the welfare of the "subjects" is very much secondary to the development of scientific knowledge. This second sense of the word research is often not compatible with professional practice.

Because of dramatic instances of abuse (particularly in physical medicine), a number of guidelines have been developed to protect research subjects. For example, institutional review boards are a federal requirement for institutions receiving federal funding. However, IRBs commonly have inherently awkward procedures for review (Hayes, Hayes, & Dykstra, 1995) and are not set up for the kind of rapid response that treatment decisions demand.

Clients are not necessarily subjects, and empirical work that puts knowledge first and client interests second is, by definition, distinct from the normal activities of a health care practitioner. Thus, in our usual use of the term, "research" is quite distinct from routine practice.

Unfortunately, in common language, people describe something as research based on its appearance. The left side of Table 10.1 presents several characteristics that appear particularly salient in making this distinction.

Note that most of these characteristics have to do with the apparent, formal, or structural characteristics of the activity. For example, if systematic data are collected, the activity is likely to be thought to be research, regardless of the goal of the activity.

The problem with this, as it applies to the clinical or educational environment, is made apparent by considering the right side of Table 10.1. Empirical practice has many of the structural aspects of formal research. The presence of any of these characteristics is likely to cause the kind of evaluation we have talked about in this book to be termed formal research. Yet the two are very different.

The goals and purposes of treatment research and treatment evaluation are quite distinct. The goal of science is to develop better organized statements of relations between events. In other words, the goal is a better verbal rule. The goal of treatment is to improve client functioning. The two are easily distinguished at the extreme. When the two goals are mixed, confusion can result, unless careful distinctions are made. Table 10.2 shows a division of activities based on the mix of scientific and treatment goals.

TABLE 10.1   Some Defining Characteristics of Research and Evaluation

Treatment Research	Treatment Evaluation
1. Systematic data collected	1. Systematic data collected
2. Intervention specified	2. Intervention specified
3. Intervention evaluated	3. Intervention evaluated
4. Subject selected on basis of scientific needs	4. Clients selected on usual clinical criteria
5. Questions selected on scientific grounds	5. Questions selected on the basis of client needs
6. Publication or presentation may result	6. Publication or presentation may result
7. Design tools used to answer scientific questions	7. Design tools used to answer clinical questions

At least four activities seem distinguishable. In pure treatment, the only goal is improved client outcome. In treatment evaluation, the primary goal is client outcome, but the practitioner would secondarily like to be able to say something about it (e.g., Did the client improve due to treatment? What was the real problem? What about treatment was helpful? How many other clients could benefit by this approach?). In treatment research, the goal is primarily the generation of better organized scientific statements. Client improvement is always hoped for, but is secondary. A specific client's needs are to be accommodated to the research project, if possible, but the individual client's needs did not start the sequence of events and are not the central issue. In pure research on applied problems, client improvement is not even a secondary goal in any immediate sense. Survey research or research in experimental psychopathology would be an example.

TABLE 10.2   The Distinction between Treatment, Treatment Evaluation, Treatment Research, and Pure Research

Valued Goals	Type of Activity			
	Pure Treatment	Treatment Evaluation	Treatment Research	Pure Research
Pursuit of better organized scientific statements	None	Secondary	Primary	Primary
Pursuit of better client outcomes	Primary	Primary	Secondary	None

The problem is that it is harder to see the goals of an activity than it is to see the form of the activity. Look again at Table 10.1. Note that it is in the areas that are easy to see (e.g., Are data collected?) that research and evaluation are similar. They differ in areas that are more difficult to discern (e.g., Why are you collecting data?). Thus, on the surface, research and evaluation look quite similar. An empirical practitioner could easily be mistakenly thought of as "doing research on clients"; it could falsely be said that "clients are being used as guinea pigs"; and so on.

There are a number of short- and long-term consequences, for both the client and the practitioner, that accrue when treatment is elevated to treatment evaluation or to treatment research. Since, in treatment research, increased client functioning is only a side effect of the main goal of generating better organized scientific statements, treatment research would seem to decrease the probability that an individual client would be helped by participating. In treatment evaluation, however, scientific goals are subsumed under the goal of increasing client functioning. Thus, treatment evaluation seems to increase the likely benefits of treatment with little increased risk.

As we have argued throughout this book, treatment evaluation is a matter of adopting an empirical approach to treatment. It seems likely to make interventions more systematic, with better information supporting clinical decisions. It would seem that this would help therapy (although this assumption has not yet itself been tested empirically). Indeed, our current societal posture at times seems to assume that if the intervention is poorly specified, if goals are unclear, and if measures are weak, infrequent, or nonexistent, then there is *less* of an ethical worry, when surely there should be *more*. Our own cultural ambivalence about science can turn vice into virtue, and sloppiness into safety.

Every client can be viewed as an opportunity to conduct a new experiment, to ask new questions, and to increase our knowledge about behavior and its treatment, all in the context of actual professional work. In light of the above, the scientist practitioner must be careful not to let this work be considered treatment research. It is treatment evaluation. This is the case despite the fact that it might yield publications, or presentations; despite the fact that it involves the refinement of scientifically important statements. If this activity is allowed to be termed research and if this label then leads to the application of the legitimate protections given to research subjects, then the strangulation of empirical clinical work is not far behind. We could very easily find ourselves in a position in which the conduct of empirical intervention is discouraged, by virtue of the immediate negative consequences occurring to a practitioner attempting to conduct it; and treatment that failed to specify its target, its procedures, or its outcome could become the officially encouraged mode of intervention.

The Ethics of Experimental Therapy

It frequently happens that clients present problems for which there are no known, demonstrably effective interventions. Normally, the practitioner will make an educated guess about what might work. The treatment might be known to be effective in similar areas, or it might seem to be logically related to the problem at hand, or it may simply be common. In this situation, the client is receiving an experimental therapy—one of unknown effectiveness.

In normal applied practice, this is often not obvious. Practitioners tend to have considerable faith in their approaches, and it is only with careful questioning that it might be clear that there are little or no data to support the intervention.

When clinical intervention is evaluated using single case evaluations, the experimental nature of such treatment may be more obvious, precisely because it is well defined. In a way, this can be disconcerting because careful evaluation may help us to see what we do not know as well as what we do. Thus, on-line evaluations of experimental therapies may be discouraged on the grounds that clients should not be subjected to experimental interventions. But it is not the evaluation procedure that makes the therapy experimental. It just keeps us from fooling ourselves when it is.

If an experimental treatment is being used because of scientific interest (not client needs), then this is a different matter. At that point the enterprise is formal treatment research, not treatment evaluation, and the full protections given research subjects are required.

It is sometimes said that evaluation is only truly needed when treatment is experimental. If it is well developed, goes the argument, why evaluate it?

Actually, evaluation of interventions of known effectiveness is worthwhile for several reasons. First, there are instances when treatment will not be maximally effective with a specific client. In such a case, treatment modifications or alternatives can be implemented when there are reasons to believe that these modifications may be more effective. In this way, the techniques we use can gradually be refined, and questions on client-treatment interactions, or on which forms of treatment are most effective with which clients, can be addressed. Second, other questions about the intervention, such as the degree of generalization across responses or situations, will emerge naturally. Third, accountability alone is a good reason for evaluation. Finally, repeated replication across many clients is the primary way we determine the generality of results for a specified population. Population-based intervention is at the very core of a modern health care delivery system because it is at this level that more consistent quality and increased efficiency is possible.

Ethical Issues Raised by Evaluation

Evaluation does not relieve the practitioner of the need for general ethical conduct. Issues of informed consent in applied practice, competence, proper professional relationships, and so on, are not reduced one iota by evaluation. These topics, however, are beyond the scope of this book.

Evaluation does raise three major classes of additional ethical concerns, however. First, the empirical practitioner must take care to avoid confusion between research and evaluation. For example, if a practitioner selects a treatment target because of its scientific interest and not clinical need, this is research—not evaluation—and the full procedural protections of research subjects are needed.

Table 10.3 describes several issues that should be examined. The practitioner must be honest in answering these questions. If the evaluation process is not fostering good practice, then it is not really evaluation.

The second major issue raised is confidentiality. Careful evaluation increases our knowledge of the client. If we then present our results, it is critical that the client's confidentiality be protected. This is a general problem in applied fields. An anecdotal case report presents the same difficulties. The solution is to ensure absolute confidentiality or, if that is not possible, to secure client consent for any possible breaches of confidentiality. One way to do this is to have the client sign a "consent for services," which describes what information will be collected and how it will be used. Alternatively, if data are presented that might allow the client to be identified, nonessential information can be removed or changed. If needed information might allow client identification, the client should be asked to consent in writing to its use.

A third and final area of concern is that an empirical approach to intervention may take more time, effort, or money, particularly in the early stages of intervention. Usually, a person raising this issue will view these costs as needless, and therefore unethical. If expenditures are in the service of a client, however, they may actually be required for effective intervention. If quality intervention requires more work, then saving a client this effort may be pennywise and pound-foolish.

TABLE 10.3 Questions to Ask Oneself to Prevent Doing Research in the Name of Evaluation

Practical Issues	Treatment Research	Treatment Evaluation
How did the client come to be in treatment?	Sought for project	Routine clinical channels
Why is the client being kept in therapy?	To be evaluated	Client need
Why was the target behavior selected?	Scientific interest	Client need
Why are these measures being taken?	To make a better case to the scientific community	To assess client progress
Why is intervention being timed this way?	Research purposes	Client need
Why is this intervention being used?	Scientific interest	It seems most likely to be of aid
Why is this intervention being changed?	Scientific interest	To help the client or to clarify client need
Why are control conditions used?	To establish a scientifically valid effect	To help understand the client's needs

Additional protective devices may need to be generated that are unique to treatment evaluation. For example, the decreased privacy entailed by the publication or presentation of treatment evaluations may require some examination by persons other than the practitioner. Agencies interested in encouraging treatment evaluations could set up committees that would review presentations or publications of treatment evaluations with the specific goal of diminishing reasonable threats to invasion of privacy. They might also encourage practitioners to obtain consent for the kind of evaluations that are being performed. The same committees might review the work of practitioners doing no evaluations and design methods to encourage more evaluation. It would be important to arrange conditions so that it is harder to be sloppy than to be systematic.

The Necessity of Evaluation

There is a flip side to the ethical coin. Do practitioners have an ethical obligation to promote treatment evaluation? If so, how?

There are strong ethical arguments to be made for evaluation. Without repeated, systematic measurement how can a professional really know if the client is progressing? Isn't there an ethical need to be sure of this? Similarly, without careful specification of treatment, how can a practitioner really inform the client or others of its nature? Is not this ethically required?

Fortunately, the ethical need for evaluation is being supplemented by a financial need. Health care delivery systems must evolve to compete and win in the emerging health marketplace. There is simply no better way ever invented to develop service delivery systems than empirical evaluation. It is increasingly in the economic interests of agencies and managed care companies to encourage or even require evaluation and to provide the resources it needs. This linkage between science and business has happened before in engineering, biological technology, information processing, and other fields. It has never before occurred in behavioral health care. In these other fields, tremendous benefits rapidly emerged from the marriage: practically, scientifically, and financially. There seems to be little reason to imagine a different outcome for clinical science.

11 General Strategies in Assessment and Data Collection

Introduction

While other sections of this book focus on evaluation methodologies, this section focuses on the measures or dependent variables that are the focus of evaluation. This chapter describes general strategies in assessment and data collection that may be helpful to scientist practitioners in clinical environments. The next two chapters describe specific types of measures used in assessment and data collection: first, various self-report and psychophysiological measures; and second, observational and self-recording measures of behavior.

The object of measurement that is of special interest to scientist practitioners are clients' problems—that is, the specific presenting problems and/or treatment goals for each individual client expressed in quantifiable and measurable ways. In addition, measures of certain aspects of treatments themselves, such as treatment integrity, are often important (Yeaton & Sechrest, 1981).

Quantification of clients' problems is no small task. Such quantification requires conceptual and practical ingenuity. For example, nearly half of the behavior therapists (43.87%) who responded to a survey indicated that a disadvantage of behavioral assessment techniques was their impracticality in applied settings (Wade, Baker, & Hartmann, 1979), even though such techniques do lead to quantified data. Naturalistic observations, which are often cited as the *criterion* measure in behavioral assessment with which the accuracy of all other measures is compared, are thought to be particularly difficult to obtain. Professionals rated several barriers to the use of naturalistic measures (Ford & Kendall, 1979). Time and expense (mean of 3.6 on a 5-point scale, where 5 equals the most formidable barrier), lack of cooperation from clients (3.0), and unavailability or unfeasibility of requisite assessment methods (2.9) are all considered to be relatively difficult barriers to overcome.

The task of problem measurement may be especially challenging for therapists who tend to formulate treatment goals in terms of changes in clients' self-perception or intrapsychic functioning (Nelsen, 1981). Some specific suggestions for this situation are presented in a subsequent section.

Assessment techniques that are used during the course of an assessment vary, depending on the stage of assessment. One framework summarizing the stages of assessment has been proposed by Hawkins (1986), who views these stages as a funnel. During the first broad phase, several potential problematic areas may be screened, with a broad range and scope of information. Treatment decisions at this time include whether treatment is indicated, and whether another referral should be made. During the second phase, the focus of assessment begins to narrow, culminating in the specification of a client's problematic responses and a diagnosis. During the third phase, the focus of assessment narrows considerably, with target behaviors selected and assessment used as a basis of treatment selection. Intervention options are considered, including what class of psychosocial intervention strategies might be most useful and whether a medication evaluation may be desirable. In the fourth phase, the impact of intervention strategies on the target behaviors is continuously assessed. In the fifth and final phase, follow-up assessments of the target behaviors are done to assess the maintenance of treatment gains.

Different assessment techniques are more or less useful at different stages of this assessment funnel. In the first two broad stages of assessment, unstructured and semi-structured interviews are probably most widely used. The former are especially useful in helping to confirm a diagnosis or in providing detailed information about a client's behavior within a specific diagnostic category. Interviews are useful not only because of the information provided by the client's verbalizations, but also as a context in which to perform a mental status examination. Measures for personality assessment, both projective and objective measures, might also be used during these first two stages. During the third phase, the selection of target behaviors, other assessment devices might be more useful, such as questionnaires designed for specific purposes (see Fischer & Corcoran, 1994, for information about a wide variety of questionnaires) and role-playing of various interpersonal behaviors. During the fourth and fifth stages, when the funnel is very narrow, specific behaviors are monitored, perhaps through self-monitoring, direct observation, role-playing, questionnaire responses, or physiological measures. This range of measures is described in this and the two subsequent chapters.

Assessment in the Era of Managed Care: A Population-Based Approach

The development of managed behavioral health care is described in Chapter 2 of this volume. In the age of managed care, all assessment and intervention practices must be cost-justified and contribute to the effectiveness and efficiency of behavioral health care, conceived of as a total system. The hallmark of a modern industrialized health care system is a population-based approach appropriate to the information age. This approach, however, must walk a line between nomothetic and idiographic domains.

Clinical assessment is typically designed: (a) to select a target behavior or behaviors and make a diagnosis; (b) to select a treatment; and (c) to evaluate treatment outcome. In the age of managed behavioral health care, assessment is characterized by a population-based or nomothetic approach. The primary goal is to identify treatment-responsive collections of people—that is, to identify the needs of distinctive populations within the delivery system. To make this approach work, assessment and intervention must be standardized and be of known quality. There has also been an increase of assessment methods linked to treatment manuals, complete with measures of treatment adherence and therapist competence. The populations that were initially identified were largely synonymous with clinical syndromes, but increasingly the health care system is dealing with less topographically defined groups such as "high utilizers of health care," or "emotional avoiders," or "chronic, multiple-problem patients."

As this population-based system develops, the available scientific information is increasingly being tied to the needs of individuals in the form of flexible treatment guidelines. A population-based approach thus does not ultimately mean the homogenization of human beings into groups that ignore individuality. Instead, assessment that helps identify what is uniquely important and functionally distinct about individuals will come to dominate over time, provided only that these distinctions be empirically verified and tied to treatment outcome and client satisfaction.

In this chapter, we discuss the three main goals of assessment from this vantage point. Several guidelines are then suggested for use in collecting measures: (a) consider idiographic versus nomothetic measures; (b) state client's problems in specific terms; (c) choose measures consistent with one's theoretical orientation; (d) specify several target behaviors; (e) obtain multiple measures for each problem behavior; (f) select measures that are both sensitive and meaningful; (g) collect measures early and repeatedly in the course of treatment; (h) make comparisons within a specific measure only if the data are collected under similar conditions; (i) graph the data; (j) record inconvenient measures less frequently than more convenient measures; (k) select "good" and accurate measures; (l) obtain clients' informed consent when necessary; and (m) use institutional means to encourage the collection of measures.

Goals of Assessment

As noted above, there are three main goals of assessment: (a) select target behaviors and make a diagnosis; (b) choose a treatment strategy; and (c) evaluate the effectiveness of the chosen treatment or of the treatment delivery system. Each of these goals is considered below.

Select Target Behaviors and Make a Diagnosis

The first goal of assessment is to identify the appropriate target behavior or behaviors to be modified in treatment. Target behaviors are those that need to either decrease in frequency (e.g., noncompliance in a child; panic attacks in an adult), to increase in frequency (e.g., social contacts in a socially phobic person, pleasant events and reports of positive affect in a depressed person), or to change in stimulus control (e.g., change urination from a bed to a commode in an enuretic person, change sexual responding from a child to a consenting adult in a pedophiliac).

Clients generally come to therapy with somewhat vague complaints (e.g., I feel like I'm having a nervous breakdown, or I'm just not as happy as other people) or with somewhat vague goals (e.g., I'd like to increase my self-confidence, or I want to start enjoying life again). Several suggestions for transforming these vague presenting problems into target behaviors are described within a subsequent section on guidelines for collecting measures. One example is the "rules of evidence," that is, asking clients how they or someone else would know that their goal has been accomplished? In other words, what would be different in their lives if their goal had been accomplished. A client who wanted to increase self-confidence might give as evidence that she would start applying for employment outside the home, or that she would enroll in a college course.

Various nonempirical and empirical guidelines have been proposed to help select target behaviors. These have been summarized by Nelson and Hayes (1986). Examples of nonempirically based or philosophical guidelines for target behavior selection include the following. First, behavior should be changed that is physically dangerous to the client or to others; thus, it is self-evident that suicidal or aggressive behavior has a premier place among target behaviors. Second, select for modification only those behaviors that the individual's natural environment will continue to maintain (Ayllon & Azrin, 1968). An example would be the difficulty in targeting nonassertive behavior in a woman who is physically abused for expressing her views to her spouse; prior to assertiveness training, the woman may need case management help in actually leaving the abusive situation. Third, target behaviors should be selected that are treatable; "when intervention strategies are not available, the behavioral analysis becomes an academic exercise of no consequence" (Kanfer & Grimm, 1977, p. 9). An example here would be attempting to treat manic behavior only through psychosocial treatment—this strategy is unlikely to be successful.

Various empirically or data-based suggestions have also been made for the selection of target behaviors, also summarized by Nelson and Hayes (1986). An example here is comparing a client's behavior to normative data, including developmental data. Especially for children, it is difficult to determine if a potential target behavior is indeed problematic without knowledge of the child's age and developmental norms. Another empirically based strategy is the known groups method, where two groups are compared (usually a diagnosed group and a "normal" group) on specific behaviors. The behaviors that differentiate the two groups are good candidates for target behaviors for the diagnosed group. For example, research has shown that depressed college students differed from their nondepressed peers by inappropriate timing of self-disclosures and by excessive negative self-statements (Jacobson & Anderson, 1982); the latter two behaviors could be considered as target behaviors in a college student client presenting as depressed.

In addition to selecting target behaviors, many clinical situations also require the generation of a diagnosis. Usually this is a syndromal classification using DSM-IV diagnostic criteria. In the abstract, diagnoses have obvious utility in some areas. Diagnoses facilitate communication in the professional community, for example, in making referrals or in writing grant proposals. Diagnoses are also useful for record-keeping, whether in a local site like a clinic or hospital or in an epidemiological catchment area. Diagnoses communicate the types of problems that are presented for treatment in a certain site, and that are occurring within a certain area in epidemiological research. The use of some kind of classification is essential within clinical science in order to generalize across individuals with problems and to access the findings of clinical science. Indeed, the empirically validated treatments listed by the Task Force on Promotion and Dissemination of Psychological Procedures (1995) and presented in Chapter 3 of this volume are generally listed as effective for specific disorders (e.g., group cognitive behavioral therapy for social phobia).

There is no necessary incompatibility between the use of syndromal diagnostic categories and the selection of specific target behaviors. Syndromal diagnostic criteria, if they are empirically sound, can be thought of as responses that covary nomothetically across a certain group of individuals (Nelson & Barlow, 1981). If a client presents with a few of the responses that comprise diagnostic criteria for a particular category, then it is wise for the clinician to assess the presence of other diagnostic criteria within that category. The polythetic nature of DSM-IV acknowledges that all individuals who merit a certain diagnosis do not inevitably manifest all behaviors listed in the diagnostic criteria; nonetheless, there are sufficient data to indicate that a client who has a subgroup of the diagnostic criteria within a certain category is likely to meet other diagnostic criteria, thus expanding the list of potential target behaviors for the individual. With certain limitations, diagnosis can also be useful in treatment selection, as is described in greater detail below.

Select Treatment

In addition to the selection of target behaviors, the second major goal of assessment is to select what is likely to be the most effective treatment. This is the single most important issue for applied systems that hope to save health care costs by delivering effective and efficient treatment, and a great deal of research and evaluation is being dedicated to the problem. At the present time, however, the literature showing a positive treatment impact for assessment and diagnosis is still relatively underdeveloped.

There are four main strategies by which assessment can be helpful in selecting treatment: diagnosis, identification of problematic response classes, the functional analysis (Nelson, 1988), and other case formulations.

Diagnosis as a Basis of Treatment Selection   The most crucial question for any clinical assessment process or diagnostic label is "in what way and to what extent does this . . . information help us in treating the patient?" (Meehl, 1959, p. 117). Meehl called this question "ultimately the practically significant one by which the contributions of our [assessment] techniques must be judged" (1959, p. 116).

As described in Chapter 3 of this book, empirically validated treatments are generally listed as efficacious for problems within specific diagnostic categories by the Task Force on Promotion and Dissemination of Psychological Procedures

(1995). For example, for a client with unipolar depression, well-established psychosocial treatments include cognitive therapy (e.g., Beck, Rush, Shaw, & Emery, 1979) and interpersonal therapy (Klerman, Weissman, Rounsaville, & Chevron, 1984). This provides some support for the view that the diagnostic label assigned to a client's configuration of problems can be useful in selecting an efficacious treatment.

The assumption in using diagnosis as a basis for treatment selection is that many clients within that diagnostic category will respond well to the selected treatment; of course, it is not inevitable that every client within that diagnostic category will benefit from the selected treatment. Moreover, many effective treatments, both psychological and pharmacological, have impact on a number of DSM disorders. For example, cognitive therapy has been demonstrated to be successful in the treatment of depression (Beck et al., 1979), but has also been utilized with anxiety disorders (Michelson & Ascher, 1987) and with personality disorders (Beck & Freeman, 1990) (although it should be recognized that cognitive therapy is not monolithic, and has many useful variations). In addition, there seems to be a great deal of functional variability within many syndromal groupings.

In fully capitated managed care organizations, a very large percentage of clinical visits will be for such problems as marital difficulties, problems at work, or problems with raising children (Strosahl, 1994). These kinds of problems are not clinical syndromes, although these problems may be suitable for V-codes in DSM-IV. Data may exist on how best to treat these problems, for example, through parent training or through social skills training. These empirical data on the likelihood of successful intervention for specific problematic behaviors are thus quite relevant.

The treatment implications of syndromal diagnosis are thus somewhat limited. Consistent with recognition of these limitations, some managed care organizations are now using treatment guidelines that put much greater emphasis on the treatment of presenting complaints rather than syndromal distinctions, or on broad-spectrum but inexpensive treatment packages rather than highly focused treatments.

Haynes (1986) argues that a diagnostic strategy in treatment selection is effective if (1) clients within a particular diagnostic category are relatively homogeneous; (2) a powerful treatment is available for the disorder; and (3) the cost of an idiographic assessment outweighs its additive benefits. To illustrate Haynes's first point, if a client is diagnosed with mental retardation, that diagnosis is an insufficient basis for treatment planning. Even though the Task Force on Promotion and Dissemination of Psychological Procedures (1995) lists "behavior modification" as a well-established treatment for developmentally disabled individuals, further assessment is necessary to identify specific target behaviors and behavior modification procedures for the individual client. Others (Fensterheim & Raw, 1996; Nezu, 1996) have also argued that diagnostic categories are an insufficient basis for treatment selection because they do not capture variability across clients in problem configurations and in controlling variables. Three treatment selection strategies that are more idiographic than the diagnostic strategy are described next.

Response Class or Keystone Behavior Strategy in Selecting Treatment   A second strategy in selecting treatments is to give a diagnosis, but also to assess for problematic response classes that are associated with the particular diagnostic category. Using the example of unipolar depression, response classes that have been associated with this diagnosis include dysfunctional thought patterns, social skills difficulties, and an unfavorable ratio of pleasant and unpleasant events (Beck et al., 1979; Lewinsohn & Arconad, 1981). In this strategy, the response classes that are problematic for the individual, or that are a "keystone" to the individual's depression, are targeted for treatment. This metaphor of a keystone (usually attributed to Wahler, 1975) is used to designate target behaviors that are central for the individual, or even crucial in effecting more widespread behavior change.

There is some evidence that treatment that is matched to an individual's problematic and keystone response classes is more efficacious than is mismatched treatment. For example, McKnight, Nelson, Hayes, and Jarrett (1984) found that depressed women with assessed problems in social skills improved significantly more in both social skills and depression after receiving the matched treatment of social skills training as compared with the mismatched treatment of cognitive therapy. Conversely, depressed women with assessed problems in irrational cognitions improved significantly more in both cognitions and depression after receiving the matched treatment of cognitive therapy as compared with the mismatched treatment of social skills training. These results showed that identification and treatment of the correct keystone behavior was critical in ameliorating each woman's depression. Overall, however, the evidence is mixed regarding advantages of matched treatment for depression over mismatched treatment; in fact, in some studies, depressed subjects improved more if they had strengths rather than deficits in areas targeted for treatment (Rude & Rehm, 1991).

In the context of the health care delivery system, the question is not merely whether treatment matching is more effective: It is also whether it is more efficient. This is a complex question. Individually tailored treatment may require more therapist training, more time and expense in assessment, more supervision and monitoring, and higher-level (and thus more expensive) therapists, and may lead to more variability in quality across therapists in applying individually tailored treatment. Conversely, broad treatment manuals may hit enough of the "high spots" to be effective even if they are not individually tailored, and may be able to be used by a broad range of therapists with reasonable consistency (Wilson, 1996). The jury is still out on this question. Many of these "services research" questions are only now being asked and answered, since the arrival of managed care organizations has provided the economic interest in seeing them solved. The robust tradition of psychotherapy outcome research, while a significant component of these issues, will not alone provide the information needed.

Functional Analysis   Functional analysis has a long and distinguished history within assessment, especially behavioral assessment (e.g., Kanfer & Phillips, 1970). The focus of the functional analysis is to identify "important, controllable, causal functional relationships applicable to a specified set of target behaviors for an individual client" (Haynes & O'Brien, 1990, p. 654). Basic elements of a functional analysis include the identification of clinically relevant target behaviors or responses, the stimuli or antecedents that precede the target behaviors, the consequences (e.g., reinforcers and/or punishers) that follow target behaviors and which function to influence the frequency of those behaviors, and a delineation of relevant organismic or individual difference variables such as physiological states or past learning that may be useful for developing an understanding of the client's present problems (Goldfried & Sprafkin, 1976). Once such an analysis has been performed, an intervention is devised that is conceptually linked to assessment findings. Treatment is then implemented, and change in the target behaviors is continuously assessed.

Linehan (1993a; 1993b) presents an example of the use of functional analysis in the treatment of borderline personality disorder, specifically as it relates to the display of parasuicidal acts (e.g., wrist cutting), which are common among members of this group. In the event that the client has engaged in a parasuicidal act since the previous session, a detailed functional analysis is performed to identify the context in which this behavior was performed. For example, a client may have cut her wrists following an argument with her boyfriend (antecedent). Possible consequences following wrist-cutting that may influence its frequency might include relief from guilt and feelings of emptiness (negative reinforcement), the refocusing of attention away from unpleasant cognitions about the self (negative reinforcement), statements of support and apology from the boyfriend (positive reinforcement), a new scar (delayed punishment), and a sizable hospital bill following emergency room treatment (delayed punishment). This functional analysis is then followed by a solution analysis to identify alternative behaviors that may produce similar desirable consequences as the target behavior (i.e., relief from aversive emotions and cognitions, evocation of support from others). Linehan's treatment package, which includes the functional analyses of parasuicidal acts, has been found to result in fewer incidents of parasuicidal behavior and fewer inpatient days than standard therapies (e.g., Linehan, Heard, & Armstrong, 1993).

A diagnosis can sometimes be useful in suggesting nomothetic controlling variables that assist in choosing a treatment using a functional analytic approach. For example, if a person is diagnosed with unipolar depression, a nomothetic controlling variable is loss (of either stimulus control or positive reinforcers for normal behaviors). To illustrate, a woman may suffer a major depressive episode consequent to divorce; her typical stimulus control for many daily household behaviors is now gone, as is the positive reinforcement for doing those normal behaviors. Treatment may focus on establishing new environmental control for a repertoire of normal behaviors—for example, enjoying a single life, returning to work, establishing other relationships. Of course, it would need to be determined that a nomothetic controlling variable suggested by a diagnosis is applicable to a specific person's situation.

The same specific behavior, however, can be controlled by different functional conditions. For example, Carr and Durand (1985) categorized the disruptive behavior of developmentally delayed children as having either an attention-seeking or task-relief function. Some children showed high levels of disruption during task performance because it brought adults into contact with their performance on the task; others did it to escape the task. This distinction was shown to have treatment implications. For instance, teaching the children to say "how do you like my work?" (followed by adult attention) decreased disruptiveness in the attention-seeking group, but not the task-relief group. Conversely, teaching the children to say "this is too hard" followed by adult assistance helped with the task-relief group but not the attention-seeking group (see also Durand & Carr, 1991).

The problem with functional analysis is twofold. First, it has not yet been shown empirically to be cost effective. Second, the entire process is ill-defined. The "assess, formulate, intervene, evaluate" structure of classical functional analysis is highly abstract when compared to the actual analytic behaviors employed by a given therapist in a given case conceptualization. Within a specific case, a myriad of analytic behaviors could be said to follow this functional analytic structure, and they could do so in a wide variety of ways (see Hayes & Follette, 1992, for a more detailed analysis of this problem). This second problem also means that functional analysis is probably not sufficiently replicable to be tested empirically.

At least three solutions have been proposed to this second problem (Hayes & Follette, 1992): (a) develop expert systems (e.g., through nomological nets) that allow the decision-making styles of well-known functional analysts to be replicated, (b) develop theoretically driven logical decision trees that constitute a kind of functional analysis, and (c) develop functional diagnostic categories (much as did Carr and Durand above). None of these solutions has yet advanced sufficiently to be broadly applicable; but in limited areas, some such solutions already exist.

Case Formulation Approach to Treatment Selection   A fourth assessment strategy by which to select treatment is a case formulation approach. In some ways, a case formulation is similar to the response class or keystone behavior strategy, described above. Case formulation has been defined as the identification of "the patient's central underlying psychological problem" (Persons, Curtis, & Silber-schatz, 1991, p. 608). In other ways, case formulation is a kind of functional analysis.

Turkat (1990) has outlined a case formulation approach for the personality disorders that includes the development of a case formulation, a controlled evaluation of that formulation, and the linkage of case formulation to treatment selection. Case formulation generally occurs through an interview, resulting in a hypothetical formulation of the interrelationship among the client's various presenting problems. This hypothetical formulation is then tested by within-session experiments. The most probable formulation is then the basis for treatment selection. For example, Turkat and Maisto (1985) present a case of a client with histrionic personality disorder whom the therapist formulated had empathy deficits. To test this hypothesis, the therapist asked the client to engage in two tasks that involved the judgment of moods and thoughts of others. Treatment selection, implementation, and evaluation followed.

Persons (1989) has modified Turkat's case formulation approach to emphasize the role of cognitions as causal determinants of psychopathology. Persons' formulations distinguish between overt difficulties in the behavioral, cognitive, and emotional realms, and underlying psychological mechanisms that generally are maladaptive beliefs about the self that are hypothesized to produce and maintain the client's overt difficulties. Since the latter cannot be directly observed or assessed, they are best viewed as working hypotheses to be tested in the course of therapy—for example, through Socratic dialogue. Treatment includes both the reduction of overt difficulties and the modification of underlying pathological beliefs.

Evaluate Treatment Delivery and Outcome

Once treatment has been selected, the manner of its implementation and the client's response to the treatment is evaluated. There are several good reasons for practitioners to collect quantified measures of their clients' problems and progress. Five reasons are elaborated below.

Improve Treatment by Measuring Problems   The first practical reason to collect quantified measures of clients' problems, progress, and satisfaction with their course of treatment is to improve treatment and behavioral health care delivery systems. Measures of clients' problem(s) should be taken before treatment begins, several times during the course of treatment, and at short- and long-term follow-up when treatment ceases. Client satisfaction should be collected periodically, but especially at termination and follow-up. When measures are collected at regular temporal intervals, they provide feedback to the therapist about the client's progress. If the treatment procedures are not producing desired results, then the procedures can be modified. Frequent measurement allows timely revision in unproductive therapeutic strategies. Client and therapist time and effort and client fees are not wasted on ineffective techniques. If the treatment procedures are producing desired results, the therapist can continue the procedures with renewed confidence.

While the above statements may seem obvious, experimental verification is needed to corroborate them. In other words, it makes sense that the collection of objective measures can improve clinical efficacy. But applied science has yet to provide experimental support for this claim. To remedy the situation, a between-subjects design might be employed, with two groups of clinicians. An assessor collects repeated measures on all client–subjects. Half of the clinicians view the results during treatment, while the other half do not. The relative improvement in the clients treated by the two groups of clinicians is determined. Alternatively, and more in keeping with the spirit of this book, a single-subject research design might be used to determine if the collection of objective measures produces improved treatment, for example, a multiple baseline across several problems in an individual client. An assessor collects measures on all problems each week. The quantified measures are revealed to the therapist, however, at successive weeks in a multiple-baseline format. The hypothesis would be that each client problem would receive better treatment, as evidenced by improvements in measures of his or her problem, when the data about the problem was shared with the therapist.

Until such experiments are performed, it is a common-sense statement that the collection of repeated measures improves therapeutic efficacy. The measures provide feedback to the therapist on the effectiveness of the treatment, so that the current treatment can be altered or maintained. The data on the impact of client satisfaction measures are better developed since this approach has been used for many years in a wide variety of businesses. Measures of client satisfaction are relevant to the increasingly industrialized health care system of today (Strosahl, 1994), although such assessment in medical or mental health is not always routine.

Measure Aspects of Treatment and Treatment Integrity   Treatment may also be improved when aspects of treatment are measured. Clinicians and clinical researchers are recognizing that measuring certain aspects of treatment can be very important in clinical practice. Two aspects of particular importance are the strength and integrity of treatment (see Yeaton & Sechrest, 1981, 1992, for detailed discussions). In most instances, practitioners choose treatments because they think these treatments will be effective. As our technology improves, it is necessary to pay some attention to the particular strength or "dosage" of treatment that should be used. For example, in treating a medical problem by pharmacological means, a physician generally recommends a particular dosage of a given drug. This decision is based on some prior knowledge of what dosage is usually effective with the particular type of patient presenting with a given problem. Strength or "dosage" of psychological treatment, then, would have to do with the intensity of the treatment (e.g., duration of time-out needed to affect a child's undesirable behavior) and the frequency of administration (e.g., weekly vs. semi-weekly vs. bi-weekly therapy sessions).

The more important concept is *treatment integrity,* the degree to which treatment is delivered as intended. As described earlier in this book, the bare minimum for treatment integrity is the availability of a treatment manual that outlines in some detail the components of each therapy session. In addition, the success of the therapists in following the treatment manual must be monitored and reported. For example, in a recent series of nine case studies with depressed persons with different personality disorders (Nelson-Gray, Johnson, Foyle, Daniel, & Harmon, 1996), treatment manuals were created for each treated personality disorder. All sessions were taped, and half were compared against the treatment manuals to assess treatment integrity.

To take another example that occurred recently in one of our clinics, two agoraphobics were administered a treatment package consisting of cognitive restructuring and detailed instructions on gradually approaching a hierarchy of feared situations. These clients self-monitored a variety of items, including the amount of "practice" exposing themselves to feared situations that occurred between sessions. In many cases, this self-monitoring was corroborated by a spouse. Measures of the problem, specifically the avoidance behavior and amount of subjectively reported anxiety, indicated that one client improved, while one client did not. Measures of treatment integrity—that is, how much treatment was actually experienced by each patient based on the amount of practice between sessions—revealed that the client who got better had practiced, while the other client had not. In this case, one can conclude that the treatment is probably effective, but one client simply did not receive it in its intended form. Alterations may then be made in the treatment approach that will improve treatment and make it more effective for such clients.

Another crucial aspect of measuring treatment integrity is to assess intermediate or process-related dependent variables. The number of possible behavioral problems and interventions is far too vast for applied researchers to determine who will respond to what kind of treatment by simply trying out different treatments and measuring their effectiveness. Functional theories are needed that suggest not only what treatment might work, but why and how it might work. These theoretical notions are as important to progress in the applied arena as is treatment outcome per se. For example, suppose one delivers cognitive therapy as intended to change severe depression, but only depression—not changes in dysfunctional cognitions—are monitored. Even if treatment works, one does not know why. If treatment does not work, one cannot be sure if this was due to the failure to change cognitions or to the lack of a relationship between measured cognitive changes that occurred and depression in this client.

Thus, many of the strategies suggested in subsequent chapters can be used not only to measure problems, but also to measure the integrity of treatment. In each instance, this should improve treatment. In most cases, measures of treatment integrity are different from measures of treatment outcome. This is obvious when assessment is done to determine if a treatment manual were properly implemented. In the example above, measuring the amount of practice in feared situations is not the final outcome that one desires, which is reduction of subjective and behavioral aspects of fear. Taking blood levels to determine if a patient with bipolar affective disorder has reached an adequate level of lithium is not the same as observing changes in the client's manic behavior. Monitoring the implementation of a contingency contract between a disruptive adolescent and his parents is different from decreasing the disruptive behavior itself. Practitioners can monitor depth of relaxation through portable physiological monitoring equipment as a measure of treatment integrity when using relaxation or biofeedback as a treatment for headaches, hypertension, or some other stress-related physiological syndrome. Additional measures would be used, however, to assess desired changes, such as self-monitoring of headache pain.

Measures of treatment integrity can be further broken down into two domains. *Adherence* refers to the degree to which a treatment protocol was followed. For example, if the treatment package includes deep muscle relaxation training, the intervention actually delivered can be examined to see if the specific components of deep muscle relaxation training have been implemented. *Competence* refers to the level of practical skill with which an individual therapist applies the specified treatment. The two concepts are not synonymous. For example, relaxation training might be done in a formally correct but incompetent manner: A therapist might use an irritating, staccato voice, or may giggle at odd moments. Conversely, it is important not to confuse adherence with general social and clinical skill. A therapist who is warm and confident but who does not follow the needed treatment protocol may have good outcomes, but not in a fashion that is specifiable and replicable—which are hallmarks of assessment and intervention in the era of managed care. Adherence is a necessary but not sufficient condition for competence (see Waltz, Addis, Koerner, & Jacobson, 1993), and both domains should be measured.

Provide Accountability   The third reason for practitioners to collect quantified measures of their clients' problems, progress, and satisfaction is to enhance accountability. As noted in Chapter 2, there is increasing pressure from a variety of sources, namely, insurance companies and other third-party payers, for evidence that therapy is actually helping clients.

There are different categories of measures used to assess treatment (Panzarino, 1995): (a) changes in client level of functioning; (b) changes in client's perception of the quality of life; (c) changes in initial presenting problems; and (d) degree of satisfaction with treatment services. Client level of functioning is frequently assessed by Axis V of DSM-IV (1994), the GAF, or the Global Assessment of Functioning scale, which is a 0–100 clinician rating of client functioning. A myriad of other measures of social functioning, however, are also available (see review by Goldman, Skodol, & Lave, 1992). Quality of life, or patient life satisfaction, is sometimes assessed using the Quality of Life Inventory (Frisch, Cornell, Villanueva, & Retzlaff, 1992). There is a large variety of ways to assess changes in initial presenting problems, which seems to be at the heart of treatment outcome. These measures include: therapist ratings of client improvement regarding specific problems; the use of questionnaires specific to certain diagnostic categories; and the use of more idiographic measures tailored to the individual client. Client satisfaction measures are still predominantly idiosyncratic measures, often using Likert scales in domains of interest.

Comprehensive systems have been proposed by which all areas of clinical practice can be quantified and available to accountability evaluations. Two examples are provided here, one from the private sector and one from the commercial sector. From the private sector, Clement (1996) has proposed a comprehensive system useful for evaluation in private practice. Within that plan, treatment plans would be evaluated in terms of their specificity regarding treatment setting, agent of change, goals, intervention, intensity and duration of treatment, and criteria for termination. Compliance with the treatment plan would also be monitored, as would the quality of professional and financial record-keeping. In addition, public relations would be assessed by satisfaction of patients, satisfaction of referring professionals, and absence of ethical and legal complaints. Time and money consumed by administration would also be monitored. Most importantly, perhaps, changes in initial presenting problems are evaluated based on formulating individualized goals using goal attainment scaling (Kiresuk & Sherman, 1968) and by the Global Assessment of Functioning (American Psychiatric Association, 1994).

From the commercial sector, Systems Management, Inc. (1995) has available a fully comprehensive accountability system that includes terminals in the provider's office, a processing center set up in consultation with Systems Management, Inc., and access to data by insurance companies. All aspects of office functioning are computerized, including but not limited to narrative and process notes of therapy sessions, patient and provider information, treatment plans, and psychological, disability, and lethality reports. Changes in client presenting problems are evaluated mainly by clinician ratings of either frequency or severity of specific target behaviors, using a 5-point Likert scale, at intake and to measure treatment progress. Computerized graphs of these ratings are available.

One of the difficulties with both these private and commercial systems is that the main outcome measure of change in client problems is clinician ratings, which are readily subject to bias—in this case, especially positive bias (Nezu, 1996). It has been suggested (Nelson-Gray, 1996; Nezu, 1996) that such subjective ratings be supplemented by more standardized measures that are suitable to specific diagnostic categories, for example, the Beck Depression Inventory (Beck, Ward, Mendelson, Mock, & Erbaugh, 1961) to assess depression, and the State-Trait Anxiety Inventory (Spielberger, Gorsuch, & Lushene, 1970) to assess anxiety. A large range of outcome measures are reviewed by Ogles, Lambert, and Masters (1996). In addition, Nelson-Gray (1996) proposes that idiographic measures designed for the individual client and his or her life circumstances be utilized as an adjunct to more nomothetic measures. The next two chapters describe in detail many of these measures, such as self-monitoring, observational measures, and physiological measures, that can be used idiographically.

Enhance Clinical Science   The fourth reason for practitioners to collect quantified measures of their clients' problems and progress is to enhance clinical science. The thesis of this book is that data collection and experimentation by practitioners who bridge the scientist–practitioner gap expand our armamentarium of effective techniques and our knowledge of therapeutic processes (Azrin, 1977; Barlow, 1980; Barlow & Hersen, 1984; Jayaratne & Levy, 1979; Meehl, 1978). As elaborated earlier in this book, practicing clinicians can enhance the work of clinical research centers in at least two important ways: (a) create hypotheses to be tested in clinical research centers through clinical innovations, that is, data suggesting that a new or modified treatment technique might be effective with clients with a particular problem or a particular diagnosis; and (b) engage in clinical replications and extend the external validity of research findings, either by practitioners publishing independently or through contributions to practice research networks.

Accurate measurement of the problem is a prerequisite for internal validity. Hence, the scientist–practitioner, in contributing to clinical science, must utilize accurate measures. Of course, accurate measurement by itself does not ensure internal validity. More is said about internal validity and accurate measurement in the section in this chapter labeled "Select 'Good' and Accurate Measures." Internal validity is also discussed in this book's chapters on single-subject experimental design.

Improve the Behavioral Health Care System   The final reason to collect data on client problems, progress, and satisfaction is that these are the data, when combined with other data on program cost and efficiency, that assess the functioning of the behavioral health delivery system itself, be it an office, clinic, hospital, provider network, or health care company. What is new and important about the current environment is that the industrialization of health care provides opportunities for improvement of client care and for comprehensive assessments of such improvements. For example, suppose it is decided that all clients referred to behavioral health providers in a large managed care organization who have panic disorder will first receive an empirically validated manualized group treatment for panic (e.g., Barlow, Brown, & Craske, 1994; Barlow, Craske, Cerny, & Klosko, 1989) by providers specifically trained to provide this treatment. If the levels of client progress and satisfaction improve overall, this system change has lead to a better health delivery system. If as a result of this improvement, fewer clients show up in the emergency rooms with a false "heart attack," the managed care firm that made this change may have a greater degree of financial success.

In summary, there are at least five good reasons for scientist–practitioners to collect repeated measures on clients' problems: (a) to improve treatment offered to clients, (b) to assess treatment integrity, (c) to provide accountability, (d) to enhance clinical research, and (e) to improve the behavioral health care system itself. The remainder of this chapter focuses on guidelines for quantifying clients' problems and progress as well as for measuring treatment. While most guidelines are provided in the context of measuring problems, these guidelines are equally applicable to assessing the integrity of treatment, as illustrated in examples given above.

Guidelines for Collecting Measures

The following suggestions may help practitioners in implementing data collection procedures in their settings.

Idiographic versus Nomothetic Measures

The current trend in managed care is the development of outcome measures that are nomothetic, that is, applicable to all clients within a system. Examples of groups developing such nomothetic systems of outcome measures are: National Alliance for the Mentally Ill, the Minnesota Council of Child Caring Agencies, Compass Information Services, Inc., the Joint Commission on Accreditation of Healthcare Organizations (Mental Health Weekly, 1995), the Australian National Mental Health Information Strategy Committee (Andrews, 1995), the Massachusetts Medicaid program (Nelson, Hartman, Ojemann, & Wilcox, 1995), and the American Managed Behavioral Healthcare Association (Panzarino, 1995). Even though each of these systems is striving for uniform outcome measures across clients, there is a call for even greater uniformity, that is, a single accepted system of outcome measures: "Providers and delivery systems will be driven to a House of Babel if required to use multiple instruments and protocols to satisfy various payers, contracts, and regulators" (Sederer, 1995, p. 43).

One difficulty with nomothetic measures is that successful treatment outcomes are more difficult to obtain with some disorders than with others. When a nomothetic system is used, particular hospitals, agencies, or individual clinicians might appear to be more or less effective because the majority of their clientele presents with disorders that are relatively easy versus difficult to treat unless the diagnosis is used as a "covariate" of sorts.

Alternatively, different sets of nomothetic measures may be appropriate with different diagnostic categories. The best measures for each diagnostic category could be determined by experts who perform clinical research with clients bearing that diagnosis. For example, to determine improvement following treatment for social phobia, Turner, Beidel, and Wolff (1994) recommend using the Index of Social Phobia Improvement, which is comprised of five individual measures, including self-report, clinician rating, and behavioral performance. Researchers have also indicated their preferences for certain measures within diagnostic categories by their high frequency of usage. For example, in Lambert and McRoberts's (1993) review of 116 studies of psychotherapy with adults, the Beck Depression Inventory (Beck et al., 1961) was the most frequently used measure of depression, and the State-Trait Anxiety Inventory (Spielberger, Gorsuch, & Lushene, 1970) was the most frequently used measure of anxiety.

An alternative to relying solely on nomothetic measures, whether across clients or specific to diagnostic categories, is to supplement nomothetic measures with idiographic measures. Idiographic measures are those tailored to the individual client and his or her presenting problem. The advantages of idiographic measures are that they may be readily implemented in the specific situation and that they may be more sensitive to changes in the client's problems. One disadvantage of most idiographic measures is that there are no norms available against which to compare the client's progress. When such norms are available, they provide a basis against which to evaluate the substantive or clinical significance of the client's progress. A second disadvantage of most idiographic measures is that their psychometric properties have not been investigated or established.

More globally, encouragement of idiographic measures assists clinical science by fostering the development of novel and potentially better outcome measures. Relatedly, "the risk of standardization is that it may freeze the creative development of improved measures and methodologies in a young field" (Trabin, 1995, p. 6).

At the moment, idiographic outcome measures are popular. In Froyd and Lambert's (1989) review of 348 outcome studies published in 20 selected journals from 1983 through 1988, a total of 1,430 outcome measures were identified for a wide variety of patient diagnoses, treatment modalities, and therapy types. Of these, 840 different measures were each used in just one published study. In the age of managed health care, it is likely that idiographic measures will supplement nomothetic measures in the future.

In summary, the first guideline in creating measures is to balance the need for nomothetic measures, which may be required by third-party payers, with the advantages of idiographic measures, which may be more sensitive to a particular client's problems. As clinical science develops, these two may be balanced by the development of well-evaluated assessment systems that include idiographic components.

State Client's Problems in Specific Terms

The presenting problems of each individual client must be stated in specific terms. Clients' problem behaviors and desired therapeutic objectives should be defined with clear behavioral referents (Mischel, 1968). Clients and some therapists may initially conceptualize presenting problems in global terms, such as "the reduction of nervousness" or "improvement in self-concept." The following questions have been useful in intake sessions to help concretize presenting problems and to establish treatment objectives. One question is to ask the client for "acceptable evidence" of having attained the desired global goal. For example, if the client wants to improve his self-concept, acceptable evidence of that improved self-concept might include: being able to speak in front of groups without one's voice faltering, saying fewer negative statements to oneself (e.g., "I'm such a bore."), and being able to decline invitations that are momentarily not appealing.

A second useful question to help define client problems in specific terms is to ask the client for his or her "three wishes." In other words, if any three of the client's wishes could be granted, what would they be? For example, a schizophrenic in remission might wish that he could have a girlfriend, be able to study without intrusive fantasies, and be able to obtain a part-time job.

Another strategy in specifying client problems is to ask the client about a "typical day or week." Describing a current typical day or week helps to specify current problems. Describing an ideal typical day or week helps to establish therapeutic goals. For example, an ideal typical week for a currently depressed female client might be to get up and go to work in the mornings, to go out with a male partner a few evenings a week, and to receive calls or visits from her grown children on the weekends.

It may be especially challenging for practitioners to describe clients' problems or therapeutic objectives in specific terms, especially when the client's long-term goals are rather global and distant. In these cases, Nelsen (1981) suggests that clinicians specify partial or instrumental goals. According to Nelsen, partial goals involve part of a final goal or doing something that builds up the skills needed to accomplish the final goal. Nelsen provides the following example of a partial goal. A client's long-term final goal is being less socially isolated. Partial goals may be saying hello to a stranger, speaking briefly to a neighbor, and calling up a friend. According to Nelsen, instrumental goals lead indirectly to a final goal. Nelsen provides the following example of an instrumental goal. A client's final goal is experiencing higher self-esteem. One instrumental goal may be getting a raise at work.

As noted above, another source of suggestions for specific behaviors or goals is the operational criteria of the DSM-IV. The diagnostic labels themselves are too global to serve as the targets of therapeutic intervention. The operational criteria or diagnostic criteria that define each diagnostic category, however, may provide useful suggestions for specific therapeutic goals.

Practitioners who have been using the Problem-Oriented Record (POR) (Katz & Wooley, 1975; Weed, 1968) have a head start in specifying client problems. The problem list of the POR generally requires a specification of problems to be treated. Strategies or techniques to measure progress in treating these problems can serve as measures and can be reported in the "subjective" and "objective" portions of the SOAP notes. The SOAP notes are the portion of the POR in which progress is recorded under the format of subjective data (S), objective data (O), assessment (A), and plan (P).

Another rather well-known strategy by which problem behaviors and treatment goals are specified is *goal-attainment scaling* (Kiresuk & Sherman, 1968). Individual goals for each client are selected, goals that will ameliorate his or her problems. For each goal, a scale is created, composed of a series of likely treatment outcomes varying from *least favorable* (–2), to *most likely* (0), to *most favorable* (+2). An objective event is tied to each scale point. In an example provided by Kiresuk and Sherman (1968), a goal was "dependency on mother." The least favorable outcome (–2) was "lives at home; does nothing without mother's approval." The most likely outcome (0) was "chooses own friends, activities, without checking with mother; returns to school. " The most favorable outcome (+2) was "establishes own way of life; chooses when to consult mother."

In summary, the second guideline in creating measures is to specify the client's problem and treatment objective in terms of specific behaviors. This specification can be accomplished with the help of particular interview questions, partial or instrumental goals, DSM-IV, the Problem-Oriented Record, and goal attainment scaling.

Choose Measures Consistent with One's Theoretical Orientation

Many of the examples provided in this chapter are focused on changing specific behaviors or symptoms, especially if behaviors are broadly defined to include behaviors across the triple response system first outlined by Lang in relation to anxiety (Lang, 1968). The three response systems are overt motoric behavior, cognitive-verbal behavior, and emotional-physiological behavior.

Psychodynamically oriented therapists may also be interested in the dynamic functions that the symptoms serve, along with the symptoms themselves. Barber and Crits-Christoph (1993) have reviewed a number of reliable and valid measures of psychodynamic formulations. There is no reason these measures could not be used in a repeated fashion (at least, pre- and posttreatment) by psychodynamically oriented therapists, within a scientist–practitioner framework. One example is the Core Conflictual Relationship Theme (CCRT) (e.g., Luborsky & Crits-Christoph, 1990), which abstracts interpersonal relationship patterns from narratives told during psychotherapy sessions. The CCRT describes the relationship pattern or conflict in terms of three components: (a) wishes, needs, or intentions expressed by the subject; (b) expected or actual responses from others; and (c) responses of self, which can include emotions, behaviors, symptoms, and so forth. Procedures to quantify these components are being developed in terms of rating each of these three components.

In summary, the third guideline is to choose measures consistent with one's theoretical orientation. Although all of the measures presented in this book may be useful, regardless of the theoretical orientation of the clinician, some clinicians may wish to supplement these universal measures with measures that are unique to a specific theoretical orientation.

Specify Several Target Behaviors

This fourth guideline, of measuring multiple problem behaviors per client, is implicit in the preceding discussion. Most cases are sufficiently complex that several intervention goals can readily be identified.

In some cases, these various intervention goals comprise a recognizable syndrome. To illustrate, a client may display several of the diagnostic or operational criteria outlined in DSM-IV as typical of a particular disorder. A depressed woman, for example, cries excessively, has difficulty sleeping through the night, has recurrent thoughts of suicide, has difficulty concentrating on a task, and has lost interest in usual pastimes. It would be useful to take quantified measures of each of these problems. Even though they are characteristic of the depressive syndrome, it is not certain that they covary or change at the same rate in any individual client.

In other cases, the combination of intervention goals is more idiosyncratic. For example, Humphreys and Beiman (1975) describe a case in which six problem areas were specified: uncertain vocational goals, inadequate social skills, unassertiveness, marital difficulties, fear of crowded places, and public speaking phobia. Quantified measures should be obtained for each of these problems.

When listing several therapeutic goals, it is not critical that they be comparable in importance. Using Nelsen's terminology (1981), at times, several therapeutic goals may be established that are all final or terminal goals. At other times, however, some of the multiple goals may be partial or instrumental goals, that help attain a final goal.

Upon occasion, it may be critical to measure some behaviors that will not be subjected to treatment. An example might be a pedophiliac who showed normal sexual arousal toward his wife. Pedophiliac arousal would, of course, be measured to demonstrate that treatment was effective in reducing deviant arousal. In this case, however, it would also be advisable to measure heterosexual arousal to determine that it was not adversely affected by the treatment. Although Brownell, Hayes, and Barlow (1977) demonstrated a functional independence among these types of arousal, it is nevertheless a useful precaution to measure both deviant and normal arousal during the course of treatment.

In summary, the fourth guideline is to specify several target behaviors. These may be the range of behaviors that are targeted for treatment, a combination of final and partial goal behaviors, or a combination of targeted behaviors and untreated but important ancillary behaviors.

Obtain Multiple Measures for Each Problem Behavior

In addition to measuring several different problem behaviors or treatment goals per client, it is also advisable to obtain several different measures for each problem or goal. One reason for multiple measurement is that there is no one "true" measure of the client's problem. This issue is also discussed in Chapter 12.

Let us suppose that a clinician was treating a person with deviant sexual arousal. The clinician obtains physiological measures of sexual arousal, a self-report measure of arousal, and a self-report measure of deviant sexual activity. The various measures may not agree (Barlow, 1977). Since there is no prior basis on which to decide which is the "best" or "true" measure, the various types of measures should continue to be collected. Similarly, a clinician treating a phobic client might measure avoidance or approach behavior, obtain a physiological measure of fear (e.g., heart rate or galvanic skin response), and obtain a self-report of fear. Again, the measures might not agree (Rachman & Hodgson, 1974). But, since there is no basis on which to select the one true or best measure, the various types of measures may all be relevant measures that together are useful in painting a broader picture of the client's status.

Moreover, even if synchrony (or agreement) were found among various measures for a particular client at a particular point in time, there is no guarantee that this synchrony would be maintained as treatment progressed. The relationship between simultaneous measures of heart rate and approach behavior was examined during treatment of nine phobic cases by Leitenberg, Agras, Butz, and Wincze (1971). In some cases, heart rate increased as phobic avoidance behavior decreased. In other cases, there was a parallel decline. In still others, there was a decline in phobic avoidance without any accompanying change in heart rate. And, finally, in several cases heart rate decreased only after phobic avoidance had declined. The point is that accurate conclusions about clients' progress necessitated the measurement of both heart rate and avoidance behavior. Similar asynchrony (lack of agreement) among behavioral measures, heart rate, and self-reports of anxiety was reported in three agoraphobic women, over the course of therapy, by Barlow, Mavissakalian, and Schofield (1980). Again, all three measures were needed to form a complete picture of client progress.

Inconsistency among different measures of the same problem is generally attributed to method variance—that is, variability due to the use of different methods of measurement to measure the same problem (Campbell & Fiske, 1959; Cone, 1979). In Hartshorne and May's classic research (1928) on children's moral behavior, for example, there was substantial inconsistency in children's honesty as measured in actual situations and on questionnaires. This inconsistency can be attributed to method variance.

Not only is method of measurement frequently varied, but so is the content of what is measured. Cone (1979) argued that the frequently reported asynchrony among motoric, physiological, and self-report measures is due to a confound between the method of measurement and the content being measured. In other words, self-report methods are used to measure cognitive content ("Tell me what you are thinking"), but direct observation methods are used to assess motor or physiological content. Cone (1979) proposed that if only method and not content were varied, more consistent relationships might be obtained across physiological, motor, and self-report responses. Typically, self-reports of fear would be compared with direct observation of a physiological response, like perspiring during a behavioral avoidance test, with resultant asynchrony. If Cone's suggestion were followed, self-reports of perspiring would be compared with direct observations of perspiring during a behavioral avoidance test. Indeed, as Cone would have predicted, when subjects are asked to report what they would do and then are asked to perform those tasks, the correlations between self-report and overt behavior are often very high (Bandura & Adams, 1977; McReynolds & Stegman, 1976).

Relationships are frequently inconsistent, however, not only across different response systems, but also in measures taken from the same response system. Different measures of change in obesity status produced by weight-loss treatment, for example, are imperfectly correlated (Rogers, Mahoney, Mahoney, Straw, & Kenigsberg, 1980). Also, inconsistent responding on different questionnaires purporting to measure depression or assertiveness would not be surprising.

In light of these data, consistency cannot be assumed among different measures of the same problem behavior or treatment goal, especially across different methods of measurement. Multiple measures, including different methods of measurement, are thus recommended to obtain converging evidence of the client's progress or lack thereof.

Select Measures That Are Both Sensitive and Meaningful

Measures can vary on a molecular–molar dimension as related to the presenting problem. Some measures may be very molecular, very precise, and very sensitive to weekly therapeutic change. These measures, however, may be weak in construct validity; that is, they may not provide a meaningful measure of the presenting problem. To illustrate, assume that the presenting problem is a deficiency in social skills ("I can't get along with anybody; nobody seems to like me"). Molecular, precise measures might be selected, such as smiles displayed or percentage of eye contact made during weekly role-playing sessions in the clinic. If the client is taught through behavioral rehearsal to smile more and to increase eye contact, these measures may show weekly improvements. It is unclear, however, in what way smiles and eye contact relate to global social skills. Over the course of therapy, these precise, molecular measures might change, while the presenting problems remain intact. Thus, it may not be sufficient to rely on molecular measures as the sole criterion of client improvement.

Conversely, if only molar measures are taken, they may have good construct validity; but they may be difficult to measure precisely and may be insensitive to weekly therapeutic progress. To continue with the social skills example, a molar measure might be to ask significant others in the client's environment to rate his or her social skills on a 1–7 rating scale. Such ratings may have good construct validity, but may be insensitive to small therapeutic changes.

In addition to good construct validity, another advantage of some molar measures is the normative data available for them. In other words, for some molar measures, there are published means and standard deviations of how particular samples of subjects scored on these molar measures. Such normative data are useful as a standard of comparison against which to measure a particular client's score. Before treatment, the comparison helps to gauge the severity of the client's complaint; after treatment, the comparison helps to gauge the degree of improvement, relative to a "normal" sample (Kazdin, 1977; Nelson & Bowles, 1975).

The ideal, then, may be to take both types of measures—molecular measures that can be measured with precision and that are sensitive to gradual therapeutic progress, and molar measures that relate to the presenting problems in a meaningful way. Since it is not likely that a single measure can fulfill both roles, it may be necessary to rely on multiple measures for each presenting problem.

In another example, a child may be referred because of academic achievement that is below grade level. A global achievement test like the Woodcock-Johnson-Revised (Woodcock & Johnson, 1989, 1990) may have good construct validity, but such tests may be insensitive to small, gradual therapeutic changes. As a solution, such tests might be given two to four times per year, or at the beginning and end of treatment; but other more sensitive and molecular measures might be more frequently administered. Examples of the latter might be daily homework assignments that are completed correctly or grades on weekly in-class quizzes.

Another example relates to the presenting problem of depression. Molar measures like the Depression Scale of the Minnesota Multiphasic Personality Inventory (MMPI) (Hathaway & McKinley, 1951) or the Beck Depression Inventory (Beck et al., 1961) may have good construct validity. In other words, if a client's scores on these measures improve dramatically, it is believable that the client is truly less depressed. These measures, however, may be less sensitive to gradual therapeutic improvement. A client's depression may be related to problems in several different response classes (Craighead, 1980); for example, an unfavorable ratio of pleasant and unpleasant events, a deficiency in social skills, or an excess of irrational cognitions (Lewinsohn & Arconad, 1981). More molecular measures may be selected that are sensitive to changes in these individual response classes, for example, role-play measures of social skills, or questionnaire responses on the Pleasant Events Schedule (MacPhillamy & Lewinsohn, 1975). The molecular measures may be administered weekly or biweekly, while the more molar measures may be administered monthly, bimonthly, or at pre- and posttreatment.

Thus, both molar and molecular measures have their advantages and disadvantages. Molar measures generally have good construct validity and frequently have normative data; molecular measures generally are more sensitive to gradual therapeutic improvement.

Collect Measures Early in the Course of Treatment

In most cases, a reasonable hypothesis about the nature of the problem behaviors can be constructed during the initial, or intake, interview. Thus, the collection of some measures can begin immediately. For example, a depressed client may cry and complain during the intake interview, report weight loss, inability to sleep, and inability to complete routine duties. As measures, the assessor may count the number of crying episodes and of complaints during a portion of the intake session (e.g., the last 30 minutes), and weigh the client before he or she leaves. The client may also be given a weekly activity schedule to complete for homework. The schedule lists the days of the week and the times of the day. The client is asked to record sleeping and waking times and duties completed during the forthcoming week.

If data collection has begun early enough, as in the above example, the assessment phase may be concluded with a substantial baseline in hand (Hayes, 1981). Baseline, of course, consists of a quantification of the problem behaviors prior to intervention. Early collection of measures precludes unnecessary delays prior to treatment implementation, delays that are sometimes cited as an objection against the collection of baseline data.

It is advisable to collect data initially on a rather large number of possible measures of the client's problems. As assessment and intervention proceed, irrelevant measures can be discarded and relevant measures retained. In order to do this in the context of actual practice, assessment procedures must be routine and ready. Some practitioners have clients come in early for computerized assessment; the actual instruments administered are specified in advance by the practitioner.

The bare minimum to determine if the client changed during the course of treatment is to measure the client's problems before and after treatment. Even if an improvement is noted by such pre–post measurement, the causal efficacy of the treatment has not been established, unless proper experimental controls have been employed, as discussed elsewhere in this book. Nonetheless, a pre–post objective measure of client change is, of course, superior to no measure, especially for accountability purposes.

Repeated measurement prior to, during, and following treatment is better than pre–post measurement for two reasons. First, repeated measurement provides feedback to the therapist about the effectiveness of the treatment strategy at an opportune time. If the treatment is effective, it should continue to be employed. If the treatment is not effective, however, the therapist has received feedback at a time when the treatment can be changed. The ineffective treatment can be replaced with one that is potentially more effective. If repeated measurement is continued, effectiveness can be empirically determined.

The second advantage of repeated measurement over pre–post measurement is in enhancing clinical science. If repeated measures are obtained, marked changes or variability in the data may be noted. The scientist–practitioner uses such variability to formulate hypotheses about the independent variables or factors that are controlling the dependent variables or the client's problems. As an example, let us say that a client keeps daily records of the duration and severity of his or her tension headaches. These headaches seem to be worse on some days more than others. The clinician can explore with the client the factors that make these particular days different from other days. Identification of those factors may provide suggestions for more effective treatment. In this example, let us say that headache severity and duration are related to increased job demands. Depending on the circumstances, the clinician may intervene by teaching the client better organizational skills, appropriate assertiveness toward the boss, or relaxation coupled with coping statements. If headache severity and duration now change, assuming that appropriate experimental controls have been utilized, then the causal link has been established with greater certainty between job demands and worsening of headaches, and between a particular treatment and improvements in headaches.

In summary, pre–post objective measures of client problem behaviors are helpful in determining whether or not a client changed during the course of treatment. Repeated measures, prior to, during, and after treatment are superior to pre–post measures for two reasons. First, timely feedback is provided to the therapist so that the treatment strategies may be altered or maintained. Second, variability in the data can be explored to help identify the factors or independent variables contributing to the client's problems or dependent variables. Whether measurement is pre–post only or if repeated during the course of treatment, it is advisable to begin baseline data collection early in the course of treatment.

Make Comparisons within a Specific Measure Only If the Data Are Collected under Similar Conditions

Repeated measures should be obtained under similar stimulus conditions if valid comparisons are to be made across the measurements. As an example, let us say that the therapist is counting the number of complaints that a depressed client makes in each therapy session. Obviously, the number of complaints could be influenced by the content of the therapy session, or by how much the therapist talks in relation to how much the client talks. In this example, the therapist may attempt to keep such factors constant by beginning each session with the same instruction: "Tell me about your week," and by counting client complaints made in the first 10 minutes. In other words, the therapist attempts to keep "irrelevant" factors constant, such as the content of the conversation or therapist talk time, so that the number of client complaints can be controlled by "relevant" factors, such as the actual events of the week or the client's reactions to those events.

As another example, a mother brings her adolescent daughter to the clinic, complaining that the daughter is overly dependent on the mother and shows no initiative of her own. One way that lack of initiative is operationalized is that the daughter will do household chores only if the mother instructs her to do so and will not initiate those chores herself. As a measure, the therapist and mother draw up a list of chores; the mother is to mark each chore daily if the daughter undertakes the chore at her own initiative. Obviously, these daily measures of chores undertaken can be compared only if the stimulus situation is relatively constant. In this example, if the family goes on vacation, if the daughter is ill, or if relatives come to visit for several days, the data may be altered by these factors. Thus, the daily data will not accurately reflect therapeutic progress or lack thereof. In this instance, the "atypical" days' data may either be discarded or be noted as atypical.

The main point is that the measures should be influenced by relevant independent variables, such as treatment or life events. The influence of irrelevant independent variables, such as alterations in the measurement conditions, should be minimized or at least noted, so that the influence of the relevant independent variables can be better detected.

The underlying principle here is that behavior tends to be situation-specific (Mischel, 1968). In other words, the immediate stimulus situation has some influence on the observed behavior. For example, in the classic Hartshorne and May research (1928) on children's moral behavior, children's honesty varied depending on the stimulus situation—for example, home, party games, classroom, athletic contests. The more dissimilar the situations, the lower was the correlation between measures of moral behavior taken in those situations.

The measures of interest to a scientist–practitioner are also subject to situation specificity. To be useful, these measures should reflect relevant situational changes due to treatment or to life events, rather than irrelevant situational changes such as alterations in the measurement circumstances. The latter has been conceptualized as measurement error, variance that should be minimized if accurate measurement is to be obtained.

Graph the Data

As a scientist–practitioner collects repeated measurements for a particular client, it becomes necessary to synthesize and to store the data. This is especially true when several different client problems are measured in several different ways. It is necessary to synthesize the data not only for practical storage reasons, but also for purposes of meaningfully interpreting the data.

A convenient way to store and interpret repeated measurement is by graphing the data, either by hand or by using a convenient computer program (Barlow & Hersen, 1984; Parsonson & Baer, 1978). Time from baseline through treatment and follow-up is indexed on the abscissa. Depending on the type of data being collected, the time on the abscissa may be in terms of weeks or days. For example, if observations of a particular behavior are made in the clinic at a weekly therapy session, the abscissa for such data would be in weekly temporal units. Conversely, if a client conscientiously recorded on a daily basis the duration of time spent in compulsive rituals, the abscissa for such data would be in daily temporal units.

The measure is indexed on the ordinate. The unit of measurement must be appropriate to the type of measure taken. For example, if a questionnaire is administered on a weekly basis in the clinic, the unit of measurement on the ordinate is possible scores on the questionnaire. For another example, if typical sex-role motor behavior is observed weekly in the clinic waiting room using an appropriate checklist (Barlow, Hayes, Nelson, Steele, Meeler, & Mills, 1979), then the unit of measurement on the ordinate is possible checklist scores.

If several types of measures are taken for the same problem behavior, as is recommended above, it is usually desirable to store the different measures of the same problem on the same graph. The same abscissa can be used for all types of measurement, although entries may be on a daily or a weekly basis for different measures. Different ordinates will probably be necessary, since the different types of measures will probably have different units of measurement. The purpose of storing the different measures of the same problem on the same graph is to determine how and if the different measures covary. In other words, do the measures respond in a similar or dissimilar fashion to the same intervention? Dissimilar responding, asynchronous responding, or lack of covariation implies that the different types of measures are functionally controlled by different independent variables, or respond to the same independent variables in a different manner.

Another item to enter on the data graphs is any significant event that might account for alterations in or variability in the measures. The beginning of a new treatment program is an example of a significant event that is expected to produce a change in the data. Other significant events may not be planned, but may nonetheless markedly alter the data. Examples might include a visit by a relative or an unpleasant change in job status.

Apparently, the clinical impact of graphing client data has itself never been examined. Thus, we do not yet know if clients are more likely to improve if clinicians consider their cases in this fashion. This is the kind of delivery system question that may eventually be asked by the research and development arm of an interested managed care system. Until such data are available, however, the scientific and evaluative benefits seem clear.

In summary, as the data accumulate for several different measures of several different problems, it is necessary to store the data, for practical reasons and for purposes of understanding the data. Graphs provide a convenient means of storage. On these graphs, time is quantified on the abscissa and the measures are quantified on the ordinate.

Record Inconvenient Measures Less Frequently Than More Convenient Measures

Although it is recommended that several different types of measures across different methods of measurement be taken of several different client problems, it is not necessary to obtain all these measures with the same frequency. Measures that are inconvenient to record may be taken on a less frequent basis than more convenient measures. It is better to take the inconvenient measures on an infrequent basis than not at all, because these measures may provide different or additional information about the client's problems. Recall that there is no one "true" measure of a specific problem, but rather that different measures across different methods provide converging evidence about different aspects of the problem.

To illustrate, self-ratings of sexual arousal and physiological measures of sexual arousal do not necessarily covary (Barlow, 1977). Since self-ratings are more convenient to obtain than physiological measures, self-ratings of sexual arousal to deviant and heterosexual stimuli could be taken at every treatment session, whereas physiological measures of arousal could be taken on a monthly basis.

As another example, self-monitored data and direct observation by a trained observer do not always agree (Lipinski & Nelson, 1974). In naturalistic settings, self-monitored data are more convenient to obtain, given a cooperative client, than are data taken by a trained observer. Hence, the client may be asked to self-monitor on a daily basis, whereas a trained observer may enter the naturalistic setting only occasionally. For example, in a case study reported by Katell, Callahan, Fremouw, and Zitter (1979), an overweight client completed a daily food diary in which she recorded the antecedents of eating and facts about her eating. On a *weekly* basis, the client was asked to eat a meal in a small on-campus dining area while being video-taped; her eating behaviors were subsequently coded from the videotapes. Also on a *weekly* basis, an observer entered the home and coded her eating behavior during a family supper. Presumably, self-monitoring was a more convenient measure and hence was undertaken on a daily basis. Since the direct observations of eating in both the analogue and naturalistic settings were probably more inconvenient, these measures were obtained on a weekly basis.

In a similar example, Eyberg and Johnson (1974) requested that parents keep daily data on their children's behavior problems. Home observation data by trained observers were collected for five days during baseline and for five days at the conclusion of treatment. Again, the more convenient measure was obtained on a more frequent basis.

Select "Good" and Accurate Measures

So far, a broad recommendation has been made that multiple methods of measurement should be employed for several problems for each client. There are, however, a great many available measures within each method of measurement. How is the scientist–practitioner to select among them? By what criteria are "good" and accurate measures to be selected?

One criterion is the measure's psychometric properties (i.e., its reliability and validity). The scientist–practitioner encounters two problems, however, when employing psychometric properties as central criteria in selecting measures. The first problem is that psychometric calculations are nomothetic, that is, they depend on data from groups of individuals. Psychometric data do not provide idiographic information about individuals. For example, even if the concurrent validity between role-playing in the clinic and observed behavior in the natural environment were determined to be high or low, such information would not indicate whether a particular client's role-playing and naturalistic behavior were similar. Psychometric data may provide some nomothetic "good guesses" for the scientist–practitioner about which measures to use or to avoid, but some idiographic validation would be needed to determine if these are reliable and valid measures for the individual client.

A second problem with psychometric criteria for the scientist–practitioner are the assumptions underlying psychometric procedures. Among these assumptions is that there is a true score for an individual on a particular test or assessment device that is somewhat difficult to detect because of measurement error.

Consistency of measurement is thought to be a desirable quality of tests or of assessment devices because consistent scores indicate that more of the true score is being assessed than error variance. Consistency of measurement is demonstrated by high correlation coefficients in investigations of reliability and validity.

A problem here is that inconsistency may be a characteristic of client behavior, rather than an indicator of an inferior assessment device. Clients within certain diagnostic categories (e.g., borderline personality disorder, for example, with accompanying impulsive behavior or unstable interpersonal relationships) are known for their erratic or rapidly changing behavior. Other client behavior may be inconsistent due to therapeutic change, different situational factors (Mischel, 1968), different response modes being measured (e.g., verbal, motor, physiological; Lang, 1968), or different methods of measurement (e.g., self-report, direct observation, physiological measures; Campbell & Fiske, 1959). Thus, inconsistent measurement may nonetheless be very accurate measurement. The measurement may be inconsistent—not due to a poor measuring device but rather due to actual changes in client behavior.

Part of the problem in translating psychometric criteria to clinical measures is that many clinical questions require an individual level of analysis, whereas psychometric questions typically utilize a group level of analysis. For example, consider the relationship between reports of sexual arousal and actual physiological arousal. To establish that relationship by the usual means, many individuals would be assessed once in both areas, and the two measures would be correlated. This correlation would show how these measures related across individuals at a single point in time. But as a practical matter, clinicians might be interested in this relationship between two assessment areas because they need to know if self-reported *changes* in sexual arousal indicate corresponding *changes* in physiological arousal. This is an entirely different question based on within-subject patterns that would require that many individuals be assessed in both areas many times. The two measures would then be correlated within individuals across time, and these many correlations would be combined into a nomothetic generalization.

The two questions (how do these measures relate across individuals at a single point in time versus how do they relate across time within individuals) are completely different, and the results for one kind of analysis do not necessarily predict the results for the other. For example, imagine that the sexual arousal of a group of one hundred males is assessed twenty times and that changes over time in self-reported sexual arousal closely track changes in physiological arousal, with the average within-subject correlation being .83. When these same data are examined across individuals at any give point in time, one person may call an 80% full erection "moderate arousal," while another may call it "high arousal." These differences in set points for self-report could greatly reduce the correlations observed, even though changes over time in one domain closely track changes in the other. A study quite similar to this hypothetical one has provided empirical support for this idea (Turner & Hayes, 1996). Correlations between domains of sexual arousal within subjects were significantly higher than between subjects, and the two kinds of correlations were even differently responsive to experimental manipulations such as the type of sexual stimuli viewed or the degree of public knowledge of the responses shown. Our point is that a great deal of thought should be given to the kind of assessment question actually of interest. If the question is one that emphasizes nomothetic generalizations about within-subject processes, current psychometric methods will not apply without modification.

The yardstick of concurrent or predictive validity presents another problem in selecting measures because there is no universally accepted criterion measure against which to evaluate other measures. Some assessors may believe that the criterion measure is motor behavior in the naturalistic setting. In other words, the "real" measure of behavior is what the client *does* in the natural setting, as measured by trained observers. Exceptions are apparent. To illustrate, according to DSM-IV, chief characteristics or operational criteria of depression are: "depressed mood most of the day, nearly every day . . . (and) markedly diminished interest or pleasure in all, or almost all, activities most of the day, nearly every day" (1994, p. 327). Given the subjectivity of these experiences, depression may be better assessed by self-report methods than by direct observations of client motor behavior.

What alternatives to psychometric criteria are available to the scientist–practitioner in selecting a "good" or accurate assessment device? One alternative is to use some psychometric procedures without their underlying assumptions (Cone, 1977; Jones, 1977). For example, consistency or reliability of measurement should be expected of a good assessment device under certain circumstances—when the behavior under examination is somehow "captured" or "frozen." To be more specific, let us say that two observers are coding the same videotape or the same live interaction. Since the observers are watching the same behaviors, any inconsistency in coding would be due to measurement error rather than to actual changes in behavior.

Another useful extrapolation from psychometric procedures is to use the multitrait-multimethod approach (Campbell & Fiske, 1959), as suggested by Cone (1977). For example, a group of subjects could be assessed by two questionnaires and by two observational coding systems. These comprise two different *methods* or measurements. One questionnaire and one observational coding system, in this example, are purported to measure depression, while the other questionnaire and the other observational coding system are purported to measure social skills. These comprise two different *traits* or sets of behaviors to be measured. It should be expected that if the questionnaires and the observational coding systems really measure depression and social skills, respectively, then the trait correlations should be higher than the method correlations. The point is that construct validity is a reasonable expectation for the measures that are to be employed—the measures should *measure something.* Construct validity can be established by the convergent and discriminant validity that can be assessed by the multitrait-multimethod matrix. Again, no one measure is the "true" measure. Several must be taken to provide converging evidence about the client's problems or progress.

In addition to limited use of psychometric procedures, the quality of measures can be assured by monitoring the circumstances in which the measures are employed. Previous research has discovered at least some of the controlling variables that contribute to the quality of data produced by different assessment devices. For example, the quality of self-monitored data is improved if the self-recorder is aware that his or her reliability can be determined (Lipinski & Nelson, 1974). Thus, if a practitioner chooses to use self-monitoring as a measure, it is wise to arrange occasional reliability checks for the self-recorder. As another example, it is known that performance on the behavioral avoidance test is influenced by the amount of "demand" in the approach instructions (Bernstein & Nietzel, 1973). Therefore, in order to compare a client's performance across different points in time, the amounts of demand in the approach instructions must remain constant. In other words, questions such as "Is self-monitoring a good assessment device?" or "Is the behavioral avoidance test a good assessment device?" have no generic answer. Instead, there are certain circumstances, established in part by past research, that make the data collected by the assessment device of higher or lower quality. The practitioner who employs the device should employ the optimal circumstances possible to ensure data of high quality.

Finally, one criterion that the scientist–practitioner can use in selecting an assessment device is its functional utility (Nelson & Hayes, 1979). Initially, the assessment device should help to determine the treatment that should be provided for the client. That is, a better treatment should be selected by utilizing the assessment information than by not utilizing it. Later, the assessment device should help to determine if the treatment is effective. That is, use of the assessment device should provide better feedback to the therapist about client progress or lack thereof than not using the assessment device.

In order to draw valid conclusions from the work of the scientist–practitioner, the work must have internal and external validity. Internal validity allows the reasonable conclusion that the treatment (independent variable) produced the results seen in the measure of change (dependent variable). Alternative hypotheses about the causes of treatment outcome must be ruled out.

In addition to selecting a "good" measure, there are traditional flaws in research design that should be avoided when implementing the chosen measurement (e.g., Kazdin, 1992). There are many threats to internal validity. These threats are events other than the independent variable (treatment as specified) that occur within or outside of therapy that may account for the results (Kazdin, 1992). One of the threats to internal validity is changes in the measuring instrument or measurement procedure over time. An example might be a practitioner's rating of the severity of a client's depression. On the first visit, the therapist rates the client's depression as severe. Several visits later, while the client's depressed symptomatology may, in fact, not have changed, the demand characteristics may be such that the therapist rates the client's depression as moderate. To do otherwise may endanger the therapist's self-esteem, continued access to third-party payments, and so on. This change in the way the therapist is making the rating is a threat to internal validity. It endangers the validity of conclusions that the scientist–practitioner may draw between the therapy (the independent variable) and the depression (the dependent variable). Research has shown that rating scales are more susceptible to bias than are observational measures of more molecular behaviors (e.g., Shuller &

McNamara, 1970). Using both types of measures reduces threats to internal validity produced by the exclusive use of rating scales.

Another example of a traditional flaw in research design related to measurement is reactivity—that is, changes in behavior produced by measurement itself. Another chapter in this book describes reactivity related to self-monitoring and to external observation, methods to reduce this reactivity, and therapeutic uses of such reactivity. The problem with behavior changes due to reactivity is that they are generally short-lived. To elaborate, since some reactivity is due to social desirability, when the social contingencies of therapy or of an experiment are removed, then the reactivity may cease. Moreover, incorrect conclusions that an independent variable is effective may be drawn from changes in measurement that are due mostly to reactivity.

A third example of a traditional flaw in research design related to measurement is the sensitization or practice effects due to repeated measurement. Repeated measurement is certainly espoused here as integral to the scientist–practitioner model. Care must be taken, however, in attributing change to treatment as the independent variable, instead of changes due mostly to practice or familiarity effects, or demand characteristics associated with repeated measurement. For example, if the same measure is given repeatedly, the client might respond in a more positive way over time because of demand characteristics to show the therapist that he or she is improving. In a practical example to reduce the threat to internal validity produced by repeated measurement, the Depression Adjective Check List might be a good repeated measure of dysphoric or depressed mood because it has several parallel forms and is intended for repeated measurement (Lubin, 1967).

In summary, it is desirable for scientist–practitioners to use "good" or accurate measures. Psychometric criteria cannot be used alone to make this determination because of the nomothetic nature of psychometric data and because of the psychometric assumption that inconsistent measurement implies poor assessment. As alternatives, the scientist–practitioner can employ as criteria in selecting good measures: psychometric procedures under limited circumstances, particularly reliability and multitrait-multimethod matrices; modification of controlling variables so as to optimize the quality of data produced by a particular assessment device; and evaluation of the functional utility of the assessment device and the data that it produces.

Scientist–practitioners must also guard against threats to internal validity, such as biased, reactive, or practiced measurement, which limit conclusions about the effectiveness of treatment.

Obtain Clients' Informed Consent When Necessary

With most methods of measurement, client awareness of and cooperation with the measurement procedure is essential. As examples, a client is provided with questionnaire instructions and is asked to complete the questionnaire; or a client is provided with role-playing instructions and is asked to participate in role-playing.

Many such obtrusive methods of measurement are, however, reactive. *Reactivity* refers to changes in the client's behavior that are due to the measurement process per se. The problem with reactivity is that it interferes with external validity; that is, it is difficult to generalize from measurement to nonmeasurement circumstances. In other words, the client's behavior while he or she is being assessed may not be the same as when he or she is not being assessed. Reactivity produced by self-recording and by observation is discussed in another chapter in this volume.

One proposed solution to the problem of reactivity is the use of unobtrusive measures (Kazdin, 1979). For example, let us say that a transsexual is coming to a clinic to help make a male-to-female adjustment. In one aspect of treatment, the therapist is teaching the client more feminine motor movements. The therapist asks the receptionist to code the client's motor behavior unobtrusively, while the client is in the waiting room, using a sex-role motor behavior checklist (Barlow et al., 1979). In a second example, the husband of a depressed woman is asked to record unobtrusively her crying episodes and her complaints in their home.

While these unobtrusive measurement methods may reduce the problem of reactivity, they introduce ethical concerns about the client's informed consent (Kazdin, 1979). One solution might be to explain to the client beforehand the need for unobtrusive assessment and to ask the client's permission to obtain some unobtrusive, unspecified measures. In the above examples, release of information to the clinic staff might be assumed, but a release to the husband would have to be procured.

Institutions Can Encourage the Collection of Measures

As noted earlier in this chapter, many clinicians complain of the impracticality of collecting quantitative measures. There are some steps that institutions can take to facilitate or encourage this undertaking.

First, appropriate models of science-based practice can be taught in university and internship training programs (Conte & Levy, 1979). Of course, many training programs claim to espouse the scientist–practitioner model; but a true integration of research and practice, in the manner described in this book, may be too seldom taught.

Second, the national movement toward accountability by third-party payers may require clinicians to collect quantified measures, as noted earlier in this chapter and in Chapter 2. While such requirements would be looked upon with alarm by some clinicians, the requirements would certainly increase the use of such measures.

Third, clinic administrators can arrange the clinic setting to encourage the collection of measures. One way to do this is to provide necessary assessment materials, such as a file of questionnaires, self-monitoring devices, video equipment to tape role-played interactions, computerized assessment stations, or physiological recording equipment. Another way to do this is to require that case staffings be data-based and to reward practitioners who comply. Another way is to provide in-service training workshops on the collection of measures for scientist–practitioners.

Especially as assessment becomes necessary for monitoring and modifying the functioning of health care delivery systems, appropriate assessment is being built into the work role of behavioral health providers. Commercial assessment systems that include methods for establishing successful staff use are already quite popular in managed care organizations. As practice guidelines become more dominant, careful and repeated assessment of client problems, progress, and satisfaction will be the routine expectation of both providers and system administrators.

Summary and Conclusions

Quality assessment is a hallmark of the population-based approach of the modern health care delivery system. The present chapter identifies three primary goals of assessment: (a) select target behaviors and make a diagnosis; (b) choose a treatment strategy; and (c) evaluate the effectiveness of the chosen treatment or of the treatment delivery system. Treatment can be selected using one or more of several strategies: diagnosis, response class or keystone strategy, functional analysis, or case formulation. Evaluation of outcome is important to improve treatment, provide accountability, enhance clinical science, and improve the behavioral health care delivery system. Suggestions are also given regarding measurement of treatment integrity, including therapist adherence and competence. The chapter also suggests several guidelines for use in collecting measures: (a) consider idiographic versus nomothetic measures; (b) state client's problems in specific terms; (c) choose measures consistent with one's theoretical orientation; (d) specify several target behaviors; (e) obtain multiple measures for each problem behavior; (f) select measures that are both sensitive and meaningful; (g) collect measures early and repeatedly in the course of treatment; (h) make comparisons within a specific measure only if the data are collected under similar conditions; (i) graph the data; (j) record inconvenient measures less frequently than more convenient measures; (k) select "good" and accurate measures; (l) obtain clients' informed consent when necessary; and (m) use institutional means to encourage the collection of measures.

Remaining chapters present descriptions of specific measurement strategies for practitioners. Each of these strategies incorporates the guidelines described above. The next chapter discusses collection of measures by using interviewing, questionnaires, and other self-report methods. The final chapter discusses collection of molecular measures of behavior by direct observation and self-monitoring.

12 Self-Report and Physiological Measures

WILLIAM J. KOROTITSCH and

ROSEMERY O. NELSON-GRAY

Self-Report Measures

The first part of this chapter focuses on measurements obtained through client self-report. A somewhat arbitrary distinction is drawn here between self-report and self-monitoring, the latter being discussed in another chapter. In self-monitoring, the client observes his or her own behavior and records the behavior at the time of its occurrence. In self-report, the client also observes his or her own behavior, but reports these observations in a more retrospective and global fashion. For example in a self-report questionnaire, a client may be asked to reflect on his or her own behavior and to record how he or she may generally feel, using global, summative responses such as ratings of true or false.

Self-report may pertain to any of the three behavioral content systems (Cone, 1978). To elaborate, a person can provide reports of motoric activity/motor content (such as "I left my house only once last week"), physiological activity (such as "My heart races when I am driving"), and cognitive content (such as "I think I am worthless"). Typical self-report methods include: (a) interviews and rating scales; and (b) questionnaires and cognitive assessment methods. Each of these methods is discussed in the following sections.

Self-report is often thought of as a relatively indirect measure of behavior (Cone, 1978) because it usually provides a more filtered account of clinically relevant activities than would more direct measures such as direct observation. Particularly in managed care settings, however, client reports of progress and satisfaction are critically important even if they are indirect. Client perception of progress and satisfaction can make the difference between the success and failure of a health care delivery system.

The Clinical Interview

The clinical interview is the most widely used method of assessment, both in clinical research settings and among private practitioners. For example, in a recent survey of 412 clinicians in private practice, 95% reported the use of interviews to collect assessment information (Watkins, Campbell, Nieberding, & Hallmark,

1995). There are several advantages to the use of interviews over more "objective" forms of assessment, the most salient of which is their flexibility. Interviewers can adjust their methods to the specific needs of the client. Questions can be rephrased if the client does not understand, and inquiry can be focused to obtain more detailed information relevant to particular hypotheses regarding the client.

There is little consensus regarding methods for conducting assessment interviews (Johnson, 1981), with one exception being the basic goals of the initial interview. Broadly stated, the goals of an initial assessment interview are: (a) the establishment of a working alliance and therapeutic relationship with the client and (b) collection of information relevant to conceptualization of the client's current difficulties and to the formulation of effective interventions (Reiser, 1984). Information that is acquired during the interview can be broadly divided into retrospective self-reports and behavioral observations.

Retrospective Self-Report   Information obtained in interviews largely consists of retrospective accounts of the client's experience and behavior. The widespread use of interviews in clinical assessment provides incontrovertible evidence of their importance and utility. However, the use of retrospective reports as a method of data collection has historically been a topic of debate and criticism (e.g., Rogler, Malgady, & Tryon 1992). Concerns regarding this method are often based on substantial research revealing inaccuracy in retrospective accounts (e.g., Bradburn, Rips, & Shevell, 1987) and misleading effects that can occur in the course of questioning (Loftus, 1993). Demonstrations of memory errors, and the sometimes profound effects of contextual variables on verbal reports, have been difficult to reconcile with frequent demonstrations of impressive accuracy of recalled information (Alba & Hasher, 1983). Not surprisingly, similar mixed findings are found in literature concerning the accuracy of retrospective accounts of clinically relevant information (see Brewin, Andrews, & Gotlib, 1993, for a review). Obviously, verbal reports are generated often in the context of therapy, and a preoccupation with the objective accuracy of these reports may be unnecessary and even counterproductive. Accuracy becomes more important when verbal reports are utilized as a method of data collection and valid, reliable measurement is desired.

Problems faced when attempting to establish the validity of retrospection within clinical assessment are compounded by the difficulty of obtaining objective data for comparison with a given account. Within clinical assessment, many of the accounts of interest concern experiences for which no objective criterion is possible (e.g., "Have [you] ever been bothered by thoughts that didn't make any sense?"; Spitzer, Williams, Gibbon, & First, 1990). A number of studies have evaluated the consistency of retrospective reports through comparison with assessment data collected over the course of longitudinal research or data generated more recently through self-monitoring methods. Although the "accuracy" of these criteria is often indeterminate, these studies do address the stability of self-report and the correspondence between retrospective reports and those obtained more temporally proximate to the reported experiences.

An example of this temporal consistency approach to evaluating retrospective reports is provided by Henry, Moffit, Caspi, Langley, and Silva (1994). These authors compared the agreement between information obtained in interviews with young adults and information from multiple measures collected at two-year intervals as part of a longitudinal study conducted since their births. Subjects were asked to recall physical attributes such as height and weight, life events such as residence changes, and major injuries, as well as a number of more global variables often considered of use to clinicians, such as attachment to parents, family conflict, maternal depression, internalizing symptoms, hyperactivity, and delinquent behavior. The correspondence of retrospective accounts obtained in early adulthood to assessment data obtained during the subjects' later childhood and during adolescence was generally poor. Specifically, retrospective reports of global psychosocial variables showed poor relative agreement with earlier assessment. Also, reports of early behavior problems such as anxiety, depression, and hyperactivity demonstrated little correspondence with earlier measures. Agreement for reports of delinquent behaviors was moderately good, with better agreement for reports of arrests and court appearances. The results of this and other studies underscore the need for caution when interpreting long-term retrospective accounts, particularly of global and summative psychosocial variables.

Parkinson, Briner, Reynolds, and Totterdell (1995) compared retrospective reports of mood with ratings obtained through self-monitoring. This study examined the effects of mood at the time of retrospective ratings as well as the potential influence of peak or extreme mood states (attributable to their salience and memorial availability) on global ratings. Subjects self-monitored mood over a two-week period by making momentary mood ratings at the beginning and end of each day and at two-hour intervals throughout the day. Weekly ratings were also obtained for the two-week period. Ratings were made using a pocket computer that provided no record for subjects to reference when making more summative daily and weekly ratings. Daily retrospective mood ratings showed greater correspondence to the average of momentary ratings made at two-hour intervals than to the peak mood rating made over the course of the day. Similarly, weekly ratings demonstrated better correspondence to average daily ratings than to peak daily ratings. However, peak levels of mood at the time of momentary recordings did account for a smaller but significant portion of the variance in daily ratings. Additionally, a general tendency of subjects to systematically overestimate positive affect in daily and weekly ratings was noted. The authors describe some methodological weaknesses of previous studies and conclude that daily and weekly mood ratings provide reasonably accurate information regarding the overall affect experienced across these time periods.

A number of researchers have focused on strategies for improving the accuracy and reliability of retrospective reports. This work has taken place primarily within the domains of survey research (see Tanur, 1992), and courtroom testimony (e.g., Geiselman, & Fisher, 1989). While little research has been focused on improving the accuracy of reports for more clinically relevant phenomena, some empirically validated "recall enhancement" strategies might be evaluated in this context.

One example that integrates several strategies is the cognitive interview method (Geiselman et al., 1984). The cognitive interview provides a framework for inquiry that is based on multiple strategies derived from memory research and applied toward enhancing the accuracy of retrospective reports. For example, the concept of "context reinstatement" suggests that an event will be better remembered to the extent that the individual is in the same psychological environment as when the event occurred (Tulving & Thomson, 1973). In order to reinstate the psychological environment within the cognitive interview, the respondent is encouraged to think about the environmental context of the original event as well as his or her feelings at the time. The cognitive interview method has been demonstrated to improve the accuracy of retrospective reports of a variety of recently experienced and objectively observed events without increasing intrusions of incorrect information (e.g., Ascherman, Mantwill, & Kohnken, 1991; Fisher & Quigley, 1992). The paradigms used to evaluate the interview essentially expose subjects to a particular verifiable experience either live or videotaped. After a period of time has elapsed, subjects are randomly assigned to a standard interview or cognitive interview regarding the event. Although this method has not yet been applied and evaluated within the area of clinical interviewing, these comparative procedures could be used to evaluate variables that influence retrospective reports of events such as role-plays, social interactions within the clinic setting, and events for which observational data are available. Additional research regarding the influence of interview procedures on the accuracy of verbal reports may show promise in enhancing the validity of clients' retrospective reports. However, the applicability of accuracy-enhancement procedures from other research domains to clinical assessment awaits such validation. A number of "recall-enhancement" strategies historically used in clinical settings (e.g., hypnosis) have little or no current empirical support for their use (see Miller & Fremouw, 1995, for a review).

Clinician Observations during Interviews   The interpersonal nature of the interview provides the clinician with the opportunity to observe the behavior of the client. Many authors have emphasized the importance of assessing the client's behavior and the clinician's reactions during the interview (e.g. Linehan, 1977, Mahl, 1968). One widely used methodological framework for collecting observational data within the interview is the mental status exam. Rather than a standardized method of assessment, the mental status exam is a heuristic framework for guiding the observations of the clinician. As pointed out by Nelson and Barlow (1981): "The essentials of the mental-status exam are ongoing in almost any interpersonal encounter, as when one observes 'He looks really down today,' or 'His clothes are out of date,' or 'He talks very fast.'" Mental status examination typically involves observations of five major classes of the client's behavior (Nelson & Barlow, 1981): (a) appearance and overt motoric behavior, (b) thought processes (inferred from the client's speech), (c) mood during the session and affect (referring to the range of emotional responses as well as their concordance with the content of the client's report), (d) intellectual functioning, and (e) sensorium (orientation to person, place, situation). Thorough discussions of each of these classes are provided by Nelson and Barlow (1981), Crary and Johnson (1975), and Morrison (1993).

As a measure of treatment change, results of mental status exams have been most frequently used in inpatient psychiatric settings as a global measure of change (e.g., Zubenko et al., 1994). Alternatively some studies have attempted to measure specific change, particularly in overt motoric behavior of the kind observed during mental status examination. For example, Fisch, Frey, and Hirsbrunner (1983) assessed movement patterns of 13 depressed patients during the first three minutes of clinical interviews at the beginning of hospitalization and prior to discharge. Movements of the head, trunk, shoulders, upper arms, hands, upper legs, and feet were coded according to the three parameters of mobility, complexity, and dynamic activation. Upon recovery, patients spent more time in motion, displayed more complex movements, and initiated movement more rapidly than during assessment while they were depressed. Other frameworks for coding observations of a range of nonverbal behavior are described by Davis and Hadiks (1990), Fisch, Frey, and Hirsbrunner (1983), and Schelde and Hertz (1994). A method for quantifying videotaped observations of eye contact is described by Hinchliffe, Lancashire, and Roberts (1971). While these assessment approaches could be applied in any setting where videotaped interactions with clients are available, they provide examples of methods that could enhance objectivity in quantifying some components of mental status examination.

Interview Methods

Despite the commonalities in the goals of assessment interviews and in the range of information that can be obtained, suggested methods for conducting assessment interviews can vary considerably. A common approach to the classification of interviews is according to the degree of structure imposed by the interviewer. Some authors suggest free-form, open-ended interviews in which content is largely guided by the client and direct questioning is minimized. Others have characterized the initial interview and assessment as an investigatory process in which the clinician progressively focuses inquiry from general areas toward detailed examination of the client's difficulties (e.g., Hawkins, 1979; Linehan, 1977; Morrison, 1993). Guidelines for areas to assess are often recommended for the interviewer. Finally, the greatest degree of structure is provided by standardized structured interviews, which provide a format for the course of the interview, specific areas to be assessed, specific questions to be asked, and scales for quantification of responses. Semistructured interviews share these features while allowing the interviewer to probe for additional information where appropriate. For this reason, semistructured interviews are more commonly used in clinical and research settings. Unstructured and semistructured forms of the clinical interview are discussed in more detail in the following sections.

Unstructured Interviews   The greatest flexibility for the interviewer is afforded by the unstructured interview. The goal of unstructured interviews is often problem identification and/or target behavior selection. The degree of structure that the interviewer provides is often associated with theoretical orientation. For example, a number of psychodynamic guidelines for the interview advise against the use of specific questions to elicit information and emphasize a nondirective approach (e.g., Auld & Hyman, 1991; Leon, 1982). Behavioral approaches to the assessment interview tend to be more structured and provide guidelines to interviewers for the pursuit of relevant information. Goals of the behavioral interview include the identification of target behaviors and their controlling variables. While the idiographic nature of such assessment may preclude the use of standardized formats and questions, a number of general formats for collecting information in behavioral interviews have been suggested. While the form of these guidelines may differ, the emphasis on identification of controlling variables for problem behaviors is consistent. For example, Kanfer and Saslow (1969) propose that information be obtained in seven areas: (1) an initial analysis of the problem situation; (2) clarification of the problem situation, including delineation of the antecedents and consequences of problem behaviors; (3) a motivational analysis; (4) a developmental analysis; (5) an analysis of self-control; (6) an analysis of social relationships; and (7) an analysis of the social-cultural-physical environment. This format has been criticized for being overly comprehensive for typical assessment purposes (Stuart, 1970), but remains highly influential in behavioral assessment.

Goldfried and Davison (1976) provide a format for the initial interview that includes a physical description of the patient; observations of the patient's behavior; and collecting information regarding the presenting problem (including current situational determinants, consequences, historical information, and organismic variables), other problems, personal assets, targets for modification, recommended treatment, motivation for treatment, prognosis, and expectancies.

At the present time, there are no data showing whether highly targeted interviews are more or less effective in fostering clinical outcomes than more wide-ranging interviews. Managed care settings, however, often require that practitioners move through initial assessment phases quickly, and thus the initial clinical interview may need to be more highly focused on the presenting problem and its context.

Reliability of Unstructured Interviews   As mentioned previously, unstructured interviews afford the clinician with a high degree of flexibility. As a consequence, considerable variability is likely to be present across interviews, which results in generally poor potential for reproducibility of results. Reliabilities for unstructured diagnostic interviews have historically been poor, while improvements in reliability have generally been associated with the use of standard diagnostic criteria as well as structured and semistructured interviews (see Matarazzo, 1983, for a review). This matter is crucial in the design of health care delivery systems, since high variability in case analysis necessarily means both variability in quality and difficulties in designing effective delivery systems of known cost and impact. Thus the interviews that are playing a role in empirically validated systems of assessment and intervention are generally quite structured.

Semistructured Interviews Interviews commonly categorized as structured or semistructured are those with standardized formats. Helzer (1983) described standardized interviews as those with specific formats dictating: (a) the symptoms or information to be obtained; (b) the manner in which information is elicited; (c) the order of questions; (d) the wording of, or definitions for, symptom questions; and (e) guidelines or verbatim wording for probing of responses in order to obtain codable responses. Standardized forms of interviews emerged, along with standardized diagnostic criteria, in response to poor diagnostic agreement that plagued early clinical research. The goal of semistructured interviews is to arrive at a reliable and valid diagnostic classification of clients' difficulties. Studies examining diagnostic agreement associated with the use of semistructured interviews suggest they are highly useful for obtaining reliable diagnoses (see Matarazzo, 1983). Standardized semistructured interviews have become invaluable assessment tools in research settings in which reliable diagnostic classification is important for purposes of generalization across persons with a particular diagnosis and communication of findings to other professionals.

Structured and semistructured interviews are almost invariably designed for diagnostic purposes. In principle, semistructured interviews could also be used to determine functional dimensions of client behavior. This is a more difficult empirical task than syndromal diagnosis because the criteria used to validate the interview methods would not be topographical but functional. When functional distinctions are well developed (for example, Carr and Durand's 1985 distinction between attention-seeking and task-relief disruptive behavior), there is no reason that semistructured interviews might not be developed that would aid in making such distinctions.

Currently, standardized interviews are available assessing nearly every diagnostic category of the DSM. One primary variable that distinguishes among semistructured interviews is the scope of their content. Some interviews survey large numbers of diagnostic categories, while others limit themselves to more particular diagnostic categories.

One broad-based semistructured interview is the Schedule for Affective Disorders (SADS; Endicott & Spitzer, 1978) The SADS covers more than twenty diagnostic categories based on the Research Diagnostic Criteria (RDC) published by Spitzer, Endicott, and Robins (1978). The RDC represents a modification and elaboration of the Feighner Criteria (Feighner et al., 1972). In addition to the regular version of the SADS, a lifetime version (SADS-L) and a version for measuring change (SADS-C) were also developed. The interview contains standard questions as well as suggested rephrasings. Each symptom is rated on a Likert-type scale with explicit anchors provided for each rating.

A semistructured interview developed to correspond to DSM-IV criteria is the Structured Clinical Interview for DSM-IV Axis I Disorders (SCID-I; First, Gibbon, Spitzer, & Williams, 1996). The SCID-I assesses the major categories of Axis I disorders. The interviewer proceeds through decision trees for diagnosis approximating those outlined in the DSM-IV. If specific criteria are not met within a particular diagnostic category, the interviewer is instructed to skip to other areas.

Each diagnostic criterion is rated on a 1–3 scale, where a rating of one indicates that the criterion symptom is absent, two indicates a subthreshold presence of the criterion, and three indicates that the threshold for the criterion is met. A similar interview, the Structured Interview for DSM-IV Personality Disorders, which assesses Axis-II disorders (SCID-II), is also widely used (First, Spitzer, Gibbon, & Williams, 1996).

Another interview that assesses a range of Axis I disorders is the Anxiety Disorders Interview Schedule (ADIS-IV; DiNardo, Brown, & Barlow, 1994). The ADIS-IV is a semistructured interview designed to assess for anxiety disorders utilizing DSM-IV criteria. The interview also contains sections assessing mood and somatoform disorders as well as substance abuse. Each diagnostic section contains initial inquiry questions and instructions to continue within the section or move to other sections based on the client's responses.

One example of a more specific semistructured interview is the Revised Diagnostic Interview for Borderlines (DIB-R; Zanarini, Gunderson, Frankenburg, & Chauncey, 1989) which contains 186 questions. Answers to the questions are utilized in rating 22 summary statements describing features of borderline personality disorder. The revised version was developed in order to maximize discrimination between borderline personality disorder and other personality disorders.

Rating Scales   In addition to semistructured diagnostic interviews, a large number of rating scales have been developed to quantify clinicians' impressions of the severity of a client's symptoms assessed during the interview. One example is the Brief Psychiatric Rating Scales (BPRS; Overall & Gorham, 1962). Following a brief interview, the clinician is asked to make judgments of the severity of 18 symptom areas on a 7-point scale. Examples of symptom areas include: anxiety, somatic concern, emotional withdrawal, depressive mood, and hostility. Scores across areas are summed to yield four factor scores: thought disturbance, withdrawal-retardation, hostility-suspiciousness, and anxiety-depression. A total "pathology" score is also obtained.

Another well-known rating scale for clinicians is the Global Assessment of Functioning Scale for Axis V included in the DSM-III-R and DSM-IV (GAF; American Psychiatric Association, 1994, p. 32). The GAF is a modified version of the Global Assessment Scale (GAS; Endicott, Spitzer, Fleiss, & Cohen, 1976). Clinicians rate the overall social and occupational functioning of the client on a 100-point scale. Scale anchors are provided for each 10-point interval, with higher ratings reflecting better general functioning.

Issues to Consider in the Use of Interviews

As described above, interviews can vary widely in their format and the degree of structure inherent in their administration. Despite these differences there are a number of common issues that should be considered in their use. These issues can be divided into sources of variance associated with the interviewer and the respondent.

Issues Associated with the Interviewer The interviewer is both the primary source of questions, as well as the person who collects and evaluates client responses. The pronounced effects of interviewer-related variables are to some extent reflected in the wide variability in interviewer diagnostic agreement described for interviews above. The often poor reliability associated with different interviewers is not limited to the product of diagnostic categorization, but can also be found with regard to selection of specific target behaviors. For example, Hay, Hay, Angle, and Nelson (1979) compared the conclusions of four graduate student interviewers regarding the number and types of problem areas identified in behavioral interviews that each conducted with the same four clients. Interviews were audiotaped and transcribed. Following each interview, therapists dictated summaries of interview findings that were evaluated for agreement. While the overall number of problem areas identified for each client was similar across interviewers, agreement for particular problem areas or responses within those areas was much lower. This attenuated reliability was not attributable to client responses, which were highly consistent across interviews, but appeared to be associated both with differences in questions asked across interviews and with the omission of information in dictated summaries of interview results.

As mentioned earlier, contextual factors can play a prominent role in determining retrospective responses. The interviewer's selection and phrasing of questions can influence the content and accuracy of information obtained, depending on the wording and order of questions, the form of response requested, and other factors (Clark & Schober, 1992). Accuracy of retrospective accounts can also be influenced by the number of times a question is posed (Loftus, Klinger, Smith, & Fielder, 1990), as well as the time provided for the response (Reiser, Black, & Abelson 1985). In general, more accurate reporting of details is associated with repeated retrieval attempts, as well as greater time devoted to an attempt. Reduction in these sources of variance is one major advantage of semistructured interviews.

The form of interviewer questions as well as interviewer responses can additionally influence the overall amount of information provided by the client. For example, open-ended questions produce greater numbers of problem-related statements (Nelson-Gray, Haas, Romano, Herbert, & Herbert, 1989), and nonverbal responses such as head nods can increase the duration of utterances made by interviewees (Matarazzo, Saslow, Wiens, Weitman, & Allen, 1964).

In the absence of standardized formats, the course of the interview is often guided by the clinician's impressions and hypotheses regarding the client's potential difficulties. Hypothesis testing is widely considered to be the critical activity of clinicians during assessment interviews. Hypotheses serve to narrow the focus of the interview away from irrelevant areas to more central aspects of the client's difficulties. One consideration in this process is confirmatory bias. Confirmatory bias refers to the tendency to explore hypotheses by collecting verifying rather than potentially falsifying evidence, and has been repeatedly demonstrated across a wide range of contexts (Snyder & Swann, 1978). Within the interview, confirmatory biases can promote the acceptance of initial hypotheses and concomitant failure to examine alternatives. Initial hypotheses regarding clients can be formed quickly (Asch, 1946; Meehl, 1960) and often demonstrate resistance to contradictory information (Rubin & Shontz, 1960; Turk & Salovey, 1985). The result may be an incomplete formulation of the client's difficulties. A classic example of this error is provided by Lazarus (1971). A client presented with a phobic reaction when crossing bridges. Further examination revealed that the client experienced considerable anxiety regarding a new work situation, on the other side of the bridge, that related to areas of competence and achievement. Targeting the client's "phobia of bridges" in this case would have been inappropriate.

A number of other systematic errors in human reasoning have been discussed in relation to clinical judgment. More comprehensive reviews of this research and suggestions to reduce potential bias in clinical judgment are provided by Turk and Salovey (1986, 1988) and by Schwartz (1991). Semistructured interviews are intended to reduce the variance associated with clinical judgments and may decrease the likelihood of these errors, particularly with regard to reaching diagnostic conclusions (Robins, 1989).

Issues Associated with the Respondent   A number of variables associated with the client can also effect data obtained in the interview. Variables such as the client's age may influence the accuracy of retrospective reports (Weinert & Schneider, 1995). For example, the quantity of information provided in free recall has been found to increase with age (e.g., Goodman & Reed, 1986). Other variables such as educational level can raise concerns regarding understanding of the questions provided. Race and cultural factors may also influence diagnostic judgments (e.g., Martin, 1993; Solomon, 1992). Standardization with different demographic groups can help to attenuate some of these influences in semistructured interviews.

Clients may also deliberately distort responses, respond to demand characteristics (Orne, 1969), attempt to create a favorable image of themselves (Sherman, Trief, & Sprafkin, 1975), or withhold sensitive information until the therapeutic relationship is more fully established (Gilbert, 1988). Additionally, clients' retrospective reports may be influenced by their own impressions both of the nature and of the stability of their behavior (Ross, 1989). These issues are not exclusive to interviews and may also be problematic in other forms of assessment. They are elaborated later in this chapter.

Another concern that is relatively specific to clinical assessment involves the potential interaction of mood at the time of recall, and the content of recollections. Exaggerated recall of negatively toned information is a common finding in depressed groups, while the opposite bias (greater recall of positively toned information) is often demonstrated in nondepressed comparison groups (Matt, Vasquez, & Campbell, 1992). These effects have commonly been observed in recall of word lists, or feedback on task performance. A number of studies have observed depressive biases in autobiographical memories, although findings are mixed. For example, Lewinsohn and Rosenbaum (1987) sampled memories of parental involvement over a one-year interval in a community sample. Depressed persons more often reported that their parents had been more rejecting or unloving than did nondepressed persons. When assessed one year later, the reports of previously depressed persons changed in a more positive direction. Similar negative reports of parenting were observed in individuals who were not depressed at the first assessment but later became depressed. In contrast, Robins et al. (1985) found no differences in recall of childhood experiences in depressed persons as compared to nondepressed siblings. Abrahams and Whitlock (1969) found no differences in retrospective reports of home life in depressed persons when compared to their reports after their depressive episodes remitted. Brewin, Andrews, and Gotlib (1993) review the above findings and other research related to mood-congruent biases in recall of early life experiences and conclude that "What can be said with more confidence is that recall of significant past events does not appear to be affected by mood state" (p.94). Additional research is needed in order to delineate the potential effects of mood on particular types of information obtained though retrospective reports.

To summarize, interviews are probably the most widely used assessment method in clinical psychology. The form of assessment interviews can vary considerably with regard to the degree of structure provided by the interviewer. More structured interviews have the advantage of reliability, with some cost to flexibility and more idiographic assessment of the client's difficulties. Given these circumstances, the use of both semistructured and unstructured interviews may be warranted for a given client, depending on the assessment question (diagnostic categorization or target behavior selection). In either case, the initial interview is an important source of information and hypotheses that may be further explored with additional assessment methods.

Self-Report Questionnaires

The second part of this chapter focuses on additional measurements obtained through client self-report outside of an assessment interview. Typical self-report measures include questionnaires and self-ratings. As discussed earlier, self-report methods can be used to obtain information regarding any of the three response systems. Many questionnaires selectively assess these different content areas. For example, an agoraphobic client could be asked to complete the Bodily Sensations Questionnaire (Chambless, Caputo, Bright, & Gallagher, 1984) to report physiological sensations of panic, the Agoraphobic Cognitions Questionnaire (Chambless et. al., 1984) to report cognitions, and the Mobility Inventory (Chambless, Caputo, Jasin, Gracely, & Williams, 1985) to assess avoidance behavior.

The essence of self-report measurement is quantification of a client's verbal report and often comparison with available normative data. Self-report can be obtained retrospectively with regard to the client's general behavior or can be used to assess specific responses within the context of analogue settings or role-plays. Common methods for quantification of self-report can be divided into questionnaire measures, rating scales, and cognitive assessments involving the analysis of client-generated verbal material from thought listings. Each of these methods is described in the following sections.

Questionnaires Self-report questionnaires are among the most frequently employed measures of clinical change, second only to interviews in both research and clinical settings (Lambert & McRoberts, 1993; Watkins et al., 1995). As assessment tools, questionnaires have several advantages: (a) questionnaire measures can be inexpensively administered and often demand only small investments of time from both clients and clinicians; (b) questionnaire responses are objectively scored and quantified without biased weighting of particular responses, and often can be referenced to normative data; (c) questionnaires can be used to collect a broad range of information regarding the client, thereby allowing interviewers to focus inquiry on specific difficulties; and (d) questionnaires can provide the client with an opportunity to report information that he or she may initially be reluctant to disclose during face-to-face interactions with the clinician. To serve as a measure of change, a given questionnaire should be administered at least on a pretreatment and posttreatment basis. More frequent administrations are advisable if the questionnaire is sufficiently brief and if it is the primary measure of change (Bloom & Fischer, 1982).

The use of questionnaires in case analysis and evaluation is being enhanced by the wide availability of computers and computer programs. Many questionnaires are either available for computerized administration and scoring or can be readily converted to such use. Thus, it is not impractical to imagine routine evaluation through the use of questionnaires of known quality, even though the kinds of clients' problems, and thus the types of needed questionnaires, may vary widely.

The thousands of extant questionnaires can be subdivided into two general categories: broad questionnaires that seek to survey several life areas or to assess general life adjustment, and more specific questionnaires seeking to identify client responses in particular life areas or situations.

Broad Questionnaires Broad questionnaires are frequently used for initial assessment in order to obtain information regarding the client's functioning across a number of life areas. Because of their breadth, they tend to be used less frequently in evaluating more specific effects of treatment. One major problem with the use of broad questionnaires on a pre–post treatment basis is that they provide a relatively insensitive measure of change. Treatment may focus on a few patient problems, whereas, by definition, the broad questionnaires assess many life areas as well as general adjustment. Therefore, even though the client may improve in the areas that were the focus of treatment, the changes may not be reflected in the broad questionnaires. Conversely, any change that is detected by using broad questionnaires adds to the credibility that treatment "really" was effective. In other words, the treatment resulted in broad-based clinical effects. The most desirable practice may be to use frequent administrations of specific questionnaires (to provide maximal sensitivity to change and ongoing assessment of treatment effectiveness) and to administer broad questionnaires (to examine broad-based changes) on a pre–post treatment basis.

One broad questionnaire is the Symptom Checklist Revised, with 90 items (SCL-90-R; Derogatis, 1983). This broad-based questionnaire evolved from the earlier Hopkins Symptom Checklist and is intended for outpatient use. For each of the 90 items, the respondent is instructed to rate "How much that problem has bothered and/or distressed you during the past week including today," on a 5-point scale, from 0 *(not at all)* to 4 *(extremely)*. The checklist has nine factors: Somatization, Obsessive-Compulsive, Interpersonal Sensitivity, Depression, Anxiety, Hostility, Phobic Anxiety, Paranoid, and Psychoticism. Sample items include: "Feeling afraid to go out of your house alone," "Pains in heart or chest," "Sleep that is restless or disturbed," and "Feelings of guilt."

Another example of a broad questionnaire is the Social Adjustment Scale Self-Report (SAS-SR; Weissman & Bothwell, 1976). This questionnaire was derived from a structured interview (the Social Adjustment Scale [SAS; Weissman, & Paykel, 1974). The questionnaire contains 42 items assessing six major areas of functioning (work, social and leisure activities, as well as marital, extended family, and parental relationships). Item endorsements are made on a scale ranging from 1 to 5, with higher scores reflecting greater impairment.

Winston et al., (1991) utilized the SCL-90 and the SAS-SR as part of an assessment battery to evaluate treatment effects of two forms of brief psychotherapy for a group of 32 outpatients diagnosed with personality disorders. Clients were randomly assigned to a short-term psychotherapy or a brief adaptational psychotherapy condition. Seventeen additional patients served as a waiting-list control group. Both treated groups demonstrated comparable improvement in global scores of the SCL-90 and SAS-SR compared to the control group. Improvements were consistent with other outcome measures.

Another very well known broad questionnaire is the Minnesota Multiphasic Personality Inventory-2 (MMPI-2; Butcher, Dahlstrom, Graham, Tellegen, & Kaemmer, 1989). Kohlenberg and Tsai (1994) administered the MMPI to a 35-year-old depressed male as part of assessment before and after treatment with a version of cognitive therapy integrated with functional analytic psychotherapy. A general reduction in severity across clinical scales was observed following treatment. A more common practice in utilizing the MMPI to evaluate treatment effects is to administer specific subscales following treatment. For example, Zettle and Herring (1995) administered the entire MMPI-2 as part of an assessment battery for depressed persons prior to individual or group cognitive therapy for depression. The Depression scale of the MMPI-2 was administered as part of posttreatment and 2-month follow-up assessments. Improvements on the Depression scale following treatment were observed for both groups and were consistent with other measures.

Specific Questionnaires Whereas broad questionnaires assess many different problem areas and general life adjustment, specific questionnaires assess more focused areas. Recent years have witnessed a proliferation of specific questionnaires. For example Froyd and Lambert (1989), in a survey of 20 selected journals from 1983 to 1988, identified 1,430 outcome measures. A large portion of these were unstandardized questionnaires and scales. Of the total number of outcome measures, 840 were only used once in a published article. These numbers alone can make the task of selecting questionnaires daunting. Resources that list large numbers of specific questionnaires include the following: Cautela (1981), Fischer and Corcoran (1994), Hudson (1992), and McCubbin and Thompson (1991). A convenient way to classify specific questionnaires is by the functional unit that they attempt to assess. Some focus on stimulus variables, others on response parameters, and still others on different consequences. Examples of each of these types follow.

One widely known specific questionnaire that focuses on stimulus or situational variables is the Fear Survey Schedule-II (Geer, 1965), which is reprinted in Fischer and Corcoran (1994). A large number (51) of stimulus items are listed, such as spiders, auto accidents, speaking before a group, being with a member of the opposite sex, and not being a success. For each item, the respondent is instructed to rate the amount of fear that he or she feels toward each object or situation on a scale ranging from 1 *(none)* to 7 *(terror)*.

Another specific questionnaire focusing on stimulus or situation variables is the Mobility Inventory for Agoraphobia (Chambless, et al. 1985, reprinted in Fischer and Corcoran, 1994). This questionnaire contains a list of 25 places or situations (a 26th is optionally generated by the respondent). The respondent rates his or her level of avoidance for each situation on a scale ranging from 1 *(never avoid)* to 5 *(always avoid)*. For further specification of stimulus conditions, respondents are asked to make separate ratings of their degree of avoidance when accompanied by a trusted companion and when alone.

Other specific questionnaires assess consequences. The consequences of interest are often potential reinforcers that can be utilized in a behavior-management program. Technically, reinforcers can only be identified empirically—that is, by observing their effect in increasing the rate of preceding behavior. Some questionnaires, however, assist in the identification of potential reinforcers that can then be tested in an empirical manner. One questionnaire used for this purpose is the Reinforcement Survey Schedule (Cautela & Kastenbaum, 1967, reprinted in Mash & Terdal, 1976). A large number of potentially desirable consequences or activities are listed. The client is instructed to rate how much pleasure each activity currently gives him or her on a 5-point scale from "not at all" to "very much."

An example of the use of such an instrument is provided by O'Donohue, Plaud, and Hecker (1992), who integrated information derived from the Reinforcement Survey Schedule into treatment of a home-bound agoraphobic. The client completed the survey schedule, then self-monitored her participation in each pleasurable activity. Treatment involved making a number of pleasant activities contingent upon the client's leaving her house or yard (e.g., watching television only at a friend's house). Compliance was measured by self-report, self-monitoring, and reports of other family members.

The final and by far the largest category of specific questionnaires is designed to assess responses within different problem areas. These questionnaires are generally administered with the intention of specifying the responses within a particular life area that may be the focus of intervention. The initial administration can be used to identify specific target responses for treatment, with repeated administrations utilized to monitor the client's improvement. If normative data are provided for the questionnaire, the client's pretreatment score can be compared to the norms to determine if his or her responses are atypical or within a "clinical range" in relation to the standardization group. Similarly, the client's posttreatment score can be compared to the standardization group to ascertain if the client's score is now in the "normal" range. This latter comparison helps to determine the substantive or clinical significance of any treatment changes.

The sources listed earlier describe many of the specific questionnaires that assess particular problem areas and problematic responses occurring within any of the three response systems. For example, some of these questionnaires assess depressed responses. The most widely used specific questionnaire assessing depression is the Beck Depression Inventory (Beck et al., 1961, reprinted in Beck, Rush, Shaw, & Emery, 1979). This inventory consists of 21 items that focus on responses typical of depression. Each item contains four statements, and the client is instructed to pick out the one statement from each group that best describes the way that he or she has been feeling over the past week, including today. For example, one item contains these four statements: "O = I don't have any thoughts of killing myself; 1 = I have thoughts of killing myself, but I would not carry them out; 2 = I would like to kill myself; 3 = I would kill myself if I had the chance."

In addition to providing summative retrospective accounts, specific questionnaires can be used to assess responses in more specific situations or in analogue situations presented in the clinical setting. The distinction between self-reports occurring in specific situations and those that are more summative and retrospective is often subsumed within a state/trait distinction. One well-known example of a specific questionnaire that can be applied to quantify either global retrospective reports or situationally based responding is the Stait Trait Anxiety Inventory (STAI: Spielberger, Gorsuch, & Lushene, 1970). This is the most widely used specific questionnaire assessing anxiety (Lambert & McRoberts, 1993). Each version of the questionnaire consists of 20 items rated on a scale from 1 to 4. In the trait version, respondents are asked to respond to items according to how they generally feel. The state version instructs respondents to answer according to how they feel at that moment.

Walder, McCracken, Herbert, James, and Brewitt (1987) utilized the state version of the STAI in evaluating a brief exposure-based intervention for 38 individuals with a specific phobia of air travel. The questionnaire was administered during an introductory meeting, before boarding an aircraft in the second session, and (three times) in the final session: prior to boarding the aircraft, immediately prior to take-off, and midway through the return flight.

To summarize, specific questionnaires offer standardized and objectively scored assessment of stimulus situations, consequences, or the client's report regarding any of the three response systems for a given problem area. The expected sensitivity of questionnaires to behavioral change differs depending on the breadth of areas assessed, as well on the degree to which they request global and summative retrospective reports and ratings from the client.

The environment of managed care has placed increasing emphasis on assessment instruments that yield broad estimates of client functioning while monitoring more specific behavioral change. Many of these measures are based upon frameworks for conceptualizing outcome assessment developed by researchers. They are also designed to be easily administered and to suit the informational needs of clinicians and managed care administrators. For example, the Outcome Questionnaire (OQ-45; Lambert, Huefner, & Reisinger, 1996) was developed to be consistent with the conceptual scheme described by Lambert, Ogles, and Masters (1992). The questionnaire contains 45 questions with subscales assessing domains of symptom distress, interpersonal relations, and social role performance. The Symptom Distress scale assesses symptoms of frequently diagnosed disorders, with emphasis on anxiety, depression, and substance abuse. The Interpersonal Relations scale includes questions assessing problems in relationships, feelings of isolation, and withdrawal. The Social Role Performance scale assesses dissatisfaction and distress related to employment, family roles, and leisure activity. A more abbreviated form of the questionnaire (OQ-10) has also been developed as a brief screening instrument. A similar instrument, the Youth Outcome Questionnaire (Y-OQ; Burlingame, Wells, & Lambert, 1995), has been developed for children and adolescents. It assesses content areas derived from narrative and meta-analytic reviews of the child and adolescent treatment outcome literature (Wells, Burlingame, Lambert, Hoag, & Hope, 1996).

Measures of Client Satisfaction   Within the context of managed care, assessment of client satisfaction with psychological services assumes a prominent role in quality assurance procedures (Winegar, 1992). Along with frequently administered measures of behavioral change, session-by-session assessment of satisfaction can provide valuable information relevant to continuous quality improvement (Johnson & Shaha, 1996). It is advisable to avoid equating assessments of change with client satisfaction because of the often low correlation between satisfaction and outcome measures (e.g., Attkinson & Zwick, 1982; Carscaddon, George, & Wells, 1990; Pekarik & Wolff, 1996). This low correspondence is perhaps more understandable in light of the multidimensionality that can characterize the construct of satisfaction. In a review of the satisfaction literature relevant to mental health services, Lebow (1983) noted that dimensions of satisfaction can include satisfaction with the clinician, outcome, access, confidentiality, medicines, and facilities among others. Additionally, Williams (1994) notes that satisfaction ratings may represent "diverse opinions ranging from 'I've evaluated the service and I'm happy with it' through 'I don't really think I have the ability to evaluate, but I do have confidence in the staff' to 'the service was appalling but I don't like to criticize, after all they're doing their best' being collapsed into a single category of users all of whom expressed 'satisfaction'"(p. 514).

A number of specific questionnaires have been developed for the assessment of client satisfaction with mental health services. An example of a summative measure administered following treatment is the Client Satisfaction Questionnaire (CSQ; Attkinson & Zwick, 1982). A number of versions of this questionnaire have been developed. The most widely used is probably the 8-item version (CSQ-8; Larsen, Attkinson, Hargreaves, & Nguyen 1979). The questionnaire items comprise a unidimensional score reflecting satisfaction with treatment and are rated on scales ranging from one to four, with scale anchors varying with items.

Other questionnaires assess satisfaction on a session-by-session basis. An example of such a questionnaire is the Session Evaluation Questionnaire (SEQ; Stiles & Snow, 1984). The SEQ contains 24 bipolar pairs of adjectives with a seven-point continuum for ratings along each dichotomous dimension (e.g., relaxed vs. tense). Clients provide ratings for both the session just completed and their feelings following the session.

Self-Ratings   In addition to broad and specific questionnaires, another available form of self-report measure is the collection of self-ratings. In self-ratings, the client is asked to rate himself or herself on some specific dimension. The rating can be made in the presence of particular stimuli to which the client is exposed in the clinic, or a more summative and retrospective rating can be made in the absence of a particular stimulus. Self-ratings will be discussed more thoroughly in the next chapter. Some examples of rating scales are described in this section.

Retrospective self-ratings are often requested in questionnaires, but rating scales can also be used to assess responses when no appropriate questionnaire is available to assess the information of interest. The client can be asked to provide retrospective ratings for any number of behaviors, and many different scale types can be used with scale anchors tailored to the individual client. A discussion of the construction of individualized rating scales as well as of the advantages and disadvantages of this approach is provided by Bloom, Fischer, and Orme (1995).

A number of rating scales have been developed particularly for use in specific types of situations. For example, self-ratings have frequently been used to assess the subjective components of fear or anxiety. A behavioral avoidance test is often arranged in which the fearful stimulus is presented, either in vivo or representationally (e.g., slides, audiotapes or videotapes). During the behavioral avoidance test, all three aspects of the triple-response system can be assessed: motoric responses are assessed by directly observing the client's degree of approach or avoidance; physiological responses are directly assessed by physiological recording devices; and subjective responses are indirectly assessed by self-ratings. Self-ratings in the context of a behavioral avoidance test were introduced by Wolpe (1969), who devised a 1–100 self-rating scale to assess subjective units of disturbance (SUDs). A similar 1–10 Fear Thermometer had been designed by Walk (1956). An example of self-ratings used in the context of a behavioral avoidance test for clients diagnosed with obsessive-compulsive disorder is provided by Foa, Steketee, Grayson, Turner, and Latimer (1984). Each client displayed fears of contamination as well as washing or cleaning rituals. As part of assessments conducted before and after treatment and at four separate follow-up periods, clients were exposed to feared contaminants and asked to approach them in discrete steps. SUDS ratings were obtained at each step.

Informant Reports   To supplement and corroborate client self-reports, a number of questionnaires have versions designed to be administered to informants such as parents, spouses, and teachers. One example of a broad questionnaire for which informant versions are available is the Child Behavior Checklist (CBCL; Achenbach & Edelbrock, 1983). The CBCL contains 118 items reflecting behavior problems that are endorsed on a 3-point scale, with 0 rating indicating the behavior is not a problem and 2 indicating a severe problem. The CBCL yields individual factor scores as well as broad scores for internalizing and externalizing behavior problems.

An important consideration in the use of informant reports is their frequent discrepancy with client self-report. For example, Kolko and Kazdin (1993) examined the degree of correspondence between child, parent, and teacher reports for a group of children referred for treatment and a group of nonpatient children. In general, only moderate correlations were obtained between child/parent, child/teacher, and parent/teacher reports for both internalizing and externalizing scales. Additionally, the degree of correspondence between child/parent and parent/teacher ratings in the overall sample was higher for externalizing than for internalizing scales. Imperfect correspondence between collateral and client reports underscores the utility of obtaining assessment information from multiple sources and of considering the contexts in which the informants interact with the client.

Cognitive Assessment Methods

A number of assessment methods have been developed with the specific purpose of quantifying cognitive responses. Nisbett and Wilson (1977) have made a distinction between cognitive contents and cognitive processes. They argue that individuals are more able to accurately report cognitive contents such as beliefs or appraisals, but less able to accurately report the processes (e.g., attributions) or processing errors (e.g., all or none thinking) involved in their production. The distinction between products and processes is often complicated by the necessity of using systematic changes in content to infer processing differences. While a number of experimental tasks are thought to assess cognitive processes, the measurements most commonly used in clinical assessment are classified as measures of cognitive products (Hollon & Bemis, 1981).

Kendall and Hollon (1981) describe four methods for the assessment of cognitive products: (a) endorsement methods that are akin to recognition memory tasks in which the individual is provided with a list of potential thoughts provided by the assessor and is asked to indicate whether each thought occurred in a relevant target situation or time period; (b) recording methods such as think-aloud procedures in which individuals are asked to continuously verbalize their stream of consciousness and their verbalizations are recorded, coded, and quantified; (c) sampling methods in which the individual is given periodic prompts such as a tone and is asked to report what he or she was thinking during the time immediately preceding the prompt; and (d) production methods such as thought-listing, in which the individual is asked to recall thoughts from an immediately prior experience such as a role-play, a social interaction, or behavioral avoidance test.

The most frequently applied measures of cognitions fall within the category of endorsement methods, which provide the client with a list of thoughts in questionnaire form and he or she is asked to indicate whether each thought has been experienced within a particular period of time. The particular questionnaires may vary with regard to the time period being assessed. For example, the Automatic Thoughts Questionnaire (ATQ; Hollon & Kendall, 1980) contains 30 negative self-statements. The client is asked to rate the frequency of each statement over the past week. The Social Interaction Self-Statement Test (SISST; Glass, Merluzzi, Biever, & Larsen, 1982) contains 15 positive and 15 negative self-statements associated with anxiety in a social interaction. It is designed to be administered immediately following a heterosocial interaction.

Glass and Arnkoff (1982, p.51) raised a number of concerns related to equating endorsements with actual thought contents. Specifically, they suggested that: (a) endorsements may reflect the importance rather than frequency of cognitions; (b) subjects may endorse thoughts that are similar but not identical to their own thoughts; (c) individuals may respond based on the relevance rather than the frequency of the cognition; and (d) individuals may base their responses on affective experiences that they translate into the self-statement format.

Recording methods such as think-aloud and thought-sampling procedures have infrequently been utilized in assessment. One possible reason for this is that these methods tend to involve time-consuming scoring procedures (Arnkoff & Glass, 1989). Additionally, Arnkoff and Glass (1989) argued that methods requiring the articulation of thoughts could not be realistically used in naturalistic social interactions because interrupted interactions are no longer naturalistic. The same argument would seem to apply in a number of in vivo assessment procedures. Clark (1988) discusses a number of concerns that have been raised regarding these methods. These include: (a) that the methods may interfere with cognitive processing (see Blackwell, Galassi, Galassi, & Watson, 1985); (b) individuals may report only a small portion of the cognitions experienced at a given time; and (c) relevant but low-frequency cognitions may be missed by these procedures (see Cacioppo and Petty, 1981). There are other criticisms as well (e.g., see Crutcher, 1994; Payne, 1994; Wilson, 1994). Many of these criticisms have well-developed counterarguments, however (Ericsson & Simon, 1993; Hayes, 1986; Hayes, White, & Bissett, 1998).

While thought-listing may be susceptible to many of the same criticisms discussed above, it is the more widely used method for obtaining and assessing client-generated verbal responses in specific analogue situations. In thought-listing, clients are exposed to clinically relevant stimuli or situations and are then prompted either to verbalize or to write their thoughts within a certain time interval. Shorter intervals provided for listing are thought to produce the most salient thoughts. The distinctions between this method and self-monitoring are minimal. Self-monitoring is more widely applied in both naturalistic and analogue situations, while thought-listing is more exclusively utilized in contrived situations such as role-play assessments. Another distinction involves prompting responses and limiting the time during which the client generates responses. In thought-listing, clients can be prompted to generate responses for a specific duration at particular times in anticipation of, during, or following stimulus presentations, while in self-monitoring such prompting is not typically provided.

An example of the utilization of thought-listing in outcome assessment is provided by Heimberg et al. (1990). This study compared the outcome of cognitive behavioral group treatment for social phobia to a placebo treatment condition. Following a simulation of a personally relevant anxiety-provoking event (for example, talking with someone of the opposite sex), clients were given forms and asked to record the thoughts they had experienced. Thoughts were classified by independent raters as negative, positive, or neutral. Both groups evidenced a significant decrease in negative thoughts and an increase in positive thoughts following treatment, but changes remained significant at 3- and 6-month follow-up only for the cognitive-behavioral therapy group.

McKnight, Nelson, Hayes, and Jarrett (1984) used a thought-listing task to assess the presence of irrational cognitions in depressed women following three separate role-plays. Following each role-play, subjects were asked to report what they might have been thinking. Thought-listings were later classified by the experimenter through comparison with Ellis's eleven irrational thoughts (Ellis & Greiger, 1977). A decrease in the frequency of sampled irrational cognitions was observed following treatment.

Coding and scoring procedures for thought-listings have been described by Cacioppo and Petty (1981). One advantage of thought-listing procedures is that client responses are self-generated rather than generated by experimenters and endorsed on questionnaires. Thought-listings therefore allow for assessment of more idiosyncratic thoughts. Among its disadvantages are the complexity and time requirements of scoring, potential demand characteristics, and the lack of normative data. The use of stimulus conditions specifically tailored to a given client can also make comparisons across individuals difficult.

In order to facilitate comparisons across individuals, standardized stimulus situations may be used to elicit thought-listings. One example is the Articulated Thoughts during Simulated Situations method (ATSS; Davison, Robins, & Johnson, 1983). In the ATSS method, audiotaped scenarios recounting a variety of hypothetical situations are played, and subjects are asked to imagine themselves involved in each. The situations are periodically interrupted and subjects are prompted to think aloud at this point.

Lehnert, Overholser, and Adams (1996) describe an approach to assessing cognitions associated with depression that represents an intermediate between endorsement and thought-listing methods. The Cognition Rating Form (CRF) is a scoring method applied to responses on the Rotter Incomplete Sentences Blanks: High School Form (Rotter, Lah, & Rafferty, 1992). The CRF rates the presence of 25 cognitions comprising 10 categories, including negative view of the self, self-blaming, and negative view of the future, and additional categories of positive cognitions. The method exerts more structure than thought-listings, while allowing for self-generated responses rather than endorsements. The authors report that rating requires substantial training but can be done quickly by individuals, once trained. An additional advantage of this method is that it incorporates cognitive assessment with sentence-completion methods, which are widely used assessment tools reported by practicing clinicians (Watkins et al., 1995).

Issues in the Use of Self-Report

The preceding sections have described the use of questionnaire, ratings scales, and cognitive assessment methods of collecting self-report data. Because of their convenience, self-report measures tend to be quite popular. Nonetheless, a number of issues must be considered in their use. These concerns include stimulus variables, organism variables, the agreement between self-report measures, and the relationship between self-report and other methods of data collection.

Stimulus Variables

Self-report has sometimes been criticized on the grounds that self-report responses are subject to demand or expectancy, response bias, and social desirability (Haynes, 1978; Haynes & Wilson, 1979; Jayaratne & Levy, 1979). *Demand or expectancy* refers to responding to "extraneous" variables, such as "faking bad" prior to treatment and "faking good" following treatment. *Response* bias refers to the serial dependency of responses to questionnaire items (e.g., the respondent marking several items in a row as "true," or giving several items in a row a rating of "4"). *Social desirability* refers to the social value that is perceived to be associated with particular items.

One point to be noted here is that all behavior has multiple determinants. The nominal and functional stimuli controlling behavior can sometimes differ. In the case of questionnaires, even though the questionnaire item is the nominal stimulus, the client may also be reacting to other functional stimuli, such as a therapeutic program that is expected to be helpful or a therapist who seems like a pleasant person. Shifting functional stimuli contribute to response differences across time and across different measurement devices. The argument can again be made that multiple measurement within content areas and across time is desirable to help filter out the *signal* (measures of the client's problem behavior in response to the nominal stimulus of the questionnaire item) from the *noise* (the client's reply to other functional but "irrelevant" stimuli, like wanting to please the therapist or to avoid jail).

A related point is that self-report measures are not the only measures subject to demand characteristics. It has been shown that clients' approach or avoidance behavior on a behavioral avoidance test (in this instance, for claustrophobia) can be influenced by *high-demand* instructions ("If you should become fearful, please control it as best you can so you can remain for the full period. . . . Remember that it is extremely important that we get the full 10 min.") versus *low-demand* instructions ("You should stop the process at any point where you become fairly uncomfortable. . . . You should remain in the situation as long as you feel reasonably at ease") (Miller & Bernstein, 1972, p. 207).

Similarly, heart rate during a behavioral avoidance test has also been shown to be influenced by high-demand versus low-demand instructions (Odom & Nelson, 1977), although this is not a consistent finding (Miller & Bernstein, 1972).

Thus, there are no "pure" measures in which only the nominal or "relevant" stimulus controls the client's responses. Other types of assessment, in addition to self-report, can be influenced by "extraneous" stimuli.

Another issue regarding self-report measures is the relative importance of their psychometric properties. Psychometric examinations, especially of self-report questionnaires, are popular. Usually assessed are split-half reliability, test-retest reliability, and concurrent validity with other measures of the same behavior. As discussed in the previous chapter, it is our opinion that particular types of psychometric investigations produce especially useful data. Of utility are investigations of content validity and those which result in normative data. Content validity is important to determine if the problem area purported to be assessed by the questionnaire is, in fact, adequately represented. Regretfully, the content of many questionnaires has been determined on a logical basis (speculation about what items are appropriate or not) rather than on an empirical basis (generation of items by means of data collection) (Haynes, 1978). Normative data are also important for two reasons (Kazdin, 1977; Nelson & Bowles, 1975): As mentioned previously, normative comparisons can be used in pre-treatment selection of target behaviors to determine if behavior falls in the "clinical" range, and in post-treatment, to determine if scores fall within the "normal" range.

Organism Variables

One issue that is more frequently addressed in self-report methods than in other forms of data collection is the impact of organism variables. Individuals from different demographic groups may respond differently to questionnaire items; hence different norms are required for different demographic groups. Factors such as age, sex, and race are frequently areas of concern in the standardization of self-report measures. Separate normative data is often used as a reference for individuals from different demographic groups, to determine if behavior is "normal" in comparison to these more particular normative populations.

Another extraneous variable that can influence a client's response on self-report measures is the client's reading skills. This is especially true for questionnaires which often require a fairly sophisticated reading ability. Manuals or instructions that accompany some questionnaires sometimes give the minimum grade level of skills needed to read the questionnaire effectively.

Relationship between Different Self-Report Measures

Agreement between different self-report measures purported to measure similar life areas is often imperfect. One obvious factor contributing to these discrepancies is the variance in both the content and scales of measurement employed in different questionnaires and rating-scales. Different questionnaires ask different questions and require different types of responses from the client. Given this high level of variance in stimulus conditions, perfect agreement should not be expected. As mentioned earlier, agreement between self-report measures is evaluated nomo-thetically and cannot be predicted for a given client. It is crucial for the clinician to be familiar with the content and response requirements of questionnaires selected for use. Discrepancies between self-report measures do not suggest that one questionnaire is necessarily better than the other, but can often be reconciled through careful evaluations of the client's responding and the particular information being provided.

Relationship between Self-Report and Other Measures

As outlined earlier, frequently there is asynchrony in the triple-response system. However, one variable that has been demonstrated to increase the correspondence between verbal and motoric measures, and between verbal and physiological measures, is the phrasing of the questions requiring verbal responses. For example, motoric measures of snake avoidance (in a behavioral avoidance test) were correctly predicted 95% of the time by specific questions (where subjects verbally predicted their own degree of approach-avoidance in a laboratory situation), but only 61% of the time by more general questions (where subjects self-rated their degree of fear of snakes) (McReynolds & Stegman, 1976). Cone (1979) believed that the generally low correspondence among verbal, motor, and physiological measures was frequently due to a methodological confound. To illustrate, indirect measures of cognitive content (e.g., "I feel anxious") were often compared to direct measures of physiological content (e.g., galvanic skin response). Cone (1979) predicted that the low correlations produced by this measure-by-content confound could be improved if, for example, indirect measures of physiological content (e.g., "I perspire") were compared to the related direct measures of physiological content (e.g., galvanic skin response). Cone (1979) cited the results of McReynolds and Stegman (1976) to buttress his point that the correspondence between verbal reports and motoric or physiological measures increases if the verbal report is specifically about those motoric or physiological activities.

Asynchrony between response systems does not support the conclusion that self-report is a generally inferior measure, but helps to underscore that it is a unique form of measurement. Self-report assesses what the client says about what he or she is thinking, feeling, or doing. Furthermore, self-report is our most direct measure of cognitive responses (such as obsessions or negative self-statements) or of subjective experience (such as pain or sexual arousal). On a practical level, clients voluntarily seek treatment when they think that they have a problem, and they terminate treatment when they think that they do not have a problem (Tasto, 1977). On a philosophical level, Wolf (1978) has quoted Levi and Anderson (1975): "We believe that each individual can be assumed to be the best judge of his [sic] own situation and state of well-being. The alternative is some type of 'big brother' who makes the evaluation for groups and nations. World history provides many examples of such 'expert' or 'elitist' opinions being at variance with what was expected by the man in the street" (p. 213). What people think about their cognitive, motoric, and physiological behavior does matter, practically and philosophically.

Undeniably, some responses such as physiological and motoric activity can be measured through more direct means than self-report (at least with the aid of instrumentation); however, self-report methods provide the client with a forum for his or her views about those physiological and motoric behaviors. The critical advice here is not to assign global priority to particular measures, but to obtain multiple measures in order to produce a complete assessment of the client's responses. As one of several measures that are repeatedly administered over the course of treatment, self-report provides a unique assessment of client change.

Physiological Measures

The second portion of this chapter focuses on more direct measures of psychophysiological processes. These processes are generally measured with the aid of instrumentation—for example, a sphygmanometer to measure blood pressure or a cardiotachometer to measure heart rate. As mentioned previously, physiological processes can also be measured through self-monitoring or self-report. However, a number of advantages have been attributed to more direct measurement via instrumentation. Direct measurement can be highly sensitive and can often provide both discrete and continuous data with regard to physiological processes (Iacono, 1991). Intentional distortions in responding may be difficult given the unfamiliarity of psychophysiological measurement to most lay persons (Iacono, 1991). Additionally, psychophysiological assessment often requires more passive participation of the individual subject and is not dependent on the subject's communicative or verbal skills, which suggests its potential utility with specific populations such as children (Tomarken, 1995). Also, subtle changes in physiological indices can provide assessment data concerning physiological processes that are not amenable to self-report.

Recent years have witnessed advances in both the instrumentation of psychophysiology, as well as the specificity of physiological measurement with regard to psychological phenomena. The discussion provided here is, of necessity, brief. More complete discussion of the use of psychophysiological measures is provided by Andreassi (1995). Additional texts addressing the application of psychophysiological assessment for clinical phenomena in behavioral medicine, psychophysiological disorders (Gatchel & Blanchard, 1993), emotional disorders (Turpin, 1989), and biofeedback (Gatchel & Blanchard, 1993) are also available.

Issues in Direct Psychophysiological Assessment

Applications of psychophysiological measurement are widespread in the areas of psychophysiological disorders, behavioral medicine, and biofeedback. These measures are also frequently used in research and specialty clinics for anxiety, sexual disorders, and sleep disorders. However, this method of assessment is less likely to be found in general clinical settings, for a number of reasons. Among the issues to be considered in the integration of psychophysiological measurement with clinical assessment are the feasibility of their use, and the complexities involved in assessing and controlling for variables that may influence the data obtained. These latter variables can be broadly divided into organism variables and variables associated with the stimulus conditions during assessment. Each of these categories is discussed in the following sections and should be considered when using these measures.

Feasibility of Psychophysiological Measurement

The relative absence of physiological measurement in more nonspecialized clinical settings can in large part be attributed to the cost of such measures, as well as the level of technical expertise required for their implementation. However, there have been a number of technological advances in instrumentation for both laboratory assessment and ambulatory recording, as well as developments in biofeedback technology, that continue to simplify measurement and facilitate its availability in more general settings. Additionally, a number of attempts have been made to standardize assessment procedures. Detailed guidelines, recommended by the Society for Psychophysiological Research, are available for recording electrodermal responses (Fowles et al., 1981), heart rate (Jennings, Berg, Hutcheson, Obrist, & Turpin, 1981), and muscular activity (electromyography) (Fridlund & Cacioppo, 1986).

Organism Variables

Organism variables in psychophysiological research are a common source of measurement error often discussed under the category of "nuisance" variables. Factors such as age, sex, race, physical fitness, menstrual cycle, and drug use, among others, are known to exert marked effects on psychophysiological measurement (Sturgis & Gramling, 1988; Turpin, 1989). However, the specific magnitude of the effects of a particular "nuisance" variable for a given measure is often unclear (Iacono, 1991). In group research, the influence of these variables can be controlled by group selection criteria and randomization. In single-subject research, the problem can be addressed by utilizing multiple assessment tasks so that the subject serves as his or her own control. In both cases, the use of validated and potent stimuli during assessment is recommended.

Organismic systems usually work to maintain homeostasis. The organism responds and readjusts itself with exposure to each new stimulus. The implications of homeostasis for psychophysiological measurement are twofold (Epstein, 1976). First, after the client is prepared for measurement, an adaptation period must follow to allow the client to become accustomed to the measurement device and setting. Second, initial presentations of relevant stimuli may produce an initial orienting response in addition to expected physiological changes. This response should diminish with subsequent presentations of the stimuli.

Diminished responding or habituation to repeated stimulation can also be undesirable in physiological assessment. Habituation rates can vary across different psychophysiological responses and across different populations and individuals. Habituation can pose upper limits on the frequency of repeated measures, especially with the same stimulus, and therefore necessitates the use of varied stimuli within assessments. In some cases, intermixing of stimuli rather than presenting similar stimuli in blocks is advisable for delaying habituation effects (Tomarken, 1995).

Individuals can also differ with respect to their characteristic psychophysiological responding. For example, a given individual may consistently show a maximal response on a particular measure across varying stimulus conditions, making this measure insensitive for that individual. This phenomenon of intersubject inconsistency in physiological responding has been labeled individual response specificity (Lacey, Bateman, & Van Lehn, 1953). These person-specific response patterns can complicate group research because the more sensitive measures for a given individual may not be included in assessment. An implication of response specificity in single-subject research is that for a given subject the most sensitive physiological measure should be determined and utilized.

Another organism variable that presents difficulty for interpreting change in psychophysiological assessment concerns the Law of Initial Values (LIV; Wilder, 1967). The LIV describes a relationship between initial levels of responding and the magnitude of physiological responses to subsequent stimulation. The higher the initial level, the lower the magnitude of increase and the greater the magnitude of decrease that can occur to response-altering stimuli. This means that a heart rate change of 5 beats per minute from an individual's baseline of 120 beats per minute is not equivalent to the same magnitude of change in the same direction from a baseline of 80 beats per minute. Wilder (1967) asserted that the LIV primarily applies to group data and may or may not be observed in particular instances. Others have questioned the consistency of the LIV citing, for example, evidence that it appears to hold more often for some physiological measures but not for others (e.g., Hord, Johnson, & Lubin, 1964), or that it may represent more of a statistical artifact rather than a lawful description of physiological processes (Myrtek & Foerster, 1986). However, there is some evidence that it may be more evident in within-subject measurement (Scher, Furedy, & Heslegrave 1985), and the issue warrants concern when interpreting change scores. A commonly used correction technique for the LIV was outlined by Lacey (1956). Additional approaches have been suggested (e.g., Heath & Oken, 1965; Myrtek & Foerster, 1986; Stemmler & Fahrenberg, 1989). Corrections may or may not be appropriate depending on the research design and statistical analysis being used (see Geenen & Van de Vijver, 1993).

Importance of Stimulus Situations

The psychophysiological responses of interest in clinical assessment often occur in the presence of particular clinically relevant stimuli. Thus, it is critical to introduce the relevant stimulus into the measurement situation. In clinic settings, relevant stimuli can be presented in an analogue fashion. For example, slides can be used to present neutral versus phobic stimuli or appropriate versus deviant sexual stimuli.

In addition to the stimuli of interest, a number of extraneous environmental factors may affect physiological recordings. These include lighting, sound, temperature, time of day, barometric pressure, and electrode placement (Andreassi, 1989; Coles, Donchin, & Porges, 1986). Experimenter-generated stimuli such as instructions can also influence responding (Iacono & Lykken, 1979). For example, attentional instructions during exposure to phobic stimuli have been shown to influence the magnitude of heart rate and skin conductance responses (McGlynn, Rose, & Lazarate, 1994). As mentioned earlier, high-demand and low-demand instructions in behavioral avoidance tests have been shown to influence psychophysiological responses (Odom & Nelson, 1977). Psychophysiological responses to stimuli can also differ when subjects believe they are being observed (Cacioppo, Rourke, Marshall-Goodell, Tassinery, & Baron, 1990). Every effort should be made to attenuate or equate the effects of these variables across assessment sessions.

Psychophysiological measurement can also be collected in the natural environment through the use of continuous ambulatory monitoring or discrete self-measurement of pulse or blood pressure (Pickering, 1989). Self-measurement methods can be less expensive, but should be considered in relationship to the target behavior of interest. For example, while self-measurement of blood pressure at discrete intervals may be appropriate in assessment of hypertension, such recording may not be desirable for assessing in vivo responses to emotion or anxiety eliciting stimuli or situations. A concern would be that self-measurement in these cases would entail some degree of distraction or removal from clinically relevant stimuli. For this reason, a common assessment procedure is to obtain self-recorded measurements immediately prior to and following engaging in the emotion provoking activity.

Relationship between Physiological and Other Measurements of Behavior

As mentioned earlier, assessment of physiological variables can be achieved by means other than through psychophysiological instrumentation. For example, a client can be asked to monitor the occurrence and duration of headaches or to self-report sensations experienced during panic attacks. While such methods can be more easily applied in clinical settings, their concordance with direct physiological indices is notoriously low (Margraf et al., 1987; Martin, 1961). This is true both for measures that appear more loosely related, such as self-reported anxiety and heart rate, as well as those that may seem more directly related, such as those of reported sexual arousal and penile tumescence.

It seems most useful to think of motoric, physiological, and verbal responses as "separate but equal" (Lang, 1968, 1971). Measurements should be obtained reflecting each of these response systems, provided that all three are relevant in particular circumstances. Emphasis of one response system over another should be considered only in the context of the particular circumstances. For example, the verbal reports of deviant sexual arousal given by court-referred sexual deviants may be less trustworthy than measures of genital arousal in the presence of inappropriate stimuli. Indeed, Abel, Blanchard, and Barlow (1981) reported that paraphiliacs could suppress their penile arousal by only 15–20%, even when explicitly instructed to suppress their erections to inappropriate stimuli. Conversely, if self-reported headache pain is not consistent with EMG recordings (e.g., Haynes, Griffin, Mooney, & Parise 1975), the poor correlation between perceptions of pain and actual tissue damage or stress suggests that reports of pain be given significant weight unless there is evidence of malingering.

Relationship between Multiple Psychophysiological Measures

Another common dissociation observed when applying multiple measurements within psychophysiological assessment is that of response fractionation. This refers to the often observed discordance between independent measures of a given physiological system (Andreassi, 1995; Lacey, 1967). Directional fractionation refers to more particular instances in which changes in two related measures occur in opposite directions. These phenomena have helped to fuel criticism of unidimensional theories of activation or arousal (Lacey, 1967), arguing for more multidimensional models of physiological responding. Within clinical assessment, response fractionation can be a source of confusion in the interpretation of data. One direct implication of response fractionation is that employing more than one index of physiological measurement within a single physiological system is advisable within assessment.

Clinical Applications of Psychophysiological Measurement

The application of psychophysiological theories and techniques to the study of psychopathology is steadily expanding. Psychophysiological measurement has increasingly been applied to address theoretical and research questions in the areas of schizophrenia, affective disorders, and psychopathy. Physiological measurement in areas of behavioral medicine, health psychology, and biofeedback is standard and often mandatory. Although a comprehensive review of these areas is beyond the scope of the present discussion, some examples follow. Comprehensive discussions of psychophysiological disorders and biofeedback are provided by Gatchel and Blanchard (1993) and by Schwartz (1995).

Cardiovascular Measures

Cardiovascular measures typically assess the force and rate of cardiac cycles (heartbeats), as well as the pressure of arterial blood flow and resistance of blood vessels to blood flow. Heart rate is most commonly obtained though an electro-cardiogram, which provides a record of electrical activity associated with the activity of heart atria and ventricles. Blood pressure measurements reflect the degree of pressure exerted by blood flow, on the walls of arteries or blood vessels. Pressure is assessed during diastole (relaxation and dilation of the heart) and at systole (contraction).

McGrady (1994) measured blood pressure, forehead muscle tension, finger temperature, and heart rate in patients with essential hypertension. Measures were taken in three weekly sessions prior to and following treatment consisting of group relaxation training and thermal biofeedback. When compared to a no-treatment control group, the treated group evidenced decreases in both systolic and diastolic blood pressure as well as decreased forehead muscle tension and increased finger temperature following treatment.

One area in which heart rate measures have shown promise as an adjunctive measurement strategy is in assessment of post-traumatic stress disorder. Psychophysiological assessment of Vietnam veterans during exposure to combat-related stimuli has tended to yield correct discriminations between diagnosed and undiagnosed groups in the range of 70% to 100% (cf. Blanchard, Kolb, & Prins, 1991). Additionally, psychophysiological measures can provide good discrimination between combat veterans with and without PTSD when the former are directed to attenuate their response to combat-related stimuli and to a lesser degree when the latter were directed to exaggerate their responses (Gerardi, Blanchard & Kolb, 1989).

An example of the use of a heart rate measure in the assessment of therapeutic outcome for veterans diagnosed with combat-related PTSD is provided by Frueh, Turner, Beidel, Mirabella, and Jones (1996). These authors measured heart rate at 7-minute intervals during imagined combat scenes individually constructed for each of 15 patients. This was one component of a comprehensive assessment conducted prior to and following a multicomponent behavioral treatment. The therapy included education and exposure therapy, as well as social skills and anger-management training. Decreased heart rate reactivity to imagined traumatic cues was observed following treatment and was consistent with clinician and patient ratings of symptoms and overall improvement.

Plethysmography

Plethysmography involves measurement of regional changes in blood volume. One common method of plethysmography involves measuring volume changes in a body part reflected in the displacement of air or fluids. Another form of this method, photoplethysmography, involves measuring changes in the intensity of light that is passed through or reflected back from tissue. These changes in light intensity vary with the amount of blood present in the tissue. Within clinical assessment, plethysmography is often associated with measurement of sexual arousal.

Physiological measures of male sexual arousal are typically of two types: penile circumference and volumetric measures. Penile circumference measures are of two general types: electromechanical (e.g., Barlow, Becker, Lietenberg, & Agras,

1970) and resistance strain gauges (e.g., Fisher, Gross, & Zuch, 1965). Changes in penile circumference produce mechanical changes in strain gauges that alter their electrical characteristics. These alterations are measured and can be calibrated to yield both absolute circumference or circumferential changes. Volumetric measures of penile changes are of two main types: air and water plethysmographs (Fisher, et al., 1965; Freund, 1963). In both cases, the penis is enclosed in a chamber, and changes in air or water displacement are transduced and recordings are calibrated in units of volume change.

Along with laboratory measures, recent technological advances have yielded an instrument that allows male sexual arousal to be measured in the patient's home. The RigiScan monitor (Dacomed/Urohealth, Minneapolis, MN) is a small portable measuring device worn during sleep that provides measures of both penile tumescence and rigidity. A measure of rigidity has significant clinical value because men with erectile disorder are typically distressed by changes in the firmness or rigidity of their erections.

An example of the use of plethysmography in evaluating treatment effects is provided by Johnston, Hudson, and Marshall (1992). These authors assessed erectile responses of convicted child molesters to 18 color slides of nudes. Assessments were conducted prior to and following treatment with masturbatory reconditioning. There were three male and three female slides representing each of three age groups (adult, adolescent, and child). Within each of these categories, there were three accompanying types of audiotaped descriptions (cooperative, reluctant, resisting). Erectile responses were measured with a mercury-in-rubber strain gauge (Davis, Inc.). Following assessment, subjects were instructed to produce full erections, to which circumference changes during assessment were compared. There was a significant decrease in erectile responses to child and adolescent slides following treatment (although a nonsignificant decrease in arousal to appropriate stimuli was also observed, p = .13).

Electromyography

Electromyography involves the measurement of electrical correlates of muscle activity. Measurements can be made from needle electrodes inserted into muscle tissue, but is more commonly obtained using surface electrodes that record electrical activity preceding muscular contractions that is conducted to the skin. Raw EMG recordings are typically converted to an integrated surface EMG measurement that reflects overall activity within discrete time periods.

Chung, Poppen, and Lundervold (1995) utilized forearm EMG recordings to assess the effects of behavioral relaxation training for tremor disorders in two adult males. One patient was an 86-year-old male with essential tremor (ET) and the other a 63 year-old male with Parkinson's disease (PD). Tremors were assessed in four baseline sessions prior to treatment with both forearm EMG recordings and clinical ratings. Resting tremors were assessed while the subject sat quietly. Postural tremor was assessed by asking the subject to slowly extend his arm to the front and hold this posture for twenty seconds. Finally, kinetic tremor was assessed by asking the subject to extend his arm forward, touch his nose with extended fore-finger, then return his arm to a resting position. The two patients also made daily self-ratings of tremors in a variety of activities. Decreases in forearm EMG were nonsignificant for the participant with PD; however, the participant with ET evidenced significant reduction in forearm EMG as well as clinical and self-ratings.

Activity Measurement

Another promising area in which instrumentation can be a useful addition to assessment is activity measurement. Instruments for the assessment of gross motor activity come in a number of types (e.g., pedometers, actimeters, step counters) and vary in terms of the intended bodily site of attachment (e.g., wrist or waist) (Tryon, 1993). A number of these instruments are inexpensive and widely available. A thorough review of the utility of activity monitoring and methods of instrumentation is provided by Tryon (1991).

Dunne, Sanders, Rowell, and McWhirter (1991) used pedometer readings to assess the effectiveness of cognitive-behavioral intervention aimed at the management of chronic arthritic pain in three males with hemophilia. Components of treatment included relaxation training, guided imagery techniques, and interventions aimed at targeting antecedents for pain experiences. Assessments were made before and after therapy and at six-month follow up. Each of the clients demonstrated improvements following treatment.

While instrumented activity measurement is not yet widely applied in clinical settings, there is evidence for the utility of these measures in assessing clinical populations. Tryon and Pinto (1994) have applied activity measurement to the assessment of motor excess in children with attention deficit/hyperactivity disorder (ADHD). These authors argued on the basis of their findings that activity measurement can reduce potential false positive classifications made on the basis of teacher ratings. Futterman and Tryon (1994) have also demonstrated large differences in activity levels found in inpatient and outpatient depressives, as compared to community controls, utilizing wrist-worn actometers. This line of research suggests that objective forms of activity measurement may be a potentially useful addition to treatment outcome evaluation.

Composite Measures

Given the potential drawbacks of any individual assessment method, and the variance in results across methods, the most efficient and thorough assessment approach combines multiple measures both within and across response systems. However, the same variance that necessitates multiple measures can complicate their conceptual integration into a single conclusion or index of the client's difficulties. Some attempts have been made toward more quantitative integration of multiple assessment measures in the assessment of treatment outcomes. Some examples are discussed below.

One approach to combining multiple measures is the use of composite indices as reflections of end-state functioning. For example, Craske, Street, and Barlow (1989) describe a composite measure used to assess the status of agoraphobics following exposure-based treatment. Treatment included instructions to focus on or distract from internal cues during in vivo exposures. The composite consisted of: total scores on fear and avoidance hierarchies, scores on a subjective symptom scale, reported frequency of panic, clinical severity ratings, and SUDS ratings during behavioral avoidance tests. Clients were assigned one point for each improvement over a cut-off criterion reached following treatment. High end-state status was defined by composite scores of three or greater. Turner, Beidel, and Wolff (1994) describe a similar procedure for quantifying improvements following treatment for social phobia across self-report and behavioral measures as well as clinician ratings.

The advantage of composite scores is that they provide a convenient and straightforward numerical index of the client's functioning following treatment. However, Turner et al. (1994) point out some disadvantages. Among these are (a) the lack of consensus regarding measures to include in composite scores, which mirrors the general lack of consensus in choice of outcome measures, (b) the lack of psychometric examination of these indices, and (c) that the use of arbitrary cutoffs and criteria that specify improvement on some number of the total assessment measures (e.g., improvement on three of five measures) does not allow for consideration of response profiles that may reflect important individual differences. In addition to the above limitations, the use of composites often involves the implicit assumption that each measure should carry equal weight in the quantification of improvement.

Summary

This chapter has presented a brief overview of strategies for obtaining assessment data from interviews, self-report questionnaires, rating scales, cognitive assessment, and psychophysiological measurement. The initial interview provides an invaluable opportunity to collect information from the client's self-report and from observations of the client's behavior. Hypotheses regarding a client's difficulties and potential targets for treatment can be further assessed using self-report questionnaires and rating scales. These measures can provide information regarding both broad domains of a client's functioning and particular responses that are targeted in treatment. When questionnaires are used to assess responses, information concerning antecedents and consequences can be obtained, in addition to the responses of interest. Finally, cognitive assessment and psychophysiological measurement can contribute invaluable information regarding an individual client's thought content in particular situations and regarding physiological processes that are not amenable to self-report. Examples of the use of these methods within clinical assessment have been provided. Each of these assessment strategies can be used both in the initial assessment of a client's difficulties and in careful evaluation of the progress and outcome of therapeutic intervention.

The scientist practitioner must be sensitive both to potential sources of error in measurement and to the often observed discordance in data collected using different methods. In order to maximize the accuracy and utility of assessment data, the employment of multiple-assessment methods and multiple measures within a given method is advisable. By nature, no measure is globally more direct or indirect than another. The extent to which a measure can be viewed as more direct or superior depends greatly on the nature of the response being assessed (e.g., subjective experiences versus physiological responses). Utilizing the assessment methods described in this chapter, the scientist practitioner can collect information relevant to each of the three response systems (cognitive/motoric/physiological). Each assessment method can provide unique and important information to be used in a comprehensive approach to formulating treatment goals and to evaluating the effects of therapeutic intervention.

13 Direct Observation and Self-Monitoring

SUSAN BAIRD and

ROSEMERY O. NELSON-GRAY

Introduction

A first step in behavioral assessment is identifying and defining target behaviors that are intended to be reduced if problematic or increased if adaptive. Once target behaviors have been selected, it is often helpful to quantify these specific target responses as they occur in the individual's environment. This quantification allows for a baseline assessment of the occurrence of the target behaviors, evaluation of the appropriateness of the target behaviors, monitoring of changes in the occurrence of the behaviors, and finally, evaluation of treatment effectiveness and treatment integrity. This chapter focuses on methods of observing target behaviors on a molecular level: direct observation and self-monitoring. As the names imply, the primary distinction between these two methods is the person responsible for observing and recording information about the behavior: either the identified client in self-monitoring or another person with access to the identified client (e.g., parent, significant other, therapist, trained observer) in direct observation. The first part of the chapter describes direct observation, and the second part self-monitoring.

Direct Observation

The first portion of the section on direct observation provides examples of molecular measures for quantifying observed behavior. These observations may be made by either participant or nonparticipant observers in the therapeutic environment or in the client's natural environment. A discussion follows that describes procedures for selecting observers and appropriate settings. Sometimes, by-products of behaviors or archival records of behavior are measured, rather than the behaviors directly; also, specialized coding systems are available to assist in direct observation. Examples of indirect observations are described more fully in the next section. A brief discussion follows of the use of computers to aid in direct observation. The last section deals with issues related to the accuracy of observational measures, and the reactivity of individuals being observed.

Observational Approaches

There are at least six alternative ways of quantifying observed behaviors into molecular measures. These include frequency count, discriminated operant, finite response class, duration recording, interval recording, and spot-checking. Some of these approaches differ by recording method; others differ by the dimension of behavior that is recorded. Each approach is described in turn, explaining when and for what types of behavior the particular method is most suitable, how to use the method, and examples of "real-world" utilization of each procedure.

Frequency Count   A frequency count consists of recording each occurrence of a behavior during a specific interval of time. This is the method of choice when the behavior to be observed occurs at a relatively low frequency and is discrete. For example, the parents of a child who has difficulty falling asleep at night could record the frequency with which their child called out in the night before falling asleep. The spouse of a client with various checking compulsions could record the number of times the client checked to see that the stove was turned off. Finally, a therapist could record the number of suspicious complaints a paranoid outpatient made during a therapy session. In all of these examples, the behaviors could be appropriately quantified via a frequency count. If the same unit of time is used at each sampling to record the frequency of a specific behavior, the frequency counts themselves can be compared to one another. Otherwise, if different units of time are used, rates per minute, hour, or day can be calculated and compared with each other.

There are several convenient ways in which the frequency of a behavior can be recorded in the clinical environment. It is possible to record slash marks on a piece of paper when the behavior occurs, or have prenumbered data sheets with the numbers being marked out when the behavior occurs. It is also possible to keep track of the frequency of occurrences by transferring an object (e.g., a coin) from one pocket to another. In each of these cases, a final tally of the slash marks, marked-out numbers, or coins transferred provides the frequency count. Other devices such as wrist counters, pocket counters, and hand-held counters can also be used to record frequency data. Finally, more technical and precise devices to record frequency data also exist that generally involve computerized equipment (see later section).

Discriminated Operant   A second observational method involves recording discriminated operants. These are behaviors that tend to occur only in the presence of clearly specified antecedents. In such cases, a frequency count would be inappropriate because the occurrence of the behavior depends on the occurrence of the antecedent event. Discriminated operants are reported as percentages: the number of response occurrences divided by the number of presentations of the specified antecedents.

The discriminated operant method could be used in the following marital interaction. A husband complains that when he initiates conversations with his wife about the family budget, she typically changes the topic of conversation or busies herself with household chores. In this case, the denominator of the percentage would be the number of times per week that the husband initiates conversations about finances with his wife. The numerator would be the number of times in which she responds constructively and appropriately, by discussing finances. If he initiated this topic six times in one week, and she responded appropriately two times, the weekly quantified observation measure would be 33%.

Finite Response Class A third approach to gathering observational data employs the concept of a finite response class. This approach involves reducing complex behaviors into a series of response components, each of which can be recorded. A percentage is derived by calculating the total number of components of the response class successfully completed, divided by the total possible number of components.

A finite list could be constructed of socially skilled responses that occur during encounters with acquaintances. Some items on the list might be the following: greeting the acquaintance, making eye contact, smiling, using the acquaintance's name, and asking a question of the acquaintance. A client who is working on social skills might be asked to role-play several scenes that portrayed meeting acquaintances. Each scene would be observed for the presence or absence of each socially skilled behavior comprising the finite list. A percentage could be determined by dividing the numerator, the number of responses that the client was observed to make, by the denominator, the total number of responses on the list. If several role-playing scenes are used, the percentages from each scene can be averaged to produce a single observational measure of the client's social skills for that therapy session.

Duration Recording A fourth method of collecting observational data involves recording the duration of a target behavior. This method is especially appropriate for measuring continuous, rather than discrete, behaviors. The duration method involves recording the elapsed time between the initiation and termination of the target behavior. Duration is sometimes expressed as a percentage: the numerator is the amount of time that the target behavior occurred, and the denominator is the total amount of observation time. At other times, if the unit of time is a 24-hour day, simple duration is recorded without a percentage. Duration provides a more sensitive observational measure than does a frequency count for such continuous behaviors as amount of time spent speaking during a therapy session for a socially avoidant client, time spent studying for a client having problems in school, time spent on outings away from home for an agoraphobic client, temper tantrums for a child with conduct problems, or daytime sleeping for a depressed client. The main problem with the use of the duration measure to observe continuous behaviors is that it requires near-continuous attention from the observer in order to record duration properly.

Dugan et al. (1995) assessed the use of a cooperative learning group as an instructional format for the inclusion of two students with developmental disabilities into an elementary school classroom. Using the Social Interaction Code (SIC;

Niemeyer & McEvoy, 1989), length of time spent engaging in peer interactions was one measure of successful integration into the classroom. Observations were recorded using computers, which had an inner timing device to record frequency, duration of interactions, and total duration time for peer interactions.

Latency recording is a cross between a simple duration measure and the recording of discriminated operants. In this approach, a record is made of the length of time it takes to engage in the behavior following a particular stimulus that specifies the behavior. That is, the latency between the stimulus onset or presentation and the subsequent response is recorded. An example would be the number of minutes that it takes a child to get into bed after being instructed to do so by her parent; or the number of minutes late that an adolescent is for his midnight curfew; or the number of minutes that it takes a class to become quiet after the bell has rung.

Interval Recording   A fifth observational method is interval recording (also referred to as time sampling), which is appropriate for continuous or high-frequency behaviors. In interval recording, a longer unit of time—for example, 10 minutes—is subdivided into smaller units of time, for example, 40 15-second intervals. Within each shorter interval, the occurrence of one or more preselected target behaviors is recorded. The occurrence of the target behavior(s) is usually recorded in an all-or-none fashion. There are several variations of interval recording. It is possible to record single instances of the response occurring during the interval (e.g., partial-interval sampling), responses emitted throughout the entire interval (e.g., whole-interval sampling), or responses occurring at a specific moment, such as beginning, middle, or end of the interval (e.g., momentary interval sampling) (Foster & Cone, 1986).

Time-sampling data are usually expressed as a percentage: the number of intervals in which the target behavior occurs, divided by the total number of observation intervals. In time sampling, data sheets are routinely divided into a number of intervals with coded symbols in each interval representing the preselected target behavior(s). Observers mark the coded symbols as the particular behaviors occur in the observational setting. Because this time-sampling method requires a great deal of concentration on the part of the observers, nonparticipant observers trained in the use of the observation system are generally used (see below for discussion of participant and nonparticipant observers). To facilitate observation, the termination of the short intervals can be indicated to the observers by means of an auditory signal received through headphones or an ear plug (e.g., Jayne, Schloss, Alper, & Menscher, 1994). This procedure typically involves creating cassette tapes with a recording of the auditory stimulus occurring at each programmed interval. These tapes are then placed in standard portable tape players that are used by the observers. Thus, the observer can concentrate on the behaviors being observed, rather than on a timing device.

The Family Interaction Coding System (FICS) created by researchers at the Oregon Social Learning Center (Patterson, 1977; Reid, 1978) is a widely used time-sampling observational system (e.g., Hoffman, Fagot, Reid, & Patterson, 1987; Snyder, 1983). The FICS was designed to measure both aggressive and prosocial behaviors between target subjects and their family members. Typically observation sessions occur in the home while all family members are present. Trained observers are provided with a clipboard containing a built-in auditory device that produces a signal every 30 seconds. The observer focuses on each family member for a period of 5 minutes, divided into 30-second intervals. During each 30 seconds, the observer records, on a protocol sheet, symbols from the 29-category coding system that represent the behaviors of the target person and of other family members interacting with the target person. Some examples of the behaviors recorded are giving approval, ignoring, playing, teasing, and yelling.

For more detailed discussions of time-sampling procedures reviewing topics such as appropriate length of intervals and comparisons of momentary and partial interval procedures, see Adams (1991); Edwards, Kearns, and Tingstrom (1991); Harrop, Daniels, and Foulkes (1990); Harrop, Murphy, and Shelton (1994); Kearns, Edwards, and Tingstrom (1990); Murphy and Harrop (1994); and Saudargas and Zanolli (1990).

Spot-Checking   The sixth observational procedure is spot-checking, which is appropriate for continuous or high-frequency behaviors. In spot-checking, the observer is cued by a device, such as a timer, at a designated time to record the target behavior. The spot-checks can be made at either fixed intervals or variable intervals. Note, however, that conducting spot-checks at regularly spaced intervals is technically the same procedure as momentary interval sampling described above (Foster & Cone, 1986). Because spot-checking does not require continuous observation, it is a more convenient method for recording high-frequency behaviors than either duration or interval sampling. Therefore, this procedure is recommended for a participant observer who does not have time for continuous observation due to a busy schedule, for example. Data collected through spot-checking is usually expressed as a percentage: the number of spot-checks at which the target behavior was occurring divided by the total number of spot-checks made.

Selecting Observers

Along with choosing the appropriate approach for measuring the target behavior, selecting observers is also crucial when using direct observation. Foster and Cone (1986) describe the skills necessary to ensure competent observing. These include good attention and acuity skills to identify and discriminate codable behavior. Other qualities that are important for good observers include the ability to sustain attention without habituation and the ability to take in a high load of information from the environment without confusion.

Another important factor to consider when selecting observers is whether participant or nonparticipant observers should be used. Participant observers are individuals who are naturally part of the environment in which the behavior is being observed, such as a therapist, staff member, parent, or significant other. In contrast, nonparticipant observers are individuals who are not naturally part of the environment, but enter the environment exclusively for the purpose of making observations.

On the one hand, there are several advantages to participant observers. Because participant observers are naturally part of the environment, they may be less obtrusive than nonparticipant observers and, therefore, may cause less reactivity (see more in-depth discussion in Reactivity section). In addition, participant observers are less costly and are usually able to collect data over longer periods of time, thus making observations of low-frequency behavior feasible (Foster, Bell-Dolan, & Burge, 1988). Also, there are some behaviors that because of the situation-specificity of the behavior, or low-frequency of occurrence of the behavior, it would be impractical to use nonparticipant observers. Nonparticipant observers, on the other hand, are more appropriate when the behavior is continuous, difficult to detect, and/or occurs at a high rate. Observation under these demands would be impractical for participant observers, especially in conjunction with their regular schedule (Foster, Bell-Dolan, & Burge, 1988; Foster & Cone, 1986). Some examples follow that demonstrate the use of participant and nonparticipant observers.

Participant Observers   Significant others may be requested to record the occurrences of specific target behaviors that are the focus of assessment or treatment. To illustrate, using the Parent Daily Report (PDR), parents used a checklist of 34-items to record the occurrence or nonoccurrence of their child's behavior problems (Chamberlain & Reid, 1987). In another example, spouses record the frequency of their partner's behavior, as well as the pleasingness of the behavior on a 7-point scale from neutral to extremely pleasing. Spouses recorded a total of 43 possible behaviors falling into 10 categories: companionship, affection, consideration, communication process, sex, child care, household management, financial decision making, employment/education, and self/spouse independence (Volkin & Jacob, 1981). Knox, Albano, and Barlow (1996) examined the contribution of parental involvement in the treatment of four children with obsessive compulsive disorder. As a pretreatment baseline and during treatment and follow-up phases, parents recorded each observed compulsion made by the child, the date, time, location, triggering event, and their response to the child's behavior. In a final example, a mother made a spot-check of her 10-year-old son's nocturnal thumbsucking four times each night. The father or older brother occasionally made simultaneous observations with the mother to provide reliability checks (Lewis, Shilton, & Fuqua, 1981).

Although direct observation is difficult in many applied environments, therapists are always available to be participant observers if the behavior of importance occurs in the therapeutic setting. Kohlenberg and Tsai (1991) have described a therapeutic approach known as Functional Analytic Psychotherapy (FAP), in which the client–therapist relationship is considered a social environment in which there is the potential to evoke and observe the client's clinically relevant behaviors (CRB) during therapy sessions for the purpose of immediate and natural reinforcement. Kohlenberg and Tsai (1991) describe the importance of creating a functional similarity between the therapeutic situation and the client's natural environment so that CRBs will be elicited, eventually modified, and generalizable to the natural environment. CRBs include: in-session occurrence of the problematic behavior with the goal to decrease such behavior (e.g., self-punitive statements), in-session occurrence of client improvements with the goal to increase such behavior (e.g., assertive behaviors in a dependent person), and clients' verbal interpretations of their own behavior related to the CRB (e.g., identification of situations that evoke problematic behavior). In this therapy approach, the therapist is an active participant in the therapy process intending to evoke, observe, and reinforce clinically relevant behavior. Many, if not most, therapeutic approaches target at least some behaviors that occur in the therapeutic environment, so this approach could have much wider applicability.

Nonparticipant Observers   Individuals who are not typically present in the observational setting can also be utilized to observe behavior. For example, a 5-year-old girl with Down syndrome, language delay, and speech articulation difficulties was being treated for severe behavior problems. A trained observer, seated in the corner of her school classroom, observed three to four 10-minute sessions, 5 days per week. The observer recorded, on a hand-held computer, responses per minute of disruption, communication, and independent behavior (Marcus & Vollmer, 1995).

In a double-blind, placebo-controlled medication evaluation, drug response information was obtained on a large sample of hyperactive children by direct observations in the classroom, at recess, and during lunch periods (Nolan & Gadow, 1994). For the observations in the classrooms, a modified version of the Classroom Observation Code (Abikoff & Gittelman, 1985) was used. The Classroom Observation Code consists of scoring, during 15-second intervals, the occurrence of interference, motor movement, noncompliance, nonphysical aggression, or off-task behavior. In an attempt to reduce reactivity, the children were each introduced to the observers, who were described as student teachers. Also, observers sat at the side of the classroom and child–observer contact was discouraged.

Two examples follow that utilized direct observation in the course of inpatient treatment. A 12-year-old female was admitted to an inpatient unit for the treatment of severe self-injurious behavior and self-restraint (Derby, Fisher, & Piazza, 1996). Sessions occurred in a living space on the inpatient unit, and observers using computers recorded the frequency of self-injurious (hand-to-head and knee-to-head blows) behavior and the duration of self restraint (holding onto the hand of another person with both of her hands directly in front of her knees). An 11 year old male was admitted to the hospital for the treatment of aggression and destruction of property. Sessions were observed behind a one-way mirror in which trained observers recorded the occurrence of aggressive (hitting, kicking, pinching, pulling hair, biting, throwing objects at others) and destructive (banging, kicking, ripping, breaking, or overturning objects) behaviors by pressing a key on a computer keyboard (Fisher, Piazza, & Chiang, 1996).

Nonparticipant direct observation is perhaps the most practically difficult assessment method in fee-for-service applied settings. But even here, variants may be possible through the use of students or staff. For example, the secretarial staff in a psychotherapy clinic may be able to observe client behavior in the waiting room, and students and trainees may be available to observe therapy sessions.

Coding Systems   As evidenced above, nonparticipant observers frequently utilize specialized coding systems to assist in direct observations. The following examples are samples of coding systems used to monitor mother–child interactions, marital interactions, and clients' behavior in an inpatient treatment unit, respectively. Again, these systems are less feasible in applied settings, and more widely used in large university or research sites.

The Maternal Observation Matrix (MOM) yields frequency data for maternal behaviors and mother–child interactions (Tuteur, Ewigman, Peterson, & Hosokawa, 1995). During 10-minute observations, trained observers continuously rate the quality and intensity of maternal behavior on the MOM recording form, which is divided into 20 recording intervals each of 30-second duration. During each interval, the occurrence or nonoccurrence of behaviors is scored. Examples of MOM variables are the following: mother makes a positive description of the child (e.g., "You are a smart girl"), mother makes negative request of the child (e.g., "Draw a circle right now"), mother exerts positive control over the child (e.g., mother and child laugh), and mother initiates neutral uncharged body touch (e.g., mother rests her arm on the child).

The Marital Interaction Coding System (MICS; Hops, Wills, Patterson, & Weiss, 1972), recently updated to the MICS-IV (Heyman, Weiss, & Eddy, 1995), is widely used in the assessment of marital interactions. (For a detailed discussion of the history, development, and use of the MICS, see Weiss & Summers, 1983). The MICS technique typically consists of three stages of assessment (Weiss & Summers, 1983). In the first stage, the married couple is videotaped interacting about a relationship issue. Next, coders, trained in the MICS, observe and code the videotaped interactions. Behaviors are coded along a 30-second time line, with a signal presented every 30 seconds to instruct the coder to go to the next line on the record sheet (Weiss & Summers, 1983). The updated MICS-IV consists of 31 codes, such as *excuse* (denial of personal responsibility, based on implausible or weak rationale), *disengage* (requests to postpone discussion of a topic in a neutral or positive tone), *off-topic* (statements not related to the topic discussion), and *withdrawal* (behaviors that indicate that one partner is avoiding or closing off the other). These codes are further organized into nine behavioral categories: *blame, invalidation, description, propose change, facilitation, validation, irrelevant, dysphoric affect/behavior, and withdrawal* (Heyman et al., 1995). Finally, a summary of interaction behaviors is calculated in the form of a frequency (rate per minute) of codes, which could be further reduced to the categories described above.

Ward and Naster (1991) describe an observational system that is used to monitor clients' behavior in an inpatient residential treatment unit. Unit Coverage (UC) is a system that is used 24 hours a day, 7 days a week, 52 weeks a year. This system operates by having a staff member make observations every 30 minutes using a coding system of 12 mutually exclusive behaviors. UC duty rotates hourly among staff members. Some examples of the behavioral observations are *inactive:* lying in bed with eyes closed and not responding to a single name call; *seclusion:* in a seclusion room; and *interacting:* involved in any interaction with another person, staff, or visitor. The UC was found to have acceptable reliability with a kappa coefficient of 86.2%, corrected for chance.

Training Observers

Along with the important task of selecting appropriate observers, scientist–practitioners should ensure that observers are adequately trained. Hartmann and Wood (1982) outline seven steps for training observers. These guidelines typically apply to nonparticipant observers; however, slight modifications of these procedures could be applied to participant observers. Initially, observers are asked to record behaviors without the use of a standardized observation system. The purpose of this is to demonstrate the difficulties inherent in observing, and the usefulness of using standardized observation systems to aid in making observations. Observers also study research related to direct observation and ethical issues in conducting human research. After reviewing relevant literature, observers are familiarized and trained in the particular observational system being used. This is followed by paper-and-pencil tests involving the observational system and the behaviors to be coded. The next step involves using analogue samples of behavior to train accuracy and consistency of coding. During these practice sessions, observers are required to achieve predetermined accuracy levels. In addition, observers periodically have retraining and recalibration sessions during the time they are actually using the observational coding system. Finally, observers are routinely debriefed to determine if any biases might have impacted their observations.

One reason that it is important to be specific about the training of observers is that replication across sites requires such specificity. It is not uncommon for researchers to describe how they defined the observational categories, and to report interobserver reliability, but to report limited or no information regarding observer training. Yet, just as the observers probably did not originally achieve reliability through the written definitions alone, consumers of the research will not be able to apply the defined observational categories directly. If training procedures differ, the same categories can mean different things at different sites. The specification of observer training, as well as the availability of criterion training tapes or other objective benchmarks, can avoid this possibility.

Repp, Nieminen, Olinger, and Brusca (1988) also suggest precautions to be taken to increase the level of observer performance. They stress the importance of ensuring that the coding system is not overly complicated, and that the observing schedule is not so rigorous that observers become unduly fatigued. In addition, observers should be blind to the hypothesis of the study, and should be both male and female, so as not to unintentionally bias the findings. Repp et al. (1988) also discourage any interaction between the observers, and suggest that observer accuracy should be considered. Future research examining the impact of such observer training on the reliability and/or accuracy of observations would be helpful. (See the Interobserver Agreement section for further discussions of accuracy and reliability.)

Selecting an Appropriate Environmental Context

There are many different contexts in which behaviors can be observed, including work, home, school, a therapist's office, a laboratory, clinic, or hospital. Foster, Bell-Dolan, and Burge (1988) outline factors that should be considered when choosing the appropriate setting for direct observation, including available resources, type and number of behaviors to be observed, and degree of situational-specificity of the behavior. The following section provides examples of observations that have occurred in natural environments and in analog settings.

Natural Environment   Observing behaviors in the natural environment, or in vivo observation, involves collecting data in the location where the target behavior is naturally emitted. This method has been used with a wide array of target behaviors and in a variety of settings; in addition, the data can be collected by either participant or nonparticipant observers.

A treatment outcome study examining the relative and combined efficacy of cognitive therapy, relaxation training, and graded exposure for individuals with panic disorder with agoraphobia utilized in vivo exposure as an assessment and treatment of symptoms (Michelson, Marchione, Greenwald, Testa, & Marchione, 1996). The Standardized Behavioral Avoidance Course (S-ABC; Michelson, Mavissakalian, & Marchione, 1985) provided a direct measure of agoraphobia. The S-ABC involves a one-mile walk from the front of the building to a crowded public area, and ending at a congested bus stop. Subjects were asked to walk as far as they could until their anxiety reached an intolerable level. During the graded exposure treatment, subjects were assisted by the therapist and gradually exposed to increasingly more phobic scenarios, with the aid of the therapist, for 90 minutes per session. As subjects improved, they were encouraged to engage in more demanding situations, with a gradual increase in independence on these outings.

As noted earlier, parents can observe and record the occurrence or nonoccurrence of their child's behavior problems on the Parent Daily Report (PDR; Chamberlain & Reid, 1987). The Family Interaction Coding System (FICS; Patterson, 1977; Reid, 1978) allows measurement by nonparticipant observers of both aggressive and prosocial behaviors between target subjects and their family members. The Classroom Observation Code (Abikoff & Gittelman, 1985) can be used to observe the in-class occurrence of interference, motor movement, noncompliance, nonphysical aggression, or off-task behavior.

Role-Play Situations   In some instances, the scientist practitioner may not have access to target behaviors as they occur in the natural environment. Likewise, some target behaviors may not occur in the clinic unless some special arrangements are made to prompt their occurrence. When the target behaviors involve interactions with another person, a convenient way to prompt their occurrence is through role-playing. For example, a couple having problems communicating might be instructed to interact with each other about a particular topic that causes conflict. This role-play could be observed by the therapist, who could record the frequency, for example, of the use of "you" and "I" statements, with the goal being to increase the amount of "I" statements, which tend to indicate that the speaker is taking responsibility for himself or herself, and decrease the amount of blaming and provoking "you" statements (Weeks & Treat, 1992). In addition, the role-play could be videotaped for the couples to observe their own communication skills.

As an alternative to a client's role-playing with a significant other, the client may be asked to role-play with a staff member who is assuming a role. As an example, in our clinic, a female client who was having difficulty interacting with members of the opposite sex role-played an interaction with a male therapist while her therapist observed. The therapist made a frequency count of the number of client-initiated comments and client-initiated questions, as well as recorded duration of time spent engaged in conversation. Following the interaction, the therapist gave feedback and suggestions. This procedure could be continued throughout treatment as a measure of client improvement.

Bellack, Morrison, Mueser, Wade, and Sayers (1990) used the role-play test (RPT) for the assessment of social skills in chronic psychiatric patients. The RPT consists of 12 common, social encounters involving initiating conversation, resisting unfair treatment, and expressing appreciation. The following is an example of a role-play scenario: You get on a crowded bus with two heavy packages. An acquaintance of yours, who is sitting down, sees you and offers to give you her seat saying, "Hi. Why don't you take my seat?" These role-plays are videotaped and rated on a 5-point scale for overall social skills; a 3-point scale for appropriateness of gaze, affect, and meshing (smoothness of turn-taking and conversational pauses); and a 4-point scale for speech duration.

The Simulated Social Interaction Test (SSIT; Curran, 1982; Hayes, Halford, & Varghese, 1995; Mersch, Emmelkamp, Bogels, & Van Der Sleen, 1989; Mersch, Emmelkamp, & Lips, 1991) is a standardized role-play in which a narrator describes a social situation (of eight possible scenarios) to the client and a confederate with whom the client will interact. Half of the scenes involve a male and half a female confederate who delivers a prompt to the client to initiate the interaction. Following each scene, clients, confederates, and/or independent raters rate on two 11-point scales anxiety (1 = "not at all anxious" to 11 = "extremely anxious") and skills (1 = "extremely unskilled" to 11 ="extremely skilled"). In an example of an item from the SSIT involving disapproval or criticism, the narrator reads: You are at work and one of your bosses has just finished inspecting one of the jobs that you have completed. He (the confederate) says to you, "That's a pretty sloppy job. I think you could have done better." In another example involving an interpersonal loss the narrator reads: You have had an argument with a close friend. She (the confederate) says to you, "I don't want to talk about it anymore. I'm leaving."

The RPT and SSIT are examples of structured role-plays that can be used with various clients having social-skills or other interpersonal problems. These can be used by scientist–practitioners in the assessment phase of treatment or following some intervention to monitor treatment progress. Additionally, modifications can be made in these procedures to address idiosyncratic problems that a particular client may have.

Contrived Situations   Contrived situations are designed to evoke behavior(s) that may otherwise not be emitted in the current environment (e.g., therapeutic environment). By evoking these otherwise absent behaviors, these behaviors can be observed, recorded, and, ideally, modified. In the above examples, role-playing was used to prompt the occurrence of target behaviors in the therapeutic setting. Sometimes, other stimuli must deliberately be presented so that the target behavior will occur.

One well-known type of contrived situation is the behavioral avoidance test (BAT). In the BAT, a phobic or fearful stimulus is deliberately presented to the client so that his or her fearful behavior can be measured. During the behavioral avoidance test, all three aspects of the triple-response system may be assessed: the client's motoric approach or avoidance, the client's self-report of fear, and the client's physiological responses.

In a treatment outcome study for obsessive compulsive disorder (OCD), Steketee, Chambless, Tran, Worden, and Gillis (1996) used a BAT before and after treatment to assess changes in symptomatology. Three BAT tasks were chosen based on tasks clients found difficult to complete without significant anxiety or rituals. For each task, between three and seven steps were chosen that elicited increasing levels of discomfort. Examples included touching progressively more contaminated objects without washing, and driving on progressively busier streets without checking. Measures included percentages of steps completed, subjective anxiety (*subjective units of distress [SUDS] 0–100*), avoidance [*0=no avoidance, 1=partial avoidance, to 2=complete avoidance*], and rituals [*0=no rituals, 1=some rituals, 2=extensive rituals*]. Using a BAT to assess treatment outcome for OCD demonstrated good divergent and convergent validity, and sensitivity to treatment based on effect sizes.

BATs do not have to be used with direct stimuli. For example, Hayes, Nelson, Willis, and Akamatsu (1982) showed that snake phobics respond similarly in their approach to increasingly explicit visual slides as they do to live animals. This means that a standardized environment can be created that can then be readily available in the clinical situation in the form of slides, videotapes, or other material. Computers are making such materials increasingly easy to access.

Another contrived method that has been used to elicit target responses incorporates the use of computer-generated virtual reality (VR). "VR integrates real-time computer graphics, body tracking devices, visual displays, and other sensory input devices to immerse a participant in a computer-generated virtual environment" (Rothbaum, Hodges, Watson, Kessler, & Opdyke, 1996, p. 477). Three examples follow that utilize VR in the treatment of psychological disorders.

In a total of five sessions conducted over the course of 3 weeks, a 19-year-old male diagnosed with acrophobia (particularly fear of elevators) was treated using graded exposure through the use of computer-generated VR (Rothbaum et al., 1995a). This procedure was successful in reducing his fear of heights. Similarly, Rothbaum et al. (1995b) examined the effectiveness of graded exposure using computer-generated VR in individual sessions conducted over 8 weeks for ten individuals diagnosed with acrophobia. Compared to a waiting-list control group (N=7), participants in the virtual reality group had significant decreases in anxiety, avoidance, distress, and attitudes toward heights after 8 weeks. In an attempt to extend the efficacy of VR to another disorder, Rothbaum et al. (1996) used VR and anxiety management techniques in the treatment of a 42-year-old female with a fear and avoidance of flying. The VR graded exposure consisted of seven sessions in a virtual airplane. Following treatment, the client reported decreases in all self-report measures of the fear and avoidance of flying, and was able to successfully and comfortably complete a posttreatment flight.

The authors caution that although currently the hardware required to run VR applications is too costly for the majority of practitioners, and the software composition requires specialized knowledge, such systems should eventually become more feasible (Rothbaum et al., 1996). Rothbaum et al. (1996, p. 480) also note that several companies presented VR head-mounted displays ranging in cost from $400 to $1000 (*Newsweek*, 1995, p. 52). It should also be noted that while the examples given above used this computer-generated VR for treatment purposes, this procedure could be applied to the assessment of behavior.

Exposure to anxiety-provoking stimuli is also possible through the use of video images (e.g., Anderson, Taylor, & McLean, 1996). A client's reaction to blood-injury stimuli was assessed using a 30-minute videotape consisting of injections and blood extraction procedures. The videotape showed an individual graphically describing the blood donation process, and close-up images of a variety of needle injections and blood extractions. During treatment via in-vivo exposure, the client also viewed a 15-minute video of a thoracic surgery. The video images consisted of the chest being expanded, the incision into the chest cavity, and various surgical procedures on the heart and arteries (Anderson et al., 1996).

Pros and Cons of Role-Playing and Contrived Measures   Role-playing is used primarily so that interpersonal behaviors (e.g., marital or familial interactions) may be directly observed in the clinical setting. Contrived situations are used to prompt the occurrence of the target behavior. The advantages of these measures are they allow the target behavior to occur at a time and place readily accessible to the therapist, and they permit direct observation of the client's behaviors.

The central question that arises with both role-playing and contrived situations is their concurrent validity with behavior in the natural environment. This question with regard to role-playing has been subjected to many empirical tests over the last few years and has yielded mixed results. Some studies have found an association between behavior in role-plays and naturalistic analogs (Blumer & McNamara, 1982; Merluzzi & Biever, 1987). Other researchers have demonstrated only a modest relationship between role-played and naturally occurring events (Bellack, Hersen, & Lamparski, 1979; Bellack, Hersen, & Turner, 1978). However, Bellack et al. (1990) contend that role-play tests continue to be utilized because of the low cost, convenience, and adaptability of the procedure.

Regarding the RPT, Bellack et al. (1990) found strong support for the concurrent validity and reliability of the RPT. The RPT was also found to discriminate between diagnostic groups and to correlate with other measures of social functioning. The scenes from the SSIT (Curran, 1982) appeared to be an adequate sample of social situations with good generalizability, and differentiated normals and psychiatric patients. The training procedure for the judges in the SSIT resulted in high inter-rater reliability and good test-retest reliability. Judges' ratings were also significantly related to ratings from hospital personnel and interviewers, and to self-ratings.

To make the question of external validity of role-playing even more difficult to answer, it has repeatedly been shown that role-played performance is highly sensitive to situational variables. Relatively small variations in the role-played scenes or instructions can cause relatively large changes in subjects' performance. For example, Galassi and Galassi (1976) showed that role-played assertive behavior was altered if the stimulus presentation was taped or live, and if single or multiple responses were required of the subject. Role-play behaviors are also affected by variations in role-play instructions and procedures (Frisch & Higgins, 1986; Higgins, Alonso, & Pendleton, 1979). Likewise, assertive responding in role-played situations was affected by situational parameters: whether a good friend or an acquaintance made the request, whether the requesting person expressed a reason, and whether other people heard the request (Hopkins, Krawitz, & Bellack, 1981). Since situational variables affect role-played responses, it is really not possible to determine generically the external validity of role-playing (Nelson, 1983).

Another difficulty with using either role-playing or contrived situations to yield measures of change is that the resultant responses must be scored or coded to produce quantified measures. Thus, these measures are subject to the same problems as are other observational measures, problems that are delineated below. More complete discussions of the advantages and disadvantages of role-played and contrived measures have been prepared by Becker and Heimberg (1988), Bellack (1983), Haynes and Wilson (1979), McFall (1977), and Nay (1977).

Indirect Measures

The measures described above rely on direct observations of the client's behavior. Indirect measures may also be useful, either as measures in their own right or as ancillary measures to validate more direct response measurement. There are at least two types of indirect measures of behavior, behavioral by-products and archival records.

Behavioral By-Products   Behavioral by-products are measures, not directly of the target behavior as it is occurring, but rather of the effects of the target behavior. For example, body mass index or weight is a useful measure for problems of bulimia, overeating, obesity (Williamson, Prather, McKenzie, & Blouin, 1990) and food refusal (Cooper et al., 1995). Similarly, weighing food, plates, and dishes before and after meals has been used to assess the amount of food consumed (Amari, Grace, & Fisher, 1995). In the treatment of smoking cessation, one possible measure of smoking abstinence is the amount of expired carbon monoxide as indicated by a carbon monoxide analyzer (Cinciripini, Cinciripini, Wallfisch, Haque, & Vunakis, 1996; Lichtenstein, 1982). In a similar fashion, alcohol consumption can be measured using breath samples obtained from a breath-testing device (Van Houten, Van Houten, & Malenfant, 1994). In one of our own cases, one target behavior for a retarded adult client was nail biting. Instead of counting episodes of nail biting, the client's hands were photocopied each week. The length of her nails was measured on the photocopies.

Archival Records   Another indirect measure of behavior is archival records. These are generally used as ancillary measures. Following the treatment of exhibitionists, Marshall, Eccles, and Barbaree (1991) obtained outcome data by examining official and unofficial police records to determine if any subsequent charges were filed, convictions obtained, or complaints made against sexual-offender clients. Relatedly, in an assessment of risk and protective factors on overall adjustment and reoffending in a sample of 338 12- to 17-year-old delinquent youths, one outcome measure was the reoffending index. Information for this index was obtained from the youths' client information card contained in the official criminal record at the probation offices (Hoge, Andrews, & Leschied, 1996).

In the age of managed care, a particularly important behavioral by-product is work attendance and performance. Employers pay for a large majority of private health care coverage and part of the rationale for this payment is that a healthy workforce is a productive workforce. Thus, employers are interested in evidence that a health care delivery system can improve worker retention rates; decrease tardiness, absences, and sick leave; and increase productivity. At a systems level, these behavioral by-products are as important as changes in clinically targeted behaviors or client satisfaction.

Using Computers in Direct Observation

Advances in computer technology over the last 20 years have expanded the use of computers in the arena of behavioral assessment. Computers are valuable tools for collecting interview, self-monitoring, observational, and psychophysiological data, as well as training observers, and organizing and analyzing data (Farrell, 1982, 1986, 1991). Specifically, in the area of direct observation, computers have eased the process of data collection and expanded the capabilities for analyzing data, as well as improved the accuracy and reliability of observational data. Systems exist in which different keys on the keyboard represent various target behaviors (Hile, 1991; Repp, Harman, Felce, Acker, & Karsh, 1989); as well, portable bar code labels and scanners attached to clipboards are available whereby observers scan the appropriate bar code when the target behavior occurs (Eiler, Nelson, Jensen, & Johnson, 1989). Other computerized coding systems include the Portable

Computer Systems for Observational Use (Bush & Ciocco, 1992), INTRACT (Dumas, 1988), INTERACT/BLISS systems (Dumas, Blechman, & Prinz, 1992), The Empiricist (McGrath, 1991), and DATA database (Bluestone, 1995).

Interobserver Agreement

Calculating Interobserver Agreement   It is often quite difficult to assess the actual *accuracy* of observational data. Accuracy refers to "how faithfully a measure represents objective topographic features of a behavior of interest" (Cone, 1981, p. 59). The reason for the difficulty in assessing accuracy is because there is usually no "truth" criterion available against which to evaluate accuracy (Foster & Cone, 1980). When there is (e.g., comparing observations made by human observers with a mechanical record of the same behavior), the correlation between an observational system and these criteria is a main measure of observational quality. In the absence of such "truth" criteria, the most common way of evaluating the quality of observational data is by interobserver agreement. In other words, data are collected simultaneously and independently by two observers, and their records are then compared. A high degree of consistency is taken to mean that the observers are interchangeable, and that another similarly trained observer would yield comparable results (Suen, 1988). While this does not mean that the observation system is accurate (e.g., observers could agree due to shared bias), it does reduce the importance of idiosyncratic sources of variability for particular observers. In general, accuracy involves evaluating a measurement against "reality" or "truth," while interobserver agreement involves comparing the scores of one observer against another's (Hayes, Nelson, & Jarrett, 1986).

There are two general approaches to calculating interobserver agreement. The first involves calculations of percent agreement and is used mainly for time sampling and spot-checking. The frequency matrix in Table 13.1 will aid in using the formulas to calculate the following indices of interobserver agreement: overall

TABLE 13.1   Frequency Matrix to Calculate Interobserver Agreement for Interval-Recording Systems

	Observer 2	
Observer 1	1	0
1	a	b
0	c	d

1 = occurrence of behavior
0 = nonoccurrence of behavior

percent agreement, percent occurrence agreement, percent nonoccurrence agreement, kappa (Cohen, 1960), and phi (Table 13.2). Agreement refers to both observers agreeing on the occurrence (cell a) or nonoccurrence (cell d) of the behavior (see Table 13.1). Depending on such factors as chance agreement, the relative equivalence of occurrence and nonoccurrence of behavior, and the relative frequency of target behaviors, different methods of calculating observer agreement should be used (Foster & Cone, 1986). A discussion follows that will assist scientist–practitioners in determining when to use the formulas just discussed for calculating interobserver agreement.

Overall percent agreement involves summing the agreement on the occurrence and nonoccurrence of behavior, and dividing by the sum of agreements and disagreements. It is most appropriate when the occurrence and nonoccurrence of the behavior is relatively equivalent (e.g., on-task versus off-task behavior for a child with mild attention problems). If the occurrence and nonoccurrence of the behavior are not roughly equivalent, calculations of overall percent agreement are susceptible to inflation due to high rates of chance agreement. If the occurrence of the target behavior is relatively infrequent (e.g., requests of the teacher for an overly passive, withdrawn child), the best estimate of observer agreement is *percent occurrence agreement*. This is calculated by dividing the agreements on occurrence by the sum of the agreements on occurrence and disagreements. Finally, if the agreement on nonoccurrence is important (e.g., not talking during 'quiet time' for a disruptive, impulsive child), *percent nonoccurrence agreement* can be used. This is calculated by dividing the agreements on nonoccurrence by the sum of the agreements on nonoccurrence and disagreements. The *kappa coefficient* considers the agreement on occurrence and nonoccurrence of behavior and takes into account chance agreement due to base rates. It is one of the most widely used and well-defended methods, especially now that it is available as part of common computer statistical packages. Finally, another alternative is *phi*, which is equivalent to the correlation procedure for dichotomous variables to be described next (Foster & Cone, 1986).

A second approach to calculating interobserver agreement involves the computation of correlations. The data from one observer are correlated with the data

---

TABLE 13.2   Formulas for Calculating Interobserver Agreement

overall percent agreement = a + d/a + b + c + d

percent occurrence agreement = a/(a + b + c)

percent nonoccurrence agreement = d/(b + c + d)

kappa =
$$\frac{[a - (a + c)(a + b)/(a + b + c + d)] + [d - (c + d)(b + d)/(a + b + c + d)]}{[a - (a + c)(a + b)/(a + b + c + d)] + b + c [d - (c + d)(b + d)/(a + b + c + d)]}$$

phi =
$$\frac{(a \times d)(b \times c)}{(a + c)(b + d)(a + b)(c + d)}$$

from the second observer. This correlational procedure can be used with frequency counts, latencies, and the various percentage methods noted earlier. For example, both parents agree to record the latency until their child goes to bed after being told to do so at 8:00 P.M. each evening. The mother records the following minutes over the seven evenings: 35, 16, 100, 18, 25, 70, and 15. The father records the following minutes over the seven evenings: 30, 12, 90, 15, 25, 80, and 15. These seven pairs can be used to calculate a correlation coefficient that is indicative of interobserver agreement, a correlation of .98.

For discussions about selecting an appropriate observation reliability index, see Suen, 1988 and Suen, Ary, and Covalt, 1990. Other discussions of interobserver reliability include: Ary, Covalt, and Suen, 1990; Foster and Cone, 1986; Hartmann, 1977; MacLean, Tapp, and Johnson, 1985; Repp, Deitz, Boles, Deitz, and Repp, 1976; and Stine, 1989.

Enhancing Interobserver Agreement   It has repeatedly been shown that observers produce higher interobserver agreement when they know that agreement is being assessed and calculated (Weinrott & Jones, 1984; see review by Kent & Foster, 1977). Additionally, it has been found that high agreement can best be maintained by conducting random agreement checks, as opposed to not checking agreement or informing when agreement checks will be made (Taplin & Reid, 1973). It has also been demonstrated that prior exposure to subjects to be observed results in higher interobserver agreement than observation of novel subjects (Rojahn & Warren, 1991). Therefore, in collecting observational data, the primary observer should be aware that another observer will be collecting agreement data at random, unspecified times, as well as, if possible, have prior exposure to the subject being observed.

Reactivity of Observations

Observees—that is, people under observation—sometimes act differently when they are being observed than when they are not being observed. This phenomenon, labeled observee reactivity, has been reviewed by Kent and Foster (1977) and by Kazdin (1979). Observee reactivity does not always occur, but the variables that control its occurrence have generally not been empirically determined. When observee reactivity does occur, it limits the external validity of observations. In other words, it is more difficult to generalize from observed to nonobserved occasions, or to assume that observed behavior is similar to nonobserved behavior.

The reactivity of observations was first noted when nonparticipant observers were utilized. It was hoped that the use of participant observers or of significant others would reduce or eliminate observee reactivity. In fact, the few studies performed on participant observation have shown that observee reactivity can occur, at least sometimes, even with participant observers who are usually part of the natural setting (e.g., Hay, Nelson, & Hay, 1977, 1980).

One possible solution to the reactivity of observations is to take surreptitious or unobtrusive observations of which the observee is unaware. The use of such unobtrusive measures, however, raises ethical concerns since the observee is not providing informed consent (Kazdin, 1979). Some unobtrusive measures—for example, archival records that are routinely kept—may raise fewer ethical concerns (Kazdin, 1979).

Another suggestion is to allow desensitization to the observation procedures by extending the amount or duration of observations until the data stabilize. In other words, observees ostensibly habituate or adapt to the observation procedure, thereby, reducing reactivity (Foster et al., 1988; Repp et al., 1988). For example, in videotaping emotionally or behaviorally disordered children to assess appropriate and inappropriate interactions, activity sessions with videotapes were begun two weeks before collecting baseline data (Kern et al., 1995). In a similar example, involving the assessment of the effectiveness of a treatment package for the acquisition of social behaviors in language-disabled adolescents, the videocamera used for recording observations was present in the observation setting two weeks prior to baseline recording (Rasing, Coninx, Duker, & Van Den Hurk, 1994).

Introduction to Self-Monitoring

Self-monitoring, or self-recording, refers to the client's noticing and recording the occurrences of the selected target behaviors as they happen (Nelson, 1977). This is in contrast to direct observation, in which another person notices, observes, and records the target behavior. Self-monitoring is a popular means of data collection for several reasons. One is that self-recording can be used with a wide range of clients, including clients who live alone. For these clients, no "participant observer," such as a spouse or parent, is readily available to collect data. Similarly, paid and/or trained nonparticipant observers, who could enter the home, school, or work environment to collect data on the client's behavior, are generally available only in conjunction with research projects that have their own source of funding. Self-recorders, then, are an inexpensive and practical source of data.

A second reason for the popularity of self-recording is that for some types of behaviors it is the only readily available data collection procedure. For example, some target behaviors are cognitive or covert, and hence are inaccessible to external observers. Self-monitors may also be able to provide more complete data than external observers because they are aware of a wider range of their target behaviors, as compared with the sample that an observer might witness (Kazdin, 1974a). To illustrate, self-monitoring has been used successfully to provide records of obsessional thoughts (Steketee, 1993) and urges to take medication (Elsesser, Sartory, & Maurer, 1996). Other target behaviors are private by societal convention. For instance, self-monitoring has successfully been used to keep measures of domestic sexual behavior (Hulbert & Apt, 1994) and sleeping (Morin, Colecchi, Ling, & Sood, 1995).

Self-monitoring is also a popular tool, not simply as a method for collecting data, but also as a way to manage students' behavior and academic productivity in the school classroom (Webber, Scheuermann, McCall, & Coleman, 1993). Having students self-monitor academic productivity (e.g., frequency count of correct number of math problems on a worksheet), as well as collect data on their own behavior (e.g., spot-checks of on-task behavior) have been found to have reactive effects (Nelson, 1977). These may be manifested in both decreases in inappropriate behavior, as well as increases in appropriate behavior (Gardner & Cole, 1988; Nelson & Hayes, 1981; Nelson, Smith, Young, & Dodd, 1991).

The remaining portions of the chapter outline the behaviors and devices that are appropriate for self-monitoring, as well as how scientist–practitioners can incorporate self-monitoring into their clinical work. A subsequent portion of this chapter describes strategies to enhance clients' compliance with self-recording instructions, and issues related to the accuracy of self-monitored data. The final section discusses the reactivity of self-monitoring.

What and How to Self-Monitor: Behaviors and Devices

This section provides many examples of the types of problems that have been successfully self-monitored and of the devices used for self-monitoring, as reported in the research and clinical literature. The purpose of these multiple exemplars is to provide a broad perspective so that either the particular examples or their derivations will prove useful to individual practitioners in their own work.

Frequency Count

As described in the previous section on direct observation, a frequency count is an appropriate recording procedure when the target behavior is discrete and of relatively low frequency. Frequency counts are often the product of self-monitoring procedures.

Self-recording is especially useful for recording cognitive or private behaviors. Along these lines, the frequency of obsessive-compulsive behaviors has been self-monitored. A 45-year-old male recorded the frequency of ritualistic responses that he employed to reduce fears of impending heart attack, stroke, or other physical catastrophe. These rituals involved several personal hygiene tasks which he completed each morning, usually three times. Self-monitoring included recording the frequency and duration of toothbrushing, hair-washing, and earhair cutting, as well as frequency of scale use and hemorrhoid and cortisone creme use (Acierno & Last, 1995). Frequency of sexual activity defined as any sexual encounter between spouses in which either partner experienced an orgasm was self-monitored each week by married women (Hulbert & Apt, 1994).

Several medically related problems have been monitored by self-recording. A client who was the victim of bladder cancer and his wife recorded the frequency of days the patient spent in bed due to gastrointestinal pain; perfect agreement was found between the patient's and wife's recordings (Hamberger, 1982). Patients suffering from Parkinson's disease have been taught to observe and record their own symptoms by using the Parkinson's Symptom Diary. In the diary, the frequency of loss of balance and start-hesitation (difficulty in initiating a new movement), for example, are self-monitored (Montgomery & Reynolds, 1990).

Peterson and Azrin (1992) evaluated the effectiveness of three behavioral procedures in the treatment of six subjects with Tourette's syndrome. The intervention included self-monitoring, relaxation training, and habit reversal. The self-monitoring procedure consisted first of identifying the different types of motor and/or vocal tics the subject was emitting. Then, using a hand-held counter, subjects self-recorded the occurrence of each tic, yielding a frequency count. This procedure was intended to enhance the subject's self-awareness of the type and frequency of tic that was emitted.

Self-monitoring has also been used with individuals suffering from speech disorders. Three aphasic males were taught to self-monitor speech disfluencies (Whitney & Goldstein, 1989). Potential target behaviors were audible pauses (noncontentive fillers such as "uh" or "well"), word or phrase break-offs, and word or phrase repetition. Subjects recorded the occurrence of the target behavior by pressing a counter, and the clinician unobtrusively recorded with tally marks on a paper the occurrence of the target behavior. All subjects showed a decrease in the frequency of target behaviors.

Children have also been instructed to self-monitor the frequency of specific target behaviors. A fifth-grade boy self-monitored frequency of out-of-seat behavior, which he entered on a computer. A teacher also periodically entered data on the target behavior and provided a reliability check and rewards for accurate self-monitoring (Tombari, Fitzpatrick, & Childress, 1985).

Examples of forms used by self-recorders to record the frequencies of problem behaviors are shown in Figures 13.1 and 13.2. In Figure 13.1, the client records the number of cigarettes smoked in the indicated time period of each day. In Figure

	Sat	Sun	Mon	Tues	Wed	Thurs	Fri
Midnight to 6 A.M.							
6:00 to 8:00 A.M.							
8:00 to 10: A.M.							
10:00 A.M. to Noon							
Noon to 2:00 P.M.							
2:00 to 4:00 P.M.							
4:00 to 6:00 P.M.							
6:00 to 8:00 P.M.							
8:00 to 10:00 P.M.							
10:00 to Midnight							
Daily Total							

FIGURE 13.1   **Log of cigarettes smoked**

Obsessive Thoughts and Compulsive Acts	Week of: _____ Client: _____						
	Sat	Sun	Mon	Tues	Wed	Thurs	Fri
1.							
2.							
3.							
4.							
Intensity (rate daily): 1 = Not at all 100 = Extremely							

FIGURE 13.2   Log of obsessive thoughts or compulsive acts

13.2, the idiosyncratic obsessive thoughts or compulsive acts of the client are recorded. The client records the frequency of those thoughts or acts, preferably by making a slash mark in the appropriate space, immediately after the thought or act has occurred. The average daily intensity of the obsessive-compulsive urges is entered in the bottom row.

Duration

The cases described above provide examples of measuring discrete target behaviors by self-recording the frequency of their occurrence. When each occurrence of a behavior can vary considerably in length, the behavior is more appropriately measured by self-recording the duration of each occurrence. This method was reviewed in the previous section on direct observation.

The following cases exemplify appropriate uses of self-recorded duration. A time meter was activated by a college freshman for as long as she studied, yielding a cumulative record of total hours studies (Spurr & Stevens, 1980). Compulsive patients with washing rituals were instructed to self-record the duration of each washing episode (Foa, Steketee, & Milby, 1980). In addition, the length of time spent away from home for an agoraphobic patient and the time spent alone for a client anxious about staying alone are other examples of duration measures (Kirk, 1989).

An example of a form used to self-record duration is shown in Figure 13.3. The form may be useful with a depressed person or with a disorganized person, both of whom complain of not accomplishing desired goals. The task attempted is noted in the first column, with times begun and ended in the second and third columns, respectively. In the last column, the client rates his or her satisfaction with the performance.

Self-Ratings

In practice, one of the more frequent uses of self-monitoring is to provide a measure of subjective states, as they occur in the client's natural environment or in a contrived situation. The general procedure is to have the client provide a rating of his or her subjective state at some predesignated time or during a specified situation. In this way, the client's feelings can be quantified.

Barlow, Craske, Cerny, and Klosko (1989) report the results of a treatment outcome study comparing a variety of behavioral treatments for panic disorder without agoraphobic avoidance. Cognitive therapy with exposure, applied relaxation, and a combination of these techniques proved more efficacious on several measures when compared to a wait-list control group. All clients were required to monitor daily fluctuations in anxiety, depression, and the occurrence of panic attacks. The self-monitoring was to occur in the morning, afternoon, evening, and at bedtime. At each time, clients rated their current level of anxiety, depression, and pleasantness on 0-to-8-point scales.

Clients who were undergoing benzodiazepine withdrawal were treated with either complaints management training or anxiety management training to alleviate withdrawal symptoms. Treatment effectiveness was assessed through

	Task	Time Begun	Time Ended	Rating of Satisfaction (1 to 100)
Monday				
Tuesday				
Wednesday				
Thursday				
Friday				
Saturday				
Sunday				

FIGURE 13.3 **Daily record of accomplishments**

several measures, including patients' self-recorded urges to take medication on a scale from 0 (*no urge*) to 100 (*extreme urge*) (Elsesser, Sartory, & Maurer, 1996).

Self-ratings can also be taken in contrived settings. Chambless and Williams (1995) conducted a behavioral avoidance test to assess anxiety and avoidance with agoraphobic clients. For each client, individualized challenging scenarios were presented based on client's avoidance hierarchies. Clients rated their level of anxiety during each situation according to the Subjective Units of Discomfort Scale (SUDS, range 0–100). In addition, clients received an avoidance score for each situation, with 0=complete refusal, 1=partial completion, 2=full performance.

Devices can be used to cue individuals to self-monitor at specific times. For example, readily available devices, such as cooking timers or elapsed-time indicators on wristwatches, can be used for cuing purposes. Electronic, pocket calendars can also be programmed to signal at designated times. Electronic pagers or beepers are also widely available, and therapists could call the pager to cue the client to self-monitor. Many pagers or beepers provide a tactile stimulation as a cue that is less obtrusive than an auditory signal. This device could be carried in a pocket or affixed to a belt to provide a more private cue for self-rating. Audiotapes can also be created that provide a tone (e.g., Heins, Lloyd, & Hallahan, 1986) or verbal "record" cue (e.g., Blick & Test, 1987).

An example of a form for self-ratings is provided in Figure 13.4. The form was designed for a client who was both anxious and depressed. The cue to self-rate subjective experience of anxiety or depression from 0 (*calm, not depressed*) to 100 (*panic, very depressed*) could be either at predesignated times of the day or at particularly intense emotional experiences.

Diaries

One widely used self-monitoring procedure is a diary or narration in which the client is asked to record the occurrence of the target behavior, as well as descriptions of the circumstance surrounding the occurrence. For example, it can be helpful for the client to self-record the antecedents or consequences that precede or follow the occurrence of the problem behavior, such as the cognitions or feelings that accompany the problem behavior. Along with the record of the occurrence of the target behavior, the additional information provided in the narration or diary is especially useful during the gathering of intake information, early in assessment, and prior to the development of a treatment program. When recording the occurrence of the target behavior on the diary, it is possible to utilize the procedures described above such as recording the frequency or duration of the behavior; in addition, subjective self-ratings are also often recorded in the diary. These diary entries can be made in a small notebook, on a structured form, or in an appointment calendar on a hourly basis.

One widespread use of the diary or narration is in cognitive therapies for the monitoring of automatic, negative thoughts that are believed to be maintaining the problem behavior (e.g., Beck, Rush, Shaw, & Emery, 1979; Dobson, 1988). In their seminal text on the cognitive treatment of depression, Beck et al. (1979) outline uti-

| Name: _____ | Date: _____ |

Time: _____

	0	20	40	60	80	100
Nervous						
	Calm					Panic

	0	20	40	60	80	100
Depressed						
	Not at all					Very

Time: _____

	0	20	40	60	80	100
Nervous						
	Calm					Panic

	0	20	40	60	80	100
Depressed						
	Not at all					Very

Time: _____

	0	20	40	60	80	100
Nervous						
	Calm					Panic

	0	20	40	60	80	100
Depressed						
	Not at all					Very

FIGURE 13.4   Self-ratings of anxiety and depression

lization of the Daily Record of Dysfunctional Thoughts (DRDT). The columns in the DRDT correspond to (a) the situation or event that led to the unpleasant emotion, (b) the resulting emotion, (c) the automatic thought(s) that preceded the emotion, (d) the rational response to the automatic thought or other possible interpretations to the situation, and (e) the outcome. The outcome can include a subjective rating from 0–100% of the belief in the automatic thought and ratings from 0–100 of the intensity of the subsequent emotion.

Beck et al. (1979, p. 165) describe an application of the DRDT with a 24-year-old female nurse recently discharged from a hospital. At a party a male guest asked her how she was feeling. Her automatic cognitions were: he must think I'm a basket case, and I must look really bad with resulting feelings of anxiety. Other possible interpretations were that he cares, or that he thinks I look better than before and is wondering if I feel better also.

Diaries are also used as a way to self-monitor behavior in dialectical behavior therapy (DBT) for the treatment of borderline personality disorder (Linehan, 1993a, 1993b). For example, on DBT diary cards, clients list the occurrence of target behaviors (e.g., use of prescription medication, parasuicidal acts), including the frequency of the behavior, amount of medication consumed, and the degree to which desired self-harm was present. Clients also record ratings of whether behavioral skills were used to cope in these situations and the usefulness of the skills.

Other problem areas that have been monitored using diaries are sleep patterns. Five clients with chronic insomnia received cognitive behavior therapy and gradual tapering of medication to facilitate discontinuance of benzodiazepine dependence. A multiple baseline design was utilized to assess treatment effects. Clients self-monitored sleep patterns using daily sleep diaries that were kept pretreatment, during treatment, and posttreatment. From the diaries, latency to onset of sleep, wakefulness after onset of sleep, early morning wakenings, total wake time, total sleep time, number of nocturnal wakenings, time in bed, and sleep efficiency were measured (Morin et al., 1995).

Panic attacks are also conveniently monitored with diaries, as demonstrated in a treatment study of panic disorder with agoraphobia (Bouchard, Gauthier, Laberge, French, Pelletier, & Godbout, 1996). Daily panic attack diaries provided information on the date and time of the panic attack, duration from the onset of the symptoms to the reduction of anxiety, a description of the cues (or lack of cues) that preceded the attack, ratings of anxiety severity on a scale from 1–10, and a list of the occurrence of the 13 symptoms of panic attacks identified in DSM-IV. Similar daily diaries are widely used to self-monitor frequency, duration, and severity of panic symptoms (Arntz & Van Den Hout, 1996; Barlow, 1988; Clark, 1989; Gould & Clum, 1995; Williams & Falbo, 1996).

The self-monitoring of thoughts has also been used in a cognitive-behavioral program for the treatment of bulimia nervosa (Hsu, Santhouse, & Chesler, 1991). One aspect of the treatment program consists of client's completing a cognitions monitoring sheet. On this sheet, the client records the date and situation when he or she has the urge to binge or vomit. The labeled automatic thought and accompanying emotion, with intensity level from 1–10, is recorded. The client also records a rational response or plan of action until feeling comfortable with accompanying emotions, including intensity level, and the result or outcome is recorded.

The above example of daily records and diaries has been used with adult clients. Beidel, Neal, and Lederer (1991) assessed the feasibility and reliability of a daily diary completed by children to self-monitor anxiety. The diary consisted of recording the date, time, location, situation eliciting anxiety, and the behavioral response. The children completed either a printed or a picture version of the diary. The children also recorded their level of distress using the Self-Assessment Manikin (SAM; Lang & Cuthbert, 1984), which is a picture representation that depicts increasing levels of anxiety on a 5-point rating scale. Beidel et al. (1991) found compliance to diary completion ranging from 7.9 to 11.5 days for the two weeks tested. Six-month test-retest reliability was modest and approached statistical significance; however, there was little correspondence at the two assessments for severity of distress as measured by SAM. The fifth- and sixth-grade children did not differ in mean number of events recorded, or compliance for the picture or printed version of the diaries; however, the third- and fourth-grade children appeared to find the picture version more appealing. They concluded that overall children will comply with this self-monitoring procedure and that the data are reliable, but that the way in which information is presented may affect the frequency of recording.

Figure 13.5 is an example of a form that provides diary-like information about assertive behavior. The client records the antecedents in the first two columns, labeled "Date and time" and "Situation." The third and fourth columns are used to

Date and time	Situation	What were you thinking?	What did you do?	How did it end?	How do you feel about the outcome? 0 = very dissatisfied 10 = very satisfied	What should you have done?

FIGURE 13.5   Diary of assertiveness situations

record motoric and cognitive behaviors or responses to those situations. The fifth and sixth columns are used to self-record consequences, and the last column is used to record behavioral alternatives.

Computers and Self-Monitoring

Advances in computer technology over the last 20 years have expanded the use of computers in the arena of behavioral assessment. Computers are valuable tools for collecting interview data, self-monitoring, collecting observational data, psychophysiological data, and training, organizing, and analyzing data (Farrell, 1986, 1991).

As mentioned previously, Tombari et al. (1985) utilized a computerized self-monitoring system to target a fifth-grade boy's out-of-seat behavior. Each day the child entered on the computer his target behavior and goal for that behavior. He then recorded, for example, the frequency of out-of-seat behavior. At the end of the day, if he met or exceeded his goal, he was rewarded with 5 minutes of a video game on the computer.

Agras, Taylor, Feldman, Losch, and Burnett (1990) used a small hand-held computer for treating obesity. Each day clients enter goals for caloric intake and amount of exercise. Clients then record throughout the day the number of calories consumed and amount of time spent exercising. The computer could also be used to plan meals. Summary graphs were produced providing direct feedback on daily calorie intake, exercise, and weight.

Using Self-Monitoring with Clients

There are a variety of steps that can ensure that self-monitoring is successful when used with clients.

Provide Training

Before using self-monitoring with clients, clinicians have a responsibility to ensure that clients understand the rationale for self-monitoring, as well as to make sure clients are proficient at identifying target behaviors and use the proper procedure for recording behavior. Therapists should not assume that self-monitoring is self-explanatory; instead, the procedure should be explicitly taught and demonstrated. Mahoney (1977) provided suggestions for training in self-monitoring: (a) give explicit definitions and examples of target behaviors; (b) give explicit self-monitoring instructions; (c) model the appropriate use of the self-monitoring device; (d) ask the client to repeat the target definitions and self-monitoring instructions; and (e) have the client self-monitor several occurrences of the target behavior as described by the therapist.

As mentioned, Bouchard et al. (1996) used a panic attack diary with individuals diagnosed with panic disorder accompanying agoraphobia. To ensure proper use and compliance with the panic attack diary, subjects were seen individually and were given detailed information, through a written description and graphic representation of a panic attack, on how to identify, monitor, and distinguish a panic attack from simply anxiety and stress. Subjects were also given information on the importance of diaries and accurate diary completion, as well as explicit instructions regarding carrying the dairy with them at all times and recording information as soon as possible after the panic attack.

Clinicians should provide the client with the appropriate forms or small notebooks and/or counting or timing devices, rather than asking clients to obtain these devices or notebooks from a store or create the form on their own. Also, the therapist must select a self-recording response that is suitable to the problem at hand. To illustrate, it is not appropriate to measure continuous behaviors by means of frequency counts. Similarly, the self-recording device must be appropriate for the type of self-recording; that is, counting devices for frequency, timing devices for duration, diaries for antecedents–behaviors–consequences. The self-monitoring device should be sufficiently obtrusive to remind the client to self-record and sufficiently unobtrusive to save the client from public questions (Nelson, 1977).

Modification can be made in self-monitoring procedures to suit particular clients. For example, a client who refrains from self-monitoring each occurrence of a high-frequency behavior over an entire day may successfully self record when asked to do so for selected shorter daily intervals. For clients who cannot or will not write, alternative self-recording methods include talking into a tape recorder or telephoning the clinic (Mahoney, 1977). If a client does not self-monitor in the natural environment, perhaps he or she could self-monitor in the clinic, if the target behaviors are suitable. For example, clients with ruminative thoughts were asked to count the frequency of the thoughts' occurrence within therapy sessions (Leger, 1979).

Compliance

Compliance is another factor that is important for clinicians to consider when using self-monitoring with clients. The probability that a client will collect self-monitored data is enhanced if he or she makes a verbal and/or written commitment to collect such data (Kanfer, Cox, Greiner, & Karoly, 1974; Levy, 1977), and if the client provides a monetary deposit that is refunded contingent on self-monitoring (Ersner-Hershfield, Connors, & Maisto, 1981). Therapists can build in compliance with the self-monitoring assignment by requesting that the client mail self-monitored data on a daily basis (Harmon, Nelson, & Hayes, 1980), or the therapist may make telephone calls to the client at random times to obtain self-monitored data (Christensen, Johnson, Phillips, & Glasgow, 1980).

The first step if a client is not complying with self-monitoring instructions is to explore possible reasons for the noncompliance. Shelton and Levy (1981) suggest three possible reasons for noncompliance: (a) the client lacks the necessary skills and knowledge to complete some or all of the tasks in the assignment; (b) the client has cognitions that interfere with the completion of the assignment; and (c) the client's environment elicits noncompliance. Each of these hypotheses can be explored, and appropriate remedial action taken. Similarly, Shelton and Ackerman (1974) suggest two common reasons for noncompliance: (a) lack of explicit instructions and (b) lack of perceived relevance of the assignment to the client's needs. Appropriate remediation in the latter case may be to reemphasize the rationale for the task and to reassign it. Alternatively, the therapist may decide that self-monitoring is not an appropriate procedure for this particular client and other procedures may be used (e.g., direct observation).

Haley (1978) has argued that once a task has been assigned, the therapist should challenge the client if he or she has not completed it, regardless of the reasons given for noncompliance. In a similar vein, Mahoney (1977) outlines steps that he follows if a client fails to comply with self-monitoring instructions. Some of these include making the importance of self-monitoring more obvious by asking the client retrospective questions. In other words, the therapist asks the client questions about his or her activities or behaviors during the previous week that the client is unlikely to be able to answer without consulting written self-monitored data. Mahoney also tries to shape self-recording by first assigning self-monitoring tasks that place minimal demands on the client, and then by gradually increasing those demands.

The particular characteristics of the client and the case should be considered when deciding how to handle noncompliance. If the therapist genuinely believes that self-monitoring data are needed and useful, noncompliance is a clinically relevant behavior that can be handled as any other significant issue(s) impacting treatment (e.g., missing sessions, failing to raise difficult problems in therapy). But self-monitoring may not be appropriate for all clients. Some clients may be in such distress that self-monitoring might compound their stress by calling undue attention to undesirable behaviors; other clients may not have the skill needed to understand and carry out the task. Noncompliance may be an indication that one or more of such barriers is at play, and consideration should be made as to the appropriateness of self-monitoring with such clients. In the same way, noncompliance may be handled differently with a client who is not self-monitoring because the monitoring of behaviors is distressful, as compared to the client who is noncompliant because of resistance to therapy. Determination of which factors are at play with the client is the challenge to the scientist–practitioner.

Accuracy of Self-Monitoring

There are several factors that appear to increase the accuracy of self-monitoring. They include providing training in self-monitoring, making self-recorders aware that accuracy is being monitored, providing reinforcement for accurate self-monitoring, minimizing concurrent responding, self-recording after each response, and monitoring one behavior only.

Providing training in self-monitoring appears to increase accuracy. Nelson, Lipinski, and Boykin (1978) trained four retarded adolescents to self-record their appropriate classroom verbalizations. The self-recording accuracy of the trained adolescents (.914) was significantly higher than that of less trained adolescents (.784). Similarly, Bornstein, Mungas, Quevillon, Kniivila, Miller, and Holombo (1978) found that training self-recorders (by having them either self-monitor specific aspects of their own tape-recorded speeches or monitor specific aspects of others' tape recorded speeches) produced more accurate self-monitored data than not training self-recorders. Attempts have even been made to train self-recorders to self-monitor their cognitive responses (Meyers, Mercatoris, & Artz, 1976); however, there are obvious difficulties in determining the accuracy of self-monitored cognitions (Nelson, 1977).

Self-recording is more accurate when self-observers are aware that their accuracy is being monitored than when their accuracy is monitored covertly (Lipinski & Nelson, 1974; Nelson, Lipinski, & Black, 1975; Lipinski, Black, Nelson, & Ciminero, 1975). In day-to-day clinical work, the accuracy of self-monitored data can be evaluated against concurrent data collected by another person. For example, the accuracy of adolescents' self-monitored eating and exercising was evaluated against parental data that were collected one day per week (Cohen, Gelfand, Dodd, Jensen, & Turner, 1980). Likewise, the frequency of the daughter's stomachache complaints were recorded each day by both the mother and the daughter (Miller & Kratochwill, 1979). For a group of children in a classroom situation, high levels of self-recorded accuracy were maintained when the accuracy of only one child per group was checked per day (Hundert & Bucher, 1978). Similarly, for a group of children in a camp, high levels of self-recorded accuracy were maintained when the accuracy of the group was checked on an average of every third day (Layne, Rickard, Jones, & Lyman, 1976).

The observers do not have to collect data as often as the self-recorders to enhance the accuracy of self-recording, given the proviso that the self-recorder knows that his or her accuracy can be checked on a random basis. For example, as a check on a self-recorder's accuracy, a spouse or roommate monitored the self-recorder's latency to sleep onset, with the client's knowledge and consent, on at least one night in a study that lasted for 9 weeks. The spouse or roommate monitored the subject's sleep behavior by checking to see that the subject's eyes were closed, there was no voluntary movement for 10 minutes, and there was no response after whispering the subject's name (Turner & Ascher, 1979).

Self-recorders can also be informed that their accuracy can be checked against mechanical devices or behavioral by-products. For example, the accuracy of self-monitored food consumption could be assessed against weight for obese, anorexic, or bulimic clients. Similarly, the accuracy of self-monitored study time could be assessed against grades. Obviously, there is not a one-to-one correspondence between the self-monitored behavior and its by-product; but perhaps the awareness of this potential accuracy check may enhance the accuracy of self-recording.

Another variable that has consistently been found to influence the accuracy of self-recorded data is reinforcement for accuracy. Risley and Hart (1968) found that the initially low correspondence between children's verbal and nonverbal behavior could be improved when reinforcement was made contingent on correspondence, as evaluated by external observers. Fixsen, Phillips, and Wolf (1972) found that the .76 level of agreement between peer and self-reports of room cleanliness could be enhanced to .86 through contingent reinforcement. Just as positive reinforcement has been demonstrated to increase the accuracy of self-recorded data, punishment or threats of punishment have also been reported to minimize discrepant ratings (Hundert & Batstone, 1978; Seymour & Stokes, 1976). Rewards for accurate self-recorded data that are available to therapists include praise and reduction in session fees. Monetary deposits can also be refunded contingently.

The accuracy of self-recording diminishes when clients perform other tasks in addition to self-recording (Epstein, Webster, & Miller, 1975; Epstein, Miller, & Webster, 1976). Although it is impractical for clients to limit their other ongoing activities completely, perhaps overly busy clients could be asked to clear their calendars or to refuse new commitments for the duration of therapy. Alternatively, self-monitoring could be limited to less rushed times of the day, with the proviso that the target behavior occurs at those times in a typical manner.

Hayes and Cavior (1980) reported that the accuracy of self-monitoring was significantly higher when only one target behavior was self-monitored than when either two or three behaviors were self-monitored. Based on this investigation, it seems advisable to ask clients to self-monitor only one target behavior to attain maximal accuracy. Perhaps good accuracy could be maintained if other behaviors to be self-monitored were gradually introduced.

Duration of Self-Recording

One reasonable question is that of how long clients can be asked to self-monitor without decreasing their accuracy. The answer seems to be for a reasonably long duration of time, given favorable conditions. That is, it appears that accuracy can be maintained across time, given that additional safeguards are employed.

Subjects were asked to self-record the frequency of face touching behavior in a classroom situation for either 2 weeks or 9 weeks (Nelson, Boykin, & Hayes, 1982). The accuracy of their self-recording was comparable for both groups. The long-term group did not display decreases in accuracy across time. However, these subjects were aware that they were participating in an experiment, and were required to turn in their self-recorded data at the end of each class period.

Conversely, Boren and Jagodzinski's subjects (1975), who were all parents, were left to self-record independently following an initial period of contact with therapists. In a follow-up interview eight months after the cessation of weekly contacts with the therapists, only one parent out of 20 was collecting data of any kind. Most had stopped data recording soon after the cessation of regular monitoring. It seems necessary, therefore, for the therapist to show continued interest in the self-recorded data and reward the client's efforts. Also, incorporating these data into the therapy session could help with more continuous quality improvement and suggest changes in treatment strategies.

The Reactivity of Self-Monitoring

When clients self-record, the behavior that is being self-recorded changes in frequency. This phenomenon is well established and has been termed the *reactivity of self-monitoring* (Kazdin, 1974b; Nelson, 1977). Generally, this reactivity is therapeutic; that is, the direction of the reactive behavior change is in a desirable direction.

Three alternative explanations for this behavior change have been presented. Snider (1987) posits that self-monitoring creates a situation of increased *awareness,* which alone creates behavior change. This theory contends that internal cognitive processes of "awareness" lead to the regulation of one's behavior (Meichenbaum, 1983). Alternatively, it is possible that the behavior of self-monitoring acts as a discriminative stimulus for behavior that is under the control of external consequences (Rachlin, 1974). In other words, internal consequences are not needed for the occurrence of behavior change. Similarly, Nelson and Hayes (1981) suggest that the procedures involved in self-monitoring (e.g., instructions, training, monitoring device), not the targeted responses, act as antecedents that cue "the external consequences that produce reactivity" (Nelson & Hayes, 1981, p. 8). A third explanation combines a covert, cognitive component and the external antecedent of self-monitoring (Kanfer, 1977). Self-monitoring "results in self-evaluation (a judgment about performance), which, in turn, results in covert self-reinforcement or self-punishment. The self-monitoring cues the individual to engage in the covert self-evaluation, and the covert consequences motivate the behavior change" (Webber et al., 1993, p. 39).

An example of reactivity is provided by Clum and Curtin (1993). These authors demonstrate the validity and reactivity of a self-monitoring scale of suicidal ideation with a sample of severely ideating college students who volunteered for a treatment study. The self-monitoring scale measures strength, duration, and level of control of suicidal ideation. Strength was measured on a 4-point scale, ranging from 0 *(none)* to 3 *(strong),* following the prompt, "Today I have had thoughts of making an actual suicide attempt." Duration was assessed on a 5-point scale, ranging from 0 *(not at all)* to 4 *(continuously),* following the prompt, "Today I have thought about making an active suicide attempt." Control was measured from 0 *(strong; no doubt I had control)* to 3 *(absent; no sense of control)* with the prompt, "Today I have felt that the control I have over making an active suicide attempt was . . . ." Clum and Curtin (1993) found that college students with severe suicidal ideation had decreases in suicidal ideation over a two-week period between initial assessment and pretreatment. During this time period, all subjects were instructed to do was self-monitor—there was no active intervention at this time. The authors suggest that the decreases in ideation could be due to self-monitoring alone (although they caution that it might also be due to the expectation of starting treatment). They suggest that "self-monitoring of suicide ideation may serve the same function as self-monitoring of other psychological symptoms, namely, as a form of treatment early in the assessment/treatment process" (Clum & Curtin, 1993, p. 384).

For the clinical goals of scientist practitioners, the reactivity of self-monitoring is generally desirable. The reactivity enhances therapeutic effectiveness. For the research goals of scientist practitioners, the reactivity of self-monitoring must be considered in making appropriate interpretations of results. If a scientist practitioner is conducting single-subject research in which one measure is self-monitored data, any changes from A (baseline) conditions to B (treatment) conditions must be interpreted as due to an interaction between self-monitoring and any other treatment ingredient. If self-monitoring is used, changes cannot be solely attributed to other treatment ingredients.

Summary

Direct observation and self-monitoring are two methods that can be used to quantify specific target behaviors on a molecular level as they occur in the individual's environment. This quantification initially allows a baseline assessment of the occurrence of the target behaviors, evaluation of the appropriateness of the target behaviors, monitoring of changes in the occurrence of the behaviors, and finally, evaluation of treatment effectiveness and treatment integrity. All of these are important data for the scientist practitioner. The primary distinction between direct observation and self-monitoring is the person responsible for observing and recording information about the behavior: either the identified client (self-monitoring) or another person other than the subject who has access to the client (e. g., parent, significant other, therapist, trained observer).

The scientist practitioner must make careful considerations before using either direct observation or self-monitoring. With either self-monitoring or direct observation, it is important to use the most suitable measuring method for the particular target behaviors. As examples, duration should be used for continuous behaviors and a frequency count for discrete, low-frequency behaviors. In direct observation, it is also important to consider whether participant or nonparticipant observers would be more appropriate. In fee-for-service applied settings, nonparticipant direct observation is perhaps the most practically difficult assessment method. But even here, variants may be possible through the use of students or staff. With direct observation, it is also important to consider whether observations should be taken in the client's natural environment or in the therapeutic environment. When using self-monitoring, scientist practitioners must consider how to most effectively incorporate self-monitoring into their work with clients and how to enhance clients' compliance with self-recording. Finally, in either direct observation or self-monitoring, accuracy and reactivity must be carefully considered in making appropriate interpretations of results.

With the age of managed care and other health care regulations, direct observation and self-monitoring become even more critical as a way to justify the effectiveness of particular therapeutic techniques with clients. Direct observation and self-monitoring provide methods for obtaining concrete raw data as to the initial functioning of the client through quantification of target behaviors, as well as provide data regarding changes in behaviors over the course of treatment. Such raw data are often required by managed care companies before reimbursement is authorized (Cantor, 1996; 1997). This chapter has outlined basic methods of quantifying clients' behavior, providing a broad overview of both fairly simple and straightforward methods of self-monitoring, as well as some that are more complex, such as the technical computer-based coding systems. Some of what has been presented, such as these highly technical computer coding systems, may be of less utility for practitioners in applied settings. However, the majority of the methods are intended to be easily implemented by the scientist practitioner.

REFERENCES

Abel, G. G., Blanchard, D. B., & Barlow, D. H. (1981). Measurement of sexual arousal in several paraphilias: The effects of stimulus modality, instructional set, and stimulus content on the objective. *Behaviour Research and Therapy, 19,* 25–33.

Abikoff, H., & Gittelman, R. (1985). Classroom observation code: A modification of the Stony Brook code. *Psychopharmacology Bulletin, 21,* 901–909.

Abrahams, M. J., & Whitlock, F. A. (1969). Childhood experience and depression. *British Journal of Psychiatry, 115,* 883–888.

Achenbach, T. M., & Edelbrock, C. S. (1983). *Manual for the child behavior checklist and revised child behavior profile.* Burlington: University of Vermont.

Acierno, R., & Last, C. G. (1995). Outpatient treatment of obsessive compulsive disorder by self-directed graded exposure and response prevention. *Psychotherapy in Private Practice, 14*(3), 1–11.

Adams, R. M. (1991). Momentary and partial interval time sampling: A reply to Harrop, Daniels, and Foulkes (1990). *Behavioural Psychotherapy, 19*(4), 333–336.

Adler, P. T. (1972). Will the Ph.D. be the death of professional psychology? *Professional Psychology, 3,* 69–72.

Agras, W. S., & Berkowitz, R. (1980). Clinical research in behavior therapy: Halfway there? *Behavior Therapy, 11,* 472–488.

Agras, W. S., Chapin, H. N., & Oliveau, D. C. (1972). The natural history of phobia. *Archives of General Psychiatry, 26,* 315–317.

Agras, W. S., Kazdin, A. E., & Wilson, G. T. (1979). *Behavior therapy: Toward an applied clinical science.* San Francisco: W. H. Freeman.

Agras, W. S., Leitenberg, H., & Barlow, D. H. (1968). Social reinforcement in the modification of agoraphobia. *Archives of General Psychiatry, 19,* 423–427.

Agras, W. S., Leitenberg, H., Barlow, D. H., & Thomson, L. E. (1969). Instructions and reinforcement in the modification of neurotic behavior. *American Journal of Psychiatry, 125,* 1435–1439.

Agras. W. S., Schneider, J. A., Arnow, B., Raeburn, S. D., & Teich, C. F. (1989). Cognitive-behavioral and response-prevention treatments for bulimia nervosa. *Journal of Consulting and Clinical Psychology, 57,* 215–221.

Agras, W. S., Taylor, C. B., Feldman, D. E., Losch, M., & Burnett, K. F. (1990). Developing computer-assisted therapy for the treatment of obesity. *Behavior Therapy, 21,* 99–109.

Akutsu, P. D., Snowden, L. R., & Organista, K. C. (1996). Referral patterns in ethnic-specific and mainstream programs for ethnic minorities and whites. *Journal of Counseling Psychology, 43,* 56–64.

Alba, J. W., & Hasher, L. (1983). Is memory schematic? *Psychological Bulletin, 93,* 203–231.

Albee, G. W. (1970). The uncertain future of clinical psychology. *American Psychologist, 225,* 1071–1080.

Albee, G. W., & Ryan-Finn, K. D. (1993). An overview of primary prevention. *Journal of Counseling and Development, 72,* 115–123.

Allen, J. P., Hauser, S. T., Eickholt, C., Bell, K. L., et al. (1994). Autonomy and relatedness in family interactions as predictors of expressions of negative adolescent affect. Special Issue: Affective processes in adolescence. *Journal of Research on Adolescence, 4*(4), 535–552.

Allen, K. E., Hart, B., Buell, J. S., Harris, F. R., & Wolf, M. M. (1964). Effects of social reinforcement on isolate behavior of a nursery school child. *Child Development, 35,* 511–518.

Aman, M. G., Teehan, C. J., White, A. J., Turbott, S. H. (1989). Haloperidol treatment with chronically medicated residents: Dose effects on clinical behavior and reinforcement contingencies. *American Journal of Mental Deficiencies, 93,* 450–460.

Amari, A., Grace, N. C., & Fisher, W. W. (1995). Achieving and maintaining compliance with the ketogenic diet. *Journal of Applied Behavior Analysis, 28,* 341–342

American Psychiatric Association. (1994). *Diagnostic and statistical manual of mental disorders* (4th ed.). Washington, DC: Author.

American Psychiatric Association Guidelines Steering Committee and the Office of Research.

(1993). *Development of a psychiatric practice research network: Overview of the purpose and a proposed approach.* Unpublished manuscript.

American Psychological Association. (1966). *Standards for educational and psychological tests and manuals.* Washington, DC: Author.

American Psychological Association Task Force on Psychological Intervention Guidelines. (1995, February). *Template for developing guidelines: Interventions for mental disorders and psychosocial aspects of physical disorders.* Washington, DC: American Psychological Association.

Anderson, K. W., Taylor, S., & McLean, P. D. (1996). Panic disorder associated with blood-injury reactivity: The necessity of establishing functional relationships among maladaptive behaviors. *Behavior Therapy, 27,* 463–472.

Andreassi, J. L. (1995). *Psychophysiology: Human behavior and physiological response* (3rd. ed.). Hillsdale, NJ: Erlbaum.

Andrews, G. (1995). Best practices for implementing outcomes management. *Behavioral Healthcare Tomorrow, 4*(3), 19–21, 74–75.

Andrews, G., Crino, R., Hunt, C., Lampe, L., & Page, A. (1993). *A list of essential psychotherapies.* Unpublished manuscript.

Arean, P. A., Perri, M. G., Nezu, A. M., Schein, R. L., Christopher, F., & Joseph, T. X. (1993). Comparative effectivenss of social problem-solving therapy and reminiscence therapy as treatments for depression in older adults. *Journal of Consulting and Clinical Psychology, 61,* 1003–1010.

Arnkoff, D. B., & Glass, C. R. (1982). Clinical cognitive construct: Examination, evaluation, and elaboration. In P. C. Kendall (Ed.), *Advances in cognitive-behavioral research and therapy, 1* (pp. 1–34). New York: Academic Press.

Arnkoff, D. B., & Glass, C. R. (1989). Cognitive assessment in social anxiety and social phobia. *Clinical Psychology Review, 9,* 61–74.

Arntz, A., & Van Den Hout, M. (1996). Psychological treatments of panic disorder without agoraphobia: Cognitive therapy versus applied relaxation. *Behaviour Research and Therapy, 34,* 113–121.

Ary, D., & Suen, H. K. (1983). The use of momentary time sampling to assess both frequency and duration of behavior. *Journal of Behavioral Assessment, 5,* 143–150.

Ary, D., Covalt, W. C., & Suen, H. K. (1990). Graphic comparisons of interobserver agreement indices. *Journal of Psychopathology and Behavioral Assessment, 12,* 151–156.

Asch, S. E. (1946). Forming impressions of personality. *Journal of Abnormal and Social Psychology, 41,* 258–290.

Ascherman, E., Mantwill, M., & Kohnken, G. (1991). An independent replication of the effectiveness of the cognitive interview. *Applied Cognitive Psychology, 5,* 489–495.

Attkinson, C. C., & Zwick, R. (1982). The Client Satisfaction Questionnaire: Psychometric properties and correlations with service utilization and psychotherapy outcome. *Evaluation and Program Planning, 5,* 223–237.

Auerbach, R., & Kilmann, P. R. (1977). The effects of group systematic desensitization on secondary erectile failure. *Behavior Therapy, 8,* 330–339.

Auld, F., & Hyman, M. (1991). *Resolution of inner conflict: An introduction to psychoanalytic therapy.* Washington DC: American Psychological Association.

Ayllon, T., & Azrin, N. (1968). *The token economy.* New York: Appleton-Century-Crofts.

Azrin, N. H. (1977). A strategy for applied research: Learning based but outcome oriented. *American Psychologist, 32,* 140–149.

Azrin, N. H., Bersalel, A., Bechtel, R., Michalicek, A., Mancera, M., Carroll, D., Shuford, D., & Cox, J. (1980). Comparison of reciprocity and discussion-type counseling for marital problems. *American Journal of Family Therapy, 8,* 21–28.

Azrin, N. H., Nunn, R. G., & Frantz, S. E. (1980). Habit reversal vs. negative practice treatment of nail-biting. *Behavior Research and Therapy, 18,* 281–285.

Azrin, N. H., Nunn, R. G., & Frantz-Renshaw, S. (1980). Habit reversal treatment of thumbsucking. *Behavior Research and Therapy, 18,* 395–399.

Baer, D. M., Wolf, M., & Risley, T. R. (1968). Some current dimensions of applied behavior analysis. *Journal of Applied Behavior Analysis, 1,* 91–97.

Bakan, D. (1966). The test of significance in psychological research. *Psychological Bulletin, 66,* 423–437.

Balkom, A. J. L. M., van, Oppen, P., van, Vermeulen, A. W. A., Nauta, N. C. E., Vorst, H. C. M., & Dyck, R. van (1994). A meta-analysis on the treatment of obsessive compulsive disorder: A comparison of antidepressants, behaviour and cognitive therapy. *Clinical Psychology Review, 14,* 359–381.

Bandura, A., & Adams, N. E. (1977). Analysis of self-efficacy theory of behavioral change. *Cognitive Therapy and Research, 1,* 287–310.

Barber, J. P., & Crits-Christoph, P. (1993). Advances in measures of psychodynamic formulations.

Journal of Consulting and Clinical Psychology, 61, 574–585.

Barker, C., Pistrang, N., Shapiro, D. A., Davies, S., & Shaw, I. (1993). You in mind: A preventative mental health television series. *British Journal of Clinical Psychology, 32,* 281–293.

Barlow, D. H. (1977). Behavioral assessment in clinical settings: Developing issues. In J. D. Cone & R. P. Hawkins (Eds.), *Behavioral assessment: New directions in clinical psychology.* New York: Brunner/Mazel.

Barlow, D. H. (1980). Behavior therapy: The next decade. *Behavior Therapy, 11,* 315–328.

Barlow, D. H. (1981). On the relation of clinical research to clinical practice: Current issues, new directions. *Journal of Consulting and Clinical Psychology, 49,* 147–155.

Barlow, D. H. (1983). Editorial policies of behavior therapy. *The Behavior Therapist, 6,* 32.

Barlow, D. H. (1988). *Anxiety and its disorders: The nature and treatment of anxiety and panic.* New York: Guilford Press.

Barlow, D. H. (1991). Disorders of emotion. *Psychological Inquiry, 2,* 58–71.

Barlow, D. H. (1994). Effectiveness of behavior treatment for panic disorder with and without agoraphobia. In B. E. Wolfe & J. D. Maser (Eds.), *Treatment of panic disorder: A consensus development conference* (pp. 105–120). Washington, DC: American Psychiatric Press.

Barlow, D. H. (1994). Psychological interventions in the era of managed competition. *Clinical Psychology: Science and Practice, 1,* 109–122.

Barlow, D. H. (1996a). Health care policy, psychotherapy research, and the future of psychotherapy. *American Psychologist.*

Barlow, D. H. (1996b). The effectiveness of psychotherapy: Science and policy. *Clinical Psychology: Science and Practice.*

Barlow, D. H., & Barlow, D. G. (1995). Practice guidelines and empirically validated psychosocial treatments: Ships passing in the night? *Behavioral Healthcare Tomorrow,* May/June, 25–29, 76.

Barlow, D. H., Becker, R., Leitenberg, H., & Agras, W. S. (1970). A mechanical strain gauge for recording penile circumference change. *Journal of Applied Behavior Analysis, 3,* 73–76.

Barlow, D. H., & Brown, T. A. (1995). Correction to Klosko et al. (1990). *Journal of Consulting and Clinical Psychology, 63,* 830.

Barlow, D. H., Brown, T. A., & Craske, M. G. (1994). *Mastery of your anxiety and panic II.* Albany, NY: Graywind Publications.

Barlow, D. H., Chorpita, B. F., & Turovsky, J. (1995). Fear, panic, anxiety, and disorders of emotion. In D. A. Hope (Ed.), *Perspectives on anxiety, panic, and fear* (the 43rd annual Nebraska Symposium on Motivation). Lincoln: University of Nebraska Press.

Barlow, D. H., & Craske, M. G. (1994). *Mastery of your anxiety and panic II.* Albany, NY: Graywind Publications.

Barlow, D. H., Craske, M. G., Cerny, J. A., & Klosko, J. S. (1989). Behavioral treatment of panic disorders. *Behavior Therapy, 20,* 261–282.

Barlow, D. H., & Hayes, S. C. (1979). Alternating treatments design: One strategy for comparing the effects of two treatments in a single subject. *Journal of Applied Behavior Analysis, 12,* 199–210.

Barlow, D. H., Hayes, S. C., & Nelson, R. O. (1984). *The scientist practitioner: Research and accountability in clinical and educational settings.* New York: Pergamon Press.

Barlow, D. H., Hayes, S. C., Nelson, R. O., Steele, D. L., Meeler, M. E., & Mills, J. R. (1979). Sex role behavior: A behavioral checklist. *Behavioral Assessment, 1,* 119–138.

Barlow, D. H., & Hersen, M. (1984). *Single case experimental design: Strategies for studying behavior change (2nd ed.).* Elmsford, NY: Pergamon Press.

Barlow, D. H., & Lehman, C. (1996). Advances in the psychosocial treatment of anxiety disorders: Implications for national health care. *Archives of General Psychiatry, 53,* 727–735.

Barlow, D. H., Mavissakalian, M., & Schofield, L. (1980). Patterns of desynchrony in agoraphobia. *Behaviour Research and Therapy, 18,* 441–448.

Barlow, D. H., O'Brien, G. T., & Last, C. G. (1984). Couples treatment of agoraphobia. *Behavior Therapy, 15,* 41–58.

Barlow, D. H., Rapee, R. M., & Brown, T. A. (1992). Behavioral treatment of generalized anxiety disorder. *Behavior Therapy, 23,* 551–570.

Barrett, P. M., Dadds, M. R., Rappee, R. M., & Ryan, S. M. (in press). Family intervention for childhood anxiety: A controlled trial. *Journal of Consulting and Clinical Psychology.*

Barrom, C. P., Shadish, Jr., W. R., & Montgomery, L. M. (1988). PhDs, PsyDs, and real-world constraints on scholarly activity: Another look at the Boulder model. *Professional Psychology: Research and Practice, 19,* 93–101.

Battaglia, J., Coverdale, J. H., & Bushong, C. P. (1990). Evaluation of a mental illness awareness week program in the public schools. *American Journal of Psychiatry, 147,* 324–329.

Baumeister, A. A., & Sevin, J. A. (1990). Pharmacologic control of aberrant behavior in the mentally retarded: Toward a more rational approach. *Neuroscience and Biobehavioral Reviews, 14,* 253–262.

Beck, A. T., & Freeman, A. (1990). *Cognitive therapy of personality disorders.* New York: Guilford Press.

Beck, A. T., Rush, A. J. Shaw, B. J., & Emery, G. (1979). *Cognitive therapy of depression.* New York: Guilford.

Beck, A. T., Ward, C. H., Mendelson, M., Mock, J., & Erbaugh, J. (1961). An inventory for measuring depression. *Archives of General Psychiatry, 4,* 561–571.

Becker, R. E., & Heimberg, R. G. (1988). Assessment of social skills. In A. S. Bellack & M. Hersen (Eds.), *Behavioral assessment: A practical handbook* (3rd ed.). New York: Pergamon.

Beidel, D. C., Neal, A. M., & Lederer, A. S. (1991). The feasibility and validity of a daily diary for the assessment of anxiety in children. *Behavior Therapy, 22,* 505–517.

Belar, C. D. (1995). Collaboration in capitated care: Challenges for psychology. *Professional psychology: Research and practice, 26,* 139–146.

Belar, C. D., & Perry, N. W. (1992). National conference on scientist–practitioner education and training for the professional practice of psychology. *American Psychologist, 47,* 71–75.

Bellack, A. S. (1983). Recurrent problems in the behavioral assessment of social skills. *Behavioral Assessment, 1,* 157–165.

Bellack, A. S., Hersen, M., & Lamparski, D. (1979). Role-play tests for assessing social skills: Are they valid? Are they useful? *Journal of Consulting and Clinical Psychology, 47,* 335–342.

Bellack, A. S., Hersen, M., & Turner, S. M. (1978). Role-play tests for assessing social skills: Are they valid? *Behavior Therapy, 9,* 448–461.

Bellack, A. S., Morrison, R. L., Mueser, K. T., Wade, J. H., & Sayers, S. L. (1990). *Psychological Assessment, 2,* 248–255.

Belles, D., & Bradlyn, A. S. (1987). The use of the changing criterion design in achieving controlled smoking in a heavy smoker: A controlled case study. *Journal of Behavior Therapy and Experimental Psychiatry, 18,* 77–82.

Benedict, R. H. B., Brandt, J., & Bergey, G. (1993). An attempt at memory retraining in severe amnesia: An experimental study. *Neuropsychological Rehabilitation, 3,* 37–51.

Bergin, A. E., Garfield, S. L., & Thompson, A. S. (1967). The Chicago Conference on clinical training and clinical psychology at Teachers College. *American Psychologist, 22,* 307–316.

Bergin, A. E., & Lambert, M. J. (1978). The evaluation of psychotherapy outcomes. In S. L. Garfield & A. E. Bergin (Eds.), *Handbook of psychotherapy and behavior change: An empirical analysis* (2nd ed.) (pp. 139–191). New York: Wiley.

Bergin, A., & Strupp, H. (1972). *Changing frontiers in the science of psychotherapy.* Chicago: Aldine.

Bernard, C. (1865; reprinted in 1957). *An introduction to the study of experimental medicine.* New York: Dover.

Bernstein, D. A., & Nietzel, M. T. (1973). Procedural variation in behavioral avoidance tests. *Journal of Consulting and Clinical Psychology, 41,* 165–174.

Beutler, L. E. (1991). Selective treatment matching: Systematic eclectic psychotherapy. *Psychotherapy, 28,* 457–462.

Beutler, L. E., Engle, D., Mohr, D., Daldrup, R. J., Bergan, J., Meredith, K., & Merry, W. (1991). Predictors of differential response to cognitive, experiential, and self-directed psychotherapeutic procedures. *Journal of Consulting and Clinical Psychology, 59,* 333–340.

Beutler, L. E., Williams, R. E., & Wakefield, P. J. (1993). Obstacles to disseminating applied psychological science. *Applied and Preventive Psychology, 2,* 53–58.

Biglan, A. (1995). *Changing cultural practices: A contextualist framework for intervention research.* Reno, NV: Context Press.

Blackwell, R. T., Galassi, J. P., Galassi, M. D., & Watson, T. E. (1985). Are cognitive assessments equal? A comparison of think-aloud and thought listing. *Cognitive Therapy and Research, 9,* 399–413.

Blanchard, E. B., Andrasik, F., Ahles, T. A., Teders, S. J., & O'Keefe, D. (1980). Migraine and tension headache: A meta-analytic review. *Behavior Therapy, 11,* 613–631.

Blanchard, E. B., Andrasik, F., Evans, D. D., Neff, D. F., Appelbaum, K. A., & Rodichok, L. D. (1985). Behavioral treatment of 250 chronic headache patients: A clinical replication series. *Behavior Therapy, 16,* 308–327.

Blanchard, E. B., Andrasik, F., Neff, D. F., Arena, J. G., Ahles, T. A., Jurish, S. E., Pallmeyer, T. P., Saunders, N. L., Teders, S. J., Barron, K. D., & Rodichok, L. D. (1982). Biofeedback and relaxation training with three kinds of headache: Treatment effects and their prediction. *Journal of Consulting and Clinical Psychology, 50,* 562–575.

Blanchard, E. B., Kolb, L. C., & Prins, A. (1991). Psychophysiological responses in the diagnosis of posttraumatic stress disorder in Vietnam veterans. *Journal of Nervous and Mental Disease, 179,* 97–101.

Blanchard, E. B., Schwarz, S. P., & Radnitz, C. (1987). Psychological assessment and treatment of irritable bowel syndrome. *Behavior Modification, 11,* 348–372.

Blatt, S. J. (1995). The destructiveness of perfectionism: Implications for the treatment of depression. *American Psychologist, 50,* 1003–1020.

Blick, D. W., & Test, D. W. (1987). Effects of self-recording on high-school students' on-task behavior. *Learning Disability Quarterly, 10,* 203–213.

Bloom, B. L. (1992). Computer-assisted psychological intervention: A review and commentary. *Clinical Psychology Review, 12,* 169–197.

Bloom, M., & Fischer, J. (1982). *Evaluating practice: Guidelines for the accountable professional.* Englewood Cliffs, NJ: Prentice-Hall.

Bloom, M., Fischer, J., and Orme, J. (1995). *Evaluating Practice: Guidelines for the accountable professional* (2nd ed). Englewood Cliffs, NJ: Prentice Hall.

Bluestone, M. A. (1995). Computer processing of client behavioral and psychiatric data. *Journal of Behavior Therapy and Experimental Psychiatry, 26,* 133–140.

Blumer, C., & McNamara, R. (1982). The adequacy of a role play of a previous event as affected by high and low social anxiety and rehearsal. *Journal of Behavioral Assessment, 4,* 27–37.

Book, H. E. (1991). Is empathy cost efficient? *American Journal of Psychotherapy, 45,* 21–30.

Boren, J. J. (1953). *Response rate and resistance to extinction as functions of the fixed ratio.* Unpublished Doctoral Dissertation, Columbia University.

Boren, J. J., & Jagodzinski, M. G. (1975). The impermanence of data recording behavior. *Journal of Behavior Therapy and Experimental Psychiatry, 6,* 359.

Borkovec, T. D., & Costello, E. (1993). Efficacy of applied relaxation and cognitive-behavioral therapy in the treatment of generalized anxiety disorder. *Journal of Consulting and Clinical Psychology, 61,* 611–619.

Borkovec, T. D., Mathews, A. M., Chambers, A. Ebrahimi, S., Lytle, R., & Nelson, R. (1987). The effects of relaxation training with cognitive or nondirective therapy and the role of relaxation-induced anxiety in the treatment of generalized anxiety. *Journal of Consulting and Clinical Psychology, 55,* 883–888.

Bornstein, P. H., Mungas, D. M., Quevillon, R. P., Kniivila, C. M., Miller, R. K., & Holombo, L. K. (1978). Self-monitoring training: Effects on reactivity and accuracy of self-observation. *Behavior Therapy, 9,* 545–552.

Botvin, G. J., & Tortu, S. (1988). Preventing adolescent substance abuse through life skill straining. In R. H. Price (Ed.), *14 Ounces of prevention: A casebook for practitioners* (pp. 98–110). Washington, DC: American Psychiatric Association.

Bouchard, S., Gauthier, J., Laberge, B., French, D., Pelletier, M., & Godbout, C. (1996). Exposure versus cognitive restructuring in the treatment of panic disorder with agoraphobia. *Behaviour Research and Therapy, 34,* 213–224.

Bradburn, N. M., Rips, L. J., & Shevell, S. K. (1987). Answering autobiographical questions: The impact of memory and inference on surveys. *Science, 236,* 157–161.

Breier, A., Charney, D. S., & Heninger, G. R. (1986). Agoraphobia with panic attacks: Development, diagnostic stability, and course of illness. *Archives of General Psychiatry, 43,* 1029–1036.

Brewin, C. R., Andrews, B., & Gotlib, I. H. (1993). Psychopathology and early experience: A reappraisal of retrospective reports. *Psychological Bulletin, 113,* 82–98.

Brown, T. A., & Barlow, D. H. (1995). Long-term outcome in cognitive-behavioral treatment of panic disorder: Clinical predictors and alternative strategies for assessment. *Journal of Consulting and Clinical Psychology, 63,* 754–765.

Brown, T. A., Antony, M. M., & Barlow, D. H. (1995). Diagnostic comorbidity in panic disorder: Effect on treatment outcome and course of comorbid diagnoses following treatment. *Journal of Consulting and Clinical Psychology, 63,* 408–418.

Brownell, K. D., Barlow, D. H., & Hayes, S. C. (1977). Patterns of appropriate and deviant sexual arousal: The behavioral treatment of multiple sexual deviations. *Journal of Consulting and Clinical Psychology, 45,* 1144–1155.

Browning, R. M. (1967). A same-subject design for simultaneous comparison of three reinforcement contingencies. *Behaviour Research and Therapy, 5,* 237–243.

Browning, R. M., & Stover, D. O. (1971). *Behavior modification in child treatment: An experimental and clinical approach.* Chicago: Aldine.

Burke, W. H., & Lewis, F. D. (1986). Management of maladaptive social behavior of a brain injured adult. *International Journal of Rehabilitation Research, 9,* 335–342.

Burlingame, G. M., Wells, M. G., & Lambert, M. J. (1995). *The Youth Outcome Questionnaire.* Stevenson, MD: American Professional Credentialing Service.

Burns, L. E., Thorpe, G. L., & Cavallaro, L. A. (1986). Agoraphobia eight years after behavioral treatment: A follow-up study with interview, self-report, and behavioral data. *Behavior Therapy, 17,* 580–591.

Bush, J. P., & Ciocco, J. E. (1992). Behavioral coding and sequential analysis: The portable computer systems for observation use. *Behavioral Assessment, 14,* 191–197.

Busk, P. L., & Marascuilo, L. A. (1992). Statistical analysis in single case research: Issues, procedures, and recommendations, with applications to multiple behaviors. In T. R. Kratochwill & J. R. Levin (Eds.), *Single-case research design and analysis: New directions for psychology and education* (pp. 159–185). Hillsdale, NJ: Erlbaum.

Busk, P. L., & Serlin, R. C. (1992). Meta-analysis for single-case research. In T. R. Kratochwill & J. R. Levin (Eds.), *Single-case research design and analysis: New directions for psychology and education* (pp. 187–212). Hillsdale, NJ: Erlbaum.

Butcher, J. N., Dahlstrom, W. G., Graham, J. R., Tellegen, A., & Kaemmer, B. (1989) *Minnesota Multiphasic Personality Inventory (MMPI-2) Manual for administration and scoring.* Minneapolis: University of Minnesota Press.

Butler, G., Fennell, M., Robson, P., & Gelder, M. (1991). Comparison of behavior therapy and cognitive behavior therapy in the treatment of generalized anxiety disorder. *Journal of Consulting and Clinical Psychology, 59,* 167–175.

Butler, S. F., & Strupp, H. H. (1991). Psychodynamic psychotherapy. In M. Hersen, A. Kazdin, & A. Bellack (Eds.), *The clinical psychology handbook* (pp. 528–529). Elmsford, NY: Pergamon Press.

Cacioppo, J. T., & Petty, R. (1981). Social psychological procedure for cognitive response assessment: The thought listing technique. In T. V. Merluzzi, C. R. Glass, & M. Genest (Eds.), *Cognitive assessment* (pp. 309–342). New York: Guilford.

Cacioppo, J. T., Rourke, P. A., Marshall-Goodell, B. S., Tassinary, L. G., & Baron (1990). Rudimentary physiological effects of mere observation. *Psychophysiology, 27*(2), 177–186.

Camarata, S. (1993). The application of naturalistic conversation training to speech production in children with speech disabilities. *Journal of Applied Behavior Analysis, 26,* 173–182.

Campbell, D. T. (1959). Factors relevant to the validity of experiments in social settings. *Psychological Bulletin, 54,* 297–312.

Campbell, D. T. (1973). The social scientist as methodological servant of the experimenting society. *Policy Studies Journal, 2,* 72–75.

Campbell, D. T., & Fiske, D. W. (1959). Convergent and discriminant validation by the multitrait-multimethod matrix. *Psychological Bulletin, 56,* 81–105.

Campbell, D. T., & Stanley, J. C. (1963). *Experimental and quasi-experimental designs for research.* Chicago: Rand McNally.

Cantor, D. W. (1996). Lowering the standard of care. *The APA Monitor, 27*(11), 2.

Cantor, D. W. (1997). Open letter to managed care. *The APA Monitor, 28*(1), 2.

Carr, E. G., & Durand, V. M. (1985). Reducing problem behaviors through functional communication training. *Journal of Applied Behavior Analysis, 18,* 111–126.

Carscaddon, D. M., George, M., & Wells, G. (1990). Rural community mental health: Consumer satisfaction and psychiatric symptoms. *Community Mental Health Journal, 26,* 309–318.

Carter, N., Kindstedt, A., & Melin, L. (1995). Increased sales and thefts of candy as a function of sales promotion activities: Preliminary findings. *Journal of Applied Behavior Analysis, 28,* 81–82.

Carver, R. P. (1978). The case against statistical significance testing. *Harvard Educational Review, 3,* 378–399.

Cautela, J. R. (1981). *Behavior analysis forms for clinical intervention* (2 vols.). Champaign, IL: Research Press.

Cautela, J. R., & Kastenbaum, R. (1967). A reinforcement survey schedule for use in therapy, training, and research. *Psychological Reports, 20,* 1115–1130.

Cerny, J. A., Barlow, D. H., Craske, M. G., & Himadi, W. G. (1987). Couples treatment of agoraphobia: A two-year follow-up. *Behavior Therapy, 18,* 401–415.

Chadwick, P. D. J., & Lowe, C. F. (1990). Measurement and modification of delusional beliefs. *Journal of Consulting and Clinical Psychology, 58,* 225–232.

Chamberlain, P., & Reid, J. B. (1987). Parent observation and report of child situations. *Behavioral Assessment, 9,* 97–109.

Chambless, D. L. (1990). Spacing of exposure sessions in treatment of agoraphobia and simple phobia. *Behavior Therapy, 21,* 217–229.

Chambless, D. L., Caputo, G. C., Bright P., and Gallagher, R. (1984). Assessment of fear in agoraphobics: The Body Sensations Questionnaire and the Agoraphobic Cognitions Questionnaire. *Journal of Consulting and Clinical Psychology, 52,* 1090–1097.

Chambless, D. L., Caputo, G. C., Jasin, S. E., Gracely, E. J., and Williams, C. (1985). The Mobility Inventory for Agoraphobia. *Behaviour Research and Therapy, 23,* 35–44. Instrument reproduced with permission of Pergamon Press.

Chambless, D. L., & Gillis, M. M. (1994). A review of psychosocial treatments for panic disorder (pp. 149–173). In B. E. Wolfe & J. D. Maser (Eds.), *Treatment of panic disorder: A consensus development conference.* Washington, DC: American Psychiatric Press.

Chambless, D. L., Sanderson, W. C., Shoham, V., Johnson, S. B., Pope, K. S., Crits-Christoph, P., Baker, M., Johnson, B., Woody, S. R., Sue, S., Beutler, L., Williams, D. A., & McCurry, S. (1996). An update on empirically validated therapies. *The Clinical Psychologist, 49,* 5–18.

Chambless, D. L., & Williams, K. E. (1995). A preliminary study of African Americans with agoraphobia: Symptom severity and outcome of treatment with in vivo exposure. *Behavior Therapy, 26,* 501–515.

Chassan, J. B. (1960). Statistical inference and the single case in clinical design. *Psychiatry, 23,* 173.

Chiles, J. & Strosahl, K. (1995). *The suicidal patient: Principles of assessment, treatment & case management.* Washington DC: American Psychiatric Press.

Christensen, A., & Jacobson, N. S. (1994). Who (or what) can do psychotherapy: The status and challenge of nonprofessional therapies. *Psychological Science, 5,* 8–14

Christensen, A., Johnson, S. M., Phillips, S., & Glasgow, R. E. (1980). Cost effectiveness in behavioral family therapy. *Behavior Therapy, 11,* 208–226.

Chung, W., & Poppen, R., & Lundervold, D. (1995). Behavioral relaxation training for tremor disorders in older adults. *Biofeedback and Self-Regulation, 20,* 123–135.

Cinciripini, P. M., Cinciripini, L. G., Wallfisch, A., Haque, W., & Vunakis, H. V. (1996). Behavior therapy and the transdermal nicotine patch: Effects on cessation, outcome, affect, and coping. *Journal of Consulting and Clinical Psychology, 64,* 314–323.

Clark, D. A. (1988). The validity of measures of cognition: A review of the literature. *Cognitive Therapy and Research, 12,* 1–20.

Clark, D. M. (1989). Anxiety states: Panic and generalized anxiety. In K. Hawton, P. M., Salkovskis, J. Kirk, & D. M. Clark (Eds.), *Cognitive behaviour therapy for psychiatric problems* (pp. 52–96). Oxford: Oxford University Press.

Clark, D. M. (1994). Cognitive therapy for panic disorder. In B. E. Wolfe & J. D. Maser (Eds.), *Treatment of panic disorder: A consensus development conference* (pp. 121–132). Washington, DC: American Psychiatric Press.

Clark, D. M., Salkovskis, P. M., Hackmann, A., Middleton, H., Anastaiades, P., & Gelder, M. (1994). A comparison of cognitive therapy, applied relaxation and imipramine in the treatment of panic disorder. *British Journal of Psychiatry, 164,* 759–769.

Clarke, G. N., Hawkins, W., Murphy, M., Sheeber, L. B., Lewinsohn, P. M., and Seeley, J. R. (1995). Targeted prevention of unipolar disorder in an at-risk sample of high school adolescents: A randomized trial of a group cognitive intervention. *Journal of the American Academy of Child and Adolescent Psychiatry, 34,* 312–321.

Clark, H. B., Boyd, S. B., & Macrae, J. W. (1975). A classroom program teaching disadvantaged youths to write biographic information. *Journal of Applied Behavior Analysis, 7,* 67–75.

Clark, H. H., & Schober, M. F. (1992). Asking questions and influencing answers. In J. Tanur (Ed.), *Questions about questions: Inquiries into the cognitive bases of surveys* (pp. 15–48). New York: Russell Sage.

Clement, P. W. (1996). Evaluation in private practice. *Clinical Psychology: Science and Practice, 3,* 146–159.

Clum, G. A. (1989). Psychological interventions versus drugs in the treatment of panic. *Behavior Therapy, 20,* 429–457.

Clum, G. A. (1990). *Coping with panic: A drug-free approach to dealing with panic attacks.* Pacific Grove, CA: Brooks/Cole.

Clum, G. A., & Curtin, L. (1993). Validity and reactivity of a system of self-monitoring suicide ideation. *Journal of Psychopathology and Behavioral Assessment, 15*(4), 375–385.

Cockburn, J., Thomas, R. J., McLaughlin, S. J., & Reading, D. (1995). Acceptance of screening for colorectal cancer by flexible sigmoidoscopy. *Journal of Medical Screening, 2,* 79–03.

Cohen, E. A., Gelfand, D. M., Dodd, D. K., Jensen, J., & Turner, C. (1980). Self-control practices associated with weight loss maintenance in children and adolescents. *Behavior Therapy, 11,* 26–37.

Cohen, J. (1960). A coefficient of agreement for nominal scales. *Educational and Psychological Measurement, 20,* 37–46.

Cohen, L. H. (1979). The research readership and information source reliance of clinical psychologists. *Professional Psychology, 10,* 780–786.

Cohen, L. H., Sargent, M. M., & Sechrest, L. B. (1986). Use of psychotherapy research by professional psychologists. *American Psychologist, 41,* 198–206.

Coie, J. D., Watt, N. F., West, S. G., Hawkins, D. J., Asarnow, J. R., Markman, H. J., Ramey, S. L., Shure, M. B., & Long B. (1993). The science of prevention: A conceptual framework and some future directions for a national research program. *American Psychologist, 48,* 1013–1022.

Coles, M. G. H., Donchin, E., & Porges, S. W. (1986). *Psychophysiology: Systems, processes, and applications.* New York: Guilford.

Cone, J. D. (1977). The relevance of reliability and validity for behavioral assessment. *Behavior Therapy, 8,* 411–426.

Cone, J. D. (1978). The Behavioral Assessment Grid (BAG): A conceptual framework and a taxonomy. *Behavior Therapy, 9,* 882–888.

Cone, J. D. (1979). Confounded comparisons in triple response mode assessment research. *Behavioral Assessment, 1,* 85–95.

Cone, J. D. (1981). Psychometrics considerations. In M. Hersen & A. S. Bellack (Eds.), *Behavioral assessment* (pp. 38–68). New York: Pergamon Press.

Conte, J. R., & Levy, R. L. (1979, March). *Problems and issues in implementing the clinical research model of practice in educational and clinical settings.* Paper presented at the meeting of the Council on Social Work Education, Boston, MA.

Cook, T. D., & Campbell, D. T. (Eds.). (1979). *Quasi-experimentation: Design and analysis issues for field settings.* Chicago: Rand McNally.

Cooper, J. O., Heron, T. E., & Heward, W. L. (1987). *Applied behavior analysis.* Colombus, OH: Merrill.

Cooper, L. J., Wacker, D. P., McComas, J. J., Brown, K., Peck, S. M., Richman, D., Drew, J., Frischmeyer, P., & Millard, T. (1995). Use of component analysis to identify active variables in treatment packages for children with feeding disorders. *Journal of Applied Behavior Analysis, 28,* 139–153.

Cope, J. G., & Allred, L. J. (1991). Community intervention to deter illegal parking in spaces reserved for the physically disabled. *Journal of Applied Behavior Analysis, 24,* 687–693.

Cope, J. G., Allred, L. J, & Morsell, J. M. (1991). Signs as deterrents of illegal parking in spaces designated for individuals with physical disabilities. *Journal of Applied Behavior Analysis, 24,* 59–63.

Cope, J. G., Moy, S. S., & Grossnickle, W. F. (1988). The behavioral impact of an advertising campaign to promote safety belt use. *Journal of Applied Behavior Analysis, 21,* 277–280.

Cordes, S. (1989). The changing rural environment and the relationship between health services and rural development. *Health Services Research, 23,* 757–784.

Côté, G., Gauthier, J., & Laberge, B. (1992, November). *The impact of medication use on the efficacy of cognitive-behavioral therapy for panic disorder.* Poster presented at the 26th annual convention of AABT, Boston, MA.

Craighead, W. E. (1980). Away from a unitary model of depression. *Behavior Therapy, 11,* 122–128.

Crary, W. G., & Johnson, C. W. (1975). Mental status examination. In C. W. Johnson, J. R. Snibbe, and L. A. Evans (Eds), *Basic psychotherapy: A programmed text.* New York: Spectrum Publications.

Craske, M. G., & Barlow, D. H. (1993). Panic disorder and agoraphobia. In D. H. Barlow (Ed.), *Clinical handbook of psychological disorders,* (2nd ed.) (pp. 1–47). New York: Guilford Publications.

Craske, M. G., Brown, T. A., & Barlow, D. H. (1991). Behavioral treatment of panic: A two year follow-up. *Behavior Therapy, 22,* 289–304.

Craske, M., & Street, L., & Barlow, D. (1989). Instructions to focus upon or distract from internal cues during exposure treatment of agoraphobic avoidance. *Behaviour Research and Therapy, 27,* 663–672.

Crits-Christoph, P., Frank, E., Chambless, D. L., Brody, C., & Karp, J. F. (1995). Training in empirically validated treatments: What are clinical psychology students learning? *Professional Psychology: Research and Practice, 26,* 514–522.

Croce, R. V. (1990). Effects of exercise and diet on body composition and cardiovascular fitness in adults with severe mental retardation. *Education and Training in Mental Retardation, 25,* 176–187.

Cronbach, L. J. (1975). Beyond the two disciplines of scientific psychology. *American Psychologist, 30,* 116–127.

Cronbach, L. J., & Snow, R. E. (1977). *Aptitudes and instructional methods: A handbook for research on interactions.* New York: Irvington.

Crowe, M. J., Gillan, P., & Golombok, S. (1981). Form and content in the conjoint treatment of sexual dysfunction: A controlled study. *Behaviour Research and Therapy, 19*, 47–54.

Crutcher, R. J. (1994). Telling what we know: The use of verbal report methodologies psychological research. *Psychological Science, 5*, 241–244.

Cummings, J. W. (1992). Psychologists in the medical-surgical setting: Some reflections. *Professional Psychology: Research and Practice, 23*, 76–79.

Cummings, N. A. (1986). The dismantling of our health system: Strategies for the survival of psychological practice. *American Psychologist, 41*, 426–431.

Cummings, N. A. (1991). Arguments for the financial efficacy of psychological services in health care settings. In J. J. Sweet, R. H. Rozensky, & S. M. Tovian (Eds.), *Handbook of clinical psychology in medical settings* (pp. 113–126). New York: Plenum.

Cummings, N. A. (1992). The future of psychotherapy: Society's charge to professional psychology. *Independent Practitioner, 12*(3), 126–130.

Cummings, N. A. (1995). Behavioral health after managed care: The next golden opportunity for professional psychology. *Register Report, 20*(3) & *21*(1), 1, 30–33.

Cummings, N. A. (1997). Practitioner-driven IDS groups continue as the best hope for the future. *The National Psychologist, 6*(4), 10–11.

Cummings, N. A., & Follette, W. T. (1976). Brief psychotherapy and medical utilization. In H. Dorken (Ed.), *The professional psychologist today.* San Francisco: Jossey-Bass.

Cummings, N. A., & Hayes, S. C. (1996). Now we are facing the consequences: A conversation with Nick Cummings. *The Scientist Practitioner, 6*(1), 9–13.

Curran, J. P. (1982). A procedure for the assessment of social skills: The simulated social interaction test. In J. P. Curran, & P. M. Monti (Eds.), *Social skills training: A practical handbook for assessment and treatment* (pp. 348–373). New York: Guilford.

Darrow, C. W. (1929). Psychological effects of drugs. *Psychological Bulletin, 26*, 527.

Davis, M., & Hadiks, D. (1990). Nonverbal behavior and client state changes during psychotherapy. *Journal of Clinical Psychology, 46*, 340–351.

Davison, G. C., Robins, C., & Johnson, M. K. (1983). Articulated thoughts during simulated situations: A paradigm for studying cognition in emotion and behavior. *Cognitive Therapy and Research, 7*, 17–40.

Dawes, R. M. (1994). *House of cards: Psychology and psychotherapy built on myth.* New York: Free Press.

Dawes, R. M., Faust, D., & Meehl, P. E. (1989). Clinical versus actuarial judgment. *Science, 243*, 1668–1674.

Deaux, E., & Callaghan, J. W. (1984). Estimating statewide health risk behavior: A comparison of telephone and key informant survey approaches. *Evaluation Review, 8*, 467–492.

Depression Guideline Panel. (1993, April). *Depression in primary care: Volume 2. Treatment of major depression.* Clinical Practice Guideline Number 5. Rockville, MD: U.S. Department of Health and Human Services, Public Health Service, Agency for Health Care Policy and Research.

Derby, K. M., Fisher, W. W., & Piazza, C. C. (1996). The effects of contingent and noncontingent attention on self-injury and self-restraint. *Journal of Applied Behavior Analysis, 29*, 107–110.

Derogatis, L. R. (1983). *SCL-90: Administration, scoring, and procedures manual for the revised version.* Baltimore: Clinical Psychometric Research.

DeVries, J. E., Burnette, M. M., & Redmon, W. K. (1991). AIDS prevention: Improving nurses' compliance with glove wearing through performance feedback. *Journal of Applied Behavior Analysis, 24*, 705–711.

DiMascio, A., Weissman, M. M., Prusoff, B. A., Neu, C., Zwilling, M., & Klerman, G. L. (1979). Differential symptom reduction by drugs and psychotherapy in acute depression. *Archives of General Psychiatry, 36*, 1450–1456.

DiNardo, P. A., Brown, T. A., & Barlow, D. H. (1994). *Anxiety Disorders Interview Schedule for DSM-IV (ADIS-IV).* Albany, NY: Graywind Publications.

Dobson, K. S. (Ed.). (1988). *Handbook of cognitive-behavioral therapies.* New York: Guilford.

Dobson, K. S. (1989). A meta-analysis of the efficacy of cognitive therapy for depression. *Journal of Consulting and Clinical Psychology, 57*, 414–419.

Dobson, K. S., & Craig, K. D. (1998). (Eds.), *Empirically supported therapies: Best practice in professional psychology.* Thousand Oaks, CA: Sage.

Dowis, C. L., & Schloss, P. (1992). The impact of mini-lessons on writing skills. *Remedial and Special Education, 13*, 34–42.

Drum, D. J. (1995). Changes in the mental health service delivery and finance systems and resulting implications for the national register. *Register Report, 20*(3) & *21*(1), 4–10.

Dugan, E., Kamps, D., Leonard, B., Watkins, N., Rheinberger, A., & Stackhaus, J. (1995). Effects of cooperative learning groups during social studies for students with autism and fourth-grade peers. *Journal of Applied Behavior Analysis, 28*, 175–188.

Dumas, J. E. (1988). *INTERACT: Data collection and analysis software.* Unpublished manual.

Dumas, J. E., Blechman, E. A., & Prinz, R. J. (1992). *INTERACT/BLISS: A computer coding system to assess small group communication.* Unpublished coding manual.

Dunne, P. W., Sanders, M. R., Rowell, J. A., & McWhirter, W. R. (1991). An evaluation of cognitive-behavioral techniques in the management of chronic arthritic pain in men with haemophilia. *Behaviour Change, 8,* 70–78.

Durand, V. M., & Carr, E. G. (1991). Functional communication training to reduce challenging behavior: Maintenance and application in new settings. *Journal of Applied Behavior Analysis, 24,* 251–264.

Edgington, E. S. (1966). Statistical inference and non-random samples. *Psychological Bulletin, 66,* 485–487.

Edgington, E. S. (1967). Statistical inference from N=1 experiments. *Journal of Psychology, 65,* 195–199.

Edgington, E. S. (1992). Nonparametric tests for single-case experiments. In T. R. Kratochwill & J. R. Levin (Eds.), *Single-case research design and analysis: New directions for psychology and education* (pp. 135–157). Hillsdale, NJ: Erlbaum.

Edwards, R., Kearns, K., & Tingstrom, D. H. (1991). Accuracy of long momentary time-sampling intervals: Effects of errors in the timing of observations. *Journal of Psychoeducational Assessment, 9*(2), 160–165.

Eiler, J. M., Nelson, W. W., Jensen, C. C., & Johnson, S. P. (1989). Automated data collection using bar code. *Behavior Research Methods, Instruments, & Computers, 21,* 53–58.

Elkin, I., Gibbons, R. D., Shea, M. T., Sotsky, S. M., Watkins, J. T., Pilkonis, P. A., & Hedeker, D. (1995). Initial severity and differential treatment outcome in the National Institute of Mental Health treatment of depression collaborative research program. *Journal of Consulting and Clinical Psychology, 63,* 841–847.

Elkin, E., Shea, M. T., Watkins, J. T., Imber, S. D., Sotsky, S. M., Collins, J. F., Glass, D. R., Pilkonis, P. A., Leber, W. R., Docherry, J. P., Fiester, S. J., & Parloff, M. B. (1989). National Institute of Mental Health Treatment of Depression Collaborative Research Program: General effectiveness of treatments. *Archives of General Psychiatry, 46,* 971–982.

Ellis, A., & Greiger, R. (1977). *Handbook of rational-emotive therapy.* New York: Springer.

Elsesser, K., Sartory, G., & Maurer, J. (1996). The efficacy of complaints management training in facilitating benzodiazepine withdrawal. *Behaviour Research and Therapy, 34,* 149–156.

Emmelkamp, P. M. G. (1982). *Phobic and obsessive-compulsive disorders: Theory, research, and practice.* New York: Plenum.

Emmelkamp, P. M. G., & Kuipers, A. C. M. (1979). Agoraphobia: A follow-up study four years after treatment. *British Journal of Psychiatry, 134,* 342–355.

Endicott, J., & Spitzer, R. L. (1978). A diagnostic interview: The Schedule for Affective Disorders and Schizophrenia. *Archives of General Psychiatry, 35,* 837–844.

Endicott, J., Spitzer, R. L., Fleiss, J. L., & Cohen, J. (1976). The Global Assessment Scale: A procedure for measuring overall severity of psychiatric disturbance. *Archives of General Psychiatry, 33,* 766–771.

Epstein, L. H. (1976). Psychophysiological measurement in assessment. In M. Hersen, & A. S. Bellack (Eds.), *Behavioral assessment: A practical handbook.* New York: Pergamon.

Epstein, L. H., Miller, P. M., & Webster, J. S. (1976). The effects of reinforcing concurrent behavior on self-monitoring. *Behavior Therapy, 7,* 89–95.

Epstein, L. H., Webster, J. S., & Miller, P. M. (1975). Accuracy and controlling effects of self-monitoring as a function of concurrent responding and reinforcement. *Behavior Therapy, 6,* 654–666.

Epstein, L. H., Valoski, A., Wing, R. R., & McCurley, J. (1994). Ten-year outcomes of behavioral family-based treatment for childhood obesity. *Health Psychology, 13,* 373–383.

Epstein, S. (1979). The stability of behavior: I. On predicting most of the people much of the time. *Journal of Personality and Social Psychology, 37,* 1097–1126.

Epstein, S. (1980). The stability of behavior: II. Implications for psychological research. *American Psychologist, 35,* 790–806.

Epstein, S. (1983). Aggregating and beyond: Some basic issues in the prediction of behavior. *Journal of Personality, 51,* 360–362.

Ericksen, S. C. (1966). Responsibilities of psychological science to professional psychology. *American Psychologist, 21,* 950–953.

Ericsson, K. A., & Simon, H. A. (1993). *Protocol analysis: Verbal reports as data* (Rev. ed). Cambridge, MA: MIT Press.

Erskine, A., Morley, S., & Pearce, S. (1990). Memory for pain: A review. *Pain, 41*(3), 255–265.

Ersner-Hershfield, S. M., Connors, G. J., & Maisto, S. A. (1981). Clinical and experimental utility of refundable deposits. *Behaviour Research and Therapy, 19,* 455–457.

Evans, I. (1986). Response structure and the triple-response-mode concept. In R. O. Nelson & S. C. Hayes (Eds.), *Conceptual foundations of behavioral assessment* (pp. 131–152). New York: Guilford Press.

Eyberg, S. M., & Johnson, S. M. (1974). Multiple assessment of behavior modification with families: Effects of contingency contracting and order of treated problems. *Journal of Consulting and Clinical Psychology, 42,* 594–606.

Eysenck, H. J. (1952). The effects of psychotherapy: An evaluation. *Journal of Consulting Psychology, 16,* 319–324.

Eysenck, H. J. (1965). The effects of psychotherapy. *International Journal of Psychiatry, 1,* 97–178.

Fairburn, C. G., Jones, R., Peveler, R. C., Hope, R. A., O'Conner, M. (1993). Psychotherapy and bulimia nervosa: Longer-term effects of interpersonal psychotherapy, behavior therapy, and cognitive behavior therapy. *Archives of General Psychiatry, 50,* 419–428.

Falloon, R. H., Boyd, J. L., McGill, C. W., Williamson, M., Razani, A., Moss, H. B., Giulderman, A. M., & Simpson, G. M. (1985). Family management in the prevention of morbidity of schizophrenia: Clinical outcome of a two-year logitudinal study. *Archives of General Psychiatry, 42,* 887–896.

Fals-Stewart, W., Marks, A. P., & Schafer, J. (1993). A comparison of behavioral group therapy and individual behavior therapy in treating obsessive-compulsive disorder. *Journal of Nervous and Mental Disease, 181,* 189–193.

Farrell, A. D. (1982). *Microcomputer-Assisted Behavioral Assessment System* (Computer program). Richmond: Virginia Commonwealth University.

Farrell, A. D. (1986). Microcomputer as a tool for behavioral assessment. *The Behavior Therapist, 9,* 16–17.

Farrell, A. D. (1991). Computers and behavioral assessment: Current applications, future possibilities, and obstacles to routine use. *Behavioral Assessment, 13,* 159–179.

Fawzy, F. I., Fawzy, N. W., Arndt, L. A., & Pasnau, R. O. (1995). Critical review of psychosocial interventions in cancer care. *Archives of General Psychiatry, 53,* 100–113.

Fehr, A., & Beckwith, B. E. (1989). Water misting: Treating self-injurious behavior in a multiply

handicapped, visually impaired child. *Journal of Visual Impairment and Blindness, 83,* 245–248.

Feighner, J. P., Robins, E., Guze, S. B., Woodruff, R. A., Winokur, G., & Munoz, R. (1972). Diagnostic criteria for the use in psychiatric research. *Archives of General Psychiatry, 26,* 57–63.

Feinson, M. C., & Popper, M. (1995). Does affordability affect mental health utilization? A United States-Israel comparison of older adults. *Social Science and Medicine, 40,* 669–678.

Feldman, J. L., & Fitzpatrick, R. J. (Eds.). (1992). *Managed mental health care: Administrative and clinical issues.* Washington, DC: American Psychiatric Press.

Felton, J., & Nelson, R., (1984). Inter-assessor agreement on hypothesized controlling variables and treatment proposals. *Behavioral Assessment, 6,* 199–208.

Fensterheim, H., & Raw, S. D. (1996). Psychotherapy research is not psychotherapy practice. *Clinical Psychology: Science and Practice, 3,* 168–171.

Feske, U., & Chambless, D. L. (1995). Cognitive behavioral versus exposure only treatment for social phobia: A meta-analysis. *Behavior Therapy, 26,* 695–720.

First, M. B., Gibbon, M., Spitzer, R. L., & Williams, J. B. W. (1996). *User's guide for the Structured Clinical Interview for DSM-IV Axis I Disorders (SCID-I) Research Version.* New York: Biometrics Research.

First, M. B., Spitzer, R. L., Gibbon, M., & Williams, J. B. W. (1996). *User's guide for the Structured Clinical Interview for DSM-IV Personality Disorders (SCID-II).* Washington DC: American Psychiatric Press.

Fisch, H., Frey, S., Hirsbrunner, H. (1983). Analyzing nonverbal behavior in depression. *Journal of Abnormal Psychology, 3,* 307–318.

Fischer, J., & Corcoran, K. (1994). *Measures for clinical practice: A sourcebook* (2 vols, 2nd ed.). New York: Macmillan.

Fisher, C., Gross, J., & Zuch, J. (1965). Cycle of penile erection synchronous with dreaming (REM) sleep. *Archives of General Psychiatry, 12,* 29–45.

Fisher, R. A. (1925). On the mathematical foundations of the theory of statistics. In *Theory of statistical estimation.* Proceedings of the Cambridge Philosophical Society.

Fisher, R., and Quigley, K. (1992). Applying cognitive theory in public health investigations: Enhancing food recall with the cognitive interview. In J. Tanur (Ed.), *Questions about questions: Inquiries into the cognitive bases of surveys* (pp. 154–169). New York: Russell Sage.

Fisher, W. W., Piazza, C. C., & Chiang, C. L. (1996). Effects of equal and unequal reinforcer duration during functional analysis. *Journal of Applied Behavior Analysis, 29,* 117–120.

Fixsen, D. L., Phillips, E. L., & Wolf, M. M. (1972). Achievement place: The reliability of self-reporting and peer-reporting and their effects on behavior. *Journal of Applied Behavior Analysis, 5,* 19–30.

Flexner, A. (1910). *Medical education in the United States and Canada.* Boston: Merrymount Press.

Foa, E. B. (1979). Failure in treating obsessive-compulsives. *Behaviour Research and Therapy, 17,* 169–176.

Foa, E. B., Grayson, J. B., Steketee, G., Doppelt, H. G., Turner, R. M., & Latimer, P. L. (1983). Success and failure in the behavioral treatment of obsessive-compulsives. *Journal of Consulting and Clinical Psychology, 15,* 287–297.

Foa, E. B., & Kozak, M. S. (1986). Emotional processing of fear: Exposure to corrective information. *Psychological Bulletin, 99,* 20–35.

Foa, E. B., Rothbaum, B. O., Riggs, D. S., & Murdock, T. B. (1991). Treatment of posttraumatic stress disorder in rape victims: A comparison between cognitive-behavioral procedures and counseling. *Journal of Consulting and Clinical Psychology, 59,* 715–723.

Foa, E. B., Steketee, G., Grayson, J. B., Turner, R. M., & Latimer, P. R. (1984). Deliberate exposure and blocking of obsessive-compulsive rituals: Immediate and long-term effects. *Behavior Therapy, 15,* 450–472.

Foa, E. B., Steketee, G., & Milby, J. B. (1980). Differential effects of exposure and response prevention in obsessive-compulsive washers. *Journal of Consulting and Clinical Psychology, 48,* 71–79.

Follette, W. C., Houts, A. C., & Hayes, S. C. (1992). Behavior therapy and the new medical model. *Behavioral Assessment, 14,* 323–343.

Fonnebo, V., & Sogaard, A. J. (1995). The Norwegian mental health campaign in 1992. Part II: Changes in knowledge and attitudes. *Health Education Research, 10,* 267–278.

Ford, J. D., & Kendall, P. C. (1979). Behavior therapists' professional behaviors: Converging evidence of a gap between theory and practice. *The Behavior Therapist, 2,* 37–38.

Foster, S. L., Bell-Dolan, D. J., & Burge, D. A. (1988). Behavioral observation. In A. S. Bellack & M. Hersen (Eds.), *Behavioral assessment: A practical handbook* (3rd ed.) (pp. 119–160). New York: Pergamon.

Foster, S. L., & Cone, J. D. (1980). Current issues in direct observation. *Behavioral Assessment, 2,* 313–338

Foster, S. L., & Cone, J. D. (1986). Design and use of direct observation procedures. In A. R. Ciminero, K. S. Calhoun, & H. E. Adams (Eds.), *Handbook of behavioral assessment* (pp. 253–324). New York: Wiley

Fowles, D. C., Christie, M. J., Edelberg, R., Grings, W. W., Lykken, D. T., & Venables, P. H. (1981). Publication recommendations for electrodermal measurement. *Psychophysiology, 18,* 232–239.

Frank, E., Kupfer, D. J., Wagner, E. F., McEachran, A. B., & Cornes, C. (1991). Efficacy of interpersonal psychotherapy as a maintenance treatment for recurrent depression: Contributing factors. *Archives of General Psychiatry, 48,* 1053–1059.

Frank, E., & Spanier, C. (1995). Interpersonal psychotherapy for depression: Overview, clinical efficacy, and future directions. *Clinical Psychology: Science and Practice, 2,* 349–369.

Frank, P. J., Klein, S., & Jacobs, J. (1982). Cost-benefit analysis of a behavioral program for geriatric inpatients. *Hospital and Community Psychiatry, 33,* 374–377.

Frank, R. G., & Dewa, C. S. (1992). Insurance, system structure, and the use of mental health services by children and adolescents. Special issue: Child and adolescent mental health. *Clinical Psychology Review, 12,* 829–840.

Frank, R. G., McGuire, T. G., Notman, E. H., & Woodward, R. M. (1996). Developments in Medicaid managed behavioral health care. In R. W. Manderscheid & M. A. Sonnenschein (Eds.), *Mental health, United States, 1996* (pp. 138–155). Washington, DC: Substance Abuse and Mental Health Services Administration.

Franklin, J. A. (1989). A 6-year follow-up of the effectiveness of respiratory retraining, in-situ isometric relaxation, and cognitive modification in the treatment of agoraphobia. *Behavior Modification, 13,* 139–167.

Franzen, M. D., & Harris, C. V. (1993). Neuropsychological rehabilitation: Application of a modified multiple baseline design. *Brain Injury, 7,* 525–534.

Frasure-Smith, N. (1991). In-hospital symptoms of psychological stress as predictors of long-term outcome after acute myocardial infarction in men. *American Journal of Cardiology, 67,* 121–127.

Freund, K. (1963). A laboratory method for diagnosing predominance of homo- or hetero-erotic interest in the male. *Behavior Therapy 5,* 339–348.

Fridlund, A. J., & Cacioppo, J. T. (1986). Guidelines for human electromyographic research. *Psychophysiology, 23,* 567–589.

Frisch, M. B., Cornell, J., Villanueva, M., & Retzlaff, P. J. (1992). Clinical validation of the Quality of Life Inventory: A measure of life satisfaction for use in treatment planning and outcome assessment. *Psychological Assessment, 4,* 92–101.

Frisch, M. B., & Higgins, R. L. (1986). Instructional demand effects and the correspondence among role-plays, self-report, and naturalistic measures of social skills. *Behavioral Assessment, 8,* 221–236.

Froyd, J., & Lambert, M. J. (1989, May). A survey of outcome research measures in psychotherapy research. Paper presented at the meeting of the Western Psychological Association, Reno, NV. Cited in Lambert, M. J., & Hill, C. E. (1994). Assessing psychotherapy outcomes and processes. In A. E. Bergin & S. L. Garfield (Eds.), *Handbook of psychotherapy and behavior change* (4th ed.) (pp. 72–113). New York: Wiley.

Frueh, B. C., Turner, S. M., Beidel, D. C., Mirabella, R. F., & Jones, W. J. (1996). Trauma management therapy: A preliminary evaluation of a multicomponent behavioral treatment for chronic combat-related PTSD. *Behaviour Research and Therapy, 34,* 533–543.

Fuchs, C. Z., & Rehm, L. P. (1977). A self-control behavior therapy program for depression. *Journal of Consulting and Clinical Psychology, 45,* 206–215.

Futterman, C. S., & Tryon, W. W. (1994). Psychomotor retardation found in depressed outpatient women. *Journal of Behavior Therapy and Experimental Psychiatry, 25,* 41–48.

Galassi, M. D., & Galassi, J. P. (1976). The effects of role-playing variations on the assessment of assertive behavior. *Behavior Therapy, 7,* 343–347.

Gallagher-Thompson, D., & Steffen, A. M. (1994). Comparative effects of cognitive-behavioral and brief dynamic therapy for depressed family caregivers. *Journal of Consulting and Clinical Psychology, 62,* 543–549.

Gannett News Service (November 11, 1996). HMOs remain a mystery, poll says. *Reno Gazette Journal,* 7a.

Gardner, W. I., & Cole, C. L. (1988). Self-monitoring procedures. In E. S. Shapiro & T. R. Kratochwell (Eds.), *Behavioral assessment in schools: Conceptual foundations and practical applications* (pp. 106–146). New York: Guilford.

Garfield, S. L. (1966). Clinical psychology and the search for identity. *American Psychologist, 21,* 353–362.

Garfield, S. L. (1981). Evaluating the psychotherapies. *Behavior Therapy, 12,* 295–308.

Garfield, S. L. (1994). Some problems associated with "valiadated" forms of psychotherapy. *Clinical Psychology: Science and Practice.*

Gatchel, R. J., & Blanchard, E. B. (Eds.). (1993). *Psychophysiological disorders: Research and clinical applications.* Washington, DC: American Psychological Association.

Geenen, R., & Van de Vijver, F. J. R. (1993). A simple test of the law of initial values. *Psychophysiology, 30,* 525–530.

Geer, J. H. (1965). The development of a scale to measure fear. *Behaviour Research and Therapy, 3,* 45–53.

Geiselman, R. E., & Fisher, R. P. (1989). The cognitive interview technique for victims and witnesses of crime. In D. Raskin (Ed.), *Psychological methods in criminal investigation* (pp. 191–215). New York: Springer-Verlag.

Geiselman, R. E., Fisher, R. P., Firstenburg, I., Hutton, L. A., Sullivan, S. J., Avetission, I. V., & Prosk, A. L. (1984). Enhancement of the eyewitness memory: An empirical evaluation of the cognitive interview. *Journal of Police Science and Administration, 12,* 74–80.

Gelder, M. G., & Marks, I. M. (1966). Severe agoraphobia: A controlled prospective trial of behavior therapy. *British Journal of Psychiatry, 112,* 309–319.

Gerardi, R. J., Blanchard, E. B., & Kolb, L. C. (1989). Ability of Vietnam veterans to dissimulate a psychophysiological assessment of posttraumatic stress disorder. *Behavior Therapy, 20,* 229–243.

Gilbert, P. (1988). Shame and guilt. *Changes, 6,* 50–53.

Gilchrist, L. D., Allen, D. G., Brown, L., Cox, G. B., Semke, J., Thomas, M. D., Jemelka, R., Perry, R. D. & Sutphen-Mroz, J. (1994). A public-academic approach to designing a state mental health program evaluation. *Evaluation and Program Planning, 17,* 53–61.

Giles, T. (1993). *Managed mental health care.* Boston: Allyn and Bacon.

Glass, C. R., & Arnkoff, D. B. (1982) Think cognitively: Selected issues in cognitive assessment and therapy. In P. C. Kendall (Ed.), *Advances in cognitive behavioral research and therapy (Vol. 1).* New York: Academic Press.

Glass, C. R., Merluzzi, T. V., Biever, J. O., and Larsen, K. H. (1982). Cognitive assessment of social anxiety: Development and validation of a self-statement questionnaire. *Cognitive Therapy and Research, 6,* 37–55.

Glick, I. D., Hargreaves, W. A., & Drues, J. (1976). Short versus long hospitalization: A prospective controlled study. *American Journal of Psychiatry, 133,* 515–517.

Goisman, R. M., Rogers, M. P., Steketee, G. S., Warshaw, M. G., Cuneo, P., & Keller, M. B. (1993). Utilization of behavioral methods in a multicenter anxiety disorders study. *Journal of Clinical Psychiatry, 54,* 213–218.

Goldfried, M. R., & Davison, G. C. (1976) *Clinical behavior therapy.* New York: Holt, Rinehart and Winston.

Goldfried, M. R., & Sprafkin, J. N. (1976). Behavioral personality assessment. In J. Spence, R. Carson, & J. Thibaut (Eds.), *Behavioral approaches to therapy.* Morristown, NJ: General Learning Press.

Goldman, H. H., Skodol, A. E., & Lave, T. R. (1992). Revising Axis V for DSM-IV: A review of measures of social functioning. *American Journal of Psychiatry, 149,* 1148–1156.

Goltz, S. M., Citera, M.., Jensen, M., Favero, J., & Komaki, J. L. (1989). Individual feedback: Does it enhance effects of group feedback? *Journal of Organizational Behavior Management, 10,* 77–92.

Goodman, G. S., & Reed, R. S. (1986). Age differences in eyewitness testimony. *Law and Human Behavior, 10,* 317–332.

Gould, R. A., & Clum, G. A. (1993). A meta-analysis of self-help treatment approaches. *Clinical Psychology Review, 13,* 169–186.

Gould, R. A., & Clum, G. A. (1995). Self-help plus minimal therapist contact in the treatment of panic disorder: A replication and extension. *Behavior Therapy, 26,* 533–546.

Greenfield, S. (1989). The state of outcome research: Are we on target? *The New England Journal of Medicine, 320,* 1142–1143.

Group Health Association of America (1995). *Sourcebook on HMO utilization data.* Washington, DC: Group Health Association of America.

Hadorn, D. C., Baker, D., Hodges, J. S., & Hicks, N. (1996). Rating the quality of evidence for clinical practice guidelines. *Journal of Clinical Epidemiology, 49,* 749–754.

Haley, J. (1978). *Problem-solving therapy: New strategies for effective family therapy.* San Francisco: Jossey-Bass.

Hall, R. V. (1971). *Management series: Part 11.* Lawrence, KS: H&H Enterprises.

Hall, R. V., & Fox, R. G. (1977). Changing-criterion designs: An alternate applied behavior analysis procedure. In B. C. Etzel, J. M. LeBlanc, & D. M. Baer (Eds.), *New developments in behavioral research: Theory, method, and application. In honor of Sidney W. Bijou.* Hillsdale, NJ: Erlbaum.

Hamberger, L. K. (1982). Reduction of generalized aversive responding in a post-treatment cancer patient: Relaxation as an active coping skill. *Journal of Behavior Therapy and Experimental Psychiatry, 13,* 229–233.

Haring, T. G., & Kennedy, C. H. (1990). Contextual control of problem behavior in students with severe disabilities. *Journal of Applied Behavior Analysis, 23,* 235–243.

Harmon, T. M., Nelson, R. O., & Hayes, S. C. (1980). Self-monitoring mood versus activity in depressed clients. *Journal of Consulting and Clinical Psychology, 48,* 30–38.

Harris, F. N., & Jenson, W. R. (1985). Comparisons of multiple-baseline across persons designs and AB designs with replication: Issues and confusions. *Behavioral Assessment, 7,* 121–129.

Harrop, A., Daniels, M., & Foulkes, C. (1990). The use of momentary time sampling and partial interval recording in behavioural research. *Behavioural Psychotherapy, 18*(2), 121–127.

Harrop, A., Murphy, M., & Shelton, T. (1994). Momentary time sampling and partial interval recording: A rejoinder to Adams (1991). *Behavioural and Cognitive Psychotherapy, 22*(1), 97–98.

Hartmann, D. P. (1977). Considerations in the choice of interobserver reliability estimates. *Journal of Applied Behavior Analysis, 10,* 103–116.

Hartmann, D. P., & Hall, R. V. (1976). The changing criterion design. *Journal of Applied Behavior Analysis, 9,* 527–532.

Hartmann, D. P., & Wood, D. D. (1982). Observational methods. In A. S. Bellack, M. Hersen, & A. E. Kazdin (Eds.), *International handbook of behavior modification and therapy* (pp. 109–138). New York: Plenum.

Hartshorne, H., & May, M. A. (1928). *Studies in the nature of character. Vol. 1: Studies in deceit.* New York: Macmillan.

Hathaway, S. R., & McKinley, J. C. (1951). *MMPI manual.* New York: Psychological Corporation.

Hawkins, R. P. (1979). The functions of assessment: Implications for selection and development of devices for assessing repertoires in clinical, educational, and other settings. *Journal of Applied Behavior Analysis, 12,* 501–516.

Hawkins, R. P. (1986). Selection of target behaviors. In R. O. Nelson & S. C. Hayes (Eds.), *Conceptual foundations of behavioral assessment* (pp. 331–385). New York: Guilford.

Hay, L. R., Nelson, R. O., & Hay, W. M. (1977). The use of teachers as behavioral observers. *Journal of Applied Behavior Analysis, 10,* 345–348.

Hay, L. R., Nelson, R. O., & Hay, W. M. (1980). Methodological problems in the use of participant observers. *Journal of Applied Behavior Analysis, 13,* 501–504.

Hay, W. M., Hay, L. R., Angle, H. V., & Nelson, R. (1979). The reliability of problem identification in the behavioral interview. *Behaviorial Assessment, 1,* 107–118.

Hayden, M., Wheeler, M. A., Carnine, D. (1989). The effects of an innovative classroom networking system and an electronic grade book on time spent scoring and summarizing student performance. *Education and Treatment of Children,* 253–264.

Hayes, G. J., Hayes, S. C., & Dykstra, T. (1995). A survey of university institutional review boards: Characteristics, policies, and procedures. *IRB: A Review of Human Subjects Research, 17* (3), 1–6.

Hayes, R. L., Halford, W. K., & Varghese, F. T. (1995). Social skills training with chronic schizophrenic patients: Effects on negative symptoms and community functioning. *Behavior Therapy, 26,* 433–449.

Hayes, S. C. (1981). Single case experimental design and empirical clinical practice. *Journal of Consulting and Clinical Psychology, 49,* 193–211.

Hayes, S. C. (1985). Natural multiple baselines across persons: A reply to Harris and Jenson. *Behavioral Assessment, 7,* 129–132.

Hayes, S. C. (1986). The case of the silent dog: Verbal reports and the analysis of rules. A review of K. Anders Ericsson and Herbert A. Simons "Protocol analysis: Verbal reports as data." *Journal of the Experimental Analysis of Behavior, 45,* 351–363.

Hayes, S. C. (1987) A contextual approach to therapeutic change. In N. Jacobson (Ed.), *Psychotherapists in clinical practice* (pp. 327–387). New York: Guilford Press.

Hayes, S. C. (1997). National planning summit on practice guidelines: Round two. *The Behavior Therapist, 20,* 160–162.

Hayes, S. C. (1998). Scientifically-based practice guidelines in political, economic, and professional context. In K. S. Dobson, & K. D. Craig, (Eds.), *Best practice: Development and promoting empirically validated interventions* (pp. 26–42). Newbury Park, CA: Sage.

Hayes, S. C., & Cavior, N. (1980). Multiple tracking and the reactivity of self-monitoring II: Positive behaviors. *Behavioral Assessment, 2,* 283–296.

Hayes, S. C., & Cone, J. D. (1977). Reducing residential electrical energy use: Payments, information, and feedback. *Journal of Applied Behavior Analysis, 10,* 425–435.

Hayes, S. C., & Follette, W. C. (1992). Can functional analysis provide a substitute for syndromal classification? *Behavioral Assessment, 14,* 345–365.

Hayes, S. C., Follette, V. M., Dawes, R. D., & Grady, K. (Eds.). (1995). *Scientific standards of psychological practice: Issues and recommendations.* Reno, NV: Context Press.

Hayes, S. C., & Heiby, E. (1996). Psychology's drug problem: Do we need a fix or should we just say no? *American Psychologist, 51,* 198–206.

Hayes, S. C., Hussian, R. A., Turner, A. E., Anderson, N. B., & Grubb, T. D. (1983). The effect of coping statements on progress through a desensitization hierarchy. *Journal of Behavior Therapy and Experimental Psychiatry, 14,* 117–129.

Hayes, S. C., Johnson, V. S., & Cone, J. D. (1975). The marked item technique: A practical procedure for litter control. *Journal of Applied Behavior Analysis, 8,* 381–386.

Hayes, S. C., Nelson, R. O., & Jarrett, R. B. (1986). Evaluating the quality of behavioral assessment. In R. O. Nelson & S. C. Hayes (Eds.), *Conceptual foundations of behavioral assessment* (pp. 463–503). New York: Guilford.

Hayes, S. C., Nelson, R. O., & Jarrett, R. B. (1987). Treatment utility of assessment: A functional approach to evaluating the quality of assessment. *American Psychologist, 42,* 963–974.

Hayes, S. C., Nelson, R. O., Willis, S., & Akamatsu, T. J. (1982). Visual avoidance: The use of slides in a convenient measure of phobic behavior. *Behavioral Assessment, 4,* 211–217.

Hayes, S. C., Strosahl, K. & Wilson, K. (in press). *Acceptance and commitment therapy: Understanding and treating human suffering.* New York: Guilford Press.

Hayes, S. C., White, D., & Bissett, R. T. (1998). Protocol analysis and the "silent dog" method of analyzing the impact of self-generated rules. *The Analysis of Verbal Behavior, 15,* 57–63.

Haynes, S. N. (1978). *Principles of behavioral assessment.* New York: Gardner.

Haynes, S. N. (1986). The design of intervention programs In R O. Nelson & S. C. Hayes (Eds.), *Conceptual foundations of behavioral assessment* (pp. 386–429). New York: Guilford.

Haynes, S. N. (1996). The changing nature of behavioral assessment. In M. Hersen, & A. S. Bellack (Eds.), *Behavioral assessment: A practical handbook* (4th ed.). Boston: Allyn & Bacon.

Haynes, S. N., Griffin, P., Mooney, D., & Parise, M. (1975). Electromyographic biofeedback and relaxation instructions in the treatment of muscle contraction headaches. *Behavior Therapy, 6,* 672–678.

Haynes, S. N., & Horn, W. F. (1982). Reactivity in behavioral observation: A review. *Behavioral Assessment, 4,* 369–385.

Haynes, S. N., & O'Brien, W. H. (1990). Functional analysis in behavior therapy. *Clinical Psychology Review, 10,* 649–668.

Haynes, S. N., & Wilson, C. C. (1979). *Behavioral assessment.* San Francisco: Jossey-Bass.

Hays, W. L. (1963). *Statistics for psychologists.* New York: Holt, Rinehart & Winston.

Heath, H. A., & Oken, M. D. (1965). The quantification of "response" to experimental stimuli. *Psychosomatic Medicine, 27,* 457–471.

Heimberg, R. G., Dodge, C. S., Hope, D. A., Kennedy, C. R., Zollo, L. J., & Becker, R. E. (1990). Cognitive behavioral group treatment for social phobia: Comparison with a credible placebo control. *Cognitive Therapy and Research, 14,* 1–23.

Heins, E. D., Lloyd, J. W., & Hallahan, D. P. (1986). Cued and noncued self-recording of attention to task. *Behavior Modification, 10,* 235–254.

Helzer, J. E. (1983). Standardized interviews in psychiatry. *Psychiatric Developments, 2,* 161–178.

Henry, B., Moffit, T. E., Caspi, A., Langley, J., & Silva, P. A. (1994). "On the remembrance of things past": A longitudinal evaluation of the retrospective method. *Psychological Assessment, 6,* 92–101.

Hersen, M., & Barlow, D. H. (1976). *Single case experimental designs: Strategies for studying behavior change.* New York: Pergamon.

Heyman, R. E., Weiss, R. L., & Eddy, J. M. (1995). Marital interaction coding system: Revision and empirical evaluation. *Behavior Research and Therapy, 33*(6), 737–746.

Higgins, R. L., Alonso, R. R., & Pendleton, M. G. (1979). The validity of role-play assessments of assertiveness. *Behavior Therapy, 10,* 655–662.

Higgins, S. T., Budney, A. J., Bickel, W. K., Hughes, J. R., Foeg, F., & Badger, C. (1993). Achieving cocaine abstinence with a behavioral approach. *American Journal of Psychiatry, 150,* 763–769.

Hile, M. G. (1991). Hand-held behavioral observations: The observer. *Behavioral Assessment, 13,* 187–196.

Hilliard, R. B. (1993). Single-case methodology in psychotherapy process and outcome research. *Journal of Consulting and Clinical Psychology, 61,* 373–380.

Hinchliffe, M. K., Lancashire, M., & Roberts, F. J. (1971). A study of eye-contact changes in depressed and recovered psychiatric patients. *British Journal of Psychiatry, 119,* 213–215.

Hiss, H., Foa, E. B., & Kozak, M. J. (1994). Relapse prevention program for treatment of obsessive-compulsive disorder. *Journal of Consulting and Clinical Psychology, 62,* 801–808.

Hoch, E. L., Ross, A. O., & Winder, C. L. (Eds.) (1966). *Professional education of clinical psychologists.* Washington, DC: American Psychological Association.

Hodgson, R., & Rachman, S. (1974). Desynchrony in measures of fear. *Behaviour Research and Therapy, 12,* 319–326.

Hoffman, D. A., Fagot, B. I., Reid, J. B., & Patterson, G. F. (1987). Parents rate the Family Interaction Coding System comparisons of problem and nonproblem boys using parent-derived behavior composites. *Behavioral Assessment, 9*(2), 131–140.

Hofmann, S. G., & Barlow, D. H. (1996). Ambulatory psychophysiological monitoring: A potentially useful tool when treating panic relapse. *Cognitive and Behavioral Practice, 3,* 53–61.

Hogarty, G. E., Anderson, C. M., Reiss, D. J., Kornblith, S. J., Greenwald, D. P., Javina, C. D., & Madonia, M. J. (1986). Family psychoeducation, social skills training, and maintenance chemotherapy in the aftercare treatment of schizophrenia: I. One-year effects of a controlled study on relapse and expressed emotion. *Archives of General Psychiatry, 43,* 633–642.

Hoge, R. D., Andrews, D. A., & Leschied, A. W. (1996). An investigation of risk and protective factors in a sample of youthful offenders. *Journal of Child Psychology and Psychiatry, 37,* 419–424.

Hollon, S. D., and Kendall, P. C. (1980). Cognitive self-statements in depression: Development of an Automatic Thoughts Questionnaire. *Cognitive Therapy and Research, 4,* 383–395.

Hollon, S., & Bemis, K. (1981) Self-report and the Assessment of cognitive functions. In M. Hersen, & A. Bellack, (Eds.) *Behavioral assessment: A practical handbook.* New York: Pergamon Press.

Holroyd, K. A., & Penzien, D. B. (1990). Pharmacological versus nonpharmocological prophylaxis of recurrent migraine headache: A metanalytic review of clinical trials. *Pain, 42,* 1–13.

Hopkins, J., Krawitz, G., & Bellack, A. S. (1981). The effects of situational variations in role-play scenes on assertive behavior. *Journal of Behavioral Assessment, 3,* 271–280.

Hops, H., Wills, T. A., Patterson, G. R., & Weiss, R. L. (1972). *Marital interaction coding system.* Eugene, OR: University of Oregon and Oregon Research Institute.

Hord, D. J., Johnson, L. C. & Lubin, A. (1964). Differential effect of the law of initial value (LIV) on automatic variables. *Psychophysiology, 1,* 79–87.

Horner, R. D., & Baer, D. M. (1978). Multiple-probe technique: A variation of the multiple baseline. *Journal of Applied Behavior Analysis, 11,* 189–196.

Hoshmand, L. T., & Polkinghorne, D. E. (1992). Redefining the science-practice relationship and professional training. *American Psychologist, 47,* 55–66.

Houlihan, D. D., Jones, R. N., Sloane, H. N., & Cook J. (1992). An extension of the sequential alternating treatments design using reversals with subjects not available concurrently. *Behavioral Residential Treatment, 7,* 71–77.

Houts, A. C. Berman, J. S., & Abramson, H. (1994). Effectiveness of psychological and pharmacological treatments for nocturnal enuresis. *Journal of Consulting and Clinical Psychology, 62,* 737–745.

Howard, K. I., Moras, K., Brill, P. L., Martinovich, A., & Lutz, W. (1996). Evaluation of psychotherapy: Efficacy, effectiveness, and patient progress. *American Psychologist, 51,* 1059–1064.

Hsu, L. K. G., Santhouse, R., & Chesler, B. E. (1991). Individual cognitive behavioral therapy for bulimia nervosa: The description of a program. *International Journal of Eating Disorders, 10,* 273–283.

Hudson, S. M., Johnston, & Marshall, W. L. (1992). The effect of masturbatory reconditioning with nonfamilial child molestors. *Behaviour Research and Therapy, 30,* 559–561.

Hudson, W. W. (1992). *The Clinical Measurement Package: A field manual.* Chicago: Dorsey Press.

Hugdahl, K. (1981). The three-systems-model of fear and emotion–a critical examination. *Behaviour Research and Therapy, 19,* 75–85.

Hughes, G. H., Frederiksen, L. W., & Frazier, M. (1978). Carbon monoxide analyses for measurement of smoking behavior. *Behavior Therapy, 9,* 293–296.

Huitema, B. E., & McKean, J. W. (1991) Autocorrelation estimation and inference with small samples.

Hulbert, D. F., & Apt, C. (1994). Female sexual desire, response, and behavior. *Behavior Modification, 18,* 488–504.

Human, J., & Wasem, C. (1991). Rural mental health in America. *American Psychologist, 46,* 232–239.

Humphreys, K., Mavis, B., & Stofflemayr, B. (1991). Factors predicting attendance at self-help groups after substance abuse treatment: Preliminary findings. *Journal of Consulting and Clinical Psychology, 59,* 591–593

Humphreys, L., & Beiman, I. (1975). The application of multiple behavioral techniques to multiple problems of a complex case. *Journal of Behavior Therapy and Experimental Psychiatry, 6,* 311–315.

Hundert, J., & Batstone, D. (1978). A practical procedure to maintain pupils' accurate self-rating in a classroom token program. *Behavior Modification, 2,* 93–112.

Hundert, J., & Bucher, B. (1978). Pupils' self-scored arithmetic performance: A practical procedure for maintaining accuracy. *Journal of Applied Behavior Analysis, 11,* 304.

Hunter, J. E. (1997). Needed: A ban on the significance test. *Psychological Science, 8,* 3–7.

Hunter, M., & Windle, C. D. (1991). NIMH support of rural mental health. *American Psychologist, 46,* 240–243.

Hyler, S. E., Gabbard, G. O., & Schneider, I. (1991). Homicidal maniacs and narcissistic parasites: Stigmatization of mentally ill persons in the movies. *Hospital and Community Psychiatry, 42,* 1044–1048.

Iacono, W. G., (1991). Psychophysiological assessment of psychopathology. *Psychological Assessment, 3,* 309–320.

Iacono, W. G., & Lykken, D. T. (1979). The orienting response: Importance of instructions. *Schizophrenia Bulletin, 5,* 11–14.

Ingenmey, R., & Van Houten, R. (1991). Using time delay to promote spontaneous speech in an autistic child. *Journal of Applied Behavior Analysis, 24,* 591–596.

Institute of Medicine (U.S.). (1992). Committee on Clinical Practice Guidelines: *Guidelines for clinical practice: From development to use.* Edited by Field, M. J. & Gray, B. H. Washington, DC: National Academy Press.

Institute of Medicine (U.S.). (1989). Committee on Utilization Management by Third Parties: Controlling costs and changing patient care? *The role of utilization management.* Edited by Field, M. J., & Gray, B. H. Washington DC: National Academy Press.

Israel, A. C., Silverman, W. K., Slotar, L. C. (1986). An investigation of family influences on initial weight status, attrition, and treatment outcome in a childhood obesity program. *Behavior Therapy, 17,* 131–143.

Ivanoff, A., Blythe, B. J., & Briar, S. (1987). The empirical clinical practice debate. *Social Casework, 68,* 290–298.

Iwata, B., Dorsey, M., Slifer, K., Bauman, K., & Richman, G. (1982). Toward a functional analysis of self-injury. *Analysis and Intervention in Developmental Disabilities, 3,* 1–20.

Jacobson, N. S., & Anderson, E. A. (1982). Interpersonal skill and depression in college students: An analysis of the timing of self-disclosures. *Behavior Therapy, 13,* 271–282.

Jacobson, N. S., & Follette, W. C. (1985). Clinical significance of improvement resulting from two behavioral marital therapy components. *Behavior Therapy, 16,* 249–262.

Jacobson, N. S., Follette, W. C., & Revenstorf, D. (1984). Psychotherapy outcome research: Methods for reporting variability and evaluating clinical significance. *Behavior Therapy, 15,* 336–352.

Jacobson, N. S., Schmaling, K. B., Holtzworth-Munroe, A., Katt, J. L., Wood L. F., & Follette, V. M. (1989). Research structured vs. clinically flexible versions of social learning-based marital therapy. *Behaviour Research and Therapy, 27,* 173–180.

Jacobson, N. S., & Truax, P. (1991). Clinical significance: A statistical approach to defining meaningful change in psychotherapy research. *Journal of Consulting and Clinical Psychology, 59,* 12–19.

Jacobson, N. S., Wilson, L., & Tupper, C. (1988). The clinical significance of treatment gains resulting from exposure-based interventions for agoraphobia: A reanalysis of outcome data. *Behavior Therapy, 19,* 539–554.

Jamison, C., & Scogin, F. (1995). The outcome of cognitive bibliotherapy with depressed adults. *Journal of Consulting and Clinical Psychology, 63,* 644–650.

Jannson, L., Jerremalm, A., & Ost, L. G. (1986). Follow-up of agoraphobic patients treated with exposure in vivo or applied relaxation. *British Journal of Psychiatry, 149,* 486–490.

Jannson, L., & Ost, L. G. (1982). Behavioral treatments for agoraphobia: An evaluative review. *Clinical Psychology Review, 2,* 311–336.

Janosky, J. E. (1992). Use of the nonparametric smoother for examination of data from a single-subject design. *Behavior Modification, 16,* 387–399.

Jayaratne, S., & Levy, R. L. (1979). *Empirical clinical practice.* New York: Columbia University Press.

Jayne, D., Schloss, P. J., Alper, S., & Menscher, S. (1994). Reducing disruptive behaviors by training students to request assistance. *Behavior Modification, 18,* 320–338.

Jennings, J. R., Berg, W. K., Hutcheson, J. S., Obrist, P. A., & Turpin, G. (1981). Publication guidelines for heart rate studies in man. *Psychophysiology, 18,* 226–231.

Joffe, J. M., Albee, G. W., & Kelly, L. D. (Eds.). (1984). Report of the task panel on prevention. *Readings in primary prevention of psychopathology: Basic concepts.* Burlington, VT: Vermont Conference on the Primary Prevention of Psychopathology.

Johnson, L. D., & Shaha, S. (1996). Improving quality in psychotherapy. *Psychotherapy, 33,* 225–236.

Johnson, S. M., & Greenberg, L. S. (1985). Differential effects of experiential and problem-solving interventions in resolving marital conflict. *Journal of Consulting and Clinical Psychology, 53,* 175–184.

Johnson, W. R. (1981). Basic interviewing skills. In C. P. Walker (Ed.), *Clinical practice of psychology.* New York: Pergamon.

Johnston, P., Hudson, S. M., Marshall, W. L. (1992). The effects of masturbatory reconditioning with nonfamilial child molesters. *Behaviour Research and Therapy, 30*(5), 559–563.

Joint Commission on Mental Illness and Health. (1961). *Action for mental health.* New York: Science Editions.

Jones, E. E. (1993). Introduction to special section: Single-case research in psychotherapy. *Journal of Consulting and Clinical Psychology, 61,* 371–372.

Jones, R. R. (1977). Conceptual vs. analytic uses of generalizability theory in behavioral assessment. In J. D. Cone & R. P. Hawkins (Eds.), *Behavioral assessment: New directions in clinical psychology.* New York: Brunner/Mazel.

Jordan, J., Singh, N. N., & Repp, A. C. (1989). An evaluation of gentle teaching and visual screening in the reduction of stereotypy. *Journal of Applied Behavior Analysis, 22,* 9–22.

Kanfer, F. H. (1977). The many faces of self-control, or behavior modification changes its focus. In R. B. Stuart (Ed.), *Behavioral self-management: Strategies, techniques, and outcomes* (pp. 1–48). New York: Brunner/Mazel.

Kanfer, F. H. (1990). The scientist-practitioner connection: A bridge in need of constant attention. *Professional Psychology: Research and Practice, 21,* 264–270.

Kanfer, F. H., Cox, L. E., Greiner, J. M., & Karoly, P. (1974). Contracts, demand characteristics and self-control. *Journal of Personality and Social Psychology, 30,* 605–619.

Kanfer, F. H., & Grimm, L. G. (1977). Behavioral analysis: Selecting target behaviors in the interview. *Behavior Modification, 1,* 7–28.

Kanfer, F. H., & Phillips, J. S. (1970). *Learning foundations of behavior therapy.* New York; Wiley.

Kanfer, F. H., & Saslow, G. (1969). Behavioral Diagnosis. In C. M. Franks (Ed.), *Behavior theory appraisal and status.* New York. McGraw-Hill.

Kaplan, H. S. (1979). *Disorders of sexual desire.* New York: Brunner/Mazel.

Kaplan, H. S. (1987). *Sexual aversion, sexual phobias, and panic disorder.* New York: Brunner/Mazel.

Kashima, K. J., Baker, B. L., & Landen, S. L. (1988). Media-based versus professionally led training for parents of mentally retarded children. *American Journal on Mental Retardation, 93,* 209–217.

Katell, A., Callahan, E. J., Fremouw, W. J., & Zitter, R. E. (1979). The effects of behavioral treatment and fasting on eating behaviors and weight loss: A case study. *Behavior Therapy, 10,* 579–587.

Katkin, E. S., Fitzgerald, C., & Shapiro, D. (1978). Clinical applications of biofeedback: Current status and future prospects. In H. L. Pick, H. W. Leibowitz, J. E. Singer, A. Steinschneider, & H. W. Stevenson (Eds.), *Psychology: From research to practice.* New York: Plenum.

Katz, R. C., & Wooley, F. R. (1975). Improving patients' records through problem orientation. *Behavior Therapy, 6,* 119–124.

Kazdin, A. E. (1974a). The effect of model identity and fear-relevant similarity on covert modeling. *Behavior Therapy, 5,* 624–635.

Kazdin, A. E. (1974b). Reactive self-monitoring: The effects of response desirability, goal setting, and feedback. *Journal of Consulting and Clinical Psychology, 42,* 704–716.

Kazdin, A. E. (1977). Assessing the clinical or applied importance of behavior change through social validation. *Behavior Modification, 1,* 427–452.

Kazdin, A. E. (1979). Unobtrusive measures in behavioral assessment. *Journal of Applied Behavior Analysis, 12,* 713–724.

Kazdin, A. E. (1980). *Research design in clinical psychology.* New York: Harper and Row.

Kazdin, A. E. (1981). Drawing valid inferences from case studies. *Journal of Consulting and Clinical Psychology, 49,* 183–192.

Kazdin, A. E. (1982). *Single-case research designs: Methods for clinical and applied settings.* New York: Oxford University Press.

Kazdin, A. E. (Ed.). (1992). *Methodological issues and strategies in clinical research.* Washington, DC: American Psychological Association.

Kazdin, A. E. (1992). *Research design in clinical psychology* (2nd ed.). Boston: Allyn & Bacon.

Kazdin, A. E. (1994). *Behavior modification in applied settings* (5th ed.). Pacific Grove, CA: Brooks/Cole.

Kazdin, A. E., & Bass, D. (1989). Power to detect differences between alternative treatments in comparative psychotherapy outcome research. *Journal of Consulting and Clinical Psychology, 57,* 138–147.

Kazdin, A. E., & Hartmann, D. P. (1978). The simultaneous-treatment design. *Behavior Therapy, 9,* 912–922.

Kazdin, A. E., & Kopel, S. A. (1975). On resolving ambiguities of the multiple-baseline design: Problems and recommendations. *Behavior Therapy, 6,* 601–608.

Kazdin, A. E., & Wilcoxon, L. A. (1976). Systematic desensitization and nonspecific treatment effects: A methodological evaluation, *Psychological Bulletin, 83,* 729–758.

Keane, T. M., Fairbank, J. A., Caddell, J. M., & Zimering, R. T. (1989). Implosive (flooding) therapy reduces symptoms of PTSD in Vietnam combat veterans. *Behavior Therapy, 20,* 245–260.

Kearns, K., Edwards, R., & Tingstrom, D. H. (1990). Accuracy of long momentary time-sampling intervals: Implications for classroom data collection. *Journal of Psychoeducational Assessment, 8*(1), 74–85.

Keefe, F. J., Dunsmore, J., & Burnett, R. (1992). Behavioral and cognitive-behavioral approaches to chronic pain: Recent advances and future directions. *Journal of Consulting and Clinical Psychology, 60,* 528–536.

Kendall, P. C., & Hollon, S. D. (1981). Assessing self-referent speech: Methods in the measurement of self-statements. In P. C. Kendall & S. D. Hollon (Eds.), *Assessment strategies for cognitive-behavioral interventions.* New York: Academic Press.

Kent, R. N., & Foster, S. L. (1977). Direct observation procedures: Methodological issues in naturalistic settings. In A. R. Ciminero, K. S. Calhoun, & H. E. Adams (Eds.), *Handbook of behavioral assessment.* New York: Wiley.

Kern, L., Wacker, D. P., Mace, F. C., Falk, G. D., Dunlap, G., & Kromrey, J. D. (1995). Improving the peer interactions of students with emotional and behavioral disorders through self-evaluation procedures. *Journal of Applied Behavior Analysis, 28,* 47–59.

Kessler, M., & Albee, G. (1975). Primary prevention. *Annual Review of Psychology, 26,* 557–591.

Kessler, R. C., & Wethington, E., (1991). The reliability of life event reports in a community survey. *Psychology Medicine, 21,* 723–738.

Kiesler, C. A., & Simpkins, C. (1991). The de facto national system of psychiatric inpatient care: Piecing together the national puzzle. *American Psychologist, 46,* 579–584.

Kiesler, D. J. (1966). Some myths of psychotherapy research and the search for a paradigm. *Psychological Bulletin, 65,* 110–136.

Kiesler, D. J. (1971). Experimental designs in psychotherapy research. In A. E. Bergin & S. L. Garfield (Eds.), *Handbook of psychotherapy and behavior change: An empirical analysis* (pp. 36–74). New York: Wiley.

Kiresuk, T. J., & Sherman, R. E. (1968). Goal attainment scaling: A general method for evaluating comprehensive community mental health programs. *Community Mental Health Journal, 4,* 443–453.

Kirk, J. (1989). Cognitive-behavioural assessment. In K. Hawton, P. M., Salkovskis, J. Kirk, & D. M. Clark (Eds.), *Cognitive behaviour therapy for psychiatric problems.* (pp. 13–51). Oxford: Oxford University Press.

Klerman, G. L., Weissman, M. M., Rounsaville, B. J., & Chevron, E. S. (1984). *Interpersonal psychotherapy of depression.* New York: Basic Books.

Klosko, J. S., Barlow, D. H., Tassinari, R., & Cerny, J. A. (1990). A comparison of alprazolam and cognitive-behavior therapy in treatment of panic disorder. *Journal of Clinical Psychology, 58,* 77–84.

Knox, L. S., Albano, A. M., & Barlow, D. H. (1996). Parental involvement in the treatment of childhood obsessive compulsive disorder: A multiple baseline examination incorporating parents. *Behavior Therapy, 27,* 93–115.

Kohlenberg, R. J., & Tsai, M. (1991). *Functional analytic psychotherapy: Creating intense and curative therapeutic relationships.* New York: Plenum.

Kohlenberg, R. J., & Tsai, M. (1994). Improving cognitive therapy for depression with functional analytic psychotherapy: Theory and case study. *Behavior Analyst, 17,* 305–319.

Kolko, D. J., & Kazdin, A. E. (1993) Emotional/behavioral problems in clinic and nonclinic children: Correspondance among child, parent, and teacher reports. *Journal of Child Psychology and Psychiatry and Allied Disciplines, 34*(6), 991–1006.

Konarski, E. A., & Johnson, M. R. (1989). The use of brief restraint plus reinforcement to treat self-injurious behavior. *Behavioral Residential Treatment, 4,* 45–52.

Korman, M. (Ed.). (1976). *Levels and patterns of professional training in psychology.* Washington, DC: American Psychological Association.

Kornet, M., Goosen, C., & Van Ree, J. M. (1991). Effect of naltrexone on alcohol consumption during chronic alcohol drinking and after a period of imposed abstinence in free-choice drinking rhesus monkeys. *Pharmacology, 104,* 367–376.

Lacey, J. I. (1956). The evaluation of automatic responses: Toward a general resolution. *Annals of the New York Academy of Sciences, 67,* 125–163.

Lacey, J. I. (1967). Somatic response patterning and stress: Some revisions of activation theory. In M. H. Appley & R. Trumbell (Eds.), *Psychological stress: Issues in research* (pp. 14–42). New York: Appleton-Century-Crofts.

Lacey, J. I., Bateman, D. E., & Van Lehn, R. (1953). Autonomic response specificity: An experimental study. *Psychosomatic Medicine, 15,* 18–21.

Lambert, M. J., & Brown, G. S. (1996). Data-based management for tracking outcome in private practice. *Clinical Psychology: Science and Practice, 3,* 172–178.

Lambert, M. J., Huefner, J. C., & Reisinger, C. W. (1996). Quality improvement: Current research in outcome management. In W. T. Stricker and S. Sheuman (Eds.), *Handbook of quality management in behavioral health.* New York: Plenum.

Lambert, M. J., & McRoberts, C. (1993, April). Survey of outcome measures used in JCCP: 1986–1991. Poster presented at the annual meeting of the Western Psychological Association, Phoenix, AZ. Cited in Lambert, M. J., & Hill, C. E. (1994), Assessing psychotherapy outcomes and processes. In A. E. Bergin & S. L. Garfield (Eds.), *Handbook of psychotherapy and behavior change* (4th ed.) (pp. 72–113). New York: Wiley.

Lambert, M. J., Ogles, B. M., & Masters, K. S. (1992). Choosing outcome assessment devices: An organizational and conceptual scheme. *Journal of Counseling and Development, 70,* 527–532.

Lamiell, J. T. (1980). On the utility of looking in the "wrong" direction. *Journal of Personality, 48,* 82–88.

Lamiell, J. T. (1981). Toward an idiothetic psychology of personality. *American Psychology, 36,* 276–289.

Lamiell, J. T., Trierweiller, S. T., & Foss, M. A. (1983). Theoretical versus actuarial analyses of personality ratings and other rudimentary distinctions. *Journal of Personality, 51,* 259–274.

Landerman, L. R., Burns, B. J., Swartz, M. S., Wagner, H. R., & George, L. K. (1994). The relationship between insurance coverage and psychiatric disorder in predicting use of mental health services. *American Journal of Psychiatry, 151,* 1785–1790.

Lang, P. J. (1968). Fear reduction and fear behavior: Problems in treating a construct. In J. M. Shlien (Ed.), *Research in psychotherapy, Vol. 3.* Washington, DC: American Psychological Association.

Lang, P. J. (1971). The application of psychophysiological methods to the study of psychotherapy and behavior modification. In A. E. Bergin & S. L. Garfield (Eds.), *Handbook of psychotherapy and behavior change.* New York: Wiley.

Lang, P. J., & Cuthbert, B. N. (1984). Affective information processing and the assessment of anxiety. *Journal of Behavior Assessment, 6,* 369–395.

Larsen, Attkinson, C. C., Hargreaves, W. A., & Nguyen, T. D. (1979). Assessment of client/patient satisfaction: Development of a general scale. *Evaluation and Program Planning, 2,* 197–207.

Last, J. M., (1988). *A dictionary of epidemiology* (2nd ed.). New York: Oxford University Press.

Layne, C. C., Rickard, H. C., Jones, M. P., & Lyman, R. D. (1976). Accuracy of self-recording on a variable ratio schedule of observer verification. *Behavior Therapy, 7,* 481–488.

Lazarus, A. A. (1971). *Behavior therapy and beyond.* New York: McGraw-Hill.

Lebow, J. L. (1983). Research assessing consumer satisfaction with mental health treatment: A review of findings. *Evaluation and Program Planning, 6,* 211–236.

Leger, L. A. (1979). An outcome measure for thought-stopping examined in three case studies. *Journal of Behavior Therapy and Experimental Psychiatry, 10,* 115–120.

Lehnert, K. L., Overholser, J. C., & Adams, D. M. (1996). The cognition rating form: A new approach to assessing self-generated cognitions in adolescent sentence completions. *Psychological Assessment, 8,* 172–181.

Leigh, B. C., & Stall, R. (1993). Substance use and risky sexual behavior for exposure to HIV: Issues in methodology, interpretation, and prevention. *American Psychologist, 48,* 1035–1045.

Leitenberg, H. (1973). The use of single-ease methodology in psychotherapy research. *Journal of Abnormal Psychology, 82,* 87–101.

Leitenberg, H. (1974). Training clinical researchers in clinical psychology. *Professional Psychology, 5,* 59–69.

Leitenberg, H., Agras, W. S., Butz, R., & Wincze, J. (1971). Relationship between heart rate and behavioral change during the treatment of phobias. *Journal of Abnormal Psychology, 78,* 59–68.

Leitenberg, H., & Callahan, E. J. (1973). Reinforced practice and reduction of different kinds of fears in adults and children. *Behavior Research and Therapy, 11,* 19–30.

Lemere, F., & Voegtlin, W. L. (1950). An evaluation of the aversion treatment of alcoholism. *Quarterly Journal of Studies on Alcohol, 11,* 199–204.

Leon, R. L. (1982). *Psychiatric interviewing: A primer.* New York: McGraw-Hill.

Leonard, S. R., & Hayes, S. C. (1983). Sexual fantasy alternation. *Journal of Behavior Therapy and Experimental Psychiatry, 14,* 241–249.

Levi, L., & Anderson, L. (1975). *Psychosocial stress. Population, environment, and the quality of life.* Holliswood, NY: Spectrum.

Levy, R. L. (1977). Relationship of an overt commitment to task compliance in behavior therapy. *Journal of Behavior Therapy and Experimental Psychiatry, 8,* 25–29.

Lewinsohn, P. M., & Arconad, M. (1981). Behavioral treatment of depression: A social learning approach. In J. F. Clarkin & H. 1. Glazer (Eds.), *Depression: Behavioral and directive intervention strategies.* New York: Garland.

Lewinsohn, P. M., Hoberman, H. M., & Clarke, G. N. (1989). The Coping With Depression Course: Review and future directions. *Canadian Journal of Behavioural Science, 21,* 470–493.

Lewinsohn, P. M., & Rosenbaum, M. (1987). Recall of parental behavior by acute depressives, remitted depressives, and nondepressives. *Journal of Personality and Social Psychology, 52,* 611–619.

Lewis, M., Shilton, P., & Fuqua, R. W. (1981). Parental control of nocturnal thumbsucking. *Journal of Behavior Therapy and Experimental Psychology, 12,* 87–90.

Liberman, R. P. (1972). Behavioral modification of schizophrenia: A review. *Schizophrenia Bulletin, 1*(6), 37–48.

Lichtenstein, E. (1982). The smoking problem: A behavioral perspective. *Journal of Consulting and Clinical Psychology, 50,* 804–819.

Lidren, D. M., Watkins, P. L., Gould, R. A., Clum, G. A., Asterino, M., & Tulloch, H. L. (1994). A comparison of bibliotherapy and group therapy in the treatment of panic disorder. *Journal of Consulting and Clinical Psychology, 62,* 865–869.

Lieberman, M. A., & Snowden, L. R. (1993). Problems in assessing prevalence and membership characteristics of self-help group participants. *Journal of Applied Behavioral Science, 29,* 166–180.

Lieberman, M. A., & Videka-Sherman, L. (1986). The impact of self-help groups on the mental health of widows and widowers. *American Journal of Orthopsychiatry, 56,* 435–443.

Lilienfeld, D. E., & Stolley, D. D. (1994). *Foundations of epidemiology* (3rd ed.). New York: Oxford University Press.

Linehan, M. M. (1977). Issues in behaviorial interviewing. In J. D. Cone & R. P. Hawkins (Eds.), *Behavioral assessment: New directions in clinical Psychology.* New York: Brunner\Mazel.

Linehan, M. M. (1993a). *Cognitive-behavioral treatment of borderline personality disorder.* New York: Guilford.

Linehan, M. M. (1993b). *Skills training manual for treating borderline personality disorder.* New York: Guilford.

Linehan, M. M., Armstrong, H. E., Suarez, A., Allmon, D., & Heard, H. L. (1991). Cognitive-behavioral treatment of chronically parasuicidal borderline patients. *Archives of General Psychiatry, 48,* 1060–1064.

Linehan, M. M., Heard, H., & Armstrong, H. (1993). Naturalistic follow-up of a behavioral treatment for chronically parasuicidal borderline patients. *Archives of General Psychiatry, 50,* 971–974.

Lipinski, D. P., Black, J. L., Nelson, R. O., & Ciminero, A. R. (1975). The influence of motivational variables on the reactivity and reliability of self-recording. *Journal of Consulting and Clinical Psychology, 43,* 637–646.

Lipinski, D. P. & Nelson, R. O. (1974). The reactivity and unreliability of self-recording. *Journal of Consulting and Clinical Psychology, 42,* 118–123.

Loftus, E. (1993). The reality of repressed memories. *American Psychologist, 48,* 518–537.

Loftus, E. F., Klinger, M. R., Smith, K. D., and Fielder, J. (1990). A tale of two questions: Benefits of asking more than one question. *Public Opinion Quarterly, 54,* 330–345.

Loftus, G. R. (1996). Psychology will be a much better science when we change the way we analyze data. *Current Directions in Psychological Science, 5,* 161–171.

LoPiccolo, J., & Stock, W. E. (1986). Treatment of sexual dysfunction. *Journal of Consulting and Clinical Psychology, 54,* 158–167.

Lubin, B. (1967). *Depression adjective check lists manual.* San Diego, CA: Educational and Industrial Testing Service.

Luborsky, L., & Crits-Christoph, P. (1990). *Understanding transference: The Core Conflictual Relationship Theme method.* New York: Basic Books.

Luborsky, L., & DeRubeis, R. J. (1984). The use of psychotherapy treatment manuals: A small revolution in psychotherapy research style. *Clinical Psychology Review, 4,* 5–14.

Lynch, P. N., & Zamble, E. (1989). A controlled behavioral treatment of irritable bowel syndrome. *Behavior Therapy, 20,* 509–523.

Mace, F. C., McCurdy, B., & Quigley, E. A. (1990). A collateral effect of reward predicted by matching theory. *Journal of Applied Behavior Analysis, 23,* 197–205.

MacLean, W. E., Tapp, J. T., & Johnson, W. L. (1985). Alternate methods and software for calculating interobserver agreement for continuous observation data. *Journal of Psychopathology and Behavioral Assessment, 7*(1), 65–73.

MacPhillamy, D., & Lewinsohn, P. M. (1975). *Manual for the pleasant events schedule.* Unpublished manuscript.

Mahl, G. F. (1968). Gestures and body movements in interviews. In J. M. Shlien (Ed.), *Research in psychotherapy: Vol. 3* (pp. 295–346). Washington, DC: American Psychological Association.

Mahoney, M. J. (1977). Some applied issues in self-monitoring. In J. D. Cone & R. P. Hawkins (Eds.), *Behavioral assessment: New directions in clinical psychology.* New York: Brunner/Mazel.

Maletzky, B. M. (1980). "Assisted" covert sensitization in the treatment of exhibitionism. In D. J. Cox & R. J. Daitzman (Eds.), *Exhibitionism: Description, assessment and treatment* (pp. 187–251). New York: Garland.

Maletzky, B. M. (1991). *Treating the sexual offender.* Newbury Park, CA: Sage Publications.

Manderscheid, R. W., & Henderson, M. J. (1996). The growth and direction of managed care. In R. W. Manderscheid & M. A. Sonnenschein (Eds.), *Mental health, United States, 1996* (pp. 17–26). Washington, DC: Substance Abuse and Mental Health Services Administration.

Manning, W. G., & Wells, K. B. (1992). The effects of psychological distress and psychological well-being on use of medical services. *Medical Care, 30,* 541–553.

Marcus, B. A., & Vollmer, T. R. (1995). Effects of differential negative reinforcement on disruption and compliance. *Journal of Applied Behavior Analysis, 28,* 229–230.

Margraf, J., Taylor, C. B., Ehlers, A., Roth, W. T., & Agras, W. S. (1987). Panic attacks in the natural environment. *Journal of Nervous and Mental Disease, 175,* 558–565.

Marks, I. M. (1971). Phobic disorders four years after treatment: A prospective follow-up. *British Journal of Psychiatry, 118,* 683–686.

Marks, I. M. (1981). New developments in psychological treatments of phobias. In M. R. Mavissakalian & D. H. Barlow (Eds.), *Phobia: Psychological and pharmacological treatment.* New York: Guilford.

Marks, I. M. (1992). Innovations in mental health care delivery. *British Journal of Psychiatry, 160,* 589–597.

Marshall, G. N., Hays, R. D., Sherbourne, C. D., & Wells, K. B. (1993). The structure of patient satisfaction with outpatient medical care. *Psychological Assessment, 5,* 477–483.

Marshall, W. L., Eccles, A., & Barbaree, H. E. (1991). The treatment of exhibitionists: A focus on sexual deviance versus cognitive and relationship features. *Behaviour Research and Therapy, 29,* 129–135.

Marshall, W. L., Jones, R., Ward, T., Johnston, P., & Barbaree, H. E. (1991). Treatment outcome with sex offenders. *Clinical Psychology Review, 11,* 465–485.

Martick, R. P., & Peters, L. (1988). Treatment of severe social phobia: Effects of guided exposure with and without cognitive restructuring. *Journal of Consulting and Clinical Psychology, 56,* 251–260.

Martin, B. (1961). The assessment of anxiety by physiological and behavioral measures. *Psychological Bulletin, 58,* 234–255.

Martin, P. R. (1989). The scientist-practitioner model and clinical psychology: Time for change? *Australian Psychologist, 24,* 71–92.

Martin, T. W., (1993). White therapists' differing perceptions of black and white adolescents. *Adolescence, 28,* 281–289.

Mash, E. I., & Terdal, L. G. (Eds.). (1976). *Behavior therapy assessment.* New York: Springer.

Masters, W. H., & Johnson, V. E. (1970). *Human sexual inadequacy.* Boston: Little, Brown.

Matarazzo, J. D. (1983). The reliability of psychiatric and psychological diagnosis. *Clinical Psychology Review, 3,* 103–145.

Matarazzo, J. D., Saslow, G., Wiens, A. N., Weitman, M., & Allen, B. V. (1964). Interviewer head-nodding and interviewee speech duration. *Psychotherapy, 1,* 54–63.

Mathews, A. M. (1978). Fear-reduction research and clinical phobias. *Psychological Bulletin, 85,* 390–404.

Matt, G. E., Vasquez, C., Campbell, W. K. (1992). Mood-congruent recall of affectively toned stimuli: A meta-analytic review. *Clinical Psychology Review, 12,* 227–255.

Mavissakalian, M., & Barlow, D. H. (Eds.). (1981). *Phobia: Psychological and pharmacological treatment.* New York: Guilford Publications.

McCleary, R., & Welsh, W. N. (1992). Philosophical and statistical foundations of time-series experiments. In T. R. Kratochwill & J. R. Levin (Eds.), *Single-case research design and analysis: New directions for psychology and education* (pp. 41–91). Hillsdale, NJ: Erlbaum.

McCubbin, H. I., and Thompson, A. I. (Eds.). (1991). *Family assessment: Inventories for research and practice.* Madison: University of Wisconsin.

McFall, R. M. (1977). Analogue methods in behavioral assessment: Issues and prospects. In J. E. Cone & R. P. Hawkins (Eds.), *Behavioral assessment: New directions in clinical psychology.* New York: Brunner/Mazel.

McFall, R. M. (July 1996). *Panel discussion on "Consumer satisfaction as a way of evaluating psychotherapy: Ecological validity and all that versus the good old randomized trial."* Paper presented at the meeting of the American Association of Applied and Preventive Psychology, San Francisco.

McGlynn, F. D., Rose, M. P., & Lazarate, A. (1994). Control and attention during exposure influence arousal and fear among insect phobics. *Behavior Modification, 18,* 371–388.

McGonigle, J. J., Rojahn, J., Dixon, J., & Strain, P. (1987). Multiple treatment interference in the Alternating Treatments Design as a function of the intercomponent interval length. *Journal of Applied Behavior Analysis, 20,* 171–178.

McGrady, A. (1994). Effects of group relaxation training and thermal biofeedback on blood pressure and related physiological and psychological variables in essential hypertension. *Biofeedback and Self-Regulation, 19*(1), 51–66.

McGrath, M. L. (1991). The Empiricist. *Behavioral Assessment, 13,* 1

McGuire, W. J. (1973). The yin and yang of progress in social psychology: Seven koan. *Journal of Personality and Social Psychology, 26,* 446–456.

McIntyre, J. (1994, March 18). Practice research network: Pilot stage. *Psychiatric News, xxix* (6), 3.

McKnight, D. L., Nelson, R. O., Hayes, S. C., & Jarrett, R. B. (1984). Importance of treating individually-assessed response classes in the amelioration of depression. *Behavior Therapy, 15,* 315–335.

McPherson, F. M., Brougham, L., & McLaren, S. (1980). Maintenance of improvement in agoraphobic patients treated by behavioural methods—a four-year follow-up. *Behaviour Research and Therapy, 18,* 150–152.

McReynolds, P. (1979). The case for interactional assessment. *Behavioral Assessment, 1,* 237–247.

McReynolds, W. T., & Stegman, R. (1976). Sayer versus sign. *Behavior Therapy, 7,* 704–705.

Mechanic, D. S. (1996). Key policy considerations for mental health in the managed care era. In R. W. Manderscheid & M. A. Sonnenschein (Eds.), *Mental health, United States, 1996* (pp. 1–16). Washington, DC: Substance Abuse and Mental Health Services Administration.

Meehl, P. E. (1959). Some ruminations on the validation of clinical procedures. *Canadian Journal of Psychology, 13,* 102–128.

Meehl, P. E. (1960). The cognitive activity of the clinician. *American Psychologist, 15,* 19–27.

Meehl, P. E. (1978). Theoretical risks and tabular asterisks: Sir Karl, Sir Ronald, and the slow progress of soft psychology. *Journal of Consulting and Clinical Psychology, 46,* 806–835.

Meichenbaum, D. (1983). Teaching thinking: A cognitive-behavioral approach. In *Interdisciplinary voices in learning disability and remedial education* (pp. 127–155). Austin, TX: PRO-ED.

Mental Health Weekly (Vol. 5, No. 6, 1995). Providence, RI: Manisses Communications Group.

Merluzzi, T. V., & Biever, J. (1987). Role-playing procedures for the behavioral assessment of social skill: A validity study. *Behavioral Assessment, 9,* 361–376.

Mersch, P. P. A., Emmelkamp, P. M. G., Bogels, S. M., & Van Der Sleen, J. (1989). Social phobia: Individual response patterns and the long-term effects of behavioral and cognitive interventions. *Behaviour Research and Therapy, 27,* 421–434.

Mersch, P. P. A., Emmelkamp, P. M. G., & Lips, C. (1991). Social phobia: Individual response patterns and the long-term effects of behavioral and cognitive interventions. A follow-up study. *Behaviour Research and Therapy, 29,* 357–362.

Meyers, A., Mercatoris, M., & Artz, L. (1976). On the development of a cognitive self-monitoring skill. *Behavior Therapy, 7,* 128–129.

Michelson, L., & Ascher, L. M. (1987). *Anxiety and stress disorders: Cognitive-behavioral assessment and treatment.* New York : Guilford Press.

Michelson, L. K., & Marchione, K. (1991). Behavioral, cognitive, and pharmacological treatments of panic disorder with agoraphobia: Critique and synthesis. *Journal of Consulting and Clinical Psychology, 59,* 100–114.

Michelson, L. K., Marchione, K. E., Greenwald, M., Testa, S., & Marchione, N. J. (1996). A comparative outcome and follow-up investigation of panic disorder with agoraphobia: The relative and combined efficacy of cognitive therapy, relaxation training, and therapist-assisted exposure. *Journal of Anxiety Disorders, 10*(5), 297–330.

Michelson, L., Mavissakalian, M., and Marchione, K. (1985). Cognitive and behavioral treatments of agoraphobia: Clinical, behavioral, and psychophysiological outcomes. *Journal of Consulting and Clinical Psychology, 53,* 913–925.

Miller, A. J., & Kratochwill, T. R. (1979). Reduction of frequent stomachache complaints by time out. *Behavior Therapy, 10,* 211–218.

Miller, B. V., & Bernstein, D. A. (1972). Instructional demand in a behavioral avoidance test for claustrophobic fears. *Journal of Abnormal Psychology, 80,* 206–210.

Miller, C. M., & Fremouw, W. J. (1995). Improving the accuracy of adult eyewitness testimony: Implications for children. *Clinical Psychology Review, 15,* 631–645.

Miller, W. (1997). *Spirituality, religion, and the addictive disorders.* Washington, DC: National Institute for Healthcare Research.

Mischel, W. (1968). *Personality and assessment.* New York: Wiley.

Mischel, W. (1973). Toward a cognitive social learning reconceptualization of personality. *Psychological Review, 80,* 252–283.

Mishan, E. J. (1982). *Cost-benefit analysis: An informal introduction.* London: George Allen & Unwin.

Mitchell, J. E., Pyle, R. L., Eckert, E. D., Hatsukami, D., Pomeroy, C., & Zimmerman, R. (1990). A comparison study of antidepressants and structured intensive group psychotherapy in the treatment of bulimia nervosa. *Archives of General Psychiatry, 47,* 149–157.

Moncher, F. J., & Prinz, R. J. (1991). Treatment fidelity in outcome studies. *Clinical Psychology Review, 11,* 247–266.

Montgomery, G. K., & Reynolds, N. C. (1990). Compliance, reliability, and validity of self-monitoring for physical disturbances of Parkinson's disease. *Journal of Nervous and Mental Disease, 178,* 636–641.

Montgomery, R. W. (1993). The collateral effect of compliance training on aggression. *Behavioral Residential Treatment, 8,* 9–20.

Morin, C. M., Colecchi, C. A., Ling, W. D., & Sood, R. K. (1995). Cognitive behavior therapy to facilitate benzodiazepine discontinuation among hypnotic-dependent patients with insomnia. *Behavior Therapy, 26,* 733–745.

Morin, C. M., Stone, J., McDonald, K., & Jones, S. (1994). Psychological management of insomnia: A clinical replication series with 100 patients. *Behavior Therapy, 25,* 291–309.

Morrison, J. R. (1993). *The first interview: A guide for clinicians.* New York: Guilford Press.

Murphy, M. J., & Harrop, A. (1994). Observer error in the use of momentary time sampling and partial interval recording. *British Journal of Psychology, 85*(2), 169–179.

Murray, J. D. & Keller, P. A. (1991). Psychology and rural America. *American Psychologist, 46,* 220–231.

Myrtek, M., & Foerster, F. (1986). The Law of Initial Values: A rare exception. *Biological Psychology, 22,* 227–237.

The National Psychologist. (1997). Survey shows that managed care grew 19% in 1996. *The National Psychologist, 6*(4), 22.

Nay, W. R. (1977) Analogue measures. In A. R. Ciminero, K. S. Calhoun, & H. E. Adams (Eds.), *Handbook of behavioral assessment.* New York: Wiley.

Nelsen, J. C. (1981). Issues in single-subject research for non-behaviorists. *Social Work Research and Abstracts, 17*(2), 31–37.

Nelson, C. M., & McReynolds, W. T. (1971). Self-recording and control of behavior: A reply to Simkins. *Behavior Therapy, 2,* 594–597.

Nelson, D. C., Hartman, E., Ojemann, P. G., & Wilcox, M. (1995). Outcome measurement and management with a large Medicaid population. *Behavioral Healthcare Tomorrow, 4*(3), 31–37.

Nelson, J. R., Smith, D. J., & Dodd J. M. (1992). The effects of teaching a summary skills strategy to students identified as learning disabled on their comprehension of science text. *Education and Treatment of Children, 15,* 228–243.

Nelson, J. R., Smith, D. J., Young, R. K., & Dodd, J. M. (1991). A review of self-management outcome research conducted with students who exhibit behavioral disorders. *Behavioral Disorders, 16,* 169–179.

Nelson, R. O. (1977). Methodological issues in assessment via self-monitoring. In J. D. Cone & R. P. Hawkins (Eds.), *Behavioral assessment: New directions in clinical psychology.* New York: Brunner/Mazel.

Nelson, R. O. (1981). Realistic dependent measures for clinical use. *Journal of Consulting and Clinical Psychology, 49,* 168–182.

Nelson, R. O. (1983). Behavioral assessment: Past, present, and future. *Behavioral Assessment, 5,* 195–206.

Nelson, R. O. (1988). Relationships between assessment and treatment within a behavioral perspective. *Journal of Psychopathology and Behavioral Assessment, 10,* 155–170.

Nelson, R. O., & Barlow, D. H. (1981). Behavioral assessment: Basic strategies and initial procedures. In D. H. Barlow (Ed.), *Behavioral assessment of adult disorders.* New York: Guilford.

Nelson, R. O., & Bowles, P. E. (1975). The best of two worlds-observations with norms. *Journal of School Psychology, 13,* 3–9.

Nelson, R. O., Boykin, R. A., & Hayes, S. C. (1982). Long-term effects of self-monitoring on reactivity and on accuracy. *Behaviour Research and Therapy, 20,* 357–363.

Nelson, R. O., Hay, L. R., & Hay, W. M. (1977). Comments on Cone's "The relevance of reliability and validity for behavioral assessment." *Behavior Therapy, 8,* 427–430.

Nelson, R. O., & Hayes, S. C. (1979). Some current dimensions of behavioral assessment. *Behavioral Assessment, 1,* 1–16.

Nelson, R. O., & Hayes, S. C. (1981). Theoretical explanations for reactivity in self-monitoring. *Behavior Modification, 5*(1), 3–14.

Nelson, R. O., & Hayes, S. C. (1986). The nature of behavioral assessment. In R. O. Nelson & S. C. Hayes (Eds.), *Conceptual foundations of behavioral assessment* (pp. 3–35) New York: Guilford.

Nelson, R. O., Lipinski, D. P., & Black, J. (1975). The effects of expectancy on the reactivity of self-recording. *Behavior Therapy, 6,* 337–349.

Nelson, R. O., Lipinski, D. P., & Boykin, R. A. (1978). The effects of self-recorders' training and the obtrusiveness of the self-recording device on the accuracy and reactivity of self-monitoring. *Behavior Therapy, 9,* 200–208.

Nelson-Gray, R. O. (1996). Treatment outcome measures: Nomothetic or idiographic? *Clinical Psychology: Science and Practice, 3,* 164–157.

Nelson-Gray, R. O., Haas, J. R., Romano, B., Herbert J. D., & Herbert D. L. (1989). Effects of open-ended versus closed-ended questions on interviewees' problem-related statements. *Perceptual and Motor Skills, 69,* 903–911.

Nelson-Gray, R. O., Johnson, D., Foyle, L. W., Daniel, S. S. & Harmon, R. (1996). The effectiveness of cognitive therapy tailored to depressives with personality disorders. *Journal of Personality Disorders, 10,* 132–152.

Newsweek. (1995). 23 January, p. 52.

Nezu, A. (1996). What are we doing to our patients and should we care if anyone else knows? *Clinical Psychology: Science and Practice, 3,* 160–163.

Niemeyer, J. A., & McEvoy, M. A. (1989). *Observational assessment of reciprocal social interactions: Social interaction code.* Vanderbilt/Minnesota Social Interaction Project, Vanderbilt University and the University of Minnesota.

Nisbett, R. E., & Wilson, T. D. (1977). Telling more than we know: Verbal reports on mental processes. *Psychological Review, 84,* 231–259.

Nolan, E. E., & Gadow, K. D. (1994). Relation between ratings and observations of stimulant drug response in hyperactive children. *Journal of Clinical Child Psychology, 23,* 78–90.

Obler, M. (1973). Systematic desensitization in sexual disorders. *Journal of Behavioral Therapy & Experimental Psychiatry, 4,* 93–101.

O'Brien, G. T., & Barlow, D. H. (1984). Agoraphobia. In S. M. Turner (Ed), *Behavioral treatment of anxiety disorders* (pp. 143–185). New York: Plenum.

O'Brien, S., Ross, L. V., & Christophersen, E. R. (1986). Primary encopresis: Evaluation and treatment. *Journal of Applied Behavior Analysis, 19,* 137–145.

Odom, J. V., & Nelson, R. O. (1977). The effect of demand characteristics on heart rate during the behavioral avoidance test. *Perceptual and Motor Skills, 44,* 175–183.

O'Donohue, W., Plaud, J. J., & Hecker, J. E. (1992). The possible function of positive reinforcement in home-bound agoraphobia: A case study. *Journal of Behavior Therapy and Experimental Psychology, 23,* 303–312.

O'Farrell, T. J., Choquette, K. A., Cutter, H. S. G., Brown, E., Bayog, R., McCourt, W., Lowe, J., Chan, A., & Deneault, P. (1996). Cost-benefit and cost-effectiveness analyses of behavioral marital therapy with and without relapse prevention sessions for alcoholics and their spouses. *Behavior Therapy, 27,* 7–24.

Ogles, B. M., Lambert, M. J., & Craig, D. E. (1991). Comparison of self-help books for coping with loss: Expectations and attributions. *Journal of Counseling Psychology, 38,* 387–393.

Ogles, B. M., Lambert, M. J., & Masters, K. (1996). *Assessing outcome in clinical practice.* Boston: Allyn & Bacon.

Oliva, T., Oliver, R., & Bearden, W. (1995). The relationships among consumer satisfaction, involvement, and product performance: A catastrophe theory application. *Behavioral Science, 40,* 104–128.

Ollendick, T. H., Hagopian, L. P., & Huntzinger, R. M. (1991). Cognitive behavior therapy with nighttime fearful children. *Journal of Behavior Therapy and Experimental Psychiatry, 22,* 113–121.

Olton, D. S., & Markowska, A. L. (1988). Within-subjects, parametric manipulations to investigate aging. *Neurobiology of Aging, 9,* 469–474.

Onghena, P., & Edgington, E. S. (1994). Randomization tests for restricted alternating treatments designs. *Behaviour Research and Therapy, 32,* 783–786.

Oos, M. E., & Stair, T. (May 1996). Industry statistics: 68% of insured in managed behavioral health. *Open Minds—The Behavioral Health Industry Analyst.*

O'Reilly, M. F., Green, G., & Braunling-McMorrow, D. (1990). Self-administered written prompts to teach home accident prevention skills to adults with brain injuries. *Journal of Applied Behavior Analysis, 23,* 431–446.

Orne, M. T. (1969). Demand characteristics and the concept of quasi-controls. In R. Rosenthal & R. L. Rosnow (Eds.), *Artifact in behavioral research.* New York: Academic.

Osborne, K., Rudrud, E. & Zezoney, F. (1990). Improved curveball hitting through the enhancement of visual cues. *Journal of Applied Behavior Analysis, 23,* 371–377.

Ost, L. (1988). Applied relaxation vs progressive relaxation in the treatment of panic disorder. *Behaviour Research and Therapy, 26,* 13–22.

Ost, L. G., Salkovskis, P. M., & Heilstrom, K. (1991). One-session therapist-directed exposure vs. self-exposure in the treatment of spider phobia. *Behavior Therapy, 22,* 407–422.

Otto, M. W., Pollack, N. H., Sachs, G. S., Reiter, S. R., Meltzer-Brody, S., & Rosenbaum, J. F. (1993). Discontinuation of benzodiazepine treatment: Efficacy of cognitive behavioral therapy for patients with panic disorder. *American Journal of Psychiatry, 150,* 1485–1490.

Overall, J. E., & Gorham, D. R. (1962). The Brief Psychiatric Rating Scale. *Psychological Reports, 10,* 799–812.

Padgett, D. K., Patrick, C., Burns, B. J., & Schlesinger, H. J. (1994). Ethnicity and the use of outpatient mental health services in a national insured population. *American Journal of Public Health, 84,* 222–226.

Pallack, M. S. (1995). Managed care and outcomes-based standards in the health care revolution. In S. C. Hayes, V. M. Follette, R. M. Dawes, & K. E. Grady (Eds.), *Scientific standards of psychological practice: Issues and recommendations* (pp. 73–77). Reno, NV: Context Press.

Paniagua, F. A., Morrison, P. B., & Black, S. A. (1990). Management of a hyperactive conduct disordered child through correspondence training: A preliminary study. *Journal of Behavior Therapy and Experimental Psychiatry, 21,* 63–68.

Panzarino, P. (1995). Behavioral healthcare report card indicators. *Behavioral Healthcare Tomorrow, 4*(3), 49–50, 52–54.

Pargament, K., Falgout, K., Ensing, D., Reilly, B., Silverman, M., Van Haitsma, K., Olsen, H., & Warren, R. (1991). The congregation development program: Data-based consultation with churches and synagogues. *Professional Psychology: Research and Practice, 22,* 393–404.

Parkinson, B., Briner, R. B., Reynolds, S., & Totterdell, P. (1995). Time frames for mood: Relations between momentary and generalized ratings of affect. *Personality and Social Psychology Bulletin, 21,* 331–339.

Parsonson, B. S., & Baer, D. M. (1978). The analysis and presentation of graphed data. In T. R. Kratochwill (Ed.), *Single subject research: Strategies for evaluating change.* New York: Academic.

Parsonson, B. S., & Baer, D. M. (1992). The visual analysis of data, and current research into the stimuli controlling it. In T. R. Kratochwill & J. R. Levin (Eds.), *Single-case research design and analysis: New directions for psychology and education.* Hillsdale, NJ: Erlbaum.

Patterson, G. R. (1977). Naturalistic observation in clinical assessment. *Journal of Abnormal Clinical Psychology, 5,* 309–322.

Patterson, G. R., Ray, R. S., Shaw, D. A., & Cobb, J. A. (1969). *A manual for coding of family interactions,* 1969 revision. Eugene, OR: Oregon Research Institute.

Paul, G. L. (1969). Behavior modification research: Design and tactics. In C. M. Franks (Ed.), *Behavior therapy: Appraisal and status.* New York: McGraw Hill.

Payne, J. W. (1994). Thinking aloud: Insights into information processing. *Psychological Science, 5,* 241–248.

Pekarik, G., & Wolff, C. B. (1996). Relationship of satisfaction to symptom change, follow-up adjustment, and clinical significance. *Professional Psychology: Research and Practice, 27,* 202–208.

Perry, R. D., & Hanig, D. (1994). Dissemination and utilization of the mental health evaluation. *Evaluation and Program Planning, 17,* 93–96.

Perry, R. D., Hoff, B. H., & Gaither, D. S. (1994). The process study component of mental health evaluation. *Evaluation and Program Planning, 17,* 43–46.

Persons, J. B. (1989). *Cognitive therapy in practice: A case formulation approach.* New York: Norton.

Persons, J. B. (1991). Psychotherapy outcome studies do not accurately represent current models of psychotherapy. *American Psychologist, 46,* 99–106.

Persons, J. B., Curtis, J. T., & Silberschatz, G. (1991). Psychodynamic and cognitive-behavioral formulations of a single case. *Psychotherapy, 28,* 608–617.

Peterson, A. L., & Azrin, N. H. (1992). An evaluation of behavioral treatments for Tourette Syndrome. *Behaviour Research and Therapy, 30,* 167–174.

Peterson, D. R. (1968). *The clinical study of social behavior.* New York: Appleton-Century-Crofts.

Peterson, D. R. (1976a). Is psychology a profession? *American Psychologist, 31,* 572–581.

Peterson, D. R. (1976b). Need for the Doctor of Psychology degree in professional psychology. *American Psychologist, 31,* 792–798.

Peterson, G., Abrams, D., Elder, J. & Beaudin, P. (1985). Professional versus self-help weight loss at the worksite: The challenge of making a public health impact. *Behavior Therapy, 16,* 213–222.

Pfiffner, L. J., & O'Leary, S. G. (1987). The efficacy of all-positive management as a function of the prior use of negative consequences. *Journal of Applied Behavior Analysis, 20,* 265–271.

Phillips, B. N. (1989). Role of the practitioner in applying science to practice. *Professional Psychology: Research and Practice, 20,* 3–8.

Pickering, T. G. (1989). Ambulatory monitoring: Applications and limitations. In N. Schneiderman, S. M. Weiss, & P. G. Kaufmann, (Eds.), *Handbook of research methods in cardiovascular behavioral medicine* (pp. 261–272). New York: Plenum Press.

Poling, A., & Grossett, D. (1986). Basic research designs in applied behavior analysis. In A. Poling, & R. W. Fuqua (Eds.), *Research methods in applied behavior analysis: Issues and advances.* New York: Plenum.

Powell, J., Martindale, & Kulp, S. (1975). An evaluation of time-sampling measure of behavior. *Journal of Applied Behavior Analysis, 8,* 463–469.

Powell, T. J. (Ed.). (1994). *Understanding the self-help organization.* Thousand Oaks, CA: Sage.

Praderas, K., & MacDonald, M. L. (1986). Telephone conversational skills training with socially isolated, impaired nursing home residents. *Journal of Applied Behavior Analysis, 19,* 337–348.

Project MATCH Research Group (1997). Matching alcohol treatments to client heterogeneity: Project MATCH post-treatment drinking outcome. *Journal of Substance Abuse, 58,* 7–29.

Proshansky, H. M. (1972). For what are we training our graduate students? *American Psychologist, 27,* 205–212.

The Quality Assurance Project. (1983). A treatment outline for depressive disorders. *Australian and New Zealand Journal of Psychiatry, 17,* 129–148.

The Quality Assurance Project. (1984). Treatment outlines for the management of schizophrenia. *Australian and New Zealand Journal of Psychiatry, 18,* 19–38.

The Quality Assurance Project. (1985). Treatment outlines for the management of anxiety states. *Australian and New Zealand Journal of Psychiatry, 19,* 138–151.

Quirk, M. P., Strosahl, K., Todd, J. L., Fitzpatrick, W., Casey, M. T., Hennessy, S., & Simon, G. (1995). Quality and customers: Type 2 change in mental health delivery within health care reform. *Journal of Mental Health Administration, 22*(4), 414–425.

Rachlin, H. (1974). Self-control. *Behaviorism, 2,* 94–107.

Rachman, S. J., & Hodgson, R. I. (1974). Synchrony and desynchrony in fear and avoidance. *Behaviour Research and Therapy, 12,* 311–318.

Raimy, V. C. (Ed.). (1950). *Training in clinical psychology (Boulder Conference).* New York: Prentice-Hall.

Rasing, E. J., Coninx, F., Duker, P. C., & Van Den Hurk, A. J. (1994). Acquisition and generalization of social behaviors in language-disabled deaf adolescents. *Behavior Modification, 18,* 411–442.

Rasing, E. J., & Duker, P. C. (1992). Effects of multifaceted training procedure on the acquisition and generalization of social behaviors in language-disabled deaf children. *Journal of Applied Behavior Analysis, 25,* 723–734.

Rasing, E. J., & Duker, P. C. (1993). Acquisition and generalization of social behaviors in language disabled deaf children. *American Annals of the Deaf, 138,* 362–369.

Regier, D. A., Narrow, W. E., Rae, D. S., Manderscheid, R. W., Locke, B. Z., & Goodwin, F. K. (1993). The de facto US mental and addictive disorders service system: Epidemiologic catchment area prospective 1-year prevalence rates of disorders and services. *Archives of General Psychiatry, 50,* 85–94.

Rehm, L. P., Fuchs, C. Z., Roth, D. M., Kornblith, S. J., & Romano, J. M. (1979). A comparison of self-control and assertion skills treatments of depression. *Behavior Therapy, 10,* 429–442.

Reid, J. B. (Ed.). (1978). *A social learning approach to family intervention, Vol. 2: Observation in home settings.* Eugene, OR: Casting Publishing.

Reiser, B. J., Black, J. B., & Abelson, R. P. (1985). Knowledge structures in the organization and retrieval of autobiographical memories. *Cognitive Psychology, 17,* 89–137.

Reiser, D. E. (1984). The psychiatric interview. In H. G. Goldman (Ed.), *Review of general psychiatry.* (pp. 197–205). Los Altos, CA: Lange.

Repp, A. C., Deitz, D. E. D., Boles, S. M., Deitz, S. M., & Repp, C. F. (1976). Differences among common methods for calculating interobserver agreement. *Journal of Applied Behavior Analysis, 9,* 109–113.

Repp, A. C., Harman, M. L., Felce, D., Van Acker, R., & Karsh, K. G. (1989). Conducting behavioral assessment on computer-collected data. *Behavior Assessment, 11,* 249–268.

Repp, A. C., Nieminen, G. S., Olinger E., & Brusca, R. (1988). Direct observation: Factors affecting the accuracy of observers. *Exceptional Children, 55,* 29–36.

Reynolds, G. S. (1968). *A primer of operant conditioning.* Glenview, IL: Scott, Foresman.

Rice, D. P., Kelman, S., & Miller, L. S. (1991). Economic costs of drug abuse. In W. S. Cartwright & J. M. Kaple (Eds.), *Economic costs, cost-effectiveness, financing, and community-based drug treatment. National Institute on Drug Abuse Research Monograph Series, 113.* Washington, DC: Government Printing Office.

Risley, T. R., & Hart, B. (1968). Developing correspondence between the non-verbal and verbal behavior of preschool children. *Journal of Applied Behavior Analysis, 1,* 267–281.

Robins, L. N. (1989). Diagnostic grammar and assessment: Translating criteria into questions. In L. N. Robins, & J. E. Barrett (Eds.), *The validity of psychiatric diagnosis* (pp. 263–279). New York: Raven.

Robins, L., Schoenberg, S. P., Holmes, S. J., Ratcliff, K. S., Benham, A., & Works, J. (1985). Early home environment and retrospective recall. *American Journal of Orthopsychiatry, 55,* 27–41.

Robinson, P., Wischman, C., & DelVento, A. (1997). *Treating depression in primary care: A manual for primary care and mental health providers.* Reno, NV: Context Press.

Roe, A., Gustad, J. W., Moore, B. V., Ross, S., & Skodak, M. (1959). *Graduate education in psychology. Report of the conference sponsored by the E & T Board.* Washington, DC: American Psychological Association.

Rogers, T., Mahoney, M. J., Mahoney, B. K., Straw, M. D., & Kenigsberg, M. 1. (1980). Clinical assessment of obesity: An empirical evaluation of diverse techniques. *Behavioral Assessment, 2,* 161–181.

Rogler, L. H., Malgady, R. G., & Tryon, W. W. (1992). Evaluation of mental health: Issues of memory in the Diagnostic Interview Schedule. *Journal of Nervous and Mental Disease, 180,* 215–226.

Rojahn, J., & Warren, V. J. (1991). The affects of prior exposure to a subject on measures of observer performance. *Journal of Psychopathology and Behavioral Assessment, 13*, 389–403.

Rosenthal, R. (1995). Progress in clinical psychology: Is there any? *Clinical Psychology: Science and Practice, 2*, 133–150.

Ross, A. O. (1963). Deviant case analysis: Neglected approach to behavior research. *Perceptual and Motor Skills, 16*, 337–340.

Ross, A. O. (1981). Of rigor and relevance. *Professional Psychology, 12*, 319–327.

Ross, M. (1989). Relation of implicit theories to the construction of personal histories. *Psychological Review, 96*, 341–357.

Ross, M. W., Walinder, J., Lundstrom, B., & Thuwe, I. (1981). Cross-cultural approaches to transsexualism: A comparison between Sweden and Australia. *Acta Psychiatrica Scandinavia, 63*, 75–82.

Rossi, P. H., & Berk, R. A. (1990). *Thinking about program evaluation.* Newbury Park, CA: Sage Publications.

Rossi, P. H., & Freeman, H. E. (1989). *Evaluation: A systematic approach.* Newbury Park, CA: Sage.

Roth, A., & Fonagy, P. (1995, February). *Research on the efficacy and effectiveness of the psychotherapies (National Health Service Report).* Report to the Department of Health.

Rothbaum, B. O., Hodges, L. F., Kooper, R., Opdyke, D., Williford, J. S., & North, M. (1995a). Virtual reality graded exposure in the treatment of acrophobia: A case report. *Behavior Therapy, 26*(3), 547–554.

Rothbaum, B. O., Hodges, L. F., Kooper, R., Opdyke, D., Williford, J. S., & North, M. (1995b). Effectiveness of computer-generated (virtual reality) graded exposure in the treatment of acrophobia. *American Journal of Psychiatry, 152*(4), 626–628.

Rothbaum, B. O., Hodges, L., Watson, B. A., Kessler, G. D., & Opdyke, D. (1996). Virtual reality exposure therapy in the treatment of fear of flying: A case report. *Behaviour Research and Therapy, 34*, 477–481.

Rotter, J. B., Lah, M. I., & Rafferty, J. E. (1992). *Rotter Incomplete Sentences Blank: Manual* (2nd ed.). San Antonio, TX: Psychological Corporation.

Rousseau, M. K., Tam, B. K. Y., & Ramnarain, R. (1993). Increasing reading proficiency of language-minority students with speech and language. *Education and Treatment of Children, 16*, 254–271.

Routh, D. K. (1994). *Clinical psychology since 1917: Science, practice, and organization.* New York: Plenum.

Rubin, M., & Shontz, F. C. (1960). Diagnostic prototypes and diagnostic processes of clinical psychologists. *Journal of Consulting Psychology, 24*, 234–239.

Rude, S. S., & Rehm, L. P. (1991). Response to treatments for depression: The role of initial status on targeted cognitive and behavioral skills. *Clinical Psychology Review, 11*, 493–514.

Rupp, A. (1991). Underinsurance for severe mental illness. *Schizophrenia Bulletin, 17*, 401–405.

Sargent, J. D., Green, E. E., & Walters, E. D. (1972). The use of autogenic feedback training in a pilot study of migraine and tension headaches. *Headache, 12*, 120–125.

Saudargas, R. A., & Zanolli, K. (1990). Momentary time sampling as an estimate of percentage time: A field validation. *Journal of Applied Behavior Analysis, 23*(4), 533–537.

Saunders, T., Driskeil, J. E., Hall, J., Salas, E. (in press). The effect of stress inoculation training on anxiety and performance. *Journal of Occupational Health Psychology.*

Schalock, R. L., & Thornton, C. V. D. (1988). *Program evaluation: A field guide for administrators.* New York: Plenum.

Schelde, T., & Hertz, M., (1994). Ethology and psychotherapy. *Ethology and Sociobiology, 15*, 383–392.

Scher, H., Furedy, J. J., & Heslegrave, R. J. (1985). Individual differences in phasic cardiac reactivity to psychological stress and the law of initial value. *Psychophysiology, 22*, 345–348.

Schindele, R. (1981). Methodological problems in rehabilitation research. *International Journal of Rehabilitation Research, 4*, 233–248.

Schover, L. R. (1980). Clinical practice and scientific psychology: Can this marriage be saved? *Professional Psychology, 11*, 268–275.

Schulte, D., Kunzel, R., Pepping, G. & Schulte-Bahrenberg, T. (1992). Tailor-made versus standardized therapy of phobic patients. *Advanced Behavioral Research and Therapy, 14*, 67.

Schwartz, I., & Baer, D. (1991). Social validity assessments: Is current practice state of the art? *Journal of Applied Behavior Analysis, 24*(2), 189–204.

Schwartz, M. S. (1995). *Biofeedback: A practitioner's guide.* New York: Guilford Press.

Schwartz, S., (1991). Clinical decision making. In P. R. Martin (Ed.), *Handbook of behavior therapy and psychological science* (pp. 196–215). New York: Pergamon.

Scogin, F., & McElreath, L. (1994). Efficacy of psychosocial treatments for geriatric depression: A quantitative review. *Journal of Consulting and Clinical Psychology, 62*, 69–74.

Scotti, J. R., Evans, I. M., Meyer, L. H., & Walker, P. (1991). A metaanalysis of intervention research with problem behavior: Treatment validity and standards of practice. *American Journal on Mental Retardation, 96,* 233–256.

Sechrest, L. (1975). Research contributions of practicing clinical psychologists. *Professional Psychology, 8,* 413–419.

Sederer, L. I. (1995). The shift from efficacy to effectiveness research to demonstrate value. *Behavioral Healthcare Tomorrow, 4*(3), 40, 43–44.

Seligman, M. (1995). The effectiveness of psychotherapy: The Consumer Reports Study. *American Psychologist, 50,* 965–974.

Seligman, M. E. P. (1995). The effectiveness of psychotherapy: The consumer reports. *American Psychologist, 50,* 965–974.

Seymour, F. W., & Stokes, T. F. (1976). Self-recording in training girls to increase work and evoke staff praise in an institution for offenders. *Journal of Applied Behavior Analysis, 9,* 41–54.

Shadish, W. R., Cook, T. D., & Leviton, C. (1991). *Foundations of program evaluation: Theories of practice.* Newbury Park: Sage.

Shakow, D. (1969). *Clinical psychology as a science and as a profession: A forty-year odyssey.* Chicago: Aldine.

Shakow, D. (1976). What is clinical psychology? *American Psychologist, 31,* 553–560.

Shakow, D., Hilgard, E. R., Kelly, E. L., Luckey, B., Sanford, R. N., & Shaffer, L. F. (1947). Recommended graduate training program in clinical psychology. *American Psychologist, 2,* 539–558.

Shear, M. K., Ball, G., Fitzpatrick, M., Josephson, S., Klosko, J., & Frances, A. (1991). Cognitive-behavioral therapy for panic: An open study. *Journal of Nervous and Mental Disease, 179,* 467–471.

Shear, M. K., & Barlow, D. H. (1995, February). *Multicenter treatment study of panic disorder: Combination treatment of designs of the study and interim results.* Presented at the Psychiatric Research Society meeting. Salt Lake City, Utah.

Shelton, J. L., & Ackerman, J. N. (1974). *Homework in counseling and psychotherapy.* Springfield, IL: Thomas.

Shelton, J. L., & Levy, R. L. (1981). *Behavioral assignments and treatment compliance.* Champaign, IL: Research Press.

Sherbourne, C. D., Hays, R. D., Orday, L., Dimatteo, M. R., & Kravitz, R. (1992). Antecedents of adherence to medical recommendations: Results from the medical outcome study. *Journal of Behavioral Medicine,15,* 447–468.

Sherman, M., Trief, P., & Sprafkin, R. (1975) Impression management in the psychiatric interview: Quality, style, and individual differences. *Journal of Consulting and Clinical Psychology, 43,* 867–871.

Shoor, R. (1993, November). For mental health cost problems, see a specialist. *Business and Health,* pp. 59–62.

Shuller, D. Y., & McNamara, J. R. (1970). Expectancy factors in behavioral observation. *Behavior Therapy, 7,* 519–527.

Sidman, M. (1960). *Tactics of scientific research: Evaluating experimental data in psychology.* New York: Basic Books.

Silver, B. V., & Blanchard, E. B. (1978). Biofeedback and relaxation training in the treatment of psychophysiologic disorders: Or, are the machines really necessary? *Journal of Behavioral Medicine, 1,* 217–239.

Silverstein, J. M., & Allison, D. B. (1994). The comparative efficacy of antecedent exercise and methylphenidate: A single-case randomized trial. *Child Care, Health and Development, 20,* 47–60.

Singh, N. N., & Aman, M. G. (1981). Effects of thioridazine dosage on the behavior of severely mentally retarded persons. *American Journal of Mental Deficiency, 85,* 580–587.

Sintach, G., & Geer, J. H. (1975). A vaginal plethysmograph system. *Psychophysiology, 12,* 113–115.

Sisson, L. A., & Dixon, M. J. (1986). Improving mealtime behaviors through token reinforcement. *Behavior Modification, 10,* 333–354.

Sleen, J. (1989). Social phobia: Individual response patterns and the effects of behavioral and cognitive interventions. *Behaviour Research and Therapy, 27,* 421–434.

Smith, M. S., Glass, G. V., & Miller, T. I. (1980). *The benefits of psychotherapy.* Baltimore: Johns Hopkins University Press.

Snider, V. (1987). Use of self-monitoring of attention with LD students: Research and application. *Learning Disability Quarterly, 10,* 139–151.

Snow, R. E. (1974). Representative and quasi-representative designs for research in teaching. *Review of Educational Research, 44,* 265–291.

Snyder, D. K., & Wills, R. M. (1989). Behavioral versus insight-oriented marital therapy: Effects on individual and interspousal functioning. *Journal of Consulting and Clinical Psychology, 57,* 39–46.

Snyder, D. K., Wills, R. M., & Grady-Fletcher, A. (1991). Long-term effectiveness of behavioral versus insight-oriented marital therapy: A

4-year follow-up study. *Journal of Consulting and Clinical Psychology, 59,* 138–141.

Snyder, J. (1983). Aversive social stimuli in the Family Interaction Coding System: A validation study. *Behavioral Assessment, 5*(4), 315–331.

Snyder, M., & Swann, W. B. (1978). Hypothesis testing processes in social interaction. *Journal of Personality and Social Psychology, 36,* 1202–1212.

Sobel, D. (1995). Rethinking medicine: Improving health outcomes with cost effective psychosocial interventions. *Psychosomatic Medicine, 57,* 234–244.

Solomon, A. (1992). Clinical diagnosis among diverse populations: A multicultural perspective. *Families-in-Society, 73,* 371–377.

Spiegel, D., Bloom, J. R., Kraemer, H. C., & Gottheil, E. (1989, October 14). Effect of psychosocial treatment on survival of patients with metastatic breast cancer. *The Lancet,* pp. 888–891.

Spiegel, D. A., Bruce, T. J., Gregg, S. F., & Nuzzarello, A. (1994). Does cognitive behavior therapy assist slow-taper alprazolam discontinuation in panic disorder? *American Journal of Psychiatry, 151,* 876–881.

Spielberger, C. D., Gorsuch, R. L., & Lushene, R. E. (1970). *Manual for the State-Trait Anxiety Inventory.* Palo Alto, CA: Consulting Psychologists Press.

Spitzer, R. L., Endicott, J., & Robins, E. (1978). Research diagnostic criteria. *Archives of General Psychiatry, 35,* 773–782.

Spitzer, R., Williams, J., Gibbon, M., & First, M. (1990). *SCID user's guide for the structured clinical interviews for DSM-III-R.* Washington, DC: American Psychiatric Press.

Spitzer, R. L., Williams, J. B., Kroenke, K., Linzer, L., deGruy, F. V., Hahn, S. R., Brody, D., & Johnson, J. G. (1994). Utility of a new procedure for diagnosing mental disorders in primary care: The PRIME-MD 1000 Study. *Journal of the American Medical Association, 272,* 1749–1756.

Spurr, J., & Stevens, V. J. (1980). Increasing study time and controlling student guilt: A case study in self-management. *Behavior Therapist, 3,* 17–18.

Starker, S. (1988). Do-it-yourself therapy: The prescription of self-help books by psychologists. *Psychotherapy, 25,* 142–146.

Steege, W. W., Wacker, D. P., Cigrand, K. C., Berg, W. K., Novak, C. G., Reimers, T. M., Sasso, G. M., & DeRaad, A. (1990). Use of negative reinforcement in the treatment of self-injurious behavior. *Journal of Applied Behavior Analysis, 23,* 459–467.

Steketee, G. S. (1993). *Treatment of obsessive compulsive disorder.* New York: Guilford Press.

Steketee, G., Chambless, D. L., Tran, G. Q., Worden, H., & Gillis, M. M. (1996). Behavioral avoidance test for obsessive compulsive disorder. *Behaviour Research and Therapy, 34,* 73–83.

Stemmler, G., & Fahrenberg, J. (1989). Psychophysiological assessment: Conceptual, psychometric, and statistical issues. In G. Turpin (Ed.), *Handbook of clinical psychophysiology* (pp. 45–70). Chichester, United Kingdom: Wiley.

Stern, G. W., Fowler, S., & Kohler, F. W. (1988). A comparison of two intervention roles: Peer monitor and point earner. *Journal of Applied Behavior Analysis, 21,* 103–109.

Stevens, S. S. (1958). Measurement, statistics, and the schemapiric view. *Science, 161,* 849–856.

Stiles, W. B., & Snow, J. S. (1984). Counseling session impact as seen by novice counselors and their clients. *Journal of Counseling Psychology, 31,* 3–12.

Stine, W. W. (1989). Interobserver relational agreement. *Psychological Bulletin, 106,* 341–347.

Stricker, G. (1973). The doctoral dissertation in clinical psychology. *Professional Psychology, 4,* 72–78.

Stricker, G. (1975). On professional schools and professional degrees. *American Psychologist, 30,* 1062–1066.

Stricker, G. (1992). The relationship of research to clinical practice. *American Psychologist, 47,* 543–549.

Strosahl, K. (1994). Entering the new frontier of managed mental health care: Gold mines and land mines. *Cognitive and Behavioral Practice, 1,* 5–23.

Strosahl, K. (1996). Three "gold mine-land mine" themes in generation 2 of health care reform. *The Behavior Therapist, 19*(4), 52–54.

Strosahl, K. D., Hayes, S. C., Bergan, J., & Romano, P. (1998). Assessing the field effectiveness of Acceptance and Commitment Therapy: An example of the manipulated training research method. *Behavior Therapy, 29,* 35–63.

Strupp, H. H. (1987). The future for time limited dynamic psychotherapy. In N. Cheshire & Thomae, H. (Eds.). *Self, symptoms and psychotherapy* (pp. 267–284). New York: Wiley.

Stuart, R. B. (1970). *Trick or treatment: How or when psychotherapy fails.* Champaign, IL: Research Press.

Sturgis, E. T., & Gramling, S. (1988). Psychophysiological assessment. In A. S. Bellack & M. Herson (Eds.), *Behavioral assessment: A practical handbook* (3rd ed.) (pp. 213–251). New York: Pergamon Press.

Sue, S. (1995). The implications of diversity for scientific standards of practice. In S. C. Hayes, V. M. Follette, R. M. Dawes, & K. E. Grady (Eds.). (1995). *Scientific standards of psychological practice: Issues and recommendations* (pp. 265-279). Reno, NV: Context Press.

Suen, H. K. (1988). Agreement, reliability, accuracy, and validity: Toward a clarification. *Behavior Assessment, 10,* 343–366.

Suen, H. K., Ary, D., & Covalt, W. C. (1990). A decision tree approach to selecting an appropriate observation reliability index. *Journal of Psychopathology and Behavioral Assessment, 12,* 359–363.

Systems Management, Inc. (1995). *Transmittals, rating scales, and narrative reports.* 300 Vestavia Office Park, Suite 3200, Birmingham, AL 35216.

Tanur, J. (Ed.). (1992). *Questions about questions: Inquiries into the cognitive bases of surveys.* New York: Russell Sage Foundation.

Taplin, P. S., & Reid, J. B. (1973). Effects of instructional set and experimenter influence on observer reliability. *Child Development, 44,* 547–554.

Taras, M. E., Matson, J. L., & Leary, C. (1988). Training social interpersonal skills in two autistic children. *Journal of Behavior Therapy and Experimental Psychiatry, 19,* 275–280.

Task Force on Promotion and Dissemination of Psychological Procedures. (1995). Training in and dissemination of empirically-validated psychological treatments; Report and recommendations. *The Clinical Psychologist, 48,* 3–24.

Tasto, D. L. (1977). Self-report schedules and inventories. In A. R. Ciminero, K. S. Calhoun, & H. E. Adams (Eds.), *Handbook of behavioral assessment.* New York: Wiley.

Taylor, C. B., King, R., Margraf, J., Ehlers, A., Telch, M., Roth, W. T., & Agras, W. S. (1989). Use of medication and in vivo exposure in volunteers for panic disorder research. *American Journal of Psychiatry, 146,* 1423–1426.

Teasdale, J. (1988). Cognitive models and treatments for panic: A critical evaluation. In S. Rachman & J. D. Master (Eds.), *Panic: Psychological perspectives* (pp.189–203). Hillsdale, NJ: Erlbaum.

Telch, M. J., & Lucas, R. A. (1994). Combining pharmacological and psychological treatment of panic disorder: Current status and future directions. In B. E. Wolfe & J. D. Maser (Eds.), *Treatment of panic disorder: A consensus development conference* (pp. 177–197). Washington, DC: American Psychiatric Press.

Telch, M. J., Lucas, J. A., Schmidt, N. B., Hanna, H. H., Jaimez, T. L., & Lucas, R. A. (1993). Group cognitive-behavioral treatment of panic disorder. *Behaviour Research and Therapy, 31,* 279–287.

Test, D. (1994). Supported employment and social validity. *Journal of the Association for Persons with Severe Handicaps. 19,* 2, 116–129.

Thase, M. E., Simons, A. D., Cahalane, J. F., & McGeary, J. (1991). Cognitive behavior therapy of endogenous depression: Part 1: An outpatient clinical replication series. *Behavior Therapy, 22,* 457–467.

Thomas, E. J. (1978). Research and service in single-case experimentation: Conflicts and choices. *Social Work Research and Abstracts, 14,* 20–31.

Thomas, E. J., Bastien, J., Stuebe, D. R., Bronson, D. E., & Yaffe, J. (1987). Assessing procedural descriptiveness: Rationale and illustrative study. *Behavioral Assessment, 9,* 43–56.

Thomas, S., Crouse Quinn, S., Billingsley, A., & Caldwell, C. (1994). The characteristics of Northern Black churches with community health outreach programs. *American Journal of Public Health, 84,* 575–579.

Thorne, F. C. (1947). The clinical method in science. *American Psychologist, 2,* 161–166.

Thyer, B. A., & Curtis, G. C. (1982, May). *The repeated pretest-posttest single-subject experiment: A new design for applied behavior analysis.* Paper presented at the Association for Behavior Analysis, Milwaukee, WI.

Timmreck, T. C. (1994). *An introduction to epidemiology.* Boston: Jones and Bartlett.

Tischler, G. L. (1990). Utilization management of mental health services by private third parties. *American Journal of Psychiatry, 147,* 967–973.

Tomarken, A. J. (1995). A psychometric perspective on psychophysiological measures. *Psychological Assessment, 7,* 387–395.

Tombari, M. L., Fitzpatrick, S. J., & Childress, W. (1985). Using computers as contingency managers in self-monitoring interventions. *Computers in Human Behavior, 1,* 75–82.

Trabin, T. (1995). Making quality and accountability happen in behavioral healthcare. *Behavioral Healthcare Tomorrow, 4*(3), 5–6.

Trabin T., & Freeman, M. A. (1995). *Managed behavioral healthcare: History, models, strategic challenges and future course.* Tiburon, CA: CentraLink Publishers.

Trull, T. J., Nietzel, M. T., & Main, A. (1988). The use of meta-analysis to assess the clinical significance of behavior therapy for agoraphobia. *Behavior Therapy, 19,* 527–538.

Tryon, W. W., (1991). *Activity measurement in psychology and medicine.* New York: Plenum.

Tryon, W. W. (1993). The role of motor excess and instrumented activity measurement in attention deficit hyperactivity disorder. *Behavior Modification, 17,* 371–406.

Tryon, W. W., & Pinto, L. P. (1994). Comparing activity measurements and ratings. *Behavior Modification, 18,* 251–261.

Tulving, E., and Thomson, D. M. (1973). Encoding specificity and retrieval processes in episodic memory. *Psychological Review, 80,* 352–373.

Turk, D. C., & Salovey, P. (1985). Cognitive structures, cognitive processes, and cognitive-behavior modification: II. Judgments and inferences of the clinician. *Cognitive Therapy and Research, 9,* 19–33.

Turk, D. C., & Salovey, P. (1986). Clinical information processing: Bias inoculation. In R. E. Ingram (Ed.), *Information processing approaches to clinical psychology.* Orlando: Academic Press.

Turk, D. C., & Salovey, P. (1988). *Reasoning, inference, and judgement in clinical psychology.* New York: Free Press.

Turkat, I. D. (1990). *The personality disorders: A psychological approach to clinical management.* New York: Pergamon.

Turkat, I. D., & Maisto, S. A. (1985). Personality disorders: Application of the experimental method to the formulation and modification of personality disorders. In D. H. Barlow (Ed.), *Clinical handbook of psychological disorders* (pp. 502–570). New York: Guilford.

Turner, A. E., & Hayes, S. C. (1996). A comparison of response covariation viewed idiothetically and nomothetically (Una comparacion de la covariacion de repuesta vista desde una perspectiva idiotetica y nomotetica). *Psicologia Conductual, 4,* 231–250.

Turner, J. A., & Clancy, S. (1988). Comparison of operant behavioral and cognitive-behavioral group treatment for chronic low back pain. *Journal of Consulting and Clinical Psychology, 56,* 261–266.

Turner, R. M., & Ascher, M. (1979). A within-subject analysis of stimulus control therapy with severe sleep-onset insomnia. *Behaviour Research and Therapy, 17,* 107–112.

Turner, S. M., Beidel, D. C., & Wolff, P. L. (1994). A composite measure to determine improvement following treatment for social phobia: The Index of Social Phobia Improvement. *Behaviour Research and Therapy, 32,* 471–476.

Turpin, G. (1989). An overview of clinical psychophysiological techniques: Tools of theories? In G. Turpin (Ed.), *Handbook of clinical psychophysiology* (pp. 3–44). Chichester, United Kingdom: Wiley.

Tustin, R. D. (1995). The effects of advance notice on activity transitions on stereotypic behavior. *Journal of Applied Behavior Analysis, 28,* 91–92.

Tuteur, J. M., Ewigman, B. E., Peterson, L., & Hosokawa, M. C. (1995). The maternal observation matrix and the mother-child interaction scale: Brief observational screening instruments for physically abusive mothers. *Journal of Consulting and Clinical Psychology, 24,* 55–62.

Tyler, F. B., & Speisman, J. C. (1967). An emerging scientist-professional role in psychology. *American Psychologist, 22,* 839–847.

Tyler, R. W. (1931). What is statistical significance? *Educational Research Bulletin, 10,* 115–118; 142.

Ulman, J. D., & Sulzer-Azaroff, B. (1975). Multielement baseline design in educational research. In E. Ramp & G. Semb (Eds.), *Behavior analysis: Areas of research and application.* Englewood Cliffs, NJ: Prentice-Hall.

Vandenbos, G. R. (1980). *Psychotherapy: Practice, research, and policy.* Beverly Hills, CA: Sage.

Vandenbos, G. R. (1983). Health financing, service utilization, and national policy: A conversation with Stan Jones. *American Psychologist, 38,* 948–955.

Van Houten, R. (1993). Rote vs. rules: A comparison of two teaching and correction strategies for teaching basic subtraction facts. *Education and Treatment of Children, 16,* 147–159.

Van Houten, R., Van Houten, J., & Malenfant, J. E. L. (1994). The effects of low alcohol beverages on alcohol consumption and impairment. *Behavior Modification, 18,* 505–513.

Verhovek, S. H. (1997, June 5). Texas will allow malpractice suits against HMOs. *New York Times,* p. 1, c. 6.

Volkin, J. I., & Jacob, T. (1981). The impact of spouse monitoring on target behavior and recorder satisfaction. *Journal of Behavioral Assessment, 3,* 99–109.

Von Korff, M. R., & Marshall, J. (1992). High cost HMO enrollees: Health status and components of actuarial costs. *HMO Practice, 6,* 20–25.

Wacker, D., McMahon, C., Steege, M., Berg, W., Sasso, G., & Melloy, K. (1990). Applications of a sequential alternating treatments design. *Journal of Applied Behavior Analysis, 23,* 333–340.

Wade, T. C., Baker, T. B., & Hartmann, D. P. (1979). Behavior therapists' self-reported views and practices. *The Behavior Therapist, 2,* 3–6.

Wade, W. A., Treat, T. A., & Stuart, G. L. (1998). Transporting an empirically supported treatment for panic disorder to a service clinic setting: A benchmarking strategy. *Journal of Consulting and Clinical Psychology, 66,* 231–239.

Wagner, E. H. (September 1997). *Is there a role for managed care organizations?* Paper presented at the National Institute on Drug Abuse Conference on Stage III Behavior Therapy Research, Washington, DC.

Wahler, R. G. (1975). Some structural aspects of deviant child behavior. *Journal of Applied Behavior Analysis, 8,* 27–42.

Walder, C. P., McCracken, J. S., Herbert, M., James, P. T., & Brewitt, N. (1987). Psychological intervention in civilian flying phobia: Evaluation and a three-year follow-up. *British Journal of Psychiatry, 151,* 494–498.

Walk, R. D. (1956). Self-ratings of fear in a fear-invoking situation. *Journal of Abnormal and Social Psychology, 52,* 171–178.

Walter, H. I., & Gilmore, S. K. (1973). Placebo versus social learning effects in parent training procedures designed to alter the behavior of aggressive boys. *Behavior Therapy, 4,* 361–377.

Waltz, J., Addis, M. E., Koerner, K., & Jacobson, N. S. (1993). Testing the integrity of a psychotherapy protocol: Assessment of adherence and competence. *Journal of Consulting and Clinical Psychology, 61,* 620–630.

Waltz, J., Addis, M. E., Koerner, K., & Jacobson, N. S. (1993). Testing the integrity of a psychotherapy protocol: Assessment of adherence and competence. *Journal of Consulting and Clinical Psychology, 61,* 620–630.

Ward, J. C., & Naster, B. J. (1991). Reliability of an observational system used to monitor behavior in a mental health residential treatment unit. *Journal of Mental Health Administration, 18,* 64–68.

Washburn, S., Vannicelli, M., & Longabaugh, R. (1976). A controlled comparison of psychiatric day treatment and in-patient hospitalization. *Journal of Consulting and Clinical Psychology, 44,* 665–675.

Watkins, C. E., Campbell, V. L., Nieberding, R., & Hallmark, R. (1995). Contemporary practice of psychological assessment by clinical psychologists. *Professional Psychology: Research and Practice, 26,* 54–60.

Watts, F. N. (1992). Is psychology falling apart? *The Psychologist: Bulletin of the British Psychological Society, 5,* 489–494.

Webber, J., Scheuermann, B., McCall, C., & Coleman, M. (1993). Research on self-monitoring as a behavior management technique in special education classrooms: A descriptive review. *Remedial and Special Education, 14*(2), 38–56.

Weed, L. (1968). Medical records that guide and teach. *New England Journal of Medicine, 278,* 593–600.

Weeks, G. R., & Treat, S. (1992). *Couples in treatment: Techniques and approaches for effective practice.* New York: Brunner/Mazel.

Weinert, F. E., & Schneider, W. (1995). *Memory performance and competencies: Issues in growth and development.* Hillsdale, NJ: Lawrence Erlbaum Associates.

Weinrott, M., & Jones, R. R. (1984). Overt versus covert assessment of observer reliability. *Child Development, 55,* 1125–1137.

Weisbrod, B. A., Test, M. A., & Stein, L. I. (1980). Alternative to mental hospital treatment: II. Economic benefit cost analysis. *Archives General Psychiatry, 37,* 400–405.

Weiss, R. L., & Summers, K. J. (1983). Marital interaction coding systems-III. In E. E. Filsinger (Ed.), *Marriage and family assessment: A sourcebook for family therapy* (pp. 85–115), Beverly Hills: Sage Publication.

Weissman, M., & Bothwell, S. M. (1976). Assessment of social adjustment by patient self-report. *Archives of General Psychiatry, 33,* 1111–1115.

Weissman, M. M., & Paykel, E. S. (1974). *The depressed woman: A study of social relationships.* Chicago, University of Chicago Press.

Wells, K. C., & Egan, J. (1988). Social learning and systems family therapy for childhood oppositional disorder: Comparative treatment outcome. *Comprehensive Psychiatry, 29,* 138–146.

Wells, M. G., Burlingame, G. M., Lambert. M. J., Hoag, M. J., & Hope, C. A. (1996). Conceptualization and measurement of patient change during psychotherapy: Development of the Outcome Questionnaire and the Youth Outcome Questionnaire. *Psychotherapy, 33,* 275–283.

Wetzell, S. (1995, June). *Market driven reform: How payors align incentives to accelerate the behavioral outcomes/guideline agenda* (Keynote address). Presented at the Behavioral Healthcare Outcomes, Guidelines and Report Card Summit. Minneapolis, MN.

Wheeler, M. E., & Hess, K. W. (1976). Treatment of juvenile obesity by successive approximation control of eating. *Journal of Behavior Therapy and Experimental Psychiatry, 7,* 235–241.

White, G. W., Mathews, R. M., & Fawcett, S. B. (1989). Reducing risk of pressure sores: Effects of watch prompts and alarm avoidance on wheelchair push-ups. *Journal of Applied Behavior Analysis, 22,* 287–295.

Whitney, J. L., & Goldstein, H. (1989). Using self-monitoring to reduce disfluencies in speakers with mild aphasia. *Journal of Speech and Hearing Disorders, 54,* 576–586.

Wilder, J. (1967). *Stimulus and response. The law of initial value.* Bristol: John Wright & Sons.

Wilfley, D. E., Agras, W. S., Telch, C. F., Rossiter, E. M., Schneider, J. A., Cole, A. G., Sifford, L. & Raeburn, S. D. (1993). Group cognitive-behavioral therapy and group interpersonal psychotherapy for the nonpurging bulimic individual: A controlled comparison. *Journal of Consulting and Clinical Psychology, 61,* 296–305.

Williams, B. (1994). Patient satisfaction: A valid concept? *Social Science and Medicine, 38,* 509–516.

Williams, S. L., & Falbo, J. (1996). Cognitive and performance-based treatments for panic attacks in people with varying degrees of agoraphobic disability. *Behaviour Research and Therapy, 34,* 253–264.

Williamson, D. A., Prather, R. C., McKenzie, S. J., & Blouin, D. C. (1990). Behavioral assessment procedures can differentiate bulimia nervosa, compulsive overeater, obese, and normal subjects. *Behavioral Assessment, 12,* 239–252.

Wilson, G. T. (1995). Empirically validated treatments as a basis for clinical practice: Problems and prospects. In S. C. Hayes, V. M. Follette, R. M. Dawes, & K. E. Grady (Eds.), *Scientific standards of psychological practice: Issues and recommendations* (pp. 163–196). Reno, NV: Context Press.

Wilson, G. T. (1996). Manual-based treatments: The clinical application of research findings. *Behaviour Research and Therapy, 34,* 295–314.

Wilson, T. D. (1994). The proper protocol: Validity and completeness of verbal reports. *Psychological Science, 5,* 249–252.

Wincze, J. P., & Carey, M. P. (1991). *Sexual dysfunction: A guide for assessment and treatment.* New York: Guilford Press.

Winegar, N. (1992). *The clinicians's guide to managed mental health care.* Binghamton, NY: Haworth Press.

Winston, A., Pollack, J., McCullough L., Flegenheimer, W., Kestenbaum, R., Trujillo, M. (1991). Brief psychotherapy of personality disorders. *The Journal of Nervous and Mental Disease, 179,* 188–193.

Withey, S. B. (1954). Reliability of recall of income. *Public Opinion Quarterly, 18,* 197–204.

Witmer, L. (1907/1996). Clinical psychology. *American Psychologist,* 248–251. [Original article from *The Psychological Clinic,* 1907, *1,* 1–9.]

Wolf, M. M. (1978). Social validity: The case for subjective measurement or how applied behavior analysis is finding its heart. *Journal of Applied Behavior Analysis, 11,* 203–214.

Wolfe, B. E., & Maser, J. D. (Eds.). (1994). *Treatment of panic disorder: A consensus development conference.* Washington, DC: American Psychiatric Press.

Wollersheim, J. P. (1974). Bewail the Vail, or love is not enough. *American Psychologist, 29,* 717–718.

Wolpe, J. (1958). *Psychotherapy by reciprocal inhibition.* Stanford: Stanford University Press.

Wolpe, J. (1969). *The practice of behavior therapy.* New York: Pergamon.

Woodcock, R. W., & Johnson, M. B. (1989, 1990). *Woodcock-Johnson Psycho-Educational Battery-Revised.* Allen, TX: DLM Teaching Resources.

Woody, G. E., Luborsky, L., McLellan, A. T., & O'Brien, C. P. (1990). Corrections and revised analyses for psychotherapy in methadone maintenance patients. *Archives of General Psychiatry, 47,* 788–789.

Yarnold, P. R. (1992). Statistical analysis for single-case designs. In F. B. Bryant, J. Edwards, R. S. Tindale, E. J. Posavac, L. Heath, E. Henderson, & Y. Suarez-Balcazar (Eds.), *Methodological issues in applied social psychology* (pp. 177–197). New York: Plenum.

Yarrow, M. R., Campbell, J. D., & Burton, R. V. (1970). Recollections of childhood: A study of the retrospective method. *Monographs of the Society for Research in Child Development, 35,* (5, Serial No. 138).

Yates, B. T. (1994). Toward the incorporation of costs, cost-effectiveness analysis, and cost-benefit analysis into clinical research. *Journal of Consulting and Clinical Psychology, 62,* 729–738.

Yeaton, W. H., & Sechrest, L. (1981). Critical dimensions in the choice and maintenance of successful treatments: Strength, integrity, and effectiveness. *Journal of Consulting and Clinical Psychology, 49,* 156–168.

Yeaton, W. H., & Sechrest, L. (1992). Critical dimensions in the choice and maintenance of successful treatments: Strength, integrity, and effectiveness. In A. E. Kazdin (Ed.), *Methodological issues and strategies in clinical research.* Washington, DC: American Psychological Association.

Zanarini, M., Gunderson, J., Frankenburg, F., & Chauncey, D. (1989). The revised diagnostic interview for borderlines: Discriminating BPD from other Axis II disorders. *Journal of Personality Disorders, 45,* 733–737.

Zaro, J. S., Barach, R., Nedelmann, D. J., & Dreiblatt, I. S. (1977). *A guide for beginning psychotherapists.* Cambridge, England: Cambridge University Press.

Zettle, R. D., & Herring, E. L. (1995). Treatment utility of the sociotropy\autonomy distinction: Implications for cognitive therapy. *Journal of Clinical Psychology, 51,* 280–289.

Zilbergeld, B., & Evans, M. (1980). The inadequacy of Masters and Johnson. *Psychology Today, 14,* 28–43.

Zubenko, G. S., Mulsant, B. H., Rifai, A. H., Sweet, R. A., Paternak, R. E., Marino, L. J., & Tu, X. (1994). Impact of acute psychiatric inpatient treatment on major depression in late life and prediction of response. *American Journal of Psychiatry, 151,* 987–994.

NAME INDEX

SUBJECT INDEX

433